THE INSPECTORS GENERAL
OF THE
UNITED STATES ARMY
1903–1939

Maj. Gen. Eli A. Helmick Inspecting Battery A, 41st Coast Artillery,
at Fort Kamehameha, Hawaii, in June 1925

THE INSPECTORS GENERAL
OF THE UNITED STATES ARMY
1903–1939

by

Joseph W. A. Whitehorne

*OFFICE OF THE INSPECTOR GENERAL
AND CENTER OF MILITARY HISTORY
UNITED STATES ARMY
WASHINGTON, D.C., 1998*

Library of Congress Cataloging-in-Publication Data

Whitehorne, Joseph W. A., 1943–
    The inspectors general of the United States Army, 1903–1939 /
by Joseph W. A. Whitehorne.
        p.   cm.—(CMH pub : 70–68)
    Includes bibliographical references and index.
    1. Military inspectors general—United States—History. 2. United
States. Army. Office of the Inspector General—History.
    I. Title. II. Series.
    UB243.W49   1998
    355.6'85'0973—dc21   98–10976
                                                                    CIP

First Printing—CMH Pub 70–68

Foreword

As the companion work to *The Inspectors General of the United States Army, 1777–1903*, this volume continues the story of the Inspector General's Department and its corps of inspectors during the years from 1903 to 1939. The period was a time of revolutionary reform and reorganization, with the department shifting to the detail system and adapting to the newly created General Staff. The challenges it confronted were even greater as the inspection system became one of the key elements in helping the Army deal with the crises of World War I, with postwar adjustments, and, finally, with a decade of economic depression.

The Inspectors General of the United States Army, 1903–1939, recounts how the inspectorate became one of the most consistent and important agents for change within the War Department, providing the analyses, much of the criticism, and most of the description of the Army's metamorphosis. During this critical period of modernization virtually all of the principles under which the modern inspectorate operates were confirmed or established. While explaining the precedents of modern policies, this history provides a deeper insight into the need for the Army inspectorate. I urge you to read this volume, which serves not only as a tribute to the exceptional group of dedicated soldiers who sustained a proud tradition but also as an inspiration to those who carry it on.

Washington, D.C.
30 January 1998

LARRY R. JORDAN
Lieutenant General, USA
The Inspector General

Preface

Any reference to an inspector general, or "I-Gee," usually elicits little more than a polite nod and, perhaps, a perplexed look from the general public. In truth, few have heard of or know anything about the Army Inspector General System, which grew out of a recognized need for an independent inspection office, one without affiliation or responsibility for the command inspected. Yet within most military services an inspector general is a well-known figure, functioning as a confidential representative of his commander. He is responsible for making inquiries into matters affecting mission performance and the state of discipline, economy, and efficiency of the organization to which he is assigned. Because he often deals with matters of considerable sensitivity, he serves on his commander's personal staff and normally enjoys direct access to him. Most of his time, however, is spent in assisting unit members in improving organizational and individual conditions.

Traditionally, the inspectors general have been informal trainers and advisers to soldiers at every level. From the beginning they have divided their time between matters of training, efficiency, and conduct as required by their commanders. The scope of their inquiries has ranged from unit mission capabilities and funds expenditures to the welfare and morals of unit members. Commanders as different as Maj. Gen. Anthony Wayne and General William T. Sherman have called the inspectors their "alter ego," bringing to light their subordinates' various concerns that needed command attention.

Like any group with a function that has lasted over an extended period within a larger bureaucratic structure, the inspectors have developed various procedures and forms of organization both effective and precedent-setting. The growth of interest in inspection activities at every level of government has made the articulation of this body of experience increasingly important. As the oldest of its type, the Army Inspector General System has provided an example on which later inspectorates have often chosen to model themselves. To better assist such efforts, Lt. Gen. Richard G. Trefry, The Inspector General, 1977–1983, inaugurated a formal project to document the Army's extensive experience and established procedures so that it could be shared and defended. Trefry's interest was fully sustained by his successors, Lt. Gen. Nathaniel R. Thompson, Jr., 1983–1986, and Lt. Gen. Henry Doctor, Jr., 1986–1990. The result of their generous support is this second volume on the history of the inspectorate, taking the record from 1903 to 1939.

This work was written with serving inspectors general in mind. Although few are historians, certainly all recognize the value of the experience of their predecessors. This history hopefully will serve the practical purpose of explaining how the inspection system in the Army has evolved and why things are done the way they are. Above all, it explains the reasons for a separate inspectorate, for its traditions, and for its place in history, providing a guide and inspiration to meet the challenges of the present.

This study was made possible only with the assistance of many people. Special thanks go to General Trefry for reading the several drafts, including the final, and for his valuable comments. I am equally grateful to Dr. Daniel R. Beaver for his comments on the manuscript and the many fruitful discussions we have enjoyed on the era of the Great War. Additional thanks are due General Thompson, Dr. Edward M. Coffman, and Dr. Edgar F. Raines for reading and commenting on the final draft. The assistance given and interest shown by archivists Charles A. Shaughnessy, Timothy K. Nenninger, and Fred W. Purnell of the National Archives and Records Administration, Washington, D.C., and archivists John J. Slonaker, Richard J. Sommers, and David Keough of the U.S. Army Military History Institute, Carlisle Barracks, Pennsylvania, have been indispensable, sustaining me through many rough points. A very special thanks goes to Sharon M. Daugherty, Pat Smith, Susan S. Sparks, Ellen M. Whitehorne, and Shotzy Wright for superb typing and computer support. Words cannot express my appreciation for their selfless dedication. Other talented individuals deserving of recognition are Arthur S. Hardyman and Beth F. MacKenzie for their masterful design, cartographic, and desktop publishing support, as well as Florence Brodkey for her efforts in preparing the useful index. Finally, this work would never have achieved the precision, clarity, and consistency it has without the commitment and skill of Joanne M. Brignolo, one of the finest editors an author could hope for. She pulled it from the brink, for which I am most grateful.

All of these good people have made a major contribution to what merits this work may have. I alone claim full responsibility for any shortcomings.

Cedarville, Virginia   JOSEPH W. A. WHITEHORNE
30 January 1998

Contents

PART TWO
World War I and the Inspectorate, 1917–1919

PART THREE
Neglect and Privation, 1919–1939

Tables

Maps

Illustrations

Illustrations courtesy of the following sources: pp. 15, 25, 32, 78, 122, 127, 137, 319, 337, 357, 363, 385, 437, and 449, Office of The Inspector General; paperback cover/frontispiece and pp. 99 and 288, U.S. Army Military History Institute; p. 279, U.S. Military Academy Archives; pp. 411 and 419, Joseph W. A. Whitehorne; p. 345, Maj. Gen. John L. Deane, Sr.; pp. 159, 170, 174, 201, 204, 209, 302, and 306, National Archives and Records Administration; pp. 53 (oil by Irma Maduro Peixotto), 66 (ink by Charles Johnson Post), 179 (pencil by J.

Andre Smith), and 247 (watercolor by J. Andre Smith), Army Art Collection; and p. 213, Fort Sheridan Association, *History and Achievement of the Fort Sheridan Officers' Training Camps* (N.p., 1920), p. 203.

THE INSPECTORS GENERAL
OF THE
UNITED STATES ARMY
1903–1939

INTRODUCTION
Von Steuben's Legacy

Combat and planning for combat are the primary subjects that attract most students of military history. Too often they exhibit less interest in the extensive support activities that are necessary to sustain the battle and in the broad institutional developments that make the requisite support available. Yet even during wartime, armies spend far more time off the battlefield than they do in combat. In peacetime, only a small part of the soldier's day is devoted to preparing for battle. To sustain itself, any army must deal with myriad routine tasks—morale, supply, health, finances, development, and training. None of these issues are particularly dramatic, and most are difficult to document after the fact.

Despite this lack of the dramatic, it is essential that these tasks be performed well. They maintain an army in peacetime and sustain it in battle. If properly done, they are the key to its readiness to wage war when necessary. The record of any organization, but particularly a military force, is very largely a tale of its administrative and structural development. Countless dedicated professionals are necessary to keep an army functioning and focused for its rare encounters with crises. Armies have long since become too large and complex for any one man, with only a small staff, to command. They require the aid of numerous specialists, and commanders in turn need to monitor their specialists in order to obtain information on the condition of their forces.

Early in the history of the U.S. Army, the requirement for oversight resulted in the establishment of the senior position of Inspector General.[1] The Army's inspection system, first suggested by General George Washington, began in December 1777 with a resolution of the Continental Congress. Washington assessed that he needed a principal

---

[1] For a detailed study of the founding and growth of the inspectorate, see David A. Clary and Joseph W. A. Whitehorne, *The Inspectors General of the United States Army, 1777–1903* (Washington, D.C.: Office of The Inspector General and U.S. Army Center of Military History, 1987).

assistant to aid him in the training, discipline, and development of his growing forces, who had gone into winter quarters at Valley Forge after a series of humiliating defeats fought in defense of Philadelphia that summer. His generals were for the most part brave and tactically competent. However, they were inexperienced in doctrine and training, and often too sensitive to their rights and prerogatives. Washington recognized that his senior inspector had to be outside the chain of command, mindful that his often feisty subordinates would perceive that their positions were in jeopardy. At the same time, the officer had to be professionally competent so that he could meet Washington's training objectives while earning the respect of the rest of the Army.

Although Maj. Gen. Friedrich W. A. von Steuben was preceded briefly by three Inspectors General, he is credited with establishing the high standards desired by Washington—integrity, knowledge, and loyalty to conscience—that have been the measure of the inspection system ever since. Steuben developed the inspector's role as the confidential assistant of his commander. Chief tasks were training and assisting the chain of command in carrying out its mission in the most efficient manner.

However, a second tradition, conflicting with Steuben's legacy, was launched by Alexander Hamilton when he became Inspector General during the quasi-war with France in 1798. A large force was authorized by Congress to be raised in the event of a French invasion. Washington was asked to command the force. In the meantime, a senior officer was needed to attend to the various administrative preparations then under way, and Hamilton was appointed and given the title. In actual practice, Hamilton assumed the role and functions more closely associated with a deputy commander or chief of staff, and in so doing he created a tenacious tradition that competed with Steuben's version of the inspectorate throughout the nineteenth century. Normally, in peacetime the Inspectors General performed in the Steuben role, visiting units and reporting on conditions throughout the Army. But when war broke out, the senior inspectors took to the field to serve in various executive capacities, terminating the flow and processing of information so vital to the commanders' understanding of conditions within their forces.

Despite these problems, the value of the inspectorate was recognized during every early conflict. In 1821, as a result of legislation requested by Secretary of War John C. Calhoun, the Office of the Inspector General finally was made permanent, with an unbroken chain of inspectors thereafter detailed to various staff levels. Nevertheless, it had to wait some forty years, until the Civil War, before becoming an official staff component of the War Department. With the promotion to brigadier general in 1878 of Inspector General Randolph B. Marcy, the office assumed the status of a full-fledged department, equal to comparable War Department elements. In the 1890s the influence of Steuben's inspection philosophy grew, and the Hamiltonian tradition disappeared after the War with Spain in 1898. Many problems in supply, health, and transportation were identified by unit inspectors general during that brief war, and yet, with most of the Inspectors General absent performing line duties, little action could be taken. The resulting criticism of the Inspector General's Department briefly threatened its continued existence. However, it survived, partly because of the able defense mustered by Brig. Gen. Joseph C. Breckinridge, the Inspector General, and partly because of the perception of its value by members of Congress and the War Department.

The inspectorate entered the twentieth century as an object of criticism during a time of reform and reorganization throughout the Army. The detail system was used to bring it, like other staff elements, into closer contact with the rest of the Army. At the same time, the functions of the Inspector General's Department had to undergo a period of experimentation as it accommodated itself to the newly created General Staff, headed by a chief of staff. Its experience was a part of the modernization effort. Within a decade, however, the inspectorate became a powerful extension of the Chief of Staff and one of the most consistent and important agents for change within the War Department.

Throughout the period that followed, the inspectorate provided a unique view of the Army as it entered a new era with unprecedented challenges. The able group of men who came and went through the ranks of the Inspector General's Department provided the analyses, much of the criticism, and most of the description of the Army's metamorphosis. The inspectors general were often instrumental in keeping the Army's individual leaders informed about the nature and health of the overall establishment. In the words of General Breckinridge, they were "to touch most firmly those things the generals most needed to know."[2]

The inspectors general were a central force in that mass of unsung professionals who sustained the Army since its inception. They helped ready it for war. When war came, they assisted in assuring that the mission was met as effectively as possible. Their view of the Army is unique, and in many ways this work is a history written from their perspective. But, most of all, it is the story of a vital staff element that has served the Army well.

---

[2] Ltr, Breckinridge to Garlington, 19 Sep 10, Entry 35, Record Group 159, National Archives and Records Administration, Washington, D.C.

PART ONE

EXPERIMENT AND REFORM
1903–1917

1

Inspection and Reform

The era between the War with Spain and World War I was a time of dynamic change in the U.S. Army. The activities of the Inspector General's Department (IGD), the collective designation of the Office of the Inspector General (OIG) and the inspectorate, consisting of those officers detailed as inspectors general at each echelon of command, touched the Army at every point of its daily life and training. Inspectors were charged to examine staffs, units, and personnel to determine whether they could perform their wartime missions and whether they were administering themselves and their resources in the most effective manner. Throughout the period, official inspection reports traced the progress of reform.

Inspectors oversaw myriad routine tasks as well. At each level of command they devoted a large part of their efforts to the examination of supplies, animals, and equipment, determining their condition and recommending their disposition or condemnation. Extensive money accountability inspections and audits were made on all funds controlled or disbursed by War Department members. At the top, the Inspectors General performed many special inquiries or investigations into matters of discipline and justice affecting the efficiency or well being of the entire Army. The variety and scope of all this work gave them a unique perspective and potential for influence during the years when a struggle both of principles and of powerful individuals reshaped the Army into a more modern form.

The Root Reforms and the New Army

In July 1899 President William McKinley appointed Elihu Root as Secretary of War to replace the discredited Russell A. Alger, scapegoat for the Army's shortcomings as revealed in the War with Spain. Root, a successful corporation lawyer, soon became involved in Army reform, among many other activities, and played a central role in the process of reorganization.[1]

When Root took office, the Army was an administrative anomaly, violating many basic principles of the emerging science of management. The position of Commanding General had no legislative sanction, and the Commanding General's duties and relationships with the Secretary of War and the rest of the Army were unclear, particularly in peacetime. Support for line, or the Army in the field, was provided by a group of War Department technical and administrative bureaus, the Adjutant General's Department (AGD) and the Inspector General's Department among them. With few exceptions, the bureaus worked directly for the Secretary of War. While secretaries came and went, bureau chiefs remained, becoming over the course of time virtually autonomous. Their independence was further enhanced by their lifetime appointments. Thus, although drawn originally from the line, bureau chiefs, not unsurprisingly, had become increasingly unresponsive to troops in the field.

The Army's "invertebrate" structure has been likened by historians to the larger inchoate American society of the period. Root's efforts to create a more rational organization were part of a general progressive impulse that gave its name to the whole era. Root set out to eliminate the separate status of the bureaus and to form a hierarchical structure in which the Secretary of War and his senior general could manage both the bureaus and the line while anticipating the Army's future requirements.[2]

His efforts resulted in congressional passage in February 1901 of an act that significantly altered the appointment of bureau staffs. Officers were to be selected—that is, detailed—from the line to serve a specified period and then return to duty in their basic branch. The intent of the lawmakers was to link the bureaus with the rest of the Army and to eliminate the permanent members of the bureaus by attrition. The bureau chiefs fought the change, arguing that detailed officers would lack the necessary expertise. Events were to demonstrate that

---

[1] Richard W. Leopold, *Elihu Root and the Conservative Tradition* (Boston: Little, Brown and Co., 1954), p. 32.

[2] Ibid.; Philip C. Jessup, *Elihu Root*, 2 vols. (New York: Dodd, Mead and Co., 1938), 1:215; Russell F. Weigley, "The Elihu Root Reforms and the Progressive Era," in *Command and Commanders in Modern Warfare: The Proceedings of the Second Military History Symposium, U.S. Air Force Academy, 2–3 May 1968*, ed. William Geffen, 2d ed., enl. (Washington, D.C.: Office of Air Force History, Headquarters USAF, and U.S. Air Force Academy, 1971), pp. 11–13 (quoted word, p. 12).

there was some validity to their claim, and as a result the new system was slightly modified for some of the technical branches at a later date.[3]

The capstone of Root's efforts came with the General Staff bill, passed by Congress in February 1903. The new act eliminated the position of Commanding General, replacing it with the position of Chief of Staff and creating the General Staff, to be supported by a group of detailed officers. Lt. Gen. Nelson A. Miles, the incumbent Commanding General, opposed the bill strongly, forcing Root to delay submitting it for a year. Even when he resubmitted it, he was compelled to withdraw provisions eliminating the Inspector General's Department and transferring its functions to the General Staff because of Inspector General Breckinridge's eloquent defense before Congress. Additional pressure on Root also secured the continued independent existence of the Record and Pension Office, headed by Brig. Gen. Fred C. Ainsworth.[4]

When Root introduced his General Staff bill, he justified it as an effort to put the War Department on an economical, businesslike basis with a single, clear chain of command. His key word was "efficiency."[5] The General Staff was to be a vehicle to eliminate the functional constraints placed on the Army by the bureaus. Root hoped to assert the primacy of so-called professional values, as opposed to the parochial technical values of the bureaus. Although he was less than specific, all indications are that Root intended the Chief of Staff to remain aloof from daily activities, controlling them without becoming involved. The General Staff was expected to be a nerve center, providing direction for the Army while focusing on major issues and contingencies.

But Root failed to anticipate the effects of human nature and daily requirements upon his concept. It proved impossible for the General Staff to maintain its aloof position of watchful supervision over the bureaus. Many of the capable young officers detailed to the Staff did not understand the principles upon which their positions were based. As they attempted to exercise their supervisory functions, some intervened

---

[3] Otto L. Nelson, Jr., *National Security and the General Staff* (Washington, D.C.: Infantry Journal Press, 1946), p. 106; Memo, OIG, 25 Jun 01, sub: Act of February 2, 1901, Entry 24, Record Group (RG) 159, National Archives and Records Administration (NARA), Washington, D.C.

[4] Philip L. Semsch, "Elihu Root and the General Staff," *Military Affairs* 27 (Spring 63): 23; Nelson, *National Security*, p. 58. For a detailed discussion of Breckinridge's success in preserving the IGD, see David A. Clary and Joseph W. A. Whitehorne, *The Inspectors General of the United States Army, 1777–1903* (Washington, D.C.: Office of The Inspector General and U.S. Army Center of Military History, 1987)(hereafter cited as *IGs 1777–1903*).

[5] Semsch, "Elihu Root," p. 22.

in the routine affairs of the bureaus. Others, trying to avoid associating themselves too closely with the bureaus, lost control by failing to follow through on Staff directives. In the end, the Chief of Staff himself was doomed to become involved in matters that were not specifically in his charter.[6] The result was constant tension between the bureau chiefs and the Chief of Staff, manifested in power plays that were anathema to the rational hierarchical structures Root had envisioned.

Such problems were, for example, effectively exploited by General Ainsworth, who was able to have his Record and Pension Office excluded from direct General Staff supervision. Under Root's concept, the paperwork generated by the Commanding General function went to the Adjutant General while that from the planning elements moved to the General Staff.[7] Other bureau administrative functions were theoretically untouched.

However, Root was impressed by Ainsworth's administrative abilities and wanted to improve the War Department's efficiency. He thus directed that the historical and personnel records branches of the Adjutant General's Department, because of arrears in operations, be transferred to Ainsworth's office, thus eviscerating the department. The Adjutant General's remaining vestige followed on 23 April 1904, when Congress passed an act that created a Military Secretary's Office and appointed Ainsworth a major general.[8]

The result was a bureaucratic Frankenstein. The Military Secretary's Office was larger than the nine other permanent bureaus combined. Root had favored the term *Military Secretary* to stress the point that advice and control, not administration, was now a General Staff function. The justification for merging the Adjutant General's Department with the Record and Pension Office was to create an even better administrative agency, capable of lifting the burden from the General Staff. But the end result, given the Staff's unavoidable entanglement with administrative detail, produced only conflict between the Military Secretary and the Chief of Staff over areas of interest and responsibility.[9]

---

[6] Weigley, "Elihu Root Reforms," p. 20; James E. Hewes, Jr., "The United States Army General Staff, 1900–1917," *Military Affairs* 38 (Apr 74): 68.

[7] Mabel E. Deutrich, *Struggle for Supremacy: The Career of General Fred C. Ainsworth* (Washington, D.C.: Public Affairs Press, 1962), p. 81.

[8] Idem, "Fred C. Ainsworth: The Story of a Vermont Archivist," *Vermont History* 27 (Jan 59): 29.

[9] Siert F. Riepma, "Portrait of an Adjutant General: The Career of Major General Fred C. Ainsworth," *Journal of the American Military History Foundation* 2 (Spring 38): 34.

Ainsworth's power and influence were further enhanced when he received the title of Adjutant General, conferred upon him by Congress in the Army Appropriation Act of 2 March 1907. The change was also significant symbolically: The implementing general order specified that the title of the head of the resurrected department would be preceded by the word *The*—hence, The Adjutant General, which conveyed the prestige and authority of the position that was lacking in the term *Military Secretary*. Ainsworth might not have been as successful in expanding his power had not Root left office in 1904, to be replaced by the less dynamic and more pliable William H. Taft, who was also an admirer of Ainsworth's administrative expertise. What occurred was predictable: The Chief of Staff functioned in isolation, while Ainsworth, with the Secretary of War's compliance, virtually ran the Army.[10]

Root's efforts to impose modern managerial methods on the Army's traditional structure seemed to be constrained without the presence of a strong chief of staff, supported by a strong secretary of war. This condition was met with the appointment of Maj. Gen. Leonard Wood as Chief of Staff in 1910 and Henry L. Stimson as Secretary of War shortly afterward. As a showdown with The Adjutant General took shape, their best ally among the bureau chiefs was the Inspector General.

The IGD's Role in Reform

The Inspector General's Department had developed rapidly during the era of reform. When Root was appointed Secretary of War, the small department was virtually dormant because of conflict between Generals Breckinridge and Miles. Inspector General Breckinridge was a Civil War veteran with a distinguished combat record. A conservative, his focus was largely on the improvement of unit-level operations and specific items of individual equipment. He was an effective defender of the functions of his organization and consequently opposed many of the Root reforms.[11]

The relationship of the Inspector General to the War Department leadership changed as a result of Root's efforts to have the General Staff bill passed. Breckinridge successfully argued before Congress against the elimination of his department, and Root was forced to yield.

---

[10] Hewes, "General Staff," p. 69.

[11] Deutrich, *Struggle*, p. 78; "Recent Deaths: Joseph Cabell Breckinridge," *Army and Navy Journal*, 28 Aug 20, p. 1578; *National Cyclopedia of American Biography*, vol. 9, and *Who Was Who in America*, vol. 1, s.v. "Breckinridge, Joseph Cabell." For more information, see Clary and Whitehorne, *IGs 1777–1903*, and Appendix C of this volume.

Having achieved his own aims, Breckinridge accepted promotion to major general and early retirement in April 1903. His replacement, Brig. Gen. George H. Burton, was known to be more sympathetic to Root's views and the problems of the line Army. When Burton reached mandatory retirement age in October 1906, he was in turn succeeded by Brig. Gen. Ernest A. Garlington, brother-in-law to the incumbent Chief of Staff, Maj. Gen. J. Franklin Bell.[12]

Known as a cultured, considerate officer of great integrity, sensitive to the welfare of soldiers, Garlington was sympathetic to innovations that would improve conditions in the Army. Thus, at the time of the struggle for authority in the War Department, the Office of the Inspector General, charged with being the eyes and ears of the Chief of Staff and the Secretary of War, was headed by a series of general officers receptive to reform. When properly supported, the OIG proved to be a powerful instrument in assuring the accomplishment of War Department policies and unit compliance with directives.[13]

Wood and Stimson together formed a progressive team. Their intent was to modernize the Army and to clarify the role of their positions in relation to the rest of the Army. Both men were aggressive, yielding nothing to their opponents' views. General Ainsworth tenaciously defended the status quo and traditional ways of doing things, and his bureaucratic knowledge and abilities, combined with great political influence built up over the years, made him seem virtually unassailable. Yet Wood was determined to "settle the command confusion." He recognized that the best way to upstage Ainsworth was with his own weapons—administrative tactics, working through matters of routine.[14]

The conflict between the two officers reached a climax when President Taft's Committee on Economy and Efficiency reported its findings. Ainsworth led a War Department board that reviewed the committee's recommendations, the majority of which were rejected. However, a General Staff representative on the board filed a minority report, pressing for the elimination of the muster roll as a desirable administrative reform. On 15 December 1911 Wood sent a memorandum to Ainsworth requesting his views on the matter. Ainsworth's

---

[12] "Further Promotion to General Officers," *Army and Navy Journal*, 21 Feb 03, p. 607; Edgar F. Raines, "Major General J. Franklin Bell and Military Reform: The Chief of Staff Years, 1906–1910" (Ph.D. diss., University of Wisconsin-Madison, 1976), p. 148.

[13] See Appendix C.

[14] Archibald Butt, *Taft and Roosevelt: The Intimate Letters of Archie Butt, Military Aide* (Port Washington, N.Y.: Kennikat Press, 1971), p. 781; Jack C. Lane, *Armed Progressive: General Leonard Wood* (San Francisco: Presidio Press, 1978), p. 157 (quotation); Deutrich, *Struggle*, p. 112.

Brig. Gen. George H. Burton   *Brig. Gen. Ernest A. Garlington*

answer was "scorching and contemptuous," stressing the need to keep the roll and questioning the intelligence and abilities of those recommending otherwise. Stimson, considering Ainsworth's reply "grossly insubordinate," relieved him and prepared court-martial charges.[15]

Ainsworth, instead of facing trial, requested early retirement, rather than continue the struggle with his superiors. His departure assured Wood's personal supremacy in the War Department. It also appeared to reconfirm Root's concept of the governance of the Army. Stimson believed that no important challenge to the authority of the Chief of Staff could be mounted in the future. Greater harmony soon developed for Stimson began to include the bureau chiefs more deeply in the decision-making process. Wood and Stimson saw themselves as instrumental in overcoming the inertia of the old guard in the Army and Congress, and in preparing the Army for the demands of a new era.[16]

Yet the two paid a high price for their victory. Ainsworth had been popular with many officers, who maintained that he had done the Army a great deal more good than harm. He also had many congressional

[15] Henry L. Stimson and McGeorge Bundy, *On Active Service in Peace and War* (New York: Harper and Brothers, 1947), p. 34 (quoted words); Deutrich, *Struggle*, p. 119.
[16] Stimson and Bundy, *On Active Service*, p. 37.

supporters, who immediately protested his dismissal. The affair thus discredited Wood politically. Regardless of Wood's motives, his actions were viewed by many as an abuse of his authority and an example of the ruthlessness with which he frequently was charged. To some critics he seemed to be trying to achieve the sort of personal direction of the Army sought earlier by the past commanding generals. Ainsworth himself remained in close touch with key members of Congress, often foiling reform initiatives sponsored by Wood and his successors. In such matters Wood and Stimson often demonstrated remarkably little political sense, while Ainsworth displayed the opposite, wielding informal influence for many years through his congressional connections.[17]

Wood found that he was unable to push his subsequent programs through Congress, losing a battle to close marginal posts and lacking support to create an expansible Army with trained reserves. What little political influence he retained further faded with the election of Democratic President Woodrow Wilson in 1913. Despite these setbacks Wood continued to upgrade the Army's efficiency, for many of his and Stimson's objectives could be realized by using their administrative authority, without recourse to Congress. They continued to improve unit administration, schools, and training programs through the use of existing military channels, and the Inspectors General also served as a means to implement and enforce their directives.

The Inspectors General in turn appear to have been motivated by a mixture of self-interest and altruism. Beginning with Breckinridge, they all argued for the continued existence of their department, hoping to retain the prestige and trappings of a separate agency. However, they also displayed a sincere conviction that their activities were beneficial to the Army. They stressed the need for a disinterested observer within the command structure, capable of investigating a situation and having no vested interest in the conclusions to be reached. Additionally, they saw a need for competent third parties with the time to review matters, such as individual soldier amenities, which otherwise might be missed by more hard-pressed commanders and staff officers.[18]

The situation created by the Root reforms and extended by the Wood-Ainsworth struggle caused the Chief of Staff and the Inspector General to draw closer in a mutually supporting relationship. Gradually,

---

[17] Butt, *Taft and Roosevelt*, p. 780; Lane, *Armed Progressive*, p. 166; "Newton D. Baker on Executive Influence in Military Legislation," *American Political Science Review* 50 (Sep 56): 700–701.

[18] U.S. Congress, House, Committee on Military Affairs, *Hearings on a Bill To Increase the Efficiency of the Army*, 58th Cong., 1st Sess., 1902, p. 41.

the Inspector General came to be considered as an extension of the Secretary of War and the Chief of Staff, exercising considerable delegated authority in the process. This supportive lateral coordination was enhanced by an upward flow of ideas. Many of Wood's reforms originated in the reports of the inspectors in the field, which covered virtually every aspect of military operations and living, and the recommendations and findings appearing in the inspectors' reports often were quoted verbatim in the annual reports of the Chief of Staff and the Secretary of War.[19]

Beginning in 1903, the Office of the Inspector General once again monitored militia inspections, easing Wood's later efforts to impose his preparedness policy. In 1905 the OIG directed that the developing system of service schools at Forts Monroe, Riley, and Leavenworth be inspected annually. Over the years this work assisted the efforts of successive chiefs of staff to impose—independent of legislative action—standards on curricula, attendance procedures, and school organization, influencing not only individual careers and attitudes but also doctrine and programs.[20]

The effects of budget limitations were offset partially by the inspectors' concern for waste; the economy measures they recommended were often adopted, sometimes with significant results. In 1905 the Secretary of War directed that unit business practices be made a routine item of annual inspection. Wood, who in 1910 had begun his term as Chief of Staff by stressing a more businesslike, efficient way of operating, favored similar reforms. He restructured the General Staff along functional lines and streamlined numerous administrative procedures, saving money and improving effectiveness. He was able to implement many of his ideas through the Army's inspection system because of the practices and procedures that had evolved since 1903.[21]

General Wood expanded his influence further in 1911 by directing that troops be inspected in the field. Subsequently, inspectors routinely evaluated the proficiency of individuals and units in the field, as well

---

[19] Marcellus G. Spinks, "Major Problems of the Inspector General, AEF, and Their Solution" (Lecture delivered at G–1 Course No. 5, Army War College, Washington, D.C., 9 Oct 33), in Army War College Curriculum Papers, U.S. Army Military History Institute (MHI), Carlisle Barracks, Pa. See also U.S. War Department, *Annual Report of the Secretary of War, 1912* (Washington, D.C.: Government Printing Office, 1913) p. 24 (hereafter cited as *ARSW*); idem, *Annual Report of the Inspector General, 1903* (Washington, D.C.: Government Printing Office, 1903), pp. 447–48, 451 (hereafter cited as *ARIG*); *ARIG 1905*, p. 452.

[20] *ARSW 1904*, pp. 28–29; *ARIG 1905*, p. 448; *ARIG 1906*, p. 638.

[21] *ARIG 1909*, p. 293; *ARIG 1911*, p. 271; *ARIG 1914*, p. 202.

as the creation of balanced tactical divisions. Concurrently, the Army's emergency responsiveness was greatly improved by creating a structure for orderly call-ups. The success of Wood's efforts was revealed by the increasing smoothness of large-unit operations. Wood also began a successful system of civilian training camps as part of his philosophy of preparedness.[22]

These reforms made it possible to manage the concomitants of the crises of the time. They also had implications for the internal structure of the General Staff. While the role of The Adjutant General was limited largely to the mechanics of administration, the functions of the Inspector General expanded to the point that anything affecting the Army's efficiency, including the effectiveness of its leaders, became subject to the IGD's oversight and appraisal.

IGD Strength and Organization

Despite its growing influence, the Inspector General's Department remained small. The new detail system had little practical effect, although seven majors were assigned on 28 February 1901 as the first group of detailed officers. On 21 May 1903 the Chief of Staff accepted a policy that the details from the different arms, or branches, would be "equalized"—in other words, would be proportional to line strength. Whenever a vacancy occurred, the Inspector General submitted to the Chief of Staff three names in nomination, one from each branch. By 1915, however, the average strength of the department was only twenty-one, including four acting inspectors.[23]

The structure of the Inspector General's Department remained the same throughout the prewar period. Small in size, the Office of the Inspector General oversaw the activities of inspectors in the field, as well as conducted War Department–level inspections and investigations. On average, eleven OIG civilians supported the inspectorate, working in the Mail and Records Division and the Examining (later, in 1905, Money Accounts) Division. In the Examining Division an expert accountant and his clerk inspected and assisted in the management of all Army disbursements worldwide. The Mail and Records Division, whose archives went back to the 1820s, was headed by a series of chief clerks, some of whom had forty years experience. The division, in addi-

---

[22] *ARIG 1911*, pp. 265, 267; ARegs 887 and 888, 1913; Hermann Hagedorn, *Leonard Wood: A Biography*, 2 vols. (New York: Harper and Brothers, 1931), 1:126.

[23] IGD, "History for 1912," 14 Jan 13; Memo (quoted word), SofW to WDGS, 21 May 03, sub: Detail of Officers to Staff Bureaus. Both in Entry 24, RG 159, NARA.

tion to conducting the daily business of the office, monitored and processed current investigation and inspection reports.[24]

The inspectors in the field were distributed among the various geographical departments, commanded by general officers. In the United States one inspector general was assigned to each department until 1904, when the Army was divided geographically into five large divisions, each with two or more departments subordinate to it. The objective was to free the echelon of command closest to the troop units from excessive administrative requirements so that it could concentrate on training. But problems resulted in several areas, inspection among them. Inspectors were removed from department staffs, except in the Philippines, and concentrated at division levels. But this practice proved unsatisfactory to department commanders, who had their own needs for inspection and investigation. After the divisions were abolished in 1906, inspectors were once again assigned on the basis of one for each geographical department.[25]

In 1911 the division concept was revived, with a better alignment of duties. Three large divisions were headquartered at New York, Chicago, and San Francisco, while the Philippine Division continued in Manila. The Eastern Division had five inspectors, while the others each had four. The Inspector General decided where particular inspectors would be assigned, his objective being to have a balanced mix of grades and expertise. Normally, the next senior-most IG was assigned to the Eastern Division at Fort Jay, New York, after a tour as the Philippine Division senior inspector. At Fort Jay he was groomed and available to become Inspector General of the Army at the appropriate time.[26]

The Inspector General maintained standards and oversaw his inspectors by a variety of means. All newly assigned inspectors continued to be brought to the Washington office for a two- or three-week training period. There, they underwent a general orientation and exposure to numerous regulations and policy statements. The brief appren-

---

[24] File 306, Inspector General's Office, July 1903, and File 6650, IGD Organization, 1905, Entry 22, RG 159, NARA; *ARIG 1905*, p. 471; *ARIG 1908*, p. 444. The dedicated performance of OIG employees inspired both Generals Burton and Garlington to recommend the development of proper retirement, pension, and assignment plans for all War Department civilians.

[25] *ARSW 1904*, p. 5; *ARSW 1907*, p. 25; *ARIG 1906*, p. 653; WD GO 65, 22 Dec 03; IGD, "Names and Stations of Inspectors General," Entry 24, RG 159, NARA. See also copy of Eli A. Helmick, "From Reveille to Retreat: Autobiography of Major General Eli A. Helmick," MHI.

[26] Memo, Wood to TAG, 29 May 11, Entry 5, RG 165, NARA; Ltr, Mills to Chamberlain, 23 Apr 09, Stephen C. Mills Papers, MHI.

ticeship also gave them a chance to meet and work under their Washington colleagues. No less important was the 1908 publication of *A Guide for the Use of Officers of the Inspector General's Department*, a referenced compilation of all policies and regulations affecting an inspector's duties. Known as the Yellow Book, because of the color of its cover, it underwent several printings and assured a standard interpretation and training reference for inspectors. General Garlington believed that the guide would improve "the thoroughness and uniformity of the inspection service" and would compensate for the relative inexperience of officers detailed to the inspectorate.[27]

The OIG's chief clerk also kept all inspectors informed of policy changes, new regulations, and orders in the War Department. This procedure allowed the inspectors to advise their commanders often before any official word came from the General Staff—a bit of one-upmanship that enhanced the local prestige of the inspectorate. The notice of change went out under the signature of the Inspector General, who often added his own advice as to how inspectors should handle a particular situation. The Office of the Inspector General also published its own series of blank forms to serve as guides for inspecting a particular organization, such as the militia, or function, such as monetary accounts. The forms not only served as a means of standardizing inspector performance but also were in demand throughout the Army as guides for organization and administration. The OIG's requirement for monthly reports from inspectors helped to tighten central control.[28]

Improving efficiency in IGD operations brought the department increasing respect throughout the Army. General Thomas H. Barry, commanding the Army of Cuban Pacification in 1908, considered his inspector general to be one of his most important staff officers and insisted on having a fully qualified officer assigned to the post as long as he remained in Cuba. The proximity of inspectors to senior officers acted as a magnet to some ambitious individuals, who worked for appointments to the inspectorate; others, awed by the professionalism demanded of an inspector, shied away. Maj. Eli A. Helmick had just deployed to the Mexican border with his regiment in 1911, when he was notified of his detail. He hesitated to take the appointment, feeling that he lacked the professional knowledge or powers of observation that he attributed to all of the inspectors he had encountered. Eventually, on

---

[27] Helmick, "Autobiography," MHI; Ltr, Garlington to TAG, 6 Feb 09, and Memo (quotation), Garlington to CofS, WD, 16 May 08, sub: The Inspector General's Department of the Army, Entry 24, RG 159, NARA.

[28] File 46, Matters Pertaining to Blank Forms, 1916, Entry 25, RG 159, NARA.

the advice of senior officers, he took the job despite his misgivings and performed exceptionally well, ultimately passing through division command to become Inspector General in 1921. By the end of the century's first decade the inspectorate thus had established a unique role for itself. As retired General Breckinridge later told Garlington, the "department is the Army's litmus paper, making a test of our conditions and status—and the public is often the final court of appeals."[29]

Conflict With the General Staff

Despite its contribution to reform and its usefulness to the chief of staff, the inspectorate was confronted almost until World War I with attempts by staff members and their allies in Congress to transfer some or all of its functions elsewhere. General Burton set the tone for the defense of the inspectorate as early as October 1903, when a bill was under consideration in Congress to transfer the inspection of money accounts from Army officers to the Treasury Department. Burton argued that since War Department rules governed Army funds and since the War Department was responsible for the conduct of its members, it should be equally responsible for investigating them. He considered it essential to good discipline that commanders should be able to investigate their own people without having to call in an "alien agency."[30] The fundamental issues of confidentiality and command control would underlay most subsequent efforts to justify the continued existence of the Inspector General's Department.

Yet the fact that department members were forced to present the argument repeatedly indicated a lack of understanding of the inspectorate's role on the part of many General Staff members. Continued sniping at the existence of an independent inspectorate caused General Garlington in 1908 to present the Chief of Staff with an overview of his department's performance since the inception of the General Staff. He stressed that the Office of the Inspector General was the only War Department element that, because of its duties, had a comprehensive feel for unit efficiency, supply operations, and Army finances. Additionally, its performance of many delicate special investigations

---

[29] Ltr, Mills to Garlington, 27 Mar 09, Mills Papers, MHI; Ltrs, Barry to Garlington, 26 Dec 19, and Liggett to Garlington, 25 Feb 07, Entry 24, RG 159, NARA; Helmick, "Autobiography," MHI; Ltr (quotation), Breckinridge to Garlington, 19 Sep 10, Entry 35, RG 159, NARA.

[30] Memo, Burton to CofS, WD, 4 Oct 03, sub: Proposed Bill S:3917 and HR:11350, Entry 25, RG 159, NARA.

had assured the maintenance of high standards. Garlington emphasized that the Inspector General's Department touched the Army at every point of its daily life and training as no other staff element could.[31]

Despite the apparent usefulness of the department many officers did not consider it necessary, especially now that a General Staff was functioning. In 1909 Chief of Staff Bell favored merging both The Adjutant General's Department and Inspector General's Department into the General Staff. Bell claimed that the latter agency duplicated the inspection responsibility of the General Staff, which could perform the task better. The General Staff's efficiency, he opined, was impaired by its lack of direct access to the records controlled by The Adjutant General and the full power of inspection enjoyed by the Inspector General.[32]

Bell's attitude was one of frustration, influenced, perhaps, by his inability to make the General Staff as effective as he thought it should be. Seeking to create a single point of unquestioned authority, he failed to recognize the numerous activities of the two departments that were routine and administrative in nature, beyond the charter of the General Staff. Such work as IG investigations and money inspections would have buried the General Staff in daily matters, taking it further from the policy planning for which it had been established.

General Garlington stressed such duties, pointing out that, in addition to the traditional comprehensive concern for Army efficiency, the specific other responsibilities of the Inspector General's Department freed the General Staff to perform its main function. Such arguments, however, failed to persuade many line officers, from whom the General Staff membership was drawn. Many junior line officers resented the time that they were obliged to devote to pleasing the inspectors. It was their contention that they were already so burdened with administrative requirements that it was nearly impossible to conduct proper training. The stress on tactical readiness, which intensified with the 1911 mobilization of the first maneuver division, heightened their resentment.[33]

In the spring of 1911 the move to consolidate functions gained new momentum with the submission of a bill to the House Military Affairs Committee by the General Staff through Secretary of War Jacob M.

---

[31] Memo, Garlington to CofS, WD, 16 May 08, Entry 24, RG 159, NARA.

[32] Memo, Bell to SofW, 29 Nov 09, sub: The Incorporation Into the General Staff Corps of the Adjutant General's and the Inspector General's Departments, 29 Nov 09, Entry 296, RG 165, NARA.

[33] Memo, Garlington to President's Cleveland Commission [Committee on Economy and Efficiency, 1911], Entry 22, RG 159, NARA.

Dickinson. The bill proposed merging the two departments with the office of the Chief of Staff, making them a bureau and a part of the General Staff Corps. Secretary Dickinson favored this on the premise that it would result in greater efficiency by reducing personnel and costs. The plan called for the assignment of the permanent AGD and IGD members to the new bureau and the return of all those on detail to the line.[34]

Fortunately, the proposal had enemies in high places. General Wood opposed the measure, which he saw as contrary to the intent of the 1903 law creating the General Staff. Congressman James Hay, chairman of the committee and a friend of Adjutant General Ainsworth, also felt that many of the tasks performed by both departments exceeded the planning and supervision role to be played by the General Staff. New statutes, altering the missions envisioned by Secretary Root, would have been necessary. Yet the bill remained under consideration for some time, obliging General Garlington to justify his department once again. He pointed out that statutory and regulatory inspection requirements made it necessary to assign twenty-one officers, regardless of where the inspection function was placed. Passage of the bill would neither reduce the demands on the line for details nor alter the mechanics of the tasks.

An inspection service, to be of any value, had to be independent, according to Inspector General Garlington, because the Secretary of War needed an unbiased view of the Army. "In other words, the inspector making the report should be entirely independent of the men or element reported upon." Garlington believed that such a principle prevailed both in civil business and in some form in other armies. The same should hold for the General Staff. He concluded with the recommendation that the General Staff should concentrate on the higher issues for which it was created, rather than concerning itself with minor structural arrangements within the War Department. In the face of many objections, the consolidation bill faded away, in part because the crisis with The Adjutant General was climaxing at this time, overshadowing other concerns of Hay's committee while bringing the Chief of Staff and the Inspector General closer.[35]

---

[34] Ltr, Dickinson to Chair, Mil Affs Cmte, HofReps, 20 May 11, Entry 5, RG 165, NARA; U.S. Congress, House, Committee on Military Affairs, *Hearing on Staff Service of the Army, Terms of Enlistment in the Army, General Service Corps in the Army, Consolidation of Certain Branches of the War Department and the Army*, 62d Cong., 1st Sess., 1911.

[35] Memo, Garlington to CofS, WD, 6 May 12, Entry 24, RG 159, NARA.

This did not mean that General Garlington could lower his guard. A committee on the General Staff had been studying the lessons of the 1911 mobilization. The eventual result of its efforts was a detailed report, "The Organization of the Land Forces of the United States." Among many other structural changes, the report contained the perennial recommendation that The Adjutant General's Department and the Inspector General's Department be merged with the General Staff. The committee considered inspection as more appropriate to Staff planning. It recommended that military inspections be made by the Chief of Staff or subordinate commanders and routine inspections by General Staff officers or expert accountants. The strength of the General Staff would be increased permanently by direct transfer of IGD personnel and authorizations. Perhaps secure in the support of General Wood, Garlington told his staff not to be unduly concerned. Reaction to the report eventually led to several reforms in the field forces, but no major changes took place in the War Department staff structure.[36]

Despite the repeated failures of the consolidation attempts, the General Staff forwarded still another bill to Congress in February 1914. The new proposal would have appointed all permanent AGD and IGD officers to a specialist corps in the line Army. Positions in the former bureaus would be filled by General Staff detail. Reaction to the proposal was negative throughout the Army, because of the effect the movement of senior officers into the line would have had on promotions.[37] Yet the issue refused to die. Consolidation was considered during discussions in late 1915 that ultimately led to the National Defense Act of 1916. Again, the increasingly close relationship between the Chief of Staff and the Inspector General not only assured the continued existence of the Inspector General's Department but also provided for its growth under legislation enacted the next year. The inspectorate had proven its value—and much of that value rested precisely upon its independence.

The Army in the Field

The ultimate objective of many of General Wood's reforms was the development and training of large tactical units, composed of all arms and services. A series of tactical exercises began during the tenure of

---

[36] "The Organization of the Land Forces of the United States," 3 Jul 12, IG copy in Entry 24, RG 159, NARA; Charles D. McKenna, "The Forgotten Reform: Field Maneuvers in the Development of the United States Army, 1902–1920" (Ph.D. diss., Duke University, 1981), pp. 148–50.

[37] Ltr, Chamberlain to Garlington, 18 Feb 14, Entry 24, RG 159, NARA.

Troop E, 6th Cavalry, Standing for Inspection at Fort Riley, Kansas, in 1906

Secretary Root, the first in 1902 at Fort Riley, Kansas, where Col. Stephen C. Mills served as IG of the new maneuver division.[38] Limited often by funding, the maneuvers became a regular feature of the training cycle by 1909 and included elements of the National Guard. At each exercise inspectors identified weaknesses and codified remedies.

By 1910 the General Staff had developed a plan for a field army, combining both Regular Army and National Guard elements. The plan remained theoretical that year, for funds were not available to test it. But political turbulence endangering American interests, both in Mexico and along the border it shared with the United States, prompted the mobilization in March 1911 of a so-called field maneuver division, to be concentrated in the San Antonio area. This action marked the first effort to create a division-size tactical unit, a product of the concepts and lessons learned that were recorded since 1902. Under the leadership of Maj. Gen. William H. Carter, the troops embarked upon an extended training program until August, when the division was disbanded.[39]

---

[38] McKenna, "Forgotten Reform," Ph.D. diss., pp. 62–64.

[39] William A. Ganoe, *The History of the United States Army* (New York: D. Appleton and Co., 1924), pp. 434, 437, 439, 443; Clarence C. Clendenen, *Blood on the Border: The United States Army and the Mexican Irregulars* (London: Collier-Macmillan, 1969), pp. 146–50; Memo, CoS, WD, to IG, Jan 11, sub: Emergency Supply Depots, Roll 12, Microfilm 912, Indexes to War College Division Records, RG 165, NARA.

The Office of the Inspector General reported comprehensively on the mobilization. Lt. Col. George Bell, Jr., was assigned as IG of the maneuver division. He was assisted in the inspection of field artillery units by Maj. William Lassiter for the first two months and later by Lt. Col. James B. Erwin, who also covered the separate cavalry brigade for the last month of the exercise. Bell observed everything he could until the division was disbanded. Additionally, he continued to make inspections of disbursing accounts and condemned unserviceable property whenever required. Although no formal unit inspections were made, Bell paid numerous informal visits to division elements in camp and on the march. He noted not only unit performance but also problems of organization and equipment.

Many of his conclusions were necessarily tentative because of the novelty of the situation. Senior officers were for the first time dealing with units of such size. Most of the regiments arrived at half strength and spent their time assimilating an influx of recruits while conducting basic training. The resulting paperwork caused many line officers to conclude that excessive administration was one of the greatest detriments to progress. One commander estimated that from orderly room to War Department, each soldier was accounted for nineteen times before his status was finalized in The Adjutant General's records.[40]

Colonel Bell noted the negative effects of bringing in large numbers of recruits to raise units to war strength. He estimated that unit efficiency actually declined despite the increase in personnel. Bell further cited problems in strategic rail transportation, which delayed bringing some units to the mobilization sites for several weeks after being alerted. For example, bids had to be let in most cases before transportation arrangements were implemented. He also joined commanders in criticizing the elaborate administrative requirements imposed on the supply system. He recommended that all administrative procedures be simplified and made the same for peace and war. Bell further discussed issues in personnel and artillery training, which he believed adversely affected tactical readiness.[41]

General Carter, founding genius of the General Staff and no friend of the inspectorate, did not receive Bell's report with grace. He forwarded the report, citing Bell as earnest and industrious but also as one whose "mental processes tend to magnify unimportant matters into affairs of magnitude." Despite Carter's lack of enthusiasm, many

---

[40] Arthur Ruhl, "What Is the Matter With the U.S. Army?" *Collier's Magazine,* 15 Apr 11, pp. 17, 39–41.

[41] Ltr Rpt, Bell to Maneuver Div Adj, 6 Jul 11, Entry 26, RG 112, NARA.

of Bell's recommendations were adopted, especially those pertaining to the structure of medical organizations. (He especially praised the high quality of field sanitation, but suggested that the Medical Department should consider motorizing its ambulance service.) The problems he found, such as equipment variations amongst similar units and the need for better infantry training and physical conditioning, were treated seriously when brought up to the War Department. His report remains a balanced overview of the operations and problems of the maneuver division, and provided part of the substance for further changes and reforms.[42]

In 1912 the General Staff prepared an organization scheme for field armies. In case of full mobilization a large force was contemplated, consisting of four field armies of three divisions each, with two divisions in reserve. Each division would have an inspector general (lieutenant colonel), while each army would have an inspector general (colonel) and an assistant inspector (major). Inspectors were identified for service in the first field army and its elements, and a total of twenty-six more were to be authorized automatically if the units were activated. In this way, the principle recommended in 1898 by Inspector General Breckinridge—automatically authorizing at least one inspector for each senior general officer command at its activation—became established as a matter of policy.[43]

A board of officers, headed by Secretary Stimson, created the necessary divisions and component brigades. As a result, in 1913, the peacetime structure of the Army was again reorganized, this time into four large geographical departments in the United States, plus one each in the Philippines and Hawaii. Department boundaries were adjusted so that each included the units that would form a single tactical division, an effort to compensate for the scattering of forces over twenty-four states in forty-nine posts, with an average strength of 700 men.[44]

In February of that year a second concentration of troops took place along the Mexican order. It was a smooth operation by comparison with its predecessor in 1911, but problems still were noted. Although all the units assembled without difficulty, many were understrength and ineffective, the result of low manning authorizations imposed by a budget-conscious Congress as well as problems in the prevalent recruiting and reserve systems. Although horses and mules to move the field army

---

[42] Ibid. and End (quotation); *ARIG 1911*, p. 268; Ltr, SG Torney to TAG, 31 Aug 11, Entry 26, RG 112, NARA.

[43] Ltr, Mills to IG, 25 Mar 12, and Reply, same date, Entry 296, RG 165, NARA.

[44] Ganoe, *History*, pp. 444–45.

were in short supply, there were too few men available to care for those on hand.

The situation made the inspectorate one of the strongest advocates of motorization. General Garlington noted the experimental use of a truck and some motorcycles in 1911, saying they had fully proven their value. Other inspectors added their recommendations, urging that the Army replace wagons with motor vehicles to the maximum extent. The growing difficulty in procuring satisfactory horses further justified the change. These recommendations provided the necessary impetus for the Quartermaster General to begin serious testing to produce a suitable truck. By the time of the 1913 mobilization, motor vehicles had become a significant part of the Army's transportation system. Inspectors continued to push for similar improvements, such as motor ambulances and mobile kitchens, after each major field problem.[45]

The General Staff slowly began to appreciate the value of the inspectorate in the mobilization process. Indeed, the work of the inspectors had made them indispensable. One result, however, was that the planners proposed curtailing several of the traditional regulatory IG duties, such as inspections of condemned property, to allow more time for unit inspections. General Garlington, ever alert to any challenge to the scope of the Inspector General's authority, successfully warded off such proposals, arguing that procedures should not be changed because of unique temporary demands.[46]

While clinging to old duties, however, the Office of the Inspector General failed to specify the duties of tactical unit inspectors. At the time of the troop concentrations on the Mexican border in 1913 and during the occupation of Vera Cruz in 1914, the OIG had developed few guidelines or instructions for the inspectors with the field organizations. Hence, inspectors assigned to the new units were forced to develop their own methods of operation. They combined their traditional duties, such as inspecting money accounts, with an increased stress on evaluating the proficiency, or readiness, of their units.[47]

The intense activity along the Mexican border taxed the limited resources of the small IG office of the Southern Department, from

---

[45] *ARIG 1913*, p. 279; *ARIG 1916*, p. 304; James A. Huston, *The Sinews of War: Army Logistics, 1775–1953* (Washington D.C.: Office of the Chief of Military History, United States Army, 1966), p. 298.

[46] Memo, Hodges to Chief, War College Div, WDGS, 16 Feb 14, Entry 296, RG 165, NARA.

[47] Helmick, "Autobiography," MHI; *ARIG 1914*, p. 197.

which most of the tactical unit inspectors were drawn. The inspectors, who were few in number compared to the volume of their commitments and tasks, were almost continually out of the headquarters, which prevented them from developing a close relationship with the department commander. The situation was so demanding that the two department inspectors and their detailed assistants were always on the road, returning only to file their reports and then leave again. As a result, they often were not sufficiently familiar with the commander's views and policies, either to represent him properly or to present uniform standards throughout the department. Inspectors would encounter some situation in the field that seemed improper and file lengthy reports; however, their recommendations would be impracticable because higher headquarters had issued orders of which they were unaware or because the larger tactical situation was unknown to them.[48]

When Brig. Gen. Tasker H. Bliss became the Southern Department commander, he concluded that his inspectors were necessary to his command success but that they were too overworked to be fully effective. Hence, he suggested to General Garlington that IG officer strengths be increased so that an inspector could always be available at the headquarters. This way the commander would have a channel to issue new information to the traveling inspectors while also having an IG present for special inquiries.[49] Such requests by Bliss and other general officers helped keep the inspectorate intact and growing as the Army entered the final major reorganization before the World War.

The National Defense Act

Two crises the sinking of the steamship *Lusitania* by a German submarine, and continued unrest in Mexico—prompted President Wilson in July 1915 to request that more thorough military preparedness plans be developed. The War College Division of the General Staff already had worked on preparing contingency plans, which envisioned a large increase in the size of the Regular Army and the virtual elimination of the National Guard in favor of a federally controlled "Continental Army" reserve of 400,000 men. Secretary of War Lindley M. Garrison concurred in the proposal but ran into opposition in Congressman Hay's Military Affairs Committee. Hay objected to the dissolution of the

---

[48] Ltr, Bliss to Garlington, 10 Sep 14, Entry 35, RG 159, NARA.
[49] Ibid.

National Guard and believed that a legal basis existed for establishing complete federal control over the Guard in an emergency.[50]

Chairman Hay offered a counterplan that left the Guard as the mainstay of any emergency Army expansion. President Wilson ultimately accepted Hay's plan when it became apparent that the Military Affairs Committee was adamantly opposed to the Continental Army scheme. Secretary Garrison, in fact, had become so closely associated with the Continental Army idea that he resigned on 10 February 1916, and was replaced on 7 March by Newton D. Baker. The House approved Hay's plan on 23 March and it went to the Senate. There for a time the War College Division proposal seemed to be favored. However, a compromise bill emerged in May and was approved by the President on 3 June as the National Defense Act of 1916.[51]

Even during the months of debate it became evident that, regardless of the plan adopted, the Regular Army would undergo a major expansion. Hay's bill contemplated a substantial increase in line strength and an overage of 1,000 officers for duty on staffs, as instructors, and in other nonregimental slots. The Secretary of War's office sent a confidential memorandum to the bureau chiefs in October 1915, asking them to translate the bill's implications into specific manpower needs. General Garlington replied that, assuming only the increase in units with no territorial changes, his department would need five officers to fill inspection positions in new units—a departmental strength increase to twenty-six officers. It was the Inspector General's view that in wartime the character of IG duties would not change, only the volume.[52]

The passage of the National Defense Act as well as events in Mexico dominated the inspectorate's development up to the declaration of war with Germany in April 1917. The act provided for the expansion of the Regular Army from an average strength of 65,000 to 175,000 over a five-year period, its increase nearly doubling annually until the ceiling was reached. An organized reserve was authorized, and the Regular

---

[50] Arthur S. Link, *Woodrow Wilson and the Progressive Era, 1910–1917* (New York: Harper and Row, 1963), pp. 179–88.

[51] George C. Herring, Jr., "James Hay and the Preparedness Controversy, 1915–1916," *Journal of Southern History* 25 (Nov 64): 383–402.

[52] Memos, Breckinridge [Acting SofW] to Bureau Chiefs, 12 Oct 15, sub: Increase in Personnel, Commissioned and Enlisted, of Staff Departments; Garlington to Acting SofW, 14 Oct 15, sub: Increase in Personnel of the Inspector General's Department in Connection With Revision of Army Reorganization Act, etc.; and TAG to IG, 3 Nov 15, sub: War Department Organization and Administration. All in Entry 25, RG 159, NARA. See also Memo, Brewster to TAG, 5 Nov 15, sub: Organization and Administration of the IGD, Entry 296, RG 165, NARA.

Army was organized into tactical divisions and brigades. The National Guard was thoroughly integrated into a federal defense structure and authorized to expand over the five-year period to a ceiling of 425,000 men. The Guard was made subject to much closer federal control and scrutiny through a requirement for periodic IGD inspections. The act created the Reserve Officers Training Corps (ROTC) Program, as well as provided for volunteer civilian training camps patterned on a system begun by General Wood at Plattsburg Barracks, New York, in 1915.[53]

The Inspector General's Department was affected by the act in many different ways. The mere fact that it survived intact and with expanded responsibilities precluded further substantial General Staff sniping for the foreseeable future. The first and most obvious consequence of the law was a rise in authorized strength. Twelve new active-duty authorizations over five years were specified, bringing the department's strength to a maximum of thirty-three inspectors. The act also provided for an IG Reserve Corps of sixteen majors, who were required to be "of good character" and under forty-five years of age, with at least one year of active service and "sound" civilian experience. Each of the thirteen tactical divisions envisaged would be assigned an IG officer in the rank of major; higher commands, more senior officers. Within a month The Adjutant General was soliciting names for these positions.[54]

In August 1916, because of the rapid increase in IG strength, the Office of the Inspector General hired six civilian clerks, raising the number to thirteen, plus the three messengers and the expert accountant already on board. The act also prevented General Staff officers from inspecting schools with military detachments. The job of doing so reverted to the Inspector General's Department at a time when the creation of ROTC added to the number of schools requiring inspection. Every aspect of the National Guard required inspection. At General Garlington's suggestion, the accounts and records of disbursing in each state also had to be inspected annually. Citizen training camps were totally new organizations also needing careful inspection.[55]

The sudden demand for inspectors had to be met by temporary details until the number of permanent inspectors could be increased.

[53] Ganoe, *History*, p. 456; Link, *Woodrow Wilon*, p. 188.

[54] *ARIG 1916*, p. 295 (quoted words); Ltr, TAG to IG, 5 Jul 16, sub: Formation of Divisions, and Reply, 6 Jul 16, Entry 25, RG 159, NARA.

[55] Ltr, Brewster to Chief Clerk, WD, 28 Aug 16, and Memos, Garlington to TAG, 11 Jan 17, sub: History of the IGD for CY 1916; TAG to Dept Cdrs, 16 Dec 16, sub: Inspection of Records and Accounts of Property and Disbursing Officers; and Brewster to Garlington, 20 Jun 16, sub: Effect of Act Approved June 3, 1916, Upon IGD. All in Entry 26, RG 159, NARA. See also *ARIG 1916*, p. 295.

*Inspecting Battery C, 10th Connecticut Field Artillery, at Tobyhanna,
Pennsylvania, During the Mexican Border Crisis*

The situation became more urgent in light of a full-scale mobilization
going on along the Mexican border, concurrent with the passage of the
act. The rapid growth of large provisional units in the Southwest caused
local commanders to appoint their own inspectors without notifying the
Inspector General. Although their ad hoc action indicated a high regard
for inspection, it threatened IG standards and violated approved procedures. General Garlington moved quickly to curtail the practice by having a directive from the Secretary of War issued to all department commanders forbidding such appointments. As a result, commanders uni-
laterally could appoint an inspector only for the emergency destruction
of property. At the same time, the appointment of approved inspectors
was speeded up.[56]

Planning for expansion of the Inspector General's Department continued because of the provisions for a reserve in the National Defense
Act. Lawmakers envisioned the eventual training of a half-million men
annually, creating a pool of three million reservists. When such a pro-

---

[56] Memo, IG to TAG, 30 Oct 16; Ltr, SofW to Dept Cdrs, 7 Nov 16. Both in Entry
25, RG 159, NARA.

gram was realized, Inspector General Garlington determined that OIG personnel strength would need to be increased by six officers to support the thirteen who would be in the field with units. But the immediate demands of the field increasingly dominated his department's time. Even while the final expansion plans were being made, the inspectorate already had been involved in supporting serious operations along the Mexican border for over six months.

The Punitive Expedition

The continuing problems along the Mexican Border climaxed on 1 March 1916, when the town of Columbus, New Mexico, was raided by Mexican irregulars led by Pancho Villa, an opponent of the recognized government headed by Venustiano Carranza. Villa or his group had committed earlier hostile acts against Americans, apparently in the hope that U.S. intervention would bring down the Carranza government. American intervention did indeed result from the attack on Columbus, but mostly to the disadvantage of Villa.

Reaction to the raid itself by Columbus' 13th Cavalry garrison had been unexpectedly vigorous, and the Villistas lost an estimated 100 men. On 15 March Brig. Gen. John J. Pershing's Punitive Expedition, consisting of one infantry and two cavalry brigades, crossed into Mexico in pursuit. Pershing established his rear base at Columbus, with a forward base at Dublan in the Mexican state of Chihuahua. From the forward base, Pershing sent out a series of cavalry columns that slowly eroded the strength of the Villista bands in the course of a series of sharp engagements.

Beginning about June 1916, Pershing shifted his strategy by dividing his limited operational area into districts, each combed by a force of regimental size. By that time the last elements of the Regular Army mobile forces had been called to the border because of the growing hostility of the Carranza government over the presence of U.S. troops on its soil, and President Wilson had federalized the National Guards of Texas, Arizona, and New Mexico. The growing possibility of war with Mexico caused the President to call out most of the rest of the National Guard on 18 June, about two weeks after the newly signed National Defense Act authorized the move.

While most U.S. troop activities in Mexico were limited to patrols and vigorous training, an outnumbered force from the 10th Cavalry was defeated by Carranza troops at Carrizal on 21 June. The battle shocked both sides into seeking a peaceful solution, and all American units were withdrawn peacefully by 5 February 1917. Although the politico-military value of the expedition is still debated, the invaluable experience and training gained by senior officers and commanders in the Regular Army and National Guard alike is not. Among them, the inspectors who worked on both sides of the border learned important lessons while providing essential information, assistance, and evaluation to all participating units and staffs.[57]

Because of its provisional nature and the speed with which it had been constituted, the Punitive Expedition initially lacked an inspector general. Col. Lucien C. Berry was named acting inspector in the general order organizing the expedition and later, after he assumed command of the 4th Field Artillery, was replaced by Lt. Col. Henry T. Allen. In the meantime, General Garlington recommended that an IG be detailed to Pershing's command because of its size and importance. As a consequence, Lt. Col. George O. Cress, a cavalryman serving as IG of the Central Department, was sent on temporary duty to the Southern Department. There, General Frederick Funston, the department commander, assigned Cress to Pershing's headquarters, and he joined the expedition at Dublan on 15 June.[58]

One of Cress' first tasks was to investigate the battle at Carrizal, which occurred just after his arrival. Two troops from the 10th Cavalry, under the command of Capt. Charles T. Boyd, had attempted a frontal assault against a much larger entrenched Mexican force. After inflicting heavy losses on the Mexicans, the Americans were repulsed with many casualties of their own; Captain Boyd was among those killed. As his investigation developed, Colonel Cress noted several less than creditable acts by some of the fight's survivors. He also concluded that Boyd, although courageous, had stretched his orders and used bad tactical judgment. Sensing that various reputations might suffer, he wrote General Garlington, asking for guidance in case he should find someone's conduct discreditable. Garlington promptly replied in a long encouraging letter, telling Cress to discover the unvarnished facts. "The facts developed will point to your conclusions and recommendations." Doing so was the only way to be fair to the individuals and the rest of the Army.[59]

---

[57] Punitive Expedition summary based on versions in Clendenen, *Blood on the Border*, and Frank Tompkins, *Chasing Villa: The Story Behind the Story of Pershing's Expedition Into Mexico*, (Harrisburg, Pa.: Military Service Publishing Co., 1934).

[58] Ltr, Garlington to Cress, 17 May 16, and End, Garlington to TAG, 14 Jun 16, Entry 25, RG 159, NARA; Telg, Bundy to Pershing, 15 Jun 16, Entry 1187, RG 394, NARA. See also Tompkins, *Chasing Villa*, pp. 72, 257.

[59] Rpt, Cress, Aug 16, sub: Investigation of Encounter Between American and Mexican De Facto Government Forces at Carrizal, Mexico, June 21, 1916, and End (quotation), Garlington to CofS, WD, [Sep 16], Entry 25, RG 159, NARA.

Encouraged, Cress went on to produce a thorough report. He interviewed seventy-four persons, producing a 66-page narrative that realistically described what had occurred. He concluded that Boyd had exceeded his instructions and underestimated the danger of his situation. Believing the 10th Cavalry troops had fought as well as the odds allowed, he recommended no further action. His findings paralleled and corroborated the versions of other participants on both sides. The report moved through channels with little comment, and General Garlington passed it to the Secretary of War after analyzing some tactical lessons. The United States and Mexico had been at their closest point to war as a result of Carrizal, and the incident had made such an impression on President Wilson that he kept a copy of the report among his private papers.[60]

The bulk of Cress' duties were much more prosaic, but valuable in their own way. General Pershing was a strong advocate of inspection in all its forms, using his aides as his tactical eyes and ears. While he roved between elements of his force in a small motor cavalcade, he would send one or two of his aides to other places of interest or concern. The aides had the authority to give orders in his name. The inspector and the assistants periodically assigned to him were used in a similar fashion for support and logistical activities. In this way, Pershing was able to impose his direction and standards on all of his scattered command.[61]

It was routine for a vigorous program of inspection to be carried out by each of Pershing's principal staff officers in their areas of responsibility. Their findings were given to the expedition's chief of staff, who summarized and tabulated them for Pershing's use. While the staff officers looked at elements germane to their functions, such as pack trains or medical aid stations, the IG reviewed the entire command, with an emphasis on personal clothing and equipment and the care and condition of the livestock. From 20 August to 6 September Colonel Cress inspected all the units and locations within the expedition. His inspection was subjective, detailed, and unanalytical. He also continued to inspect unit funds and disbursing accounts on a regular basis. His remarks were general on the funds; apparently, he made all the minor corrections needed without listing them. Pershing himself conducted regularly scheduled command inspections, accompanied by members of his staff. On these occasions Colonel Cress, with his

---

[60] Link, *Woodrow Wilson*, p. 142.
[61] Tompkins, *Chasing Villa*, p. 156.

branch background, performed as the cavalry inspector. Weekly full inspections were made at Dublan, and Pershing directed subordinates elsewhere to make frequent inspections of their units. After each command inspection any deficiencies were reported by letter to the commanders, who were not required to respond because any failure to take corrective action would be detected in ensuing inspections.[62]

Garlington and Cress maintained an extensive formal and informal correspondence throughout the period of the Punitive Expedition's existence. Cress had only recently been detailed to the Inspector General's Department and lacked an experienced clerk to help him. Consequently, his primary concerns had to do with meeting regulatory requirements, such as funds and property inspections, and reporting them properly. Garlington told him not to be unduly concerned about such things, but rather to concentrate on improving the expedition's efficiency. Hence, Cress circulated continually between his headquarters at Columbus and the town of El Valle, Chihuahua, 176 miles away—by October the farthest outpost of the expedition. The road conditions were such that the trip took four days, despite the best efforts of the engineers. By making these exhausting treks, Cress was able to observe equipment in action, talk with the troops, sometimes prevent waste, and gather invaluable data on equipment and operations.[63]

A large part of the inspector's time was spent in evaluating equipment and assessing field maintenance operations. A great number of new items had been developed since the War with Spain, and the expedition provided a rare opportunity to test them under extended use in demanding field conditions. By September 1916 Cress had produced a detailed analysis of most of the equipment used, along with recommendations for changes in operations and support plans. He divided his report under topics pertaining to command issues and to each of the bureaus.[64] He commented on each item of clothing and personal equipment about which he had received a complaint; noted such minor matters as the need for hip pockets on field trousers, a modification later agreed to by the Quartermaster General; and pointed out that the snaps on the ammunition pouches were so tight that often the pouches could not be opened, which was unacceptable in combat and resulted in Ordnance Department testing to find a more suitable fastener. Everyone Cress inspected stated that the model 1912 cavalry equip-

---

[62] Punitive Expedition to Mexico Reports/Inspection File, Entry 1202, RG 394, NARA.

[63] Ltr, Cress to Garlington, 23 Oct 16, Entry 25, RG 159, NARA.

[64] Rpt, Cress to TAG (thru channels, 35 ends.), 16 Sep 16, Entry 25, RG 159, NARA.

ment was a disaster and no improvement over previous designs. Later a cavalry board was convened for the purpose of reviewing and correcting the problems. As a matter of interest, Cress reported that the cavalry units had left their sabers in storage at home. The general view was that they should be eliminated, with no more time wasted on training the troops to use such edged weapons.

Cress' report also treated major items of equipment and logistical procedures. He favored the use of the so-called rolling kitchens, on the grounds that they greatly enhanced the comfort and convenience of the troops. At the same time, he pointed out some design defects in existing equipment, which tended to confirm observations from other sources and precipitated further Ordnance Department testing to develop a better design. The inspector recommended adopting the repair and maintenance system developed during the expedition—forward support teams and light repair shops moving with or near the combat units—as an Army-wide standard. These forward maintenance elements were backed up by full service shops in the base areas, which were capable of performing major overhauls. The system was found to be responsive to immediate needs, keeping more material out of the pipeline and in the hands of the users. The Quartermaster General favored Cress' recommendation and later began inquiries to determine the personnel composition of the forward teams so that an appropriate table of organization and equipment could be issued.

Colonel Cress echoed his predecessor, Colonel Bell, in concluding that supply paperwork was too complex, a conclusion also reached simultaneously by his colleagues inspecting National Guard units. He urged that inspection reports or surveys be used as transfer documents at depots and that no further accountability be required. He viewed the existing supply system as functioning properly only in peacetime, when each supply officer could be near the organization requiring equipment. Field conditions prevented this, and Cress suggested a more flexible bulk issue to units whose own supply personnel would determine distribution. General Pershing agreed, saying that all peacetime systems should work unchanged in wartime or be replaced by ones that would.

A classic example of the existing system's inflexibility could be seen in the Quartermaster General's repeated queries about the disposition of the hides of government cattle. Livestock were purchased locally in the wilds of Chihuahua for immediate consumption. Normal procedure at an Army post would be to preserve the hides of slaughtered cattle and to sell them to the highest bidder within ten days. To follow this procedure in Mexico was absurd, indeed impossible, and yet bureaucrats demanded a documented explanation for each departure from normal procedure. This sort of red tape was often so harassing that many officers preferred to use their own money to feed their units. A board convened to consider the problem somewhat reduced the tight accountability requirements, but still did not go so far as Colonel Cress wished.[65]

Numerous other matters addressed by the inspection report set precedents that endured for years. For example, the War Department approved Pershing's and Cress' suggestion that officers wear their rank insignia on one collar and branch insignia on the other collar of their work shirts. Cress also proposed that vehicle drivers and other technicians not be given NCO rank, but rather special ranks of their own, with the aim of upholding the prestige of the sergeants and corporals in the line. All in all, the extensive report that emerged from the Punitive Expedition had a positive effect on many aspects of policy and logistical support, providing a stimulus for change at a critical time and proving beneficial to planners in the early phases of 1917 wartime mobilization.[66]

It also provided welcome support for an unexpected requirement imposed on the Office of the Inspector General by the Secretary of War. On 21 July 1916 Baker asked General Garlington to be the focal point for statistics concerning the operations in Mexico and along the border, requiring that his office coordinate with the chiefs of the supply corps and departments to document expenditures incurred by the Punitive Expedition and related border operations. As the project evolved, all supply elements forwarded monthly reports to the OIG, which consolidated them for the Secretary's use. The final report differentiated between National Guard and Regular Army expenditures, providing special detail on costs involving motor vehicles and aircraft.[67]

The observation of the logistical and tactical operations was the major part of the inspector's duties. But some time was also spent in investigating complaints and matters of special interest. A few complaints came from civilians concerning property destruction. The majority, however, dealt with military matters, most of which could be classified as leadership issues. The following two cases were typical. During his time as the expedition inspector, Colonel Allen investigated a problem arising essentially from a personality conflict between a battery commander and one of his lieutenants. The solution was to reassign the lieutenant and to counsel the captain on self-control. Meanwhile, Colonel Cress investigated a more serious case of miscon-

---

[65] Tompkins, *Chasing Villa*, pp. 147–48.

[66] Rpt, Cress to TAG, 16 Sep 16, Entry 25, RG 159, NARA.

[67] Ltr, TAG to IG, 21 Jul 16; Rpt, OIG, 25 Jul 16, sub: Record of Expenditures. Both in Entry 25, RG 159, NARA.

duct in response to a soldier's complaint of improper treatment. He found that a group of officers who had been drinking roughed up the soldier for no other reason than that he happened to be passing by. The officers involved were relieved and court-martialed.[68]

In a case with wider implications, General Garlington himself successfully defended Army personnel who were under political attack. New Mexico Senator Albert B. Fall claimed that poor leadership and faulty equipment had increased the vulnerability of the town of Columbus to Villa's attack. Garlington supervised the investigation and found that, on the contrary, the garrison commander, Col. Henry J. Slocum, had done all that could be expected. The Inspector General analyzed Slocum's report in light of his mission and concluded that his patrol plans and interior guard system represented sound procedures. He praised the rapid assembly and aggressive reaction of Slocum's 13th Cavalry as signs of good leadership, discipline, and training. Newspaper allegations against the machine-gun officer, Lt. John P. Lucas, were similarly shown to be without foundation. Garlington recommended that the defenders of Columbus be commended for their vigorous defense of the town.[69]

Some investigations of narrow issues proved in the long run to have benefits for the entire command. In October Colonel Cress investigated soldiers' complaints about unfair treatment while on truck train, or convoy, duty. His examination of the problems led Cress to observe that no standard policy for the operation of convoys existed; each was run on the whim of its particular commander. The inspector recommended the adoption of a uniform standard to assure efficiency and fairness for the guards and drivers, and Pershing agreed. He directed that unsafe practices be halted and required the rear base commander to evolve a standard policy to establish responsibilities for convoy procedures and roadside camp administration. Greater overall operational efficiency resulted from an initially narrow complaint investigation.[70]

---

[68] Rpt, Allen to CG, Pun Exp, 19 Jun 16, sub: Investigation of Mutual Complaint Against Capt. Edgar C. Yule and 1/Lt. C. P. George; Ltr, CO, 4th FA, to CofS, Pun Exp, 7 Dec 16, sub: In the Matter of the Complaint of Private Eliace M. Buzzard, Supply Co., 4th F. A.; Memo, Div Insp, n.d., sub: Reference Complaint of Private Buzzard, 4th FA. All in Entry 1187, RG 394, NARA.

[69] Tompkins, *Chasing Villa*, pp. 61–64; Garlington Remarks on Rpt, Slocum, 11 Mar 16, sub: Border Conditions, Entry 25, RG 159, NARA.

[70] Rpt, Cress to CG, Pun Exp, 29 Oct 16, sub: Investigation of Complaints Made by Members of Guards on Truck Train No. 63; Proceedings of a Board of Offs Convened at Base of Comm, Columbus, N.Mex., 2 Nov 16; Hq Base of Comm GO 33, 4 Nov 16. All in Entry 1187, RG 394, NARA.

Cress' useful work and the seriousness with which General Pershing viewed inspection set a precedent for the larger challenges about to be presented by the World War. The situation in the Punitive Expedition also exemplified the solid position enjoyed by the inspectorate after nearly fifteen years of adjustment to the changes begun at the start of the century. At the working level, in the field, these changes had had relatively little effect. Inspectors, detailed or permanent, continued to inspect, investigate, and perform special missions for their commanders. At the War Department level, however, the inspectorate had to adjust to pressures exerted by the Chief of Staff and the General Staff. This entailed, in part, the Inspector General having to defend the inspectorate and its independence repeatedly against the efforts of some zealous General Staff members who wanted to absorb the inspection function completely.

This hostility, however, was not reflected in the field, where most commanders appreciated a good inspector. The value and uses of an inspectorate in the presence of strong leaders was underlined once again during this era. General Wood used the inspectors as his enforcers and evaluators to ensure that his policies were being implemented. Pershing also used the inspectors to set standards for his command. In each case the IG served as the eyes and ears of his general, and in so doing acquired extensive influence. But measuring the effect of the Inspector General's Department requires a more detailed look at the inspections and investigations made between the War with Spain and World War I and their impact on the higher-level changes and reforms of that era.

2

Shaping the New Army

The inspectorate's role—enforcing the directives of War Department reformers and evaluating the results in inspection reports—evolved gradually. At the same time, the needs of commanders in the new Army structure had to be defined, the quality of units evaluated, and the safety and comfort of the men safeguarded and, where possible, improved. Army property also had to be regulated by tougher standards of efficiency. In these areas policy and practice developed together, the former often growing out of specific problems encountered in the latter.

Inspection Reports

With the establishment of the General Staff, Army regulations were revised both to clarify the relationship of inspectors to field commanders and to define the jurisdiction of the Washington inspection office. Unless otherwise instructed by the Secretary of War, inspectors assigned to the geographical commands continued to work exclusively for their commanders, to whom they submitted their inspection reports. The commanders could hold these reports as long as necessary but eventually had to retire them through channels to the Office of the Inspector General (OIG). When appropriate, the OIG forwarded the inspection reports to the Chief of Staff, recommending that the bureau in question be notified of the problem areas to be corrected.

At times, this flow of information was modified by the Inspector General himself. For example, General Burton personally notified the Chief of Engineers of problems encountered in the Corps of Engineers, forwarding the inspection reports to the Chief of Staff only after the corps had taken remedial action. Burton told his staff that special handling was necessary because of the Chief of Engineers' sensitivity to criticism. General Garlington, on the other hand, denied the less powerful Chief of Ordnance similar early notice. In July 1909 the Chief of Ordnance demanded that he be considered an intermediate commander in the routing of arsenal and depot reports and statements of remedial action. For a few months Garlington allowed depot reports to go through the Chief of Ordnance, but in September returned to the regular process, holding a report until a remedial action report was received from the inspected unit.[1]

The General Staff was barred from interfering in the inspection of excluded activities, such as depots and hospitals. Inspectors for these units were nominated by the Inspector General to the Secretary of War. The senior inspector himself, or a subordinate OIG officer, was to inspect geographical commands, civilian and military schools, and the U.S. Military Academy. The suzerainty of the Chief of Staff was recognized with the requirement that the Office of the Inspector General prepare an annual inspection plan, for review by the Chief of Staff and for approval by the Secretary of War. By the summer of 1903 the principles had been agreed to. One final change, made in November, provided that orders to inspectors be given by letter, rather than being published as had been the custom in the past. The change was intended to reduce the possibility of advance notice, allowing units to be seen "under normal circumstances."[2]

The monitoring and control of actions derived from the inspection reports were among the OIG's principal functions. Inspection reports before World War I rarely dealt with broad aspects of mission accomplishment, unless that topic was the purpose of the inspection. For the most part, the reports were factual, listing each specific irregularity noted in the conduct and appearance of personnel and in the condition of equipment and facilities. General Burton directed inspectors to stop following standard formats soon after he became senior inspector. Rather, they were to use notebooks, recording whatever they thought was important under broad topical headings. The headings were to be in the same order for all reports, to allow readers to find particular subjects more easily. Inspectors were expected to solicit ideas and opinions for improvements and to conclude with a narrative description of the unit or post inspected, specifying any immediate necessary actions.[3]

Extracts from remedial action reports constituted the most significant information circulated by the Office of the Inspector General. The remedial process was often cumbersome and time-consuming, and many

---

[1] Corresp, OIG, 19 Nov 03, 23 Jul 09, 19 Sep 09, sub: Instructions for Clerks, Entry 35, Record Group (RG) 159, National Archives and Records Administration (NARA), Washington, D.C.

[2] WD Cir 22, 28 Nov 03, Entry 24, RG 159, NARA.

[3] Ltr, Burton to SofW, 22 May 03; Memo, WD, 22 May 03, amending Memo, AGO, same date, sub: Inspections; WD Cir 22, 28 Nov 03. All in Entry 24, RG 159, NARA.

actions that were left to the end of the inspection cycle merited much quicker attention. Consequently, Chief of Staff Wood directed Garlington to come up with a faster system. Wood wanted the OIG to review each incoming report and then the Inspector General to brief him personally on any critical matters. Garlington believed that part of the problem lay in the long delays that were encountered in funneling reports out of the geographical commands. He suggested that commanders be required to explain any unusual delays in their endorsements and that they forward immediately extracts of any items that required prompt action beyond their power to correct. The Chief of Staff approved Garlington's approach, implementing it with a letter to each geographical area commander. In 1914 the expedited procedure was incorporated into Army regulations.[4]

Yet the number of inspection reports, particularly those of garrisoned posts, continued to grow as the General Staff and bureaus added more and more special subjects for which information was desired. In some cases a picture of the units emerged, but all too often the reports became long lists of irregularities and property, alternating with formal statements that requirements were being met. In 1913 a change in the regulations specified that trivial matters would not be reported, particularly those that could be corrected on the spot. The effect was to prune the growth of the inspection reports, and during the final years before the World War they were quite prosaic and trim, providing a fairly clear picture of unit and post conditions. Nevertheless, items for special inquiry continued to be added to the reporting requirements, especially those dealing with administration, logistics, training, and living conditions. The most enduring concern, however, was the conduct of proper business methods. The greatest number of special topics grew during the tenure of General Wood, reflecting his activism as Chief of Staff. By 1916, the last full year of peace, sixteen items of special inquiry had been added to the basic inspection report.[5]

---

[4] Memos, Wood to Garlington, 9 Jan 14, and Reply, 10 Jan 14, and Ltr, TAG to Dept Cdrs, 26 Jan 14, Entry 24; Memo, IG to TAG, 12 Jan 17, sub: Proposed Amendments to Army Regulations, Entry 25. All in RG 159, NARA.

[5] Memos, Wood to IG, 26 Jan 12, 28 May 13, 17 Jun 13, 27 Aug 13, Entry 24; Corresp, OIG, 1911–1912, sub: Special Instructions for Inspectors, File 15208, Entry 9; Memo, Brewster to Insps, 2 Aug 16, sub: Special Topics of Inspection, 1913–1916, Memo, OIG to Insps, 8 Jan 16, sub: Matters Pertaining to Blank Forms, and Rpt, Galbraith, 15 Jun 15, sub: Annual Inspection of Ft. William McKinley, Rizal, P.I., Entry 26C. All in RG 159, NARA. See also WD GO 23, 1912; U.S. War Department, Office of the Inspector General, *A Guide for the Use of Officers of the Inspector General's Department, 1911, Corrected to April 1, 1917* (Washington, D.C.: Government Printing Office, 1917), pp. 27–36, 38 (hereafter cited as *Guide 1911/1917*).

Inspectors often submitted a supplemental letter to the Office of the Inspector General, summarizing their general observations once they had completed a cycle of annual inspections of similar organizations or functions. The Inspector General circulated these reports to the bureau chiefs, concerned that they receive the information and take appropriate action. Each inspector in the field also was required to submit an annual report, which constituted one means of indirect OIG control over inspectors and provided another source of information to the bureaus and the General Staff. These IG reports became feeders for the Secretary of War's annual report, which was mandated by Congress. They consisted of a brief summary of activities, followed by a more detailed analysis of the year's trends, and often contained recommendations in some depth for remedial action and lessons learned from investigations. Specific investigations were cited only if findings pertained to aspects of War Department–level policies and programs.[6]

The IG reports proved to be useful for assessing Army-wide trends. In 1909 they showed that many findings over the year dealt with failures to comply with regulations and orders, primarily because of myriad policy changes then engulfing the Army. Several inspectors agreed that commanders should be alert to the changes, some appearing for the first time in the reports, but they urged the central staffs to ease up on the process, allowing the field commands to respond in a more efficient manner. Others used them as vehicles to express their own views on the effects of War Department policies. In 1911 Col. John L. Chamberlain, the Western Division inspector, criticized the excessive rotation of line officers by showing a direct ratio between good units and stable officer assignments. In short, the annual reports allowed the presentation of opinion and analyses that were out of place in the more formal and limited individual inspection reports. Collectively, they provided a sound view of the concerns of the Army, along with many useful recommendations for improvement.[7]

The information contained in the annual reports, however, was for the Army alone. The practice of keeping all inspection reports and IG investigations within official channels dated to the time of the Civil War; only the Secretary of War could direct the release of information derived from IG activities to persons outside a chain of command. This policy was upheld by the Judge Advocate General each time the issue

---

[6] Dept of East Annual Rpt, 1904, Entry 35, RG 159, NARA; Ltr, Garlington to Chief, War College Div, WDGS, 26 Mar 12, sub: Necessity for Annual Report, Entry 296, RG 165, NARA.

[7] Dept of East Annual Rpt, 1911, Entry 24, RG 159, NARA.

arose. The authority and propriety of releasing information within the official chain was often less clear. In 1914 one of the Southern Department assistant inspectors, Maj. Alonzo Gray, submitted a report critical of a cavalry brigade to the department commander, General Bliss, who forwarded the report to the War Department because, in his opinion, it contained useful information on new cavalry drill regulations. But the embarrassed brigade commander contended that Major Gray should have submitted the report to him for his disposal. General Bliss passed the complaint to General Garlington for resolution.

Garlington's decision helped to clarify the internal treatment of information. He ruled that it was Gray's duty to give General Bliss the unvarnished truth, because Bliss as commander had to know the true condition of his units. Bliss, in turn, had the right to forward the report to the War Department if he considered it worthwhile. But Garlington also ruled that the inspector had erred in not discussing his findings with the brigade commander before forwarding them, because the latter's views on the problem areas could have enhanced the report and spared him the surprise and embarrassment of learning about the criticism first from General Bliss. While he concluded that greater tact and objectivity would have made the report more palatable, Garlington nevertheless held that Gray and Bliss were technically within their rights in treating it as they had.[8]

There was no such confusion over the granting of information to persons outside the War Department. Requests for photographs or accurate copies of IG documents were screened by the Office of the Inspector General for any matters of a confidential nature before they were satisfied. This rule applied even when the requester was another federal or state government entity. Anything judged derogatory or uncomplimentary was excised before copies were made. Standards were very stringent, and the age of the document seemed to mean little. For example, in 1914 the acid remark "The commissary which stands at the foot of the hill is a monument to the false reasoning of him who erected it" was deleted from a copy of an 1828 report on Fort Mackinac sent to the Wisconsin Historical Society![9]

However excessive in individual cases, such control assured that reliable information was disseminated to those needing it within the War Department and that reputations and the confidentiality of sources

---

[8] Memo, Garlington to Lyon, 6 Oct 14, sub: With Respect to Letter Received From Major Alonzo Gray, IG, dated 2 October 1914, and Ltr, Lyon to Gray, 6 Oct 14, Entry 24, RG 159, NARA; WD, OIG, *Guide 1911/1917*, pp. 12–13.

[9] Memo, Pyne to IG, 12 Jan 14, Entry 24, RG 159, NARA.

were protected. The scale and scope of the information contained in IG reports and their revelation of the Army's strengths and weaknesses pointed to the overall wisdom of the policy.

Education and Training

No function of the inspectorate was more important than oversight of the education and training of both officers and men. Civilian colleges were becoming important sources for the increased number of trained officers that were needed. Assigning officers to college faculties and issuing government equipment to schools had been authorized since the 1880s. It was not long before the inspectors became involved in evaluating such programs.

Annual inspections of colleges began in June 1886. As a result of program expansion, the inspectorate had to share its responsibilities with specially detailed officers. The number of participating schools dropped during the War with Spain but returned to prewar levels by 1903; in that year seventy-eight detachments were in colleges, fifty-one of which were led by recalled retirees. In hopes of increasing enrollments, the War Department authorized these detachments to grant a small number of Regular Army commissions in place of the less prestigious reserve commission. Inspection of the colleges became more decentralized in late 1903, when the responsibility was transferred to the geographical commands in whose areas the schools were located.[10]

The General Staff used IG reports as the basis for planning the staffing, equipping and training of the various civilian cadet units. This unusual situation caused the Chief of Staff in November 1905 to direct that the General Staff assume the responsibility for college inspections. Annually, thereafter, four officers were designated as inspectors from the General Staff. They not only visited the schools but also functioned as a board that selected "distinguished institutions."[11] This practice persisted until 1916 when, as a result of the crisis in Mexico and other major changes in the Army, the inspection responsibility reverted to the geographical area commanders and local inspectors general.

Despite the significance of training in civilian institutions, the most important influence in upgrading the standards of the Army was its own burgeoning school system. The system closed in 1898 because of the

---

[10] Ltr, Chamberlain to AG, Dept of East, 30 Jun 09, Entry 7, RG 159, NARA. See also U.S. War Department, *Annual Report of the Inspector General, 1909* (Washington, D.C.: Government Printing Office, 1909), p. 290 (hereafter cited as *ARIG)*.

[11] Southwestern Div Annual Rpt, 1904, Entry 35, RG 159, NARA.

War with Spain, but by 1902 most schools reopened. Their reemergence reflected basic changes in the Army. The nature of the officer corps was in transition. By 1902 half of its nearly 3,000 men had entered the Army since 1898, and only a fraction of them had been trained at the Military Academy. Consequently, an expanded educational system was essential. By 1916 there were eleven major schools located in Washington, D.C., and at Forts Riley, Leavenworth, Monroe, and Sill, many of them training both officers and enlisted men. The last two schools to be formed were Aviation, at San Diego, California, in 1913, and Ordnance, at Sandy Hook, New Jersey, in 1916. All were subject to inspection by War Department inspectors, usually by General Garlington himself. His office kept inspection suspenses and received information on matters pertaining to the schools. Only the six bakers and cooks schools were the responsibility of the geographical area commanders, with inspections performed by local IGs.[12]

After a tentative beginning in the 1880s, general orders issued between 1890 and 1892 had made post and branch schools and the Military Academy subject to IG inspections. Most school inspections were made by simply observing classes and activities, whereas troops at the Military Academy and the bakers and cooks schools were formally reviewed and inspected. Inspectors sometimes included their opinions or impressions, as well as factual information. Maj. Jacob G. Galbraith, for example, in 1909 recorded the "tension" experienced by the students at Fort Leavenworth's Army School of the Line: "By tension is meant extreme strain of mind and nervous anxiety. These result from hard study and rivalry." He suggested doing away with grades or, at least, not publishing them. One of the students he interviewed was Captain Helmick, who cited his experience at Fort Leavenworth as one of the most unpleasant of his career.[13]

Not everyone agreed. Following his inspection of the Coast Artillery School in June 1909, Maj. Henry D. Todd, Jr., found no competition for grades at Fort Monroe but rather a strong desire to work hard in order to be prepared professionally. "The whole tone of the institution is a healthy one. The requirements are rigid, based upon what men well above average can accomplish in eight hours every day."

---

[12] Memos, Pyne to IG, 12 Jan 14, and Garlington to SofW, 25 Jan 17, sub: Request of Rep. William L. Igoe, Entry 24, RG 159, NARA.

[13] Insp Notes (quotation), Galbraith, 1909, File 13385, Army School of the Line Inspection, Entry 9, RG 159, NARA. See also copy of Eli A. Helmick, "From Reveille to Retreat: Autobiography of Major General Eli A. Helmick," U.S. Army Military History Institute (MHI), Carlisle Barracks, Pa.

He recommended that officers trained at the Coast Artillery School be admitted to the Army War College without any further training. The school also gave courses for senior enlisted master gunners, electricians, and artillery engineers.[14]

Few school reports were so laudatory. Those on the newly established Artillery School of Fire were sympathetic and helpful, but not uncritical. Courses offered for junior officers and NCOs generally were praised, while the field-grade course was regarded as a waste of time. Part of the problem lay in the small amount of ammunition authorized for practice (forty rounds for officers, ten for NCOs), which meant that no meaningful tactical training of any complexity could be given. Another consequence was that the school statistical section was limited in the data it could collect on the accuracy and effect of artillery fire.[15] Such discriminating and technically competent criticism was common in the inspectors' reports.

The inspectors also looked into school and personnel administration and funds management. These activities usually were well run, although occasionally the presence of unauthorized funds would be discovered, derived from the sale of books and school materials. Such accounts either were closed or diverted to authorized nonappropriated funds that were used for student welfare. The practice of maintaining unauthorized funds, however, became so widespread that in August 1915 General Garlington directed that all inspectors make a special effort to detect their existence. In addition, the inspectors evaluated not only the levels of responsibility of staff and faculty, making recommendations for grade increases and organizational changes, but also the appropriateness of school locations and available facilities. Because of student turbulence and poor facilities, the Washington Barracks Engineer School was inspected annually.[16]

A routine 1914 school inspection of the new aviation arm of the Army was unusual in that it led to an extended series of investigations and probes. The War Department established the Aeronautical Service as part of the Signal Corps in August 1907. Bids were put out for a suitable aircraft, and the Wright Brothers responded in the summer of 1908. Unfortunately, the aircraft they offered crashed during tests at

---

[14] Rpt (quotation), Todd, Jun 09, sub: Inspection of Coast Artillery School, Ft. Monroe, Va., Entry 9, RG 159, NARA. In loc. cit., see also Rpt, Chamberlain, 13 Oct 08, sub: Inspection of Ft. Monroe, Va.

[15] Rpt, Lyon, 18 Apr 14, sub: Inspection of School of Fire for Field Artillery, Entry 25, RG 159, NARA.

[16] Memo, Garlington to CofS, WD, 30 May 09, sub: Wear of Uniforms, File 15344, Inspection of Alaskan Posts and Stations, 1908–1909, Entry 9, RG 159, NARA.

Fort Myer, Virginia, killing Lt. Thomas W. Selfridge, the first of a disturbingly large number of aviator fatalities. In the ensuing years several Army officers were detailed to the service and the one aircraft it owned. They were based first at College Park, Maryland, until 1909; then, as the detachment slowly grew, it moved to several different locations, finally coming to rest at San Diego in the summer of 1913. By this time the organization had become large enough for the Chief Signal Officer, Brig. Gen. George P. Scriven, to redesignate it as the Aviation Section of his corps. In December the San Diego facility was designated the Aviation School and made part of the Army's educational system. This distinction marked it as an item for inspection.[17]

Col. John L. Chamberlain, then the Pacific Division inspector, visited the Aviation School in February 1914. What started as a routine inspection, however, soon became a detailed investigation of school operations, prompted by the death of Lt. Henry B. Post in an aircraft crash—the fifteenth of the forty-eight officers detailed to aviation duty to have died since Selfridge. The investigation uncovered serious problems. Neither the school nor the recently created 1st Aero Squadron were organized except on paper. Equipment and personnel had not been provided, and no system of accountability existed for the disbursal of funds. Most important, interviews with aviators and mechanics revealed that most of the aircraft on hand were obsolete and unfit for field service—few could be used even for training. No well defined system of training existed either for aspiring pilots or enlisted mechanics. Only a few hired civilian maintenance men were considered competent to work on the aircraft.

Chamberlain believed that poor equipment and guidance were only part of the problem with the aviation facility. The overall lack of experience among the junior officers assigned to aviation duty worsened the situation. Most were lieutenants, and the few senior Signal Corps officers involved at the War Department were not pilots and had little understanding of the school's needs. Furthermore, all of the aviators were on detail, just as in any other staff department, and as soon as they gained experience the four-year rule required them to return to their basic branch units. Hence, experience in flying not only was in short supply but, once gained, was quickly lost.

Regrettably, Chamberlain's proposals for reform were ignored. After another critical annual report, however, the Chief of Staff

---

[17] Rpt, Chamberlain, 19 Mar 14, sub: Annual Inspection of First Areo Squadron and of Signal Corps Aviation School, Entry 9, RG 159, NARA.

appointed General Garlington as president of a board to examine the Aviation School administration. Its findings confirmed the flaws pointed out by Chamberlain. Additionally, the board discovered fraud and collusion on the part of the school commandant and contracting irregularities on the part of the Army officers overseeing aircraft contracts, who were accepting substandard planes from the factories because of a lack of supervision and intense pressure to speed up delivery. The practical effect of Garlington's board was the replacement of most of the school staff and faculty and the start of a senior officers flight program to attract more seasoned officers.[18]

But problems lingered. After two pilots crashed in January 1917, a further investigation by the assistant IG of the Western Department, Lt. Col. Frank M. Caldwell, led to action on a number of his recommendations, including the appointment of Col. Alexander Dade, the former IG of the Vera Screws Expedition, as commandant, along with a new staff. Despite the changes that resulted, the case of the Aviation School inspections stands as a cautionary example. The effect of the inspections depended both on the views of key members of the chain of command and on the degree of follow-up. At the San Diego school the inspectors' findings and recommendations were long ignored, because of parochial interests and the indifference of other members of the system.[19]

Endless other examples could be cited of the interest taken by inspectors in military schooling. General Burton, for example, was a strong advocate of giving advanced training to medical corpsmen, with the aim of enabling them to act on their own in medical emergencies. In 1911 Lt. Col. Charles G. Morton, after visiting the Signal School, suggested that the Signal Corps experiment with motor vehicles as radio carriers. The idea was quickly put into effect. In time, on the basis of their extensive experience, the inspectors developed a broader view of the Army's entire school system. By 1916 General Garlington was stressing better coordination among the service schools and the creation of a formal hierarchy of education to assure a logical progression throughout individual careers. He urged that the program also should apply to National Guard officers.[20]

---

[18] Garlington, "Proceedings of a Board of Officers," 4 Apr 16, Entry 33, RG 159, NARA.

[19] Rpt, Caldwell to TAG, 17 Mar 17, sub: Investigation in Case of 'Lost Aviators' Lt. Col. Bishop and Lt. Robertson, and Secondary Report, Entry 25, RG 159, NARA. In loc. cit., see also Auxiliary Report, 26 Apr 17.

[20] Rpt, Shanks, 15 Jul 16, sub: Inspection of Department Hospital, Entry 11; Memo, CSigOff to CofS, WD, 14 Jun 11, sub: Experimental Use of Motor Vehicles, Entry 9; and Rpts, Gale, 1905, 1906, 1907, sub: Inspections of Madison Barracks, New York, Entry 7. All in RG 159, NARA. See also Helmick, "Autobiography," MHI.

His ideas could not be realized at once, however. To his dismay and that of the other inspectors, the school system collapsed under the pressures of the Mexican border crisis. The schools were closed, and both the students and the faculty were assigned to units assembling for duty in the Southwest. Inspectors criticized this shortsighted approach that ignored future needs, particularly those generated by the concurrent expansion of the Army. They urged that, at the very least, cadres be retained to provide continuity during the inevitable revival of the schools. In fact, IG criticisms helped to bring about the rapid reopening of the schools in late 1916.[21]

The Military Academy at West Point was always a special case. The Inspector General himself usually inspected the academy and the corps of cadets; when scheduling conflicts arose, the Department of the East senior inspector would make the visit for him. In either case, a narrative report for the Chief of Staff was submitted through the academy superintendent and The Adjutant General. Every West Point inspection report provided voluminous information concerning academy operations, including details on the menus in the cadet mess hall and descriptions of laundry operations. Occasionally, however, matters of greater significance came into the reports.[22]

Discipline issues at the Military Academy, as well as in the rest of the Army, were referred to the Inspector General for his review and remarks. The issue of greatest concern was hazing, which had become so serious in the 1890s that in 1901 Congress passed a law compelling the superintendent to dismiss cadets who engaged in such behavior. General Garlington objected to the law on the grounds of inflexibility and, in 1909, proposed amending it to give the superintendent the same latitude as a general court-martial authority. Garlington believed that any cadet dismissed under this reformed system should be barred permanently from returning. The law was amended later that year, incorporating his views.[23]

Garrison and Unit Inspections

Every unit and post in the Army had to be visited each fiscal year by an inspector, and this goal was normally met, except on rare occasions

[21] Rpt, Shanks, 6 May 14, sub: Inspection of Mounted Service School, Entry 9, RG 159, NARA.

[22] Rpt, Garlington, 27 Jul 08, sub: Inspection of USMA, July 16th to 20th, Entry 9, RG 159, NARA.

[23] Rpt, Shanks, 3 Aug 14, sub: Annual Inspection of USMA, Entry 11; Ltr, Garlington to CofS, WD, 29 May 09, sub: USMA Superintendent G. C. M. Authority, Entry 24. Both in RG 159, NARA.

when weather or health problems intervened. Year after year it was safe to assume that well over 1,700 places and organizations would receive thoroughgoing attention to their facilities, personnel, and operations.[24]

The inspector accounted for all personnel, listing all officers absent by name. Inspection of units stressed the appearance of soldiers, the care and condition of their uniforms and equipment, and the adequacy of their quarters. The inspectors also saw the units at various drills and parades, including a full field inspection followed by proficiency demonstrations in first aid, signaling, and similar skills. Suggestions for improvement were made, where appropriate. Inspectors were required to report all officers whose units were not properly prepared, as well as those physically, mentally, or morally incapable of performing the duties of their grade. Other concerns included the condition of livestock, conduct of garrison schools, and care of post prisoners. Funds were inevitably a matter of concern. All documentation was carefully reviewed, and any unexplained entries were referred to the custodian for written explanation. If the responsible officer had been reassigned, an inquiry was sent to him at his new station. The file on the report remained open until a satisfactory explanation was received.[25]

Inspection reports concluded with a brief, frank overall statement of a unit's or post's capacity to perform its mission. Here inspectors frequently gave their views about the effect of War Department plans or policies on the organizations inspected. Flaws in regulations or policy were sometimes detected as a result of inspections. Inspectors also continued to be strong advocates of modernization, especially in cases where morale, efficiency, or safety could be improved. Persistence by the Inspector General's Department (IGD), for example, overcame inaction, and in 1911 the War Department agreed to provide electric power to Army posts in Alaska. In the Philippines an inspector's recommendation led to a new policy of buying local horses, which were small, tough, acclimated, and inexpensive, rather than shipping animals from the United States to meet arbitrary size standards.[26]

Regardless of where they were conducted, the inspections of garrisoned posts represented a prodigious task for the team of one or two inspectors and a clerk. Aspects of the inspection had the potential to

---

[24] U.S. War Department, *Annual Report of the Secretary of War, 1904* (Washington, D.C.: Government Printing Office, 1904), p. 33 (hereafter cited as *ARSW*). See, for example, inspections of Department of the East posts in Box 154, Entry E9, RG 159, NARA.

[25] Memo, Brewster to Insps Gen, 4 Nov 11, Entry 24, RG 159, NARA.

[26] Files 15344 and 15679, Inspection of Alaskan Posts and Stations, 1908, 1909, 1911, Entry 9, RG 159, NARA. On the purchase of local horses, see Rpt, Frier, 1 Aug 13, sub: Inspection of Camp Stotsenburg, P.I., same entry.

"Picket Line Outside Brick Stables at Fort Myer." *A major IG oversight responsibility was the acquisition, care, and disposal of horses.*

reflect adversely on a unit. In all cases, extreme frankness on the inspector's part was expected and strenuous work was the norm. Major Helmick learned during his first tour the difference between an inspection versus a social visit. Other inspectors strongly advised him not to accept the hospitality offered when conducting an official inspection to avoid the possibility of embarrassment and a conflict of interest. After becoming Inspector General in 1921, Helmick adopted this informal practice as IGD policy.[27]

Tactical Inspections

In one of its most important reforms, the General Staff increased the amount of practical training beyond the simple drills required of all units and supporting services. By late 1906 garrison training had been differentiated from field training. In the latter, emphasis was placed on weapons firing and tactical exercises. At least one day each week was to be set aside for full unit training, with no excused absences. More of a unit's time was expected to be spent under field conditions. Beginning

---

[27] Helmick, "Autobiography," MHI.

in 1907, all units were required to conduct extended three- to six-day road marches each month, accompanied by all their trains and equipment. At least once a year every regiment was expected to conduct a combined practice march and three-week bivouac, with all of its elements present. The training cycle was refined even more in 1911, when Chief of Staff Wood specified that the bivouac phase would include large-scale tactical maneuvers.[28]

The capabilities of Army units and their levels of training had been a growing interest of inspectors even before the War with Spain. In 1892, at General Breckinridge's suggestion, annual inspections had begun to include tactical exercises. The era of reform transformed a practice into a requirement. The new War Department general orders specified that IGs inspect a unit's tactical training and report their findings. Usually, the annual inspection was scheduled to coincide with the bivouac, for mutual convenience. Prior to 1910 the inspection report of a garrison included comments on both the troops and the installation; however, beginning in September, a separate field report was required. The reason for the reporting change was General Wood's greater stress on preparedness. Wood wanted inspectors to assess the efficiency of the units as part of a mobile force. Troops had to be observed in the field for at least four days while they conducted tactical problems, road marches, and weapons training.

In some cases unit commanders helped devise the field problems, but most of the time the visiting inspector prepared them. Combined arms exercises, whenever possible, were conducted to familiarize the participants with each other's work. Inspectors were required to note especially the support provided by staff department troops. Saber and bayonet proficiency and the condition of soldiers' feet after marching were further items of concern. The use of motor vehicles and the standardization of equipment were stressed as a result of observations of the first large-scale bivouacs.[29]

Inspectors quickly formulated a set procedure to ensure that all required subjects were covered. Their visits were divided between gar-

---

[28] Rpt, Sanger, 7 Dec 1896, sub: Coast Artillery Inspections, Department of the East; Memo, Breckinridge to Insps Gen, 28 Nov 03. Both in Entry 24, RG 159, NARA. The emphasis on field training led the Inspectors General to recommend repeatedly that a chief be appointed for each combat arm. (Only artillery had a chief, and when the arm was divided the chief's position went to the newly formed coast artillery.) Both Burton and Garlington contended that field problems would be of greater value if branch chiefs existed to issue training doctrine and policies. See *ARIG 1905*, p. 444; *ARIG 1906*, p. 650.

[29] For policies on training and tactical exercises, see WD GO 44, 1906, GO 177, 1907, and GO 7, 1911. See also *ARIG 1911*, pp. 265, 267, 274; Memo, Garlington to Insps Gen, 29 May 11, Entry 24, RG 159, NARA.

rison and field activities. During the garrison phase they evaluated drill, athletics, equitation, and bayonet practice. The field phase was further divided into camp and tactical sections. The inspection of troops in camp emphasized organization, sanitation, and completeness of equipment. The performance of support elements, such as the kitchens and trains, was examined, as were the functions of the battalion and regimental staffs. During this time individual skills in first aid, signaling, and range finding were made by selecting men at random and running them through a series of tests. The tactical portion of the inspection concentrated on scouting, patrolling, entrenching, and battle exercises. Problems on the ground included outposts by day and night, attacks, withdrawal, and position defenses. River crossings and night movements were practiced whenever possible.[30]

Some senior officers resented the tactical inspections, fearing the effects of criticism on their careers and disliking the disruption of their routine caused by the inspector's visit. But implicit in the Root reforms were higher standards of officer performance. Some colonels, unwilling to adjust to the new situation, were forced into retirement. Inspectors frequently were involved in these actions, if only because of their evaluations of a unit's tactical proficiency. Inefficient or incompetent senior officers were most often identified through tactical inspections. Although commanders were relieved on the spot, the War Department or the particular geographical command usually would direct a follow-up inspection to see how the officer in question had reacted to earlier criticisms. An inspector, ordinarily accompanied by a senior member of the geographical command staff, would return for a second look. Few of the old colonels survived this process. Many had resisted the changes under way in the Army, almost to the point of insubordination.[31]

Despite such opposition, one of the benefits of the new system was to reduce the total number of inspections that units had to face. By the time Wood came to office, inspections had multiplied to a point that threatened to overwhelm units in the field. Even the Surgeon General, Quartermaster General, and Chief Signal Officer, as well as the geographical area commanders, assigned officers to make some sort of unit or garrison inspections. Much of what they did was duplicated by the inspectors general, who were also following regulatory requirements.[32]

---

[30] Memo, Brewster to IG, 2 Nov 11, Entry 35, RG 159, NARA.

[31] Helmick, "Autobiography," MHI.

[32] Ltr, Bell to AG, Western Div, 17 Feb 12; Memo, Garlington to CofS, WD, 28 Jun 12; Ltr, Garlington to Wood, 6 Jul 12; Memo, Pyne to Garlington, 5 Jul 12. All in Entry 24, RG 159, NARA.

Wood felt that the whole system was makeshift and that the structure needed clarification. In his view, inspectors general were to be responsible for garrison, financial, and supply accounting inspections and senior commanders for inspecting units in the field and evaluating the performance of officers. Commanders could use IGs to assist them but could not delegate the responsibility for tactical inspections. Wood wanted such inspections to be held during scheduled field training, rather than on special exercises, to reduce disruptions, and he wanted officers' annual physical evaluations to be scheduled at the same time. Secretary of War Stimson gave the Chief of Staff strong support.[33]

Wood coordinated closely with General Garlington and other OIG officers while developing his new plans for tactical inspections. Each phase of planning was mutually agreed to. The Chief of Staff intended his new policy to be tested and then refined after the first year of implementation. For his scheme to work, Wood realized that the senior commanders and their inspectors had to become competent inspectors. He thus decided that the local command IG would prepare all reports, including the one on the tactical inspection, and forward them through his commander. The modified tactical inspections program began in July 1912. Commanders were asked to coordinate inspection schedules upon receipt of Wood's instructions. The OIG field artillery inspector was required to do the same with the geographical commands. All itineraries had to be forwarded to the War Department along with requests for any General Staff support or IG personnel needed to augment local staffs.[34]

At the end of 1912 General Wood required all inspectors and division commanders to provide their views on the new system. The consensus was generally favorable, and the system was made permanent in January 1913. New regulations issued that month attempted to define command relations and procedures for the conduct of tactical inspections—changes that coincided with the reorganization of the mobile army into tactical divisions and brigades within geographical commands.[35]

The new system had problems. Some inspectors found that senior commanders failed to conduct the required inspections personally. General Garlington advised that in such cases the inspectors in the field were obliged to tell their commanders what should be done and to make

---

[33] Memo, Wood to TAG, 9 Jul 12, Entry 24, RG 159, NARA; Memo, Wood to Garlington, 13 Jul 12, Entry 296, RG 165, NARA.

[34] Memo, Wood to TAG, 23 Jul 12, Entry 296, RG 165, NARA.

[35] Ltr, TAG to Dept Cdrs and Insps, 13 Dec 12, sub: Change to Army Regulations, Entry 9, RG 159, NARA; Change 26 to Army Regulations, 20 Jan 13, Entry 296, RG 165, NARA.

recommendations as to how to conduct proper inspections. Inspectors had to avoid being made the commander's surrogate, because the regulations now specified that the commander had to perform his own tactical inspection. Garlington blamed the problem on the reluctance of some generals to accept the responsibility that came with their positions. Too many counted on inspectors and their staffs to "pull their chestnuts out of the fire when the flame is very hot," and Garlington was quite bitter about the conduct of some of the line commanders.[36]

A major concern of the field inspectors was the perception that they represented the local commander, even if they actually came from a higher staff for the event. In such cases they viewed themselves as no more than observers. This view was strengthened when, during the first inspection cycle, several brigade commanders were found to be incompetent. Clearly, this significant fact could not be made known in the proper quarters if the inspectors were subject to the command of the marginal officer. Other inspectors complained that too much of the actual conduct of the inspection was being required of them. Very few senior commanders were giving full support to the program, compounding the problems of the inspectors charged with making it work.[37]

Garlington advised the new Chief of Staff, Maj. Gen. William R. Wotherspoon, of the situation in May 1914, suggesting that the regulation more clearly state the geographical area commanders' responsibility for conducting tactical inspections. The Chief of Staff agreed, amending the regulation to specify that IGs from geographical commands would serve only as observers at infantry and cavalry field exercises but that they could assist the commander if so requested. For field artillery inspections, an OIG inspector would continue to conduct them. These changes, which appeared in June 1914, were now an established part of the Army's routine and remained in effect until wartime training requirements brought a complete revision. Exercises conducted as a part of the tactical inspections grew in scale as larger troop concentrations took place. On the whole, the emphasis on preparedness would prove exceedingly beneficial to the expanding Army.[38]

---

[36] Ltr, Garlington to Chamberlain, 17 Feb 14, Entry 24, RG 159, NARA.

[37] Ltrs, Chamberlain to Garlington, 4 Mar 14, and Mills to Garlington, 9 Mar 14, Entry 24, RG 159, NARA.

[38] Memos, Garlington to CofS, WD, 8 Jun 14; Biddle to CofS, WD, 25 May 14, sub: Proposed Changes in Army Regulations in Connection With Annual Tactical Inspections; and Lyon to Garlington, 27 May 14 and 1 Jun 14. All in Entry 296, RG 165, NARA. See also *ARIG 1914*, p. 198.

Field Artillery Inspections

The tactical inspections made clear that the Army's components were not all progressing at the same pace. The coast artillery was consistently the most efficient arm, while the cavalry and infantry were only gradually improving. On the other hand, the field artillery was so beset with problems that at times its progress seemed hopeless.

The lack of proficiency in the field artillery may best be explained by the number of changes it had undergone in the period since the War with Spain. Originally, the Corps of Artillery had consisted of both field and coastal units, scattered in battery-sized organizations throughout the country. Although regiments existed in theory, the dispersion and the diverse missions of their constituent batteries meant that regimental officers had no experience in actually commanding the massed elements of their unit—a major flaw in artillery organization. The War Department began forming two-battery battalions in 1904; activated two provisional field artillery regiments in 1905; and considered separating the field artillery from the coast artillery in 1906, which was approved in January 1907. The Chief of Artillery was left with the Coast Artillery Corps and the well-organized artillery school at Fort Monroe.[39]

The newly created Field Artillery Corps, consisting of one horse, two mountain, and three light regiments, had the immediate tasks of establishing its own schools and doctrine. In 1909 the Secretary of War directed that a thorough inspection of the entire corps be made to identify areas requiring improvement. An extensive series of tactical inspections was made by Maj. William Lassiter, the OIG field artillery inspector, to assess the progress of the reorganization and to evaluate the tactical proficiency of the units, particularly battalion and regimental headquarters. What he discovered was not encouraging. He found that the regiments were not well drilled in fundamentals, such as hitching teams or making camp, and exhibited a high level of absenteeism. Several battery commanders admitted they had never seen all their men assembled in one place for anything.[40]

The artillery inspectors tested each battery in a series of tactical exercises involving reconnaissance, the selection and occupation of

---

[39] William A. Ganoe, *The History of the United States Army* (New York: D. Appleton and Co., 1924), p. 428; Vardell E. Nesmith, Jr., "The Quiet Paradigm Change: The Evolution of the Field Artillery Doctrine of the United States Army, 1861–1905" (Ph.D. diss., Duke University, 1977), pp. 320–30.

[40] *ARIG 1909*, p. 291.

positions, and simulated fire at targets. The tests began on the drill ground and then moved to the post maneuver area. A final examination at each station was designed to evaluate regimental-level control over road marches and as many tactical situations as could be introduced— night movements, use of camouflage, and the soundness of tactical decisions. Targets were positioned at appropriate points, and live ammunition was used during fire missions.[41]

Major Lassiter concluded that the exercises showed that not a single artillery command could take to the field and be effective. All were deficient, technically and tactically, through lack of training and experience. None of the units had trained together, and many of the artillery field-grade officers were not up to the task of commanding at regimental levels. Several of them showed no inclination or flexibility to learn or to improve themselves. The inspector judged the artillery to be a "mere aggregate of batteries, devoid of intelligent direction" and incapable of performing as required in a tactical division.[42]

Lassiter believed the remedy began with the development of a coherent artillery doctrine at the War Department level, accompanied by progressive training programs designed to prepare units for field duty. He urged the appointment of a field artillery chief to provide centralized guidance and the establishment of a school of fire to give battery personnel practical, standardized experience. He stressed the need for combined arms exercises and special programs for senior officers. Proficiency could only be gained through practice and experience— and for the artillery, he pointed out, that meant budgeting at War Department levels for far more liberal ammunition allowances.

After reviewing summaries of Lassiter's devastating reports, several members of the General Staff called them "admirable" for their candidness and scope. Under pressure from General Wood, reforms along the lines of Lassiter's recommendations began to be made. The War Department established the School of Fire at Fort Sill, Oklahoma, in 1911 and expanded the mission of the Artillery Board, established in 1902 as a technical advisory board for the Secretary of War, to include operational matters. The board moved from Fort Riley to Fort Sill in 1913, and its membership expanded to include the School of Fire faculty. Although these measures never resulted in the appointment of a field artillery chief or the creation of a cohesive

---

[41] Rpt, Lassiter, Apr 09, sub: Inspection of Third Field Artillery Regiment, Entry 9, RG 159, NARA.

[42] Ltr, Lassiter to IG, 3 Aug 09, Entry 9, RG 159, NARA.

doctrine, the consolidation of the board with other artillery activities was a step forward.[43]

The War Department reorganization in February 1913 created tactical divisions subordinate to the geographical commands. The change caused field artillery inspection procedures to be modified. New regulations required the geographical area commanders to concentrate subordinate tactical divisions annually to allow senior personnel experience in handling larger units. Tactical inspections of the various arms were to be carried out by the geographical area commander with the assistance of his inspector, as was usual for cavalry, infantry, and coast artillery.[44] Regardless of the arrangement, the inspector prepared the inspection report, which he gave to his commander to forward through channels to the Office of the Inspector General.

The tactical inspections conducted after the reorganization continued to show serious problems in the field artillery. The inspectors concluded after the 1915 inspection cycle that the most serious obstacle to improvement lay in the scattering of the field artillery units among small garrisons. In the Southern Department, for example, fourteen batteries from three different regiments were assigned to eight different locations. The problem was compounded by the diversion of half of their officers to schools, other duties, and militia training. The situation meant that field artillery battalions and regiments could not perform effectively in the field. Regular and militia units alike repeated elementary gun drills but failed to go beyond them into more complicated maneuver and firing problems. The low levels of field artillery proficiency were made worse by what inspectors felt was the wrong mix of artillery units in the force. The current fighting in France was showing that many more guns were needed to support a given number of infantry formations.[45]

The Army expansion dictated by the National Defense Act of 1916 found the field artillery unprepared. New regiments quickly absorbed the small pool of experienced personnel. The effect was to make the old regiments as unfit as the newly created ones. Inspectors recommended that the subsequent mandated expansions be achieved by transferring

---

[43] Rpt Extract, Lassiter, Jun 09, sub: Artillery Commands, and Memo, Wood to IG, 10 Jan 11, Entry 9; Rpt, McNair, 2 Jun 15, sub: Inspection School of Fire, Entry 25. All in RG 159, NARA. See also G. B. McReynolds, "Notes on Some Random Activities of the Field Artillery Board," *Field Artillery Journal* 32 (Jul 42): 509 (quoted word).

[44] Ltr, Funston to Garlington, 26 Jul 15, Entry 25, RG 159, NARA; AReg 193(2)(k), 1913.

[45] *ARIG 1916*, p. 303.

small cadres of quality personnel to provide a nucleus for the newer units, thereby preserving the effectiveness of the old ones. Supply shortages also were noted, as a result of poor coordination between the General Staff and the supply departments at the time the expansion directives were issued. The inspectors concluded that staff procedures must be improved, and, even more important, that supplies must be stockpiled for unexpected requirements. Commanders and staffs at all levels were having difficulty adjusting to the organizational and logistical demands of a large modern Army. Nevertheless, the inspectors' recommendations helped provide the basis for later restructuring prompted by the declaration of war on Germany in April 1917.[46]

Business Methods

While the tactical inspections of officers, men, and units emphasized preparedness, the annual inspections of armories, depots, and hospitals focused increasingly on what the Progressive Era termed *business methods*. This phrase referred to both paperwork processing and fiscal management. Army leaders viewed the great burden of paperwork as an impediment to the organizational and tactical reforms and the reliance on business methods as a manifestation of the general effort to achieve greater efficiency and control.

Eventually, every IG report had a section devoted to business methods analyses. The inspectorate's traditional role involved oversight of disbursements and property, and about half of each inspector's annual effort was spent investigating some aspect. Secretary Root's interest brought additional emphasis. Late in his tenure he directed that a study be made of the disbursement of funds appropriated for so-called War Department civil costs. Root's successor was equally interested in improving administration. Secretary Taft directed General Burton to develop an inspection program that would review systematically the accounts and business methods of all disbursing officers. By July 1903 Burton had special inspections on all fiscal accounts and contracts scheduled worldwide.[47]

The first inspections showed that disbursing was only a small part of the Army's problems. Cumbersome administrative procedures and requirements imposed by each echelon of command often proved to be a

---

[46] Rpts, Stephens, 20 Sep and 30 Oct 16, subs: 3d Field Artillery Regiment, Entry 11; Rpt, Conner, 31 Jan 17, sub: Quartermaster Matters Observed During Annual Inspection of Field Artillery, Entry 25. All in RG 159, NARA.

[47] Ltr, Burton to Ainsworth, 26 Jul 03, Entry 24, RG 159, NARA.

greater hindrance than a help to managers and their commanders. Hence, the War Department ordered inspectors to evaluate the effects of each change in administrative procedure, and in November 1905 a general order formally added business methods as a topic in all inspections.[48]

The Inspector General's Department was required to inspect each bureau and geographical command headquarters to assure administrative uniformity and to recommend any changes to existing procedures, a requirement that demanded detailed inspections of correspondence files and voluminous comments on office paperwork, marking, indexing, and so on. The reports were obviously time-consuming and tedious, but were viewed as necessary to improve efficiency and to keep up standards. The inspections, however, went beyond the minutiae of office management. The complexity of business methods inspections increased with each inspection cycle. For example, inspectors had to examine the activities of the Quartermaster General's Department; they analyzed such matters as the size of local work forces and the appropriateness of office and depot locations and identified officers qualified for duties in disbursing and procurement.

By 1909 General Garlington considered the review of business methods to be routine. The scope was widened in 1910, in response to the work of the Secretary of War's Board on Business Methods. Based on the board's recommendations, the Office of the Inspector General had inspectors examine the operating expenses of all depots and commands, and in January 1911 the Secretary of War directed each bureau to survey its operations, with the objective of reducing the unnecessarily large amount of intricate and cumbersome paperwork in the Army. Garlington solicited the views of all OIG inspectors and forwarded a lengthy report containing numerous proposals. These included dropping the muster roll in favor of a single regimental return; discontinuing duplicate-type reports, such as the post exchange audit and monthly finance reports; and simplifying correspondence and filing procedures. The board's recommendations, including those of Garlington, were tentatively approved by General Leonard Wood in April.[49]

---

[48] Rpt, OIG, 29 Jun 09, Inspection of the Department of the Lakes, St. Paul, Minn., Entry 9; Ltr, Garlington to TAG, 6 Feb 09, sub: History for 1908, and Memo, OIG to Insps Gen, 29 Jun 09, sub: Change to AR 888, 1909, Entry 24. All in RG 159, NARA. See also WD GO 191, 1905, GO 118, 1908, GO 73, 1908, GO 92, 1908, and GO 176, 1908; *ARIG 1906*, p. 635.

[49] Rpt 2, Bus Methods Board to TAG, 9 Mar 11; Memo, Wood to SofW, 18 Apr 11; and Memo, Liggett to Sec, WDGS, 20 Apr 11, sub: Committee of Officers. All in Entry 296, RG 165, NARA. See also OIG Summary of FY 1909–1910 Business Methods Inspections; Rpt, Garlington to Offs Cmte, 26 Feb 11. Both in Entry 24, RG 159, NARA.

The period of administrative introspection was prolonged with the appointment of President Taft's Committee on Economy and Efficiency. Its preliminary report, issued in November 1911, provided an excellent overview of Army organization, finding little to criticize in the management of daily operations. The committee's research represented the last major effort to make a comprehensive overhaul of Army administration before the World War. Although inspectors remained extensively involved in financial matters, the high-level concern over improving administration was slowly overshadowed by a growing stress on tactical preparedness. The period of reform left the business methods of the staff departments in a condition that was judged to be generally sound.

Funds Management

The Inspector General's Department had been the Secretary of War's agent for the inspection of all funds and disbursing activities since the days of Calhoun. Specific responsibilities in this field had been described in an April 1874 law, which required IGs to make frequent unscheduled inspections of funds activities.

The number and variety of disbursing accounts were large. Inspecting the more important Quartermaster contracts associated with major items of government spending proved to be fairly easy, whereas supervising the numerous small-unit and installation accounts proved to be extremely time consuming. Every company-sized organization—units of 100 to 200 men—managed a morale and welfare fund of considerable complexity. Every regimental or post commander also had a small fund, as did engineer and coast artillery commands and even military bands with separate messes. In fact, the installation band was the source of income and the principal beneficiary of the fund. The proliferation of funds also included accounts managed by chaplains and others.

Unlike current unit funds, each could generate income in profit-making activities, subject to War Department approval. The inspectorate was the department's adviser and approving authority on all requests from funds managers to enter into such ventures. The line between unit fund activities and those of the post exchange, in which the funds were shareholders, was often indistinct. All issues of indebtedness to any type of government fund were submitted to the Office of the Inspector General for review before final actions were taken. This allowed uniform determinations of liabilities while it also kept the inspectorate alert to problems that might require policy or regulatory changes.[50]

---

[50] File 63, Bad Debts, Entry 25, RG 159, NARA.

Every time an officer was relieved from or given responsibility for a fund, his commander or bureau chief notified the Office of the Inspector General, initiating closeout inspections and the beginning of a new inspection cycle. The OIG reviewed all claims for and against the government to assure justice and, again, to note any problems within the system.

Inspection responsibility for funds outside Army appropriations also fell to the Office of the Inspector General, because of its experience in the field. In 1905 the OIG assumed oversight of a miscellaneous collection of small civil accounts in the District of Columbia, including the funds disbursed for the maintenance of public buildings, the Washington Aqueduct, and War Department civilian salaries. In 1906 the Secretary of War transferred to the Inspector General his responsibility for inspecting the accounts of the newly chartered American Red Cross. Additional quasi-military accounts were added in 1909, when the Chief of Staff recommended to the Secretary of War that the funds of War Department civil agencies administered by Army officers should be inspected also. The inspectorate was directed to include in its inspection schedule not only the Alaska Telegraph, rumored to be poorly administered, but also such exotic activities as the California Debris Commission and the Board of Alaska Road Commissioners.[51]

Regardless of category, the Office of the Inspector General supervised an average of nearly 2,000 account inspections in the United States and 70 in the Philippines each fiscal year during the pre-World War era. Rarely were problems encountered. But each account had to undergo a routine but thorough audit, followed by a detailed written appraisal and report. The procedures required a documentary verification of all transactions and a complete review of every check, bill, and deposit. The sources of income each had to be identified and evaluated for conformance with regulations. All vouchers and receipts were physically checked or accounted for. Everything was expected to balance. All work had to conform to the revised guide for inspectors issued in 1911, which contained twenty-eight pages of procedural guidance.

Many inspectors objected to their involvement in such a time-consuming process, and the field commands wanted more time given to issues of preparedness. Garlington recognized the problem, but felt that the Army's need to document its handling of funds to Congress and the

---

[51] Ltr, Garlington to TAG, 25 Jan 07, sub: History for 1906, and Memo, Garlington to Insps Gen, 16 May 08, sub: The Inspector General's Department of the Army, Entry 24; File 306/6650, Accounts Inspections Reports, 1905, Entry 22. All in RG 159, NARA. See also WD, OIG, *Guide 1911/1917*, pp. 37–39.

public prevented any relaxation of standards. When the revised guide for inspectors general was distributed, an accompanying memorandum stressed the necessity for the thorough inspection of all financial matters. A similar admonition was pasted inside each guide.[52]

Depot Activities

Depots, armories, arsenals, and similar facilities usually were inspected annually by the Washington office. Inspectors examined both management practices and the larger question of whether the facility was still needed. Their reports contained narrative descriptions of depot activities, a chronicle of events since the previous inspection, and a summary with detailed statistics.

The inspection of medical depots covered essentially the same ground, although closer attention was paid to the inventory and accounting of such high-value pilferable items as drugs and alcohol. The inspection of arsenals was much the same. After describing the work force, most reports focused on improvements in efficiency through technological innovation, for example, the use of motor vehicles. The inspections of supply depots were reported in equal detail, but observations and recommendations tended to be even more practical and specific. Inspectors often proposed changes in routines to aid efficiency.[53]

One inspector pointed out sources of possible savings. In his June 1908 report Colonel Chamberlain recommended that supply articles should all be of standard designs, with no unique items procured for particular individuals, and identified procedures that would enable the government to defray moving costs to families when units were reassigned. Many of these types of suggestions had beneficial effects. For example, one found in a Philippine depot inspection report resulted in a 33-percent reduction in land costs there. The inspectors were consistent advocates of the expansion of the enlisted strength in the Quartermaster General's Department a goal realized eventually with the merger of the latter and the Subsistence Department into the Quartermaster's Corps in 1908.[54]

Despite such improvements, the depot commanders appeared to have seen little value in the inspection visits. The basic operations of their facilities were controlled by the respective bureau chiefs, to whom

---

[52] Memo, Brewster to Insps, 20 Sep 16, Entry 25, RG 159, NARA.

[53] Insp Rpts, Medical Supply Depots, 1915–1917, Entry 11, RG 159, NARA.

[54] Rpt, Chamberlain, 7 Jun 08, sub: Inspection of Philadelphia Depot, Frankford, Pa., Entry 9, RG 159, NARA; *ARSW 1907*, p. 17.

"Coming Home Aboard the SS Grand Duchess." *Shipboard conditions became a special IG interest when the U.S. acquired global commitments.*

they looked for guidance; outside criticism was often unappreciated. The General Staff, for the most part, deferred to the bureaus to judge the value of the inspection comments and to take remedial action. This situation was recognized by the Inspectors General. General Burton recommended in 1906 that arsenals and depots be placed under the geographical area commanders, especially for inspection. But the suggestion was successfully fought by the bureau chiefs, and most of their facilities remained exempted. Depot inspections obviously were valuable sources of information, for they often were amplified at the request of a bureau chief concerned about one of his activities. In an effort to avoid public criticism, depot activities were reviewed repeatedly and special inquiries were conducted at one time or another in nearly every depot, generally in response to journalistic reports citing inefficiency or corruption. Garlington advised the Secretary of War that such newspaper accounts generated more excitement than they merited. Nevertheless, as the Inspector General recognized, public interest was a positive force in maintaining high standards.[55]

---

[55] *ARIG 1906*, pp. 639, 647.

Inspection of the Militia

The Inspector General's Department had been one of the first War Department elements to display an interest in the resurgent militia or National Guard. General Breckinridge had served in the Kentucky volunteers during the Civil War, and his emphasis on the importance of a citizen reserve led to an order in 1889 that made his office responsible for coordinating militia inspections.[56]

In 1892 the Adjutant General assumed the duty of preparing militia inspection instructions, and the Office of the Inspector General lost direct control over the matter. But IGs at the lower levels continued to carry out militia inspections. They monitored inspection standards; the performance of specially detailed inspectors who assisted them; and the forwarding of inspection records to the War Department. Thus in this way, even after the General Staff created the Militia Affairs Division in 1908 to administer militia inspections, the Inspector General retained considerable influence over National Guard inspections through his technical channels.[57]

The militia was also the object of legislation during the tenure of Secretary Root. Root eventually supported legislation establishing the organized militia, aware of unyielding congressional sentiment favoring the state troops. The Militia Act of 21 January 1903, generally known as the Dick Act, increased federal aid to the National Guard and laid the basic groundwork for its role as part of a total force. The first annual inspection of the National Guard occurred shortly after the law was passed. The War Department used the findings to determine the scope of its new liabilities and responsibilities. Each state's military organization was unique, tailored to its own concept of its needs. In consequence, a considerable force imbalance existed nationwide. Infantry units, cheaper to maintain and easier to fill, predominated, while very few states maintained the more expensive support units or artillery or cavalry formations. Some substantial discrepancies in actual strength as opposed to reported strength also existed. Many reorganizations and realignments thus were necessary in each state for meeting the law's requirement that the National Guard must parallel Regular Army organization within five years.[58]

Inspectors at geographical commands had conducted the first inspection, assisted by officers temporarily detailed by their comman-

---

[56] *ARIG 1883*, pp. 34–35; Memo, SofW to IG, 13 Nov 89, Entry 24, RG 159, NARA.

[57] WD, OIG, *Guide 1911/1917*, p. 19.

[58] Ganoe, *History*, p. 417; Elbridge Colby, "Elihu Root and the National Guard," *Military Affairs* 23 (Spring 59): 32; *ARSW 1904*, pp. 28–29, 258.

ders. This process was formalized in December 1903. Geographical area commanders were made responsible for the scheduling and conduct of the annual militia inspections. Each January thereafter they were to publish an inspection schedule and a roster of officers to be detailed for the duty. In actual practice, the local inspector carried out the responsibility and assured inspection standards. Units usually were visited during their five-day encampment, rather than in their armories. Typically, the inspectors looked into all aspects of Regular Army support for the militia units undergoing training and examined the units themselves for proficiency, conduct of training, and troop strength. Overall, they were to assess compliance with the provisions of the Dick Act and the resulting improvements in Guard operations. Their inspection reports went from the geographical area commanders through channels to the General Staff and, after 1908, to its Militia Affairs Division.[59]

The National Guard was brought closer to federal control when an amendment to the Dick Act on 27 May 1908 lifted restrictions on its employment following mobilization and specified that its supply and administrative procedures were to meet Regular Army standards by 1910. Thereafter, inspectors visited National Guard armories, making the equivalent of a Regular Army garrison visit. The War Department in March 1911 authorized the assignment of Regular Army inspector-instructors to the Guard units, on the basis of one officer for each regiment or separate battalion. The objective was to have 200 regulars assisting and evaluating the Guard units, but strength problems restricted the actual number to just over 100. These individuals were carefully selected and sent for special training to the Army Service School at Fort Leavenworth. Among the first officers assigned to the new duty were Lt. George C. Marshall (Massachusetts) and a future distinguished inspector general Capt. Marcellus G. Spinks (Maine).[60]

Inspector-instructors were considered to be agents of the War Department assigned to assist in National Guard training. Repeatedly, they and the state governors were advised that their relationship was one of coordination only, not direction. The regulars were encouraged to be flexible regarding adherence to regulations and enjoined to exercise tact and diplomacy. The Militia Affairs Division chief repeatedly

---

[59] Ltr, CofS, Atlantic Div, to Garlington, 15 Jun 06, Entry 24, RG 159, NARA. See also AReg 191, 1908.

[60] Ganoe, *History*, p. 438; Ltr, Wood to TAG, 15 May 11, and File 6506, Inspector-Instructors, Entry 296, RG 165, NARA; U.S. War Department, *Report of Chief, Division of Militia Affairs, 1911* (Washington, D.C.: Government Printing Office, 1912), pp. 48–51; WD GO 33, 1911, and GO 45, 1911.

emphasized to newly detailed officers the avocational, part-time nature of participation in the Guard. Inspector-instructors and IGs were warned that this did not imply a lack of zeal or military interest, for "militiamen are frequently shrewd observers, quick to detect a mere assumption of knowledge." Regular Army inspectors had to be fully knowledgeable; otherwise, they would lose all credibility.[61]

By 1913 a set formula was being used to cover all topics of interest. The Militia Affairs Division had prepared an extensive series of formats for every conceivable type of inspection by branch or by function. To assist, the Inspector General's Department produced a form for the annual inspection of National Guard armories. Despite the quantity of detail revealed through these checklists, the main areas of concern remained unit strength, property and fiscal accountability, and tactical proficiency. The two groups of inspectors complemented each other's activities, minimizing the problems that might have arisen from the fact that Guard inspection responsibilities were divided between two departments.[62]

During this period a growing number of states began to create the overhead staffs for major tactical organizations. By early 1912 ninety guardsmen were listed as inspectors general within their various commands. Their selection had been made by state officials, with no coordination with the Inspector General. Appointments to state inspectorates often were rewards for long and faithful service within the state military structure. But most functioned as additional staff officers in the state headquarters or as aides to one of the senior state officials, and rarely, if ever, performed as inspectors general. This was not always the case, however. In early 1911 the Delaware adjutant general, Brig. Gen. Ira P. Wickersham, successfully arranged for his inspector, Maj. Charles A. Short, to understudy active-duty IGs at the Eastern Division headquarters, and by the end of the year both Wickersham and General Garlington were satisfied that Short was operating at a level that was up to War Department standards.[63]

Despite instances of zeal and interest, however, the condition of the National Guard still gave many Regular Army officers cause for con-

[61] Ltrs, Mills to Insp-Instrs, Ret Offs on Duty with Militia, and AGs of States, [1915], sub: Duty of Inspector-Instructors; to Insp-Instrs, 19 Feb 15, sub: Confidential Instructions (quotation); and to Insp-Instrs, 1 Sep 15, sub: Instructions. All in Entry 35, RG 159, NARA.

[62] Rpt, Shanks, 9 Oct 13, sub: Inspection of South Carolina National Guard, Entry 24; IGD Office Memos and Blank Forms, Box 206, Entry 35. Both in RG 159, NARA.

[63] William H. Carter, *The American Army* (Indianapolis, Ind.: Bobbs-Merrill, 1915), pp. 282, 292; Ltr, AG, State of Del., to Chief, Mil Affs Div, 12 Jan 11, and Ends., Entry 296, RG 165, NARA.

cern. Strength, organization, and training levels remained low. The Guard's reliability was also questionable because of the legislative limitations on its deployability, length of service, and responsiveness. The value of the Guard as the Regular Army's main backup was challenged repeatedly with respect to the number that could be mobilized and the effect on the Army of diverting regulars to support Guard training.

The growing number of joint maneuvers and encampments observed and reported on by inspectors throughout the era allowed the National Guard's improvement to be monitored and an accurate comparison to elements of the Regular Army to be made. Joint maneuvers were carried out as early as 1902 and then in the summer of 1904 in California, the state of Washington, and Virginia. Other mixed exercises were conducted annually at coast artillery posts for units of that arm. Maneuvers and mobilizations took place every year—except 1905, 1907, and 1909 due to budgetary constraints—up through the Mexican border crisis. Mixed brigades of regular and militia units were formed into provisional divisions to conduct tactical exercises at various campsites throughout the country. Troop concentrations averaged between 5,000 and 10,000 men. The largest maneuvers were held at Manassas, Virginia, in 1904. There, a total force of over 26,000 officers and men was mobilized and organized into a provisional corps of two divisions. About 5,000 of the troops were regulars, while the remainder were militia from seventeen states. Joint maneuvers grew steadily in importance, especially as the border troubles with Mexico increased.[64]

As revealed by the inspection reports from these periodic joint maneuvers, the National Guard's major problems had to do with the maintenance of unit strength and the inexperience of senior officers. Equipment was improving at about the same rate as in the Regular Army. As indicated in the tactical inspection reports submitted on regular units, the problems of the two components were essentially the same. There was little difference in the skill levels of enlisted personnel, despite the regulars' Uptonian bias against part-time soldiers. General Garlington—surprisingly—showed a strong prejudice against the National Guard, even though he was one of the few War Department officials privy to the inspection reports that should have allowed him to make a more balanced judgment.[65]

---

[64] Ganoe, *History*, p. 420.

[65] Ltr, TAG to IG, 22 Mar 15, sub: Study Regarding Strength and Organization of Armed Land Forces, and Reply, 20 Apr 15, Entry, 25, RG 159, NARA. Secretary Root directed the posthumous publication of Col. Emory Upton's study *Military Policy of the United States*, which argued eloquently against reliance on a militia or National Guard as backup for the Regular Army. See Ganoe, *History*, p. 418.

With the passage of the National Defense Act of 1916, the inspectorate's role as the primary inspector of Guard units and activities was reestablished. Every Guard function, including finances, became subject to IG inspections. Whatever each had thought of the other, the new law required a fully professional relationship immediately, as Guard units answered the call to the Mexican border.[66]

The March 1916 raid on Columbus, New Mexico, caused the Wilson Administration to call out the National Guard of New Mexico, Arizona, and Texas to supplement the regular troops already gathered along the border or chasing Villa. Secretary of War Baker notified the respective state governors by telegram on 9 May 1916. The Adjutant General the next day sent a formal letter to each War Department bureau and department chief. General Garlington was told to ship all the necessary forms to the Southern Department and to coordinate with the officers selected to help the local inspectors muster the troops at the state mustering points. Federal recognition inspections were conducted concurrently by the mustering officers. Contingency instructions were issued to the commanders of the other geographical commands, directing them to prepare for similar call-ups in their areas. On 18 June the remainder of the National Guard was mobilized, and on the twentieth The Adjutant General directed the Inspector General to provide the same support as already given to the units activated the month before.[67]

General Garlington wanted his IGs to inspect every aspect of the National Guard concentration. On 21 June he recommended to the Chief of Staff, Maj. Gen. Hugh L. Scott, that they inspect the mobilization camps for their suitability—including sanitation, care of the sick, and the efficiency of logistical support—and that they also examine the health and equipment of the men and the mustering objectives of strength and proper organization. Garlington wanted the inspections done in accordance with instructions prepared by him, but under the authority and supervision of the respective geographical area commanders. General Scott quickly concurred, and on 23 June instructions were issued to the commanders to begin the more extensive inspections as soon as possible.[68]

---

[66] Memos, IG to Chief, Mil Bureau, 18 Jul 16, sub: Requests for Orders and Circulars; Mann to CofS, WD, 20 Nov 16; and CofS, WD, to IG, 21 Nov 16. All in Entry 25, RG 159, NARA. See also Carter, *American Army*, pp. 290–94.

[67] Ltrs, TAG to IG, 10 May and 20 Jun 16, subs: Muster in of Organized Militia, and Wood to TAG, 18 Jul 16, Entry 25, RG 159, NARA.

[68] Memo, IG to CofS, WD, 21 Jun 16, sub: Inspection of Mobilization and Concentration Camps of the National Guard; Ltr, Barry to TAG, 23 Jun 16. Both in Entry 25, RG 159, NARA.

Within days, inspectors descended on the mobilizing Guard units, preparing detailed reports on strength, personnel status, drill, organization, weapons proficiency, equipment status, and discipline. In them they were to comment on food, medical and supply services, camp operations, and unit administration; state their overall impression of unit personnel and the latter's preparedness; and to estimate the time necessary for the unit to become fully campaign ready. Appendixes to each report were to include lists of equipment not on hand and descriptions of any other logistical or medical shortcomings that impaired efficiency.

In practice, inspectors often summarized the most critical problems faced by units in their forwarding endorsements. They also commented on any other significant matters, such as the condition of troop trains, which might affect the unit. Generally speaking, the inspector-instructors and geographical area inspectors at the mobilization camps were kinder in their comments than were the IGs, who looked at the units after their arrival in the Southern Department.[69]

Early problems in supply began a series of IG investigations that added to the huge workload already thrust upon the inspectors. Almost from the beginning of the mobilization, members of Congress began to relay to the War Department the complaints of their state adjutants general about equipment shortages. Geographical area commanders also were sending wires, complaining about state interference in the supply process. On 27 June General Garlington instructed Maj. William S. McNair, a field artilleryman detailed to the OIG, to investigate the situation.

McNair's two-week study identified several major problems. The depot with the responsibility to supply all Guard units east of the Mississippi River was in Philadelphia. It had been converted recently into a multifunction facility, holding equipment that belonged to several bureaus. No single bureau chief controlled the depot any longer; instead, it responded directly to the orders of the Chief of Staff.[70]

The Chief of Staff's involvement, however, was overlooked by the General Staff in the initial excitement of the mobilization, and the depot was neither notified nor given guidance for the first three days. The depot commander exercised commendable but misplaced initiative and distributed the supplies, using a remarkably accurate Associated Press dispatch that gave mobilization locations. His problems were

---

[69] File 454, Inspection of State Mobilization, Entry 25, RG 159, NARA.
[70] Rpt, McNair, 8 Jul 16, sub: Investigation of Supply of Mobilization Camps, Entry 25, RG 159, NARA.

compounded by the unexpected speed of unit concentrations. For example, New Jersey and Pennsylvania units reported in at full peace strength on 21 June, three days after the call. They demanded full field equipment, which the depot could not issue without specific authorization. Adding to the crisis was the fact that many southern National Guards showed up without any equipment or uniforms, presuming that everything would be provided by the federal government.

Adding to the initial problems were unilateral changes of the mobilization sites, conflicts between Quartermaster and Army regulations, and the insufficiency of depot stock to meet the surge of requirements. Major McNair concluded that the problem lay with the system, rather than with the actions of any individual. He recommended that a nationwide mobilization plan, to include depot participation, be created and that Congress provide the funds to allow the stockage of sufficient reserves of materiel to sustain a full mobilization. His depot organizational recommendations were adopted in July, while the next appropriations bill addressed the need for greater equipment reserves.[71]

But broader proposals were disapproved. The inspector of the New Jersey Guard mobilization recommended that permanent mobilization sites and equipment depots be prepared for each National Guard division and that periodic practice call-ups be held to test the mobilization plans. The Quartermaster General supported the concept, saying he could begin construction using standard designs on hand whenever funds were available. The General Staff, however, turned down the idea on the grounds that another full mobilization was unlikely and that sufficient facilities existed to sustain incremental call-ups. It appeared that one of the major lessons to be learned from the 1916 mobilization had been rejected even before it was fully developed.[72]

Urged on by the chief of the National Guard Bureau, General Garlington also planned to inspect National Guard units once they had deployed to the Mexican border. While Maj. Fox Conner began a circuit of the artillery units, Lt. Col. Eli A. Helmick, the newly appointed Southern Department inspector, organized an extensive inspection program for the remaining units. The scale of the task, plus Helmick's aversion to wasting the troops' time, led him to devise a new and more efficient inspection method, consisting of a series of checklists and

[71] Ibid; WD SO 177, 1916.

[72] Memos, Johnson to Garlington, 8 Jul 16, sub: Inspection of Mobilization Camps; OIG to Insps, 19 Sep 16; and TAG to IG, 5 Jul 16, sub: Changes in Mobilization Points. All in Entry 25, RG 159, NARA. See also Rpt, Chamberlain, Jul 16, sub: Mobilization of New Jersey National Guard, and End., Entry 296, RG 165, NARA.

explanatory illustrations for each echelon within an infantry regiment. Helmick had it mimeographed, illustrated with photographs, and circulated among the inspectors on the border teams. Ultimately, the checklist became the guide and model for IGs and General Staff members responsible for inspecting the far greater number of units preparing for deployment to France in 1917.[73]

The findings reported by the inspectors were not promising. Most of the units barely had met their muster strength, and many of the men on hand were in process of receiving compassionate discharges. On the whole, inspectors felt that the social nature of many Guard units attracted older enlisted men with family and financial obligations that made them unsuitable for extended military service. Although a few units were filled with over-qualified college men, the personnel of most were comparable to those of the average regular unit. Nevertheless, inspectors considered the overall Guard personnel system to be flawed, a criticism that extended to the officers. The inspectors classified most of the Guard officers as willing and eager to learn, but on the average they were too inexperienced to fulfill the role of instructors that was expected of them in a mobilization.[74]

Not all the problems were unique to the National Guard units. The inspectors were surprised by the low level of discipline prevailing throughout the force, regardless of component, a condition which they attributed in part to the dilution of Regular Army units to form cadres for newer units and in part to lack of experience in the younger officers. Throughout both components, the overall training levels of the troops were found by inspectors to be much lower in every function than expected. Nevertheless, the magnitude of such difficulties was always greater in the state-raised formations. Some 45 percent of the men in the Guard units had enlisted after the President's call, and a slightly higher percentage had never fired a weapon. Believing that under the circumstances training could never be more than marginally successful, the inspectors were very pessimistic over any real progress being made without the National Guard being brought under complete federal control in peace and war.[75]

---

[73] File 454d, Inspection of Organized Militia and National Guard in the Service of the U.S., Entry 25, RG 159, NARA; Helmick, "Autobiography," MHI; Memo, Chamberlain to Insps, 3 Jul 17, sub: Method of Inspecting and Checking the Field Equipment of an Infantry Command, Entry 296, RG 165, NARA.

[74] Helmick, "Autobiography," MHI.

[75] Memo, Helmick to IG (through channels), 11 Nov 16, sub: Special Field Inspections of National Guard and Organized Militia in the Southern Department, Entry 25, RG 159, NARA.

Guard units began to be released from the Mexican border in the fall of 1916, mustered out by IGs and inspector-instructors in a reversal of the mobilization process. The growing tensions with Germany caused IGs in the geographical commands to give priority during early 1917 to the conduct of inspections in the armories of National Guard units not in federal service. Shortly thereafter, the inspection and muster process experienced in the summer of 1916 began to repeat itself. The Adjutant General in early March checked on the federal status of Guard units and then solicited geographical area commanders to specify what further units they needed for federal service. By the twenty-fourth units were being recalled. Additional inspectors began to be detailed and assigned to mobilization sites in the first week of April. The smoothness of this second mobilization and the promptness of the accompanying inspection effort reflected fourteen years of cumulative experience capped by the dress rehearsal on the Mexican border.[76]

In retrospect, the reports of the inspectors recorded not only the growth and maturing of the National Guard but also the impact of the Progressive Era's reforms on the Regular Army as it reshaped itself into a modern force. These documents provide insight into the differences and prejudices dividing the Regular and Guard components, and help to explain many of the problems that later developed during the deployment to France in 1917 and 1918. Colonel Helmick's unsympathetic views towards the Guard formed during the inspections in the summer of 1916 were to persist into the World War, and his experience would influence strongly his findings during the mobilization. His 1916 report presaged the policies of 1917 and sealed the fate of many senior guardsmen. Despite such prejudices, there were hard truths about the state of both guardsmen and regulars contained in the views of the inspectors—truths that the Army as a whole needed to learn quickly as the nation drifted toward war.

---

[76] Ltrs, Garlington to Dept Insps, 8 Dec 16, sub: Annual Armory Inspection of National Guard, etc., and AG, Eastern Dept, to Glasgow, 6 Apr 17, sub: Inspection of 71st Regiment, N.Y. Inf. NG," Entry 25, RG 159, NARA.

3

The Quality of Life

From the time they joined the Army until the time they died, soldiers and veterans depended upon the inspectorate to watch over the quality of life and to protect them against abuses. As the Army modernized, inspectors investigated the complaints they received and filed reports on almost every aspect of military life. The problems that they identified were many and varied, and not all would be solved rapidly.

Recruiting

Inspectors, usually those assigned to geographical commands, actively monitored the various recruiting stations scattered in cities across the country. Because the stations were War Department activities, the inspection reports were sent directly to the Office of the Inspector General (OIG), which, when necessary, referred them to the respective recruiting officers for remedial action or comment before forwarding them to The Adjutant General. These reports were quite brief, in a letter format, and covered such topics as the appearance of the recruiting personnel, administration of the office, and adequacy of the facility. The inspectors considered their visits to the stations to be one of their more important duties, both because of the need for good recruits and because the stations represented the Army in the eyes of the public.[1]

Inspectors also addressed the productivity of the station and made recommendations as to whether it should remain open. Most of the stations in northern New Mexico, for example, were closed in 1907, because the number of men recruited was too low to justify operating costs. Other areas of interest were the effectiveness of advertising and community attitudes, and any contracts and fiscal arrangements made by

---

[1] File 10583, Recruiting Station Inspection Reports, Entry 24, Record Group (RG) 159, National Archives and Records Administration (NARA), Washington, D.C.

Maj. Gen. John L. Chamberlain
(Rank as of 6 October 1917)

the station commander were scrutinized and evaluated for equitability and acceptability. However, not all IG recommendations were well received. In 1915, as the Eastern Department inspector, Colonel Chamberlain suggested that tours for recruiting NCOs be changed from indefinitely—the practice of the time—to four years. General Garlington backed Chamberlain, but The Adjutant General vigorously rejected the idea. The Chief of Staff and Secretary agreed, and Chamberlain's proposal was shelved—another idea whose time had not yet come.[2]

The inspectors' involvement with the stations also led them to deal with issues that affected the retaining or attracting of recruits. In 1913 Lt. Col. Augustus P. Blocksom successfully recommended elimination of the unpopular "2300 bedcheck." Periodically, IGs remarked on the need for adequate pay and bonuses to attract recruits with special skills. Affiliating regiments with geographical areas for recruiting purposes was sometimes suggested. Some of the problems the inspectors encountered reflected the prejudices of the era in which they lived.[3]

In 1905 Senator Redfield Proctor of Vermont proposed that a teetotaler's oath be made a condition for enlistment. Secretary of War Taft asked Inspector General Burton to explain to the senator the difficulties that would result. Burton cited the many earlier Army efforts to promote temperance, which proved to him that encouraging moderation was the best policy. Trying to make the potential soldier a teetotaler would make recruiting impossible, with no retention advantage to the

[2] Ltr, Chamberlain to Garlington, 5 Jun 15, sub: Recruiting, Entry 25, RG 159, NARA.

[3] U.S. War Department, *Annual Report of the Inspector General, 1906* (Washington, D.C.: Government Printing Office, 1906), pp. 644, 648 (hereafter cited as *ARIG*); *ARIG 1913*, p. 277; Ltr (quoted words), Blocksom to Dept Cdr, 14 Jul 13, with ends., Roll 40, Microfilm 912, Indexes to War College Division Records, RG 165, NARA.

Army. He thus suggested that the best way to achieve temperance in the Army was to restore the sale of beer and wine in post exchange canteens. The senator agreed to withdraw his proposal, but the canteens remained dry.[4]

The Army traditionally mustered new recruits at selected depots, where they were physically evaluated and given the rudiments of training before being sent to their units. Discontinued in 1894 as an economy measure, the practice was revived in 1904, when recruit depots were reactivated at Columbus Barracks, Ohio; Fort Slocum, New York; and Jefferson Barracks, Missouri. As before, the depots were placed under the control of The Adjutant General (or the Military Secretary, as he was briefly known). Additional depots later were activated at Fort McDowell, California, and Fort Logan, Colorado. Almost immediately, the depots became major items of concern for the Inspector General's Department (IGD).[5]

Numerous complaints about mismanagement and abuse of authority began to be received at the War Department. Fort Slocum was cited the most frequently. The recruit barracks were below standard, and petty rackets were rampant. With the apparent knowledge of the commander, the recruits were required to sell their civilian clothing to one of the cadre NCOs or to pay bribes to the post bandmaster to receive an easier duty assignment in the band. The impression made on the new recruits was deplorable.[6]

The flood of such complaints led the Secretary of War on 29 March 1906 to direct General Burton to inspect every recruit depot in the Army every two months, describing the actual conditions and recommending improvements. The problems Burton discovered at these locations were due largely to their hasty formation with temporary personnel and little practical guidance from the War Department. Burton assisted the local commanders as best he could and successfully won approval for the assignment of permanent training cadre and staff. He did find corruption at Fort Slocum, resulting in the relief of the post commander and several NCOs. Their replacement with permanent cadre solved the most pressing difficulties there. By May, when General Burton made his last inspection, the recruit depots had

---

[4] Ltr, Burton to MilSec, 15 Apr 05, Entry 24, RG 159, NARA.

[5] U.S. War Department, *Annual Report of the Secretary of War, 1905* (Washington, D.C.: Government Printing Office, 1905), p. 13 (hereafter cited as *ARSW*); Leonard L. Lerwill, *The Personnel Replacement System in the U.S. Army*, DA Pamphlet No. 20–211 (Washington, D.C.: Government Printing Office, 1954), pp. 140–43.

[6] Ltr, Smith to CofS, WD, 26 Mar 05, Entry 24, RG 159, NARA.

improved further. In 1907 inspection authority was passed to The Adjutant General, although in practice IGs continued to do the work at his request.[7]

The recruit depots continued to function up to 1921, remaining within the purview of the War Department inspectorate because of their exempted status. When the discharge and replacement depots took over, they were assigned to the control of the geographical area commanders and the inspection responsibility devolved to inspectors at that level.[8]

Rations and Quarters

Securing the soldier adequate rations and quarters remained an important aspect of the inspectorate's duties. In 1914 the Office of the Inspector General conducted a massive survey of leased off-post housing at recruiting stations and other areas where military personnel were not living in government quarters. The survey was undertaken because of the supposedly high cost of leased housing and the charge that enlisted personnel assigned to Washington, D.C., were profiting from kickbacks from rent paid to their landlord by the government.

Headed by Lt. Col. David C. Shanks, a team wrote to every officer known to be living off post worldwide, asking for a copy of his lease and a description of his accommodations. Each geographical area commander was similarly solicited for copies of all housing contracts on file within his command. Bureau chiefs were surveyed so that facilities leased for recruiting stations, remount depots, and warehouses would not be overlooked.[9]

The survey showed that the Army generally was competing reasonably well on the housing market. Those few quarters found to be overpriced were identified and the leases scheduled for termination or renegotiation. Colonel Shanks determined that officers usually were living within their allowances, but he described the workings of the Quartermaster lease system for enlisted men as "grotesque." Far from profiting from it, the system required married soldiers to pay from their

---

[7] *ARIG 1905*, p. 466; *ARIG 1906*, p. 649; Memo, MilSec to IG, 29 Mar 06, Entry 24, RG 159, NARA; U.S. War Department, Office of the Inspector General, *A Guide for the Use of Officers of the Inspector General's Department, 1911, Corrected to April 1, 1917* (Washington, D.C.: Government Printing Office, 1917), p. 17 (hereafter cited as *Guide 1911/1917*); WD GO 124, 1907.

[8] WD GO 55, 1921.

[9] File 16689, Leased Off-Post Facilities Inspection, Entry 24; Rpt, Shanks, 13 Apr 14, sub: Investigation Concerning Leases of Quarters for Army Nurses and Enlisted Men on Duty in Washington, DC, Entry 35. Both in RG 159, NARA.

own pockets rents that exceeded the basic allowance for nongovernment housing. Single men simply needed less to live comfortably—hence, the allegations of graft.[10]

Shanks went on to describe the situation as both frustrating and humiliating for married senior NCOs, and a frequent cause for their early departure from the Army. He concluded that the only fair way to deal with the situation was to determine a flat money commutation, based on grade and marital status, to be paid whenever government housing was unavailable, with an additional variable rate for especially high-cost areas. General Garlington agreed with Shanks' recommendations in his report to the Secretary of War, and Shanks' approach became the basis for a housing allowance policy that remained in force for the rest of the century.[11]

Just as proper housing included aspects of morale, living conditions, and business efficiency, so too did the related topic of rations and feeding. Mess hall operations were at the center of a major controversy early in the century. In 1893 Congress had approved a Quartermaster's Department recommendation to consolidate unit messes into post general messes, in an effort to make the feeding system more efficient and to use the scarce talents of the cooks and bakers just graduating from newly established schools. The act was universally deplored by line commanders. Unit mess halls had served as social focal points and were under each commander's control. The practical chore of equitably sharing unit fund improvements with other units was cumbersome if not impossible. Also, a well-run unit mess hall and its company garden often could show a profit, to be used for other morale-support activities. General Burton recommended that the Army return to the company mess system, and his proposal was adopted in 1905, general messes being retained only at recruit depots and similar installations where they were unavoidable.[12]

Inspectors also were concerned about the content and composition of field rations. In June 1906 Congress revised the Navy ration, standardizing it throughout the fleet and including dairy products as a component. Garlington stressed in his 1907 report that similar arrangements should be made for Army rations. At the time, the garrison ration was a monotonous issue of staples, supplemented by produce from the company garden and special purchases of the company fund. Garlington pointed out that a unit's location and its commander's busi-

---

[10] Rpt, Shanks, 13 Apr 14, Entry 35, RG 159, NARA.

[11] Ibid.

[12] *ARIG 1903*, p. 447; *ARIG 1904*, p. 289.

ness acumen too often determined the quality of an Army mess and its offerings. Should a unit be deployed elsewhere, soldiers could be denied many components of a healthy diet. Garlington recommended incorporating greater variety into the standard Army ration, a reform that might even help to retain soldiers in the service. His recommendation, however, was not accepted, and a modified version of the system he disliked was retained for many years.[13]

Post Exchanges

The War Department established post exchanges, originally called canteens, in 1889 to replace the post trader system, which had proven both difficult to control and often unfair to the troops. The canteens were authorized to sell beer and wines as well as light meals and sundries. By the time of the War with Spain, they were judged to be a great success. They provided a wholesome alternative to off-post saloons, and they turned a modest profit that could be channeled into other forms of welfare spending, including unit funds.[14]

Exchange operations continued to expand and, by 1901, provided an extensive blend of sales and morale-support activities. Regulations specified that a fully operational exchange would consist of a general store, a restaurant, library, game rooms, and a gymnasium. Barber, tailor, and shoe repair shops also were desirable. The regulations defined the nature of each commercial activity and prohibited any other ventures without War Department approval. The Inspector General's Department was the War Department agency that decided on both the propriety of existing activities and on exemptions.[15]

The unit, or company, funds were intended to supplement the activities of the post exchanges, as well as the items issued by the supply departments for troop welfare. The funds were limited to spending money "for the benefit of the company," but the requirement was very broadly interpreted. For example, seed purchased for a company garden and wages for the gardener were both authorized. Company funds could be used to operate profit-making facilities like barbershops if such services were not provided by the post exchange. Capital for the exchanges was derived in part from per capita shares purchased by each of the units on the post. The disposition of the

---

[13] End, Garlington, 11 Nov 07, to Ltr, Greely to SG, 1 Nov 07, Entry 24, RG 159, NARA.

[14] *ARIG 1889*, p. 131; *ARIG 1890*, p. 105.

[15] WD GO 176, 1909, and GO 113, 1910; PXReg, 1916.

funds generated by company-level enterprises was subject to OIG review, as were any changes in the regulations governing funds and other aspects of soldier welfare.[16]

A critical problem in funding the exchanges developed when Congress prohibited the sale of beer and wine. This well-intended effort to reduce soldier drinking drove the men into off-post grog shops, beyond commanders' control, and drastically reduced exchange profits, curtailing other morale-support activities.

The narrow margins of profit underscored the need for professional exchange management, which the inspectors had begun to advocate almost from the beginning of the century. In 1903 General Burton successfully suggested the allocation of appropriated funds to sustain the libraries and gymnasiums, which no longer could be supported from exchange profits. In turn, the use of appropriated funds led to an increased number of investigations to assure that the money was being spent as Congress intended.[17]

The absence of standard accountability systems as revealed by inspections led General Burton to develop a model in 1905 and to urge its adoption. The discovery in February of that year that the exchange steward at Fort Monroe, Virginia, had been guilty of embezzlement prompted a series of investigations and inquiries, which led to the complete revision of exchange operations throughout the Army. After much investigation and delay, in 1909 a general order codified a standard bookkeeping and accounting system. Initially, the General Staff refused to endorse the new system because of its concern over command prerogatives. But most officers were happy to embrace the proposed system, whose practice also continued throughout the century.[18]

The OIG's recommendation remained the final word in approving or disapproving requests from exchange or company fund councils to operate concessions or games that could generate profits. Inspectors also continued to make the final recommendations for any waivers from the regulations. Advancing technology and changing modes of entertainment increased the variety of such requests. For example, General Garlington favored running motion picture programs only on a concession basis, primarily because of the overhead costs of buying equipment and building fireproof projection booths. But his reluctance to let the silver screen come to the Army posts was not shared by the Secretary of War, who overrode his objections.

---

[16] WD Cir 6 (quoted words), 1904; AReg 343, 1913.
[17] *ARIG 1903*, pp. 450–51; *ARSW 1905*, pp. 380–82.
[18] *ARIG 1905*, p. 454; *ARIG 1906*, p. 639; WD GO 176, 1909.

The variety of activities and the unpredictable nature of a project's profitability meant that problems could arise over the disposition of assets. Local commanders usually designated their inspectors to investigate any losses or improprieties in the management of exchange funds and to determine responsibility. Negligence and procedural errors composed the bulk of these sort of inquiries. Occasionally, however, disciplinary action had to be taken by commanders. In June 1912, when an inspector determined that a chaplain was misusing exchange funds, General Garlington recommended that the officer be reprimanded and reassigned, and the geographical area commander sent him off with a blistering letter. In such unusual cases, as in the more customary ones, the Inspector General's Department was the authority on every aspect of local funds management.[19]

Discipline

The improvement of living conditions could not satisfy all men in the ranks. Inevitably, the Army endured a steady trickle of desertions. Losing trained men was costly, and the morale and leadership of the affected units also suffered.

Inspectors had long been concerned with matters of discipline throughout the Army. Any issues involving disciplinary matters were at least touched upon in regular inspections, and the attention of the inspectors extended also to the disposition of the men disciplined and the policies affecting them. Prior to the annual inspection, units were required to submit strength and discipline statistics for the inspector's use during his visit and in preparing his report. Whenever the number of desertions or courts-martial was excessive, the issue became a matter of special inquiry, conducted in conjunction with the scheduled inspection. The deserters' backgrounds and their places of enlistment were checked for any trends. Inspectors interviewed unit personnel and any apprehended deserters to determine precise causes for leaving. Early in the century the main causes were personal, such as excessive drinking or indebtedness, both believed to be partially caused by a lack of recreational alternatives. By 1906 inspectors also listed excessive turbulence in the officer corps as a major factor contributing to desertion.[20]

---

[19] File 12592, Post Exchange Policy Files, Columbus Barracks, Ohio, Case of Chaplain E. P. Newson, Entry 24, RG 159, NARA.

[20] AReg 906(7), 1908; AReg 913(7), 1910; AReg 889(7), 1913. See also *ARIG 1903*, pp. 447–48; *ARIG 1906*, p. 638; *ARIG 1907*, pp. 265–69; *ARIG 1909*, p. 295; *ARIG 1911*, p. 271; *ARIG 1915*, p. 231.

By 1907 the problem of desertions had become so acute that the Secretary of War directed a special investigation be made to determine causes and provide possible remedies. Each geographical command inspector general made the inquiry in his region. Typical of these was the one made by Maj. Zerah W. Torrey in the Pacific Division. He first reviewed the statistics on desertions by unit throughout the division. He identified eighteen units with unusually high desertion rates and others with low but steady rates. Torrey visited each of the affected units, as well as a few others selected at random that had few or no desertions. Interviewing first the post commander, the officers, and NCOs of the identified units, as well as many of the men, he then moved on to interview over 200 incarcerated for desertion in the military prison at Alcatraz.[21]

Most desertions occurred because of an excessive turnover of officers—many of the worst units had had as many as three commanders in a year—and because of harsh or unfair treatment and poor food. These conditions, Torry concluded, were directly related to the inexperience and instability of the company leadership. He suggested that the solution to the desertion problem lay in leaving the company-level officers in their units for periods long enough to give them the experience and responsibility of caring for their men. Torrey's report was received favorably throughout the chain of command and was published as a part of the Inspector General's 1907 annual report. A copy also was sent to each inspector and senior commander. Such measures and general command attention to the causes of desertion led to a modest drop in the rate the next year. Yet the problem remained a matter of concern for the Army up to the World War.[22]

Complaints and Investigations

Soldiers were authorized to make complaints to a visiting inspector, who would often investigate them while on site. The quantity of soldier complaints may have been reduced by the practice of naming each complainant and his allegations in the body of the inspection report. Such actions were nevertheless routine. Inspectors were required by regulation to verify and report on all complaints, including those by civilians, and make special note of items requiring War Department action. They also were expected to follow up on any issue raised that

---

[21] OIG, 28 Dec 07, sub: Synopsis of Major Torrey's Reports on the Causes of Desertion, Entry 24, RG 159, NARA.

[22] Ibid.; *ARSW* 1907, pp. 66–110; *ARIG* 1908, p. 260.

was not in accordance with accepted practice or regulations and to recommend a solution. For unsubstantiated innuendo, they had to prepare a brief neutral account of the allegation in a separate memorandum and then forward it to the Office of the Inspector General for filing in case any corroboratory trends surfaced in the future.[23]

General Garlington made it a matter of unbending office policy never to react to an anonymous complaint. If the general source could be determined, he would direct that the complaint be sent to the local inspector for his information—a personal policy not practiced at the geographical commands. Garlington ignored particularly vituperative complaints, saying that no good purpose could be served in trying to investigate them. Generally speaking, complaints made by soldiers with poor disciplinary records or in a convict or AWOL status received preliminary analyses and brief investigations, but no further action.[24]

Issues raised by members of Congress were handled promptly. In 1914 Congressman Charles A. Plumley of Vermont had received a letter from a soldier complaining of poor conditions in the guardhouse and erratic justice at Trinidad, Colorado, and passed it on to the Secretary of War, who ordered an immediate investigation. The Central Department inspector, Col. Charles M. O'Connor, was selected to investigate the complaint on behalf of the War Department. O'Connor noted the unique conditions in Trinidad, a temporary camp set up to monitor labor unrest, and the need for tight discipline. The inspector judged the conditions in the guardhouse to be spartan, but not unreasonable. General Garlington recommended to the Chief of Staff that the complainant be punished for making a false statement and going out of the chain of command, believing that soldiers were not allowed by the Articles of War to seek redress through a third party.[25]

Secretary of War Garrison tightened the handling of complaints on 10 November 1914, directing that all be referred to an inspector general for investigation. He had learned that a number of complaints had been investigated within units, sometimes by those against whom the complaints had been made. He agreed that commanders should and could determine whether a complaint had some basis, but he wanted all

---

[23] WD GO 87, 1911; WD, OIG, *Guide 1911/1917*, p. 24. See also Rpt, Donaldson, 17 May 15, sub: Garrison Inspection of Plattsburg Barracks, N.Y., Entry 11, RG 159, NARA.

[24] Memo, Garlington to OIG, [1906], sub: Anonymous Complaints; Ltr, Gross to SofW, Nov 14, and End, Garlington, 2 Dec 14. Both in Entry 24, RG 159, NARA.

[25] Rpt, O'Connor, 5 Dec 14, sub: Investigation of Military Conditions at Trinidad, Colorado, Entry 25, RG 159, NARA.

but the most obviously false ones referred to an IG to ensure justice and to avoid allegations of mishandling.[26]

Sometimes inspectors found themselves involved in sensitive cases equivalent to modern pretrial investigations. This was particularly so in inquiries involving officers. Other bureau chiefs often asked through channels for an IG to look into sensitive items in their own elements, rather than have a member of their own corps do so. At times the Office of the Inspector General would recommend that the investigation be made by the geographical area commander or his inspector. About two-thirds of the cases investigated typically dealt with complaints about officer or soldier conduct, ranging from allegations of the abuse of authority to the commission of crime.[27]

In 1915 the Office of the Inspector General objected to wording in the proposed bill to organize the Army. The bill said in essence that the Judge Advocate General's duties included investigations necessary to the administration of justice. The Inspector General's executive officer, Lt. Col. Andre W. Brewster, drafted Garlington's ideas in a memorandum to the Secretary of War, stating that the Judge Advocate General's Department should become involved in IG investigations only upon their completion and when probable grounds for a criminal charge were evident. Garlington and the Secretary agreed. A new definition was prepared, stressing the paramount role of the Inspector General's Department in investigations.[28]

The tight grip on investigations was not quite as complete in practice as it was in principle. Commanders could appoint other officers to conduct investigations when IGs were unavailable. This practice was not encouraged, however. The chance that an investigation might not be sufficient or that confidentiality could be compromised was greater when an investigation was made outside IG channels. Further, the War Department risked embarrassment if a reply to a complainant was based on an incomplete report.

This problem was illustrated by a 1915 officer conduct case. The local commander recommended sending an investigation made by one of his officers directly to the Congressman who had forwarded the initiating complaint from one of his constituents. General Garlington

---

[26] Memo, Garrison to CofS, WD, 10 Nov 14, Entry 296, RG 165, NARA; ibid., 11 Nov 14, Entry 25, RG 159, NARA.

[27] For a listing of typical investigations, see Rpt, Bailey to IG, 30 Jun 03, Entry 35, RG 159, NARA.

[28] Memo, Brewster to SofW, 10 Nov 15; Telg, IG to SofW, 15 Nov 15; Memo, Brewster to CofS, WD, 27 Nov 15. All in Entry 25, RG 159, NARA.

rejected the proposal firmly, stressing that it was the "unbroken rule" of the Office of the Inspector General not to furnish investigation reports to outside parties, regardless of the status of the Army investigator. In this particular case the investigating officer happened to be a former IG, designated as a special inspector for the investigation but not a member of the Inspector General's Department.[29]

Race Relations

Investigations touched upon virtually every aspect of the soldier's life and activities. None were more sensitive or more politically charged than those involving race, especially in what can only be termed a racist age. The best known of the many cases investigated before the World War involved the soldiers of the 25th Infantry, a black regiment. In late July 1906 a regimental battalion deployed from Fort Niobrara, Nebraska, to Brownsville, Texas. The troops encountered strict Jim Crow laws after their arrival and were not well received by the white citizens of the town, who had vehemently opposed their assignment.[30]

In this tense environment a number of racial incidents occurred. Then on the night of 13 August a party of unknown men rampaged through the town, firing rifles. One white civilian was killed and two others were wounded. The community immediately suspected the black troops as being the perpetrators, although the circumstantial evidence available could as easily have been levied against white rowdies. Major Blocksom, the assistant inspector for the Southwestern Division, conducted the initial Army investigation of the incident, beginning his inquiry on the eighteenth. He interviewed the battalion officers, NCOs, and many of the men, as well as many civilians and federal officials. The major also visited the various places where other significant incidents had taken place.

In his report Blocksom briefly summarized the record of tensions between the community and the newly arrived black troops. He then recorded the specific events of the so-called raid as reported to him. Apparently, he had begun the investigation without questioning the

---

[29] Rpt, Helmick to CG, 2d Div, 8 Sep 15, sub: Investigation of Charges Against 2Lt J. A. Davies, 27th Inf, with encls.; Rpt (quoted words), Winn to TAG, 18 Feb 16, sub: Accusations Against 2Lt Jasper A. Davies. Both in Entry 25, RG 159, NARA.

[30] There are several studies of the Brownsville incident. See Marvin Fletcher, *The Black Soldier and Officer in the United States Army, 1891–1917* (Columbia: University of Missouri Press, 1974), and John D. Weaver, *The Brownsville Raid* (New York: W. W. Norton and Co., 1970.)

guilt of the black troops. His only question was their identity and the degree of responsibility of their leaders. He concluded that the battalion officers had done nothing that could have contributed to the incident and that they had acted reasonably in its aftermath. Unable to discover any perpetrators, Blocksom assumed that the soldiers had entered into a conspiracy of silence. He recommended that the whole unit be discharged without honor and barred from any further federal service if the guilty parties remained unknown. Blocksom ended his report listing the names of the men arrested by civil authorities, most of whom he presumed to be the culprits, and stating that they would be released because of a lack of evidence.[31]

By the time the report was submitted on 29 August, the battalion had been moved to Fort Reno, Oklahoma. There the men were watched closely, in the hope that further information could be obtained about the raid. Up to this point, with the initial exception of the battalion commander, the entire chain of command assumed that some of the soldiers had been involved in the shooting.

In late September 1906 Blocksom's superior, Lt. Col. Leonard A. Lovering, who, like Blocksom, was a West Point graduate from a northern state, initiated a follow-up investigation because of the continued lack of information from the troops and because two officers, stationed in Brownsville just before the arrival of the black troops, had stepped forward with sworn affidavits. The officers charged that some of Brownsville's citizens had conspired to discredit the blacks, with the aim of having them sent away. Colonel Lovering accumulated a large number of sworn affidavits from the officers and men. From this he was able to build an accurate list of unit members present at Brownsville or out of the area. He further substantiated some of the community hostility towards the black soldiers. But Lovering, who also presumed that the black soldiers were guilty, came no closer to discovering the truth.[32]

The work of both inspectors had far-reaching results. President Theodore Roosevelt used the inspectors' recommendations as the basis for his decision to discharge the entire battalion without honor as conspirators, unless the guilty were identified. On 4 October Assistant Secretary of War Robert Shaw Oliver gave a letter of instruction to General Garlington. Clearly implying the guilt of some members of the 25th Infantry, the letter directed the Inspector General to resume the investigation and to present the troops the President's

---

[31] *ARSW 1906*, pp. 225–85 (Blocksom Rpt).
[32] Ibid., pp. 287–356 (Lovering Rpt).

ultimatum at a moment of his choosing after he had interviewed them at Fort Reno.[33]

Before going to Oklahoma, Garlington discussed the case with Lovering and Blocksom in their office at Fort Sam Houston. Nothing new came out of the conference. Garlington then interviewed a group of soldiers still held at Fort Sam Houston, against whom Texas charges had been made and dropped; he talked with each informally in private and concluded that they were intentionally reticent when the subject of Brownsville came up. Proceeding to Fort Reno, Garlington next interviewed battalion members—officers and selected NCOs, as well as enlisted, questioning mostly the older men on the premise that their loyalty and discipline would make them less likely to cover anything up.[34]

Here again, the Inspector General found the soldiers to be uncommunicative about anything to do with Brownsville and concluded that some sort of conspiracy existed among the men. He soon decided that he could make no further progress. He had the battalion assembled, read them the President's ultimatum, and gave them twenty-four hours to think it over. At the end of the waiting period he endorsed the recommendation that all men in the battalion be discharged without honor and barred from federal employment. Garlington was convinced that some of the soldiers had participated in the incident and that their guilt was being covered up by all the others. He felt that example and good discipline for the rest of the Army required such a severe measure, although he recognized that some innocent men might be hurt. President Roosevelt approved the discharges on 5 November, and the order was carried into effect four days later.[35]

The President's order aroused a storm of protest in the black press and became a matter of growing controversy in Congress. The plight of the soldiers was championed by Senator Joseph B. Foraker of Ohio, who welcomed the opportunity to assail the President for political reasons but also was genuinely outraged by the blanket discharge. The agitation stirred the administration to further action. Secretary of War Taft wrote Garlington in December to say that, although the President considered the IG reports "entirely sufficient" for his decision, he felt it expedient to reopen the investigation because of the political interest. Taft accordingly directed that Major Blocksom return to Brownsville to gather up any further information that might be available. He closed his letter with the odd observation: "The President has

---

[33] Ltr, Oliver to Garlington, 4 Oct 06, Entry 24, RG 159, NARA.

[34] Ltr, Garlington to Ainsworth, 14 Dec 06, Entry 24, RG 159, NARA.

[35] *ARSW 1906*, pp. 357–62 (Garlington Rpt).

reached a conclusion as to what the facts are, but this should not influence Maj. Blocksom."[36]

Blocksom went back to Brownsville, accompanied by Assistant Attorney General Milton D. Purdy. The two men conducted still another investigation, even more complete. Their findings in part led the President to cancel the portion of his order barring the discharged soldiers from getting civil service jobs. Roosevelt also authorized that any of the discharged soldiers who could prove they were not involved in the incident could be reconsidered for reenlistment. As a result, on 21 January 1907 Secretary Taft directed General Ainsworth, who was responsible for recruiting operations, to screen those from the 25th Infantry who were applying for reenlistment. Each applicant was to be queried on the extent of his involvement in the Brownsville incident and what he had done to uncover the culprits. Other witnesses could be interviewed if necessary for fact-finding purposes. The interviewer further was to determine the veracity and quality of each applicant and decide whether he could reenlist.[37]

A week later Ainsworth forwarded a roster of applicants to General Garlington, requesting that an IGD member who was not involved in any of the Brownsville investigations perform the examinations. Recruiting officers already had been told of the requirements and procedures in a circular issued earlier. Major Galbraith conducted most of the interviews, traveling from Washington to wherever a member of the 25th applied for reentry. Yet his inquiries seemed more focused on gathering additional information about the incident than on clearing any of the soldiers, and his 11 February report resulted in very few of the discharged men being allowed to return. In the meantime, Major Blocksom remained in Brownsville until late April, searching for more information, a diversion of effort that completely upset his command's inspection plan and necessitated nearly all inspections being deferred or passed to IGs from other regions.[38]

This activity deflected some of the criticism aimed at the President, but Senator Foraker continued to pursue the matter. In January 1907 the Senate Military Affairs Committee agreed to investigate the raid. While that was going on, the battalion commander and officer of the day were

[36] James A. Tinsley, "Roosevelt, Foraker and the Brownsville Affray," *Journal of Negro History* 41 (Jan 56): 46, 50; Ltr (quotations) Taft to Garlington, 22 Dec 06, Entry 24, RG 159, NARA.

[37] Memo, Taft to MilSec, 21 Jan 07, Entry 24, RG 159, NARA.

[38] Ltrs, Ainsworth to IG, 26 Jan 07, and Galbraith to MilSec, 11 Feb 07, Entry 24, RG 159, NARA.

acquitted in separate courts-martial. Their cases raised doubts as to whether the soldiers had been the perpetrators or whether the culprits had been racist local citizens. The Senate investigation was not completed until March 1908, when the findings were released. The majority concurred with the inspectors and the President that some of the soldiers were guilty, although unidentified, and recommended a bill to extend the President's discharge review authority in case new evidence appeared. A minority view, spearheaded by Foraker, proposed a bill authorizing the reenlistment of all of the discharged men on the premise that they were innocent until proven guilty. Senator Foraker also produced considerable circumstantial evidence that weakened the government's case by pointing away from the soldiers to some sort of conspiracy by the local white citizens.[39]

The debate over the two bills caused considerable concern in the Senate. Senator William E. Borah, newly elected from Idaho, wrote a personal letter to Garlington, asking his views on Foraker's interpretation of the evidence. The Inspector General's lengthy reply only served to indicate that he remained fully convinced that some members of the battalion were guilty. He offered a rebuttal to each of Foraker's points, essentially saying that the confusion during the night in question made it possible for any number of men to have gone into town while appearing to be accounted for in barracks. He then reviewed a series of proven riot cases involving black units, insinuating that such conduct was typical. His circumstantial counterargument quelled the senator's doubts as to the justice of the government's case.[40]

A compromise was reached in February 1909, when Congress approved the appointment of a military court of inquiry that President Roosevelt convened a few days before he left office. This body ended its deliberations in March 1910, essentially corroborating the earlier findings but judging that fourteen of the men were eligible for reenlistment. President Taft's approval of the court's findings closed the case.[41]

The Brownsville case severely affected President Roosevelt's relations with Congress, accelerating the growing differences between the two and eventually leading to confrontations over other issues. The

---

[39] Tinsley, "Brownsville Affray," p. 56.

[40] Ltr, Borah to Garlington, 4 Apr 08, and Reply, 7 Apr 08, Entry 22, RG 159, NARA.

[41] Tinsley, "Brownsville Affray," pp. 59–61; Weaver, *Brownsville Raid*, p. 283. In 1971 Congressman Augustus F. Hawkins successfully sponsored legislation to convert the discharges to honorable and to make restitution. On 28 September 1972, when Secretary of the Army Robert F. Froehlke issued the order to change the record, only one member of the 25th Infantry was alive.

President's quick acceptance of the inspectors' findings seemingly reflected the implicit racial perspective of the era, when stereotyping clouded even the most liberal views. Roosevelt in other situations had accomplished a great deal in advancing black interests. Similarly, all of the inspectors involved were men with a reputation for fairness and integrity. They were, however, products of their time, unknowingly carrying its prejudices.[42]

The Army's and the inspectorate's record in racial matters was not always so questionable. An incident with remarkable parallels to Brownsville took place in 1909 at Madison Barracks, New York, with far different results. The case involved the 25th's sister black regiment, the 24th Infantry, commanded by Col. William Paulding. The barracks was located next to the small town of Sacketts Harbor, whose citizens also reacted against the news of a black regiment being assigned in their area. They were aware of the Brownsville incident and feared a repetition.[43]

Their apprehensions were soon allayed when the regiment arrived. The soldiers were cordial and well behaved, and their presence significantly boosted the local economy. Unfortunately, this promising beginning was marred by a number of incidents. None were particularly important in themselves, but the local sensitivity to any racial tensions, combined with overzealous newspaper reporting, resulted in deteriorating community relations.

The situation worsened in February 1909. In that month General Wood, then the Department of the East commander, received a letter from one "James White," with a clipping from the *Watertown Times* attached. The article was a highly dramatic description of a black soldier's attack on a village girl on the eleventh. The letter writer demanded that General Wood do something about the presence of black troops in Sacketts Harbor.[44]

General Wood referred the letter to Colonel Paulding, asking him to investigate and advise him as quickly as possible. Paulding, in turn, ordered Capt. William B. Cochran, Company B commander, to conduct the investigation. The captain was able to piece together the sequence of events with some accuracy. He found that on 11 February

---

[42] For another exposition of attitudes, see Memo, SG to President, 24 Dec 04, sub: Undesirability of Colored Contract Surgeons, Entry 242, RG 112, NARA; Handlist of Brownsville Material, OTIG files, Pentagon (SAIG-ZXH).

[43] Testimony of Dr. Arthur J. Hodge, Mar 09, an. to File 30361, Entry 1486, RG 393, NARA.

[44] Ltr, "James White" to Wood, 12 Feb 09; "Colored Soldier Attacks White Girl—Struck Down by Infantryman," *Watertown Times*, 12 Feb 09. Both in File 30361, Entry 1486, RG 393, NARA.

the young woman in question had been hit and knocked down by a black man wearing a soldier's hat and overcoat. When the girl screamed, the man ran away and managed to escape his pursuers in the darkness. Initially, Cochran was unable to find any suspects. After a reward was offered on the twentieth, the local tailor came forward and identified Pvt. James Richardson, stating that the latter had appeared to be in an agitated state when he came to ask for a loan on the night of the assault. The tailor claimed to have given the soldier a receipt for an earlier loan, and a part-time painter at the barracks later produced a receipt made out to Richardson, claiming he had found it in the snow near the assault site. With this information, Captain Cochran thought that he had his man. Private Richardson, however, had a solid alibi: A lieutenant, his wife, and their cook all said that he had been working on the furnace in the officer's quarters at the time of the assault. Cochran found other grounds for doubt. He later said he did not think that the alleged victim had been frank with him and pointed out that the letter to General Wood was really anonymous—there was no "James White" in the area.[45]

Meanwhile, community relations continued to deteriorate. After one of his men was sentenced by an obviously biased judge to three months confinement on a minor charge, Colonel Paulding on 26 February put Sacketts Harbor off limits. The same magistrate was alleged to have granted blanket authority to the townspeople to not only carry weapons but also arrest any black soldier they deemed suspicious. General Wood reacted to these events by reopening the investigation, assigning the task to his inspector general, Colonel Chamberlain. Wood told Chamberlain to investigate all incidents so far reported, to examine the conduct of the garrison, to determine the causes for community hostility, and to propose a solution.[46]

Chamberlain left for Madison Barracks on 9 March, arriving that evening. There he found many citizens already protesting the economic effects of the off-limits order, and he began his investigation immediately. He interviewed a remarkable number of people in three days, including most of the prominent townspeople, regimental officers, key enlisted men, and the principals in the assault and court cases. He took

---

[45] Cochran Investigation, Encl 2 to Corresp 3440, 7 Mar 09, and Cochran Testimony, File 30361, Entry 1486, RG 393, NARA.

[46] Note (pencil), Wood to TAG, 4 Mar 09; Ltr, Paulding to Wood, 28 Feb 09; and "Colored Soldier Sent to Jamestown," *Syracuse (N.Y.) Post Standard*, 26 Feb 09. All in File 30361, Entry 1486, RG 393, NARA. See also Ltr Order, Dept of East, 8 Mar 09, File 6046, Entry 22, RG 159, NARA.

an additional ten days to organize his report before submitting it to General Wood.

According to Chamberlain, part of the difficulties lay in Colonel Paulding's failure to specify social guidelines for whites and blacks to follow. He also concurred with Captain Cochran's position that a large part of the problem arose from the toleration of vice in the village and the lack of municipal control. He judged the entire village government to be corrupt. With a population of 1,000, it had six saloons and a hotel bar, none of which paid any attention to state laws specifying closing hours and Sunday operations. Additionally, there was an illegal gambling house and at least two houses of prostitution, the most profitable of which was operated by the town constable. The arrest and trial of the jailed soldier were characterized by Chamberlain as a miscarriage of justice, revealing the bias and incompetence of the judge. The soldier was picked up on unverifiable suspicion and convicted on unprovable charges over the protests of his lawyer. The judge's post-trial inflammatory remarks had led to Paulding's decision placing the town off limits.[47]

But the most telling part of his report related to the original incident. Chamberlain's inquiries into the assault case uncovered a clumsy frame-up on the part of the town tailor and the part-time painter to collect the reward money while discrediting the black troops. It turned out that the painter had forged the "James White" letter to General Wood. Although Chamberlain was suspicious of many aspects of the assault story, he felt that some soldier was guilty on the grounds that he could think of no reason why a civilian would do it. Despite this conclusion, he considered Colonel Paulding justified in placing the town off limits in order to avoid any possible trouble.

Chamberlain surmised that the universal local animosity toward the black soldiers alleged by the newspapers did not exist. Instead, it was limited to a rowdy minority. Contrary to the views expressed by this element and the press, Chamberlain found that the 24th's conduct had been exemplary. He interviewed local police officials, reviewed arrest records, and talked with officials of the railroad and trolley lines used by the soldiers. They all agreed that the soldiers were among the best behaved of any ever stationed at the barracks. Of course, every unit had its rough element. It was these few who caused the problems in the village, taking advantage of its tolerance for corruption.

Chamberlain informed the village council of its responsibility to clean up the town, especially if the citizens wanted protection from the

---

[47] Rpt, Chamberlain, 22 Mar 09, sub: Investigation, Sacketts Harbor, File 30361, Entry 1486, RG 393, NARA.

rowdy few. Until the council did so, he would recommend to Colonel Paulding not to lift his restriction. The soldiers were not deprived, since they could take the short train ride to nearby Watertown for shopping and entertainment or go on pass to Syracuse. He passed his comments to Paulding, suggesting that he cooperate with the village officials and perhaps establish courtesy patrols to restore civilian confidence. He further told Paulding that in his view he was also partially responsible for the crisis and that he should have been more vigorous in investigating and prosecuting reports of soldier misconduct. He predicted that should the town begin to reform as expected after elections scheduled for 16 March, there would be no further trouble, given the regiment's record for excellent behavior.[48]

The investigation raised another problem for Colonel Paulding, caused by Private Richardson's alibi that he was working in the lieutenant's quarters. The soldier had added that he waited on tables, did other domestic duties, and was excused from most drills to do so. Apparently, the practice of employing soldiers as servants and permitting them to almost completely disregard their military duties was widespread among officers. Colonel Chamberlain mentioned his findings informally to Colonel Paulding, who pledged he would correct the situation.[49]

Despite this, General Wood learned of the practice and decided more formal action was necessary. He instructed Paulding to assure that his troops were performing only proper duties and that any personal work was done after duty hours and for proper pay. He formalized his views in a department circular, specifying the conditions under which a subordinate could work for a superior. The work could not be demeaning, must be performed after duty hours, and must be completely voluntary and remunerative.[50] Thus, from a seemingly obscure incident and investigation, a major Army policy emerged, establishing a long-standing precedent.

The situation began to improve in Sacketts Harbor as well. As Chamberlain predicted, the elections brought in a new regime, whose efforts largely cleaned up the town. Colonel Paulding ended the off-limits restriction in April. Then, in October, General Wood received a letter from retired Maj. James H. Durham, a reporter for the *Syracuse*

---

[48] Ibid.

[49] Memo, Chamberlain to Paulding, 23 Mar 09, sub: Disregard of Military Duties; Madison Barracks Cir 2, 11 Mar 09. Both in File 30361, Entry 1486, RG 393, NARA.

[50] Dept of East Draft and Cir 14, 14 Apr 09; Ltr, TAG to All Cdrs, 17 May 09. Both in File 30361, Entry 1486, RG 393, NARA.

Post-Standard. He was a 25-year Army veteran and a local native. His editor had picked him to cover the assault case because of his background. He told Wood that in the course of his own investigation he had become convinced that the young woman in question was not telling the truth. Several months after Chamberlain's visit, she finally admitted that the incident had been contrived to discredit the black soldiers and have the 24th Infantry reassigned. Her co-conspirators had lost their nerve to follow up the incident with a riot and shooting as planned.[51] The confession supported the suspicions of many of the investigators, and the regiment was vindicated. Until its return to the Philippines in December 1911, the unit enjoyed amicable relations with the community.

Corruption in the Army

A few investigations turned up evidence of extensive corruption and led to the criminal conviction of military personnel. Such was the case of the supply operations in the Division of the Philippines. Established during the Insurrection, the depots seemed unable to organize themselves properly. Colonel Garlington served as the local division inspector from April to June 1900, when he went on extended sick leave, and Col. Joseph P. Sanger thereafter until Garlington's return in February 1901. As early as 1901 Garlington cited the Manila Commissary Depot for stockpiling more material than necessary, causing much unnecessary and expensive spoilage. When General Breckinridge visited the capital the following year, he began an investigation of the Manila Medical Depot because the amount of damaged stores being condemned indicated similar stockage problems. Recognizing that overseas logistics represented a new challenge, both directed their efforts to improve the new "imperial" logistics system.[52]

As a result of their interest, the Division of the Philippines developed specific policies for handling stores and condemning perishables. In addition, a court of inquiry was convened in May 1902 to find out how such enormous excesses could have been accumulated and whether specific responsibility should be fixed. Colonel Sanger, the division inspector and acting chief of staff as of April, headed the court. According to the court's findings, the excesses resulted from pardonable misjudgment on the part of the responsible officers. Their desire

---

[51] Ltr, Durham to Wood, 11 Oct 09, File 30361, Entry 1486, RG 393, NARA.
[52] Rpt (quoted word), Garlington, 5 Apr 01, sub: Extravagance in Manila Commissary Depot; Memo, Breckinridge, [1903]. Both in Entry 24, RG 159, NARA.

not to be caught short had combined with the novelty of the situation to create the surplusage.[53]

Thus the first problems that surfaced at the depots were found to result from inefficiency rather than turpitude. But those found at the Manila Quartermaster Depot were of a different nature. A growing scandal surfaced in January 1906, when Colonel Garlington, once again the division inspector, performed a routine inspection. Probing accusations that the depot commander had had furniture made in the carpentry shop for his own use at government expense, he found a broad pattern of similar work done for many others, along with evidence of collusion, cover-up, and graft. Because of his findings, the depot was closed and its responsibilities were transferred to other facilities. In May, following Garlington's return to the United States because of illness, General Wood, the division commander at the time, appointed the deputy inspector, Lt. Col. William T. Wood, to continue the investigation, directing him to look into every aspect of the defunct depot's operations.[54]

Colonel Wood's efforts extended into November, as he pieced together seven years of questionable activities. He requested that several former depot commanders and their civilian assistants return to Manila to give personal testimony, for their own sake as well as for that of the government. Over several months the inspector was able to reconstruct numerous examples of every type of transaction made at the depot. During the investigation he interviewed over 100 individuals.[55]

The depot shops had been established in May 1899, under the depot quartermaster. In September 1901 they were reorganized, becoming a separate agency directly under the division chief quartermaster, Col. Charles F. Humphrey, later the Quartermaster General of the Army. The investigation revealed that irregularities in shop operations had begun by the summer of 1901. Wood first worked on the furniture issue, since that was what had precipitated the whole case. Finding three different sets of books kept by the carpentry shop, he concluded that over $25,000 worth of work had been performed for nearly 200 officers and organizations, with no payment to the Treasury. In some cases, the recipients of the work had paid in good faith and the shop employees and depot commander had pocketed the funds. In other cases, officers were unaware

---

[53] Div of Phil GO 23, 1902, and SO 102, 1902, Entry 24, RG 159, NARA.

[54] Memo, Wood to Div Insp, 26 May 06, with encl. (Garlington Rpt), Entry 24, RG 159, NARA.

[55] Discussion in this and the following six paragraphs from Ltr, W. Wood to MilSec, Phil Div, 10 Nov 08, with encls., Entry 24, RG 159, NARA.

that they were supposed to pay, assuming they were entitled to the service. Still others had had items made for themselves, fully aware of the impropriety.

As a result, individuals both high and low had become witting or unwitting participants in a fraud, and some had incurred substantial bills to the government. Even Brigadier General Humphrey, while he was the Quartermaster General, had ordered lacquered chests to be made, which he gave as presents—one of them to President Roosevelt. Colonel Wood reconstructed the liability of each officer. Debts ranged from a high of $6,252.99, owed by a former Adjutant General, to a low of 44 cents, owed by a captain in the Subsistence Department.

Brig. Gen. William T. Wood
(Rank as of 18 February 1918)

But such irregularities were only the beginning. He also discovered private sales of public property, with no accounting for the funds received. Procedures required that all worn or potentially useless property be inspected before disposal. This had not been done at the depot shops. Rather, scrap metal, lumber, and worn items were sold openly to private individuals and the proceeds split between the depot commanders and several senior civilian employees. Wood estimated that the government had lost $15,000 in five years.

Another irregularity consisted in padding payrolls with fictitious names, enabling the conspirators to draw extra pay. This fraud required an elaborate multiple bookkeeping arrangement involving the depot commander, his chief clerk and the timekeeper. Two different commanders had pocketed about $11,000 by this means. Official paperwork had to be fabricated so that visiting IGs would not detect the discrepancies during their periodic audits of employee time cards. The time books had to be correlated with the payrolls. Some individuals were shown in higher paying jobs than they were performing; personal servants of the depot commander and his officers were listed as carpenters and welders. False vouchers were prepared to hide the purchase of items for private use.

There were other frauds. An outrageous rent was paid for some dock facilities. In return, the dock's owners paid $2,000 into the depot commander's personal bank account, allegedly in payment for dock maintenance. The roster of employees was amended to exempt many from recently initiated civil service examinations; the carpentry shop secretary, for example, was listed as a machinist, and expert Japanese woodcarvers were carried on the rolls as carpenters. Their carving work was done in a secluded area so as to avoid visits from inspectors, and an elaborate warning system was developed to alert them whenever IGs happened on the premises. It was these carvers who had turned out the beautiful furniture accepted unquestioningly by so many persons.

Work orders were rarely filed, although, strangely, they were retained in most cases. The carpentry shop also operated an unauthorized printing press, sanctioned by the division quartermaster general, Col. John L. Clem. Clem, in addition, failed to monitor the purchase of large items, such as coastal vessels that were bought for interisland traffic, merely authorizing expenditures on request. The inspector discovered that a gambling partner of the shop commander received sales commissions on these overpriced ships. In Colonel Wood's view, the whole atmosphere of the establishment was amoral, characterized by a lack of responsibility or accountability. Honest workers shunned the depot shops, and Wood agreed that the depot's closing had been the only solution to solve the immediate problem. Based on Wood's recommendation, six successive depot commanders were court-martialed and Clem,[56] one of the last Civil War veterans on duty, was disgraced.

In December, after Secretary of War Taft, the late governor of the Philippines, read Wood's report, he wrote a carefully reasoned letter to General Garlington, now the Inspector General. In Taft's view, Wood's identification of the improper property disposal and funds and payroll manipulations was so thorough that it established the groundwork necessary for the judicial proceedings soon to get under way. The Secretary was disturbed, however, by the furniture bills and wished them to remain an IG, rather than a criminal, matter. He was quite confident that some of the men on the list had committed no criminal act, that others might be due a return of funds, and that still others owed the government. This specific matter, he believed, should be cleared up quietly.

The Secretary gave Garlington a suggested line of inquiry and asked him to devise a system for resolving the bills. He cautioned

---

[56] Early in the investigation Clem was reassigned to a post in the United States, where he served until he retired in 1916.

against any premature publicity, as the accusations involved many prominent officers. Determining an equitable settlement took longer than expected; Garlington eventually had to go to Manila. The amounts recorded by the depot were mixed with its other operations and had been padded. The only recourse was to review completely all the paperwork. In some cases, testimony from former employees of the carpentry shop on the actual prices charged and on the amount of markup was the only hard evidence available. A new set of corrected bills was prepared, each containing a best estimate of the actual costs to the government, which Secretary Taft approved in November 1907. He further agreed to Garlington's plan to refund overpayments to those who had paid in good faith the first, inflated, billing. By June 1908 only General Humphrey had failed to pay.[57]

The Office of the Inspector General functioned as the collection agent, placing the money in an account in a Washington bank from which the refunds were made. Meanwhile, the courts-martial ran their course in Manila, and all six depot commanders involved received fines and jail sentences. The refund account was closed on 30 June 1908, and with its passing, a delicate problem, fraught with the potential for extended scandal, was resolved. So ended one of the most prolonged and far-reaching investigations conducted before World War I. In retrospect, the criminals' fear of discovery by inspectors had compelled them to develop such an elaborate system of fraud, involving so many people, that it virtually collapsed of its own weight. The case itself demonstrated the professionalism and integrity of the inspection system, which ultimately assured that justice was served while protecting the rights of the innocent involved.

Military Prisoners and Prisons

Many aspects of the military justice system drew the inspectors' attention. When Leonard Wood was Chief of Staff, he became concerned with the practice of armed guards escorting all garrison prisoners. Wood was worried over the images such practices gave to post visitors. Consequently, in May 1911 he encouraged post commanders to place "good risk" prisoners on parole when they performed duties in public. In February 1912 Wood asked General Garlington to make the execution of this program an item of special inquiry during inspections. Until

---

[57] Ltr, SofW to IG, 20 Dec 06; Memo, Garlington to TAG, 19 Jun 08. Both in Entry 24, RG 159, NARA.

1917 each inspection report thus contained a section giving related statistics and an assessment as to whether Wood's intent was being achieved. The reports were generally positive.[58]

The War Department also reviewed other military justice policies. Beginning in 1901, dishonorable discharges had been authorized for soldiers with five or more court-martial convictions. This policy was amended in June 1905. The change specified that to qualify for such discharges, soldiers had to have been convicted of offenses meriting large fines and confinement—in other words, major crimes. This modification raised a storm of protest. Commanders argued that they would no longer be able to dismiss marginal soldiers who were habitually in trouble for minor offenses. Others retorted that the commanders had been getting rid of too many people without first trying to reform them. The Judge Advocate General rejoined that discharges for prior convictions had dropped by 19 percent since 1901.

In March 1907 the Secretary of War asked General Garlington to assess the true effect of the policy and to determine whether it was beneficial as it stood or whether it should be modified. Garlington passed the requirement to inspectors at the geographical commands, asking them also to survey the officers on the situation. They found that about 60 percent of the nearly 300 company commanders surveyed disliked the 1905 amendment, claiming that it reduced their ability to eliminate problem soldiers. However, nearly 80 percent of the field-grade officers favored it, arguing that company-level officers were younger and less experienced than their pre-Spanish War counterparts. They felt that company officers often used courts-martial to avoid having to deal with the undesirable in any constructive manner. The inspectors concluded that the courts had become in many cases substitutes for leadership. Garlington agreed, stating that the senior officers' views should prevail. As a result, the 1905 amendment was retained, but special provisions were added to handle administratively soldiers who were chronic disciplinary problems.[59]

The inspectors were equally involved in reporting on the operations of the U.S. military prisons. The Army had begun its own prison system in 1873, and inspections began shortly thereafter. Because the Secretary of War had responsibility for prison operations, War Department inspectors usually performed the inspections unless scheduling prevented them. However, in 1895 the central Army facilities

---

[58] Memo, CofS, WD, to IG, 3 Feb 12, Entry 24, RG 159, NARA.
[59] Ltrs, TAG to IG, 8 Mar 07, and IG to TAG, 5 Aug 07, Entry 24, RG 159, NARA.

were turned over to the Federal Bureau of Prisons as an economy measure. This arrangement meant that while a few military felons went into the federal penitentiaries, most military prisoners were in local stockades administered by garrison commanders, imposing a great burden on them.

The Inspectors General supported the garrison commanders consistently in urging that a military prison system be resurrected. In 1903 General Burton noted that most post stockade facilities were inadequate and the requirement detracted from organizational efficiency. The task of guarding prisoners was distasteful and burdensome for units that also were trying to train. Units received no additional equipment or personnel for the job. Burton was delighted when, due to a change in policy, the Army regained control of the prison facilities at Fort Leavenworth in February 1906. While repairs began, inspectors continued to make welfare visits to military convicts in other federal prisons.[60]

During their prison visits inspectors were concerned with food, troop conduct, living conditions, staffing, and the facility in general. When necessary, they also dealt with issues unique to the individual prisoner. For example, during an inspection in October 1906 Colonel Chamberlain, who was assigned to the Office of the Inspector General, encountered a former ordnance private first class who was convicted of pilfering some minor items for his own use. The man had served with distinction for twenty-four years in the same unit and his court-martial board had recommended clemency. But the recommendation had been ignored, and the man was given a two-year sentence, with a dishonorable discharge. Chamberlain concluded that the prisoner was slow-witted and recommended that the remainder of the sentence be remitted and the man be pardoned. The Secretary of War agreed, and at the end of November the President remitted the sentence and upgraded the man's discharge.[61] Not only was he now free but also eligible for residence in the Soldiers' Home in Washington, D.C.

Inspectors recommended the assignment of chaplains to the prisons and later clerk typists to assist them. After the 1907 inspection of the Leavenworth prison, the inspector came to the conclusion that the prisoners, instead of splitting rock and doing crude roadwork, should be kept busy in meaningful labor that would enable them to learn a trade. He suggested that they repair tools and furniture for the Army. The Quartermaster General agreed in principle, and directed that the prison

---

[60] *ARIG 1903*, pp. 450–51; *ARIG 1905*, p. 453; *ARIG 1906*, pp. 650–51.
[61] Ltr, Chamberlain, thru IG, to SofW, 23 Oct 06, and Reply, 23 Nov 06, Entry 7, RG 159, NARA.

provide furniture repair support to the Fort Leavenworth garrison. Preparing for their inspections also made the inspectors aware of the outdated and conflicting policies on prisons then in print, and a revised set of policies was published in February 1908.[62]

General Garlington's personal interest in penology remained high. When he represented the United States at the Imperial German Maneuvers in 1911, he delayed his return in order to visit England, where he received an extensive tour of the British Detention Barracks. He expressed a particular interest in efforts to rehabilitate military offenders. On his return, his detailed report on the conditions and procedures in the British system was considered so important that the Secretary of War had it published as part of his annual report.[63]

Garlington's report gave impetus to reform and rehabilitation in the prison system, joining a similar move in the civilian sphere. The regulations were changed to differentiate between criminal and military offenders, and the latter were placed in disciplinary companies to undergo additional strict training aimed to rehabilitate and ultimately return them to duty. The program was a matter of interest whenever inspectors visited the prisons or their branches. At first, the military offenders spent their full sentence in a disciplinary company. This policy was amended in early 1915 at the inspectorate's suggestion. The new concept allowed offenders with good records to be restored to duty after completing a training course at the disciplinary barracks as soon as the commandant judged that they could be productive—a more humane and sensible approach to rehabilitation.[64]

Homes and Cemeteries

Even on issues relating to retirement and death benefits the inspectorate continued to guard the individual soldier's interests. The homes for regular and volunteer troops and the national cemeteries received special attention from the Secretary of War, and the homes were unique in that their inspection was required by act of Congress, rather than by War Department policy.

---

[62] Rpt, Galbraith, 4 May 07, sub: Inspection, Leavenworth Military Prison, Entry 7; Ltr, T. Wood to IG, 15 Sep 08, Entry 9. Both in RG 159, NARA. See also WD GO 131, 1890, GO 13, 1895, and GO 16, 1908.

[63] *ARSW 1911*, pp. 23, 68–74. See also prison escape files, Box 151, Entry 24, RG 159, NARA.

[64] *ARSW 1913*, p. 9; *ARIG 1915*, p. 232; WD GO 56, 1913. See also prison inspection files, Box 166, Entry 9, NARA.

The Soldiers' Home in Washington, D.C., had been established in the 1850s as an asylum for disabled Regular Army soldiers, with membership later broadened to include all retired regular enlisted men. The Inspector General, acting for the Secretary of War, began to inspect the home in 1883, when Congress directed that he visit the home annually to investigate alleged financial inefficiencies on the part of the board of managers. As required by the March 1883 law, the Secretary provided the inspection report to Congress.[65]

The inspection reviewed every aspect of the home thoroughly, including its operation and accounts. The Inspector General was accompanied by an assistant and the OIG expert accountant, who examined all transactions and disbursements and listed them in great detail. Half of the report presented data on salaries, expenditures, and costs; the remaining half included a thorough description of the living quarters, with remarks on all facilities, such as the library and hospital. Compliments as well as recommendations for improvement were given in the narrative remarks. The conduct, appearance, and morale of the residents also was discussed and suggestions made where appropriate. During this period the reports showed that the home was generally well run by able retired officers. The inspection usually took two days, and the report served mainly as a means to publicize the home's needs and to justify expenditures.[66]

Such judgments were not the case with the more complex and decentralized organization set up to care for the Civil War volunteers. The National Home for Disabled Volunteer Soldiers (NHDVS) had been organized in 1865 under the direction of a civilian board of managers. Membership originally was limited to war-disabled veterans, but in 1884 it was opened to all veterans incapable of earning a living. By then the NHDVS consisted of a growing number of branches scattered throughout the United States, plus a headquarters in New York City. The organization suffered from serious mismanagement, which erupted in a series of scandals in the late 1880s. As a result, between 1891 and 1893 the War Department inspectorate assumed a growing role in the inspection of NHDVS fiscal activities. Finally, in 1893 the Inspector General's Department was given the responsibility to make an annual inspection of all elements of the NHDVS.[67]

---

[65] WD GO 24, 1883.

[66] See Soldiers' Home Insp Rpts, 1883–, Entry 35, RG 159, NARA, as well as those published in *ARSW*.

[67] Maria B. Butler, "The National Home for Disabled Volunteer Soldiers," *Harpers New Monthly Magazine* 73, no. 47 (1886): 683–95; Act of Congress, 3 Mar 93, copy in Entry 24, RG 159, NARA.

Because of the high degree of assumed congressional interest, the first few inspections were exceptionally stringent. As a result, the per capita cost of members actually dropped at a time when the resident population was increasing. General Breckinridge estimated that in the first decade of IG inspection, the government had saved about $500,000 annually. The need to make full audits ended in 1901, but inspectors continued to look closely at all NHDVS financial activities. In the meantime, minor complaints against various elements of the organization became so routine that a form letter was developed to acknowledge receipt to the complainant and to initiate action. The Secretary of War forwarded all correspondence to the Office of the Inspector General, which tasked the president of the NHDVS Board of Managers for the actions necessary to address the complaint.[68]

The annual inspections of the NHDVS required a large portion of an inspector's year. Major Brewster, along with expert accountant William T. Kent, conducted the 1909 inspection between 11 August and 27 October. The two men visited the organization's nine branches, sanitarium, depot, and general offices, giving each a thorough inspection and audit. Each branch's administration, records, membership qualifications, and internal operations were analyzed and improvements or changes recommended.[69]

In 1909 the NHDVS received and disbursed about $16 million. A unique part of its operation was the NHDVS Depot at Dayton, Ohio, whose purpose was to manufacture blank forms, issue bedding and clothing throughout the system, and store Army surplus items that would be used to replace old NHDVS equipment. Payrolls for the entire system were prepared at the depot, which also arranged all major open purchases or contracts. Brewster considered the facility to be superbly run by its superintendent, Mrs. D. L. Miller, a woman who obviously could hold her own in a male-dominated age. Brewster judged her to be "far more than average in ability" and responsible for creating a tone of integrity throughout the NHDVS system.[70]

The inspection of national cemeteries was another task precipitated by post–Civil War congressional concern for veterans. Authorized by Congress in 1862 to handle the growing number of Civil War casualties, the cemeteries initially were located near hospitals and battlefields to

---

[68] Memo, Breckinridge, [1903], Entry 24, RG 159, NARA. For complaints, see File 3100, Entry 29, RG 159, NARA.

[69] Rpt, Brewster to SofW, 1 Dec 09, sub: Inspection of the Several Branches of the National Home for Disabled Volunteer Soldiers, Entry 22, RG 159, NARA.

[70] Rpt, Brewster to SofW, 1 Dec 09, Entry 22, RG 159, NARA.

meet emergency needs. After the war the Quartermaster General began a consolidation program, during which land titles were validated, headstones placed, and remains accounted for. By 1870 there were nearly 300,000 graves in seventy-three cemeteries. A February 1867 law provided for the care and maintenance of the cemeteries and mandated that the Secretary of War appoint officers to conduct annual inspections. The subsequent findings formed the basis for justifying appropriations to maintain the cemeteries. By 1873 legislation had expanded burial rights in a national cemetery to all veterans. This led to a further expansion of the system throughout the country, particularly in the Western states, where reburials from the cemeteries of closed posts further fueled the growth.[71]

The inspection requirements grew as the cemetery system expanded. Quartermaster officers had the responsibility to make the inspections until 1876, when the job was assumed by local IGs. It reverted again to the quartermasters in 1879, only to be resumed by IGs in 1882. The requirement was again modified the next year to allow acting inspectors detailed from the Quartermaster's Department to inspect the cemeteries. Their reports still had to go through IG channels. Finally, in 1903 supervision over cemetery inspection was placed at the War Department inspectorate and visits were required once every two calendar years, which remained the practice until the national cemeteries were transferred to the Veterans Administration in 1973.[72]

The reports indicated that the cemetery inspections, although usually routine, were thorough. They provided a good picture of cemetery conditions, as well as information on records, administration, and physical appearance. A summary of each report was prepared at the Office of the Inspector General and, once the Secretary of War had a briefing, was forwarded to the Quartermaster General for his use and action. Inspectors' recommendations were divided fairly evenly between policy suggestions and proposals for local improvements. The latter included such things as providing memorial tablets or recording the knowledge of long-term superintendents before they retired.[73]

Occasionally, an inspector's suggestion led to substantial improvements, as in 1915, when the War Department decided that water and

[71] Erna Risch, *Quartermaster Support of the Army: A History of the Corps, 1775–1939* (Washington, D.C.: Quartermaster Historian's Office, Office of the Quartermaster General, 1962), pp. 463–68.

[72] WD GO 68, 1876, GO 61, 1879, GO 17, 1882, and GO 73, 1883; Memo, Breckinridge, [1903], Entry 24, RG 159, NARA; AReg 20–10, various dates beginning 27 Jan 21. On the transfer, see PL 93–43, 18 Jun 73.

[73] For examples of cemetery inspections, see Boxes 96 and 154, Entry 9, RG 159, NARA.

sewage systems were to be installed in all cemeteries . Major Gray, the assistant inspector of the Southern Department, felt the measure was necessary to aid in improving the foliage, providing modern restrooms for the public, and helping in fire prevention. The Quartermaster General agreed and began the project the next year.[74]

There was a great similarity in the cemetery reports. The minor deficiencies were routinely passed to the Quartermaster General, who saw to it that they were corrected promptly. When larger problems concerning the care and condition of a cemetery were reported, often involving unexpected expenditures, the Quartermaster General was hampered by the slow appropriations process, which often took years. Cemetery inspections also included a thorough audit of the superintendent's disbursing records. Rarely were major problems encountered on these inspections, which, while conscientiously performed, must have been a pleasant break from more rigorous requirements.

---

[74] Rpt, Gray, 10 Nov 15, sub: Port Hudson Cemetery, Entry 25, RG 159, NARA.

PART TWO

WORLD WAR I AND THE INSPECTORATE, 1917–1919

4

The Great War Approaches

The development of the War Department General Staff and command staffs during the era of reform and the stress on preparedness, schools, and training created a generation of officers who proved capable of meeting the vast challenges presented by World War I. Yet the United States Army as a whole was at best marginally prepared for the great modern conflict in which it found itself when the nation declared war on the German Empire on 6 April 1917.

Girding for War

Other nations had been fighting since August 1914, and at first it seemed unlikely that the United States would be able to make an important contribution to the struggle. Limits on the nation's potential for success had been imposed unwittingly by the Wilson Administration and Congress. Before the outbreak of hostilities, government policy discouraged any interest in the European war; the President's desire to remain neutral in "thought as well as action" precluded taking any measures that would help to prepare for involvement in the war. The National Defense Act of 1916 was intended to make America capable of repelling an invader, not of projecting its power overseas.[1]

Even after war was declared, President Wilson remained indifferent to the need for a strong Chief of Staff and delegated most of his authority to Secretary of War Baker and to General John J. Pershing, Baker's

---

[1] Edward M. Coffman, *The War To End All Wars: The American Military Experience in World War I* (New York: Oxford University Press, 1968), pp. 10–11, 17; Harvey A. DeWeerd, *President Wilson Fights His War: World War I and the American Intervention* (New York: Macmillan Co., 1968), p. 394; Ernest R. May, *The World War and American Isolation, 1914–1917* (Cambridge, Mass.: Harvard University Press, 1959), p. 44 (Wilson's quoted words).

choice as commander-in-chief of the American Expeditionary Forces (AEF). Baker, an able administrator, focused on the administrative and logistical aspects of creating the huge Army needed for the war and left the strategic and operational planning to Pershing.[2]

Meantime, an uncoordinated procurement program began, characterized by highly optimistic manpower goals and misplaced priorities as each bureau went into direct competition with each other for available resources. American war potential was at first in danger of being frittered away in ambitious, unrealistic procurement programs propelled by uninformed guesses of War Department officials or the overly pessimistic estimates of allied advisers.[3]

By December 1917, because of the severe winter in Europe and the shifting military picture, the inefficient and cumbersome procedures at the War Department came under intense scrutiny by the Senate Committee on Military Affairs. The committee was highly critical of War Department organization. In response, Secretary Baker undertook a number of reforms in early 1918. He centralized War Department activities, gradually strengthening the Office of the Chief of Staff; created supervisory agencies, such as the War Industries Board, which exercised tighter control over purchasing and policy decisions; and replaced several bureau heads with more aggressive but flexible administrators. In March Baker also appointed a new Chief of Staff, General Peyton C. March, who possessed the authority and personality necessary to organize and centralize War Department activities into a coherent unit.[4]

A final product of the reorganization was the Overman Act of May 1918, which gave the President much wider war powers. Henceforth, the chief executive had the authority to create, alter, or abolish any agencies that affected any aspect of the war effort. For the Army the practical result was to give the Secretary broad control over industrial mobilization and the Chief of Staff the power to restructure bureau activities, particularly supply and procurement.[5]

---

[2] Warren W. Hassler, Jr., *The President as Commander-in-Chief* (Menlo Park, Calif.: Addison-Wesley Publishing Co., 1971), p. 98; Daniel R. Beaver, *Newton D. Baker and the American War Effort, 1917–1919* (Lincoln: University of Nebraska Press, 1966), pp. 87, 180.

[3] DeWeerd, *Wilson Fights His War*, pp. 394–95.

[4] Peyton C. March, *The Nation at War* (Garden City, N.Y.: Doubleday, Doran and Co., 1932), pp. 40–43, 49–51, 369–70; Beaver, *Baker and the War Effort*, pp. 96–97. March actually served as Acting Chief of Staff from March until 19 May 1918, when he received his permanent appointment.

[5] James E. Hewes, Jr., *From Root to McNamara: Army Organization and Administration, 1900–1963* (Washington, D.C.: U.S. Army Center of Military History, 1975), p. 41.

General March used the General Staff as both a directing and a planning agency, with the technical bureaus in a clearly subordinate position. He streamlined the logistics system, concentrating it under the direction of Maj. Gen. George W. Goethels, the builder of the Panama Canal. Ultimately, he established a system under which the Chief of Staff was recognized as paramount, and all bureaus reported to him through elements of the General Staff. March's primary objectives were to synchronize the training and logistical systems in order to allow the greatest possible flow of troops to France.[6] Inevitably, some tension developed between himself and General Pershing, whose status as the AEF commander-in-chief enabled him to enjoy the independence allowed him by Wilson and Baker. But both, beyond doubt, were focused on the same goal—victory in Europe.

That end entailed a far greater effort than anyone had anticipated. When the United States entered the war, very few of its leaders expected to see millions of Americans fighting in Europe. Rather, the vague anticipation was that American participation would consist of considerable financial aid, some naval cooperation with the Royal Navy, and perhaps a token ground force sent "over there." As late as the end of May 1917 the country's leaders were still reluctant to recognize that a large land force would have to be raised and deployed overseas. The realization began to sink in as the allies frankly described their situation, which was very difficult: Russia was in collapse; Great Britain was scraping the bottom of the manpower barrel; and a wave of mutinies afflicted the French Army.[7]

General Pershing's small expeditionary staff arrived in France in June and, training with a separate United States commission headed by Col. Chauncey B. Baker, already in Paris, gave Washington planners their first realistic picture of the size army that was needed. At a minimum, a force of thirty divisions, with support troops in a suitable separate line of communications, would be required; an estimated three million men would have to be called to the colors. Obviously, reliance on volunteers for such a huge force was not possible. Within days the Secretary of War ordered the Judge Advocate General to produce a reasonably equitable conscription law, which was almost immediately enacted.[8]

---

[6] March, *Nation at War*, pp. 70, 76, 188, 372.

[7] Ronald Spector, "You're Not Going To Send Soldiers Over There Are You!" *Military Affairs* 36 (Feb 72): 1–4 (quoted words, p. 1).

[8] Hugh S. Johnson, *The Blue Eagle From Egg to Earth* (Garden City, N.Y.: Doubleday, Doran and Co., 1935), pp. 75–82; Marvin A. Kreidberg and Merton G. Henry, *History of Mobilization in the United States Army, 1775–1945*, DA Pamphlet No. 20–212 (Washington, D.C.: Government Printing Office, 1955), p. 254.

The two groups also proposed a new infantry division, designed to endure the attrition expected on the Western Front. Much larger and differently organized from the few then existing, the so-called square division consisted of two infantry brigades, each with two regiments; a field artillery brigade, with three regiments; an engineer regiment; machine gun and signal battalions; and support units, to include medical. The huge unit had over 28,000 men and 6,000 horses and mules, twice the size of European divisions. Pershing planned from the start to create a force large enough to operate independently. Consequently, the AEF personnel requirements and the subsequent equipment demands remained extremely high throughout the war. Changes in either allied or enemy numbers seemed to have little effect on AEF manpower planning. The consistently high demands for men and materiel later prompted a frustrated Secretary Baker to say that Pershing "saw his own problem, but seems wholly to have failed to grasp ours."[9]

IGD Expansion

The Inspector General's Department (IGD) was no better prepared than the rest of the War Department for handling the demands of a major war. Yet, like other parts of the Army it was obliged to set a hectic pace. The focus of its work was assessing the quality of the men and units being readied to go to France, and yet all the customary and statutory duties of peacetime had to be carried on despite the emergency. The force available for this double duty was at first hopelessly small.

The effects of the National Defense Act of 1916 were only barely being felt when war was declared. Three additional officers were on board, the first of the expected five annual increments; existing legislation did not provide automatically for strength increases. With each restructuring or new nontactical unit, Brig. Gen. John L. Chamberlain, the Inspector General, was required to reapportion his personnel assets up until passage of the Overman Act, which allowed his department to expand more rapidly. In 1917 the department had 23 officers at the time war was declared in April and 37 by the end of June. A year later, after the Overman Act eased restrictions on expansion, the number of officers had increased to 129. The peak strength of the inspectorate was 216 officers on 12 November 1918.[10]

---

[9] DeWeerd, *Wilson Fights His War*, pp. 208, 241–42, 394–95; Coffman, *War To End All Wars*, p. 185 (Baker's quoted words).

[10] Rpt, IGD, Jan 19, sub: Historical Data, War of 1917–1918, Entry 26, Record Group (RG) 159, National Archives and Records Administration (NARA), Washington, D.C.

Organizationally, the Inspector General's Department had component elements located in the War Department, in each geographical command and port of embarkation, in each combat division and higher tactical unit, and in the General Headquarters (GHQ) of the AEF in France. The Office of the Inspector General (OIG) in Washington mainly was concerned with the selection and allocation of inspectors and the coordination and standardization of inspection efforts throughout the Army. It consisted of several tactical unit inspection teams, a growing number of accountants, and a matrix of inspector-investigators to provide support wherever needed. The six U.S. and three overseas geographical commands provided area support to the installations and organizations permanently in their regions. Each had a small staff of officers who inspected or investigated as required. The port and GHQ AEF inspectorates developed functionally, having distinct inspection and investigation elements.

At first, the Inspector General's Department functioned as before the war, with the local inspectors covering everything in their geographical areas, augmented only by inspectors in the new infantry divisions. General Chamberlain's later adjustments reflected a growing centralization of the stateside inspection system, seeking to achieve uniform standards and efficiency in order to meet urgent War Department needs for evaluation and information. A growing number of Washington inspectors dealt with matters concerning units training for overseas. A smaller number remained on the staffs of the geographical commands, focusing on installation and procurement matters.[11]

The demand for high-quality inspectors caused Chamberlain to change his initial reluctance to use only regulars, and in May he told the Chief of Staff that he agreed to the appointment of "well equipped" National Guard officers to division inspection positions. Instead of farming out his inspectors to the tactical units, as he had first planned, Chamberlain retained some of his best talent, eventually bringing the officers under his direct control. This, in turn, increased the importance of OIG activities, making the office the focal point of the inspection system, both from the perspectives of those in the field and in Washington. Nevertheless, there were some losses to the Washington office, notably Col. (later Brig. Gen.) Andre W. Brewster, who was selected by General Pershing to be his inspector general. Brewster was a distinguished infantry officer, with nearly eight years of experience

---

[11] Rpt, IGD, Apr 17, sub: Establishment of Changes in Department, Districts, etc., Entry 25, RG 159, NARA.

as an inspector. Cited for gallantry in Cuba and the Philippines, he had received the Medal of Honor for his bravery at Tientsin, China, during the Boxer Rebellion. Highly regarded by Generals Garlington and Chamberlain, and a personal friend of Pershing, he had an Army-wide reputation for professionalism and high personal standards.[12]

Original estimates for IG manpower continued to climb as the work load in the newly forming units became clearer. Originally, the War Department had authorized one lieutenant colonel inspector for each division. The burgeoning requirements necessitated additional person-nel, and each local commander began to augment his IG office within weeks of his unit's activation. Chamberlain recommended that a major be authorized in each division as an assistant inspector. The proposal initially lacked support from The Adjutant General; however, Chamberlain persisted, his effort augmented by comments from offi-cers overseas. The increase was approved in March 1918, making offi-cial what was by that time established practice.[13]

Not all augmentations came as easily, despite a strong consensus regarding their necessity. General Chamberlain was an early and strong advocate of having senior War Department inspectors appointed for each arm and for aviation matters. He was able to bring experts from the field, such as Col. (later Brig. Gen.) Eli A. Helmick in infantry, to achieve this aim. The officer selected to be the artillery expert was Major Conner, who had been an artillery inspector during the Mexican Border mobilization. But no sooner had he been detailed than he was picked by General Pershing for overseas duty as Brewster's assistant at the new AEF headquarters. (Capt. George S. Patton, Jr., had been offered the job first, but he turned it down, saying that service on the staff was "the cemetery of ambition.") As a result, there was no inspec-tor in the branch considered the most critical by Chamberlain.[14]

The procurement of officers from other branches posed a different problem. Chamberlain had begun by adding a few Regular Army offi-cers to the Inspector General's Department, only to see them siphoned off to other staff jobs or to commands where they were critically need-ed. The turbulence persuaded Chamberlain to request the recall of

---

[12] Memo (quoted word), IG to CofS, WD, 29 May 17, sub: Detail of Inspectors for the National Guard Infantry Divisions, Entry 25, RG 159, NARA; File 5728 ACP 1884, Andre Walker Brewster, Box 941, RG 94, NARA. Brewster was promoted to brigadier general on 17 June 1917.

[13] Ltr, CG, 29th Div, NG, to IG, 11 Sep 17, sub: Detail of Officers, Entry 26A, RG 159, NARA.

[14] Martin Blumenson, *The Patton Papers*, 2 vols. (Boston: Houghton Mifflin Co., 1972–74), 1:463. Helmick was promoted to brigadier general on 17 December 1917.

retired regular officers with inspection experience; many such officers had written Chamberlain to express their willingness for recall in any capacity. Within two weeks after entry into the war, Chamberlain was soliciting those eligible with a personal letter. He intended to accept only those willing to serve as inspectors for the duration, rather than to see them use the IGD recall as a vehicle to get into some other part of the Army. He remarked in a May 1917 note to Capt. Walter L. Reed, who became The Inspector General in 1935, that there was no dearth of applicants but that very few "promised well."[15]

Most bureaus and departments established boards or panels to review the qualifications of applicants for reserve or emergency commissions. General Chamberlain opted for a formal board of two IG officers and a medical officer when appropriate. The first appointments were made to fill positions in the IGD's Officer Reserve Corps, established by law on 3 June 1916. Under the provisions of the law, all applicants had to have served at least one year on active duty and be under forty-five years of age. The first man to receive an IGD reserve appointment was Robert S. Clark, a New York civil engineer who had left the Army in 1903. Within ten days of applying for a temporary commission, he was boarded and accepted into the Inspector General's Department. Reporting for duty as a major on 28 May 1917, Clark was quickly tagged to be part of the AEF inspectorate.[16]

Manpower from any source was most welcome by the summer of 1917. Statistics gathered in July showed that the IGD case load had increased by more than 360 percent in one year and by 65 percent in the three months after the declaration of war. But 20 experienced officers were pulled out of the department in the summer of 1917 to fill critical jobs in the National Guard and National Army divisions. None were assigned as inspectors. Their replacements had never served as inspectors before, yet Chamberlain felt lucky to get them because of the great demand for good officers throughout the Army.[17]

By September the authorized strength of the inspectorate had grown to only 34, despite the fact that 89 officers—30 regulars, 10

---

[15] Ltr, Chamberlain to Byrne, 18 Apr 17; Ltr (quoted words), Chamberlain to Reed, 14 May 17, sub: Officers of the National Guard for Service in the IGD. Both in Entry 25, RG 159, NARA.

[16] Memo, IG to TAG, 23 Apr 17, sub: Appointment of Board To Examine Applicants for Appointments in ORC; Memo, IG to TAG, 28 May 17, sub: Appointment, Robert S. Clark. Both in Entry 25, RG 159, NARA.

[17] Ltr, W. Wood to Donaldson, 22 Aug 17, Entry 11; Memo, Scofield to IG, 23 Jul 17, and Reply, 26 Jul 17, Entry 26. All in RG 159, NARA. See also Ltr, Chamberlain to Brewster, 14 Sep 17, Entry 588, RG 120, NARA.

recalled regulars, 49 reservists—were detailed to IG positions in the United States and France. Thirty-six of the total were serving in tactical units. In November Chamberlain proposed an authorized increase to 158 officers. These were intended for the most part to fill higher level tactical headquarters and to meet the requirements of the greater number of divisions being formed than first anticipated. His request was approved, with a few modifications in the branch requirements of senior inspectors. The practice of expanding automatically as tactical units were activated was again confirmed.[18]

Chamberlain felt that his authorizations were not the only things out of pace with reality. He also considered the grades of his senior inspectors to be unrealistic when the scale of their duties and the importance of their recommendations were considered. In October 1917 he successfully brokered promotions to brigadier general for the senior OIG infantry and cavalry inspectors, on the grounds that the judgment of these men determined whether a unit should embark or not, and for the Deputy Inspector General, Col. William T. Wood, who was recalled from retirement. Wood remained in Washington, filling the role of Acting Inspector General because Chamberlain spent most of his time traveling, and his elevation to flag rank facilitated his dealings with senior War Department and government officials during Chamberlain's absences. Chamberlain also recommended that all bureau chiefs be made major generals. This would, of course, include himself. He pointed out that he was often called upon to investigate senior officers and that "officers generally, at least inwardly, resent being inspected or investigated by their juniors in rank." His point was well taken. Chamberlain and all those bureau chiefs who were not major generals were promoted that month.[19]

This flurry of promotions led to a growing surplus of senior officers in the department, as officers below the brigadiers were elevated to colonel. Chamberlain's plan was to build a surplus of senior inspectors in order to staff the headquarters of senior tactical units as they were activated. A serious problem was encountered in this scheme in October, when the decision was made at General Pershing's request that all unit staffs above a division would be formed in France from personnel selected by him within the theater. The colonels that Chamberlain had groomed for these positions were not only surplus but seemed

---

[18] Memo, Lochridge to CoS, WD, 28 Nov 17, sub: Increase in Personnel and Advanced Grades of Inspector General's Department, Entry 296, RG 165, NARA.

[19] Ibid.; Memo (quotation), Chamberlain to CofS, WD, 18 Sep 17, Entry 296, RG 165, NARA.

doomed to Stateside tasks. The decision and its implementing order upset all his plans, leaving him with several first-rate colonels suddenly sidetracked. Chamberlain asked Brewster to intercede with Pershing. Brewster was able to persuade the AEF commander to select corps- and army-level inspectors from among the senior officers already designated by Chamberlain. Thus, in practice, Pershing deferred the choice of corps and higher inspectors to Brewster and Chamberlain, retaining the right to veto their decisions, a power he was never to exercise.[20]

In November authorized IG strength rose to 164 officers and 125 enlisted men, an increase in part premised on a 44-division force. Automatic increases above that strength again were allowed if the number of divisions exceeded that level. The Chief of Staff directed that the new IG positions not be filled with regular line officers except as a last resort. Reserve, National Guard, or emergency officers had to be considered first and justification made for not selecting them. As a result of this decision, most of the officers brought into the Inspector General's Department in 1918 before the armistice were nonregulars. Almost all Stateside positions came to be filled by them, while most tactical units overseas also had nonregulars assigned. By the beginning of the year the department had 179 inspectors and 14 commissioned accountants, with 73 of the former and 9 of the latter assigned to Stateside organizations and with the remainder of each either in the AEF or in units designated for deployment to France. In February, despite General March's policy, General Chamberlain's strong plea for 9 additional Regular Army officers to inspect troop units was approved. Experience had shown that, no matter how well intentioned, temporary officers did not have the depth and background to judge tactical units preparing for deployment.[21]

One category of specialist—that of expert accountant—was so rare and desperately needed that temporary officers had to be used. The proliferation of funds and the vast amounts of money involved necessitated expert oversight on a continuous and large scale. Brewster requested in August 1917 that Chamberlain find two experienced accountants for assignment to the AEF as quickly as possible. The Inspector General had

---

[20] Ltrs, Chamberlain to Brewster, 22 and 27 Oct 17, and Brewster to Chamberlain, 15 and 25 Nov 17, Entry 588, RG 120, NARA. See also War College Division Coordination Sheet, 7 Dec 17, and Ltr, Chamberlain to TAG, 27 Oct 17, sub: Officers of the Inspector General's Department for Duty in France, Entry 296, RG 165, NARA.

[21] Memo, Biddle to TAG, 27 Dec 17, sub: Increase in Personnel and Advanced Grades of the Inspector General's Department; Memo, TAG to IG, 16 Feb 18, sub: Increase of Regular Officers for the Inspector General's Department. Both in Entry 296, RG 165, NARA.

some difficulty finding men who met his standards, unwilling to commission anyone in the department unless they showed the potential to perform all of the inspector's duties, and he resisted successfully an effort to "open up the Department to a corps of expert accountants." His compromise was to procure the appointment of selected individuals as majors in the National Army, with duty to the Inspector General's Department. The first two men so appointed were Wallace A. Streater, the War Department auditor, and Arthur L. Webb, assistant to the auditor of the Panama Canal. Delighted to get both, Brewster agreed that their government background made them immediately useful without much additional training. The need for accountants continued to grow, however, as the size of the Army and its financial operations expanded. In July 1918 two Treasury Department auditors and the Panama Canal collector were commissioned as majors to sustain the IG's effort, which grew steadily throughout the war and even beyond the armistice.[22]

In late October 1918 specific plans were made to expand the Army to eighty divisions in France and eighteen divisions in the United States. The concept had been approved in principle in June and some increases had commenced. An additional 99 inspectors would have been added to the 215 already serving when the anticipated full mobilization was to be reached on 30 June 1919. Chamberlain pointed out a growing problem intrinsic to this continued expansion. In October twenty retired or former regulars were serving with the Inspector General's Department. Few more could be absorbed, because all further strength increases were against units overseas or otherwise expected to meet the physical demands of line organizations. In other words, the source of qualified manpower was pretty well consumed. In practical terms, this meant that the expansion contemplated leading to an eighty-division AEF would require filling from Regular Army assets. Chamberlain felt that temporary officers did not have the depth of experience necessary to perform satisfactorily in tactical units. Consequently, he warned, the burden to fill these positions would fall on the Regular Army element of the AEF.[23]

As matters turned out, the armistice in November 1918 canceled the need to carry out the planned expansion, and the dilemma broached

---

[22] Ltr (quotation), Chamberlain to Brewster, 14 Sep 17, and Reply, 8 Oct 17; Ltr, Brewster to Chamberlain, 20 Aug 17. All in Entry 588, RG 120, NARA. See also Memo, Brown to CofS, WD, 18 Nov 18, sub: Limited Service Men for Accountants in the Inspector General's Office, Entry 296, RG 165, NARA.

[23] Memo, Chamberlain to CofS, WD, 23 Oct 18, sub: Commissioned Personnel, Entry 296, RG 165, NARA.

by General Chamberlain, like many other manpower issues, could be ignored rather than resolved. Chamberlain was able, however, to use the expansion plan to achieve some of his other objectives. He won approval for immediate promotion of the senior field army inspectors from colonel to brigadier general and also for a flag rank inspector of artillery. Earlier, General Pershing took care of one of his own, approving the promotion to brigadier general of Colonel Spinks, the AEF assistant inspector general. Just weeks before the war's end, the senior IG grades conformed to aims Chamberlain had expressed shortly after the declaration of war.[24]

Confronting Chaos

Despite the small number of inspectors available at the beginning of the war, the Inspector General's Department had an important role to play in mobilization, training, and deployment. Inspections of the new divisions revealed a great deal about the Army of 1917–18, and tactical inspections helped to explain many of the problems experienced by the AEF during the fall offensive of 1918. IG reports, in short, formed a comprehensive and detailed picture of the Army as it struggled to ready itself for its first major war overseas.

Soon after the declaration of war, Regular Army regiments were concentrated to form a first provisional division-sized unit and hasty measures were made to have what became the 1st Division sent on its way to France. Meanwhile, National Guard units still returning from the Mexican border were retained in federal service, and those already discharged were recalled to carry out local security measures, guarding bridges and other facilities against possible sabotage. As soon as the training camps neared completion in August and September, National Guard units were redeployed to begin their training cycle. At the same time, the first waves of draftees began to fill the camps designated for the new National Army divisions.[25]

The plan was for the units to begin their training in the United States and to complete it in France under expert allied tutelage. Once in France, they would first participate in weapons and tactical exercises up to division level. Thereafter, to gain experience and seasoning under the

---

[24] Memo, Brown to CofS, WD, 23 Oct 18, sub: Personnel, Entry 296, RG 165, NARA.

[25] Frank Tompkins, *Chasing Villa: The Story Behind the Story of Pershing's Expedition Into Mexico* (Harrisburg, Pa.: Military Service Publishing Co., 1934), p. 230.

*Inspecting 27th Division Troops at Camp Wadsworth,
South Carolina, in 1917*

guidance of allied commanders, division elements would go into a quiet
sector of the front for a month and then undergo combined training with
all arms before deployment as a division. Because Pershing considered
the allied training philosophy too defensively oriented, he added extensive open order attack training and—what proved to be of questionable
value and very time consuming—individual marksmanship practice. A
program this elaborate was experienced only by the early arrivals. As
pressures increased in 1918, it will be seen that AEF training was curtailed well below minimums and was the source of considerable command concern.[26]

The War Department's immediate problem was the care and training of the thousands of draftees and guardsmen being called up. A
month before the declaration of war, the Quartermaster General's
Department had developed plans for the housing of a million-man
force. A Cantonment Division was created to supervise the actual
construction. Once war was declared, the plans were activated. By
the end of May sixteen barracks sites, mostly in the northern states,
were selected to house the National Army divisions and sixteen tent
camps, all in the southern states, for the National Guard divisions.

---

[26] DeWeerd, *Wilson Fights His War*, p. 214.

Work was begun immediately. Unlike some other bureau actions, the whole program was carried out with considerable urgency. Speed was so essential that contracts were let to single bidders on a cost-plus arrangement. Later review revealed surprisingly little unjustifiable expenditure. Schools, depots, and ports were built at the same time with equally creditable records.[27]

At the new barracks and camps confusion greeted the first large influx of men and units. Many things still needed completion. The problems of adjusting to the often primitive physical facilities were aggravated by numerous personnel changes. National Guard units had to reorganize to conform to the new organizations desired by General Pershing. Regular Army formations had to spread themselves thinner and thinner as their elements and personnel were split off to form new units. Concentrations of experienced men were diluted in an effort to reassign existing talent throughout the growing force. Promising NCOs who could have held the units together were sent to officer candidate schools to receive a modicum of training before returning to the National Army as captains and majors.

The lack of experience and the shortage of equipment and facilities severely impaired training. The little progress achieved was vitiated by the practice of reassigning large numbers of unit personnel to serve as replacements in higher priority units. In some cases fully trained men with other civilian specialties were reassigned to functions using their civilian skill, rather than in the one in which they had been trained and which was needed within their unit. The tone and pace of the training camps were frenzied and frustrating, clearly indicating the need for coherent War Department guidance.[28]

As soon as they could be fielded, teams of inspectors, first from the geographical commands and later from the Office of the Inspector General, began a cycle of visits to wherever units could be found mobilizing or in training. The teams inspecting deploying units were staffed with some of the strongest inspectors in the system; the team chiefs were always distinguished senior officers of their branch, with many years of experience as commanders and inspectors. The latter inspected the tactical units, observing the more experienced regulars, whereas

---

[27] Clarence H. Cramer, *Newton D. Baker: A Biography* (Cleveland: World Press, 1961), p. 98; Erna Risch, *Quartermaster Support of the Army: A History of the Corps, 1775–1939* (Washington, D.C.: Quartermaster Historian's Office, Office of the Quartermaster General, 1962), pp. 606–08.

[28] Coffman, *War To End All Wars*, pp. 64, 66–67; Wayne S. Jones, *Ben: The Life of Benjamin Seth Jones, 1877–1943* (N.p., 1984), pp. 83–85.

the reserve or temporary officers usually covered such areas as troop facilities, mess halls, and remount activities. Assignment of the reservists to ports or overseas organizations often followed this initial training and inspection.[29]

The Inspector General's Department completed its first inspections of the National Guard camps just before Christmas 1917 and began work on the National Army and aviation camps immediately afterward. All combat divisions and most support units were inspected at least twice prior to being sent overseas, and the findings of the inspectors determined the priority of division deployment to France. Their reports on unit efficiency and the quality of officers were frank. However, despite generally good coordination and cooperation among War Department elements, reaction to the IG reports was not as "prompt or radical" as General Chamberlain had hoped or as General Pershing had urged.[30]

The Inspector General himself stayed on the road, particularly after Colonel Wood was assigned as his deputy. The only limitation on his travel was Secretary Baker's request that Chamberlain remain in Washington on those occasions when he himself was absent. Chamberlain set a strenuous pace for himself, observing his teams in action, conducting inspections and investigations on his own, and maintaining a steady flow of memoranda to the Chief of Staff and the principal staff members. The 59-year-old Chamberlain paid a price for his constant activity, being hospitalized for exhaustion during most of November and December 1917.[31]

The inspection system developed by Helmick on the Mexican border in 1916 provided the basis for the way in which divisions were inspected during the World War. But a constant theme running through the comments of inspectors old enough to remember 1898 was the desire to avoid the failures of the War with Spain. Considerable emphasis was thus placed on matters concerning clothing issues, sanitation, and mess conditions, as well as on troop conduct and basic discipline. The previous war served as a sort of negative standard to evaluate the conditions of 1917 and 1918.[32]

---

[29] Rpts, Helmick to TAG, 19 Jun and 1 Jul 18, subs: Morale Inspections, 6th Division and Camp Meade, MD, Entry 26, RG 159, NARA; David Lewis, "A Short Account of My Experiences in the American Expeditionary Forces in France, 1918–1919," OTIG files, Pentagon (SAIG-ZXH).

[30] Ltr, Chamberlain to Brewster, 30 Jan 18, Entry 588, RG 120, Entry 588, NARA.

[31] Ibid., 20 Jan and 22 Nov 18, Entry 588, RG 120, NARA.

[32] Ltr, Helmick to Simmons, 31 May 34, Entry 26, RG 159, NARA; U.S. War Department, *Annual Report of the Inspector General, 1918* (Washington, D.C.: Government Printing Office, 1919), p. 222 (hereafter cited as *ARIG*); *ARIG 1919*, p. 650.

The dilution of experienced officers and men was perhaps the Army's greatest manpower problem. Inspectors reported that the influx of recruits reduced even established Regular Army units to the lowest levels of training, and the influx of National Guard and temporary officers contributed to a rapid decline in efficiency and standards. Lack of coordination and clarity at the War Department level added to the confusion of new men attempting to run new organizations. For example, the War Department ordered two major units to Camp Jackson, South Carolina, although the camp could accommodate only one of them. Elsewhere, commanders received orders to move nonexistent units or to perform missions with units that had never been assigned to them. In other cases they were directed to form units or staffs but were not given the necessary personnel or equipment. In one instance a major headquarters was assigned to one post, while its subordinate elements were assigned hundreds of miles away.[33]

Examples of chaotic conditions could be multiplied almost at will. Regiments lost their field-grade officers just before advanced field training. In one case the officers of a machine gun battalion were formed as a faculty, leaving the enlisted men to fend for themselves, and they were not scheduled to rejoin their unit until a week before it was programmed to go overseas. Specialists were moved about so often that they rarely learned their duties or were integrated into their units. One inspector suggested that War Department staff officers visit the units in training both to learn their problems and to confront reality.[34]

The effects of personnel turbulence noted by every inspector seriously affected the readiness of new divisions trying to meet deployment dates. Although efforts were made to rationalize the replacement system, the demands for units in France and the rapid pace of deployment prevented the establishment of a coherent system. The original replacement concept had called for several large depots to receive, train, and dispatch draftees to the divisions, but the press of events prevented the depots from functioning as intended. Most replacements were taken from major units in training and added to others that were closer to deployment; draftees often were sent directly to combat units for training, and the local depot units assumed the role associated with modern reception stations. While the depots languished, some units in training continued to be drained to fill those nearing their deployment overseas.

---

[33] *ARIG 1917*, p. 211.

[34] Memo, Landis to IG, 21 Jun 18, and OIG handwritten comment, 22 Nov 19, Entry 26, RG 159, NARA.

And divisions often arrived in France and entered action with little time for additional training.[35]

Inspecting the New Divisions

Inspectors assigned to the divisions in the various cantonments devoted the bulk of their time to discipline, morale, and training. Each developed his own approach in accordance with his own views and those of his commander. For some, this meant essentially a teaching role designed to complement the work of the commanders. By contrast, some preferred a competitive system of inspection in which inspection results were published for unit comparison, and units competed against each other and their own earlier ratings to show improvement. Regardless of their approach, inspectors found that most temporary officers were able to master basic technical skills fairly rapidly and pass these on to their subordinates. The new officers' inexperience continued to show, however, in matters of discipline, and inspectors at the division level always had their hands full in this area.[36]

As seasoned officers, the inspectors were generally well respected by the commanders of the reviewed units. Additionally, those assigned to the Regular and National Army units spent several weeks in Washington for orientation at the Office of the Inspector General and were consequently aware of the most current policies. The inspectors also found themselves intimately involved in important aspects of overseas preparations, going far beyond their usual duties. For example, when Lt. Col. Joseph A. Baer became inspector of the 15th Cavalry Division, forming at San Antonio in January 1918, he quickly became a primary assistant to the division chief of staff. In this capacity Baer helped prepare plans for the organization and training of the division and then inspected training and facilities to assure that the plans were being implemented. He also assisted in the preparation of training and movement schedules and equipment checklists for overseas service, in this way fully integrating his own inspection responsibilities with the division's operational staff.[37]

---

[35] Leonard L. Lerwill, *The Personnel Replacement System in the U.S. Army*, DA Pamphlet No. 20–211 (Washington, D.C.: Government Printing Office, 1954), pp. 178–86.

[36] Rpt, Parker, 30 Sep 19, sub: Annual Report of Inspector, Camp Funston, Kansas, Entry 26, RG 159, NARA; *ARIG 1919*, p. 648.

[37] Ltr, Baer to IG, 8 May 19, sub: Personal Service in the IGD, Entry 26, Entry 159, NARA.

"General Helmick's Guide for the Rapid Inspection of Large Units"

PLATE 1

The equipment assumed is equipment "A" with or without rations and with surplus kits.

1. FORMATION: Columns of companies at half company distance; baggage and combat wagons on right flank of column where companies can easily obtain equipment.

2. PREPARATION AND INSPECTION:
(a) Have flaps to ammunition pockets and first aid pouches unsnapped and folded back so contents of pockets and pouches can be inspected and marking of pouches observed.
(b) Have identification tags exposed, the tape passing out between first and second buttons of shirt. If the tape comes out between buttons lower down, the tag is liable to be drawn back in and hidden from view.
The preparation described in (a) and (b) should be made immediately after the column has been formed so that all organizations may be in absolute readiness for the inspection at the hour designated.
(c) Cause rifles to be brought to the position of port, bolts to be removed and held in right hand by the side. (See plate 1.)

PLATE 2

(d) As soon as the inspector has passed him, cause each man to bring rifle to right shoulder (changing bolt to left hand) and depress the muzzle so that barrel may be looked through from the rear. (See plate 2.)

PLATE 3

(e) When the inspector has passed the rear of each man, have bolt replaced, position of fix bayonet assumed, bayonet drawn and held horizontally in the right hand, point to left, ring up and inclined to front. The bayonet should be held lightly between the thumb and fingers, back of the hand down, in order not to cover slot and ring of bayonet. (See plate 3.)

PLATE 4

When the inspection of bayonets is completed, cause them to be fixed and unfixed to see whether all can easily be attached and detached from the rifle.

(f) When the bayonets have been unfixed, have oiler and thong cases and spare part containers removed and prepared for inspection as follows: Partially insert brush in the muzzle of the rifle, thong with weight attached hanging beside the barrel, the muzzle of which leans against the belt; remove the cover of oiler, and holding oiler in left hand, insert the dropper into the oil with the right hand, and hold up, point of dropper down so a drop of oil will depend from the point as the inspector passes.

Remove the contents of spare parts container and hold them in the left hand so the inspector can see them as he passes. (See plate 4.)

In order that there may be no delay, the inspector should inspect the succeeding company as to (a), (b), (c), (d) and (e), while the preparation described in (f) is being made. Position (f) should be retained until checking officer has completed the checking to be done in ranks. This should begin as soon as inspection of the battalion is completed.

PLATE 5

3. As soon as the checking in ranks of a battalion is completed, shelter tent camp is made and preparation for further inspection and checking carried out as follows:

(a) Field Kit (less poncho): Arranged by each man immediately in front of his own half of shelter tent so marking on each article can be seen. (See plate 5 for arrangement.) NOTE: Plate shows bacon and condiment cans empty; if these are to be inspected filled, the lid of the bacon [can] should be removed. The tooth brush holder shown in the cut is not a prescribed article of the equipment.

PLATE 6

(b) Surplus Kit: Spread poncho on ground about one yard in front of the personal kit, marking of poncho exposed; display the clothing on the poncho as follows: O.D. shirt spread out, buttons up with sleeves folded to show elbows; breeches spread out with waist band on waist of shirt, flap unbuttoned and button-hole side turned back to show button holes and buttons; shoes, soles up, at foot of breeches, extra shoe strings across shoes; undershirt and drawers similarly displayed at side of outer clothing with socks spread out at feet of drawers. (See plate 6.)

PLATE 7

(c) Have company property displayed for inspection. In this display the water-bag should be hanging up; fire irons erected and kettles and hooks attached; G.I. cans and bake pans separated and tops removed so they can be thoroughly inspected and quickly checked. All containers, including field desk, should be open and ready to open promptly when the inspector appears. (See plate 7.)

PLATE 8

(d) Have property of regimental and battalion headquarters displayed, and the personal property of all officers arranged so that it can be quickly inspected and checked. (See plate 8.)
(e) Have picket lines stretched and animals unsaddled or unpacked and ready for inspection of backs and feet.

PLATE 9

(f) As soon as the shelter tent camp has been completed and property displayed for inspection, have the men sit on the ground in front of and facing their tents, remove their shoes and socks, drawing the latter, bottoms up, over their hands and placing the former, soles up, beside their bare feet which rest on their leggins. (See plate 9.)
This is the position of inspection of feet. The above description applies to Headquarters and Machine Gun Companies and Sanitary Detachment of the regiment.

PLATE 10

PLATE 11

    (g) Have baggage and combat wagons, as soon as unloaded, assembled with remainder of train and held in readiness for such maneuvers in driving as the inspector may desire. At termination of this maneuvering, cause the train again to be assembled and spare parts and accessories to be displayed for inspection and checking, and the clothing and personal equipment of members of the Supply Company, including surplus kits, to be made ready for inspection. (See plates 10/11.)

The visit of one of the OIG inspection teams to a division in training was a major event for the unit. The press of time and sense of urgency required that these inspections be businesslike and as brief as possible. The senior team inspector would consult with the division inspector and then pay a courtesy call on the commander if possible. The other inspectors on the team, in the meantime, would familiarize themselves with the cantonment, possibly also inspecting post facilities and veterinary activities. During the courtesy call, the senior inspector would give the division commander a detailed letter listing the information required by the inspection team to complete its inspection. The information desired was broken down by topic and passed down to the appropriate staff sections or units for action.[38]

Replies were usually forthcoming within twenty-four hours. Most were narratives, with the appropriate statistics appended. In combination, they gave a fairly good picture of an organization's conditions and its training levels. Inspectors used the replies to supplement their own findings in assessing a unit's proficiency; however, they did not wait for them before they began their own inspection. Normally, the senior inspector would spend a half-day with each line regiment, while others on his team would begin similar visits with combat support units and nondivisional organizations. Deficiencies detected in the course of the inspection were reported through unit channels to those responsible for immediate correction.[39]

The inspections of the National Guard divisions were thorough and generally critical, reflecting in part the Regular Army bias of the inspectors. But the inspectors were also aware that these units would be the first to deploy and, in consequence, had to conform quickly to realistic standards. Further, the inspectors themselves were still developing their own mass inspection techniques and perhaps were more severe than they would be later, after establishing a routine and gaining more experience.

The inspection of the 28th Division (Pennsylvania National Guard) was a typical if scathing example. The inspectors—Helmick and Reed, now a major, a remarkable team at the time for each would serve as The Inspector General—concluded that training levels were far from satisfactory; that the fundamentals of individual training had not been stressed; and that many of the officers and NCOs, while putting on a good show of activity, failed to perform satisfactorily in many impor-

---

[38] Memo, Miller to Surg, 82d Div, 30 Jan 18, Entry 26, RG 159, NARA.
[39] Memo, Helmick to IG, 6 Apr 18, Entry 26, RG 159, NARA.

tant areas. Sanitary conditions were deplorable, kitchens and latrines were in poor condition, and the commanders from division down had ignored the reports of the division inspector and surgeon. Discipline throughout the division was "totally unsatisfactory," and the inspectors identified a long list of officers, including three generals and two regimental commanders, to be considered for discharge. (In fairness, they also identified several officers of high quality, including the division surgeon and inspector.) Chamberlain agreed, saying the division's condition was "unpardonable" and that sending "the Division to France in its present state of unpreparedness would be criminal."[40]

After each of the National Guard divisions in training had been inspected, the senior inspectors returned to Washington and discussed their findings. A product of their meeting was an annotated ranking of divisions. Each unit was rated from most to least deployable, with the reasons given for the particular placement. The ratings included evaluations of training, strength, administration, discipline, and the quality of the commander and staff. The 40th Division, with a "very good" commander and administration, "fair" discipline, and "good to very good" training, was rated first. Last was the 39th Division, with a "poor" in everything. The report was then forwarded to the Chief of Staff for use in General Staff deployment planning.[41]

The inspectors appeared more sympathetic to the National Army organizations, possibly because of their own knowledge and experience gained in criticizing National Guard units. The report from the five senior inspectors on the sixteen National Army divisions, which was forwarded to the Chief of Staff on 25 March 1918, was much more generous. They used the same criteria in giving each unit a ranking, the 83d Division coming first and the 88th Division last, but unanimously praised "the very high character of the commissioned and enlisted personnel of these divisions and the spirit and ardor with which they have taken up and pursued the work of training." They reported that "the War Department can, without injury to the service . . . determine the order of sailing."[42]

Each National Guard and National Army division was inspected at least twice, and inspectors made an effort to schedule their final inspec-

[40] Rpt (quoted words), Helmick to IG, 7 Dec 17, sub: Inspection of the 28th Division, NG (Pennsylvania); Memo (quotations), Chamberlain to CofS, WD, 10 Dec 17, sub: Conditions in the 28th Division, Camp Hancock, Georgia; and File 333, Foreign Officers. All in Entry 26, RG 159, NARA.

[41] Memo, W. Wood to CofS, WD, 10 Jan 18, Entry 26, RG 159, NARA.

[42] Memo, Insps to IG and CofS, WD, 25 Mar 18, Entry 26, RG 159, NARA.

tion as close to the unit's shipping date as possible. Predictions of combat readiness and training assessments formed part of the final inspections made on the deploying units. Some proved tragically accurate. The findings of the last stateside inspection of the 27th Division (New York National Guard) indicated "a lack of that definite control on the part of the officers which is an index of good discipline." The inspectors judged the 106th Infantry as headed for disaster without drastic changes in command, which did not appear to be forthcoming, and warned that the division would require extensive additional training before it could be trusted in combat—predictions borne out at Bellicourt and Bony on the Hindenburg Line that autumn.[43]

Whenever possible, another inspection was made just before boarding ship. Port inspectors monitored the company officers and followed up on the shortages reported in the cantonment inspection to make sure they had been made up. The objective of these final inspections was to assure that the men going overseas left as fully equipped as possible with new or at least fully serviceable clothing and equipment. Intuitively evolved by the inspectors, this procedure was later formalized in a War Department circular and its amendment.[44]

Field Artillery Problems Continue

Artillery units usually were inspected separately by the special IG artillery team of Col. Alfred A. Starbird and Maj. Dawson Olmstead. Often, divisional artillery brigades were located apart from their parent units, because of the need for extended firing ranges. In general, these units did not make the same training progress as other arms and services, principally for lack of equipment and an insufficient number of qualified instructors. Conditions in the divisional artillery brigades were described as "deplorable" after the first cycle of inspections in November and December 1917.[45]

The field artillery for some period of time had problems, which promised to become even more critical as it tried to expand to meet the requirements of the war. Reports from overseas attaches, especially Lt. Col. Spencer Cosby in Paris, underlined the huge scale and technical requirements necessary for an effective field artillery system on the Western Front. General Chamberlain consequently saw the requirement

---

[43] Rpt, Helmick to TAG, 5 May 18, sub: Methods and Results of Training in the 27th Division, Entry 296, RG 165, NARA.

[44] WD Cir, 11 Jul 18, amended 21 Sep 18, Entry 26, RG 159, NARA.

[45] *ARIG 1919*, p. 652.

27th Division Field Artillery Trains

for an urgent focus on artillery in the American mobilization, emphasizing the need for a senior field artillery inspector who specialized in the inspection of units of his arm and who, in the absence of a branch chief, served as an "instrumentality" to provide doctrine and guidance. But no one on the General Staff believed it was appropriate for the inspectorate to perform such a role. Competent field artillery officers were so scarce that in the summer of 1917 only one lieutenant colonel or colonel of that branch served in the Office of the Inspector General at any one time.[46]

By September Chamberlain felt that the artillery inspector positions were so important that one senior inspector in the United States and one in Europe should be at least a brigadier general. He stressed to the Chief of Staff that throughout the Army the field artillery was in "a demoralized condition," needing all the help it could get. Equipment to train soldiers was practically negligible; artillery officers and NCOs in newly formed National Army units were almost entirely ignorant of their specialty; and the National Guard units were in even worse shape.[47]

In October inspection of field artillery units began in earnest. Colonel Starbird and Major Olmstead began to make a circuit of field

---

[46] Memo (quoted word), Chamberlain to CofS, WD, 28 Nov 17, sub: Increase in Personnel and Advanced Grades of Inspector General's Department; Memo, ACofS, WD, to TAG, 24 Aug 17. Both in Entry 296, RG 165, NARA.

[47] Memo, Chamberlain to CofS, WD, 18 Sep 17, Entry 296, RG 165, NARA.

artillery brigades in training. Their findings soon began to confirm Chamberlain's worst suspicions. The information sent back by the two inspectors established the dimensions of the problem and enabled Chamberlain to have three more field artillery officers temporarily detailed to the Inspector General's Department. With support from Generals Pershing and Brewster in Europe, approval was finally granted in November 1917 for inspectors of artillery with the rank of colonel to augment IG offices of corps and higher units, to include the AEF and War Department inspectorate. The augmentations were valuable, but they came almost too late to influence the artillery programs of the first wave of divisions shipping to Europe.[48]

Starbird's and Olmstead's inspection of the National Guard field artillery brigades revealed an absence of any training standardization and minimal unit discipline. The difficulties of artillery training were exemplified by the 157th Field Artillery Brigade at Camp Gordon, Georgia. Organized in August 1917 as part of the 82d Division, in early February 1918 the unit was still suffering from impossible equipment shortages. Two battalions had no equipment at all, while the third had only one battery's worth, which it shared. Thus the eighteen batteries of men were trying to train with one battery of guns. Wooden mock-ups had to be used for gun drill. The limited training that one of the unequipped regiments, a six-inch-gun unit, received on the available three-inch guns was of marginal value. Equally critical was the fact that the other two unequipped regiments were supposed to be motorized. Without equipment, none of the drivers and mechanics could be trained, rendering any learning by the gunners of doubtful value.[49] The situation was common among most of the newly forming artillery organizations.

The inspection reports were so universally bleak as to make it apparent that unusual measures would be necessary to achieve even minimum levels of artillery proficiency. In early January 1918 the Chief of Staff directed that more Regular Army officers be assigned to each unit. Many were not artillerymen but cavalrymen—like Col. William C. Rivers, who would become The Inspector General in 1927. At least they could provide discipline. Additionally, experienced regular NCOs were ordered on temporary duty to serve as instructors in the newly formed National Guard field artillery units. An artillery school for brigade and field officers was opened at Fort Sam Houston, Texas, and a senior officers refresher program was begun at the School of Fire

[48] Ltrs, Brewster to Chamberlain, 8 and 18 Oct 17, Entry 588, RG 120, NARA.
[49] Rpt, McDonald to TAG, 5 Feb 18, sub: Inspection of the 82d Division at Camp Gordon, Georgia, Entry 26, RG 159, NARA.

at Fort Sill, Oklahoma. Provisions were made to attach qualified Regular Army officers to National Guard and National Army units, whose officers then were sent to the school.[50]

At Starbird's suggestion, the General Staff developed an improved equipment distribution scheme to provide each National Guard brigade enough equipment for one field battery in each of its battalions. The earlier practice of trying to equip battalions fully, one at a time, was too inefficient. Schools were given a high equipment priority to assure that they had sufficient weapons by type to provide thorough training in a reasonable time. Finally, in March 1918, fourteen field-grade and twenty-three company-grade officers with experience in France were brought back to act as trainers at the schools and in selected units.[51] But, despite the best efforts of inspectors and unit members on both sides of the Atlantic, artillery was to remain a problem throughout the war.

The Inspection System Matures

The inspections became more efficient and systematized as inspectors gained more experience and developed a sense of what was critical in assessing a unit. Their reporting also became more structured as War Department elements and the Office of the Inspector General developed their own sense of what was needed to respond to issues identified in the course of the inspections.

The inspection reports initially were narrative in format, organized by topics that reflected the prioritized importance assigned by the team chief. Subsequent reports essentially mirrored the first ones made, their organization informally standardized by the areas of interest in each unit: training and instruction, including schedules, use of films, and target practice; field exercises; sanitation; discipline and punishments; personnel; clothing; equipment; medical care; and commendations. Each report ended with some sort of conclusion or evaluation of the unit.

The similarity in report contents and format derived not only from the developing experience of inspectors at all levels but from the training given inspectors at the Washington office and the existence of various references already in circulation. The Army field service regulations provided general guidance as to the measurement of unit proficiency under field conditions, and Army regulations and the Yellow Book for inspectors offered some general statements on the

---

[50] File 9600, Artillery Inspection, Entry 296, RG 165, NARA.

[51] Ibid.

proper means of making field inspections. Collectively, this guidance allowed most inspectors to carry out reasonably satisfactory inspections. As a growing number of major units were activated, the pace of inspections quickened and the need for accurate, moderately standard information became critical. Consequently, General Chamberlain began an overhaul of the available inspection guidance to provide uniform standards, procedures, and formats for reporting inspections. In October 1917, "as information and guidance" for his inspectors, he disseminated a draft compilation of his published verbal instructions given in the past. On the twelfth an advance copy of his latest instructions was issued preliminary to Special Regulation Number 69. The regulation summarized the authority and responsibility of an inspector to look into anything affecting unit efficiency, with emphasis on determining individual proficiency in combat skills and the knowledge of unit drills and procedures. "The object of all inspections of troops is to determine their readiness and preparation for war."[52]

Unfortunately, the special regulation did not clarify fully every facet. Inspectors were expected to make a complete assessment of the units—including tactical—that they visited. The new policy confirmed the inspector's role; however, the field service regulations still specified that an inspector could not make tactical inspections, which was the responsibility of division commanders. When this conflict was pointed out to General Chamberlain in March 1918, he recommended that the authority for conducting tactical inspections be granted clearly to inspectors.[53]

The War Plans Division director of training, Maj. Gen. John F. Morrison, differed, explaining that the intent of the field service regulations was to make senior commanders personally aware of the tactical condition of their units. The War Plans Division already had agreed to authorize division commanders to allow their own inspectors to make tactical inspections. Morrison felt that any further authorization was unnecessary and would dilute the intention of the original policy. The Chief of Staff compromised by modifying the requirement to allow

---

[52] Neo-style 265 of SReg 69, and End (quotations), Chamberlain to IG [blank], 2 Oct 17, Entry 588, RG 120, NARA. Neo-styles were an early form of mimeographing. A large part of the regulation addressed procedures to be followed during inspections of financial accounts. Its circulation helped to standardize the inspection process, with inspectors providing more information and analyses than routinely required. See GS File, Inspection Service of Armies in the Field, With GO 134, 12 Oct 17, Entry 296, RG 165, NARA.

[53] Ltr, IG to TAG, 30 Jan 18, sub: Tactical Inspections, Entry 26; 1st End, TAG to IG, 5 Mar 18, sub: Tactical Inspections, Entry 34A. Both in RG 159, NARA.

commanders to delegate tactical inspection responsibilities to their inspectors. But commanders were still considered responsible for the tactical proficiency of their units through their own independent observations.[54] Nothing changed from a practical point of view.

The inspection report became increasingly complex as a growing number of items of concern requiring special comment were added to the list—for example, unit strength shortages and overages. A narrative summary of the unit's background was given, along with a summary of the unit's training level and progress. Training topics were discussed generally and later related to the Army's master training schedule for divisions once it was issued in August 1918. The quality of training facilities and their location also were assessed.[55]

The personnel and equipment status of all deployable units was checked thoroughly. Court-martial cases were reviewed as indicators of discipline, as were the appearance and courtesy of the soldiers. Clothing and equipment inventories were assessed and critical shortages reported. The inspection report also included remarks on the health of the command and the quality of the cantonment facilities to sustain it. Following requests by the Surgeon General in January and August 1918 that inspectors report on medical personnel and operations, including the medical training program run by hospital commanders, the topics were covered on a regular basis. Reports of remedial actions by hospital commanders inspected were forwarded with the inspection reports. Matters requiring immediate action were extracted from the report and forwarded separately to the Office of the Inspector General, which passed it to the agency responsible.[56]

The unit inspection and training reports were put to many uses by the War Department. They represented a reliable source of information on the developing combat units, their training facilities, and their problems. The inspectors were the first to note the need for a separate cantonment staff to free combat commanders from camp administration.

---

[54] Memo, Morrison to CofS, WD, 1 Mar 18, sub: Division Inspectors Not Authorized To Make Tactical Inspections; Memo, Graves to TAG, 4 Mar 18. Both in Entry 296, RG 165, NARA.

[55] Rpt, Dade, 6 Oct 18, sub: Inspection of the 11th Division, Camp Meade, MD, Entry 11, RG 159, NARA.

[56] Telg, Chamberlain to Senior Insps, 27 Jan 18, sub: Surgeon General Request; Ltr, Shanks to W. Wood, 30 Aug 17, and Reply, 31 Aug 17. All in Entry 26, RG 159, NARA. See also War College Division Rpts, Microfilm 912, Roll 12, Indexes to War College Division Records, RG 165, NARA. Incidentally, in June 1917, General Chamberlain recommended to the Surgeon General that an enlisted school of nursing be established, as opposed to just current hospital on-the-job training.

They were virtually the only source of information on the largely successful use of allied officers as training supervisors. Inspectors continually stressed that War Department officials should be more aware of the consequences of personnel turbulence on unit morale and progress in training.

The reports also formed a primary source of information on the soundness of War Department programs, and as such they provided a useful guide for correcting errors. For example, in February 1918, an inspector's observation that not enough time was allotted for preliminary marksmanship training and dry firing resulted in General Morrison amending the training schedule and, in a letter to senior commanders, requesting their support for the change. Many reports noted the lack of discipline in the units—"a delinquency throughout the Army." The result was a March 1918 letter from the Chief of Staff to all senior commanders, urging their attention to the problem and enjoining them to use their inspectors to assist them in eradicating indiscipline.[57]

The War Plans Division made a number of abstracts to assist in its planning. Observations detailing progress were placed on separate sheets. The Office of the Inspector General periodically supplied the War Plans Division, through the Chief of Staff, with an updated list of the divisions that had been inspected, ranked in order of their relative preparedness for combat. This, of course, was helpful in movement planning. Another sheet abstracted issues of a systemic nature, such as the optimum number of officers that should be authorized in a supply company. Flaws in training programs were always sought when analyzing reported training deficiencies. The inspection reports were useful to the Chief of Staff as a means for responding quickly to inquiries from Congress and elsewhere on conditions in various units. On occasion, for example, when a unit's readiness or training became an issue or when an allegation had to be answered, he asked that the Inspector General conduct a special inspection to gather the facts.[58] Surprisingly, it did not occur to the General Staff at first that this mass of information would be invaluable to the forces in France.

Originally, the inspection reports on units deploying to France did not leave the War Department. Then at the end of May 1918 Brig. Gen.

---

[57] Extract (quoted words) from Helmick Rpt, 4 Feb 18; Extract from TAG Ltr, 4 Mar 18. Both in File 10754, Entry 296, RG 165, NARA.

[58] Rpt Abstract, WPD, 13 Apr 18, sub: Inspection of the 8th Division, Camp Fremont, Palo Alto, CA, 22–28 February 1918; Memo, March to IG, 18 May 18. Both in Entry 296, RG 165, NARA. See also War College Division Rpts, Microfilm 912, Roll 12, Indexes to War College Division Records, RG 165, NARA.

Lytle Brown, the new War Plans Division director, realized that the AEF was not on the distribution list, even though it had the greatest need for the information the reports contained. Time was being lost in France as inspectors and trainers there unknowingly repeated exercises already practiced in the States. Brown discussed the matter with Chamberlain, and on the twenty-ninth the Chief of Staff formally authorized the Inspector General to forward to France "parts of inspector's reports he deems necessary for the staff of the AEF."[59]

Communications on training improved quickly, and by the summer the process of reciprocity was in motion. The Office of the Inspector General forwarded to the War Plans Division extracts of the AEF inspection reports on divisions in France. The information provided more data on the effectiveness of training in the United States, and particularly allowed better evaluation of discipline and morale programs. The division, in turn, used extracts from inspection reports as part of a periodic report to the GHQ AEF, required for assessing the progress of units in the States and for anticipating more accurately those ready to be deployed overseas. Specific problems in training were identified to allow the AEF Training Division (G–5) to modify its training program in France. The data sent to the AEF consisted of a War Plans Division summary and evaluation of a division's training status, the inspectors' comments, and a unit's strength and equipment status. In a few cases, a division commander's remarks on his unit's level of readiness and its training deficiencies would be appended also. By this time the reports had assumed a vital role in the training, movement planning, and organization of all elements of the Army.[60]

The depth and frequency of the OIG team visits, combined with the flow of information along the IG technical chain, made the Office of the Inspector General one of the most knowledgeable agencies at the War Department level. The observations of inspectors were respected by the General Staff, which frequently translated them into formal policy. The trend toward training standardization was an example. While on a visit in December 1917, Colonel Wood noted the 32d Division commander's comment criticizing the vagueness of current infantry training policies issuing from the General Staff Training Division. He

---

[59] Memo, Brown to CofS, WD, 29 May 18, sub: Inspection Reports To Be Sent to the AEF; Memo (quotation), TAG to IG, 29 May 18, same sub. Both in Entry 296, RG 165, NARA.

[60] Memo, Brown to CofS, WD, 29 Oct 18, sub: Report on Training of the 8th Division, Entry 296, RG 165, NARA. See also War College Division Rpts, Microfilm 912, Roll 12, Indexes to War College Division Records, RG 165, NARA.

concurred and recommended that curricula be developed at the War Department level for each type of school desired.[61]

General Morrison disagreed, arguing that the guidance was intentionally vague to allow local commanders to develop the schools and courses they deemed necessary. The General Staff did not want to develop specific doctrine, which would be forthcoming from the various service schools once they were established. Inspectors, on the other hand, became strong advocates of training standardization at the War Department level, after seeing in the field the variety of interpretations placed upon the guidance provided by the General Staff. Many senior inspectors began to urge programs in which training moved from simple to complex topics in a sequential manner, rather than randomly packing subjects into the time available. They also advocated the reservation of periods each day exclusively for training, with the maximum number of unit members participating.[62]

At length, in the summer of 1918 the War Department succumbed to a barrage of comments from inspectors. In June the first wave of National Guard and National Army divisions had been inspected at least twice, giving inspectors a unique view of recurrent systemic problems that could be deferred no longer. The Office of the Inspector General submitted a detailed series of recommendations for improving infantry training, emphasizing that leisurely prewar practices were no longer possible. "The soldier must be trained and the NCO made within a period of months, instead of a few years." A simplified drill manual and training program was needed, and the inspectors recommended producing an easy-to-read illustrated manual, distributing a soldier's handbook, and establishing a school for NCOs in each camp.[63]

As a result, drill and training were standardized throughout the Army. Training instructors relied more on demonstrations and training films. Complete modification of the drill regulations was deferred by the General Staff, however, because of the turbulence it would cause, and the idea for NCO schools was referred to a War Department committee for development.[64]

[61] Memo, W. Wood to TAG, 30 Dec 17, sub: Infantry Training Document 656, Entry 296, RG 165, NARA.

[62] Rpt, Helmick to TAG, 5 May 18, sub: Methods and Results of Training in the 27th Division, Entry 296, RG 165, NARA.

[63] Memo, Helmick to IG, 19 Jun 18, sub: Suggestions and Recommendations for Improving Disciplinary Drill in Our Army, Entry 296, RG 165, NARA.

[64] Memos, Brown to CofS, WPD, 16 Jul 18, and Brown to TAG, 16 Jul 18, Entry 296, RG 165, NARA.

The inspectors were equally critical of one specific aspect of infantry training, referred to by them as musketry. Their inspection of the mobilized divisions revealed insufficient emphasis placed on range estimates, fire distribution, and fire discipline, as well as little time spent on target practice. Their steady drumming on the inadequacies, combined with substantiating statistics, finally led to changes in the training program. A small arms firing school was established at Camp Perry, Ohio, in May 1918, to train marksmanship instructors. In addition, the General Staff began to develop a standard training course in riflery for all recruits. In such ways, the positive contributions made by the inspectors to improve training were at least as important as their negative accounts of unit failings.[65]

Officer Evaluations

Inspectors' comments on officers eventually were incorporated as a formal annex to the inspection report. In July 1917 officer efficiency reporting was suspended for the duration of the war and not resumed until June 1920. But when visiting deployable units, inspectors were directed to observe and evaluate all unit field-grade officers. As a result, some were promoted but many more were either relieved for inefficiency, demoted, or discharged.[66]

At first glance, this would appear to be a responsibility fraught with the potential for excesses. In operation, however, the practice had internal limits and was further ameliorated by the restraint and fair-mindedness displayed by the inspectors themselves. Officer evaluation began with the arrival of the inspection team at a camp or division. One of the items requested by the division commander in the opening briefing was a list of all officers who were either undergoing, or being considered for, efficiency board proceedings. Unit commanders usually submitted a single memorandum, listing all of their officers regardless of grade, with a brief comment on each. Any adverse actions were indicated.[67]

Evaluations on officer fitness were varied. Some were as simple as "an excellent officer." Others were complex, such as one inspector's

---

[65] Memo, Caldwell to IG, 20 May 18, Entry 26, RG 159, NARA; Rpt, Helmick to IG, Jan 18, sub: Inspection of the 83d Division, Entry 296, RG 165, NARA.

[66] *ARIG 1919*, p. 652; Memo, Wright to CofS, WD, 3 Jul 20, sub: Report by the Inspector General Upon the Efficiency of Officers of the Army Above the Grade of Captain, Entry 26, RG 159, NARA. Captains were included on 5 February 1920.

[67] Memo, HQ, 11th Div, to Regt/Sep Unit Cdrs and Unit Surgs, 26 Sep 18, Entry 1291; Ltr, Sessions to AG, 11th Div, 28 Sep 18, sub: Information Required by Inspector General, Entry 2144. Both in RG 120, NARA.

rating of a brigade commander as "didactic; not responsive to recommendations. Does not inspire me with confidence." And others were simply enigmatic—or at least too brief to be of immediate value. A division commander, for example, rated one of his colonels as "Good. Now before a court martial for immorality, other than that, is energetic and intelligent." All in all, however, the estimates seemed to be fair reflections of the officers inspected. Developments once the units deployed to France bore out the judgments made by commanders and IGs with reasonable consistency.[68]

Division commanders were expected to take action on those officers reported by inspectors to be unsuitable candidates for retention in their current jobs. The inspectors included in their evaluation of each officer a recommendation as to his disposition, ranging from discharge through reassignment to reclassification. In some cases, medical evaluations to assess duty capabilities and transfers to less demanding jobs were made as a result of the inspectors' remarks. Shortly after a senior inspector had rated one of the 78th Division's brigade commanders as "too fat for active field service," the officer was reduced to permanent grade and sent to a depot. In each case involving a negative action, inspectors were required to personally observe the officer in question and to verify or alter the comments made by those in the man's chain of command. Inspectors found very few cases meriting reversal of the immediate commander's views.[69]

On the other hand, the inspectors' officer evaluations were themselves subject to review, especially those critical of senior division officers. A division commander, or any other senior officer with knowledge of the criticized officer, could rebut the critical assessment. In one case, General Helmick characterized Brig. Gen. Julius Penn of the 85th Division as ineffective and better suited for a staff job. The division commander, Maj. Gen. Chase W. Kennedy, disagreed. He said Penn had been so overextended with multiple training and command responsibilities that he had been unable to give adequate attention to any one task. General Kennedy felt that Penn would make a good commander when given the chance, and asked that he be retained. The Army Chief of Staff agreed, and Penn remained in command of his brigade.[70]

---

[68] Rpt, Helmick to TAG, 26 Feb 18, sub: Estimate of Efficiency of Officers Above the Grade of Major in the 82d Division and in Other Organizations Stationed at Camp Gordon, Georgia, Entry 296, RG 165, NARA.

[69] Memo, Graves to TAG, 26 Feb 18, sub: Report Regarding Incompetent Officers of the 78th Division, Entry 296, RG 165, NARA.

[70] Extract of Rpt, Helmick, 9 Apr 18, sub: Inspection of 85th Division, Entry 296, RG 165, NARA.

In fact, the Chief of Staff reviewed all officers' reports, which were sent to him as soon as they were received by the Office of the Inspector General. Any unfit medical officers were reported directly to the Surgeon General. The Chief of Staff provided the Secretary of War his recommendations on the fate of flag officers. Regular Army officers found wanting were reduced to their permanent grades; those in other categories were given a lower temporary rank. Officers serving in combat units often were reassigned to administrative positions at regional or training commands.[71]

Evaluation boards on field-grade officers were formed as needed, using officers from the War Department when men of suitable rank, senior to those being boarded, could not be found locally. The Secretary of War directed the Chief of Staff to follow through on the fate of all junior officers with poor evaluations and to submit a report regarding the action that had been taken on each. As a result, a follow-up report was forwarded through command channels to the Chief of Staff. An information copy was sent to the Office of the Inspector General, whose task was to ensure that no officer was overlooked.[72]

Although commanders at every level could influence the ultimate fate of particular officers and rebut report findings, the inspectorate became identified with the program. This alone explained why inspectors' visits were so feared and why the inspectorate came to be disliked and, in some cases, mistrusted by elements of the officer corps. Eventually, the Office of the Inspector General was responsible for investigating all reported instances of poor performance by officers. Special investigations outside the cycle of unit visits were made whenever required, especially in the case of nondeployable organizations whose officers were not evaluated routinely.

As may be imagined, many of the officers culled from the tactical units and sent to depots and garrisons continued to perform marginally. The effect of reassigning rather than discharging them often did more harm than good, causing serious morale problems and adversely affecting local operations. Such a case might surface as a result of a court-martial, a congressional complaint, or local mission failure. General Chamberlain commented in response to an inquiry from the

---

[71] Memo, OIG to Insps, 22 Mar 18, sub: Inefficient and Unfit Officers, Entry 34A; Memo, Graves to TAG, 19 Mar 18, sub: Report of Inspectors General Relating to Deficiencies of Officers, Entry 26. Both in RG 159, NARA.

[72] Memo, Lochridge to CofS, WD, 12 Dec 17, sub: Appointment of Military Boards To Pass Upon the Qualifications of General and Field Officers of National Guard Divisions; Memo, March to SofW, 8 Mar 18, sub: Disposition of Officers Reported as Inefficient by Inspectors General. Both in Entry 296, RG 165, NARA.

Quartermaster General that the commander of the San Francisco Depot would have to go. "He is a pleasant gentleman with courteous manners and agreeable address, but markedly inefficient as has been already explained. He means well and desires to please. His inefficiency is due to lack of mentality, not unwillingness to try, but he is not a student of his duty." At Chamberlain's recommendation, the officer in question was invited by The Adjutant General to retire and he accepted the invitation.[73]

Morale and Welfare

The War Department's increasing concern with the influence of marginal leadership on morale indicated its growing interest in an aspect of troop welfare that hitherto had been largely ignored. Before the war ended, morale and morale-related activities were to become a major issue throughout the Army.

At the time of the 1916 mobilizations along the Mexican border, the Secretary of War had asked Raymond B. Fosdick to look over the troops' living conditions at their isolated bases. Fosdick, a former Princeton student of the President's, was a lawyer with an established reputation for fair investigation into social problems. Initially, he found the usual saloons and bawdy houses around the posts and a laissez-faire command atmosphere of "boys will be boys." Both he and Baker believed that most of the men were intrinsically decent, would welcome more wholesome entertainment, and were patronizing the honky-tonks only because they lacked alternatives. The two concluded that the Army was responsible for providing suitable recreational and welfare activities, in their opinion a practical means for lowering the number of venereal and alcohol casualties.[74]

The concept was novel. Since the Army hierarchy was slow to respond, the first organizations to meet the need for morale-support activities were civilian agencies, such as the Red Cross, YMCA, Knights of Columbus, and similar charitable groups. In April 1917 Fosdick was appointed by the Secretary to head the Commission on Training Camp Activities, formed as a temporary organization to coordinate the ongoing actions of many groups interested in improving the

---

[73] *ARIG 1919*, p. 653; Rpt (quotation), OIG, 12 May 17, sub: Change Station, Col. Wallace, QMC, on Account Alleged Use Intoxicants and Incompetency, Entry 25, RG 159, NARA.

[74] Raymond B. Fosdick, *Chronicle of a Generation: An Autobiography* (New York: Harper and Brothers, 1958), pp. 136–40.

lot of the soldier. In the early stages of the war private agencies funded much of the welfare activities. Club furnishings, recreation rooms, even the hospital ship in the port of New York, often came from the donations of private citizens. The Red Cross and the church-affiliated associations donated most of the sundries needed by the soldiers.

Eventually, the activities of these organizations pervaded the entire Army structure. Red Cross units supplemented Army ambulance and nursing capabilities. YMCA officials managed overseas canteens— which might now be considered small post exchanges—and served as recreation directors on board each Army transport ship. Fosdick's commission was able to coordinate and channel most of this activity fairly smoothly in the Stateside cantonments. Yet even here, he deplored the sectarianism and duplication of effort that developed. Overseas, the presence of paramilitary organizations would be a source of serious problems, ultimately leading to one of the largest IG investigations of the war.[75]

Fosdick's position was advisory, not directive in nature. Within the first year of the war it had become apparent that the morale-support activities were generally well accepted but in need of much firmer control. Additionally, it was Fosdick's view that "either through timidity or inability to get the doughboy point of view, the reports of Army inspectors frequently failed to reflect the whole situation." To become better informed on morale issues, the Secretary appointed Frederick P. Keppel, dean of Columbia University, to become the Third Assistant Secretary of War for Personnel. Within a few weeks Keppel informally approached General Chamberlain. Based on their meeting, Keppel began to receive IG inspection report extracts on a routine basis. After a brief review, he specified such topics as health care, recreation, services, and community relations as being of special interest to him. Chamberlain, in turn, directed that inspectors carry out a morale and welfare inspection along with their regular unit and training inspections and that they prepare a morale report, submitting it separately from the others.[76]

From its inception, the morale report had a standardized format, consisting of a list of the inspection team members and those inter-

---

[75] Ibid., p. 143; Coffman, *War To End All Wars*, p. 77; Cramer, *Newton D. Baker*, p. 98; Beaver, *Baker and the War Effort*, pp. 220–23; David C. Shanks, *As They Passed Through the Port* (Washington, D.C.: Cary Publishing Co., 1927), pp. 296–98. On the postwar IG investigation, see Chapter 7.

[76] Fosdick, *Chronicle*, p. 176 (quotation), and in Entry 26, RG 159, NARA, see: Memo, Keppel to Chamberlain, 14 May 18; Ltr, Chamberlain to Keppel, 18 May 18; Memo, 3d ASofW to IG, 16 May 18; and Neo-style 321, Information Desired by 3d Assistant Secretary of War, 20 May 18.

viewed and a number of topical paragraphs that reflected the Secretary's areas of concern—the general health of the command, religious activities, community relations, and conscientious objectors. The first topic on the health of the command dealt with the incidence of disease (to include venereal cases, quarantine, and treatment procedures) and, because of a serious epidemic in the autumn of 1918, the handling of those with communicable diseases, as well as the efforts of such charitable organizations as the YMCA and Knights of Columbus. The second topic discussed the breadth and type of religious activities available, to include the extent of cooperation among military chaplains, the quality of each, and the interaction with local clergy—who, as of the summer, were banned from posts because unit commanders had found that their proselytizing and stance of pacifism were too disruptive. The third topic on community relations covered the degree of cooperation with local police and the extent of their control over houses of prostitution, plus an overall assessment of morale based on such indicators as the venereal rate and the number of disciplinary actions. The final topic on conscientious objectors described the local program and identified the officer in charge, usually from the Judge Advocate General's Department, and the number and types of objectors. An assessment of the officer's suitability for such a job and the objectors' amenability to noncombat duties were included. A separate analysis of the objectors' viewpoints, whether religious or personal, was sometimes appended.[77]

This concern over conscientious objectors and their treatment was another novelty. The objectors numbered about 4,000 out of the nearly 5 million men drafted into service. About 1,300 of them were willing to fill noncombat military positions. What to do with the remainder was a serious problem. General March insisted that the objectors be subject to military discipline and liable to court-martial for failure to obey an order. Secretary Baker sought a less drastic alternative. The issue appears to have climaxed as the result of a letter sent to President Wilson from the Church of the Brethren, requesting that consideration be given to furloughing conscientious objectors "to noncombatant occupations in agriculture and other constructive pursuits." The President forwarded the letter for comment to the Office of the Inspector General.

---

[77] Ltr, Helmick to TAG, 1 Jul 18, sub: Information Desired by the Third Assistant Secretary of War Regarding Camp Meade, MD, Entry 26; Ltr, Chamberlain to Insps, 20 May 18, sub: Information Desired by the Third Assistant Secretary of War, Entry 34A; Ltr, Helmick to TAG, 19 Jun 18, sub: Information Desired by the Third Assistant Secretary of War Regarding the Sixth Division Regular, Entry 26. All in RG 159, NARA.

Chamberlain replied by memorandum through the Secretary of War on 24 May 1918. He shared General March's hard line. "It is my conviction that any policy contemplating granting furlough . . . would be a fertile and just cause for charges of discrimination against other persons who, for any cause, may desire to avoid military service." He recommended that conscientious objectors be assigned to noncombatant military duties and be subject to "the same treatment . . . [as any other] citizen if he shirked his duty or disobeyed orders."[78]

Secretary Baker, given the job of resolving the issue, did not agree fully with either Chamberlain or March. As he told the Inspector General a few days after receiving his views, "After careful consideration of the whole question, I have decided to permit conditionally the furloughing of certain conscientious objectors, but only in approved cases, after a searching investigation as to their sincerity." Policy letters were issued 1 June and 1 July, establishing procedures for handling objectors and making the issue a special item for inspection and, once developed, coverage in the morale report. Assistant Secretary Keppel monitored the program and attempted to see that the men were treated fairly. In the course of the war about 1,300 were furloughed while another 371 were jailed for a military offense. Inspections revealed that their treatment varied at each location but with few exceptions was generally decent. The last objector in jail was not to be released until November 1920.[79]

In October 1918 coverage of chaplain activities was expanded in the morale report. At the time no corps of chaplains existed to provide guidance to its officers in the field; each chaplain's duties depended on his own initiative and the desires of his commander. The brief surveys in the body of the morale report showed a wide variation in both duty performance and scope. Assistant Secretary Keppel desired to gain a broader feel for what chaplains were doing and to compile data for developing specific policies on what they should be doing. To accomplish this, he asked inspectors, both in the United States and overseas, who visited posts with assigned chaplains to add to the regular report comments on chaplain activities in several general categories.

The data on chaplains was statistical in nature and usually quite short. Items listed included the number of men the chaplain personally

---

[78] Ltr, Wilson to IG, n.d., and Encl (first quotation); Memo (remaining quotations), Chamberlain to SofW, 24 May 18, sub: Conscientious Objectors. All in Entry 34A, RG 159, NARA. See also DeWeerd, *Wilson Fights His War*, p. 242.

[79] Ltr (quotation), Baker to Chamberlain, 27 May 18, Entry 34A, RG 159, NARA; Coffman, *War To End All Wars*, pp. 75–76; DeWeerd, *Wilson Fights His War*, p. 242.

knew and the number of pastoral visits he had made. Duty performance also was summarized—whether the chaplain accompanied the troops to the field and what additional unit duties he had to perform. The report described his relations with chaplains of other faiths, and whether any organization of chaplains existed within the unit or its chain of command. In some units, inspectors had the chaplains fill in questionnaires, which they consolidated; in others, inspectors wrote their own summaries after visiting the chaplains. A great deal of data was accumulated, showing clearly the variety of tasks the chaplains performed and demonstrating that their efficiency suffered because of the absence of any central guidance or specific training to instruct them in their duties. No practical use was made of the information, however, and shortly after the war ended the tasking was discontinued.[80]

Also in October the General Staff established the Morale Branch. Its mission was to coordinate myriad morale-support activities and to formalize the morale and welfare system after Commission on Training Camp Activities ceased operations at the war's end. Headed by Brig. Gen. Edward L. Munson, the branch was soon to prove invaluable during the demobilization, assuring smooth transition of morale-support activities and programs from civilian to Army control. The formation of the branch marked the advent of the final requirement on the morale report. Munson asked for recommendations on policies and procedures. His request became still another item of special interest, and was institutionalized as a part of the report.[81]

Army Schools

Inspectors became involved in another aspect of training by reporting on the various schools that were being established at the cantonments. Often, these were associated with the divisions in training and were mentioned in the body of the unit inspection report. However, a growing number were formed by the bureaus to train the specialists needed for supporting the combat divisions or the new services, such as aviation or motor transport.

Inspectors found that most of the schools run by recalled retirees and later supplemented by officers called home from France specifi-

---

[80] Memo, W. Wood to Insps, 17 Oct 18, Entry 34A; Neo-style 349, Report on Chaplain Activities, 17 Oct 18, Entry 26; Rpts, 2d Army Corps, AEF, Oct–Dec 18, Entry 26. All in RG 159, NARA.

[81] March, *Nation at War*, pp. 212, 215; Ltr, Munson to IG, 25 Nov 18, sub: Inclusion of Morale Items in Reports of Inspectors General," Entry 34A, RG 159, NARA.

cally to serve as cadre were functioning reasonably well. Equipment shortages and training standardization problems were common difficulties noted in reports. For the most part, however, few major irregularities were discovered, except in the system created by the Signal Corps to train its aviation personnel.[82]

The Signal Corps aviation training program exhibited the same weaknesses as its aircraft procurement programs. It was badly conceived, poorly organized, overly ambitious, and virtually uncontrolled. As a result, the aviation schools were a magnet for inspectors, ultimately involving General Chamberlain himself. The system was built around eight flight schools and one balloon school. Feeding them were military aeronautics schools for ground or preflight training, established at eight universities with training contracts. Additionally, the Signal Corps created nine squadron stations, but only one was located near a flight school.[83]

These various schools were only a few of the many places that General Chamberlain had planned to visit on a nationwide tour in July 1917, but soon they became the focus of his attention. Indeed, the work that Chamberlain devoted to Signal Corps aviation training problems was the principal cause of his physical collapse. Between July and November he inspected all the aviation training sites and operational fields. Normally, he was on the road for two or three weeks, returning to Washington to report his findings and discuss them with the Chief Signal Officer and then immediately repeating the cycle without respite. His findings were so dire that they led the Chief Signal Officer to request, in September, that the Office of the Inspector General dedicate at least one inspector to Signal Corps matters. Yet Chamberlain continued to fulfill this role until February 1918, when an entire IG team was committed to it.[84]

In his concluding aviation report to the Chief of Staff in November 1917, General Chamberlain noted that aviation training

---

[82] Coffman, *War To End All Wars*, p. 193.

[83] The aviation schools were in San Diego, California; Mineola, New York; Chicago, Illinois; Newport News, Virginia; Miami, Florida; Chanute Field, Illinois; Selfridge Field, Minnesota, and Wright Field, Ohio. The balloon was at Fort Omaha, Nebraska, and an experimental field was at Langley, Hampton, Virginia. The preflight campuses were Massachusetts Institute of Technology, Princeton University, Cornell University, Georgia Institute of Technology, Ohio State University, University of Illinois, University of Texas, and University of California, Berkeley. See File 354.1, Aviation, Entry 26, RG 159, NARA.

[84] Memo, Chamberlain to CofS, WD, 18 Sep 17, Entry 296, RG 165, NARA; Ltr, Chamberlain to Brewster, 27 Oct 17, Entry 588, RG 120, NARA.

lacked "organization, system and coordination and a total lack of uniformity in the methods pursued." He went on to observe that the tendency at the schools was to "neglect the training of officers except in flying" and to ignore completely their training in discipline and basic military subjects. Sudden policy changes from the Chief Signal Officer had hindered the development of a coherent program. Construction of training facilities was defective because of a lack of supervision and unclear requirements and specifications. The selection of sites themselves was often questionable. Spare parts requisitioning was unsystematic and expensive, causing delays in training. Some of the training aircraft acquired were of very poor design and should not have been purchased.[85]

Well before his report was filed, changes began to be made as the result of his verbal interim reports to the Chief Signal Officer. Disbursing officers were assigned to each school to handle finances and to attend to unusual student financial needs. In late September 1917 school commandants were authorized to discharge "any student who evidences unfitness by reason of his habits, lack of character, inefficiency, or who is guilty of misconduct."[86] Thus the Inspector General's visits had an almost immediate effect, bringing improvements to many aspects of student morale and camp administration. These, however, formed only a small part of the Signal Corps' problems.

Shortly after Chamberlain's unflattering final report in November, the aviation school commanders were called to a meeting in Washington. There the Chief Signal Officer set the training goals for the future and directed the adoption of a standard program. He also appointed a board of experts to visit each school and to assure training quality and uniform standards. Aircraft and parts procurement procedures were reviewed and, as a result, centralized; vehicle use policies were determined and vehicle allocation tables were developed for each airfield. Finally, the Signal Corps coordinated with the Quartermaster General's Department to facilitate the timely issue of adequate winter clothing and to prevent the unauthorized issue of popular flight jackets.[87]

Although still marginal, the aviation training program was pulled from the brink of disaster. General Chamberlain had identified spe-

---

[85] Memo, Chamberlain to TAG, 13 Aug 17; Memo (quotations), IG to CofS, WD, 13 Nov 17, sub: Aviation Schools. Both in Entry 26, RG 159, NARA.

[86] Memo, CofS, WD, to TAG, 14 Sep 17, Entry 296, RG 165, NARA.

[87] Memo, IG to CofS, WD, 13 Nov 17, and 2d End, Arnold, 22 Nov 17, Entry 26, RG 159, NARA.

cific problems relatively early and provided both the recommendations and the motivation for improvement. What began as a routine
training inspection had evolved into a thorough analysis and reform
of a major program.

In more general terms, the Inspector General's Department association with unit training played a central role in the objective assessment
of nearly every organization in the Army—its strengths, weaknesses,
and readiness for deployment. Every cantonment, school, and combat
unit was visited by inspectors. In their inspection reports they investigated or analyzed unique unit problems and made recommendations for
their resolution, many of which resulted in improvements in overall
conditions, including morale, and in the training of combat units and
their supporting specialists. Nowhere in the Army was there a group
with a better understanding of the status and problems of units and programs. The inspectorate became the fulcrum for the War Department
decisions leading to the buildup of the AEF in France.

5

The Inspectorate in France

Although General Chamberlain in Washington and General Brewster overseas enjoyed a close cooperative association throughout the war, their IG organizations developed quite differently. The first wave of personnel increases and policy decisions created a fairly stable Inspector General's Department (IGD) in the United States. This was not the case in France, where the inspectorate underwent continual alterations and expansion as the American Expeditionary Forces (AEF) and its subordinate elements adjusted to many unanticipated demands and the problems intrinsic to growth.

Adjusting to Overseas

For over a two-year period, until the AEF was inactivated, Generals Chamberlain and Brewster maintained regular contact with each other through personal letters, written, on average, nearly every two weeks. Each kept the other fully informed as to policy changes and personnel needs, exchanging views on the abilities and duty performance of inspectors and men they desired for assignment. Brewster generally deferred to the views of Chamberlain as the Inspector General of the Army, who, in turn, exerted every effort to meet Brewster's needs. By this means, IGD standards and policies were uniform throughout the inspection system. At the same time, Chamberlain was able to maintain an unobtrusive influence over the flow of events in France as they affected the department, treating the AEF's IG office essentially as if it were another subordinate element of his own organization.[1]

---

[1] File 73, Guidance for IG, AEF, Entry 588, Record Group (RG) 120, National Archives and Records Administration (NARA), Washington, D.C.; Ltr, Brewster to IG, 16 Feb 18, sub: Tables of Organization, Entry 26A, RG 159, NARA.

The inspectorate's role in the AEF was shaped by both General Pershing's command style and his personal relationship with General Brewster. Pershing often relied on Brewster when making decisions on professional matters, such as training and the maintenance of personal standards, and apparently used his IG as a sounding board and source of advice. References to Brewster throughout Pershing's memoirs reflect the commander-in-chief's esteem for his inspector and suggest a close and continuous working relationship. But Pershing also made extensive use of his inspector general system because of his own unwillingness to delegate authority beyond his personal staff and his tendency to attempt to control too much himself.[2]

Pershing recognized Brewster's command potential, briefly considering him for command of the 4th Marine Brigade of the 2d Division shortly after the unit arrived in France. In the end, Pershing decided not to assign him to the post only because "the services of . . . Brewster cannot be spared." The AEF commander went on to note that "it has become necessary to confer considerable authority on the Inspector General and there is no one who can take his place. He possesses the personal and military qualifications that make him of exceptional value, especially in determining the efficiency and fitness of officers for command." Throughout the war Pershing continued to list Brewster as one of the officers he considered capable of commanding a division or higher unit.[3]

Pershing demonstrated his professional respect by ensuring that his IG retained access to him. The general order announcing the creation of the AEF staff divided it into general and administrative and technical components, including the inspector among other bureau and department chiefs in the Administrative and Technical Staff. Initially, the heads of each staff element, twenty in number, had access to General Pershing. The arrangement proved to be increasingly unworkable, and much of the administrative history of the General Headquarters (GHQ) revolved around efforts to improve it. However, restructuring in July 1917 and again in February 1918 left the IG as one of the few staff officers, other than members of the General Staff, to remain in Pershing's headquarters.[4]

---

[2] File 12, Commander-in-Chief Reports, Entry 22, RG 120, NARA; John J. Pershing, *My Experiences in the World War*, 2 vols. (New York: Frederick A. Stokes Co., 1931), 1:20, 50, 263, 333.

[3] Frederick Palmer, *Newton D. Baker: America At War*, 2 vols. (New York: Dodd, Mead and Co., 1931), 2:231; Telg (quotations), Pershing to TAG, 9 Dec 17, Entry 588, RG 120, NARA.

[4] Department of the Army (DA), Historical Division (HD), *The United States Army in the World War, 1917–1919*, 17 vols. (Washington, D.C.: Government Printing Office, 1948), 16:1–2 (GO 1, 1917), 13–24 (GO 8, 1917), 216–25 (GO 31, 1918).

Under Brewster the AEF inspectorate became highly centralized. At first, subordinate inspectors were allowed to operate under their commanders, with a minimum of interference from Brewster's office. This policy began to change, however, as the AEF grew in size and complexity and increasing numbers of questions were referred to Brewster and his staff. The absence of uniformity and standardization within the divisions, as well as the inexperience of many inspectors, argued for more central control. Ultimately, Brewster closely monitored the activities of all inspectors through a detailed reporting system, and in time his office

Maj. Gen. Andre W. Brewster

expanded in size, becoming the largest IG staff in the AEF. Because of his growing responsibilities, Brewster received his second star as a major general in the National Army on 1 December 1917.

The unusual demands placed upon Brewster's office were attributable to the inexperience of not only unit inspectors but virtually all personnel. By the fall of 1917 inspectors routinely were expected to instruct new leaders and suggest remedies for deficiencies. The experience in France showed that the number of inspectors required in a force depended not only on its size but on its condition, mission, location, and state of training. After the war Brewster suggested that future AEF IG authorizations reflect minimums but allow for expansion in case of need. Although the maximum authorized strength rose to only 35, in fact 80 officers were serving as inspectors at the time of the armistice, with most of the overstrength in the tactical units. Later, in May 1919, to undertake a series of comprehensive investigations or to assist in facilitating embarkation and demobilization, 216 inspectors were detailed or attached to Brewster's office and to the AEF's Services of Supply (SOS).[5]

---

[5] Memo, Brewster to AG, AEF, 20 May 19, sub: Report of a Board of Officers Appointed in Compliance AG AEF Memorandum of May 5, 1919, Entry 591, RG 120, NARA.

The inspectorate did not only grow at the top. Commissioned strength in the tactical units nearly always exceeded authorizations, and late in the war division commanders routinely augmented their inspectors' one-man offices because of overcommitments. Thus Lt. Gen. Robert L. Bullard, in command of the Second Army since its activation on 10 October 1918, informed Brewster that "practically every Division and Corps commander recently desired to double the number of his inspectors." Pleased with the "efficient work" done by inspectors, and realizing that no further authorizations were forthcoming, he wrote to tell Brewster that he was allowing the IG offices at every level to be augmented by officers from other elements within the command.[6] The steady growth resulted from a process of discovery throughout the command of the AEF's inherent weaknesses and the manifold ways in which the inspectorate could strengthen and compensate for them.

The Evolution of the Inspectorate

When General Brewster and his small staff landed in France, expansion on the scale just described was unthinkable. Coping with planning problems of immense importance to the future of the AEF took first priority, after which inspection methods and procedures evolved on the basis of experience. Brewster's first job upon arrival was to serve as a senior member of a board that developed AEF port and reception procedures for all debarkation points in Europe. Following the initial press of special planning, however, Brewster spent much of his time conducting general inspections or observing allied operations.[7]

Brewster and Major Clark, newly assigned to the AEF, carried the burden alone for most of 1917, because Pershing had diverted Brewster's assistant, Major Conner, and a detailed inspector to other duty assignments. The burden left on Brewster was even heavier than it seemed, for Clark, although an able investigator, lacked the necessary background to inspect tactical units effectively. To compensate for the lack of manpower, Pershing authorized Brewster to use officers from the General Staff, and Brewster took advantage of this policy, especially by using field artillerymen to check artillery units that, here as in the United States, were most in need of assistance.[8]

---

[6] Ltr, Bullard to IG, AEF, 27 Jan 19, sub: Inspector General, Entry 26A, RG 159, NARA.

[7] Ltr, Brewster to Chamberlain, 8 Oct 17, Entry 588, RG 120, NARA.

[8] Ibid., 25 Nov 17, Entry 588, RG 120, NARA.

Despite this outside help, Brewster found it difficult both to inspect and to carry out the administration and headquarters liaison expected of him as the AEF IG. Inspection difficulties were exacerbated by the steady siphoning off of competent division-level inspectors as soon as command and key staff positions opened. Brewster did not want to deny these men any opportunities, releasing them with a plea for replacements, but an ever-growing number of new units meant that Brewster's office was mired in routine. By November most of his and Clark's time was being consumed by special investigations. Hence, Brewster asked Chamberlain to send an additional officer of "experience and rank" to be his assistant.[9]

As a result, three officers were assigned to France from the War Department inspectorate: Col. John H. Hughes, Col. John S. Winn, and Major Olmstead. They were the first of what was to become a steady flow of officers picked by the Office of the Inspector General (OIG) for European duty and allowing Brewster to finally fill the IG offices of higher-level units. When new inspectors arrived, they were immediately put to work as assistants to inspectors already on the staff. At the same time, they were given copious amounts of reading to familiarize themselves with the unique aspects of AEF organization. Colonel Baer's experience suggested the frenetic pace at which Brewster was operating. Reporting on 27 July 1918, he set out only three days later with the medical inspector on a three week inspection of facilities in the District of Paris. Immediately afterward, he conducted two major investigations on his own and then departed from the GHQ AEF to an advanced element, where he worked every day until the armistice. Between 27 July and 11 November he enjoyed only three days off, and that brief rest was attributable to his car breaking down.[10]

Problems sometimes resulted when those selected as inspectors lacked maturity or experience. Although bureau inspectors performed much useful work in their own specialties, the proliferation of non-IGD inspectors also led to a series of distracting, uncoordinated visits. The First Army IG complained that one of his units was visited by medical, veterinary, remount, G–3, G–5 and IG inspectors—all on one day. Often new inspectors merely recapitulated the findings of those who had preceded them, while the inspected units got little assistance in overcoming their problems. Inspectors had different standards, some letting a situation pass that others cited as a deficiency. The overall impact was to reduce the effectiveness of inspections and to lessen their credibility.

---

[9] Ibid., 7 (quoted words) and 10 Nov 17, Entry 588, RG 120, NARA.

[10] Ltr, Baer to IG, USA, 8 May 19, sub: Personal History of Service in the Inspector General's Department, Entry 26, RG 159, NARA.

Hence, General Brewster consolidated inspections at the field army level. He set up an informal coordination system at AEF level, either establishing working arrangements or, in some cases, taking actual control over the inspection efforts of the other bureaus and departments. The AEF General Staff, however, was not amenable to his control, and its inspection activities led to common complaints about overinspection from field units.[11]

Quality and Turbulence

The officers who eventually passed under Brewster's supervision were either reservists, like Major Clark, or regulars detailed to the Inspector General's Department. Guardsmen accompanying their divisions overseas also began to enter the system. Aware of the needs of the General Staff and the line, Brewster asked Pershing for no assignment priority and released any inspector for troop duty as ordered. The inspectorate thus continued to experience considerable turbulence. Brewster reported that between 1 July and 31 December 1918 "the personnel of the IGD has changed practically twice."[12]

For the same causes, quality declined because of the inexperience of those who were available for an IG assignment. Brewster maintained reasonable standards by retaining some senior regulars and by exploiting the limited expertise of others; he always ensured that at least one good medical and one legal officer were assigned to him. Despite the dilution of the Inspector General's Department, many exceptional officers saw service with it. One who impressed Brewster was the first tactical unit inspector to arrive in France—Maj. Conrad L. Babcock of the 1st Division, who turned down a Stateside emergency promotion to go overseas. Babcock's division commander assigned him early to the division general staff and later gave him command of a regiment. Other men who were well qualified to perform their task were Majors Webb and Streater, now serving as expert accountants, and the overworked Colonel Baer. The dedication shown by Babcock was paralleled by the enthusiasm and professionalism of the ebullient Maj. Edward E. Britton, who left the Hoboken piers to work in the AEF's Services of Supply late in the war.[13]

These men formed one side of the coin. The other consisted of a significant number of inspectors who lacked both the desire and the

---

[11] Memo, Baer to CG, 3d Corps, 7 Feb 19, Entry 590, RG 120, NARA.
[12] Memo, Brewster to CofS, AEF, 7 Jan 19, Entry 588, RG 120, NARA.
[13] Ltr, Brewster to Chamberlain, 8 Oct 17, Entry 588, RG 120, NARA.

qualifications to perform their IG duties. Many of the senior Regular Army officers selected in France did not welcome an IG assignment. Although they accepted it reluctantly, they expressed their displeasure and their desire to find a combat job. Some even tried to avoid the IG assignment all together—and, when successful, bragged about it. Once he became Brewster's assistant, Colonel Spinks tried to motivate the disgruntled officers, usually writing each a letter that stressed the importance of the IG's function. And as he pointed out in one letter, "In war some men sacrifice their lives, others their careers. We all have to give up something."[14]

Despite such encouragement, Regular Army officers regarded IG duty as detrimental to their careers, and inspectors felt overlooked by promotion policies favoring officers on the General Staff and technical bureaus. The rapid promotion rate for Adjutant General and Ordnance officers was notorious. Many officers in the Inspector General's Department thus viewed their work as demanding, thankless, and personally unrewarding. Lt. Col. Philip Lauber, on duty in the Services of Supply at Tours, told Colonel Spinks that he noted in many of his fellow inspectors "a bitter feeling toward their organization instead of one of loyalty." He felt that the lack of recognition during the war was an omen of things to come once the war was over. A few officers manifested so poor an attitude as to require immediate relief.[15]

The situation grew worse when American forces suffered unprecedented losses in the summer of 1918. The need for experienced Regular Army officers was so acute that in August General Pershing directed that by 1 October all regulars serving as division or corps adjutants, ordnance officers, quartermasters, commanders of military police or inspectors would be assigned to command combat units. Major unit commanders received instructions to plan accordingly and to be prepared to select and assign National Guard and reserve officers as staff replacements.

General Brewster prevailed upon Pershing to modify his order to allow a Regular Army officer to remain as senior inspector on each

---

[14] Ltr (quotation), Spinks to Fleet, 1 Nov 18, Entry 591, RG 120, NARA. The attitude of some inspectors is strange to understand given that many of the senior AEF commanders, from Pershing down, expressed their appreciation and admiration for the inspectorate. General Bullard, for example, later attributed the success of the 33d Division commander, Maj. Gen. George Bell, to his prewar experience as an IG. He "was known to the whole Regular Army as perhaps the most exacting inspector general that was ever in it." See Robert L. Bullard, *Personalities and Reminiscences of the War* (Garden City, N.Y.: Doubleday, Page and Co., 1925), p. 268.

[15] Memo, Lauber to Donaldson, 16 May 19, and Ltr (quotation), Lauber to Spinks, 16 May 19, Entry 588, RG 120, NARA.

corps staff. Senior inspector vacancies at corps headquarters were filled with one of the regulars being reassigned from the divisions. Pershing also approved the immediate identification and assignment of the nonregular division replacements, in an effort to provide for some cross-training with the departing officers. By the end of September only division- and corps-level staffs, with a few exceptions, had Regular Army officers.[16]

The end result was a widespread assignment of so-called temporary officers to tactical unit IG positions, but the real effect on the inspectorate was that its reliability and effectiveness was doubted by Regular Army officers. This was attributable partly to the prevailing lack of confidence in the replacements and partly to the fact that many of them did not have the experience necessary to be of full value to their commanders. Justifying the change as a necessary evil, General Brewster later said that the situation proved the truth of the adage that "men are not disposed to cheerfully and willingly accept criticism from those whom they may have cause to believe not fully qualified to criticize."[17]

Yet the problems that developed were not always the fault of the new inspectors. Some found their ability to do their jobs impaired by the absence of help or encouragement from their superiors. On 31 October 1918 Maj. David Lewis, a former Pennsylvania guardsman, was assigned as inspector to the 6th Division, at the time stationed close to units fighting in the Argonne. Lewis reported to the division chief of staff, whose sole guidance to him was "to keep one foot on the ground," an instruction that Lewis felt was "quite needless." The division commander was only marginally more helpful, telling his nervous new inspector to "look after the care of animals, transportation and observation of all troop movements on the march, or otherwise." Lewis was able to make a productive contribution only as a result of help from an infantry captain who had been assigned as the assistant division inspector.[18]

Other division inspectors were moved about or given inappropriate duties by their commanders. Sometimes Brewster heard of such cases only when replacements for the reassigned men were requested. Another practice was to substitute an untrained officer chosen by the local commander for an experienced inspector. Commonly, a division

---

[16] Ltr, AG, AEF, to CGs, 13 Aug 18, sub: Availability of Regular Officers; Ltr, Spinks to Johnson, 14 Aug 18; and Ltr, IG, AEF, to CGs, 17 Aug 18, sub: Detail of Division Inspectors. All in Entry 588, RG 120, NARA.

[17] Rpt, Brewster to CinC, AEF, n.d., Entry 588, RG 120, NARA.

[18] David Lewis, "A Short Account of My Experiences in the American Expeditionary Forces in France, 1918–1919," OTIG files, Pentagon (SAIG-ZXH).

staff officer would be ordered to fill in for an inspector who was ill or away at school, to prevent IG cases from accumulating. This practice was often the source of poor investigations or reports. Although technically improper because the replacement was not on detail, it was tolerated on the grounds that it did more good than harm. Some units, however, seemingly forgot that the permanent detailing of inspectors was not their prerogative. In one case, a corps chief of staff diverted an officer sent for regimental command to be the corps IG, ousting the assigned IG without informing either Brewster or his own commander. Both were furious when they discovered the change; the inspector was reinstated and the erring chief of staff was reassigned.[19]

Not all the difficulties that developed, however, could be blamed on the misuse of inspectors. An inexperienced or rash IG officer could make many problems for himself. A Regular Army corps inspector acknowledged that the broad charter given to IGs had motivated several of his inexperienced division inspectors to "overstep a bit." He urged them to behave with tact and to keep their commanders informed of what they were doing. He suggested to his army-level counterpart that the word be spread to IGs at all levels to be more circumspect, fearing the development of "a wide breach between the line and the staff which will be very difficult to heal."[20]

Examples of such friction were all too frequent. It was easy to sympathize with the rage of the 82d Division commander, whose machine gun company had been written up for having dirty wagons on the tenth day of the fighting in the Meuse-Argonne. In another case, "one of these Reserve Corps inspectors skinned the company officers of a certain unit for being around the mess hall at dinner time, evidently being afraid they would try to eat some of the men's rations." He ignored the officers' explanation that they were assuring proper mess procedures by their presence. The tendency of some inspectors to look always for something wrong alienated many commanders, particularly in the heated atmosphere of the final offensives, when the slightest error by a commander usually meant summary relief. Under pressure both from the enemy and from their own commanders, some officers began to view their inspectors with extreme hostility.[21]

---

[19] Telg, Baer to IG, AEF, 9 Feb 19, and Memo, Brewster to CinC, AEF, 27 Sep 18, Entry 590, RG 120, NARA. See also Hines Interv, 7 Nov 47, Army General Staff Interviews, Cater Files, OCMH Collection, U.S. Army Military History Institute (MHI), Carlisle Barracks, Pa.

[20] Memo, Peck to Johnson, 23 Oct 18, Entry 799, RG 120, NARA.

[21] Ltr, Baer to Spinks, 8 Dec 18, Entry 590, RG 120, NARA.

There were many other points of friction. Brig. Gen. Hugh A. Drum, the First Army chief of staff, criticized the lack of imagination shown in the numerous IG reports he reviewed. Inexperienced inspectors at the division level slavishly stuck to their checklists, commenting on each topic whether any changes had occurred or not. Drum pointed out that replacement problems and the condition of animals were generally recognized as critical and that commanders needed no endless "harping" on the fact. Drum also urged IGs to refrain from tactically second-guessing commanders and to assess operations only when specifically tasked to do so. Drum further cautioned inspectors to be discreet when assessing the battle-worthiness of troops and units. "It is undesirable and psychologically damaging to attract attention to such matters as fatigue, time on line, and replacement quality without any real cause. A unit often only has the problems it perceives are problems."[22]

Tactlessness and pedestrianism were not the only problems of the less able inspectors. On rare occasions their actions in the field made them laughingstocks, discrediting the entire inspectorate. One such case involved a guardsman who was assigned as the 37th Division IG. During the Meuse-Argonne offensive this inspector drew his pistol on some soldiers he presumed were stragglers. Refusing to hear their explanations, he escorted them to the front lines. Later, they were able to identify themselves as members of a signal wire team setting up lines from the rear. On another occasion the same inspector drew his pistol again while trying to clear up a traffic jam. The division commander reprimanded the IG for his rash conduct; however, acknowledging that the inspector had rendered "excellent service" overall, he judged that he should not be punished further for actions made under "extremely aggravating circumstances" that might have been avoided by a more experienced officer. Nevertheless, the errant IG was reassigned to a division returning to the United States, for his usefulness in the 37th Division had ended.[23]

Brewster attempted to counsel the inspectors, urging that their questions should be positive, "helpful, calculated to build up the morale

---

[22] Ltr (quotations), Drum to IG, First Army, 20 Oct 18, sub: Comments on Inspectors' Reports, with pencil notes by A.W.B. attached; Ltr, McIlroy to Spinks, 9 Nov 18, sub: Circular Letter to All Inspectors. Both in Entry 590, RG 120, NARA.

[23] Memo, McKenney to IG, AEF, 3 Nov 18, sub: Lt. Col. B. J. Barger IG; Ltr, Larimore to CG, 37th Div, 4 Nov 18, sub: Lt. Col. Barger; and Ltr, Barger to CG, 37th Div, 14 Nov 18, sub: Accusation That I Pointed a Pistol at a Lieutenant in the Argonne Drive, and End (quoted words), Farnsworth, same date. All in Entry 588, RG 120, NARA.

and esprit de corps of the command." He prepared an encouraging letter to each inspector, specifying items of concern and directing them to work with their corps inspectors when they were in doubt. He also pointed out that it was command policy to hold them responsible for not reporting unsatisfactory conditions. He stressed that IGs should enter units as in the chain of command, from "the top down," explaining their purpose to everyone and, upon completion of their task, reversing the process as they identified matters that needed correction.[24]

As Brewster's field assistant, Col. Joseph A. Baer, admonished inspectors to "assume the attitude of an instructor and an importer of information and orders," and both he and Brewster noted that a helpful attitude could achieve cooperation. Baer made it a practice never to use his authority to give orders except in an emergency. "My policy was to force the officer concerned to see the need for correction and to issue the orders himself." This method sustained the authority of local commanders and avoided the tendency to attribute their shortcomings to IG meddling. Baer observed that an inspector should always tell the inspected commander what he had found, never letting him find out after the fact in a directive from above.[25]

The steady criticism of IG performance affected morale, especially, that of the lower-level inspectors. They bristled particularly at the statement that they would be held responsible for unreported deficiencies. One inspector pointed out to General Brewster that he was already working fourteen hours a day with no assistance, mostly on special projects for his commander, and asked for guidance on his priorities to avoid any criticism. Another inspector expressed similar sentiments, saying much of what he reported went no further than his commander, who decided what to do with it. He wanted to know what deficiencies Brewster deemed critical. Guidance, however, consisted merely of the typical checklists, the source of Drum's complaint that many IG reports were filled with the obvious. The pressure placed on new inspectors explained their excesses, at least in part, and added to the supervisory burden of IGs at corps and higher levels.

By exercising tact, able GHQ inspectors soothed but never completely overcame the resentment caused by circumstances and their own inept brethren. As soon as hostilities ended, the divisions that still had reserve officers assigned as inspectors requested that they be replaced by regulars. Regular Army officers were authorized by General

---

[24] Memo, IG, AEF, to Insps, 4 Sep 18, sub: Responsibility of Division Inspectors, Entry 588, RG 120, NARA.
[25] Ltr, Baer to IG, USA, 8 May 19, Entry 26, RG 159, NARA.

Pershing to be detailed again to the Inspector General's Department on 2 December 1918, and despite continuing difficulties in finding experienced men, the quality and experience of inspectors had for the most part returned to satisfactory standards by April 1919.

Nevertheless, the personnel problems in the lower echelons of the inspectorate had been a difficult extra burden at a critical time of frenetic activity. The positive side of the experience was the revelation of the kind of people needed by the inspectorate to succeed. But the problems of wartime cast long shadows. Many senior inspectors feared that the IG system had suffered permanent damage by allowing inexperienced or marginal officers to serve in it. The policy unquestionably had created a legacy of bias against the inspectorate among many officers destined for positions of influence in the postwar period.[26]

Training Inspections

Despite the tensions, General Pershing and the GHQ staff relied extensively on the AEF inspectorate to gauge conditions within the expeditionary force. Conformity with the GHQ training programs was stressed heavily, in part because of the low training level of the divisions arriving in France. Inspectors monitored AEF policies for avoiding overreliance on the British and French officers, which accorded with General Pershing's desire to keep the AEF as American as possible. They also reported on the effects of strength and equipment shortages. Inspectors were asked to comment on unit march discipline, including proper conduct of rest halts, appearance of the troops, correct pace, and the ability to keep a portion of the road open at all times. Finally, the ever-present officer evaluations had to be carried out, at least partly in reaction to allied reports about the limited staff capabilities of the American units.[27]

General Pershing insisted that this sort of information continue flowing from those American units that passed under allied control. Regardless of where a unit was, he kept close tabs on it through inspection visits and personal contact. The inspectors' duties were varied. IGs carried out, with tact and diplomacy, special inquiries on unit relations with allied officials, as well as reviewed transactions and

---

[26] Memo, Brewster to AG, AEF, 20 May 19, Entry 591; Ltr, Magruder to Helmick, 3 Jan 27, Entry 1360. Both in RG 120, NARA.

[27] Memo, Fiske to IG, AEF, 25 Jun 18, Entry 588, RG 120, NARA; John Toland, *No Man's Land: 1918—The Last Year of the Great War* (New York: Doubleday and Co., 1980), p. 189.

agreements executed by American units with Allies to ensure compliance with AEF policy. Specific information requests increased steadily. For example, inspectors were asked by the AEF ordnance chief to investigate the serious abuse of machine guns, which machine gunners were wrecking at an alarming rate; by the AEF G–3, to be alert to the misuse of aviation marking panels; and by the AEF chief quartermaster, to informally note the number of garbage cans in use during unit inspections and provide recommendations for a standard basis of issue.[28] The list seemed endless.

The normal AEF field inspections lasted four to seven days. During this time inspectors observed activities, interviewed unit members and most key personnel, and gathered and correlated statistics on discipline. Control of venereal disease was a major concern of General Pershing, who made it a special item of inquiry for every visit or inspection. IGs learned to check a unit's venereal rate for trends and to seek explanations for any variations. Service records and pay cards kept in the units had to be spot-checked in response to complaints about delays and errors in pay.[29]

The major portion of an inspection report, however, dealt with tactical efficiency and the exercise of command. In June 1918 Pershing directed all inspectors to make frequent training observations and assist in assuring the quality of training and the best use of time. Typical of the inspections that resulted was Col. Jacob C. Johnson's visit on 26–30 August 1918 to the 82d Division, then occupying a quiet sector in Lorraine. Although the 82d was one of the better units, and was theoretically in its final stages of training, Johnson found that its troops had no experience in open (free from the trenches) offensive warfare. Practice in attack, liaison, and fighting in woods and villages was just beginning at the time of Johnson's visit. Indeed, the 82d had received so many replacements that even its level of basic training was low. Most men needed training in infantry crew-served weapons and grenades; one brigade commander reported that the closest his men had gotten to such weapons was at demonstrations. None had any experience in dealing with artillery, for the division artillery brigade had been trained sep-

---

[28] Memos, Brewster to Insps, 28 Jan 18, sub: Observance of Official and Social Courtesies; Ovenshine to Insps, 20 May 18, sub: Injury to Machine Guns; Spinks to All Insps, 15 Oct 18, sub: Misuse of Marking Panels; Spinks to Insps, 5 Oct 18; and Olmstead to Insps, 8 Jul 18, sub: Training. All in Entry 588, RG 120, NARA. See also Bullard, *Personalities and Reminiscences*, p. 140.

[29] Edward M. Coffman, *The War To End All Wars: The American Military Experience in World War I* (New York: Oxford University Press, 1968), p. 132; Memo, Ovenshine to Insps, 23 Aug 18, sub: Payment of Soldiers, Entry 588, RG 120, NARA.

Col. Jacob C. Johnson

arately, only joining the division on 24 August. The turnover of key personnel had been constant and damaging, despite conscientious efforts to retain the best officers and NCOs.[30]

High sick rates, caused by poor sanitary practices, and a serious transportation problem also lowered the division's combat readiness and overall proficiency. Johnson discussed the situation with the division IG and chief of staff, who agreed to pursue a more aggressive sanitation program. The unit's acute shortage of vehicles, with only 45 percent of its rolling stock and eleven of its fifty authorized motor ambulances on hand, virtually doomed any effective medical evacuation during heavy combat. And the lack of the necessary spare parts for the vehicles exacerbated the whole situation. If the division were required to redeploy quickly, it would have to abandon most of its unserviceable vehicles, further reducing its already deficient transportation capability.[31]

The division commander, Maj. Gen. William P. Burnham, impressed Colonel Johnson, as did the brigade and regimental commanders and the division IG. Burnham was confident that the division could do whatever was required of it, warning, however, that "without the training we may have 2, 3, or 4 casualties where we ought to have only one." (His prophetic comment also had application for the entire AEF in the offensives launched in the autumn of 1918.) Johnson judged the commanders and staff to be ready "for the test of battle," pressed for a resolution of the division's transportation problem, and recommended that the division be required to accelerate its training.[32]

Units on the march often were observed by corps and Army IGs, who were dispatched to assess their march discipline, equipment status,

---

[30] Memo, Johnson to CG, First Army, 1 Sep 18, sub: Report of Inspection, 82d Division, AEF, Entry 588, RG 120, NARA.

[31] Ibid. The 1917 TO&E authorized 544 wagons and 731 motor vehicles.

[32] Ibid.

and degree of organization. Upon arriving in the unit area, the inspectors would first make their presence known to the commander. If the unit was on the road, they would then go down the line or observe the unit as it moved past. One inspector said he never reviewed infantry while he was in a car. "I made it a rule never to drive past troops and splash them with mud," or to ride while they walked. Inspectors might accompany the organization, watch it go into bivouac, and spot-check the condition of its equipment. The vehicle shortage was always extreme, and inspectors sometimes suggested reducing cargo loads. Inspection reports revealed that a surprising number of units, theoretically in the final stages of readiness, were ill-organized and short of equipment even as they moved to the front.[33]

As a matter of policy, inspectors from the AEF's IG office tried to be present whenever a major unit disembarked at one of the ports, to gather information on its training status. One visit had unexpectedly lasting consequences. In August 1918 Colonel Baer had the duty of watching the 81st Division disembark at the port of St. Nazaire. Upon seeing that the troops were wearing the silhouette of a wildcat on their sleeves or caps, he made an inquiry through channels if the practice was proper. Eventually, his report reached the division commander, Maj. Gen. Charles J. Bailey, who replied that he had noted the practice in allied units during his orientation tour of the Western Front. When his unit was marking its cargo for overseas shipment, the men selected a wildcat. Bailey allowed the use of the symbol on uniforms and, because it enhanced unit cohesion and morale, urged that the practice be authorized throughout the AEF. His recommendation was approved by General Pershing in October 1918, and shoulder sleeve insignia have been a part of the U.S. Army uniform ever since.[34]

Inspection teams soon discovered that inspectors assigned to divisions had varied roles to play, according to their commanders' wishes. Lt. Col. Matthew H. Taggart, the 28th Division IG, stated that he had no authority over training but visited training areas to ensure that unit programs and policies were being carried out. He spent most of his time inspecting billets and messes for adherence to health requirements. He

---

[33] Lewis, "Short Account," quotation, OTIG files, Pentagon (SAIG-ZXH); Rpts, Insp, First Army Arty, to CG, Army Arty, 20 Sep and 14 Oct 18, subs: Inspection of 60th Artillery, CAC, and Inspection of 57th Artillery, CAC, Entry 588, RG 120, NARA.

[34] Memo, Baer to IG, AEF, 5 Sep 18; Ltr, CinC, AEF, to Cdr, 81st Div, 28 Sep 18, and 1st End, Cdr, 81st Div, to CinC, AEF, 4 Oct 18; Telg, AG, AEF, to All Div CGs, 8 Oct 18; and Ltr, IG, AEF, to IG, SOS, AEF, 12 Dec 18. All in Entry 588, RG 120, NARA.

also devoted considerable interest to the care, treatment, and condition of the division livestock. His commander had delegated him the authority to order corrective actions in his name whenever necessary, which became normal practice by the summer of 1918. Taggart conducted investigations of officer efficiency, damage claims, and self-inflicted wounds, and he reviewed and made recommendations on all requests for discharge or compassionate reassignment. Taggart's relationship with his commander was cordial, close, and fully supportive.[35]

The 5th Division commander gave his inspector, Lt. Col. Robert G. Peck, a substantially different role. Peck spent his time almost exclusively in the field, inspecting unit conditions and training progress, visiting troops, assessing their activities, and helping commanders where he could, while a captain was attached to the division IG office to handle administration and conduct routine investigations. At first Peck experienced a lot of hostility from the division general staff, but he overcame the situation through sheer perseverance, the support of the division commander, and his own helpful contributions to the staff's efforts to train the division and ready it for combat. By the time the regulars were pulled out of special staffs in September 1918, the division IG was considered one of the keys to assuring division readiness and discipline.[36]

Discipline and Race Relations

In April 1918 General Pershing decided to add a "disciplinary feature" to the inspectorate, with the aim of imposing high standards of appearance and conduct throughout his growing expeditionary force. He hoped to see the AEF's IG office become "something of the nature of a court of equity." Brewster soon became responsible for overseeing discipline in the AEF and for adjudicating discipline matters in Pershing's name. A similar approach was recommended at all other levels of command.[37]

---

[35] Memo, Taggart to IG, AEF, 1 Jul 18, sub: Inspection of 28th Division; Taggert, IG, 28th Div, Annual Rpt, 1917–18. Both in Entry 588, RG 120, NARA. See also Lewis, "Short Account," OTIG files, Pentagon (SAIG-ZXH).

[36] Ltr, Peck to Brewster, 23 Sep 18, Entry 588, RG 120, NARA.

[37] Memo (quotations), Pershing to Brewster, 14 Apr 18; Ltr, Brewster to W. Wood, 8 Apr 18; Memo, Brewster to CofS, AEF, 12 Apr 18; Memo, Brewster to CinC, AEF, 16 Apr 18, sub: Duties of Inspector General's Department; Memo, Brewster to CinC, AEF, 1 May 18, sub: Draft of Order on Discipline; and Memo, Olmstead to Insps, 16 Apr 18, sub: Supervision of Discipline by IGD. All in Entry 588, RG 120, NARA. See also Marcellus G. Spinks, "Major Problems of the Inspector General, AEF, and Their Solution" (Lecture delivered at G–1 Course No. 5, Army War College, Washington, D.C., 9 Oct 33), in Army War College Curriculum Papers, MHI.

Shortly afterward, inspectors in the field received instructions to submit, using a form supplied by the AEF's IG office, a monthly report on any disciplinary issues. They did not welcome the new responsibility, regarding the tasking as a burdensome addition to an already full schedule. Nevertheless, GHQ AEF considered the discipline reports as critical information, giving staff members a means to identify trends, to fix responsibilities, and to make recommendations to the proper commanders. A general order, issued on 5 June 1918, formally assigned the responsibility for discipline oversight to Brewster and confirmed the requirement for the monthly report. Commanders were ordered to give the same responsibility to their IGs, subject to their own policies, and the discipline report was expanded to include any lack of follow-through on irregularities noted in unit inspections.[38]

The biggest problem encountered by inspectors everywhere, but especially in line units, continued to be inexperienced personnel. Too many green junior leaders had difficulty supervising troops, which in turn led to failures in discipline. Inspectors offered constructive criticism while using discipline as a measure of progress, if only evidenced by such outward signs of military conduct as saluting and appearance. But more important indicators were AWOL and venereal rates and, although less measurable, the prompt execution of orders and policies.

The AEF inspectorate conducted numerous special investigations whenever indiscipline appeared related to unit inefficiency. The high standards set by Pershing, combined with the growing urgency and intolerance for error brought on by the German offensives, allowed little latitude for honest error. The black combat units then in training suffered as a consequence, for many senior AEF officers, including those in the inspectorate, had a strong bias against such organizations, especially if they had black officers. In these cases the black leadership conveniently became scapegoats for any failures experienced by the units.[39]

Reflecting this attitude were the inspectors who visited the black 92d Division and the four black infantry regiments organized for the never-completed 93d Division and training with the French. In June 1918, after the regiments had been fully incorporated into French divisions and were using French equipment and rations, Col. Alexander T.

---

[38] Ltr, Brewster to W. Wood, 16 Apr 18; Rpt, Johnson, 5 May 18, sub: Discipline, I Corps; Ltr, Olmstead to Johnson, 7 May 18; Memo, Brewster to Insps, 25 Jun 18, sub: Reports. All in Entry 588, RG 120, NARA. See also Lewis, "Short Account," OTIG files, Pentagon (SAIG-ZXH); DA, HD, *World War*, 16:337 (GO 87, 1918).

[39] Coffman, *War To End All Wars*, pp. 317–19; Memo, Brewster to CinC, AEF, 31 Jul 18, Entry 588, RG 120, NARA.

Col. Alexander T. Ovenshine

Ovenshine from the AEF's IG office visited them. Ovenshine spent a day with each regiment, after which he submitted a report. According to his report, the unit he considered best was commanded by a white Regular Army colonel and had no black officers. His ratings of the others dropped as the numbers of black officers on their rolls increased, with the all-black 370th Infantry rated the worst. Ovenshine recommended the removal of all black officers and their replacement by white officers as the only way to upgrade discipline and efficiency.

But careful review of his few substantive comments failed to justify his findings. The units, on the contrary, all appear to have been reasonably well disciplined and trained and to have high morale. A balanced assessment would have compared them favorably to most of the other new AEF units. However, Ovenshine's fixation on commissioned blacks completely warped his vision. The apparent problem prompted General Pershing in July 1918 to direct a special investigation of the black field-grade officers in the 370th and 372d Infantry. Apparently considered to be the AEF IG's authority on black units, Colonel Ovenshine conducted the investigation, which coincided with the relief of Col. Franklin A. Denison, the black commander of the 370th Infantry, for health reasons.[40]

Denison's replacement was Col. Thomas A. Roberts from the AEF G–1, an officer who had reported adversely on the commander of the 372d Infantry two months before. Ovenshine viewed the appointment as a good one, likely to improve the regiment. Turning to the other black field-grade officers, he was frank in saying there was no basis for boarding them for incompetence. However, he persisted in recommending their gradual elimination and replacement with whites, first

---

[40] Memo, Ovenshine to IG, AEF, 24 Jun 18, sub: Inspection of 369th, 370th, 371st, and 372d Infantry Regiments (Colored), Entry 588, RG 120, NARA.

on the staff and then throughout the line. As matters turned out, Roberts proved to be a good commander, although he was greatly resented by the men for having replaced their black colonel.[41]

The consistency of the bias shared by the inspectors and the officers on the GHQ staff was exposed by an incident in the midst of the Meuse-Argonne offensive. The four independent black regiments had acquitted themselves well while fighting with the French in the summer and early fall of 1918. During the unprecedented attrition of mid-October, however, the AEF staff discussed the desirability of their return to American control. Brewster told Pershing that he did not consider any of the units to be in good condition, maintaining that so long as they had any black officers they would not make satisfactory combat units. Yet three of the units by this time had earned at least one *Croix de Guerre*. Notwithstanding, Brewster offered two scenarios for consideration once the units came under U.S. control: breaking them up and using them as replacements for the 92d Division, or forming them into labor units after taking out the best men for the 92d.[42] No amount of evidence to the contrary was able to shake the prevailing racial bias against black troops.

Fortunately for the AEF, the inspectors remained more open on other problems. Their concern over matters of discipline brought them into duties traditionally associated with the military police. The Provost Marshal General of the command at first lacked the capability to carry out all such functions, and as a result his sphere was limited to confinement of prisoners, some traffic control, and planning for the maintenance of order. A formal Military Police Corps was not organized until the summer of 1918. Until then, each division detailed a group of its own men to serve as police, and each field army headquarters possessed a traffic and police regiment.[43]

The first function picked up by the inspectors was the investigation of criminal matters. Vandalism or theft, so-called depredations,

---

[41] Arthur E. Barbeau and Florette Henri, *The Unknown Soldiers: Black American Troops in World War I* (Philadelphia: Temple University Press, 1974), pp. 123–28; Rpt, Ovenshine to IG, AEF, 20 Jul 18, sub: Investigation of Colored Field Officers in the 370th and 372d Infantry, Entry 588, RG 120, NARA.

[42] Memo, Spinks to Brewster, 18 Oct 18; Memo, Brewster to CofS, AEF, 19 Oct 18, sub: Recommendation as to 369th, 370th, 371st, and 372d Infantry Regiments (Colored). Both in Entry 588, RG 120, NARA.

[43] Memo, Groome to CofS, AEF, 9 Jun 18, sub: Recommendation for a Military Police Corps; Memo, Brewster to CofS, AEF, 11 Jun 18, sub: Military Police Force; and Ltr, Elmore to IG, AEF, 25 Jun 19, sub: Report From Observations of AEF. All in Entry 588, RG 120, NARA.

became more prevalent as the AEF grew in size. New activity also seemed to coincide with the AEF chief of staff's referral of IG investigations to the appropriate command. Even after a police capability was developed, many inconclusive or dead-end investigations were referred to the IGs for review. The scale of IG activity remained large also because the newly formed police were not authorized to investigate anything connected with the efficiency of a unit. Because the term *efficiency* was interpreted broadly, almost every misdemeanor went to the inspectors first.[44]

From the beginning, General Brewster perceived the nature and scope of what was being thrust on the inspectorate, and in June 1917 asked General Chamberlain to authorize assigning Secret Service investigators to the AEF's IG office. Chamberlain turned down the request promptly, instructing Brewster to refer undercover actions to military intelligence and to cope as best he could with the numerous but simple criminal conduct cases that he anticipated. As matters turned out, traffic-related actions comprised the bulk of them, and included not only serious cases involving death or injury but also minor incidents of property damage. Eventually, IG findings led to the formulation of vehicle-use policies and their enforcement by unit provost guards with local IG support.[45]

Services of Supply Established

The rapid accumulation of diverse functions made it imperative that a division of effort be made within the inspectorate. Army field service regulations provided for the establishment of a line-of-communications (LOC) organization to provide support for forward units. As an increasingly elaborate logistical infrastructure developed in France, mounting inefficiencies and control problems appeared as the pace of events quickened and the high command concentrated on preparations for combat. General Brewster observed the trend as early as August 1917, when he wrote to General Chamberlain that the huge shipments of unnecessary equipment from the United States were compounding the severe congestion problems at the ports. Apparently, some supplies were shipped automatically under peacetime authorizations, which no one had canceled. Other supplies were sent that, in fact, could have

---

[44] File 281, Depredations, and Ltr, Pershing to Chief, French Mil Mission, 21 Jan 19, Entry 588, RG 120, NARA.

[45] Ltrs, Chamberlain to Brewster, 14 Sep 17, and Brewster to Chamberlain, 8 Oct 18, Entry 588, RG 120, NARA.

been procured locally, thus preventing ships from transporting more critical items.[46]

These conditions and his increasingly unwieldy span of control led General Pershing to direct Brewster in December 1917 to survey the whole situation. The purpose of the study was to examine the means to decentralize GHQ activities by relegating as many functions as possible to the LOC. Other General Staff elements studied aspects of the problem throughout the month and on into January 1918. Their recommendations led to the February appointment of a restructuring board under Col. Johnson Hagood. Hagood proposed that a distinct logistical command, with broad operational responsibility, be created. General Pershing gave his approval on the eighteenth. By the end of the month the structure and relationships between the reconstituted General Staff and the newly created Services of Supply, successor to the LOC, were also defined.[47]

The incumbent commander of the old LOC, Maj. Gen. Francis J. Kernan, presided over a complete restructuring of the rear areas. Before February the LOC had consisted of the port of St. Nazaire, a headquarters area in the city of Nevers and various facilities scattered throughout France behind the front. This rather vague arrangement was changed to a much more formal organization. Advanced and Intermediate Sections were set up behind the front, with separate base sections organized around each major port—six in France and one in England. An eighth section was organized in Italy a few days before the armistice. Each contained a varying number of depots, support facilities, hospitals, and training centers. Separate SOS commands were set up in the District of Paris and at the SOS headquarters near Tours (see Map 1).[48]

The Services of Supply ultimately engaged over 670,000 men, performing every conceivable support task. But serious problems soon appeared. Rear area troop morale was one, as SOS soldiers suffered from a second-class image. Conditions worsened because of the generally poor unit leadership that resulted when the Services of Supply

---

[46] Ltr, Brewster to Chamberlain, 20 Aug 17, Entry 588, RG 120, NARA.

[47] Memo, Pershing to IG, AEF, 15 Dec 17, and Rpt, Brewster to CinC, AEF, 31 Dec 17, Entry 588, RG 120, NARA; Erna Risch, *Quartermaster Support of the Army: A History of the Corps, 1775–1939* (Washington, D.C.: Quartermaster Historian's Office, Office of the Quartermaster General, 1962), p. 649; Johnson Hagood, *The Services of Supply: A Memoir of the Great War* (Boston: Houghton Mifflin Co., 1927), pp. 134, 139–40, 151; DA, HD, *World War*, 16:216 (GO 31, 1918).

[48] Risch, *Quartermaster Support*, p. 657n42; American Battle Monuments Commission, *American Armies and Battlefields in Europe* (Washington, D.C.: Government Printing Office, 1938), pp. 437–38.

MAP 1

became a dumping ground for unsatisfactory combat-unit officers. These problems and others led Pershing to relieve Kernan in July 1918 and replace him with the 2d Division commander, Maj. Gen. James G. Harbord, who had participated in the first battles along the Marne. As one of Pershing's most trusted subordinates, Harbord allowed Pershing

"Saint Nazaire"

to focus on the problems of diplomacy and the front, secure in the knowledge that the Services of Supply was in able hands.[49]

Harbord's appointment marked the opening of a period of broad autonomy for the Services of Supply, which was reflected in the methods and organization adopted by the inspectorate. When first created in July 1917, the LOC lacked an inspector, with coverage provided as far as possible by Brewster and Clark from the AEF headquarters. The arrangement proved increasingly unworkable, and by August Brewster was pressing Chamberlain to identify and send over suitable officers. After some experimentation, he secured the services of the energetic Col. Robert Alexander and then Colonel Hughes on 7 January 1918. Shortly thereafter, Alexander was promoted and departed for command of a division, to be replaced on 2 February by Colonel Winn, another detailed IG. Within a week of arriving, Winn was in turn promoted to brigadier general but was retained as senior

---

[49] Coffman, *War To End All Wars*, p. 129; Hagood, *Services of Supply*, pp. 301, 310; James A. Huston, *The Sinews of War: Army Logistics, 1775–1953* (Washington, D.C.: Office of the Chief of Military History, United States Army, 1966), pp. 365–66; SOS, AEF, GO 29, 32 1/2, and 33, 1918, OTIG files, Pentagon (SAIG-ZXH).

LOC inspector, despite being overgrade, on the assumption that sooner or later his position would be authorized flag rank. General Winn was a respected cavalry officer with several years experience as an inspector. Both Brewster and Harbord considered him a strong leader with a "forceful personality," fully qualified to command a brigade. Brewster also reassigned Major Streater to the new Services of Supply to begin financial inspections, allowing Winn to concentrate on other issues.[50]

The creation of the sections led to an immediate need for more inspectors. Both Brewster and Winn wanted to have at least one at each of the major SOS subordinate commands, as well as several at the headquarters near Tours. The first officers so assigned were Maj. Richard I. McKenney, in the Advanced Section; Maj. J. Ryan Devereaux, at St. Nazaire; Maj. Owen T. Kenan, at Brest; and Col. James B. Mitchell, at London. Colonel Spinks became Winn's deputy on 12 April, where he remained until 11 June, when he took over similar duties in Brewster's office. Seven more Regular Army officers were assigned from General Chamberlain's informal pool by the end of June, and all were sent to base sections, except Maj. Lloyd B. Magruder who became an assistant inspector at Tours. By Armistice Day eleven officers were serving as inspectors on duty with the staffs at each base section and district command, with eleven more at the Tours headquarters available for general support.[51]

As might be expected, the duties of the SOS inspectors were focused mostly on inspections and investigations related to the base ports, depots, and other facilities set up in the SOS area. Inspections of troops were limited to those assigned to the Services of Supply; the combat units arriving and going through the training areas were served by their own assigned inspectors or IGs from GHQ. Similarly, every-

---

[50] Ltr, Kinnison to Brewster, 19 Nov 17, and Reply, 21 Nov 17, Entry 588; Memo, Howard to Kinnison, 23 Nov 17, sub: Regarding Installation of Records, Entry 588; Ltr (quoted words), Harbord to CinC, AEF, 13 Dec 18, sub: Report on General Officers, Entry 6; Ltr, Farnsworth to CinC, AEF, 12 Dec 18, sub: Confidential Report on General Officers, Entry 6; Ltr, Brewster to Winn, 26 Jan 18, Entry 1360. All in RG 120, NARA. See also Rpt, Lauber, n.d., sub: The Inspector General's Department, S.O.S, November 1918, Entry 26B, RG 159, NARA.

[51] Memo, Lauber to Donaldson, 16 May 19; Ltr, Brewster to W. Wood, 8 Apr 18; Historical Record of the Office of the Inspector General, S.O.S., from June 1st to December 31st 1918, n.d.; and Rpt, Donaldson to IG, AEF, 14 Mar 19, sub: Report of the Inspector General. All in Entry 588, RG 120, NARA. See also Info Memo, March to IG, USA, 24 Jun 18, Entry 26A; Miller, IG, Base Sec 1, Annual Rpt, 30 Jun 19, Entry 26. Both in RG 159, NARA.

thing connected with combat training, including schools, remained the province of officers sent out by GHQ. Disbursing accounts began to be inspected from the SOS headquarters following the assignment of Major Streater, while base section inspectors examined the company, hospital, and welfare funds of organizations in their areas that lacked assigned inspectors. The section inspectors periodically checked on property salvage operations, although no longer required to do so by regulation, in order to detect excessive turn-ins. Wherever they visited, they emphasized all aspects of sanitation and Pershing's venereal disease prevention program. The relative inexperience of these units led most SOS inspectors to see their role as one of providing guidance to enthusiastic young leaders—"to encourage or suppress as tendencies are right or wrong."[52]

General Winn, however, departed from the model set by General Brewster by operating a decentralized inspection system, under which inspectors outside his own headquarters were left alone except for technical advice. The result was friction with Brewster, who judged the SOS inspection operations to be somewhat ineffective, in part because so many of the SOS inspectors worked for the base commanders beyond the direct control of Generals Harbord and Winn. For this reason, among others, General Winn was relieved as the SOS IG and assigned to command a brigade on 9 September. His replacement was another cavalryman, Brig. Gen. Thomas Q. Donaldson. General Harbord judged Donaldson to be knowledgeable and active, but not as strong a personality as his predecessor.[53]

The Services of Supply now became increasingly centralized. Several inspectors were reassigned to Tours; troop inspections came under Donaldson's control, in partial compensation for the inexperience of the inspectors in the field. By the end of October Donaldson felt that he had his operation under fairly tight control. All inspections were conducted henceforth from his office in General Harbord's name, and units and staff departments at all levels were put on a periodic visit schedule. By then the Tours office was averaging 78 troop and 152 money inspections and 40 investigations each quarter. The Tours office also prepared a compliance guide or manual patterned after the prewar Yellow Book. Its concentration on transport underlined the command's paramount concern with all forms of ship, motor, and rail movement. The manual was a useful reference, but was structured in such a way

---

[52] Miller, IG, Base Sec 1, Annual Rpt, 30 Jun 19, Entry 26, RG 159, NARA.
[53] Ltr, Brewster to Donaldson, 15 Sep 18, Entry 588; Ltr, Harbord to CinC, AEF, 13 Dec 18, Entry 6. Both in RG 120, NARA.

that it could be turned into a grinding checklist by an inexperienced or lazy inspector.[54]

Funds Inspections

Following the reorganization that created the Services of Supply, the important responsibility for funds inspections was divided. The accounts of tactical units remained under the supervision of their assigned inspectors, while the AEF IG retained general supervision. Along with the transfer of Major Streater to the Services of Supply, General Brewster at the same time consolidated the inspection of accounts and related fiscal matters under the agency.

Emergency legislation in November 1917 had authorized disbursing officers to entrust their funds to other officers, and the practice became widespread in large-scale Quartermaster and Ordnance activities in France. Brewster alerted all inspectors to check for abuses, particularly in receipt systems. Unit fund management also was made somewhat less formal. The accounts were expected to be inspected whenever units were not at the front or engaged in training. Disbursing officers' money accounts were checked as often as possible without interfering with combat operations. Reports went directly to the AEF's IG office, rather than through channels.[55]

The unit funds proved to be a continual problem for inspectors, even though very few cases of embezzlement were uncovered. There were, however, numerous irregularities in both company- and hospital-type funds, leading Brewster to direct that all such funds be reconciled and inspected monthly. The problems emanated from the custodians' inexperience and the senior unit officers' lack of time to instruct or supervise. The regulations themselves made things no easier. Only unit commanders were allowed to be the funds custodians, and normally they had no place to secure such funds except on their person. Many thus went into battle carrying large amounts of cash, and often the money was lost when the officer became a casualty. In

---

[54] Memo, Lauber to Donaldson, 16 May 19, and Ltr, Donaldson to Brewster, 2 Nov 18, Entry 588, RG 120, NARA. See also Manual for IGs, SOS, AEF, Nov 18, and Ltr, Spinks to Insps, 22 Jul 18, sub: Points for Consideration of Inspectors Concerning Operations of 4th Sec. Gen. Staff, OTIG files, Pentagon (SAIG-ZXH).

[55] Ltr, IG, AEF, to All Insps, 25 Nov 17, sub: Funds of Disbursing Officers, Entry 588; Ltr, Chamberlain to Dept Insps, 15 Jun 17, sub: Company Fund Balances (Neostyle 255), Entry 588; Ltr, IG, AEF, to All Div Insps, 6 Nov 18, sub: Inspection of Company Funds and Money Accounts, Entry 590. All in RG 120, NARA.

cases where officers had access to French banks, different national procedures prevented conformity to American requirements. Ironically, the American bank in Paris proved hopelessly inefficient; it was late in processing checks, and more often than not gave inaccurate information to custodians and inspectors alike. Almost universally, IGs urged that a more flexible system be developed to reduce the burden of administering funds in combat. But reforms had to wait until well past the end of the war.[56]

The technical performance of unit IGs in matters of finance was evaluated by AEF and SOS inspectors. This was a field in which many line officers could not be expected to excel even in the best of circumstances. One of the SOS expert accountants would make the rounds of a command, not only inspecting its accounts but also assessing the quality of the work done by the local inspectors. A basic purpose of these trips was to educate both accountable officers and unit inspectors. The accountant often had a member of the local IG office accompany him, which ensured good accountability and proper follow-up on any adverse findings. In addition, the practice allowed commanders some insight into local IG and unit performance.[57]

Bases, Districts, and Depots

Growing centralization throughout the SOS inspection offices did not diminish perceptibly the work load of the inspectors who were left at the base section ports and headquarters. Expanding duties and new responsibilities were the rule at the local level. Typical was the experience of officers at Base Section No. 1. Originally established at the great port of St. Nazaire when American forces began to arrive, the base section subsequently expanded its operation throughout the Loire Valley and the north coast of the Bay of Biscay. By July 1918 it encompassed two other ports, three hospital centers, three veterinary centers, a forestry district, four major depots, and five school or training centers. But only two inspectors were assigned, one who concentrated on port activities and another who roamed the inland bases. Between them, they averaged eight major inspections and five investigations each month until the armistice. At this time their work load increased even

---

[56] Memo, Brewster to CinC, AEF, 31 Aug 18; Ltr, Haskell to IG, AEF, 5 Apr 19, sub: Report on Operation of the Inspector General's Department in France; Ltr, Vestal to GHQ AEF, 25 Apr 19, sub: Report; and Ltr, Elmore to IG, AEF, 25 Jun 19, sub: Report From Observations of AEF. All in Entry 588, RG 120, NARA.

[57] Webb Trip Diary, n.d., IAW par. 97, SO 2, Entry 590, RG 120, NARA.

more, necessitating the assignment of thirteen more inspectors for dealing mostly with problems of embarkation.[58]

Base Section No. 3 was centered in London, with responsibility for all the British Isles. The command was scattered, with 15,000 aviation personnel located at some seventy British bases and several thousand medical personnel assigned to British hospitals. Discipline was poor, in part because of the absence of sufficient staff to supervise the command's varied activities. Under these circumstances, Colonel Mitchell, in his role as IG, became the command troubleshooter. Moving from place to place, either advising, reprimanding, or teaching, he functioned much more like a deputy commander. After the armistice Mitchell determined the sequence and timing for the closing of American facilities.[59]

Port activities were the most important at each base section. The inspection of transports continued under the same procedures that had been established before the war. Inspectors en route to or from France assisted unit commanders during the voyage, conducting safety drills and monitoring troop welfare and medical support. They filed their reports with the base section inspection office upon arrival, but remedial action on the part of the Transportation Service was often slow. Consequently, port inspectors spent considerable time following up on remediation. Other transport-related inspections or investigations were made whenever ships had accidents, such as rammings or fires. Special attention was given to the conduct of personnel in a disaster, and conditions and procedures at dockside were closely monitored.[60]

Inspectors at this level found their work shaped by the unique aspects of their area. The District of Paris came into the SOS IG orbit in August 1918, when a major inspection of conditions in the city was prompted by complaints about brutality in the Army prison system. The inspection resulted in the relief of the district commander, and the appointment of a new staff, including an inspector for the first time. Lt. Col. Henry W. Fleet was transferred from the Advanced Section in October and was joined by Lt. Col. Lloyd B.

---

[58] Miller, IG, Base Sec 1, Annual Rpt, 30 Jun 19, Entry 26, RG 159, NARA; Lewis, "Short Account," OTIG files, Pentagon (SAIG-ZXH).

[59] Mitchell, IG, Base Sec 3, Annual Rpt, 22 Jul 18, Entry 26, RG 159, NARA. See also Rpt, Janney, n.d., sub: Official History ARC Convalescent Hospital No. 101, Entry 2136, RG 120, NARA.

[60] File 12, Transport Activities; Rpt, Div Insp to 1st Div Cdr, 13 Jul 17, sub: Inspection of Transport McClellan. Both in Entry 588, RG 120, NARA.

Magruder in November, who became chief of the inspection office until its closing.[61]

Colonel Magruder's observations about the city explain fully the need for the growth of his office: "Of the nearly two million Americans who visited France during the years 1917 and 1918, about 99.9 percent had one supreme desire—see Paris. As it was manifestly not possible to permit this desire to be satisfied and still continue military operations, visits to the capital were not encouraged. The result was that many, in whom the power of inhibition was not developed, went anyhow. These, together with others who, having permission, did not make the best of it, furnished the material that made detail of an inspector necessary."[62]

Depot division IGs worked closely with their unit commanders, but eventually they too came to be viewed as part of the SOS inspectorate. The activities of an IG in a depot division were similar to those in a combat division. Depot divisions were former line units that had been converted to serve as replacement regulating commands. They were used to control and forward the unexpectedly large numbers of men needed to sustain the units at the front. The first unit so transformed was the 41st Division, a National Guard unit from the western United States. Functioning as the I Corps Replacement Division and later as the 1st Depot Division, the division lost its combat units and personnel. During its Stateside phase, when the division had trained as a combat unit, its inspector had performed the usual duties relative to mustering and overseas deployment. When the division was restructured after its arrival in France in January 1918, the IG's duties underwent a considerable shift.[63]

The division elements were distributed over a 100-square-mile area, divided into five districts for administrative and training purposes. Each area contained about five sites, where division troops were on duty. Replacements assigned to the division remained with it for an average of only four or five days before going forward. A systematic inspection schedule was developed, and once it went into effect inspectors saw each organization and location at least five times a month. A record card system was developed in the IG office to keep track of all these visits and to record observations and findings. The IG sent a weekly activity report to the division commander, in which he summarized conditions encountered during the previous week.

---

[61] File 27, Weekly Reports, and Memo, Magruder to CG, Dist of Paris, 29 Jan 19, sub: Historical Data, Entry 588, RG 120, NARA.

[62] Memo, Magruder to CG, Dist of Paris, 29 Jan 19, Entry 588, RG 120, NARA.

[63] Memo, Rich to CG, 1st Depot Div, 24 Jul 18, sub: Operations of IGD Within the 1st Depot Division, AEF, FY 1918, Entry 588, RG 120, NARA.

The greatest part of the inspector's time in depot divisions was consumed by aspects of supply and property management. Physical security for equipment was a paramount concern; proper storage and guarding were checked continually. Control had to be maintained over the vast amounts of equipment stored for issue to the thousands of men processing through. Accountability and responsiveness to the needs of individuals were watched closely. A related issue was that of salvage and property disposal. The handling of expendable items and perishables, such as rations, required constant attention to avoid waste.

Motor transportation was supervised for proper use and for control over spare parts. Vehicle maintenance remained a critical issue throughout the war, mostly because of inadequate supplies of repair parts. Consequently, inspectors made every effort to promote efficiency and to economize on vehicle operations. Schools for drivers and motor officers also were monitored. A related topic was the care of animals. Each organization in the division was required to submit a weekly report on its animals to the inspector's office. There the data was consolidated, analyzed for trends, and forwarded to the division commander for his information. As a result, few substantial complaints or problems were encountered.[64]

The Burden of Routine

Despite the quickening pace of combat, 1918 saw no reduction in the burden of routine borne by inspectors in the AEF. Inspection results showing unusual amounts of excess property in some units and critical shortages in others led to an AEF-wide crackdown on hoarders. The intention was to have a complete equipment review and redistribution before the fall offensives opened. Genuine shortages were identified, and numerous organizations were brought to better equipment levels in the weeks before the St. Mihiel offensive of September 1918.[65]

Personnel losses as the result of injuries from nonhostile causes, in particular, self-inflicted wounds, also became an item of concern as the buildup progressed. Not only were these accidents a manpower drain, they reflected possible underlying disciplinary problems. On 13 July and 8 August the AEF adjutant general instructed all division and hospital commanders to report such cases to the AEF's IG office following investigation by the unit inspector and unit medical personnel. Cases

---

[64] Ibid.

[65] Memo, Spinks to IG, First Army, 3 Sep 18, sub: Excess Property in Possession of Troops, Entry 588, RG 120, NARA.

were to be classified as "unavoidable," requiring no further action; as "gross negligence," requiring a summary court-martial; or as "intentional," requiring a general court-martial. Suspect cases were treated only in division hospitals, and not evacuated further to the rear. Any soldier sentenced to hard labor as a result of court-martial was ordered to serve his sentence at the most dangerous places on the line, wearing a brassard displaying the letters SIW (self-inflicted wound).[66]

Special investigations on every conceivable topic threatened to overwhelm unit inspectors, who were often obliged to sacrifice inquiries into operational matters to examine special cases. The 28th Division inspector, for example, estimated that he spent half his time looking into cases of self-inflicted wounds or the condition and treatment of animals. He was required by his commander to investigate all requests for compassionate discharge; all allegations of indebtedness brought against division officers or unit funds; and any complaints dealing with aspects of division administration, such as lost mail, unjust promotions, or reductions in rank. At the GHQ level the treatment of prisoners of war and other aspects of the Geneva Convention were recurring topics handled with urgency. After they became a matter of personal interest to General Pershing in August, IGs were expected to interview prisoners to determine whether they had been treated fairly.[67]

Some of the more difficult and time-consuming IG investigations had to do with aspects of personal conduct—breach of promise, bigamy, nonsupport, and "ungentlemanly" conduct by officers. Such complaints primarily came from wives in the United States, as well as from French females who had developed liaisons with American suitors. The reason for IG involvement was General Pershing's desire to maintain high moral character in the officer corps. Standards were so high that officers were court-martialed for escorting so-called loose women to unit social events. There were, however, more serious allegations to be examined as well. Brewster or Spinks handled those cases involving allegations against an officer's loyalty to the United States; unit inspectors investigated lesser security breaches, such as losing

---

[66] Memo, Davis to Div Surgs and All Hosp Cdrs, 13 Jul 18, sub: Report of Self-inflicted Wounds; Ltr (quoted words), AG, AEF, to CGs, 8 Aug 18, sub: Self-inflicted Wounds; and Memo, Jones to Div CGs, 5 Sep 18, sub: Report of Self-inflicted Wounds. All in Entry 588, RG 120, NARA.

[67] File 20, OIG, 28th Div, Investigations and Inquiries, Entry 1241; Rpt, Brewster to CinC, AEF, n.d., Entry 588; Memo, McAndrew to IG, AEF, 8 Aug 18, Entry 588; Memo, Peck to Johnson, 12 Oct 18, Entry 799; and Rpt, Peck to IG, AEF, 19 Oct 18, Entry 590. All in RG 120, NARA.

maps or papers. Pershing insisted on personal responsibility being established whenever possible.[68]

One of the most peculiar small investigations of the war merits detailing because of the later prominence of the officers involved. Lt. Col. Richard I. McKenney from the AEF's IG office responded to a complaint that Lt. Kingdon Gould, an Intelligence Corps officer and a well-known New York millionaire, had eaten flies in public. The source of the allegation was the director of the Army Intelligence School. The director urged that Gould, then a student at the school, not be allowed to graduate, and the Army Schools commandant and the AEF G–2 seconded his recommendation. The incident occurred when Gould was dining in a hotel with some prewar friends—Capt. Hamilton Fish, Maj. E. Alexander Powell, and Lt. Andre Roosevelt, New Yorkers of nearly equal distinction. Apparently, Fish found some flies in the bottom of his wine glass. Since the evening's conversation had been about exotic things to eat, someone in the group bet Gould that he would not eat the flies. Thereupon, he brought the glass to his lips and seemed to quaff the contents. He immediately wiped his mouth with a napkin so that no one could say whether he really had eaten the flies. This was the act that the school director found so disturbing.[69]

Colonel McKenney classed the whole thing as "ludicrous" and deemed it "fortunate that thus far it has not reached the too eager hands of the New York press." He cited the fact that Gould spoke five languages fluently and two others reasonably well. His value to the Intelligence Corps could not justify his loss for a youthful prank. He successfully recommended that Gould be allowed to complete the course and that the case be closed. All of the men involved went on to render valuable wartime service. Yet the fact that a senior inspector could be diverted for four days on such an absurd mission at the height of the St. Mihiel attacks reveals the importance the AEF placed on officer conduct.[70]

More serious cases along this line dealt with abuse of authority. The investigation of senior officers usually was the responsibility of the principal inspector of the major command. For example, General

---

[68] Memo, Brewster to AG, AEF, 15 Nov 17, sub: Report of Investigation of Alleged Deceit on Part of A. L. Helwig, Entry 588; Ltr, AG, AEF, to CG, 89th Div, 1 Nov 18, sub: Lost Secret Documents, Entry 588; OIG, AEF, Officer Conduct, Entry 588; IG, V Corps, Special Investigations (quoted word), Entry 1138. All in RG 120, NARA.

[69] Ltr, Catron to Comdt, Army Schools, 27 Aug 18, sub: Conduct of 1st Lt. Kingdon Gould; Rpt, McKenney, 14 Sep 18, sub: Investigation Concerning Conduct of Lt. Kingdon Gould at Hotel du Cheval Blanc Evening of 27 August. Both in Entry 588, RG 120, NARA.

[70] Rpt, McKenney, 14 Sep 18, Entry 588, RG 120, NARA.

Brewster asked General Winn to investigate allegations against the commander of an artillery training area located in Base Section No. 2. The colonel was accused of being a tyrant, closing hotels, chasing suspected loose women out of town, and trying to regulate civilian conduct. Winn made a thorough investigation, interviewing French officials, regimental commanders, and numerous civilians. He found that the colonel was being blamed for exaggerated stories about the enforcement of French rules by French officials and quickly concluded that there was no basis for the allegations. Brewster briefed Pershing, who personally clarified the situation with the senior French official who had passed on the allegations.[71]

Many such cases derived from misunderstandings or distortions, but each represented an imposition on the overworked inspectors' time. A typical division-level investigation occurred in October 1918 at the 28th Division. The commander had received a written complaint through channels, in which a corporal claimed a colonel had used profane language toward him. The unit inspector interviewed numerous eyewitnesses and concluded that the corporal had exaggerated greatly. The colonel had not used profanity, but had verbally reprimanded the man—justifiably—for his lack of judgment in operating a motor vehicle in a bivouac area. The upshot was that the soldier received a written reprimand from the division commander.[72]

Unit inspectors in particular also had another large portion of their time consumed by investigation of property-damage claims, filed by civilians with French government officials. Cases included pilferage of fruit from orchards and vineyards, looting and destruction of housing in the war zone, and unauthorized hunting and fishing. The problems were often another manifestation of the lack of discipline throughout the command. Troop conduct in billeting and training areas usually was irresponsible. Damage was inflicted carelessly on civilian property wherever the troops went, and there were occasional cases of deliberate vandalism. Disciplinary action was severe. As the tempo of combat quickened, the number of these cases declined.[73]

Unit inspectors also carried out investigations to determine responsibility when billets evacuated by a unit were damaged or left in unsan-

---

[71] Rpt, Winn, 18 Apr 18, sub: Investigation of Colonel Fredrick B. Hennessy, Entry 588, RG 120, NARA.

[72] Rpt, Taggart, 28 Oct 18, sub: Investigation of Complaint Against Language of "Captain" Prescott, Entry 1241, RG 120, NARA.

[73] Ltr, Johnson to IG, AEF, 22 Mar 19, sub: Information for Report on American E. F., Entry 588, RG 120, NARA.

itary condition. Complaints could come from units that inherited the mess, as well as from civilians upset over the condition of their property. The pursuit of those responsible obviously did not make inspectors objects of popularity. However, if the AEF had not been disciplined on this topic, the entire American sector could have become one vast slum, with the United States shouldering the burden of liability. After the armistice unit commanders were required to make inventories of the condition of the facilities they were to use before moving their troops into them, a practice that reduced false claims while also fixing responsibility for damages.[74]

Such were the manifold duties of inspectors behind the fighting lines. As American participation in the struggle moved from scattered contacts with the enemy to hard fighting in the summer of 1918 and finally to full participation in the final allied offensive, the inspectorate faced even more pressing work among the combat units.

---

[74] Ibid.

6

The AEF in Combat

In 1918 AEF and tactical unit inspectors focused increasingly on combat operations, for all the preparations in the rear areas had meaning only in the payoff of battle. The same basic problems of inadequate training and inexperienced commanders appeared again in one inspector's report after another. Thus, the 2d Division inspector noted that the majority of soldiers joining his division lacked the rudiments of field craft and soldiering and that the division suffered excessive combat losses as a consequence. The need to continue training informally was noted by Colonel Johnson, when he assumed I Corps inspection duties in February. However, he also faulted the division inspectors for merely repeating accounts of common deficiencies, without doing enough to correct the problems they uncovered. He consolidated the division lists to show the inspectors the degree of overlap and provided suggested solutions to each problem, asking inspectors to hand out copies to the units they visited. Johnson continued this practice, which he called "preventive assistance," when he became First Army inspector in July. His inspection standards were eventually published as an AEF pamphlet.[1]

First Stresses

Poor and inexperienced unit leadership raised graver questions. One case involved the 7th Machine Gun Battalion in the 3d Division's first large-scale engagement at Chateau-Thierry. On the night of 1 June

---

[1] Edward M. Coffman, *The War To End All Wars: The American Military Experience in World War I* (New York: Oxford University Press, 1968), p. 219; Lay, IG, 2d Div, Annual Rpt, 8 Aug 18, Entry 588, Records Group (RG) 120, National Archives and Records Administration (NARA); Memo (quoted words), Johnson to IG, AEF, 13 Jul 27, sub: Scope of Policy No. 1, Be Helpful, Entry 26, RG 159, NARA.

1918 the two platoons of the battalion's Company B hastily withdrew from its position along the Marne River. The 3d Division IG, Lt. Col. Ernest H. Agnew, directed by his commander to make an immediate investigation, found that the withdrawal had been unnecessary. The units had sustained no casualties. Yet, at the first sign of the enemy artillery, the two inexperienced lieutenants who were in charge had requested permission to withdraw and, without personally checking the situation, the company and battalion commanders immediately granted it. Further, the commanders lost contact with and control of the platoons as they pulled out, allowing them to escape the battle entirely. Investigation showed that the battalion commander had been noticeably under the influence of alcohol for several days. The division commander forwarded the investigation to General Headquarters (GHQ), AEF, with the information that the battalion commander was being court-martialed, the company commander transferred to the Services of Supply (SOS), and the two lieutenants given another chance. General Brewster reviewed the case in his discipline oversight capacity and approved the decisions.[2]

Hoping to derive general lessons from the first heavy combat, inspectors interviewed commanders and principal staff officers about their tactical decisions, logistical support, and equipment and forwarded the results to Brewster's office. Summarized by subject, the collected data became a ready reference for Pershing and for the GHQ and SOS staffs. Although most commanders' comments were favorable, some serious problems turned up that had to be resolved.[3]

The degree of disarray in the Air Service was noticeably greater than elsewhere. Pershing had separated the service from Signal Corps control the summer before, and it evidently was undergoing extended birth pangs. Problems included organizational adjustments, the clash of personalities, and the traditional indiscipline of an individualistic service. The major American tactical unit in June and July was the I Corps, commanded by Maj. Gen. Hunter Liggett. On Liggett's staff was the Air Service chief, Brig. Gen. Benjamin D. Foulois, who exercised operational control over the air observation units. The fighter aircraft, known as Pursuit Service, were under the operational control of the French Sixth Army and received only administrative support from Liggett's corps. Subordinate to the corps, another command had been inserted, the 1st Air Brigade, headed by Col. William "Billy" Mitchell.

---

[2] Memo, IG, AEF, to CinC, AEF, 12 Jun 18, sub: Co B, 7th MG Bn, Entry 588, RG 120, NARA.

[3] Memo, IG, AEF, to CofS, AEF, 14 Aug 18, Entry 588, RG 120, NARA.

Determined to play a dominant role despite the fact that he had no units specifically assigned to him, Mitchell had behaved with a tactlessness, zeal, and aggressiveness that strained relations with his superior, General Foulois, and drew a strong letter from the corps chief of staff, Brig. Gen. Malin Craig. Mitchell's behavior precipitated a G–3 investigation at GHQ AEF. The G–3 recommended that Mitchell's position be eliminated. Because of the seriousness of the situation, the AEF chief of staff directed that General Brewster himself investigate and recommend a solution.[4]

On a scheduled visit to Liggett's headquarters to observe operations at the height of the Soissons counterattack in July, Brewster interviewed all of the senior Air Service officers. He quickly concluded that Mitchell's position was redundant, that many of the problems came from Mitchell's efforts to create a job where none existed, and that his "aggressiveness and peculiar temperament" had contributed to the friction and confusion. Despite this, Generals Liggett and Craig felt that Mitchell was a strong leader who could be a great asset commanding air units, and Brewster therefore successfully recommended the reassignment of General Foulois to the AEF air staff as deputy for logistics. Mitchell's old position was eliminated, and he was assigned to command the First Army's air units as they were formed.[5]

Although Mitchell was admired for his action-oriented style, toleration of such antics may have fostered many of the adverse traits already noted in Army aviation by the prewar investigations. In France General Brewster found that discipline and military courtesy were lacking in some air units. This lack of discipline, in his estimation, promoted a cavalier approach that had serious negative effects on maintenance and repair. As a result, SOS inspectors made aviation maintenance operations an item of special interest. On an inspection visit during the Chateau-Thierry fighting Colonel Johnson found that two-thirds of the aircraft on hand were out of commission because of maintenance problems, with critical effects on air operations.[6]

---

[4] Memo, Gorrell to ACofS, G–3, AEF, 12 Jul 18, sub: Inspection Air Service, 1st Army Corps, Entry 588, RG 120, NARA.

[5] Memo (quoted words), Brewster to CofS, AEF, 27 Jul 18, sub: Investigation Air Service, 1st Army Corps; IG, AEF, Synopsis of Report on Investigation Air Service, 30 Jul 18. Both in Entry 588, RG 120, NARA. See also John F. Shiner, *Foulois and the U.S. Army Air Corps, 1931–1935* (Washington, D.C.: Office of Air Force History, United States Air Force, 1983), pp. 9–11. Mitchell went on to enjoy great success as an air commander and fame as a martyr for air power in the 1920s.

[6] Johnson, IG, First Army, Annual Rpt, 16 Jul 18, Entry 588, RG 120, NARA.

The personal conduct of many aviators was incorrigible. Writing after the war, General March—whose son, a pilot, had been killed in training—declared that the special status given the Air Service made its members feel they were above the constraints imposed on others. The result was serious individual indiscipline and a drift away from a tradition of military teamwork. General Donaldson, the SOS IG, seconded these sentiments, citing Air Service conduct as a continuous nagging problem for his inspectors. In his view the Air Service fostered a notion that the nature of its mission required special treatment for the aviators, who were alleged to be intrinsically temperamental. Donaldson termed this claim ridiculous, for "no healthy normal male is naturally temperamental, but each one will take advantage of laxity." His views mirrored those of Pershing and Brewster, all of whom stressed the need for a single standard of discipline, with no exceptions.[7]

The issue came to a head in August 1918 during the preliminaries of the American buildup for the St. Mihiel attack. One of Brewster's assistants, Lt. Edgar Scott, was directed on the fifteenth to go to Nancy and Toul to investigate rumors that General Pershing had heard regarding the conduct of aviators visiting those cities. Scott interviewed civilian and military police authorities and U.S. medical personnel. He concluded that nearly all the officers visiting the towns were boisterous, freely drinking, and associating with loose women. Although everyone interviewed agreed that the behavior of the 82d Division officers had been the wildest, they also concurred that the pilots were the most consistent in heavy drinking and carousing. Scott heard of one case where eight pilots out on a spree flew their planes over German lines, never to return. (Scott surmised that they had flown over enemy terrain until they ran out of gas and were forced to land; a later writer attributed the incident to inexperience and poor navigation in poor weather.) Uncovering several other tales of alcohol-related accidents and tragedies in and out of combat, the inspector concluded a serious behavior problem existed, resulting from an image of bravado on duty and idleness during off-duty time.[8]

Brewster sent the report to the Air Service chief for his review and comment. Within three weeks General Foulois returned a memorandum

---

[7] Peyton C. March, *The Nation At War* (Garden City, N.Y: Doubleday, Doran and Co., 1932), p. 209; Rpt (quotation), Donaldson to CG, SOS, 14 Mar 19, Entry 588, RG 120, NARA.

[8] Rpt, Scott to IG, AEF, 20 Aug 18, sub: Investigation Concerning Conduct of Aviators in Nancy and Its Neighborhood, Entry 588, RG 120, NARA; Coffman, *War To End All Wars*, p. 206.

outlining the actions he had taken. Believing that the main problem was the absence of wholesome diversions at the air bases, he initiated a comprehensive program with the Red Cross and YMCA to provide each depot and airdrome with a clubhouse containing a library, snack bar, theater, and classrooms. He further arranged with the AEF G–4 and the Red Cross to supply athletic gear, and he directed commanders to devise full programs of games and exercises. He and other senior officers visited units to talk with the younger pilots about the effects of drinking and flying. Foulois also began a program of "systematic medical supervision of all flying personnel," something he had been urging for several years. He told Brewster that these measures already had developed a marked improvement in aviator behavior and performance, and the decline and ultimate elimination of investigations on the subject tended to validate his claim.[9]

Medical Crisis

Other problems revealed in the midsummer fighting were not so easily resolved. Complaints about logistical support during the Soissons offensive prompted several investigations from various levels. Pending his reassignment to the III Corps from the AEF's IG office, Colonel Ovenshine conducted a thorough overview for General Brewster. Ovenshine interviewed key members of the 1st and 2d Divisions and gathered written statements from those he was unable to interview, including the British division commander under whom the American units had trained. The officers were in agreement that both units were tactically proficient. Their greatest concern was the need for improvement in medical support.[10]

Inefficient medical operations already had come under considerable scrutiny. GHQ AEF became interested in July, when a *New York Tribune* reporter submitted a scathing criticism of the Medical Department to the censor. The censor notified the AEF chief surgeon, Maj. Gen. Merritte W. Ireland, MC, who requested an immediate investigation. The case was passed to General Brewster, who took the reporter with him on a preliminary inquiry. At the same time Ovenshine began a more detailed investigation. The conclusions of both were much the same.

---

[9] Memo, Foulois to IG, AEF, 9 Sep 18, sub: Efficiency of Air Service Personnel, Entry 588, RG 120, NARA.

[10] Memos, Ovenshine to IG, AEF, 7 and 28 Aug 18, and Spinks to CofS, AEF, 14 Aug 18, Entry 588, RG 120, NARA.

Ovenshine corroborated Brewster's finding that, because of security reasons, medical personnel lacked knowledge of the planned attacks until just before the troops were committed. As a result, field hospitals were hastily deployed, often too far to the rear. The insufficient lead time imposed an inordinate strain on the hard-pressed evacuation system. Casualties were far higher than expected, overrunning the understaffed and ill-equipped unit medical detachments. Litters and medicines on hand proved to be inadequate at every echelon. Deployment of corps and field army ambulance units was delayed, and heavy road congestion slowed the movement of the available ambulances.[11]

The upshot was a medical evacuation disaster. Some casualties remained on the battlefield for hours or days, and at the regulating stations they often lay without medical attention or food because of the shortage of corpsmen. Combat troops and supply vehicles filled in as best they could. The field hospitals experienced similar problems. Inundated with casualties from the front, they were unable to evacuate them promptly because hospital trains were either diverted or unavailable. Like the field hospitals, they too had not been notified in time.[12]

Concern over the medical situation resulted in a medical officer being detailed to the AEF inspectorate in June 1918. Col. Henry Beeuwkes, MC, a graduate of the Johns Hopkins Medical College, joined Ovenshine, placing his emphasis on the treatment of personnel after they had reached the field hospitals. Beeuwkes recommended that regimental medical units be doubled in size and authorized to carry greater quantities of hospital supplies; that American surgeons practice the French system of triage to better manage battle casualties; and that the number of hospitals near the front be increased. Both inspectors pointed out that one of the main causes for the crisis was an excessive concern for secrecy on the part of tactical planners, emphasizing that medical personnel had to know as early as possible when a large operation was scheduled to occur. The problems with ambulances also showed a need for much greater rear area traffic control. As a result of their findings, regimental medical detachments were doubled in size and the need for better medical planning, coordination, and deployment was recognized.[13]

---

[11] Rpt, Brewster, 17 Jul 18, sub: Investigation Concerning Charges of Inefficiency on the Part of the Medical Department Contained in Cablegram Prepared by Mr. Casper Whitney of the *New York Tribune*; Memo, Brewster to CinC, AEF, 31 Jul 18; Memos, Ovenshine to IG, AEF, 7 and 28 Aug 18. All in Entry 588, RG 120, NARA.

[12] Rpt, Lay, 2 Sep 18, sub: Investigation Concerning the Care of the Wounded at Crepy-en-Valois, Entry 2144; Memos, Ovenshine to IG, AEF, 7 and 28 Aug 18, Entry 588. All in RG 120, NARA.

[13] Memo, Brewster to CinC, AEF, 31 Jul 18, Entry 588, RG 120, NARA.

Given high priority by General Pershing, the investigation was thorough and searching, with special emphasis on the evacuation of casualties from the field hospitals rearward to the great medical centers in the Services of Supply. Throughout, the relationship between Generals Brewster and Ireland and their respective departments was cordial and supportive, and the AEF chief surgeon credited the inspectorate's considerable help as being pivotal to improving medical conditions.[14]

The Final Push

Not only in the medical arena but throughout the command every effort was made to apply the lessons that had been learned at great cost during the summer fighting in 1918. The hardest battles for American units lay ahead. The fall offensives would determine whether they were ready to participate in the war as a full-fledged army, their days of learning and experimentation now over, or whether they remained journeymen warriors.

Preparations for the concentration of U.S. forces into a field army for operations against the St. Mihiel salient proceeded even while the Aisne-Marne battles approached their climax. Orders were issued for the creation of the First Army headquarters in late July, and the staff assembled at Neufchateau in time for the command to begin to function on 10 August. The headquarters deployed on 28 August to the town of Ligny-en-Barrois, southwest of St. Mihiel, while completing the plans for the September offensive.

By 1 September the First Army included four American and one French corps a total of sixteen American and three French divisions. Until October General Pershing continued to command the new organization while also commanding all U.S. forces in France. The First Army staff, however, was distinct from the GHQ AEF; no officer but the commander served in a dual capacity. Pershing brought with him a small advance element to ensure timely coordination on events with GHQ, now located at Chaumont. In addition to maintaining liaison with GHQ, the so-called Advanced Headquarters monitored aspects of the preparations for the September offensive that were of greatest interest to Pershing. General Brewster and Colonel Baer formed the IG element at Advanced Headquarters, and Colonel Beeuwkes and three field clerks soon joined them. Brewster continued to keep in close touch with the AEF's IG office at Chaumont, which was under the direct control of

---

[14] Memo, Ireland to Brewster, 9 Oct 18, and Rpt, Donaldson to CG, SOS, 14 Mar 19, Entry 588, RG 120, NARA.

General Spinks. The work done there was normally passed to Brewster at the Advanced Headquarters for his approval and information.[15]

Baer served as the forward IG executive and later as Pershing's special troubleshooter. After command of the First Army was transferred to General Liggett on 12 October, Baer took over from Brewster at the Advanced Headquarters, while Brewster continued with Pershing at Chaumont. Soon after the inspectors came forward in August, Pershing told them that he expected them to set up a "continual inspection" system to enforce traffic and march discipline, as part of an effort to achieve a secret concentration of forces preparatory to the St. Mihiel attack. Inspectors in the tactical units were subject to Brewster's direction and were authorized to correct problems wherever they arose.[16]

Brewster, Baer, and Beeuwkes, soon joined by Maj. Charles H. Rice, began to visit unit areas. Brewster established the policy that at least one division in each corps must be visited daily. Inspectors who were not involved in the effort were to exercise more general observation over corps and field army activities, a practice that persisted until the end of hostilities. By the end of the St. Mihiel operation Brewster had developed a tight hierarchical control over the tactical unit inspectors, especially during unit movements, to assure that AEF requirements were being met.[17]

Antagonism to this system was quick to develop, both among the First Army staff and among the corps and division commanders. With few exceptions, these officers resented the direct link, outside the chain of command, between Pershing and the roving inspectors. An exception was the cordial relationship between Baer and Col. Robert McCleave, the First Army G–3. Each night Baer gave the G–3 information on the problems and tactical lessons he had noted and on the status and location of units. In return, McCleave provided Baer with summaries of the next day's orders, enabling him to place inspectors at the most critical locations.

As time went by, other members of the First Army staff began to appreciate the value of the information gathered by IGs at all levels, particularly those from the Advanced Headquarters. The number of IGs

---

[15] U.S. Army War College, Historical Section, *The Genesis of the American First Army* (Washington, D.C.: Government Printing Office, 1938), pp. 50–51; Department of the Army, Historical Division, *The United States Army in the World War, 1917–1919*, 17 vols. (Washington, D.C.: Government Printing Office, 1948), 16:393 (GO 120, 1918); Memo, Spinks to Baer, 1 Nov 18, Entry 588, RG 120, NARA.

[16] Rpt, Brewster to CinC, AEF, n.d., Entry 588, RG 120, NARA.

[17] Ibid.; Memo, IG, AEF, to CinC, AEF, 19 Sep 18, Entry 588; Ltr, Brewster to Spinks, 21 Sep 18, Entry 590. All in RG 120, NARA.

at Advanced Headquarters was increased by seven as more and more requests for information in greater detail were received. The coordination of this larger group eventually obliged Colonel Baer to remain at the headquarters, where he worked to assist tactical unit inspectors in overcoming their commanders' suspicions.[18]

Gradually, the inflow of data was organized and standardized. Inspectors of units that had been in the summer fighting were requested in August to submit special reports to the General Brewster, giving observations and recommendations based on their recent experiences. The idea was to derive a compilation of lessons learned from those in a position to observe. Inspectors were asked to submit similar reports after each future engagement. Formal tactical reports seemed even more desirable. During the St. Mihiel offensive Colonel Johnson, in his role as the First Army IG, prepared a summary of the various problems evident throughout the battlefield, identifying issues that affected combat success. Brewster found Johnson's report so useful that he informally requested all inspectors to submit similar observations on tactical developments in their units.

As a result, some corps-level inspectors required that division inspectors submit to them a daily summary. Many of them dealt with the near-insoluble problems of traffic management that had developed behind the front. Typically, Maj. T. Charlton Henry, the 79th Division IG, discussed at length the chaos on the roads in the division zone. No one appeared to be in control. Military police were too few and too ill-informed to be helpful to those who were lost. Part of the problem was the absence of any system to handle vehicle breakdowns and to repair road sections destroyed by constant use.[19]

The growing number of reports flowing in also began to show Colonel Johnson that some commanders were not using their inspectors to the full advantage that his headquarters had intended. Some IGs were stationed with unit rear echelons, while others worked as liaison officers. A few had failed to disengage from routine duties, such as billets inspections, in order to concentrate on field operations. Johnson began a program requiring daily reports on items he knew were of concern to Pershing, forcing the inspectors to perform. This practice also had the secondary effect of circumventing limitations imposed on unit IGs by

---

[18] Ltr, Baer to IG, USA, 8 May 19, sub: Personal History of Service in the IGD, Entry 26, RG 159, NARA.

[19] Rpt, Johnson to IG, AEF, 23 Sep 18, sub: Delinquencies During Recent Operation in St. Mihiel Salient, Entry 588; Henry Daily Rpts, 26–30 Sep 18, Entry 1138. All in RG 120, NARA.

their commanders. Johnson and the corps inspectors continually stressed the need for IGs to take immediate corrective action and to suggest solutions to problems they observed.[20]

The daily reports were considered useful enough to be made a formal requirement on 10 October. Ideally, the reports from the divisions were intended to be a record of the improvements being made in the line units. Inspectors were supposed to review the questionnaires and checklists sent out by GHQ AEF, to recognize the areas in which they knew their units to be weak, and to go out and check on them. If their suspicions were confirmed, they were to report on what was being done to make the situation better. The daily reports were not intended to be lists of mistakes or errors, the so-called skin lists. Rather, Pershing wanted them to be an honest appraisal of combat and administrative capabilities. The reports quickly came to be viewed by First Army and GHQ staffs as more accurate and useful than data from any other sources, as well as primary sources for information on casualties, POWs, and ammunition expenditures. Pershing later asked Brewster confidentially to monitor the effectiveness of the General Staff in the same way. His findings and those of the roving Advanced Headquarters inspectors were to be consolidated with the daily reports and presented along with them.[21]

The importance of the information coming from the inspectors may be seen in Pershing's 4 October directive that inspectors be used only as IGs, performing no other staff duties, and that they be assured adequate transportation to do their job. Army and corps inspectors tried to help subordinate IGs whose reports were unsatisfactory. Most reports quickly reflected the new emphasis. Those provided by Maj. G. Edward Buxton, Jr., the 82d Division IG, were typical. After describing tactical operations, he summarized his division's ammunition status and commented on innovations in the use of weapons. Buxton took seriously the requirement to make specific recommendations to improve operations. He helped groups of stragglers to find their units, watched traffic movement throughout the area, and carried out special inquiries sent him from every echelon, division and above.[22]

---

[20] Rpt, Dallam to CG, Fifth Army Corps, n.d., sub: Argonne-Meuse Operations, Fifth Army Corps, 26 September to 11 November, Entry 588, RG 120, NARA; Ltr, Elmore to Helmick, 12 Apr 22, Entry 26, RG 159, NARA.

[21] Ltr, Baer to Lay, 13 Nov 18, Entry 590; Memo, Buxton to IG, 1st Corps, 18 Oct 18, Entry 590; Ltr, Brewster to Chamberlain, 30 Dec 18, Entry 588; Rpt, Brewster to CinC, AEF, n.d., Entry 588. All in RG 120, NARA.

[22] Memo, Johnson to Corps Insps, 4 Oct 18, sub: Proper Use of Inspectors, Entry 590; Ltr, Baer to Taggart, 8 Nov 18, sub: Report, Entry 588; Buxton Daily Rpts, 7–19 Oct 18, Entry 590. All in RG 120, NARA.

Despite their value, however, division inspectors strongly resented the daily required report, which was an additional burden to their already heavy work load. Most believed that daily reports fueled the tendency of the corps and army IGs to intrude into unit affairs, at a time when their own commanders were also placing urgent requirements on them. The only time for preparing the report was late at night, after exhausting days with units under fire, and the report format seemed to encourage a kind of mindless repetition of problems, without any solutions. One inspector characterized the reports as "impractical while on the march, impossible to render without typewriter or field desk—the time to

Maj. G. Edward Buxton, Jr.

make a report is when you have something to report." A chorus of complaining inspectors pressed for a modification of the requirement. Finally, on 1 November Brewster and Pershing changed the reporting frequency to once every ten days, effective the tenth of the month.[23]

Part of the problem with the daily report requirement and senior IG supervision lay in the fact that the system had grown informally, almost experimentally, without fully advising corps and division commanders. Brewster and Pershing liked the way IG functions had evolved, and in early October Pershing directed Colonel Baer to prepare specific guidance for the entire force. At the end of the month the small unnumbered pamphlet *Inspection of Armies in the Field* was published. The document reaffirmed existing policy and became the basic directive for IG operations in the AEF. The policy it embodied was a direct reflection of Pershing's views that IGs were "aides, not only to myself but to the commanders of the units inspected, and are in a position to observe and call attention . . . to defects and irregular-

---

[23] Memo, Boyd to Brewster, 1 Nov 18, Entry 588; Buxton Daily Rpts, 20–23 Oct 18, Entry 590. All in RG 120, NARA. See also David Lewis, "A Short Account of My Experiences in the American Expeditionary Forces in France, 1918–1919," quotation, OTIG files, Pentagon (SAIG-ZXH).

ities." He also referred to them as a source of information that was "most helpful" to his conduct of the war.[24]

St. Mihiel (12–16 September)

A few days before the First Army began to concentrate its forces against the St. Mihiel salient, its chief of staff, General Drum, sent a detailed letter of instruction to the corps commanders on secrecy and deception—that is, denying information to the enemy. Drum designated the movement zones in which no daytime traffic was allowed; specified the hours for night movement; stressed the use of concealment, camouflage, and light discipline; and, in particular, emphasized the dangers of enemy air reconnaissance. Each corps headquarters had orders to detail an officer to enforce the requirements of the letter, to monitor the enforcement of the Army security plan, and to correct any violations. The commanders assigned this duty to their corps inspectors.[25]

Methods varied from one command to another. The IV Corps IG, Col. Edward Carpenter, volunteered for the assignment, believing that he could carry out the task without any sort of extensive organization. Only four officers were made temporary assistant inspectors; they were divided into two teams, which alternated in twelve-hour shifts, one officer covering the rear areas and another the front. The corps military police were directed to cooperate with them. On the other hand, the V Corps IG, Col. S. Field Dallam, received direct orders to supervise the program. A military police detachment of four officers and fifty men was assigned to assist him. Dallam and the provost marshal worked out an elaborate system of control, with checkpoints on the battlefield approaches.[26]

Typically, the corps inspectors found little understanding or appreciation of the security requirement. An August general order making the discussion of troop movements in public a serious offense apparently had made no impression. Colonel Dallam, in particular, had to stress repeatedly to the senior commanders in the V Corps the need to enforce security measures to assure some surprise in the forthcoming attack. He and his counterparts also discovered that the troops disre-

---

[24] Memo (quotations), Pershing to CofS, AEF, 20 Oct 18; Memo, Spinks to Brewster, 31 Oct 18. Both in Entry 590, RG 120, NARA.

[25] Ltr, Drum to CGs, 1st, 4th, 5th Army Corps, 25 Aug 18, sub: Secrecy in Troop Movements, Entry 588, RG 120, NARA.

[26] Memo, Carpenter to CofS, IV Army Corps, 28 Aug 18; Ltr, Ulio to All Org Cdrs, IV Army Corps, 28 Aug 18; Memo, Dallam to PM, V Army Corps, 28 Aug 18, sub: Instructions; and Ltr, Carpenter to IG, AEF, 27 Sep 18, sub: Observations on the Offensive for the Reduction of the St. Mihiel Salient. All in Entry 588, RG 120, NARA.

garded camouflage and many other concealment measures, even in the last days before the attack. For example, units were drilling and training in the open; off-duty soldiers were visible in the streets of the towns in which they were billeted; bivouacs and vehicles kept lights burning at night; ammunition and equipment dumps were left in the open; and convoys picking up or dropping off supplies in the daytime pinpointed otherwise camouflaged unit locations. Whenever possible, such failings were corrected on the spot, and improvements followed as the troops' experience convinced them of the wisdom of concealment.[27]

The corps inspectors also remained heavily involved in coordinating traffic flow, especially the forward movement of ammunition and the evacuation of the wounded. Sometimes they served, in effect, as medical regulators, by diverting streams of ambulances to empty hospitals when others were reaching capacity. They continued to monitor traffic control even after the programs they had developed passed nominally to the corps G–1s. This was because of General Brewster's association with the foundering military police and his oversight responsibility for discipline and combat efficiency.[28]

Traffic, however, remained a daily headache. Military police often were insufficiently briefed to give directions. Vehicles traveled too fast, causing accidents that blocked the roads. In other cases, units would not pull over during halts. One of the worst practices was "double-banking"—occupying both lanes of a two-way road while going in the same direction. Lack of coordination over all the various units moving throughout the sector contributed to congestion. French units withdrawing after being replaced routinely ignored American traffic rules. Nevertheless, staffs at every level worked desperately to keep things flowing; Colonel Carpenter reported seeing a division chief of staff personally unsnarling traffic at a particularly critical road junction. During combat the slow forward deployment of the military police and the slowness of engineers to repair road damage compounded the congestion on the roads, but the main problem continued to rest with the indiscipline of the drivers.[29]

Mindful of the medical problems in July, inspectors at all levels were careful to note conditions during the St. Mihiel fighting.

---

[27] SOS, AEF, GO 39, 24 Aug 18, OTIG files, Pentagon (SAIG-ZXH); Rpt, Dallam to CG, 5th Army Corps, n.d., and Ltr, Carpenter to IG, AEF, 27 Sep 18, Entry 588, RG 120, NARA.

[28] Cdr, Co A, 4th MP Co, Daily Rpts, 2–9 Sep 18, Entry 1138, RG 120, NARA; Ltr, Baer to IG, USA, 8 May 19, Entry 26, RG 159, NARA.

[29] Ltr, Carpenter to IG, AEF, 27 Sep 18, Entry 588, RG 120, NARA.

*General Brewster With His
Assistant, Col. Joseph A. Baer,
During a Field Inspection*

Fortunately, the number of casualties was relatively light and the hospitals were never overtaxed. Despite this, long delays were again the rule as ambulances tried to work their way rearward through the traffic jams. Because of the traffic problem, ambulances were in short supply on the first day of fighting. Additional units were deployed to alleviate the situation by the evening of the second day, when the main fighting was pretty much over. The handling of wounded animals was better than in July, but prompt treatment was still unavailable in numerous cases. Burial of the dead also was accomplished more quickly than before, due in part to the low casualties and the rapid advance. But, again, as the corps inspectors noted, the division burial teams had no backup, and when they moved forward with their units, the corpses of men and animals they had missed often went unattended—sometimes for days.[30]

Despite their preoccupation with matters directly behind the front, the corps inspectors on occasion became involved in tactical activities. Colonel Dallam made it a point to observe special actions, going forward to witness a 4th Division reconnaissance in force and to comment on its execution. He noted that infantry-artillery coordination was a persistent problem because of the unfamiliarity of the two arms with each other. As a result, the inspectors became increasingly involved in facilitating better liaison. The major problems, however, remained in the rear areas, and by the third day of the attack IGs and every other staff officer available were back trying to regulate traffic.[31]

Colonel Baer, roving the battle area at all echelons of command, concluded that the Army's biggest problem was difficulty in having

---

[30] Ibid.
[31] Rpt, Dallam to CG, 5th Army Corps, n.d., Entry 588, RG 120, NARA; Coffman, *War To End All Wars*, p. 344.

orders obeyed. "Perfectly beautiful" orders often were issued, but the junior officers receiving them merely interpreted them as guidelines. Senior commanders were too busy to check, and control was lost on the battlefield.[32] The indiscipline on the roads reflected attitudes and habits that pervaded the entire AEF.

Meuse-Argonne (26 September–3 October)

Even as the St. Mihiel fighting reached its successful conclusion, preparations for the major effort in the Meuse-Argonne were under way. AEF planners had envisaged a three-phase offensive for pushing the Germans northward through the dense forest and hills west of the Meuse River. With the most experienced units committed at St. Mihiel, less experienced divisions had to carry the burden during the first phase. But a series of crises, brought on by the cross-movement of troops in the new sector (200,000 Frenchmen leaving, 600,000 Americans entering), compelled General Pershing to halt opening operations and to realign his forces, redeploying some of the veteran units and ruthlessly pruning incompetent commanders. Even as the fighting continued, the arrival of fresh German units assured intense future actions for the Americans. Each day posed new challenges to troops, commanders, and inspectors alike as the Iron Commander insisted on keeping the pressure on the staggering enemy (see Map 2).[33]

Colonel Baer's roving mission from the Advanced Headquarters was so useful to General Pershing that he assigned an IG, or one of his aides, to each corps as his personal liaison for the Meuse-Argonne operations. The AEF commander expected to be briefed daily on the actual conditions in the battle area. He specifically told the so-called rovers to collect information on road and railway repairs, artillery movement, traffic discipline, evacuation of wounded and prisoners, engineer and tank activities, unit liaison and communications, and food and ammunition resupply. Later the new First Army G–3, Col. George C. Marshall, Jr., asked the inspectors to rate each division's combat capability, commander and staff, equipment, and clothing.

The Advanced Headquarters inspectors tried to keep each echelon of command advised of their activities. They called first at the corps headquarters to see its chief of staff, obtaining information on current activities, and to give him their itinerary. The inspectors also offered to

---

[32] Ltr, Baer to Brook, 24 Sep 18, Entry 591, RG 120, NARA.

[33] R. Ernest Dupuy and Trevor N. Dupuy, *Military Heritage of America* (New York: McGraw Hill Book Co., 1956), pp. 385–87.

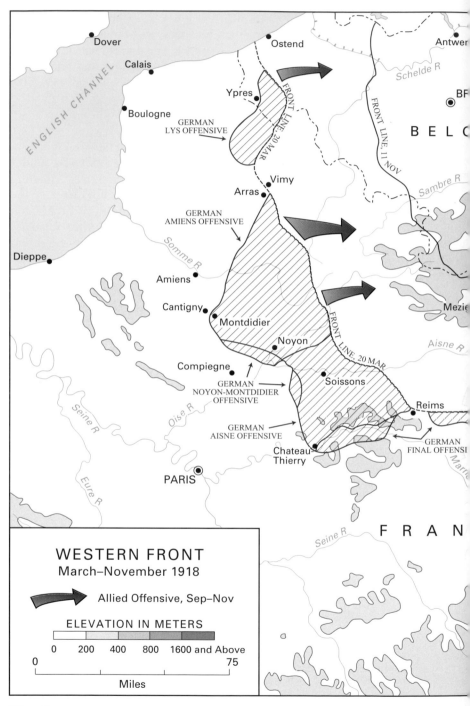

Dover

Calais

ENGLISH CHANNEL

Boulogne

Dieppe

Ostend

Antwer

Schelde R.

BF

FRONT LINE, 11 NOV

Ypres

FRONT LINE, 20 MAR

GERMAN
LYS OFFENSIVE

B E L G

Sambre R.

Vimy

Arras

GERMAN
AMIENS OFFENSIVE

Somme R.

Amiens

Cantigny

Montdidier

Noyon

FRONT LINE, 20 MAR

Mezie

Aisne R.

Compiegne

GERMAN
NOYON-MONTDIDIER
OFFENSIVE

Soissons

Reims

Seine R.

Oise R.

GERMAN
AISNE OFFENSIVE

Chateau-
Thierry

GERMAN
FINAL OFFENSI

Eure R.

PARIS

Marne

Seine R.

F R A N

WESTERN FRONT
March–November 1918

Allied Offensive, Sep–Nov

ELEVATION IN METERS

| 0 | 200 | 400 | 800 | 1600 and Above |

0   75

Miles

MAP 2

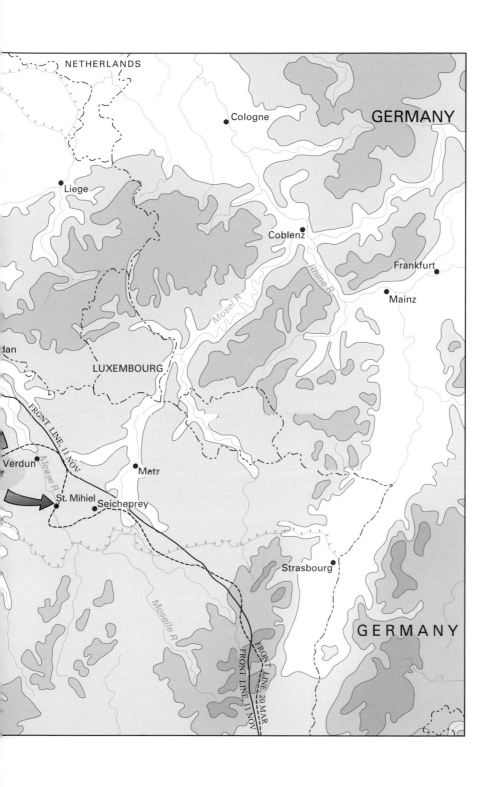

investigate any items of corps interest. The same routine was followed at division level. When the inspector left a unit, he briefed the commander or a senior staff officer on his findings or assessments. If time allowed, he visited units adjacent to the division to check on liaison procedures. Normally, the inspector ate his supper at corps headquarters, where he could brief the corps staff, monitor reports from other elements of the corps, and coordinate activities with the corps IG.[34]

The army inspectors usually convened late at night at the Advanced Headquarters to discuss their evaluations with the AEF rovers and to consolidate their findings. General Brewster or Colonel Baer subsequently briefed the First Army G–3 and, at the earliest opportunity, General Pershing. In the meantime, other inspectors coordinated with responsible staff officers and followed through on specific problems they hoped to resolve during their visits. Always, any supply deficiencies were noted. Inspectors then personally worked with the staff to find items reported as unavailable by the inspected division. Army and corps inspectors operated in similar fashion whenever they were not on assignments specified by their commanders.[35]

A division of labor evolved between Baer's post at the Advanced Headquarters and Spinks' office at GHQ AEF. Baer's immediate staff concentrated on issues directly related to combat operations, such as supply to the front, traffic control, and the care of animals, and eventually assumed responsibility for investigating cases of officers relieved in combat. Spinks' office took care of nearly all other personnel matters, including cases of self-inflicted wounds, conditions and assignments in combat units, and issues not related to combat operations.[36]

Division inspectors usually were based at the equivalent of the division rear headquarters (second echelon). The experiences of the 79th Division IG, Major Henry, were typical. His division went into the attack on 26 September and was withdrawn on the thirtieth, after taking the German strongpoint at Montfaucon in heavy fighting. On the first day of the attack Henry monitored road movements but concentrated on the developing tactical situation, being especially interested in the use of tanks and in liaison between units. His second daily report showed a growing concern with traffic conditions and their effect on evacuation of the wounded. The third and fourth days again found him preoccupied with the traffic situation. Then he returned to the front,

---

[34] Ltr, Baer to IG, USA, 8 May 19, Entry 26, RG 159, NARA.
[35] Ibid.
[36] Memo, Spinks to CinC, AEF, 10 Nov 18, Entry 588, RG 120, NARA.

Discussing Training With the 77th Division Inspector,
Col. George D. Moore (right)

investigating allegations, which he discovered to be false, that friendly air support was lacking. Each day during the course of the offensive Henry briefly met with either the division commander or the chief of staff to discuss his findings.[37]

Once their units went into combat, division inspectors functioned for the most part as expediters and problem solvers. Higher-level inspectors might be sent to monitor unusual situations. This was the case with the famous "lost battalion" of the 77th Division. The 1st Battalion, 308th Infantry, along with Company K, 307th Infantry, and Companies C and D, 306th Machine Gun Battalion, were cut off from the rest of the division during an attack on 2–3 October. Under the command of Maj. Charles W. Whittlesey, the battalion defended itself until

---

[37] Henry Daily Rpts, 26–30 Sep 18, Entry 1138, RG 120, NARA.

the night of the seventh, when division elements reached the isolated units after five desperate attacks.

The incident gained considerable romantic notoriety in the American press. General Drum at First Army, learning of the developing situation from a division inspector's daily report, asked Brewster to send an inspector to the 77th Division to monitor events. Lt. Col. Albert T. Rich was dispatched, arriving on the scene the morning of 6 October. Rich remained with the division until contact was made with Whittlesey's unit, sending back periodic summaries of events to Generals Drum and Brewster, some obviously in response to specific questions probably received over the telephone. He also looked into the circumstances concerning the unit's isolation, and the direction of his effort and the nature of his findings allow the inference that he had been instructed to investigate who was at fault.[38]

In doing so, Rich focused on the mental collapse of the commander of the 308th Infantry, Col. Cromwell Stacey. The inability of Stacey's regiment to keep pressure on the Germans allowed the enemy to infiltrate behind Whittlesey's 1st Battalion and to cut it off. The division commander, Maj. Gen. Robert Alexander, relieved Stacey; the 154th Infantry Brigade commander, Brig. Gen. Evan M. Johnson, then became the senior officer on the ground, leading the assaults to link with the battalion. Rich believed that the root of the crisis was Alexander's 2 October order to advance without regard to flank security. He exonerated Johnson, feeling that he had deployed his troops correctly and provided inspiring leadership during the relief attacks, and concluded that, while no one was censurable for the situation, Stacey should be evaluated by a disability board. That unfortunate officer was evacuated for neurasthenia, returning eventually to the United States to be discharged for disability.[39]

While Colonel Rich was serving as a reporter and investigator, the bulk of the First Army was enjoying a brief pause and reorganization preparatory to renewing the assault against stubborn German resistance. Colonel Johnson went over the problems noted in the first phase of the attack and issued guidance to the corps and division IGs on ways

---

[38] 77th Division Association, *History of the Seventy-seventh Division, August 25th, 1917–November 11th, 1918* (New York: 77th Division Association, 1919), pp. 72–76, 150–51; American Battle Monuments Commission, *American Armies and Battlefields in Europe* (Washington, D.C.: Government Printing Office, 1938), pp. 337, 362–65; Rpt, Rich to IG, First Army, 8 Oct 18, sub: 77th Division Cutting Off of Seven Companies and One Machine Gun Company, Entry 588, RG 120, NARA.

[39] Rpt, Rich to IG, First Army, 8 Oct 18, and Memo, Rich to CofS, First Army, 8 Oct 19, Entry 588, RG 120, NARA.

they could improve their own operations. Reminding them that "an inspector must be where things are happening," he stressed that they should keep one another constantly informed while covering as much of their units' operations as possible. Johnson also urged them to stay in close touch with the rest of the staff to gain and transmit information. He admonished the inspectors to avoid getting trapped by routine administration and audits and to concentrate on "bigger things"—above all, winning the battle.[40]

Many problems needed to be solved. The Meuse-Argonne offensive began to lose its momentum early because of traffic management and command-and-control difficulties. Initially, General Pershing exercised too much control over advancing divisions, causing them to miss unexpected opportunities by holding them too rigidly to the original plan. Communications breakdowns eventually made it impossible to impose any direction after the first day. Some units, such as the 35th Division, lost all cohesion. Transportation bottlenecks exacerbated the situation. The three marginal roads designated as main supply routes could not handle the flow, generating massive traffic jams. Artillery, medical, and logistical elements, plus combat units of the attacking divisions, were all crammed together, frantically trying to get their jobs done.[41]

Road discipline had been virtually nonexistent during the first phase of the offensive. Motorized and horse-drawn trains were placed on the same routes. Military police were unfamiliar with their responsibilities and, when questioned by inspectors, did not know what types of vehicles or what units could use which roads and could not give proper directions. Double-banking remained a serious impediment to traffic flow, while numerous accidents due to poor and inept driving added to the chaos. Lack of coordination with the French resulted in innumerable roadblocks, especially when French convoys were trying to go against the stream. The poor condition of the roads themselves was a contributing factor, but repairs were never adequate.[42]

The chaos was so severe that efforts by senior officers were sometimes necessary to induce any movement at all. The traffic jams in the III Corps area literally threatened to halt the assault before the Germans did. General Bullard, then the corps commander, finally "devoted all my spare military police, a battalion of infantry, and some 50 officers to regulate the traffic and prevent blockades." He eventually ordered his personal aides to help undo the tie-ups. These efforts did not preclude

---

[40] Memos, Johnson to Corps Insps, 1 and 2 Oct, Entry 590, RG 120, NARA.
[41] Coffman, *War To End All Wars*, pp. 313–14.
[42] Rpts, Henry to Insp, 5th Corps, 1 Oct 18, Entry 1138, RG 120, NARA.

Premier of France Georges Clemenceau from getting caught in one massive jam near Montfaucon on 29 September. He was so infuriated by his experience that he wrote Marshal Ferdinand Foch urging that as Generalissimo he relieve General Pershing for incompetence. Foch calmed him down and politely ignored the suggestion. The French attributed the American transportation crisis to a beginner's tendency to try to fit too many units into the front. They also cited American inexperience as an explanation for poor reconnaissance and coordination, although the stiff German resistance was acknowledged to be a contributing factor.[43]

Preliminary to the second phase of the offensive, traffic control remained an issue because of the relatively small number of military police (MPs) available. However, all inspectors agreed that traffic discipline had improved. Corps and army inspectors then became focused on a second major problem, communications, both within organizations and to adjacent and rear units. Considerable attention was paid to the use of telephones, radios, runners, and other means of liaison and control. In early October four corps and army inspectors tested the use of artillery pieces well forward, under the direct supervision of infantry commanders. Interviews with artillerymen showed that they were little used, while being dangerously exposed, and the IGs joined with them in recommending that all guns remain under artillery control.[44]

Inspectors also were required to assess the condition and attitude of senior commanders to see, in Pershing's words, how much "push and punch" they had left. When the 28th Division called for relief, saying that its regiments "were shot to pieces and down to 600 men," Brewster was sent to verify the claim and to assess the combat effectiveness of the officers. Even though the division had lost about half its frontline strength, he concluded that the survivors were in good spirits, well fed, and well equipped; "they are not asking to be taken out," he reported. Brewster felt that the artillery brigade commander had lost his drive and was the source of the pessimism pervading the division's leadership levels, and he identified several other senior officers who likewise merited evaluation. However, his visit apparently provided sufficient inspiration to the division officers. No one was relieved, and the performance of the 28th remained steady or better.[45]

---

[43] Coffman, *War To End All Wars*, pp. 338, 340; Robert L. Bullard *Personalities and Reminiscences of the War* (Garden City, N.Y.: Doubleday, Page and Co., 1925), p. 272 (quotation).

[44] Rpt, Peck to IG, AEF, 1 Oct 18, sub: Observations, Entry 588, RG 120, NARA.

[45] Memo, IG, AEF, to CinC, AEF, 3 Oct 18, sub: 28th Division, Entry 590, RG 120, NARA.

Corps and army inspectors believed that one of the best ways to gauge the combat effectiveness of a division was to observe it on the march as it was pulled from the line. Typical were Colonel Peck's observations of the 35th Division. The unit had taken part in hard fighting around the town of Cheppy; on its first day in combat, fourteen field-grade officers had become casualties while leading their units from the van, much like Civil War heroes. Unfortunately, the division's discipline was also reminiscent of earlier armies of citizen soldiers.

Lt. Col. Robert G. Peck

Peck observed routine disregard of AEF policies. March discipline and camouflage were poor, wagons were improperly loaded, and the troops failed to clear the right-of-way at halts. The men had made no effort to clean their weapons, and many appeared to have abandoned their personal equipment. Peck felt that few of the division officers were enforcing standards, and cited the division's National Guard origins as one of the reasons for the laxness—a judgment that division members greatly resented. While Peck's blunt remarks provoked some criticism in Congress when someone in the division violated the confidentiality of his report, high-level AEF officers tended to view the 35th's problems as typical of new units in battle for the first time. In fact, the division, despite the failings noted by the inspector, had acquitted itself reasonably well in combat.[46]

---

[46] Rpt, Peck to CG, 35th Div, 12 Oct 18, Entry 588, and Ltr, Jackson to McAndrew, 1 Feb 19, Entry 15, RG 120, NARA; Congressman Little in U.S. Congress, House, *Congressional Record*, 65th Cong., 3d Sess., 1919, 57, pt. 3:2557–59; Clair Kenamore, *From Vauquois Hill to Exermont: A History of the Thirty-fifth Division of the United States Army* (St. Louis: Guard Publishing Co., 1919), pp. 244–45, 251–53; Marcellus G. Spinks, "Major Problems of the Inspector General, AEF, and Their Solution" (Lecture delivered at G–1 Course No. 5, Army War College, Washington, D.C., 9 Oct 33), in Army War College Curriculum Papers, MHI; Coffman, *War To End All Wars*, pp. 311–12; Bullard, *Personalities and Reminiscences*, p. 327; Hunter Liggett, *A. E. F.: Ten Years Ago in France* (New York: Dodd, Mead and Co., 1928), pp. 180–81.

Inspectors at all levels also were called upon to study the employment of tanks. Problems with the new weapons were many. Tanks had to operate in the extremely rough terrain characteristic of the Argonne Forest, and limited communications capabilities and a lack of combined-arms training meant they could expect little infantry support. The tank brigade, equipped with 141 tanks, went into battle on 26 September with 70 officers and 657 men. By 14 October it had a total of 330 casualties and 62 tanks out of action. The survivors were grouped into a provisional company, and Lt. Col. Thorne Strayer from the First Army IG office was sent to determine whether the tanks should be committed again.[47]

He found the morale of the provisional company to be high and the remaining equipment in good condition. He noted, however, that the French had pulled out their tanks because the harsh terrain made maintenance nearly impossible, concluding that the probable personnel and equipment losses "were not commensurate with the offensive advantages" to be derived from the use of the tanks. He recommended that the company and its equipment be withdrawn to the First Army's tank center, where they could be of greater value in speeding the organization and training of newer armored units. Despite these recommendations, however, the provisional company was used in one more attack on 16 October, losing about half of its remaining strength. This action contributed more to infantry morale than to tactical success.[48]

The attack led to a First Army special inquiry by the V Corps IG, Colonel Dallam. The tanks, committed to support a brigade of the 42d Division, had arrived two hours late because of terrain difficulties, and within an hour all had been eliminated by enemy fire or mechanical failure. Those that could be salvaged were held in defensive positions against a possible counterattack until they could be withdrawn. Dallam felt that tanks had great potential, but stressed that combined training with infantry was necessary. He faulted tank leaders for not making adequate map and ground reconnaissances before going into battle and both infantry and tank commanders for failing to develop proper liaison for exploiting changing situations. Finally, he emphasized the need for near-perfect maintenance in tank units, to avoid battlefield breakdowns, and made several recommendations for changes in tank design.

---

[47] Rpt, Strayer to IG, First Army, 14 Oct 18, sub: Tank Units With First Army, Entry 797, RG 120, NARA; Martin Blumenson, *The Patton Papers*, 2 vols. (Boston: Houghton Mifflin Co., 1972–74), 1:620.

[48] Rpt, Strayer to IG, First Army, 14 Oct 18, Entry 797, RG 120, NARA.

His views, though valid and perceptive, came too late to be of practical value in the Argonne.[49]

Meuse-Argonne (4 October–11 November)

As the fighting extended through October, senior command inspectors were drawn once again into the problems of combat support. Growing chaos in the rear areas prompted General Liggett on 22 October to suspend inspection requirements at the front, ordering the First Army IG to concentrate on the inspection of units and facilities behind the division areas. Convinced that the rear areas were neither well organized nor fully productive, Liggett wanted labor units to be inspected and evaluated at railheads, hospitals, remount depots, supply dumps, and so on.[50]

Meanwhile, AEF-level inspectors continued to monitor combat effectiveness. The morale and physical condition of the troops and their junior leaders remained a paramount concern. Men at all levels were questioned, and occasionally an inspector's findings led to immediate improvements. This was the case when 82d Division soldiers complained to Major Rice that nightly rotation of battalions from the front line prevented them from sleeping. Rice reported the situation to the division chief of staff, and the unit's relief schedule was changed to allow the troops more time to rest.

The fact that an inspector was obliged to raise so basic an issue underlined the enthusiastic amateurism still pervading much of the force. Other problems pointed to the same underlying difficulty. In early November, as the war drew to an end, inspectors continued to note fundamental weaknesses in staff procedure and leadership born of inexperience and overwork. New leaders were still unable or unwilling to enforce policies and follow through on orders. Just holding things together at division level was an achievement for the staff and its inspectors.[51]

The demands on division IG offices increased greatly once units were committed to battle. Part of the problem was handling the number of outside inspection requirements. The 82d Division, for example, between 6–11 October had one visit from the Advanced Headquarters,

---

[49] Memo, Dallam to IG, First Army, 28 Oct 18; 83d Bde Daily Log, 15 Oct 18; and Lenihan Notes on Tanks From Experiences in Champagne, St. Mihiel Salient and Before St. Georges, 27 Oct 18. All in Entry 797, RG 120, NARA.

[50] Memo, Drum to IG, 1st Army, 22 Oct 18, Entry 799, RG 120, NARA.

[51] Rpt, Rice to IG, AEF, 23 Oct 18, and Memo (pencil notes), McIlheny to Baer, 3 Nov 18, Entry 590, RG 120, NARA.

two from the First Army, and one from the I Corps added to, of course, the daily rounds of its own inspector. In the 26th Division in late October the two inspectors found themselves stretched to the limit. They oversaw numerous small issues of interest to their commander, tried to complete the reports required by corps or army IGs, audited two "badly tangled" financial accounts, and conducted four full-scale inquiries on topics ranging from the efficiency of the division veterinarian to dereliction of duty and disregard of division road-march policy. A particularly complex investigation involving friendly artillery fire consumed two weeks of one inspector's time, reflecting also hours spent enforcing corrective measures. Continued disregard for concealment measures caused the division commander to direct his IG to enforce the regulations. No one else seemed able to do so.[52]

While the pressures prevented the inspectors from completely satisfying either their commanders or their counterparts at higher headquarters, most continued to enjoy command support. Many had direct access to their commanders, and even when the IGs were placed under the division G–1s, the practical effect often was much the same. In the 6th Division, for example, the IG served under the G–1 because the division chief of staff did not want a "free lance inspector" reporting directly to the division commander. In practice, however, the division commander used his inspector as a personal staff officer and the G–1, recognizing this, kept a very light rein on the officer, working closely with him to assure that no conflict arose between the commander's needs, those of the chief of staff, and any G–1 requirements.[53]

American MPs had begun to improve their performance in traffic control, but major problems on roads were still encountered, particularly during darkness when traffic volume increased. On 13 October, after a week in battle, the 82d Division experienced critical congestion on its main route. The division IG and G–1 spent two hours trying to straighten it out. They then were joined by the division provost marshal and several other staff officers, sent by the division commander with orders to stay until the traffic was flowing properly. The inspector successfully proposed that French-speaking soldiers or French military police be used to augment the Americans.[54]

Each division handled the traffic crisis in its own manner, but in each case the unit inspectors exercised some degree of oversight. In

---

[52] 82d Div File, Box 6563; Ltr (quoted words), Foote to Johnson, 5 Nov 18; Buxton Daily Rpt, 18 Oct 18. All in Entry 590, RG 120, NARA.

[53] Lewis, "Short Account," OTIG files, Pentagon (SAIG-ZXH).

[54] Buxton Daily Rpts, 8–16 Oct 18, Entry 590, RG 120, NARA.

many divisions they were actually put in charge. For example, the 28th Division IG was authorized to be "in charge of traffic and have control of MPs, directing their activities in traffic control, straggling and prisoners." The operations of the 6th Division IG were more in line with standard practice. There, Major Lewis worked with the division provost marshal to try to ease the road congestion. At times each would take a crossroads and actually direct traffic, with Lewis claiming that he now understood something of the work of a traffic cop. The division commander expected his inspectors to be on the road whenever any division element was en route to correct problems, to police stragglers, and to do whatever was necessary to reduce traffic congestion. In some cases the IGs trained new young MPs on the spot on how to regulate road traffic, developing the maxim: "In inspecting on roads, nothing must be done to interfere with the progress of the march, but an inspector can question all he likes at the various halts."[55]

Despite improvements wrought by much effort, traffic control remained a problem until the shooting stopped. The enduring practical problems were exemplified by those confronting the 2d Division during its attack in the first week of November. The division IG and provost marshal thought they had implemented a well-conceived plan. They trained division MPs and placed them along all of the unit's main routes and at every key point. They discovered, however, that seven other divisions were using the same roads and, generally, refused to obey 2d Division personnel who were trying to keep order. Nearly three days passed before the V Corps responded to requests for additional MPs. The new men arrived without briefings, maps, or information sufficient to do their job. With the division forced to divert the equivalent of a company to assist in traffic control, the division IG rated traffic flow as the major problem the unit faced because of its effect on the conduct of the battle and the crisis it imposed once more on medical evacuation.[56]

Indeed, throughout the Meuse-Argonne the effect of traffic problems on evacuation was tragic. Ambulances took as long as ten hours to make a short trip back to the field hospitals, and casualties arrived in poor condition. On some, wounds were not dressed, going unattended for almost two days; on others, tourniquets on injured limbs had shut off the blood flow for so long that the limbs could not be saved. Tie-ups

[55] Taggart Daily Rpt (first quotation), 7 Oct 18, Entry 590, RG 120, NARA; Lewis, "Short Account," second quotation, OTIG files, Pentagon (SAIG-ZXH).
[56] Rpt, Lay to IG, AEF, 14 Nov 18, and Ltr, Lay to Baer, 16 Nov 18, Entry 590, RG 120, NARA.

were so bad that it was not unusual for litter-bearers to be forced to carry the wounded 5 miles before they could find an ambulance. As reported by the 79th Division IG, one ambulance team spent fifteen hours traveling just 4 miles. Major Henry estimated that hundreds of deaths resulted from the delays imposed by the massive congestion in his division area alone.[57]

The evacuation problems were compounded by the unexpectedly high number of casualties. Apparently, actuarial predictions had not factored in the consequences of inadequate training. Hence, insufficient numbers of medical personnel were available, despite the increase authorized after the lessons of the Aisne-Marne. To augment corpsmen, a number of divisions trained line personnel in first aid and made them available as litter-bearers whenever needed. But some corps forbade this practice, requiring that ambulance personnel be used—a solution that shifted the evacuation problem without solving it. The number of medical corpsmen was never sufficient, and the additional strength increases urged by inspectors and surgeons did not go into effect until after the armistice.

Another factor complicating evacuation was the nature of the battlefield itself. The stationary battle lines limited the recovery of casualties and extended their exposure to artillery fire, forcing them to seek refuge in trenches, shell craters, and similar positions for hours, sometimes days, until evacuation to battalion or regimental aid stations was possible. Artillery fire often prevented ambulances from moving forward to the regimental areas, which in turn added to the burden of the weary litter-bearers who had to trek even greater distances back to an ambulance station or an advanced dressing station. Army-level ambulance units and their French counterparts were brought in to help offset division and corps shortages. Nevertheless, the wounded frequently had to be hauled on primitive flatbeds, compounding their suffering. While some were fortunate enough to receive stabilizing care at the front, the average time from wounding to initial treatment at an aid station was five hours and then five to ten more hours for definitive care at an evacuation hospital.[58]

Minor medical problems helped to clog the system. In the newly arrived units a large number of evacuees identified as gas cases were found to be suffering more often than not from exhaustion or a virus. Yet some were lost to their units for long periods, even permanently.

---

[57] Henry Daily Rpts, 26–30 Sep and 1 Oct 18, Entry 1138, RG 120, NARA.

[58] Brewster Notes . . . During Active Operations From 12 Sep 18 to 11 Nov 18, n.d., Entry 26B, RG 159, NARA.

After inspectors pointed out the problem, the policy was adopted of retaining all mild or indefinite cases at division aid stations until they could be diagnosed properly. In this way many evacuees were returned to their units after a few days' rest, which sustained unit strength and also discouraged malingering. The inspectors remained critical of the practice of placing convalescents into the general replacement pipeline, and some efforts were made to return them to their original units. However, this rarely could be done if an individual had moved all the way back to a base hospital. The IGs cited rigid evacuation policies as detrimental to morale and a serious manpower drain.

The inspectors were also critical of several other medical practices. They cautioned against mobile medical units settling too firmly into permanent facilities and surgeons performing complex operations too far forward, in contravention to what was prescribed by regulations. They also emphasized the need for accurate treatment records, especially the proper use of diagnostic tags, noting some improvement toward the end of the fighting. IGs who visited base hospitals to evaluate the treatment given to casualties as they moved through the medical system found the care to be generally sound at every level. Administrative weaknesses, however, still required attention, such as safeguarding personal property and salvaging government equipment.[59]

Burial of the dead was a worse problem in the Argonne than at St. Mihiel or along the Marne. As a result of the IG findings after the Aisne-Marne fighting, earnest efforts were made to improve the system. Various concepts were tried. For the St. Mihiel offensive most divisions had organized a squad of ten or more men, drawn from the reserve battalion in each regiment. Equipped with the necessary picks and shovels, the squads were attached to their respective regimental aid stations and placed under the supervision of their chaplains. The chaplains worked under the general supervision of the division burial officer, who was responsible to the division G–1 in most cases. Designated "sub-inspectors" of cemeteries, they continued to supervise actual burials and graves identification and maintained burial records until picked up by Graves Registration Service personnel—a problem in itself, for they rarely appeared. The chaplains also were responsible for collecting the personal effects of the deceased and moving them into quartermaster channels for return to the next of kin.[60]

---

[59] Ibid.

[60] DA, HD, *World War*, 16:210 (GO 30, 1918, quoted word); Memo, Buxton to Burham, 11 Sep 18, Entry 2144, RG 120, NARA.

Burial sites usually were located adjacent to civilian cemeteries. Each graveyard was for the use of a specific unit, which detailed to the site small burial teams organized from its reserve. If any Red Cross or YMCA members were attached to the division, they came under the supervision of the division chaplain, who assigned them wherever he felt they could be most useful in the identification and burial process. All of the burial teams were expected to bury dead animals and otherwise police the battlefield when not dealing with friendly and enemy dead. Even though the casualty total for St. Mihiel was not particularly high, problems persisted. A large number of isolated, unrecorded burials were made. In some cases mass graves were used in violation of policy. Too much was expected of the hard-pressed chaplains, who could not supervise every aspect of the system as thoroughly as necessary.[61]

Administrative problems added to their difficulties. A unit's casualty reports were often simply the surgeon's admission and disposition reports, which, of course, reflected only the injured in medical channels. Combat conditions and the swiftness of unit reliefs prevented a proper sweep of the battlefields, and new units coming in often inherited corpses from their predecessors. These problems caused the system to be altered for the Meuse-Argonne attack in late September, when it became apparent that the initial reforms could not handle the human and animal casualties. A company of pioneer infantry was detached from corps control and assigned to each division; at division, officer-led platoons were attached to each regiment. Each was equipped with digging implements, markers, and maps to record burial sites. The division sanitary inspector, a medical officer, was brought in to assist the burial officer and the chaplains in planning and supervising burial operations.[62]

Even after these changes, the only area in which army and AEF inspectors noted any improvement was in the wearing of identity disks. Burying the dead promptly and properly eluded those responsible. The problem lay in the dual use of the pioneer infantry, who were expected to continue to perform the corps salvage mission as well as division burials. When they were performing the graves mission, salvage suffered; when the emphasis shifted to salvage, burials

---

[61] Memo, Hollis to Surg, 82d Div, 1 Oct 18, Entry 2144, RG 120, NARA; Brewster Notes . . . During Active Operations From 12 Sep 18 to 11 Nov 18, n.d., Entry 26B, RG 159, NARA.

[62] 82d Div File, Boxes 6563–65; Memo, McIlroy to IG, AEF, 22 Oct 18, sub: Report of Inspection in Sector of 42d Division. Both in Entry 590, RG 120, NARA.

suffered. Overall, burials continued to be haphazard. Inspectors at the front often reported seeing the same remains lying unattended at the same spot for several days. The situation was even worse with the remains of horses and mules.[63]

The prolonged exposure of the dead led to the scandalous practice of corpse-robbing during the Argonne fighting. An extended investigation of the 28th Division was prompted by a 29 September letter to the AEF chaplain from one of the division chaplains, who wrote that he was having trouble identifying German and American remains because the bodies had been rifled; even identity disks had been taken as souvenirs. Only American troops had been in a position to commit these acts. General Brewster directed Lt. Col. James G. McIlroy to investigate. Colonel McIlroy interviewed the complaining chaplain and most of the division burial teams and also toured the area. He concluded that in two places within the division area several hundred German and American bodies had been robbed completely of all valuables and identification. Although unable to identify those responsible, McIlroy judged that 28th Division personnel were unquestionably at fault and recommended that all citations for gallantry within the unit during the period 26 September–7 October be disapproved.[64]

General Brewster largely agreed with McIlroy's findings; however, he believed that such conduct was not limited to the 28th Division. Brewster estimated that 95 percent of the German and 50 percent of the American dead on the battlefield had been robbed. Rejecting the idea of denying valor awards, which punished the innocent as well as the guilty, he suggested that Pershing send only a letter of reprimand to Maj. Gen. Charles H. Muir, the division commander at the time of the incident. This was done on 29 October. Muir protested the findings, but a new investigation, carried out in February 1919, produced even more convincing evidence that the 28th Division was at fault.[65]

The robbery of the dead by wandering troops was symptomatic of a growing problem of straggling, which began to plague the combat units almost from the beginning of the attack. The decline in frontline

---

[63] Rpt, McIlroy to IG, AEF, 22 Oct 18, Entry 590; Buxton Daily Rpts, 8 and 14 Oct 18, Entry 590; Memo, Brewster to CinC, AEF, 10 Nov 18, sub: Investigation 36th Division Burial of Dead, Entry 588; Memo, Brewster to CinC, AEF, 20 Nov 18, sub: Investigation 2d Division Burial of Dead, Entry 588. All in RG 120, NARA.

[64] Rpt, McIlroy to IG, AEF, 14 Oct 18, sub: Investigation Concerning Alleged Robbing of German Dead, Entry 588, RG 120, NARA.

[65] Ibid.; Brewster Comments on McIlroy Rpt, 18 Oct 18; Ltr, AG, AEF, to CG, 28th Div, 29 Oct 18, sub: Robbery of Dead; Weekly Rpts Extract, OIG, AEF, Feb 19; and Memo, Baer to CinC, AEF, 14 Oct 18. All in Entry 588, RG 120, NARA.

strength, caused by the unexpectedly high casualties, increased interest in retaining manpower by every means possible. The effect of straggler control requirements on inspectors may be seen in the experience of the 37th Division IG, Lt. Col. Byron L. Barger. During the fighting at Montfaucon on 28 September, the division commander told Colonel Barger to drop everything else he was doing, to collect all the stragglers he could, and to get them to the front.

As a result, Barger roamed the areas immediately behind the attacking regiments. At one time he gathered nearly 180 men, whom he organized into temporary squads and led forward to place under regimental control. He continued doing the same things each day the division was in the attack, forming groups that he occasionally turned over to military police but more often led forward himself. Dealing also with traffic problems as he moved about the battle area and subject to artillery and sometimes small-arms fire, he formed an impression of a frenzied situation on the edge of chaos.[66]

By mid-October straggling was a major discipline problem. Over 100,000 men were estimated to be away from their units, some on proper business, others lost or shirking. General Liggett cracked down hard on the situation when he assumed First Army command, supported by Pershing who went so far as to authorize summary execution of anyone running away in combat. The AEF required all division inspectors to report what their units were doing to control straggling and keep men at the front. In some units military police were stationed at key crossroads and sites, such as dumps and hospitals, where they gathered unattached men into groups and periodically escorted them forward.[67]

The 82d Division, operating in the Argonne Forest, embarked upon such a vigorous and elaborate straggler control program to cause the First Army to investigate. Shortly after becoming engaged, the division estimated that about 1,000 of its line troops were unaccounted for. The commander required a daily physical count. Military police circulated through all rear area facilities around villages, dugouts, and YMCA canteens; unit patrols swept from the division rear forward, picking up 140 in the first two days. Many of the stragglers were truly lost. Whenever units moved at night, large numbers inevitably turned up missing the next day. Many of them, too, were replacements. Surprising numbers could barely speak English and had failed to understand their

---

[66] Ltr, Barger to CG, 37th Div, 14 Nov 18, sub: Accusation That I Pointed a Pistol at a Lieutenant in the Argonne Drive, Entry 588, RG 120, NARA.

[67] Coffman, *War To End All Wars*, pp. 332–33; Memo, Barker to Brewster, 14 Oct 18, sub: Report on Straggler Posts, Entry 590, RG 120, NARA.

commanders' instructions on the location of the rallying points. The First Army investigator approved the system, judging that the division's vigorous actions to minimize straggling had given a false impression that an unusual problem existed. The 82d's approach so impressed Colonel Johnson and General Liggett at First Army that its program was recommended to other units.[68]

The V Corps inspector also recommended that corps MPs begin a series of patrols in towns, around depots, and at YMCA and Red Cross canteens, because "stragglers, like flies, require food and warmth." This earthy aphorism hinted at another problem indirectly shown by straggling: a breakdown in logistical support. Prompted by General Brewster, an I Corps investigation showed that some of the 77th Division stragglers actually were wandering in search of food. On 8–9 October over 100 soldiers, representing most of the units in the 78th Division, straggled into the 82d Division rear headquarters, asking for food and saying that they had not eaten for two days or more. Rough, unshaven, and dirty, they had been trucked in to a replacement rendezvous and apparently forgotten. The 82d division IG talked with many and found them "intelligent and uncomplaining." He and the division provost marshal saw to their feeding and made arrangements to return them to the 78th, located more than 12 miles away.[69]

Inspectors attributed such breakdowns in support to the inexperience and frequently low quality of unit logistical officers, whose positions were often a haven for the less competent officers in a line unit. Supply and transportation were particularly affected. Senior logistical officers were for the most part able, but their numbers were so few that their influence was fatally diluted by the scale of operations. Logistical success was left to the poorly prepared temporary officers, and their experience was so limited that they accepted intolerable situations as necessary evils rather than trying to correct them.

This attitude was especially noticeable in unit supply officers, who often contented themselves with submitting requisitions and then awaiting delivery. This passive approach and frequent unit moves led to extended delays, as depots tried to find units to arrange an issue. Those divisions with supply officers who searched out the depots and pursued

<hr>

[68] Memo, Rice to IG, AEF, 18 Oct 18, sub: Investigation of Straggling in 82d Division, Entry 590, RG 120, NARA.

[69] Memo (quotation), Dallam to CG, 5th Army Corps, 24 Oct 18, sub: Report on Stragglers, Entry 1138; Ltr (quoted words), Buxton to IG, AEF, 9 Oct 18, sub: Condition of Troops From 78th Division, Entry 590; Memo, McIlroy to Peck, 10 Nov 18, sub: Stragglers, Entry 590. All in RG 120, NARA.

their requests usually got what they needed. The main difficulty was finding the depot with the desired supplies. To ameliorate such conditions, inspectors suggested automatically issuing consumables, such as rations and fuel, without waiting for any requests. Items known to be rapidly consumed would be stockpiled closer to the front, but still under army or SOS control, without making them an extra burden for combat units lacking storage or transportation capabilities.[70]

Since the chief difficulty in the system lay in a lack of coordination between the unit logistical and depot officers, First Army and Advanced Headquarters staffs used the IG daily reports to keep the depots current on shortages existing in each unit. The depots, in turn, dealt directly with the units. This ad hoc system evolved into a modified form of automatic supply in every class. The elimination of most requisition paperwork sped up the process as long as tactical unit logisticians could keep the inspectors informed of their needs. Eventually, ammunition resupply was managed the same way.[71]

Transport and Supply Problems

Blame for supply problems by no means rested exclusively on the tactical units. Inspectors also found serious deficiencies in SOS policies, compounded by a lack of discipline and supervision. No SOS priority system existed for the issue of equipment; available items were handed out to whomever asked. Units in the combat zone received what they needed only if their requisitions coincided with what was on hand. The movement of supplies in the intermediate and advanced zones proved a serious problem, especially at the railheads. Complaints about lack of care in handling supplies, waste, and black-marketeering eventually led to an investigation by both field-army IGs.[72]

A thorough inspection of army depots and railheads by the regulating officer responsible for field-army support resulted in the appointment of a railhead inspector. Assigned a vehicle, this inspector spent his entire time going from railhead to railhead identifying problems, expediting solutions, and training troops. He further identified incompetent officers for relief and generally kept the regulating officer informed.

---

[70] Ltr, Vestal to IG, AEF, 25 Apr 19, sub: Report, Entry 588, RG 120, NARA.

[71] Brewster Notes . . . During Active Operations From 12 Sep 18 to 11 Nov 18, n.d., Entry 26B, RG 159, NARA; Ltr, Elmore to IG, AEF, 25 Jun 19, sub: Report From Observations of AEF, Entry 588, RG 120, NARA.

[72] Ltr, Johnson to IG, AEF, 22 Mar 19, sub: Information for Report on American E. F., Entry 588, RG 120, NARA.

This practice was so effective that it was soon duplicated throughout the Services of Supply.[73]

Even with this oversight, the flow of supplies continued to be unsatisfactory because of the lack of coordination between SOS units and the field forces. Those responsible far to the rear were unaware of many of the difficulties affecting supplies moving forward to the front—such things as pilferage; rough or unsanitary handling of supplies, resulting in major waste; and the absence of salvage and storage facilities. Inspectors took it upon themselves to provide the information necessary for those in the system to implement corrective measures.[74]

Despite every effort, however, the logistical system could endure no further pressure. The attrition experienced in the Meuse-Argonne taxed all forms of supply and medical service to their limits. The rear areas were swept clean of men, animals, and vehicles in a "now or never" decision to sustain the offensive. Ammunition handling, engineer activities, and vehicle repairs slowly wound down because of the lack of people. The decision was a gamble, and the system was beginning to show signs of fatal stress at the time of the November armistice. The SOS would have been unable to sustain the units at the front if they had continued fighting at the levels of intensity characteristic of October and November.[75]

One of the problems encountered by the Salvage Service was unexpectedly high waste on the part of the American troops, rooted in a policy of tolerating reduced accountability because of combat losses. In other cases, the absence of transportation forced units to abandon serviceable equipment when they were redeployed. Few combat officers could be bothered over matters of salvage. Since none of the officers or men were held pecuniarily liable, quantities of usable equipment were discarded for convenience alone. Some threw away their clothes when they were dirty, knowing they could draw more with no questions asked, and others did the same with weapons.[76]

The crisis in salvage and equipment was paralleled by an even more critical situation—the supply and care of animals, considered by

---

[73] Ibid.; Memo, Johnson to IG, AEF, 8 Nov 18, Entry 590, RG 120, NARA.

[74] Ltr, Johnson to IG, AEF, 22 Mar 19, Entry 588; Memo, Johnson to IG, AEF, 8 Nov 18, Entry 590. Both in RG 120, NARA.

[75] James A. Huston, *The Sinews of War: Army Logistics, 1775–1953*, (Washington, D.C.: Office of the Chief of Military History, United States Army, 1966), p. 386; Johnson Hagood, *The Services of Supply: A Memoir of the Great War* (Boston: Houghton Mifflin Co., 1927), pp. 314–17 (quoted words, p. 314).

[76] Ltr, Ovenshine to IG, AEF, 28 Mar 19, sub: Report; Ltr, Elmore to IG, AEF, 25 Jun 19. Both in Entry 588, RG 120, NARA.

Pershing to be "one of the biggest, if not the biggest problem" in France. A total of 243,360 horses were issued to the AEF, a ratio of about 1 horse to 8 men. They represented the Army's basic transportation unit at the time. Initially, the animals were shipped from the States; then the French undertook to supply horses, many of which, however, proved to be in poor condition. Their condition and the ignorance of most of their American handlers promised a disaster. When it became apparent that the French could not fill AEF requirements, horses again were procured from the States during the period November 1917 to April 1918. Then other priorities stopped further shipments. Purchases in Spain and France could not offset the steady consumption of animals thereafter. Shortages became so critical that some key units had to be motorized. At times, the allies loaned large numbers of animals so that AEF combat divisions could carry out essential deployments.[77]

Beginning in April 1918, the state of care and general condition of animals was made an item of special inspection interest. In May General Winn of the SOS conducted an inspection of the entire Remount Service. At the time, he found conditions to be unsatisfactory, and a follow-up check in July revealed little improvement. Mange and other diseases, overwork, and frequent breakdowns in the supply of forage took their toll on the health of most of the livestock. Many succumbed to sickness and died, while many others needed extended rest and recuperation before they could go back into service. The largest part of the problem lay in the continued disregard by officer and soldier alike of the rudiments of animal care. Inspectors tried to change conditions in their units through informal training programs; however, as they had feared, the marginal health of a large proportion of the livestock worsened during the fall offensives. This further deterioration was due primarily to continued poor care, the lack of supervision, and no command emphasis on standards.[78]

Greater command support for veterinarians soon brought change. As a rule, animal evacuation was carried out whenever appropriate. The Remount Service was more responsive, allowing reasonably prompt replacement of animal losses. Remount officers were attached to each field army to expedite animal supply and to train personnel in proper

---

[77] Memo, Hewitt to Surg, 82d Div, 31 Mar 19, Entry 2144, RG 120, NARA; Erna Risch, *Quartermaster Support of the Army: A History of the Corps, 1775–1939* (Washington, D.C.: Quartermaster Historian's Office, Office of the Quartermaster General, 1962), p. 681 (Pershing's quoted words).

[78] Brewster Notes . . . During Active Operations From 12 Sep 18 to 11 Nov 18, n.d., Entry 26B, RG 159, NARA.

animal care. Inspection of animal evacuation hospitals verified that rear area veterinary support was working well. IG observations led to the increase of veterinary unit strengths and to the authorization of sufficient rail transport for more efficient animal evacuation. By the end of November each field army and the Services of Supply had a senior animal inspector to educate everyone involved in the care, management, and administration of their livestock. Because of this intense effort, animal deaths were a rarity and diseases were fully under control by the end of February 1919.[79]

Replacement Flow

Like the logistical system, the AEF manpower system teetered on the brink of disaster. U.S. forces sustained an estimated 35,000–45,000 casualties in the first four days of the Meuse-Argonne attack. By early October the need for replacements was so great that two depot divisions and two newly arrived infantry divisions had to be broken up to fill the gaps in the line. Despite this expedient, shortages remained so severe that authorized unit strengths had to be reduced.[80]

As a result, the movement of individual replacements and recovered casualties through the remaining depot divisions was accelerated. The speed with which the men were hustled into combat units during 1918 was phenomenal. In August, while visiting a hospital in Mars-sur-Allier, General Chamberlain encountered a soldier who told him that he had been drafted in May, sent to France in June, wounded in July, and then had his leg amputated and received his port call to the United States in August. By the time of the fall fighting, replacements were sometimes equipped, interviewed, and assigned in less than a day.[81]

Even the earlier three- to four-day training sessions were curtailed in face of the urgent need for manpower at the front. Many replacements were held only a few hours at the Le Mans classification center to receive the rudiments of gas training. The center commander

---

[79] Ltr, Johnson to IG, AEF, 22 Mar 19, Entry 588; Ltr, Woolfolk to CGs, 15 Mar 19, sub: Inspection and Supervision Re Animals and Transport, Entry 588; Lay, IG, 2d Div, Annual Rpt, 1 Mar 19, Entry 590; Memos, C. Helmick to IG, 2d Div, 24 and 28 Feb 19, Entry 590. All in RG 120, NARA. See also Interv, author with C. Helmick, 3 Feb 83, Inspector General Collection, MHI.

[80] Daniel R. Beaver, *Newton D. Baker and the American War Effort, 1917–1919* (Lincoln: University of Nebraska Press, 1966), pp. 196, 202; John J. Pershing, *My Experiences in the World War*, 2 vols. (New York: Frederick A. Stokes Co., 1931), 2:238.

[81] Patterson Diary, 11 Aug 18, Entry 26B, RG 159, NARA.

requested that he be allowed to keep them an additional eight hours for basic rifle training, but GHQ AEF denied his request, stating that they were needed too urgently to allow any delay. By late September numerous inspectors were citing appallingly low levels of training among the replacements. General Brewster reported the situation to the AEF G–3 and G–5 and offered to investigate, but the staff was already aware of it, having directed the assignment of the replacements as a military necessity.[82]

The poor quality of replacements was investigated, nevertheless, in order to measure the combat effectiveness of units at the front. One of the most notorious cases involved the 77th Division in late September. The 77th received about 1,250 replacements, men whom unit commanders described as "almost entirely uninstructed . . . and very poorly disciplined." Of these, 850 were assigned to the division's 307th Infantry, which was at the time short some 1,500 soldiers. The replacements arrived the day before the 77th attacked in the Argonne. Company commanders reported that 90 percent of them had never fired a rifle, thrown a grenade, or undergone any kind of tactical drill; yet, because strength was so low, the regimental commander felt that they had to be employed. Company leaders encountered great difficulty in trying to keep these troops moving in rough terrain. They had to be herded from place to place and physically put into position. Each man had to be told what to do and when to do it. One battalion commander told an inspector that he learned in talking with the replacements that they had spent most of their time since being inducted traveling to France.[83]

The strain on junior officers was intense, as they tried to use such men without committing them to their own slaughter. Leaders were obliged to take more risks, increasing their own chances of becoming casualties. By October the replacements were arriving with so little training that they could not be used at all. On the twelfth Brewster's office petitioned—although unsuccessfully—the AEF G–1 to slow down the flow of replacements, to allow adequate time for them to undergo minimum training.[84]

The replacement picture darkened with reports of a worldwide epidemic of influenza. Major Britton, writing about his voyage to France

---

[82] Hagood, *Services of Supply*, p. 291; MFR, Spinks, 14 Oct 18, Entry 588, RG 120, NARA.

[83] Memo (quotation), Read to Spinks, 11 Oct 18; Intervs, Rich with Haughton, 6 Oct 18, and Rich with Jenkins, 6 Oct 18. All in Entry 590, RG 120, NARA.

[84] Memos, Read to Spinks, 11 Oct 18, and Baer to ACofS, G–1, AEF, 12 Oct 18, Entry 590, RG 120, NARA.

in October, graphically portrayed the ravages of the epidemic on troop-ships. About 2,400 soldiers had set sail on a converted passenger liner. Thirty influenza cases appeared after the first day at sea. The number grew to sixty-four by the third day and to eighty-two by the fifth day. During this period ten cases of pneumonia also were reported. By the sixth day 19 soldiers had died, and topside cabins had to be converted into medical wards. Britton attributed part of the problem to the lack of thorough medical screening at embarkation; many of those who became ill were showing symptoms before they came aboard. His report not only described the growing medical crisis but also hinted at the condition of men and units rushed to the front on arrival in France.[85]

A case cited by Colonel Beeuwkes reflected both the urgent need to move troops and the too frequent disregard for their welfare. On the night of 7 October 1,700 replacements for the 79th Division were crowded into boxcars, about 10 more per car than regulations pre-scribed. All were wet from a rainstorm. When they arrived at the divi-sion railhead on the tenth, 45 were transferred immediately to the hos-pital with flu or mumps; another 155 were hospitalized with flu with-in the next two days. Beeuwkes felt that the poor transportation arrangements helped to incubate the disease and, even more critical, that the men were now carriers, spreading influenza where it had not existed before.[86]

Culling the Officer Corps

Unfortunately, the condition of the troops was not improved by an able commissioned officer corps. A variety of problems in officer procure-ment and promotion brought many unsatisfactory individuals to the AEF, and the situation was worsened by the arbitrary relief of able men because of personality clashes and other difficulties unrelated to com-bat efficiency. At Pershing's order, the inspectorate became deeply involved in assessing officer efficiency and the pace of senior officer reliefs quickened greatly as the levels of combat rose in the fall of 1918.

Numerous postwar writers described General Pershing's policy as "ruthless." The AEF commander wanted dynamic leaders, tactically proficient and decisive, who also were strong disciplinarians. If an officer faltered or did not produce quick results, he was finished.

---

[85] Rpt, Britton to CG, Base Area [Sec] 3, SOS, 19 Oct 18, sub: Observations Concerning Embarkation and Transport of Troops During Epidemic of Influenza, Entry 26, RG 159, NARA.

[86] Memo, Beeuwkes to IG, AEF, 12 Oct 18, Entry 588, RG 120, NARA.

Between 1 September and 20 November 1918 General Brewster's office dealt with the cases of 152 relieved officers, 33 of whom were generals. In the first week of October alone, Pershing fired four brigade commanders. The summary relief of so many key people was characterized by Maj. Gen. William G. Haan, the 32d Division commander, as an "epidemic" conducted by the high command with little justification, and the demoralizing effects at battalion and regimental levels were severe.[87]

The situation almost went out of control. Following perfunctory investigations by division IGs, the administrative system took over, hustling the hurt and bewildered officers to a camp at Blois. As a result, the AEF chief of staff directed General Brewster to make the Advanced Headquarters IG office the controlling point for all such investigations, bringing those done at corps or at GHQ under its purview. Brewster and Baer immediately screened all IG levels to gather the cases under way and to identify any others needing action. By 15 October they had built a complete roster of all generals relieved in the AEF since its activation. Beginning 6 November, relieved officers were notified by wire and held at their senior headquarters until interviewed by an inspector. In this way, just before the armistice a semblance of order was restored to the unseemly sacking of the AEF leadership.[88]

Yet administrative attrition continued to be high until the end of hostilities. The stultifying effect of the ruthless policy adopted by Pershing unquestionably limited initiative. More tangibly, the movement of senior personnel impaired cohesion and damaged unit efficiency. The summary relief of so many senior officers was cited by inspectors as doing more harm than good, especially when it was discovered later that some had been cashiered undeservedly. Many others were fired for transient difficulties that might, in the long run, have led to their becoming better commanders. But men were given no latitude to learn. The VI Corps IG, Col. Samuel C. Vestal, summed up cogently: "The famous fighting units of past history were not made up of con-

---

[87] Coffman, *War To End All Wars*, pp. 330–31 ("ruthless" on p. 330). See also Box 2260, Officers Relieved, Entry 6; File 406, Relief Investigations, Entry 588; and Ltr ("epidemic"), Haan to CofS, AEF, 11 Mar 19, sub: Morale of Troops, Entry 15. All in RG 120, NARA.

[88] Memo, A.W.B. to Baer, 9 Oct 18, Entry 588; Memo, Spinks to ACofS, G–5, AEF, 12 Oct 18, Entry 590; Ltr, Baer to Spinks, 18 Oct 18, Entry 590; Memo, IG, III Army Corps, to [blank] Div Insp, 14 Oct 18, Entry 590; Memo, Brewster to CofS, AEF, 23 Oct 18, sub: Relief of Officers, and Replies, 25 Oct and 3 Nov 18, Entry 590; and Ltr, AG, AEF, to IG, AEF, 6 Nov 18, sub: Relief of General Officers, Entry 590. All in RG 120, NARA.

stantly changing personnel . . . transferred into them one day out the next, and when the history of this war shall have been written, the same things will be found true."[89]

The impact of officer turbulence on the already shaky discipline of the force was reported by inspectors every day. The operations of late 1918 exposed the high degree of inexperience and little knowledge that characterized the officer corps as a group. Inspectors agreed in their final reports that poor discipline, limited training, and officer turnover were constant concerns and formed the root of most of the other problems they observed. The men's good character could not compensate for the lack of discipline and experience. Leadership deficiencies had to be "made up by using men in greater numbers with consequent greater losses."[90] Cumulatively, IG reports reflected the woefully low levels of competence throughout the American forces, which achieved success largely through the bravery of the soldiers. Victory was gained by the sacrifice of good men, often poorly led, who had had no opportunity to learn how to soldier and survive.

---

[89] Ltr (quotation), Vestal to IG, AEF, 25 Apr 18, sub: Report; Ltr, Haskell to IG, AEF, 5 Apr 19, sub: Report on Operation of the IGD in France. Both in Entry 588, RG 120, NARA.

[90] Rpt, Brewster to CinC, AEF, n.d., Entry 588, RG 120, NARA.

7

From War to Peace

By agreement between the allies and the German government, an armistice went into effect at 1100 hours, 11 November 1918. Division inspectors moved through their units, making sure the cease-fire was being observed. In some cases, providing the proper instructions to the fighting men proved to be difficult; some units of the 2d and 89th Divisions continued hostilities for an hour or more after 1100. All such events were documented, to counter any German charges of armistice violations.[1]

Armistice Aftermath

Once the cease-fire was in effect, American divisions established examining posts to assist returning French refugees and allied prisoners of war, delivered by truck to the allied lines and released. There the liberated prisoners were organized, interrogated, and evacuated via proper channels. Field army inspectors checked procedures and made sure that the troops understood their duties. However, ten days of intensive inspections and visits to various division headquarters were required before the system ran satisfactorily.[2]

With the end of the fighting, inspectors at all levels saw old duties replaced with new ones. Their burden of camouflage and light-discipline requirements was removed. But because lapses in troop discipline

---

[1] Edward M. Coffman, *The War To End All Wars: The American Military Experience in World War I* (New York: Oxford University Press, 1968), p. 355; Oliver L. Spaulding, *The Second Division: American Expeditionary Force, in France, 1917–1919* (New York: Historical Commission, Second Division Association, 1937), p. 224.

[2] Rpts, IGs, 1st and 2d Army, to IG, GHQ, AEF, 11–22 Nov 18, subs: Patrol and Examining Posts for Receiving Returning Prisoners of War, Entry 590, Record Group (RG) 120, National Archives and Records Administration (NARA), Washington, D.C.

were expected in the aftermath of the armistice, they now had to be alert for signs of trouble and to take immediate corrective measures. The IGs also were to include in their reports their views on how to maintain discipline.[3]

One immediate problem was fraternization with the enemy. The practice was strictly forbidden, and inspectors were required to include in their reports their suggestions on how to prevent it. But issuing the order proved to be easier than enforcing it. Colonel Ovenshine, inspecting division outposts in the center of the Second Army front on 12 November—the morning after the armistice—found German troops panhandling for food inside the 28th Division lines. At one outpost he encountered a crowd of forty Americans and even more Germans laughing, talking, and exchanging souvenirs. While he was there, several groups of Americans were seen returning from the German lines. None of the sentries carried their rifles. Neither the guards nor the other Americans knew of any fraternization prohibitions; the guards had been given no special instructions. The troops reluctantly complied with the inspector's orders to break up their gatherings and remove the Germans from the American lines.[4]

Colonel Ovenshine found the same situation in the adjacent sector held by the 33d Division. Officers in charge of various outposts claimed to have received no guidance, and they were doing nothing to prevent the former enemies from mixing. Nearly everywhere guards went unarmed. A German officer approaching an outpost under a flag of truce was not noticed until Ovenshine called attention to him. Division inspectors seemed to be making little effort to inform the troops of their duties, as required by General Brewster at Advanced Headquarters and General Spinks at General Headquarters (GHQ). Ovenshine brought the problem to the attention of the respective division chiefs of staff. He also briefed the Second Army commander, General Bullard, who directed his own chief of staff to assure that the nonfraternization policy was disseminated properly.[5]

The apparent failure of unit inspectors to monitor nonfraternization might be explained at least in part by the press of more familiar duties. Investigations begun before the cease-fire had to be concluded properly, and command problems, burial of the dead, cases of POW abuse, and the animal inspection program demanded their attention. General

[3] Memo, Johnson to Corps Insps, 10 Nov 18, Entry 590, RG 120, NARA.

[4] Memo, Ovenshine to Brewster, 12 Nov 18, sub: Daily Report of Inspector General, 2d Army, Entry 590, RG 120, NARA.

[5] Ibid., and 15 Nov 18, same sub, Entry 590, RG 120, NARA.

Pershing also ordered a special investigation into casualty reporting, in an attempt to correct the questionable existing reports. But combat deaths continued to be discovered and reported well into December. Complicating the picture was a reorganization that caused the strong hand of Brewster's office to relax temporarily.[6]

As the Advanced Headquarters prepared to move forward into occupied Germany, all IG personnel briefly returned to Chaumont as, once again, GHQ AEF became the focal point of all inspection activities. Colonels Baer and McIlroy moved with a more streamlined Advanced Headquarters to Trier, where they served as IG liaison between GHQ and the occupation forces, forwarding daily reports on their observations for the use of Pershing and his staff. Meanwhile, Brewster's AEF inspectors continued to oversee items of interest to Pershing, such as senior officer conduct. Most of their efforts, however, were directed to problems affecting the withdrawal of the AEF from Europe, which necessitated a series of trips to the seaports involved. Another area of concern was the care and evacuation of wounded and sick. In January 1919 the AEF inspectors checked all convalescent camps, hospitals, hospital trains, and hospital ships in France. During subsequent months they concentrated on medical facilities and embarkation centers. They maintained such a rigorous schedule until Pershing and Brewster were satisfied that the system was working well.[7]

Beginning in December 1918, the AEF's IG office began to refer increasing numbers of cases requiring investigation to the commands where the incidents occurred. As a result of the growing work load, additional officers were attached to IG offices at all levels. Field army inspectors took the lead in matters directly affecting their organizations, such as monitoring troop discipline and animal care. The quality of life for the troops was a pressing concern, as the First Army IG, Colonel Johnson, made plain. Many of the troops in his command were in poor health, still living in the crudest field conditions, and lacking both the leadership and the discipline that were needed to improve their lot. Johnson predicted a major scandal unless inspectors took action. He believed that they should become directly involved in training battalion-level officers in the elementary tasks of caring for their men and strongly pressed for a vigorous effort to ameliorate the appalling conditions he described.[8]

---

[6] Memos, Brewster to CinC, AEF, 20 Nov and 10, 31 Dec 18, Entry 588; Memo, Johnson to IG, AEF, 21 Nov 18, Entry 590. All in RG 120, NARA.

[7] File 406, IG, AEF, Selected Schedules, 1 Jan–31 May 19, Entry 588, RG 120, NARA.

[8] Ibid.; Ltr, Johnson to Spinks, 23 Dec 18, Entry 590, RG 120, NARA.

Organizational Inspections and Reports

In 1918, while serving as a corps and army inspector, Colonel Johnson observed that several divisions had established their own extensive internal inspection systems to supplement the activities of their overworked assigned inspectors. In one regiment of the 26th Division the executive officer also functioned as the "organization inspector," monitoring all unit supply and administrative matters. The 42d Division also formally set up a similar practice as early as May 1918. The division commander required that each subordinate unit appoint an experienced officer—usually the unit's executive officer—to function as the organization inspector. The latter's supervision rested with the division inspector, who held weekly conferences to answer questions, give instructions, and discuss issues of current concern. As a result, in this atmosphere of cooperation and uniform practices, division problems were identified and solved quickly.[9]

Colonel Johnson, at the time the I Corps IG, was favorably impressed by the system and recommended it to other senior-level inspectors, some of whom were reaching similar conclusions from their own experiences. The IV Corps IG, Colonel Carpenter, wrote to the AEF's IG office in August 1918, urging adoption of a similar system throughout the AEF. He had observed inspection systems in nine different divisions as they came under the IV Corps' control. In some, inspection was systematic and well organized; in others, haphazard and limited. Carpenter felt that uniform inspection practices throughout his corps were essential to efficiency and discipline. A method already existed: AEF Bulletin No. 44, 7 July 1918, required that an officer in each regiment and separate smaller unit be made responsible for all administrative and logistical matters in the unit, in order to give commanders more time to lead their units. Carpenter judged that making these officers the equivalent of the 42d Division's organization inspectors would be a simple matter of modifying the existing bulletin. The imminence of the St. Mihiel attack prevented implementation of Carpenter's idea at the time. However, his proposal kept the concept prominent among senior inspectors.[10]

Thoughtful about the expected decline in troop discipline and the demonstrated inexperience of junior leaders, Colonel Johnson, now the

---

[9] Memo (quoted words), Johnson to CofS, AEF, n.d.; 42d Div, AEF, Memo 165, 4 May 18, and Memo 191, 30 May 18; Memo, Jenkins to Insp, 1st Army Corps, 19 May 18. All in Entry 799, RG 120, NARA.

[10] Memo, Johnson to CofS, AEF, n.d., Entry 799; Ltr, Carpenter to Spinks, 26 Aug 18, Entry 588. Both in RG 120, NARA.

First Army IG, sought to revive the concept in a more comprehensive form. On 10 November he proposed that AEF policy require an officer in every unit, from the battalion level upward, be designated to serve as the organization inspector to monitor conditions affecting discipline. As a group, they would become part of a coordinated inspection chain, extending from their level up to GHQ AEF. Johnson's subordinate IGs favored the idea, as did Generals Brewster and Pershing.[11]

Johnson's scheme became policy in the First Army's General Order 38, issued on 24 November 1918. The formal order mandated not only the appointment of an officer in each regiment, battalion, and company to assist the commanders in developing "soldierly qualities" but also weekly regimental-level meetings of the officers, with the division inspector in attendance. A sixteen-page questionnaire, which covered activities within the unit area—such as kitchens, latrines, and billets—and, of growing concern to commanders, more sensitive issues of animal care and motor transport, was attached as an enclosure. The elementary nature of the questions reflected Johnson's low opinion of leadership at small-unit levels. Inspectors were expected to find out if mess sergeants could cook, if troops were using proper latrines, and if soldiers were being required to bathe. Weapons were to be examined for rust and the stables checked to ensure that the horses were being fed regularly.[12]

The officers designated under General Order 38 usually were the executive officers or adjutants, who were to be trained or at least assisted by the division inspector and his staff. The concept called for having the respective chain of command involved to the greatest extent possible in detecting and correcting unit problems. Since division IGs hitherto had been encountering the same or similar deficiencies repeatedly, Johnson believed that the new approach would give commanders the information and motivation necessary to stop the cycle of recurring defects. The plan was based ultimately on establishing a thoroughgoing system of responsibility from the NCO level upward, and training unit NCOs in the new standards and requirements was to be the first step. Ideally, Johnson hoped that IGs eventually would become teachers and observers of those doing the actual checking, freeing them to concentrate on major problems rather than revisiting the minor ones again and again.[13]

---

[11] Note, Johnson to Brewster, with Baer comment and encl., 10 Nov 18, Entry 590, RG 120, NARA.

[12] First Army, AEF, GO 38, 24 Nov 18, OTIG files, Pentagon (SAIG-ZXH).

[13] Ibid.

The ultimate goal was to make the chain of command function as it should, by giving commanders the chance to make their own corrections rather than receive endless adverse reports from outsiders. Close supervision by the inspection chain was necessary, however, until unit personnel gained confidence and experience. Each regimental commander was briefed on the factors that indicated good or poor discipline, such as sanitation and appearance. In turn, he and his organization inspector, with IG help, were expected to train their subordinate leaders. The IGs assisted as required, discussing the purpose of the inspection with junior leaders and pointing out ways of correcting deficiencies.[14]

General Liggett, commanding the First Army and later the Third Army, stressed to division commanders and their IGs that the key to the system's success was the quality of the unit personnel selected and the degree of supervision given them. Some units saw General Order 38 as an opportunity to offset the inexperience of their officers by making nearly all of them an expert in something. Assistants to the organization inspector were appointed, and each developed expert knowledge in one or two areas of concern. The result was a marked improvement in unit conditions and attitudes as many officers, for the first time, became aware of War Department and AEF requirements. The scheme was embellished in some divisions by rotating the topical responsibilities among unit officers, gradually broadening their understanding and expanding their expertise.

Implementation of the new program, however, was slow. Johnson reported that few concrete changes had taken place by mid-January 1919. The high-quality officers needed to make the program work often were not appointed. Some officers proved reluctant to exercise their authority to correct deficiencies. As Johnson bitterly wrote, "There is a more conscientious effort on the part of the average enlisted man to properly perform his duties than is apparent in some officers." In other cases, unit commanders failed to give the program the support it needed to be successful. Although inspection reports showed that most units were making efforts, 90 percent of the deficiencies noted were the same old recurring ones. Nevertheless, many people proved amenable to instruction, and Johnson told subordinate inspectors to make their visits into training sessions to help junior leaders understand what was expected of them.[15]

---

[14] Ltrs, Johnson to Dallam, 28 Dec 18, and Johnson to IG, AEF, 22 Mar 19, sub: Information for Report on American E. F., Entry 588, RG 120, NARA.

[15] Memo, Johnson to Corps Insps, 15 Jan 19, Entry 1138, RG 120, NARA.

Johnson's own role consisted primarily in briefing division and corps commanders on the value of the system. In his opinion, gaining the major commander's support and training the unit inspectors so that they could train others knowledgeably and tactfully were critical. He shared with Colonel Dallam of V Corps his positive experiences with division commanders, many of whom offered to support their inspectors' efforts to implement an effective system. In one case, a division commander promised his inspector as many assistants as he needed. Johnson urged the corps inspectors to carry on a steady program of senior-officer education to assure ever-widening support for the developing program.[16]

In the V Corps Colonel Dallam personally conducted classes for inspectors in all corps units and other units that were tenants within the corps area. He briefed commanders on the meaning and intent of the new inspection program and agreed to an arrangement intended to reduce the danger of over-inspection. The corps G–3 kept a roster of all staff officers making inspections, including the IG. The object was to have every division in the corps visited daily by someone from the headquarters. Colonel Dallam saw this rule as a limit on his flexibility, but went along with it in the name of harmony and to sustain the evident command interest in promoting the inspection program. As he told Colonel Johnson, "Keeping everlastingly at it brings success."[17]

Outside the First Army, old problems festered. When Colonel Baer led an AEF team on a routine inspection to the 32d Division in mid-February 1919, the inspectors encountered numerous small problems, especially in the so-called discipline indicators; apparently, the division IG had not been performing as required. Other inspectors made the mistake of confusing carping with constructive criticism and suggestions with commands. Criticism without correction too often led to demoralization and resentment, defeating the whole purpose of the program. Baer admitted in May that "young and inexperienced inspectors who delighted to show off by giving orders to their seniors or by running in, making notes and running away without acquainting the commanding officer of the mistakes noted, occasioned much irritation and adverse criticism."[18]

---

[16] Ibid.

[17] Memos, Dallam to IG, First Army, 16 (quotation) and 19 Jan 19, and Dallam to G–1, V Corps, 22 Jan 19, sub: Conference, Entry 1138, RG 120, NARA.

[18] Memo, Baer to CG, 3d Army Corps, 7 Feb 19, sub: Inspections, Entry 590; Memo, Baer to Brewster, 7 Feb 19, sub: Inspection of 32d U.S. Division Stationed With Headquarters at Ringsdorf, Entry 590; Memo, Baer to IG, AEF, 11 Feb 19, Entry 590; and Ltr, Haan to CoS, AEF, 11 Mar 19, sub: Morale of Troops, Entry 15. All in RG 120, NARA. See also Ltr (quotation), Baer to IG, USA, 8 May 19, sub: Personal Service in the Inspector General's Department, Entry 26, RG 159, NARA.

The frustrations from this sort of inspection can easily be imagined. Unquestionably, some IGs showed more zeal than sense while making inspections, creating bitterness towards inspectors and the Inspector General's Department (IGD) in a generation of officers. Senior commanders were angered. In March 1919 Maj. Gen. John L. Hines, then commanding II Corps, wrote to General Pershing, expressing his resentment of developments in the inspectorate. He disliked the growth of Brewster's oversight and the proliferation of inspectors. He disapproved of their authority to give orders, rather than simply to inspect and report their findings. Hines said he feared that if the trend continued there would be "a usurpation of functions of the General Staff." His view was shared by several other senior officers who would carry their dislike into postwar reorganization debates.[19]

General Pershing believed that most of the shortcomings coming to his attention were due to inexperience and a "want of instruction," not intentional neglect. He saw the inspectors' main role as training and instructing the units they visited, for they "had exceptional opportunities for imparting useful information and instruction," and he urged that they establish a good relationship with young officers and NCOs to allow the easy flow of information. He cautioned that criticisms should always be accompanied by explanations and remedial suggestions, judging that by the "exercise of courtesy, tact and patience, inspectors would be welcomed, even sought." Directed to implement Colonel Johnson's First Army program in the other two field armies, Brewster sent his inspectors a letter, in which he summarized Pershing's views and to which he attached a copy of the First Army's General Order 38 reissued as an unnumbered AEF pamphlet. Brewster warned: "The prestige of the department and of inspectors depends entirely on the personality of the inspectors."[20]

Some problems remained. The periodic reports, although changed from daily to once every ten days, continued to be required so long as General Pershing was in Europe. The continuing problems of discipline and control prompted GHQ AEF to attempt to use the reports to fix responsibility for the failures noted by inspectors. Maj. Gen. James W. McAndrew, the AEF chief of staff, wanted the reports to do more than to indicate general conditions: "We want to know where the fault lies." This, of course, would have destroyed the deli-

---

[19] Memo, Hines to CinC, AEF, 16 Mar 19, Entry 15, RG 120, NARA.

[20] Ltr (Pershing quotations), Brewster to IGD, AEF, Offs, 18 Feb 19, Entry 588, RG 120, NARA.

cate relations of helpful confidentiality being built under General Order 38.[21]

Colonel Baer at the Advanced Headquarters IG office in Trier successfully resisted the requirement. He pointed out that the purpose of the reports was only to give impressions and to record corrections or improvements made. Many were extracts from reports made by inspectors for their own commanders. Time would be needed to accord blame in what essentially would be a small investigation, and the delay would erode the greatest value of the reports, which was their timeliness. Gross irregularities already were investigated as a matter of course, and Baer proposed to keep the headquarters more fully informed on such investigations. His proposals were accepted, and the reports were modified accordingly.[22]

Beginning in February, all irregularities cited in the periodic reports had to be corrected at the proper unit level. The local inspector and one superior were required to monitor the situation until rectified and the army inspector to maintain oversight on the progress of any corrections. Issues beyond the control of subordinate units and IGs were the responsibility of the army inspector. Some he referred to other army elements. Most, however, were personnel and supply matters, for example, complaints about rest billets and the distribution of bloodstained clothing from salvage units, which the army IG referred to the Services of Supply (SOS) after coordinating with the G–1 and G–4. Problems of an overlapping nature, such as coordinating with railroads to synchronize troop leave with train schedules, received the attention of the army IG himself because of his connections and comprehensive views.[23]

The monthly discipline report continued to be required. As of March 1919, army inspectors also included comments on what the local IG and other officers in the command had done to improve the morale of the troops. By then the report had become a formatted survey, which could be filled in within a few minutes. Its major topics were officers' duties, courts-martial, sanitation and health, training, and general discipline (including morale). The perfunctory aspects of the form appar-

---

[21] Memo, Spinks to All IGs, 11 Dec 18, Entry 590; Telg (quotation), McAndrew to ACofS, Adv Hq, Treves [Trier], 5 Jan 19, Entry 590; Ltr, Gordon to Johnson, 20 Dec 18, Entry 799. All in RG 120, NARA.

[22] Memo, Conger to IG, AEF, 5 Jan 19; Memo, Baer to ACofS, Adv Hq, 7 Jan 19; and Memo, Baer to IG, 2d Army, 10 Jan 19, sub: Daily Reports. All in Entry 590, RG 120, NARA.

[23] Memo, Johnson to IG, AEF, 23 Feb 19, sub: Action on 10-Day Reports, Entry 590, RG 120, NARA.

ently minimized its value, considering the amount of work it represented. Nevertheless, General Pershing wanted to see the report, along with summaries of the periodic reports, and his marginalia and requests to Brewster and Spinks for more information are evidence that he perused them seriously.[24] The commander-in-chief's effort to exert control through his inspectors remained as strong as ever.

Complaints and Grievances

The underlying cause of many of the problems faced by inspectors was a general deterioration of morale among the American forces that resulted, not from specific failings, but from the armistice itself. The decline manifested itself in a general slackening of discipline and responsiveness on the part of the soldiers. "Men were not as willing to suffer as they were in the movement forward. Their packs grew heavy, their shoes hurt their feet."[25]

The troops had expected to defeat the Germans on the field of battle, and a sense of anticlimax followed the cease-fire. Personal problems suddenly seemed more pressing, and complaints at all levels became more numerous. Inspectors attempted to compensate by paying more attention to morale issues, such as rations, pay, and mail. But in the atmosphere of disillusionment and homesickness other issues loomed large. An order to stop all promotions on the day of the armistice upset many soldiers, especially those recommended for advancement because of their demonstrated performance on the job. A powerful incentive was withdrawn at one blow. At the same time, both officers and men complained bitterly about the excessively rigorous training program launched after the armistice, which in their view no longer had any purpose.[26]

The high command, on the other hand, believed that the deteriorating state of discipline justified the extensive training program. The armistice was seen at first as just that—a break in the hostilities rather than the end. It apparently was a godsend to those who had observed the AEF disintegrating in the Argonne, giving them another chance to transform what seemed little better than an armed rabble into a manageable force. Thus the program was adopted both to sustain disci-

---

[24] Memos, Spinks to Insps, 28 Mar 19; Memo, Spinks to Sec, GS, AEF, 5 Apr 19; and Memo, Spinks to CinC, AEF, 10 Jun 19. All in Entry 588, RG 120, NARA.

[25] David Lewis, "A Short Account of My Experiences in the American Expeditionary Forces in France, 1918–1919," OTIG files, Pentagon (SAIG-ZXH).

[26] Ibid.

pline and to provide the training most American soldiers had never been offered.[27]

But as the weeks passed and the likelihood of renewed hostilities diminished, resentment of the training program grew steadily. Most men had no objection to "a reasonable schedule of disciplinary drills and exercises" to keep them busy, but they had little tolerance for the rigorous program required by their leaders. Raymond Fosdick, now General Pershing's special assistant for morale, labeled the program as the biggest morale problem in the AEF. The policy, in his view, failed to take into account the need for constructive recreation and the dissatisfaction of the soldiers in the aftermath of the armistice.[28]

Although the troops had more sports and educational programs starting in early 1919, their living conditions remained poor and their commanders seemed indifferent. In December 1918 Maj. Edward C. Sammons, the 79th Division inspector, asked General Spinks for assistance, describing the dreary existence being led by the men of the division: They drilled outdoors in the wet until darkness fell at about 1600 and after supper sat around in their billets, with no lights and no heat, awaiting the next day. Reporting that the assigned YMCA representative was doing the best with what little he had, he petitioned Spinks to let the Red Cross and the YMCA know of the need for candles, reading matter, and indoor games. General Spinks complied, and the YMCA immediately sent the desired articles. Both agencies told Spinks that they assumed the 79th Division was not unique and began preparations to send similar items to other units requesting them. In retrospect, it is remarkable that an informal IG action was needed to obtain this kind of support, and even more surprising that the request did not originate in command channels.[29]

For the soldier, redress of grievances was expected to be handled through military channels. Paragraph five of the 1913 regulations, still in effect, prohibited going outside Army command channels regarding such matters. Complaints written by soldiers directly to General Pershing were passed to Brewster's office for action. Many of the cases,

---

[27] Coffman, *War To End All Wars*, p. 358.

[28] Eli A. Helmick, "From Reveille to Retreat: Autobiography of Major General Eli A. Helmick," quotation, U.S. Army Military History Institute, Carlisle Barracks, Pa.; Raymond B. Fosdick, *Chronicle of a Generation: An Autobiography* (New York: Harper and Brothers, 1958), pp. 180–82.

[29] Ltr, Sammons to IG, AEF, 14 Dec 18, sub: Morale of Troops; Ltr, Spinks to Carter, YMCA, 16 Dec 18, and Reply, 21 Dec 18; and Ltr, Semans, ARC, to Spinks, 15 Jan 19. All in Entry 588, RG 120, NARA.

whatever the source, dealt with minor abuses of authority and were found to be justified. Disciplinary actions were taken against the complainants only when it could be verified that their chain of command had publicized proper grievance procedures.

One case involved the many inductees who, after the armistice, sent unsigned letters to the newspaper *Stars and Stripes* in an effort to get some action on their complaints. Concerned with the pay problems and embarkation delays detailed in these stories, the AEF G–2 section, which had staff supervision over the newspaper, collected the letters in January 1919 and sent them to the AEF's IG office, where each allegation was checked. General Brewster, upset that the soldiers should have chosen to seek redress through the newspaper, questioned the propriety of a semiofficial journal condoning their action by publishing the letters. Hence, he recommended disciplinary action against the anonymous writers, and every effort was made to identify them.[30]

A similar issue was raised when a group of officer patients at Base Hospital No. 44 sent a joint letter to the AEF's adjutant general, complaining about poor food. An SOS inspector eventually looked into the matter and concluded that the hospital was doing the best it could under the circumstances. Citing the officers' action as unmilitary and a violation of the regulation, he recommended that each signatory to the letter be told to submit only individual complaints through channels in the future.[31]

As a rule, inspectors attempted to handle complaints processed by soldiers through the chain of command as informally as possible, even those posing court-martial charges against their superiors. Most problems derived from the mutual inexperience of the complainant and his superior. Even when complaints were justified, the conditions encountered in the combat zone were usually beyond anyone's control, no matter how unsatisfactory. Whenever a valid grievance was found, it was corrected and the case referred to the AEF judge advocate general if necessary. Complaints passed to inspectors during a visit were resolved whenever possible on site. Any of a general nature, which was the usual case at hospitals and casual camps, where food and inprocessing were

---

[30] Memo, Nolan to CofS, AEF, 13 Jan 19; Memo, Thomas to IG, AEF, 15 Jan 19, sub: Complaints Received by the Stars and Stripes. Both in Entry 588, RG 120, NARA. See also AReg 1913, par. 5.

[31] Memo, AG, SOS, to CO, 18th Inf, 22 Jan 19, sub: Officers' Mess Base Hospital No. 44, Entry 588, RG 120, NARA. The first time the lodging of complaints was condoned outside channels came after the regulations were changed in January 1921. See AReg 20–10 (11), 1921.

frequent sources of soldiers' ire, the inspector would defer to local command channels.[32]

Another source for complaints was information provided by officers. An example was an investigation in February 1919 of the Casual Officers Camp at Angers. A medical colonel on his way home wrote a description of his outprocessing experience to a colleague at GHQ AEF, who in turn showed it to a G–4 logistics officer. The latter then forwarded it to the AEF's IG office, with the comment that similar rumors were circulating about Angers. Shortly thereafter, Colonel McIlroy verified the allegations: Officers languished for up to a month before securing homeward-bound transportation; discipline in the company-grade barracks was excessive; quarters were in an abandoned hospital complex, with ten to a room and the floor a sea of mud; venereal checks were mandatory regardless of grade; and there was even an officer punishment pen. Such humiliations compounded the indiscipline of many of the temporary officers, and virtually guaranteed postwar enmity toward the Army. Although a new commander was brought in to ameliorate conditions, the physical and organizational conditions were part of a greater problem pervading the Services of Supply.[33]

Complaints about conditions came from the civilian sector as well, lodged by friends and relatives of the soldiers. The Office of the Inspector General in Washington reviewed all submissions. Those that appeared to have substance were referred to the AEF for investigation, and the remainder were handled with a polite explanatory letter to the complainant. Inquiries from members of Congress generally went first to the Secretary of War and then to the Inspector General. Senator Joseph S. Frelinghuysen of New Jersey, as the head of a committee investigating the treatment of soldiers, was a particularly prolific source.[34]

Discharged soldiers also related stories to their hometown newspapers, which were often published in embellished form with no attempt at verification. Some issues raised in this way entered Army channels as a result of a congressional or War Department inquiry. Regardless of the source, each case was investigated. In a few

---

[32] Ltr, Bacharach to SofW, 26 May 19, sub: Investigation of William Miller Who Reported Mistreatment in Letter to His Sister; Ltr, Green to TAG, 26 Feb 19, sub: Complaint Against Officers. Both in Entry 588, RG 120, NARA.

[33] Lewis, "Short Account," OTIG files, Pentagon (SAIG-ZXH); Ltr, Shirley to Philips, with encls., 26 Jan 19, Entry 588, RG 120, NARA.

[34] Ltr, Miller to CG, Base Sec I [1], 10 Apr 19, sub: Report of Investigation of Col. James K. Parsons on Letter of James King; Ltr, Frelinghuysen to Keppel, 18 Mar 19; and Ltr, Robert to Pershing, 3 Apr 19. All in Entry 588, RG 120, NARA.

instances a responsible editor might forward a proposed item prior to publication to either Secretary Baker or General Pershing himself. For example, the editor of the *Chicago Tribune* asked the AEF to look into a veteran's claim that hundreds of gas victims were dying because of deplorable hospital conditions at Le Mans. Hospital operations were investigated thoroughly; detailed statistics were gathered on admissions and deaths at all facilities in the huge hospital center; and disabilities, diseases, and lengths of treatment were tabulated. No evidence of any of the alleged mistreatment or abuse could be found. In fact, it was proven that only eleven gas casualties had died over the entire period. The accusations were labeled as being completely unfounded. This information was passed to the *Tribune* editor, who— perhaps weary of waiting—had published the spurious story a few days before learning the facts.[35]

Welfare Organizations

A major source of complaints was the civilian welfare organizations, especially the YMCA. Problems with their overseas activities had been simmering for some time. In the months following the outbreak of hostilities the YMCA and, to a lesser extent, the Red Cross increasingly became the objects of aversion and criticism, and by the time of the fall offensives in 1918 relations between the these two agencies and the War Department were decidedly cool.

Before America's entry into the war in the spring of 1917, the YMCA had its representatives in Europe working with the allied forces. At the recommendation of Edward C. Carter, who was in charge of the YMCA's overseas operations, several of them were diverted to support the first U.S. military contingents to arrive in France. In May a recreation center was opened in Paris. From this base the YMCA secured a foothold in AEF welfare activities, and, along with several smaller charitable groups, ultimately assumed responsibility for all such activities in the command. Unfortunately, this useful and indeed necessary support began to breed problems, for the organizations, having their own overhead and logistical demands, competed—not cooperated— with each other. Their uncoordinated work for the troops resulted in a chorus of complaints throughout 1918. The soldiers charged a lack of command support. The commanders, who viewed military morale and welfare as an Army problem, objected to the usurpation of their respon-

---

[35] Memo, Burleson to IG, AEF, 5 May 19, sub: Investigation of Le Mans Area, Entry 588, RG 120, NARA

"Y.M.C.A." *The recreation tent was one of the YMCA's few field facilities for the troops in France.*

sibilities. Some even complained that YMCA's practices were conducive to poor morale and indiscipline.[36]

By November the complaints and criticisms led General Chamberlain to conclude that the civilian organizations could not sustain their operations indefinitely and that it was more appropriate for the Army to assume responsibility for the support of its own welfare and morale services. He advised inspectors overseas to be prepared to monitor the establishment of theaters and exchanges. He suggested in a letter to General Brewster that the issue be raised with General

[36] Jameson Ltr to the Editor, *New York Times*, 13 May 22, p. 12; Daniel R. Beaver, *Newton D. Baker and the American War Effort, 1917–1919* (Lincoln: University of Nebraska Press, 1966), pp. 223–24; Fosdick, *Chronicle*, p. 182; Peyton C. March, *The Nation at War* (Garden City, N.Y.: Doubleday, Doran and Co., 1932), pp. 213–16.

Pershing and the AEF G–4 so that contingency plans could be made to establish accounts and sign over property.[37]

Meanwhile, on 28 December the general secretary of the YMCA National War Council, John R. Mott, wrote to the War Department, requesting an official investigation of his organization's European operations. He enclosed a number of critical letters and asked that they be submitted to the AEF's IG office. At the same time, Carter asked Katherine Mayo, an author known for her investigative reporting on state government, to come to France to conduct her own review. Although Mott alleged only a desire to improve the YMCA's operations, he and Carter probably hoped to see their organization exonerated, both officially and before the public.[38]

Secretary Baker's office forwarded the letters through channels to the AEF IG's office, with the request that General Brewster investigate the validity of the allegations. Brewster assigned the task to Brig. Gen. John J. Bradley, an 1891 graduate of the U.S. Military Academy serving as commander of the 163d Infantry Brigade. As a member of the Washington State Bar since 1908, he had gained considerable experience as a judge advocate before the war. Accordingly, Bradley formed an inspection team, which reviewed the letters and decided to focus its inquiry on fifteen general topics. But the team soon had to broaden its original scope. Complaints from veterans and their families about the YMCA's overseas activities had not abated, and in January and February Secretary Baker passed on the new allegations through General Pershing, requesting that they be added to the original directive. The result was a massive effort that involved virtually every inspector in the AEF between February and June 1919.[39]

Upon assuming direction of the YMCA investigation, General Bradley quickly refined its scope, directing that inquiries would be made down through company level. He then detailed special investigators to units lacking inspectors of their own and disseminated information to the troops. Shortly after the investigation was under way, Mott requested that the amount and value of work performed by the YMCA also be evaluated—evidently an attempt to add a positive note to the original, almost purely negative focus on complaints. General Brewster agreed to Mott's request, although Pershing emphasized that the inves-

---

[37] Ltr, Chamberlain to Brewster, 22 Nov 18, Entry 588, RG 120, NARA.

[38] Book review of Katherine Mayo, *That Damn Y: A Record of Service Overseas* (Boston: Houghton Miffin Co., 1920), *New York Times*, 27 Jun 20, pp. 9, 30; Ltrs, Bradley to Brewster, 9 and 13 Apr 20, Entry 588, RG 120, NARA.

[39] YMCA Investigation Records, Boxes 57–58, Entry 588, RG 120, NARA.

tigation should still deal principally with grievances. Once again, Bradley's inspection team had to broaden its approach.[40]

Both Brewster and Bradley understood the wider significance of the investigation. From the outset Bradley grasped the fact that it would supply the Army with vast amounts of data that could serve as a guide for developing welfare and morale activities in future emergencies. But the individual inspectors conducting the actual investigation saw it in simpler terms. They had three objectives: to ascertain the attitudes of the welfare workers and determine the efficiency and value of their operations to the soldiers; to develop a broad overview of the opinions of military personnel toward the agencies; and to express their own views on the type of morale and welfare organizations they felt would be the most appropriate to a force like the AEF. At unit level, the heaviest emphasis was on interviews with military personnel—in most cases, with individuals selected at random from men with good records in order to avoid the so-called chronic gripers. Welfare workers also were interviewed extensively, but their testimony was regarded as somewhat self-serving and not as significant as that of the soldiers.[41]

On 21 April General Brewster added the American Red Cross to the list of agencies to be investigated. Its unusual status was responsible for the delay. Unlike the other welfare organizations, the Red Cross formed an integral part of the AEF medical services. Its officers enjoyed equivalent-rank commissioned status and its ambulance corps members enlisted status. Each division had a Red Cross staff. Assigned throughout the Services of Supply, the Red Cross officers supervised the issue and distribution of medicines and materiel supplied by the organization; they also served as casualty representatives, gathering details on the killed and injured to keep families informed. Although Red Cross finances already were included in IG oversight, General Brewster decided that the entire organization should be examined to avoid the charge of favoritism. However, by the time of the decision, most of the inspectors had finished their welfare organization inspections or were close to doing so. In some cases, demobilization was by then taking place so quickly that no investigation could be made.[42]

---

[40] Bradley Conclusions of Final Report of YMCA Investigation, 30 Jun 19, Entry 588, RG 120, NARA.

[41] Ibid.; Rpt, Haskell to Brewster, 30 Jun 19, sub: Welfare Activities Covering All Observations in the AEF, Entry 588, RG 120, NARA.

[42] Department of the Army, Historical Division, *The United States Army in the World War, 1917–1919*, 17 vols. (Washington, D.C.: Government Printing Office, 1948), 16:424 (GO 139, 1918); Rpt, Morris to CG, 9th Corps, 25 Apr 19, sub: Investigation of Red Cross, Ninth Corps Troops, Entry 588, RG 120, NARA.

While Bradley's special inspectors were completing their overview of the activities of the welfare organizations and the soldiers' attitudes toward them, Fosdick was conducting an independent review for Pershing on the same subject. After visiting American units throughout Europe, he identified some morale issues—such as back pay—that were the Army's responsibility alone. However, he also developed strong views on the inappropriateness of having civilian organizations primarily responsible for the Army's morale and welfare activities. He cited the variation in service, particularly for frontline troops, and the unnecessary duplication of effort among the agencies. Fosdick submitted his report through Pershing to Secretary Baker in early June, which conveniently set the stage for General Bradley's YMCA investigation report published at the end of the month.[43]

The tone of Bradley's 1,300-page report inevitably was critical of the YMCA, reflecting both the genuine failings of the organization and also the exaggerated expectations it had raised but had failed to satisfy. While the YMCA had done a great deal of good work in France, its overall rating was found to be mediocre if not poor. Its most egregious mistake was operating the canteens—the equivalent of small post exchanges or ship's stores. YMCA officials had volunteered for the duty, telling General Pershing they could do it more efficiently than anyone else; they had persisted even when cautioned about the need for an increase in personnel, saying they could obtain the qualified staff. The YMCA apparently saw the canteen operation as a chance to increase its influence and prestige with the soldiers, to its own postwar advantage, but the results were quite different. The mismanagement of the canteens—surly clerks, inconvenient store hours, overpricing, and the sale of items originally marked as gifts—created a negative image of the YMCA in the minds of the troops.[44]

Fueling the soldiers' ire was the perception that the YMCA said one thing but did another. Despite the millions of dollars collected at home on the promise of providing aid and service to the soldier at the front and despite the commitments given to GHQ AEF, YMCA personnel showed little desire in cooperating with the military and supporting the

---

[43] Fosdick, *Chronicle*, pp. 182–84; Rpt, Fosdick to SofW, 1 Jun 19, sub: Activities of Welfare Organizations Serving With the AEF, OTIG files, Pentagon (SAIG-ZXH).

[44] Bradley Conclusions, 30 Jun 19, and Ltr, Bradley to Brewster, 9 April 20, sub: Comment on Letters to Mr. E. C. Carter Concerning Report of Investigation of Inspector General of the YMCA in the AEF by Avery D. Andrews and Warren Motley, Entry 588, RG 120, NARA. The YMCA was the only welfare organization that sold, rather than gave, sundries to the troops. The fact that it gave away supplies—and on a large scale—went unnoticed amid the charges of mismanagement.

frontline troops. Only 20 percent of the YMCA's overseas strength served with combat units. By comparison, 25 percent were on duty in Paris and the remainder on duty at base sections or leave areas. Thus, the soldiers were disappointed, many feeling that their families at home who had made contributions to the YMCA had been duped.[45]

The negative image also extended to YMCA personnel, whose healthy physical appearance caused many soldiers to judge membership on the YMCA staff as a way to evade military service and thus, rightly or wrongly, to perceive them as shirkers. Very few had the skills needed to handle their jobs and a significant number saw their job to be proselytizing Christianity, which the majority of the troops resented. Other compounding factors for the YMCA were its inefficient personnel system, which at one point had no record of 20 percent of its workers overseas, and its unrealistic and inadequate personnel selection or management procedures. An adjunct to this was the lack of initiative shown by YMCA officials in the field. Too often, they gave the impression that the Army was there to serve them, further aggravating the mistrust between the two organizations.

General Bradley's huge IG report verified most of the original allegations against the YMCA, but he cautioned that its purpose was not to malign the many sincere workers who had helped the soldiers. He judged his findings to be "honest and conscientious," demonstrating in the final analysis that the YMCA had asked for and been given too heavy a job to do. He believed that the experience of the civilian welfare agencies in France clearly illustrated the need for the military to have its own services. More significantly, Bradley's report provided the basis for the development of the Army's own organization to take care of its recreational and welfare needs. In fact, the AEF was obliged to take over welfare programs as the civilian groups scaled down after the armistice; each major command appointed a welfare officer, usually one of its chaplains, to monitor all welfare, morale, and education activities. The completion of the report marked the end of the YMCA investigation, which proved to be one of the largest consumers of IG manpower in the period after the armistice.[46]

---

[45] Ltr, Bradley to Brewster, 9 Apr 20, Entry 588, RG 120, NARA. In contrast to the front, the YMCA's work at base sections was unquestionably good.

[46] Ibid (quoted words). On 25 January 1919, following the practice in the United States, chaplain activities in AEF units became an item of IG interest. On 17 February a special survey was begun on chaplain activities. See Memo, Spinks to All Insps, 17 Feb 19, sub: Report on Chaplains, Entry 588, RG 120, NARA.

Problems of Peace

Even while the YMCA investigation was going on, inspectors continued to deal with a growing variety of issues—some familiar but some peculiar to the postwar period. A large number of investigations concerned damage to civilian property, and in many cases the complaints lodged by the French were justified. Beehives, in particular, were frequent victims of the doughboy's attention (and his sweet tooth). However, inspectors had to be alert to the fact that the French were not always scrupulous about their claims for reimbursement, some of which were for amounts as little as 50 centimes. According to one inspector, "the old peasant merchant looked upon the sometimes extravagant American soldier as his natural prey."[47]

The movement and departure of units again raised the old problem of maintaining billeting and bivouac areas. AEF general orders covered the proper clearing and salvaging of such sites, but the matter became a special item of inquiry after the armistice. IGs were expected to implement corrective measures as soon as they identified any abuses or violations and were required to report units that did not comply so that disciplinary action could be taken. The task did little to endear them to unit officers. In the First Army IGs systematically checked out troop billets, then stables, depots, grounds, and unit transportation; departing units left details behind under the inspector's control to correct any problems that might be found. The program was considered essential to prevent the hopeless deterioration of sites that had to be used countless times by a variety of units.[48]

A problem profoundly affecting morale was the erratic AEF mail service. A matter of great concern to Secretary Baker throughout the war, its failings were not improved by the coming of peace. When the AEF first reached France, delivery of mail was the responsibility of U.S. Post Office Department civilians who accompanied the units overseas. Service was poor from the outset, in part because the civilian clerks could not cope with the rapid moves of the military units and refused to accept the austere field conditions. The volume of mail that they had to handle in the field overwhelmed the establishment of an effective organization. Afterward, the postal service was placed in the position of permanently—and unsuccessfully—trying to catch up.[49]

---

[47] Lewis, "Short Account," OTIG files, Pentagon (SAIG-ZXH).

[48] Memo, Johnson to All Insps, 20 Nov 18, Entry 590; Rpt, Burr to IG, AEF, 18 Apr 19, sub: Supplemental Report 7th Div. AEF, Entry 797. Both in RG 120, NARA.

[49] Frederick Palmer, *Newton D. Baker: America at War*, 2 vols. (New York: Dodd,
Continued

Relatively few complaints were received at IG offices about neglect or failed accountability. The major issue was misdirected or late mail. Numerous investigations revealed the causes to be a lack of postal personnel and inefficient procedures. Neither the postal service nor the AEF adjutant general maintained a central locator file for the routing of mail, and consequently a soldier's letters would follow him from place to place, rarely catching up. New York port authorities became painfully cognizant of the real magnitude of the problem in January 1919, when 22 million pieces of undelivered mail for soldiers were dumped at a port of Hoboken warehouse for rerouting or return.[50]

Some improvements were seen in mail management. Inspectors recommended locating division post offices at railheads, rather than with the headquarters, allowing the breakdown and distribution of mail along with rations. Better unit locator cards were adopted, becoming an item of inspection, and each company was authorized a mail clerk to handle postal and locator problems. Even though inspectors called attention to the low priority given mail leaving the United States in relation to other cargoes, little changed. By the summer of 1918 the Army had assumed full operation of the mail system in Europe, but the complaints over delays and damage continued, making mail service a constant IG item of interest at all echelons. As late as September, General Chamberlain was still advising Secretary Baker that the "mail problem has not yet been satisfactorily solved." The difficulty posed by the rapid movement of men and units and the consequent delays in mail delivery was never really overcome while the fighting lasted.[51]

After the armistice, when soldiers found little if any justification for inconvenience, complaints over late or undelivered mail increased. Even inspectors were not immune. A corps IG told General Brewster that his wife had received only 20 percent of the letters he had sent her, and he warned of the effect of such an unreliable system on the troops' morale. An exhaustive investigation of the Postal Service, begun immediately after the armistice, suggested that accurate personnel accountability was the key to improvement. However, by this time the

---

Mead and Co., 1931), 2:404; David C. Shanks, *As They Passed Through the Port* (Washington, D.C.: Cary Publishing Co., 1927), pp. 275–76; Ltr, Read IG, AEF, 27 Mar 19, sub: Report in Compliance With Instructions in Your Letter of February 23, 1919, Entry 588, RG 120, NARA.

[50] Ltr, Read to IG, AEF, 27 Mar 19, Entry 588, RG 120, NARA; Shanks, *As They Passed*, pp. 275–76.

[51] Ltrs, Read to IG, AEF, 27 Mar 19, and Elmore to IG, AEF, 25 Jun 19, sub: Report From Observations of AEF, Entry 588, RG 120, NARA; Palmer, *Baker*, 2:404 (Chamberlain quotation).

issue had begun to solve itself, at least in part. Under the conditions of peace, units became more stable and the mail backlog was eliminated. Once the occupation forces were in place, an express rail system brought further improvements. Indeed, with the system functioning at an acceptable level, an IG was reprimanded for exaggerating the problems that remained.[52]

But by January 1919 some of those problems had begun to take on a more sinister aspect. Theft, pilferage, and a general mishandling of the mails were new areas of IG concern in the ensuing months. No sooner were mail bottlenecks solved at the unit level than others appeared in the pipeline between the ports and the major commands. As late as March some 85,000 Christmas packages were still on hand and undeliverable, which inspectors attributed in part to the poor training of the postal clerks. At the same time, however, the ransacking of the mail added an unsettling dimension and pointed to growing indiscipline and crime along the rail system.[53]

Railroads After the Armistice

During the fighting General Spinks' office had handled a number of railroad-related cases, most involving such disciplinary problems as troops riding on top of railcars or vandalizing the rolling stock. More ominous cases began to appear in December 1918, when an Italian supply train was held up and plundered. The IG investigation found that no Americans were involved, but the same could not be said of later cases. Eventually, four GHQ inspectors formed a team that did nothing but investigate systematic looting on American supply trains in France.

The first week of February brought eleven railroad-related cases: five for looting and pilferage, three for vandalism, and another three for rail security failures. By the end of the month nearly half of the GHQ investigations were concerned with aspects of misconduct or criminal acts, many of them connected with the railroads. The situation was so critical that inspectors put special emphasis on railroad crime throughout March and April 1919.[54]

---

[52] Ltr, Haskell to IG, AEF, 5 Apr 19, sub: Report on Operation of the IGD in France; Memos, Brewster to CinC, AEF, 10 and 20 Nov 18; and Rpt, Baer to ACofS, Adv Hq, 23 Jan 19, sub: Non-receipt of Mail in 3d Division. All in Entry 588, RG 120, NARA.

[53] Ltr, Donaldson to IG, AEF, 15 Mar 19; Memo, Brewster to CinC, AEF, 20 Mar 19; and Ltr, Ovenshine to IG, AEF, 28 Mar 19, sub: Report. All in Entry 588, RG 120, NARA.

[54] Memos, Brewster to CinC, AEF, 10 Jan and 10, 20 Feb 19; File 406, IG, AEF, Selected Schedules, 10 Jan–20 Feb 19. All in Entry 588, RG 120, NARA.

Criminal activities were particularly rife among SOS troops in the Second Army area. The army loaned one of its inspectors, Lt. Col. Clyde R. Abraham, to the Services of Supply to observe and report on measures the Transportation Service was taking to safeguard goods in transit. After discussing the situation with the AEF G–4 and SOS officials and then checking the routes from the main regulating point at Liffolle-Le-Grand through occupied Germany and back, Abraham reached some disturbing conclusions. Nearly everyone in the Transportation Service appeared to be indifferent to safeguarding official property. Standard measures—such as sealing boxcars, convoying trains, inventorying cargo, and adopting antitheft policies—were ignored.[55]

In a few instances Abraham found that his presence was resented. Officers of the 21st Railroad Engineers Regiment stationed at Conflans openly avoided him. His requests for information were ignored, and the prevailing indifference and incompetence that he found was "unlike anything I had ever seen in the military service." Yet this was the exception, not the rule. In general, Abraham was courteously treated, and his recommendations were well received. Most problems, he discovered, were a result of inexperience and the virtually complete lack of military training among both officers and enlisted men. When the railroad units were first organized, those civilians with the necessary skills were rushed to France with little or no introduction to military life or military requirements.[56]

The indiscipline at Conflans was well known to inspectors. Train robberies and black-market activities were particularly bad in the area, and many members of the 21st Railroad Engineers Regiment were found to be involved in the crimes. As a result of earlier IG investigations, some regimental personnel were convicted of looting quartermaster rail cargoes and pilfering wine and rations from French and American trains. Because of Abraham's report, General Bullard loaned one of his best investigators to the Services of Supply, Lt. Col. George C. Lewis, with the mission of helping him to clean up the situation.[57]

Colonel Lewis immediately began to follow through on the cases uncovered by earlier inspectors. He, too, felt handicapped by the marked lack of cooperation from the regimental officers, which he characterized as collusion to protect the guilty. Lewis performed "a

---

[55] Rpt, Abraham to IG, SOS, AEF, 13 Feb 19, sub: Conditions in Transportation Service, Entry 588, RG 120, NARA.

[56] Ibid.

[57] Memo, Davis to TAG, 20 Oct 19, Entry 588, RG 120, NARA.

prodigious amount of work" in seeking to restore discipline and identify those who had broken the law, and he was not always gentle in doing so; his frustrations were sometimes apparent in the harshness of his questioning. Later, complaints about his manner became the basis of an IG investigation from General Chamberlain's Washington office. A lieutenant in the regiment, apparently something of a guardhouse lawyer, complained of unnecessary arrests and detentions. In the end Lewis was not only exonerated but commended for completing a difficult job under adverse conditions. More important, the special inspections were credited with reducing substantially the losses in railroad shipments.[58]

Because of the problems revealed by these special inspections, GHQ AEF directed commanders to take a greater interest in preserving and protecting property. Inspectors were required to report on how well depots complied with the policy, which stressed proper storage, accountability, security, and rail movements—the time of greatest vulnerability for government property. A daily report of the condition of freight cars arriving at the main rail depot at Is-sur-Tille was submitted through channels to the AEF's IG office. Each report listed the cars broken into, the kind of damage, and the type of stolen cargo. Using the reports, the AEF IG staff recorded any major thefts and maintained statistics, which facilitated a thorough analysis of the problems within the rail cargo system and the identification of defects. This information was passed to the SOS headquarters for remedial action. By March 1919 cargo security had improved to the point that pilferage ceased to be important. Individual larceny cases, however, continued to be investigated until the final American withdrawal from Europe.[59]

Beyond the realm of crimes was another trouble spot that bedeviled inspectors, namely, the enmity of French and German railway personnel servicing duty trains running between France and Germany. Numerous complaints were received about the hostility, which sometimes seemed to reverse the roles of friend and foe. The duty trains were made up in Germany with German equipment, but on their arrival in France the French habitually removed the cars that were in good condition and substituted broken or inferior units. French engineers refused to heat the cars so that American soldiers often were compelled to ride

---

[58] Ibid (quoted words); Rpt, Abraham to IG, SOS, AEF, 13 Feb 19, Entry 588, RG 120, NARA.

[59] AEF Bul 15, 21 Feb 19; Memo, Spinks to All Insps, 7 Mar 19, sub: Bulletin No. 15; and Memo, Spinks to ACofS, G–4, AEF, 6 Mar 19, sub: Daily Reports, Regulation Stations 1918–19. All in Entry 588, RG 120, NARA.

in windowless, heatless carriages in the middle of winter. Further, the French refused to recognize the German's baggage checking, and as a result all baggage on the France-bound trains was dumped at the border, creating a wild scene as the passengers tried to find their belongings in order to continue the journey. There was no problem going in the opposite direction.[60]

Beginning in January 1919, AEF inspectors gathered many statements about the difficulties of traveling on duty trains. Working through the SOS IG, they achieved a distinct improvement by early February. American Railway Transport officers rode the trains and served as conductors, while NCOs took charge of the baggage cars, supervising the French civilians and assuring greater cleanliness and reducing incidents in which poor equipment was substituted for good. No one, however, could persuade the French engineers to hook up their engine to the German cars to provide heat. To the end, a trip on the duty train remained something of an adventure.[61]

Special Administrative Inquiries

Confusion, indiscipline, and administrative disarray in the AEF led to a number of special inquiries by the inspectorate in the months following the armistice. A special inspection of all personnel records in the AEF was necessary both to tighten accountability and to identify AWOLs and deserters. Problems with records also could delay embarkation, because the War Department required that soldiers have up-to-date records, fully documented, before being sent home. Division and corps commanders were authorized to detail extra inspectors to get the job done quickly. The AEF adjutant general informally asked that all IGs make compliance with service record policies a special item of inquiry. When this approach proved unsuccessful, General Spinks issued a memorandum requiring all inspectors to make the necessary investigations to assure compliance.[62]

Faulty records keeping contributed to the unauthorized wearing of insignia and decorations, a practice that blossomed after the armistice. The situation became so flagrant that it brought a complaint to General Brewster from Col. George S. Patton, Jr., then a brigade commander

---

[60] Ltrs, Baer to Spinks, 7, 26 Jan and 10 Feb 19, Entry 590, RG 120, NARA.

[61] Memo, Wimberly to Spinks, 14 Feb 19, Entry 590, RG 120, NARA.

[62] Memo, Fifth Army Corps to Cdrs, 30 Nov 18, sub: Personnel Accountability, Entry 799; Memo, Davis to Brewster, 28 Oct 18, Entry 588; and Memo, Spinks to All Insps, 20 Nov 18, sub: Service Records, Entry 588. All in RG 120, NARA.

in the Tank Corps. Having encountered both officers and enlisted men whose chevrons showed more overseas service than they actually had and having heard rumors that the wound chevron and other awards were being similarly abused, Patton requested that action be taken before the wearing of such items became a "joke." Brewster and Spinks agreed, and the latter issued a memorandum on the subject in mid-December.[63]

Sheer carelessness precipitated a rather unusual and prominent IG investigation in the postwar period. The 305th Infantry of the 77th Division, which had acquitted itself well in combat, lost track of its colors while preparing to redeploy. The flags were left temporarily with a graves registration unit for a ceremony, then never reclaimed. Word of the loss led to an extensive special investigation that spread from Europe to the United States. An AEF inspector spent two weeks trying to track down units and individuals scattered throughout France and Germany, but the trail was cold. The case then passed to the War Department inspectorate, where several former 305th and graves personnel, civilians by then, were interviewed without success. U.S. Customs records for 1918 and 1919 were scanned to see if someone had mailed the colors home. General Chamberlain reviewed the case and closed it in February 1920. The fate of the colors remained a mystery.[64]

At the same time an even odder case, with considerable international notoriety, was under investigation. In January 1919 six U.S. artillery officers on leave in the Netherlands created a scandal when they tried to visit the ex-Kaiser, who was living there in exile. The leader of the group was Col. Luke Lea, a Tennessee guardsman and former U.S. Senator. General Bullard later speculated that Lea was trying to duplicate Frederick Funston's exploit in capturing guerrilla leader Emilio Aguinaldo during the Philippine Insurrection. However, the visit seemed in fact to be a spontaneous indiscretion on Lea's part. The men were traveling through the low countries with no specific destination, and when Colonel Lea learned that the Kaiser's place of exile was nearby, he apparently made a quick decision to call on him. Lea's action

---

[63] Ltr (quoted word), Patton to Brewster, 6 Dec 18, sub: Service and Wound Chevrons; Memo, Spinks to All Insps, 18 Dec 18, sub: Unauthorized Wearing of Chevrons, Badges, etc.; and Ltr, Donaldson to CG, SOS, 14 Mar 19, sub: Report of the Inspector General. All in Entry 588, RG 120, NARA.

[64] Ltr, Geyelin to IG, AEF, 14 May 19, sub: National and Regimental Colors of 305th Inf., 77th Division; Memo, Brewster to Chamberlain, 14 Feb 20. Both in Entry 588, RG 120, NARA.

flared into a major international incident, even briefly threatening the peace talks going on in Paris. A Dutch investigator more reasonably concluded that "the affair could be treated as a joke and would be of no consequence," except that one of the visitors stole an expensive ashtray from the Kaiser's estate as a souvenir.[65]

General Brewster selected Colonel Johnson to investigate the incident for the AEF. Johnson traveled throughout Belgium and Holland, carefully reconstructing the entire sequence of events. His findings portrayed a rather wild group of artillerymen out for a good time, using Army cars and drivers on their meandering jaunt and bending rules by their entry into neutral Holland. Johnson felt that Lea's status as a colonel and former senator merited his being court-martialed for behavior that could have had serious international consequences. General Pershing, however, settled for a sternly written reprimand and an immediate return to the United States, a prescription that abruptly ended the publicity surrounding the case.[66]

Embarkation

The postwar process of demobilization and its attendant problems dramatically increased the work load of the AEF inspectorate, especially in the area of the withdrawal from Europe. Soon after the armistice General Pershing sent General Brewster on a tour of the port facilities to get a firsthand feel for their condition and capabilities. He made a complete circuit during December, accompanied by an aide, his son Lt. Daniel B. Brewster, USMC, and Major Britton from the staff of Base Section No. 5. It was well for the Services of Supply that Pershing had relented and agreed to allow the overage but energetic Britton to serve in Europe. Britton's background in international shipping and his apprenticeship inspecting port activities at Hoboken made him invaluable at a time when an embarkation system had to be set up quickly to manage the flow of soldiers back to the United States. His linguistic abilities had enabled him to establish cordial relations with the French Transport Commission officials in New York, which he expanded while in France. These connections proved useful as he and the Brewsters

<hr/>

[65] Robert L. Bullard, *Personalities and Reminiscences of the War* (Garden City, N.Y.: Doubleday, Page and Co., 1925), p. 312; Memo (quotation), Bethel to CinC, AEF, 15 Feb 19, sub: Case of Col. Luke Lea, Entry 588, RG 120, NARA.

[66] Ltr Order, Brewster to Johnson, 16 Jan 19, and Rpt, Johnson to Brewster, 5 Feb 19, sub: Investigation Concerning Conduct of Colonel Luke Lea, 114th FA, AEF, and Party in Holland, Entry 588, RG 120, NARA.

made their rounds, advising the base section and port commanders on what was expected of them.[67]

Major Britton fast became the AEF IG expert on port activities and embarkation procedures from France. In December the AEF G–1 sent a wire to port commanders, specifying that each departing transport would be inspected for adequacy by a board of officers headed by an IG. Major Britton returned a detailed letter on this, with SOS concurrence, to General Brewster. He described at length the evolution of the Stateside port inspection system, emphasizing that special arrangements already had been made as far as inspection of Navy transports and suggesting that they be continued in France. Britton rejected the concept of a formal inspection board as too cumbersome and time-consuming, recommending instead that an IG and a medical officer make independent inspections, compare notes, and immediately see that deficiencies were remedied. The object of inspections in French ports should be to "determine deficiencies, if any, on incoming; to notify proper authority for remedy; take cognizance of progress of remedy; verify such by subsequent outgoing inspection; [and] make [a] report to the C.O. of the base." He also stressed that inspection procedures should be tailored to the idiosyncrasies of each port rather than be directed inflexibly from the higher headquarters.[68]

While he was getting the method of inspection changed, Britton developed thorough guidance for the St. Nazaire and Brest IGs at their request. His advice closely reflected the systems used at U.S. ports and obviously were the product of considerable experience. Critical areas were developing with local port authorities a system for the routine exchange of information on arrivals, departures, and loading schedules; checking and verifying ship capacities and lifesaving equipment, based on the criteria used by each nation; and assuring clean and adequate sleeping, lavatory, medical, and mess facilities. Britton also offered some pointers on dealing with a ship's officers , for example, the purser on a large liner or the chief officer on a commercial transport.[69]

The AEF Surgeon General's Department asked Britton for his views on the types of medical inspection appropriate to sea transportation. A few days later General Brewster told him to draft IG guidelines

---

[67] Ltr, Brewster to Donaldson, 24 Dec 18, and File 27, Reports, Entry 588, RG 120, NARA.

[68] Telg 203, Cavenaugh to CO, St. Nazaire, 4 Dec 18; Ltr (quotation), Britton to IG, SOS, 6 Dec 18, sub: Inspection of Transports. Both in Entry 588, RG 120, NARA.

[69] Memo, Britton to IGs Concerned, 6 Dec 18, sub: Notes for Inspection of Transports, Entry 588, RG 120, NARA.

for the movement of the sick and wounded. By then, it had become standard procedure for Navy commanders to give both the "rated invalid capacity" of their vessels and the patient category (ambulatory, mental, etc.) to Army port officials, who in return supplied a categorized patient roster of those being embarked. A copy of each roster was given to the IG overseeing the embarkation. After verifying it, he retained it as a passenger record until receiving confirmation that the voyage was completed safely and subsequently turned it over to the theater adjutant general for filing. With this as the basis, Britton prepared an entire embarkation medical inspection program, outlining several steps for IGs and medical inspectors to follow.[70]

According to Britton, port medical regulating officers, not IGs, were responsible for determining a patient's evacuation status. They were to select the stretcher and ambulatory cases that could be treated as "progressed convalescents" (beyond any need for intensive care), because of the limited medical facilities aboard ship. The selection and designation of units and casuals and their medical examination was made preferably at interior points; but, regardless, no one in theory sailed without a full health check. Britton stressed that port medical facilities had to be enlarged not only to handle the larger transient population but also to hold personnel rejected for travel for medical reasons. IGs were to oversee port reception arrangements and procedures, ensuring that the departing soldiers had proper clothing, equipment, and documentation, as well as adequate food and shelter. And to avoid crowding and waiting exposed at dockside, Britton suggested that inspectors facilitate the sequencing of ground transportation arrangements to coincide with the arrival of ships in port.[71]

A final medical check was required at embarkation, when inspectors, whether dealing with medical cases or healthy passengers, performed essentially the same duties. Admittedly, more technical knowledge was necessary to judge the adequacy of a ship's sleeping, lavatory, mess, medical, and other facilities for the wounded. Britton recommended that IGs make a final inspection of the loaded vessel to assure that there was no overcrowding, that proper equipment was on board, and that no last-minute deficiencies had developed. In his judgment, with which Brewster concurred, the inspectors' main objective should

---

[70] Memo (quoted words), Fiske to CO, USS *Mallory*, 15 Nov 18, sub: Transportation of Disabled Soldiers to the U.S. on Ships of the Navy Acting as Transports (T-53-40(9)E); Memo, Britton to Brewster, 9 Dec 18, sub: Transportation and Handling of Convalescent, Sick and Wounded to the U.S. Both in Entry 588, RG 120, NARA.

[71] Memo, Britton to Brewster, 9 Dec 18, Entry 588, RG 120, NARA.

be to head off complaints before they start or, if all else failed, to be in a position to offer solutions.[72]

Thus, in less than a month embarkation policies were fully on their way to final form. It was well that they were because Brewster and Britton were not encouraged as they visited the ports, finding many ill-prepared for handling the ever-growing influx of cargo and departing troops. Transport inspections were not being made unless specifically requested. Port officials and IGs were not coordinating information, nor did the latter have a familiarity with many aspects of port operations. In a few cases, U.S. Marine Corps (USMC) officers had been attached as transport inspectors. Most of them knew little about their duties, and Britton spent much of his time training them.

Britton had prepared his guidelines with these and similar augmentees in mind. He and Brewster made a thorough survey of each port visited, assessing the capacity of not only the facilities but also the officials. Britton also paid goodwill visits to the U.S. Navy and French officials and their facilities. He reported on their degree of cooperativeness and the quality of their operations. Both inspectors were confident that the ports had the potential to meet embarkation requirements; however, they foresaw a prodigious effort on the part of the whole Services of Supply to do so.[73]

Concurrent with Brewster's tour, the 2d Depot Division at Le Mans was redesignated the American Embarkation Center. It expanded into a vast enterprise by taking over eight divisional areas, each with its own subdepot and a billeting capacity of about 30,000 men, and by converting the original camps and training areas to handle casuals, convalescents, and small units. The center's capacity approached 250,000 men. Its troop population never went below 100,000 for the first six months of 1919.

Several other smaller centers, located near ports, handled nondivisional units. Inspectors at these centers assured that the departing troops were paid and properly clothed; that they had up-to-date records; that they did not take any as souvenirs government property or explosives on board ship; and that they had converted their foreign money, which had to be confirmed by their unit commanders. When division inspectors were unavailable, center IGs checked unit funds and resolved accountability issues. Each departing soldier also had to submit to a final examination by a surgeon. Before departure, both the sur-

---

[72] Memo, Britton to Chief, Labor Bureau, SGD, 4 Dec 18, sub: Embarkation of Troops for the U.S., Entry 588, RG 120, NARA.

[73] Memo, Britton to Brewster, 19 Dec 18, Entry 588, RG 120, NARA.

geon and the center IGs had to certify that the organizations and individuals they inspected were ready for embarkation.[74]

Assisting the center IGs was a large number of combat arms officers. Most served as acting inspectors for troops and equipment; a few, as administrators for the enlarged inspection staffs. The detailed IGs coordinated the embarkation program and dealt with funds and disciplinary issues. When units were inactivated or moved to the ports, their inspectors were not released until they had completed all inspections in progress, forwarding their reports to the AEF's IG office, and, as a final act, had inspected the areas, billets, and facilities used by their units to assure they were left in good condition and to minimize future claims. Many Regular Army inspectors opted to take positions in the SOS inspectorate once their units had left rather than return to the United States.[75]

Occasionally, the behavior of even an experienced inspector proved embarrassing to the inspectorate. In one such case, Col. Harry T. Matthews, recently assigned to Brewster's office after being the I Corps inspector, unnecessarily upset the officers of the 1st Replacement Depot at St. Aignan, causing considerable resentment. The depot was one of several overwhelmed by the large numbers of troops being sent for embarkation processing. The overcrowding made conditions there deplorable, and the depot cadre had been working hard to ameliorate the situation. Colonel Matthews paid a three-day visit to the camp in response to a congressional inquiry. He made little effort to learn what the cadre had done to improve things or what their plans were. Instead, he immediately began an inspection of the admittedly poor facilities. Disdainful and critical, he openly berated the cadre for tolerating such conditions and, at one point, profanely shouted down an officer who tried to explain.[76]

After Colonel Matthews left the depot, Brig. Gen. Paul B. Malone, the depot commander, wrote General Spinks. He criticized Matthews' conduct, saying he merely had discovered that which was known already about camp conditions. His attitude and conduct had lowered the morale of the permanent party and had created discipline problems

[74] Rpt, IG, AEF, AEC, to Brewster, 1 May 19, sub: American Embarkation Center, Le Mans (Sarthe), France, 1 May 19, Entry 588; SOS, AEF, Embarkation Instrs 13, 4 Jan 19, Entry 591; and, Rpt, Camp Covington Insp to IG, SOS, n.d., Entry 2691. All in RG 120, NARA.
[75] Rpt, Camp Covington Insp to IG, SOS, n.d., Entry 2691; Memo, AG, AEF, to CG, 2d Army, 7 Apr 19, sub: Inspections, Second Army, Entry 588. All in RG 120, NARA.
[76] Ltr, Spinks to CO, 1st Replacement Depot, St. Aignan, 3 Mar 19, sub: Request for Information, and Reply, 13 Mar 19, Entry 588, RG 120, NARA.

among the casual personnel. Spinks already knew about the incident, learning some details from another general who had visited the depot after Matthews' inspection. He thus asked Malone for all the facts so that some action could be taken against Matthews. Malone responded with a series of sworn statements, but asked Spinks to drop the case as he and his men were too busy to follow up. The incident is illustrative of the pressured atmosphere under which everyone was working to cope with their giant task and limited resources. Colonel Matthews had been a sound corps inspector, but must have met his limit with the situation at St. Aignan. His loss of control shows the harm such actions on the part of an inspector can achieve.[77]

The port inspectors also found the pressures of their job increasing as Major Britton's inspection schemes went into effect. The experience of Base Section No. 1 at St. Nazaire was typical of those with embarkation missions. The IG section was enlarged and organized along functional lines. The troops coming from places like Le Mans staged into camps in the base section area. Inspections for each camp were organized, as were teams to make final inspections at the docks. A small troop transport inspection team was formed under the direction of one of the USMC officers, and a larger team was dedicated to the inspection of the sick and wounded being prepared for evacuation from hospitals in the base section area.[78]

Prior to moving to the base section, most of the troops were processed for embarkation either at Le Mans or at their own billeting areas. The inspections performed there consisted only of checking on the correction of the deficiencies identified in reports of the preceding inspectors. Units coming from Le Mans initially required closer scrutiny because of the incompleteness of its inspection program, but by March 1919 the Le Mans operation had improved so much that few deficiencies were noted in units. This reduced the base section inspector's work load merely to spot-checking certain items, thus speeding up a unit's movement to the docks.[79]

The inspection of personnel, finance, and related records for those units not processed at interior sites was performed in full in the base section billeting areas. Unit adjutants could certify that corrections were made to the deficiencies noted. These certificates were accepted in lieu of further inspection, although the section inspectors still were

---

[77] Ibid.

[78] Rpt, Miller to CG, Base Sec 1, 30 Jun 19, sub: Annual Report as Required by 880 A.R., Entry 26, RG 159, NARA.

[79] Ibid.

held responsible for the condition of records. The time so saved was judged worthwhile, particularly when balanced against the few complaints about administrative or financial issues directed at the base section from receiving agencies in the United States. Formal inspection reports were made only when units permanently assigned to the base section were being processed for home. For the most part, inspectors gave verbal instructions to correct the problems they found. Their objective was to get the units ready for embarkation as quickly as possible. This was noted and appreciated by the troops with whom there was generally a friendly, cooperative relationship. The IGs were seen as assisters, rather than critics. A side benefit of this informal approach was the reduction in IG paperwork, which, in turn, gave the inspectors more time to be with the units. A great deal of effort went into establishing the system and its accompanying facilities. It was during its developing phases that most of the embarkation complaints and horror stories were made.[80]

The sudden surge of soldiers at base section ports soon after the last shots were fired caught the Services of Supply off balance, its efforts and resources still committed to supporting the fighting front. Many of the ports had neither the facilities to house nor the organizations to support adequately the departing troops. As a consequence, those processing out in the first weeks after the armistice endured considerable hardship and inconvenience. This situation gave rise to the inevitable complaints and stories that resulted in political and newspaper inquiries. The preponderance of them concerned the great port of Brest in Base Section No. 5, through which more than half of the those returning home processed.

Base Section No. 5

Brig. Gen. George H. Harries, a D.C. National Guard officer, had presided successfully over the expansion of Brest during the buildup. He early had improved the city water supply, but was given few resources for housing and transportation. Harries mentioned this problem to General Pershing during the latter's inspection visit in August 1918, pointing out that it would be particularly critical when the flow of men started going the other way. Approval was given for additional construction the next month. However, delays were encountered because of the flu epidemic and the continued absence of transportation

---

[80] Ibid.

to move building material. Progress was marginal until the Services of Supply redirected the necessary resources within days of the armistice. By then, the crisis General Harries predicted had developed. The situation became so bad that Harries was relieved and replaced by Maj. Gen. Eli A. Helmick.[81]

General Helmick had arrived in France on 9 November with the advance elements of his 8th Division. Shortly thereafter his friend and former protege General Harbord, the SOS commander, approached him, recommending that he take an assignment in the Services of Supply. Helmick deferred making a decision until 21 November, when he learned that the 8th Division was going to be deactivated. "Inside of an hour" of his phone call to Harbord, he was en route to Brest to assume command of Base Section No. 5. He took with him most of the 8th Division staff members who had accompanied him to France. As Helmick later wrote, his brief stop at Brest in early November had shown him that the port had some big problems. The facilities were spartan because of the aforementioned priorities. Loading, out-processing, and shipping requirements mandated far greater housing, dockage, and transportation than were presently available.[82]

A month after assuming command of Base Section No. 5 Helmick sent General Brewster a memorandum, in which he summarized the conditions that he found and the actions he was taking to correct them. Brewster had availed himself of Helmick's old IG ties to ask him to keep him posted because of the great number of complaints that were coming in about Brest. Helmick emphasized throughout his summary that no one was to blame for the problems cited, which he attributed to the sudden mission reversal, and admitted that correcting what he found wrong was posing an enormous challenge. As a first step, he placed Brig. Gen. Smedley Butler, USMC, in command of the embarkation camp at Pontanezen, 3 miles from the port, and Brig. Gen. Alfred A. Starbird, the War Department's senior artillery inspector before assuming command of the 8th Field Artillery Brigade, in charge of port operations and permanent-party personnel and units.[83]

Helmick told Brewster that the key to understanding all of the problems lay in the fact that expansion of the embarkation camp had not

---

[81] James A. Huston, *The Sinews of War: Army Logistics, 1775–1953* (Washington, D.C.: Office of the Chief of Military History, United States Army, 1966), pp. 366, 391; Johnson Hagood, *The Service of Supply: A Memoir of the Great War* (Boston: Houghton Mifflin Co., 1927), p. 181.

[82] Helmick, "Autobiography," MHI.

[83] Memo, Helmick to Brewster, 22 Dec 18, Entry 588, RG 120, NARA.

begun until the armistice. Even then, supplies, labor, and materials were difficult to obtain, primarily because there were no rail facilities between the city station, docks, or campsites. Consequently, all materials had to be transferred to trucks and moved over very poor roads. The ground was so boggy that vehicles could not get off the road once in the camp area. The situation was made more acute by the 1918–19 winter being one of the wettest and coolest on record. At Camp Pontanezen "an impervious clay subsoil retained the rainfall near the surface, converting the soil . . . into deep stratum of muck which for ages had been permeated with human and animal waste." A railroad spur was built to overcome this problem. By the end of December this spur made it possible for materials to be brought right to the camp, thus speeding up the building process, and for departing troops to ride to the docks instead of hiking the muddy 3 miles.[84]

When General Butler took over, the camp lacked sewage and water systems. Water carts, drawn by the troops, were the only source. Under Butler's general direction, various camp projects received a high construction priority. A dam had to be constructed and a pipeline installed, which by the end of January 1919 provided sufficient drinking and bathing water. Delousing and disinfecting facilities, as well as tent platforms, kitchens, and hardstands, were essential for ensuring minimum health standards and comforts. The capacity of the Brest facilities had nearly trebled by the end of December 1918, when each of the nine kitchens at Pontanezen was feeding 5,000 men at a meal. Helmick later said that nearly 17,000 structures were erected, with a cost in lumber alone of nearly seven million dollars. In addition to the construction projects, General Butler also organized the processing of casuals and units on their way to the port.[85]

At the port General Starbird established order amongst the diverse permanent-party elements—labor, motor transport, military police, and guard troops. He assumed control over their campsites and was responsible for troop discipline and medical care. To improve dock operations, Starbird implemented a property checking system, under which quartermaster and transportation officials coordinated closely. Previously, because no controls were in place as goods moved from ship to dock and then to warehouse or transport, pilferage and untraceable losses were high. This new coordination permitted a more efficient use of transportation, thus improving the movement of goods and speeding up

---

[84] Helmick, "Autobiography," MHI.
[85] Ibid.; Memo, Helmick to Brewster, 22 Dec 18, Entry 588, RG 120, NARA.

the requisition cycle. Expecting an acceptable operation by the end of January 1919, Helmick suggested to Brewster that he could use "another good inspector" to keep up the pace of improvements.[86]

While trying to improve port operations, the onslaught of more troops from the interior and supplies from the United States, which were no longer sent inland, exacerbated the already deplorable living conditions. It was not until late February that adequate vehicles were available to move the men and cargo around the port with any efficiency. The embarking troops were used as unskilled labor while at the port, to support the frantic construction efforts of the engineers. The mud and penetrating chill added to the misery. "To get out at 5 O'clock in the morning and march in the dark to the kitchen for breakfast, eat it standing in the wet and mud, then march three miles through the sloppy streets to the port, work there all day with a cold lunch at noon, return to camp for supper, to be eaten again in the dark and mud, and then back to their unfloored tents for a night in wet, muddy clothing—that was not a pleasant life in a Rest Camp." As might be expected, numerous complaints began to surface through every possible medium.[87]

Helmick took a personal approach as base section commander, spending considerable time visiting the port, observing progress, encouraging the workers and transients, and overseeing that the best possible was being done. Under his guidance, reception procedures, such as feeding arriving troops at the railheads before marching them to billets, and the quality of military police, whose inexperience and arbitrariness had been a major source of complaints, were improved. He characterized his job as "inspection work over again, but no tedious reports to work up for my superiors." He considered his experience as an inspector as invaluable in contributing to his ability to cope with the situation at Brest. The progress of construction and improving weather ended the worst of the problems by March 1919. Ironically, by then a large portion of the AEF had already staged through the port.

By March, however, Brest already had become a cause celebre among the press and members of Congress. Reporters in New York gathered horror stories of conditions at Brest from disgruntled doughboys as they came off the ships. Soon, there was criticism throughout the country of the entire chain of command for apparently condoning

---

[86] Helmick, "Autobiography," MHI; Memo (quoted words), Helmick to Brewster, 22 Dec 18, Entry 588, RG 120, NARA.

[87] Helmick, "Autobiography," MHI. Subsequent paragraphs, including quotations, are from this source.

the situation. At first this had the salutary effect of making the resources available to Helmick and his staff much more rapidly. But the constant carping about the problems that the Brest cadre was trying to improve eventually became discouraging. Reporters and government officials "gloried to find things to criticize and gave us no credit for the efforts we were making to correct them." Stories were rarely verified and completed corrections were never reported.

Some were fair, others were not. A U.S. Senator and his wife, who toured the base and dined with the troops, was less than candid. Overall, they were complimentary on what they had seen. But once they were back in New York, they granted a critical newspaper interview and decried the deplorable "suffering" of the soldiers. After doing some damage control, Helmick and Butler resolved that they would no longer waste their time or good food on political visitors. Some reporters, notably Mary Roberts Reinhart, were objective and fair in their comments. A series of inspectors sent to Brest in response to the complaints consistently praised the improvements in operations. Later, Chief of Staff March made a public statement supporting Helmick and his staff for their efforts. Finally, Secretary Baker and Secretary of the Navy Josephus Daniels separately issued praise for the improvements. By April the scandal over the "Hell-Hole of France" had faded away as the press sought other sensations. At the end of June measures were begun to slowly draw down the operation.

When Base Section No. 5 officially closed in September, nearly 1.1 million U.S. troops had processed through it on the way home. In other words, thirty-one divisions and numerous casuals had embarked from Brest. The average time at Camp Pontanezen was about six days, although one division, the 2d, had gone through in less than two. The port's peak embarkation month was July, when 176,000 soldiers had embarked and sailed for the United States. Despite its early reputation, its health rate was comparable to the AEF average, while its disciplinary incidents were lower. General Helmick praised many of his staff officers for the base's successful role in embarkation. He particularly singled out Col. Walter L. Reed, his inspector "who did more than any other staff officer to bring order out of the chaos that existed in the camp during the early days." With the closure of the base, a modest AEF headquarters in Paris monitored the last phases of withdrawal from France and the completion of arrangements for the occupation of Germany.

The problems faced by the inspectors at home and overseas were, however, only one part of the story. World War I had brought the United States briefly into the arena of international responsibilities and great-power conflicts. With the demobilization process under way in France, other American forces were taking part in the occupation of defeated Germany and, although unwillingly, in the civil war in Russia that followed that country's revolution. In these places, too, the inspectorate faced new and unexpected challenges.

8

The Inspectorate in Germany and Russia

One provision of the armistice agreement established an occupation zone to be held by the allies on the west bank of the Rhine, along with three bridgeheads on the east bank. In consequence, American forces were committed to occupation duty in Germany at least until the peace treaty was signed, and, as it turned out, for several years after that. The area held by the United States consisted of, for the most part, a slice of the Rhineland between Luxembourg and the German city of Coblenz. On 15 November 1918 General Pershing activated the Third Army, under Maj. Gen. Joseph T. Dickman, to control the occupation forces. Dickman selected Brig. Gen. Malin Craig to be his chief of staff and began gathering the nearly 200 staff officers necessary to form the headquarters. The Third Army was to monitor compliance with the armistice terms, and by 15 November it was directing the eastward movement of several corps following the withdrawal of German forces.[1]

An Army of Occupation

Initially, the new field army headquarters controlled about 240,000 U.S. troops. While the III Corps, with three U.S. divisions, moved across the Rhine and into the Coblenz bridgehead, the IV and VII Corps, with five divisions, occupied the Moselle valley along the line of communications back to Luxembourg. The III Corps units immedi-

---

[1] Keith L. Nelson, *Victors Divided: America and the Allies in Germany, 1918–1923* (Berkeley: University of California Press, 1975), pp. 26–27, 29; Department of the Army, Historical Division, *The United States Army in the World War*, 17 vols. (Washington, D.C.: Government Printing Office, 1948), 10:101–02.

ately began marking the boundaries of the bridgeheads, to prevent allied soldiers from wandering into the neutral zone between U.S. and German forces and to control civilian movement in and out of the American zone.[2]

The IV Corps divisions west of the Rhine were centered around the towns of Andernach, Ahrweiler, and Cochem. The VII Corps occupied a rear area centered on Trier, where the Advanced Headquarters was located. By 15 December the Third Army headquarters was in place at Coblenz, the capital of Germany's Rhine Province and a major administrative center. For the duration of the occupation General Dickman and his successors, with their staffs, were housed in the massive Ehrenbreitstein Fortress, which towers over the city on the east bank of the Rhine. The U.S. forces were well established by Christmas, and the entire command was brought up to full strength with personnel from units being disbanded in France *(Map 3)*.[3]

Discipline and standards were maintained through a rigid program of command and general inspections. In January 1919 General Brewster made a full inspection of U.S. units in their new billets in Germany, visiting every corps and division headquarters in the Third Army, as well as many of the regiments and battalions. He paid special attention to the appearance and equipment of the troops and the effects of American civil affairs policies toward the Germans. He reported favorably to Pershing regarding discipline, civil-military relations, and training, citing the 1st Battalion, 28th Infantry, 1st Division, as especially commendable. Pershing followed with his own thorough inspection a month later.[4]

By February a routine had been established, in which unit training ended at noon and the troops engaged in sports the rest of the day. One of the great events for the month was a football game between the 4th and 89th Divisions, witnessed by 20,000 officers and men. (The 89th won, 14 to 0.) Third Army schools opened, as did others at the unit level, to train or refresh personnel in needed military skills. About 1,800 officers and men attended courses at British and French universities. The

---

[2] American Battle Monuments Commission (ABMC), *American Armies and Battlefields in Europe* (Washington, D.C.: Government Printing Office, 1938), p. 489.

[3] Ernst Fraenkel, *Military Occupation and the Rule of Law: Occupational Government in the Rhineland, 1918–1923* (New York: Oxford University Press, 1944), p. 7.

[4] Rpt, Brewster to Pershing, 9 Feb 19, sub: Field Inspection of the Third Army, 13–28 January 1919, Entry 588, Record Group (RG) 120, National Archives and Records Administration (NARA), Washington, D.C.; Memo, Woolfolk to OIG, 26 Mar 19, sub: Points Covered by the General of the Armies in Inspections, OTIG files, Pentagon (SAIG-ZXH).

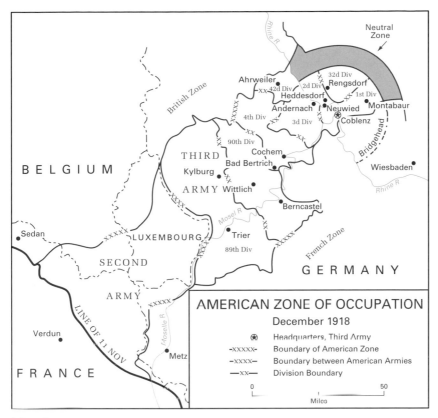

Map 3

civilian welfare organizations continued their work until April 1919, when the Third Army G–1 took over most of their operations. The army quartermaster purchased the Red Cross' and YMCA's surplus stocks and sold excess items to the hard-pressed local populace.[5]

Political turmoil and the possible need to use military force should the armistice or peace negotiations break down kept all of the Third Army's staff elements working at levels far beyond normal peacetime training activities. The G–2 continued an active Order of Battle Section to identify German units capable of opposing American move-

---

[5] Third Army G–1 Rpt, Historical File 193–11.4, Entry 931, RG 120, NARA; Irwin L. Hunt, "American Military Government of Occupied Germany, 1918–1920: Report of the Officer in Charge of Civil Affairs," mimeographed, 4 vols. (Coblenz, 1920), 1:141, copy in Army Library, Washington, D.C.

ment eastward from the bridgehead. It also monitored civilian activities within the American zone, sharing its information with the inspector general, the provost marshal, and the chief of civil affairs. Through the intelligence-gathering activity, considerable political and labor unrest was averted.[6]

The G–3 and the G–5 continued the planning and preparations that would be needed if military force again had to be used against the Germans. Personnel turbulence, however, aggravated their efforts. Gains and losses of individuals and units began almost as soon as the Third Army entered Germany; by the end of June 1919 almost 130,000 men had been sent home. Gradually, the major combat units were withdrawn and replaced by smaller organizations. Immediately after the peace treaty was signed, a further massive reduction of units required complete restructuring within the staff and the command. The G–3 and G–5 were merged, and control of the occupation zone was centralized, rather than entrusted to unit commanders in their own areas.[7]

The huge surge of units out of the command required the Third Army to become deeply involved in demobilization, mainly a G–4 and ordnance activity. Units and equipment had to be staged through Services of Supply (SOS) facilities either at Brest, Rotterdam, or Antwerp. Surplus equipment was transferred to remaining units or sold through the U.S. Liquidation Commission. Refurbishment of the dilapidated German railway system by Third Army engineers was critical for meeting use demands. A related logistical problem of major proportions was the disposition of German war materiel abandoned or given up under the terms of the armistice. Whatever was not desired by the Liquidation Commission was destroyed, including millions of artillery rounds and hundreds of aircraft, while signal equipment, arms, and vehicles often were shipped to other nations, such as Belgium and Poland.

The Liquidation Commission itself became the object of an IG investigation, carried out by General Chamberlain at the special request of Secretary Baker. An independent agency established in February 1919 to dispose of the property, facilities, and equipment that were no longer needed to support the U.S. Army's overseas activities, it was completely separate from the AEF. The commission consisted of four members, the best known of whom was Charles G. Dawes, a financier, diplomat, Republican politician, and old friend of General Pershing

---

[6] Third Army G–2 Rpt, Historical File 193–11.4, Entry 931, RG 120, NARA.
[7] Nelson, *Victors Divided*, p. 126; ABMC, *American Armies*, p. 493; Third Army G–3 Rpt, Historical File 193–11.4, Entry 931, RG 120, NARA.

who served as a National Army brigadier general in the Services of Supply and who would become vice-president of the United States in 1925. When the strong-willed Dawes resigned to join Warren G. Harding's 1920 campaign for the presidency, three members and a small staff remained, working under great pressure on a vast scale in a turbulent period. Competitiveness and rancor generated by the goals and ambitions of profiteers and newly created governments ultimately led to accusations of improper conduct by the commission, which in turn had led to Secretary Baker's request.[8]

General Chamberlain ordered his financial expert, Major Streater, to pursue the specific allegations. Following his review, Streater reported that the Liquidation Commission had entered into several questionable arrangements with a holding company acting for the Polish Government. The chairman of the holding company was a former commission staff officer, whose possible proprietary knowledge seemed to expose the commission to charges of favoritism. The commission, too, sold goods directly to the Polish Army, although a German company had entered a higher bid. This, however, was within the commission's prerogative, provided that its members believed it to be in the best interests of the United States. Major Streater also noted that the speed with which American surplus items were sold made it necessary to repurchase some of them, an embarrassing inconvenience. Both he and Chamberlain agreed that this represented poor planning but was hardly criminal. In conclusion, the Inspector General told Secretary Baker that the commission could have been better managed but that its operations merited no further investigation while it phased itself out.[9]

By March 1919 the occupation forces in Germany were no longer dependent upon the Services of Supply in France for logistical support. Operations were fully established in Antwerp, with forward bases at Andernach and Bendorf and a regulating station at Trier. Subsidiary facilities were also set up at Rotterdam under the control of the Antwerp port commander, who took his orders from the Third Army G–4.[10]

---

[8] Memos, Baker to Chamberlain, 1 Jun 20, and Streater to IG, USA, 10 Jul 20, Entry 1360, RG 120, NARA. See also Erna Risch, *Quartermaster Support of the Army: A History of the Corps, 1775–1939* (Washington, D.C.: Quartermaster Historian's Office, Office of the Quartermaster General, 1962), pp. 698–99.

[9] Memo, Streater to IG, USA, 10 Jul 20, Entry 1360, RG 120, NARA; Memo, Chamberlain to Baker, 27 Nov 20, Entry 26, RG 159, NARA. See also Frederick Palmer, *Newton D. Baker: America at War*, 2 vols. (New York: Dodd, Mead and Co., 1931), 2:397–98.

[10] Hunt, "Military Government," 1:214–15; Henry T. Allen, *My Rhineland Journal* (Boston: Houghton Mifflin Co., 1923), pp. 14, 86.

When the U.S. forces entered Germany, civil affairs was a top priority at each level of command. Operating at the Advanced Headquarters in Trier, the newly assigned civil affairs officer dealt directly with General Pershing. His deputy was placed in charge of civil affairs at the Coblenz headquarters, where he served until March 1920; he was responsible for policies and broad supervision over matters involving public works and utilities; fiscal affairs; public health; schools; charities; and political, legal, or penal activities. Each corps and division also had an officer on its staff performing similar duties. In June 1919, as distance and organization made the Advanced Headquarters increasingly superfluous, it was finally phased out, with all remaining functions transferred to the Third Army's Coblenz headquarters.[11]

Administering the American zone by tactical area proved to be increasingly difficult and unnecessarily turbulent for the Third Army because of the constant shift of key personnel and units. The overall result was the near-impossibility of implementing uniform civil affairs policies. As major units began to depart, whole regions of the zone were completely ungarrisoned and unsupervised. To rectify this awkward situation, the Third Army established a territorial organization in May 1919. One or more civil affairs officers, with a small staff consisting of a provost court officer, a sanitary inspector, and an executive, were assigned to each county (*Kreis* in German), and military police units of appropriate size were detailed to patrol each district and maintain order. Completed by the end of June, the new structure successfully weathered the uproar over the signing of the Versailles Treaty, in part because the investigations carried out by IGs for the Third Army civil affairs officer restored the German's faith in the good intentions and essential fairness of U.S. policies.[12]

After the signing of the treaty, there was little possibility of a renewal of hostilities, and the withdrawal of U.S. personnel that had begun in May became torrential. On 2 July the Third Army was deactivated, and its remaining personnel and equipment were transferred to the newly created American Forces in Germany (AFIG) headquarters, which remained at Coblenz. In the nearly eight months of its existence, the Third Army had created the framework of the occupation, with missions, functions, and standards that would endure until

---

[11] Hunt, "Military Government," 1:58–60; Ltr, Grier to Oberpresident, Rhine Prov, 8 Jun 20, sub: Civil Affairs Functions, Entry 1360, RG 120, NARA; Rpt, Brewster to Pershing, 9 Feb 19, Entry 588, RG 120, NARA.

[12] Hunt, "Military Government," 1:71–72.

the last American soldier was withdrawn. When Dickman's replacement, General Liggett, returned to the United States in July 1919, Maj. Gen. Henry T. Allen, the commander of the 90th Division on the Western Front, became the AFIG commander, serving until the AFIG was deactivated. Meanwhile, AEF headquarters remained in Paris, merging with the Services of Supply in September 1919 to form the fast-fading American Forces in France (AFIF). This temporary organization ceased to exist with the departure of General Pershing in January 1920. While in the United States, Pershing closed out final AEF matters until the time of his appointment as Chief of Staff in July 1921.[13]

Long before that, General Allen had set the pattern for the remainder of the occupation in Germany. Obviously, the presence of U.S. troops was more diplomatic than operational. AFIG strength had totaled 110,000 in July 1919 but only 11,000 in September and then, with the addition of the 8th and 50th Infantry in a brigade intended for peace-keeping service in Silesia but never deployed, about 15,000 in October, remaining at this level until the final withdrawal began in the fall of 1921. The drastic reduction of U.S. troops in 1919 necessitated a corresponding reduction in the size of the American zone, which ultimately consisted of only a part of the Coblenz bridgehead and an area north of the Moselle on the west bank of the Rhine. French forces took over the areas abandoned by the United States, creating the potential for friction both with the Germans and the doughboys.[14]

General Allen was forced to spend most of his time as the American representative on the Allied High Commission, dealing with political and diplomatic issues that affected the Rhineland or relations with Weimar Germany. Despite his focus and his diminished force, Allen insisted on the highest standards of military conduct and training. In his opinion, his showcase units made up in proficiency and appearance what they lacked in relative size. Consequently, as a matter of policy, and also to keep the troops busy, the half-day schedule ended and field training and tactical exercises became the norm for the occupation soldier.[15] The combination of issues that arose concerning soldier conduct, diplomatic needs, and civil-military relations created a challenging situation for the staff of the occupying forces.

---

[13] Allen, *Rhineland Journal*, pp. 6–7; Rpt, Reed to CG, AFIF, 20 Dec 19, Entry 588, RG 120, NARA.

[14] Nelson, *Victors Divided*, pp. 126, 211; Allen, *Rhineland Journal*, pp. 43, 46.

[15] Allen, *Rhineland Journal*, passim.

Organizing the Inspectorate

The inspectorate in Germany evolved with the army of occupation. Inspectors arrived on the Rhine on the staffs of the Third Army and its major tactical units. With their return to the United States in the summer of 1919, the small AFIG staff in Coblenz was forced to assume the functions of inspection for the entire occupation zone. Three officers were authorized, but until January 1920 only two were assigned full time. They were assisted by one army field clerk and one enlisted clerk until October 1921, when a chief clerk, an enlisted file clerk, two army field clerk stenographers, and an interpreter joined the office. The Coblenz office serviced not only the 15,000 men of the AFIG but also the nearly one million Germans in the zone and small groups of U.S. forces in Poland, Belgium, and several other European countries.[16]

The first senior inspector in the occupation force was Col. Alvan C. Read, a U.S. Military Academy graduate and an infantry officer. As a young man, he had seen action in Cuba and the Philippines; later, he served as the 1st Division senior inspector and then as the First Army assistant inspector before being assigned to the Third Army on 13 November 1918. He was assisted by two other infantrymen, Col. Robert G. Peck and Lt. Col. Charles H. Rice, until August 1919, when they returned to the United States. Read was then alone until 3 September, when he was joined by Major Magruder, a coast artilleryman who had been an inspector at the SOS headquarters and at the District of Paris. Magruder remained in the office until its closing, ultimately serving as senior inspector of the force.[17]

Another officer important to the success of the inspectorate in Germany was Lt. Col. (later Col.) Louis Van Schaick, who reported on 24 November 1919. As a permanent member of a General Court-martial Board, Van Schaick at first performed few IG functions. Then tragedy struck. In late December Colonel Read contracted influenza, which was later compounded by pneumonia. He died in Coblenz on 19 January 1920 and was buried there a few days later in an impressive international ceremony. Thus Van Schaick became the senior inspector by default, until his reassignment home in July. Col. William H. Hay, a cavalryman, succeeded him as the senior inspector on 19 August. A wartime major general who had commanded the 28th Division, he was

---

[16] Memo, IG, AFIG, to CofS, AFIG, 4 Oct 21, sub: Clerical Personnel, Entry 1360, RG 120, NARA.

[17] See Roster of Inspectors, AFIG, Entry 1360, RG 120, NARA.

a conscientious and efficient officer, admired greatly by General Allen. On 9 May 1921 Hay was selected to be the AFIG chief of staff, and Major Magruder then replaced him as senior inspector.[18]

No less burdensome were the consequences of an upheaval in organization. The Third Army commanders and, later, General Allen all believed firmly in the need for frequent command inspections of every element of their organizations. Allen conducted periodic full-scale inspections and reviews of the AFIG, continually emphasizing the need for the very best levels of appearance and performance in personnel and equipment alike. He preferred to concentrate units into formations as large as possible for his inspections. Movement to the concentration site was in itself a test of mobility and equipment, serving almost as a major field problem and an opportunity for drill on a large scale.[19] The entire procedure was very much in the style of General Pershing, to which all personnel were accustomed.

Col. Alvan C. Read

So long as General Craig was chief of staff, the heavy emphasis on command inspections remained in balance with the traditional staff relationships that developed in the AEF in 1917 and 1918. However, when Brig. Gen. William W. Harts took over as Craig's successor at the AFIG on 20 July 1919, the result was a heavy shift toward complete dominance by the general staff. Prior to that date the senior inspector, recognized as an independent member of the personal or special staff, had reported directly to the chief of staff and attended all staff conferences. General Harts made the inspectors general, along with the Signal Corps staff, service sections of the G–3. In similar fashion, he subordinated the provost marshal and adjutant and judge advocate generals to

---

[18] Ibid.; Allen, *Rhineland Journal*, pp. 72–73. Hay was later promoted to brigadier general. He left Germany in June 1922 to command a brigade on the Mexican border.

[19] Allen, *Rhineland Journal*, pp. 40, 83.

the G–1, as well as the surgeon, ordnance officer, quartermaster, and the Antwerp base section commander to the G–4. Harts transformed the G sections into operational, rather than planning, elements. Needless to say, "there was a distinct under current [*sic*] of dissatisfaction among the officers in Germany."[20]

One effect of the reorganization was an uncontrolled and uncoordinated flurry of inspections, carried out by a variety of staff officers who frequently gave conflicting instructions to confused and frustrated unit commanders. Practically all inspections—routine, tactical, or preembarkation—were made by general staff officers and not by inspectors general. The arrangement contravened the intent of the National Defense Act of 1920, which stressed that the War Department General Staff—and thus its officers—should restrict itself to planning and coordinating functions.[21]

It was not until Colonel Hay arrived in August that any changes were made. Hay insisted that he be given the independence necessary to carry out his functions in a direct relationship with the commander. He asked for and was given direct access to the AFIG chief of staff and the authority to attend staff conferences in his own right. And when he took over as chief of staff, he ended the inspectorate's subordination to the G–3 by directing that Major Magruder report to him directly.[22]

Prior to Hay's intervention, however, Harts' experiment caused myriad difficulties. Typical were those that developed in the Antwerp Base Section. Maj. John L. Parkinson was the base inspector when the base was still a service section of the AFIG G–4. G–4 policy restricted Parkinson's contact with the command inspector general, and his reports never found their way into IG channels. No problems resulted so long as his duties were limited to routine activities, such as the inspection of Army transports or the handling of local complaints. However, on issues of greater importance that could affect the entire command, the possibility existed that his reports would not be utilized to allow prompt and proper resolution.

In July 1920 General Chamberlain pointed out the potential problem in a report to General Allen, offering the solution that he assign Parkinson to the AFIG's IG office with duty station at Antwerp. Allen

---

[20] Memo, Reed to IG, USA, 16 Feb 20, Entry 26, RG 159, NARA.

[21] Ibid.; James E. Hewes, Jr., *From Root to McNamara: Army Organization and Administration, 1900–1963* (Washington, D.C.: U.S. Army Center of Military History, 1966), pp. 50–51.

[22] Ltr, Magruder to Chamberlain, 23 Aug 20; Memo, Chamberlain to Allen, 10 Jul 20. Both in Entry 1360, RG 120, NARA.

directed that a study be made, but quickly encountered strong opposition from his G–4, Lt. Col. Brehon Somervell. Somervell argued that the inspector at Antwerp should deal exclusively with the port commander and his superior, the G–4. The AFIG chief transportation officer, Capt. Abbott Boone, agreed with Somervell; however, he believed that Parkinson should be allowed access to the AFIG's IG office for technical matters. Neither officer saw any harm in Parkinson providing copies of his reports to the command inspector general. Hence, General Harts' immediate successor as chief of staff, Col. John C. Montgomery, directed that Parkinson keep the AFIG inspector informed of his activities and authorized direct coordination between the two offices.[23]

Under the new arrangement inspection reports from the Antwerp Post were sent to the AFIG G–4, who provided an information copy to the AFIG inspector. The change, however, proved to be insufficient. The British consul general in Antwerp requested that allegations of mistreatment of a British subject by U.S. military police be investigated. Major Parkinson, after a thorough investigation, found that the military police had in fact used excessive force. Yet the report, because it reflected unfavorably on some G–4 policies, was filed quietly by that office. No copy was provided the inspector general, no follow-up was carried out, and no corrective action was taken. As a result, General Allen eventually had to offer his apologies to the Allied High Commission for discourtesy shown to one of its member states. Shortly afterward, Allen shifted the subordination of the port inspector from the G–4 to the command inspector general and directed that his reports would go through IG channels for appropriate action. In this way, after Parkinson's formal reassignment on 14 November, Colonel Hay was able to reestablish fully the status of the inspectorate as it had been when the Third Army entered Germany nearly two years before.[24]

The small inspection staff remained extremely busy throughout these upheavals, despite the fact that opposition by some members of Congress to any American presence in Germany made the AFIG's future perpetually uncertain. Some inspectors played a role in the drawdown. For a time, overstaffing by officers typified the command. Many

---

[23] Memo, Chamberlain to Allen, 10 Jul 20; Rpt, IG, AFIG, to CofS, AFIG, 26 Oct 20, sub: Inspection Concerning the Complaint of Mr. E. C. Preston; Memo, CofS, AFIG, to IG, AFIG, 23 Jul 20, sub: Status of Captain [sic] J. L. Parkinson. All in Entry 1360, RG 120, NARA.

[24] Memo, IG, AFIG, to Parkinson, 26 Jul 20, sub: Status in Relation to Port Commander, Port of Antwerp; Memo, AG, AFIG, to IG, AFIG, 2 Nov 20, sub: Reports From Port Inspector. Both in Entry 1360, RG 120, NARA.

who had held wartime jobs in the numerous short-lived organizations related to the armistice, peace agreements, and relief work simply transitioned into AFIG positions, often supernumerary and frequently overgraded, in the postwar period. An additional surplus arrived from the AEF units rapidly demobilizing in France. Continued duty in Europe was desirable for many reasons. Temporary wartime grades remained in effect until the end of 1919; the dollar was very strong, compared to the declining European currencies; no Volstead Act–imposed prohibition existed; and life in an occupation force was safe and appealing.

An inspector visiting the AFIG from the American headquarters in France in June 1919 reported that he had encountered infantry companies commanded by field-grade officers and one infantry regiment with three colonels. He considered the AFIG staff "exceedingly large and somewhat top-heavy," concluding that it was too easy for an officer to secure a position in Germany. Colonel Reed, then the AFIF inspector, reported his observations to General Chamberlain when he returned to the United States. Shortly afterward, the War Department began to pressure Allen to reduce the number of officers in the command. Between October 1919 and May 1920 the headquarters trimmed nearly 450 officers out of an original total of 850.[25]

Thereafter, the strength of the command stabilized until November 1921. Then an Army-wide reorganization, mandated by Congress, reduced the command to about 6,000 of all ranks, 5,500 of whom served in a single infantry brigade. No sooner had the drawdown been achieved than another directive arrived in February 1922, reducing the command to about 3,200, with a single regiment. Each time the reduction axe fell, the small IG office anticipated losses from its own ranks. However, it remained fully manned with three officers and the supporting staff until May 1922. In Major Magruder's view, General Allen understood the need for an adequate number of inspectors to handle the personal and financial aspects of the ongoing withdrawal.[26]

By June 1922 all but 1,200 troops had departed. Two inspectors went home at that time, leaving Major Magruder and a field clerk to maintain the office until the final withdrawal in January 1923. In the course of its existence, the AFIG's IG office conducted nearly 200 so-called special investigations along with many more of a routine nature.

---

[25] Memo (quoted words), Reed to IG, USA, 16 Feb 20, Entry 26, RG 159, NARA; Allen, *Rhineland Journal*, pp. 41, 108.

[26] Memo, AG, AFIG, to CG, AFIG, 15 Oct 21, sub: Reduction of American Forces in Germany; Ltr, Magruder to Helmick, 8 Mar 22, Both in Entry 1360, RG 120, NARA. See also Allen, *Rhineland Journal*, pp. 277, 301, 320.

It also completed several special inquiries for General Allen that profoundly influenced the organization and policies of the command.[27]

Inspectors' Duties

The inspectors general held a broad area of responsibility that was limited only briefly and partially by General Harts' policies favoring the general staff. The authority to resolve deficiencies and to oversee discipline that General Pershing had vested in them continued throughout the occupation phases of the Third Army and the AFIG.[28]

All investigations and inquiries made by other agencies in the occupation force, such as the Provost Marshal's Department or a staff section, were expected to be referred to the IG office for information, additional action, or trend analysis. On occasion, the inspectors would recommend follow-up actions by other members of the headquarters. They had extensive influence over legal questions, for AFIG policy required that IGs investigate all instances of abuse, neglect, or irregularity brought out at general courts-martial.[29]

The IG office also continued to use court-martial data to indicate trends as part of its periodic analyses of discipline. Problems in soldier attitudes and conduct were not the only issues detected. For example, an inspector reported that soldiers accused of assaulting allied soldiers were never convicted, despite valid witnesses, and that long delays seemed to be the norm for bringing these types of cases to trial. The situation was an embarrassment to the AFIG, forcing General Allen to make excuses and offer apologies to his colleagues on the Allied High Commission. An inquiry found that the problem lay with one of the court-martial presidents, a crusty old colonel who was "not in sympathy for punishing soldiers becoming involved with foreigners." He was given other duties, which brought about an improvement in the judicial process and international relations.[30]

Flawed administration in the AFIG was all too common, with the commander having to rely on his IG staff for solutions. On two occa-

---

[27] Allen, *Rhineland Journal*, pp. 366, 493, 506, 508, 513; AFIG IG File 201, Entry 1360, RG 120, NARA.

[28] Rpt, Hay to CG, AFIG, 13 May 21, sub: IG History, Entry 1360, RG 120, NARA.

[29] Rpt, Robert to IG, AFIG, 19 Feb 20, sub: [Complaint] Against U.S. Soldiers, Entry 1360, RG 120, NARA.

[30] Rpt, IG, AFIG, to CofS, AFIG, 28 May 20, sub: Case of Sgt. T. J. Vrana, 28 May 20; Memo (quotation), Allen to TAG, 19 Mar 20, sub: Case of Private S. B. Gerace. Both in Entry 1360, RG 120, NARA.

each had known the combination of a safe from which money had been stolen. Colonel Hay felt that penalizing all for the loss of funds for which only one was responsible was unfair to the point of absurdity. He recommended that the accountable officer alone be held liable, on the grounds that he had put the money in an unsecured place. General Allen agreed, amending the board's decision to conform with the inspector's recommendation.[35]

Although the drudgery of finance accounts and related matters consumed a great deal of time, civil affairs placed further heavy demands on inspectors. The United States ruled its zone as a military occupier, albeit benignly. Until the United States and Germany signed a peace treaty in 1921, the AFIG authorities retained their theoretical autonomy while cooperating with the Versailles signatories. Authority over civilian activities was extensive. There were separate military tribunals established to try and imprison German violators of military rules imposed on the population—such offenses as entering the zone without a pass, engaging in black market trade, and committing vagrancy for immoral purposes (prostitution). The German judicial and penal systems also were monitored for compliance with U.S. and AFIG standards and policies. Inspectors visited German jails and health facilities, accepting complaints as if they were on a routine unit inspection.[36]

The AFIG's IG office also received complaints from private German citizens and civilian police, mostly about the behavior of American soldiers in public places. In a typical case, an American officer was rude to a German woman while traveling on the Coblenz–Frankfurt train. She complained to the assigned inspector, who tracked down the offender and then referred the case to his commander. IGs also looked into complaints from civilians concerning unsatisfactory police investigations of offenses committed by U.S. soldiers against Germans. These generally resulted from jurisdictional or procedural misunderstandings between local police and their American counterparts and normally were resolved quickly.[37]

The number of domestic issues, such as breach of promise and paternity, grew as the years of occupation went on and became a del-

---

[35] Memo, Hay to G–4, AFIG, 19 Oct 20, Entry 1360, RG 120, NARA.

[36] Ltr, Hay to OIC, Civ Affs, 23 Feb 20, sub: Complaints of German Prisoners; Rpt, Hay to CofS, AFIG, 23 Nov 20, sub: Crowded Condition of City Prisons. Both in Entry 1360, RG 120, NARA. See also Hunt, "Military Government," 1:320.

[37] Memo, Talbot to CofS, AFIG, 5 Oct 21, sub: Complaint of Henry Bohn, Czecho-Slovak Civilian; Memo, Magruder to PM, AFIG, 18 Dec 20, sub: Stolen Necklace of Countess d'Armil; and AFIG IG File 201, Misconduct of Lieutenant Whitley. All in Entry 1360, RG 120, NARA.

uge in its final days. Regardless of topic, each complaint was followed up by the AFIG's IG office through either provost marshal or civil affairs channels until resolved. Most complaints against the German courts and the American military tribunals, such as injustice and overly long sentences, were found to have no basis. However, prison conditions were often judged to be below U.S. standards and required improvement, leading to the construction of a new prison in Coblenz to ease congestion.[38]

Foreign civilians employed by the AFIG or subject to its regulations provided additional work to the inspectorate. Such people were allowed to file complaints with the AFIG's IG office. Whether German or citizens of some third nation, civilians with an extended record of misdemeanors could be deported from the occupied zone, an action that required approval from the Allied High Commission. Those marked for expulsion could appeal their deportation through inspector general channels in the American zone. Of the several hundred appeals reviewed, no High Commission decisions were overturned by the inspector general.

Officers and Soldiers

The occupation forces in Germany faced a heavy dose of command and staff inspections, not only from their own inspectors but from a steady flow of foreign and American dignitaries. In June and July 1920 Generals March and Chamberlain each inspected the AFIG within a few weeks of each other. As Allen later remarked, such scheduling was sufficient to "take the edge" off both inspections.[39]

March apparently intended to see the troops, evaluate their tactical efficiency, and size up their leaders. He was generally pleased with what he saw, but, as General Allen later noted, he did not "overdo" his praise.[40] General Chamberlain, arriving just as Chief of Staff March was leaving, concentrated on the internal functions of the command. Yet, like March, he could not resist presiding over several large field inspections, including a mounted review in the shadow of the Ehrenbreitstein Fortress. He

---

[38] Rpt, Hay to CofS, AFIG, 23 Nov 20, Entry 1360, RG 120, NARA.

[39] Allen, *Rhineland Journal*, p. 120 (quoted words). Allen's biographer suggests that the AFIG commander invited the Chief of Staff's inspection in a letter to March sent the previous December. See Heath Twichell, Jr., *Allen: The Biography of an Army Officer* (New Brunswick, N.J.: Rutgers University Press, 1974), p. 277.

[40] Allen, *Rhineland Journal*, p. 117 (quoted word); Ltrs, March to Allen, 17 and 23 Jun 20, Entry 1360, RG 120, NARA. After leaving Europe, March told a *Chicago Tribune* reporter that the AFIG was the best unit in the Army.

General Chamberlain Inspecting an AFIG Unit at Coblenz

visited each location where American troops were stationed and made a critical inspection of their facilities and how they were caring for them. He laid particular emphasis on guardhouses, prisons, and mess halls, but focused on the many problems with the Transportation Service, mostly in the areas of management and lack of adherence to War Department policies. Despite five closely typed pages of critical observations, Chamberlain concluded, to Allen's surprise, that the AFIG was the "most magnificent" command he had inspected. Later, in July 1921, both Chamberlain and March returned for a visit that was more a grand tour than a serious inspection.[41]

Although the visits of dignitaries generally were productive, AFIG officers, for the most part, dreaded them as they did those of inspectors. General Allen used IG reports as one of his sources for not only evaluating senior commanders but also determining the state of the command, and the effect of inspections in exposing the deficiencies of marginal units were sometimes devastating to their leaders. In June 1920

---

[41] Allen, *Rhineland Journal*, p. 128; Ltr (quoted words), Chamberlain to CG, AFIG, 10 Jul 20, Entry 1360, RG 120, NARA.

Allen relieved the commander of the 5th Infantry, largely as a result of problems shown in a series of IG inspections and investigations. In comparison to other units, the regiment consistently received the lowest rating in the monthly discipline report, having the highest number of incidents and courts-martial and the greatest number of cases returned for improper preparation. Two special investigations had revealed unit administration to be poor, and several tactical inspections had shown unit training to be the worst in the command.[42]

Not only commanders suffered. Special investigations often targeted members of the officer corps. At least 75 percent of the cases had to do with some form of personal misconduct. General Allen took a severe view of any abuse of alcohol. Any allegation of overindulgence was investigated and, if found to have substance, referred to a court-martial. A few other forms of personal misconduct, such as paternity, indebtedness, and brawling, occasionally appeared in IG reports. The remaining 25 percent of the cases concerned professional rather than personal failings—taking bribes, abuse of authority, and dereliction of duty.

Gambling was viewed with a jaundiced eye. In September 1919 Colonel Read investigated allegations of big-money gambling that supposedly had taken place in the 1st Signal Battalion Officers Club. Although Read found that nothing of substance had gone on, General Allen informally asked him to survey the entire command to see whether gambling was an extensive problem. The AFIG's IG office sent a survey to the commanders of all organizations having clubs and canteens, asking their views on whether gambling was a major occupation among the troops and whether they viewed it as prejudicial to good order. The survey led only to the conclusion that gambling was not a problem. Because most commanders tolerated it, officers were personally moderate. In some cases, commanders had issued orders banning gambling in their own units. Poker was not particularly popular; officers preferred playing bridge for low stakes, while soldiers favored dice. Gaming between men of different ranks was not condoned. General Allen was pleased, remarking how careful one had to be to keep the conduct of a few from tainting the image of the whole command.[43]

The form of gambling that Allen found most distasteful was speculation in the wildly fluctuating German mark. He directed the AFIG's IG office to investigate, and Major Streater, the finance expert, looked

---

[42] Ltr, CG, AFIG, to TAG, 19 Jun 20, sub: Relief of Colonel Edgar Fry, Entry 1360, RG 120, NARA.

[43] Memo, IG, AFIG, to ACofS, G–3, AFIG, 11 Dec 19, sub: Gambling in American Forces in Germany, Entry 1360, RG 120, NARA.

into manipulations of the June 1920 payroll. American troops were paid in dollars, but disbursing officers also were given a sum of marks to allow the troops to meet their obligations on the local economy. Some pay officers interpreted this provision very liberally, permitting the men to exchange funds in their possession in excess of the pay they drew. The practice contravened the intent of published orders; the pay officers apparently were not aware of restrictions on the amount a person could exchange. The investigation resulted in tighter controls and audits, which prevented that particular form of speculation. However, money was still to be made by currency manipulation, and when Allen learned in November that some officers were still speculating, he had them court-martialed and returned to the United States.[44]

Cases involving enlisted men differed in some respects from those involving officers. For one thing, such cases did not feature the same high proportion of alcohol-related investigations, perhaps because of greater command tolerance for such behavior among the soldiers. At least half of the complaints received from enlisted men had to do with allegations of improper actions on the part of the military police, including brutality, false arrest, and unnecessary use of deadly force. There were a few breach of promise and paternity cases. The remainder of the cases largely involved petty crimes, such as barracks thefts and abuse of government property, while a few related to disrespect to allied officers. Many of the special investigations concluded with a recommendation for court-martial. If such a recommendation was approved, the AFIG adjutant general would paraphrase the IG report in a directive to the individual's commander to begin the judicial process.[45]

In many cases, the inspectors were called upon to conduct inquiries more appropriate for a criminal investigative service or a police organization. The military police had begun to perform such duties by the time of the armistice in 1918. However, over time the combination of inexperienced leaders and the lack of firm direction from the AFIG G–2, under whom the military police had been placed, produced a drop in efficiency and a hopeless mixture of police and intelligence functions. By the fall of 1920 the situation had deteriorated to an unacceptable level. General Allen directed Colonel Hay to investigate the

---

[44] Rpt, Streater to CG, AFIG, 29 Jul 20, sub: Investigation of Money Exchanges by Paying Officers, Entry 1360, RG 120, NARA.

[45] AFIG IG File 201, Boxes 3–6 and 10, Investigations, Entry 1360; Ltr, AG, VI Corps, to IG, VI Corps, 1 Apr 19, sub: Investigation Discipline, Headquarters Troop, Entry 1149. Both in RG 120, NARA.

Provost Marshal's Department because of allegations that evidence was being manipulated to help friends of the military police.

The investigation took four weeks—all of October—and revealed many problems in addition to the suspected favoritism. Young military police officers were not technically knowledgeable and often showed poor judgment in their management of cases. Their organization did not control its discretionary funds properly, allowing unauthorized or questionable expenditures. The Provost Marshal's Department was understaffed and overworked, a fact that partially accounted for its poor performance and the unprofessional conduct of its personnel. Colonel Hay concluded that the department needed a complete overhaul, with new personnel and some reorganization, and recommended that an experienced officer be put in charge of the task of rebuilding command confidence in it.[46]

International Complications

Even before the reform could begin, however, amateurish efforts at criminal investigation created an international crisis that took all of General Allen's energies to subdue. On their own initiative, two young investigators had gone out of their jurisdiction into unoccupied Germany to apprehend a deserter, Pvt. Grover C. Bergdoll. In the ensuing fracas, shots were fired and a German woman was wounded. German police arrested the Americans, who were tried and sentenced to a jail term. Both the German and American governments were incensed at what they each viewed as infringements on their prestige and sovereignty. Allen was forced to resort to strong diplomatic threats to have the men released. He eventually got his way by warning the Germans that he might not mediate between them and the French as he had done in the past.[47]

The Bergdoll crisis begged for a further analysis of the entire G–2 police arrangement. In November 1920 the AFIG's IG office received a broad directive to evaluate the relationship between the G–2 and the Provost Marshal's Department and to recommend improvements. Colonel Hay examined every element of the counterintelligence and criminal sections under the G–2, defined each of their missions, and turned up much evidence both of incompatibility and duplication. He

---

[46] Rpt, Hay to CoS, AFIG, 30 Oct 20, sub: Investigation Into Certain Phases of the Provost Marshal's Department, Entry 1360, RG 120, NARA.

[47] Twichell, *Allen*, pp. 243–44; Allen, *Rhineland Journal*, pp. 178, 182, 193, 195, 197.

concluded that intelligence and police activities should be entirely distinct and that the investigation of criminal activities should be vested solely in the Provost Marshal's Department, with the G–2 removed from any direct involvement. Hay also was able to show how a better organization of the two functions would reduce personnel requirements. General Allen approved his recommendations on 31 January 1921.[48]

The Provost Marshal's Department finally was given the opportunity to realize its potential. Because of improved operations, the number of complaints of police misconduct—and, concomitantly, the number of IG special investigations of criminal conduct—declined. All involved benefited from a change that marked a significant advance in efficiency and command morale.

The Bergdoll crisis was not the first time that General Allen and his IG were involved in a case with high international interest. On occasion, AFIG inspectors handled delicate issues involving the improper use of government facilities by unauthorized civilians from allied countries. Sometimes entertainers, politicians, and businessmen unconnected with the U.S. Army or the Allied High Commission would foist themselves on unsuspecting billeting and transportation officers to secure treatment and benefits for which they were ineligible. Summaries of IG reports on such cases were sent to allied representatives, with a request for remedial action. American citizens who tried similar tricks were simply confronted with a request for reimbursement.[49]

More significant was a soldier's death that for a time seemed likely to have wide ramifications. In September 1919 Pvt. Howell Madson, 8th Infantry, had been shot and killed near Rosbach in the neutral zone between U.S. and German forces. The senior inspector at the time, Colonel Read, investigated the case and represented General Allen in dealing with the Germans. Madson had been poaching with a companion in an area patrolled by the Germans. When they encountered a group of German soldiers and failed to surrender, Madson was shot and his companion, bound with his own puttees, was forced to jog behind a mounted German NCO nearly 10 miles to the German guard station, where he was interrogated with considerable roughness.

---

[48] Memo, Johnston to IG, AFIG, 11 Jan 21; Memo, Bagby to IG, AFIG, 25 Jan 21; and Memo, Hay to CG, AFIG, 26 Jan 21, sub: Investigation of the Organization, Functions and Duties of the Personnel of Intelligence Section, General Staff and Provost Marshal's Department. All in Entry 1360, RG 120, NARA.

[49] Rpt, IG, AFIG, to CofS, AFIG, 28 Feb 20, sub: Complaint of J. L. Frohlick Submitted by Coblenz Landrat; Rpt, IG, AFIG, to CofS, AFIG, 16 Oct 20, sub: Case of Mrs. Ethel Gastrell. Both in Entry 1360, RG 120, NARA.

In the affair there was blame enough to go around. Colonel Read recommended that the dead man's NCO be court-martialed for allowing him to cross the line into a forbidden area. He also concluded that the Germans had used unnecessary force in making the arrest and that their treatment of their prisoner had been gratuitously harsh. Hence, he recommended that all members of the German patrol be interrogated and that its NCO be tried for brutality.[50]

Read discussed the matter with the senior German military representative, who agreed to send his men into the American zone to be interviewed. In the meantime, General Allen sent his judge advocate general to Marshal Foch, the allied forces commander, to find out if he would support a demand to try the German soldiers. Foch, after reviewing Read's report and agreeing with its findings, stated that he believed the American soldiers were in the wrong but that he would support Allen in whatever he did. Further discussions, however, produced a face-saving compromise. The Allies requested that the German government try its NCO for misconduct and report the action taken. This was done, and by late November 1919 the issue had faded away. Colonel Read's diplomatic handling of the case had made a large contribution to its successful conclusion.[51]

Other problems developed in eastern Europe. In August 1920, shortly after his arrival at the AFIG, Colonel Hay was obliged to put aside his many IG duties to go to Poland. The U.S. Army had several thousand soldiers in that country. Some were members of the advanced party of the so-called Silesian Brigade, which was beginning to withdraw after the American government decided not to participate in the plebiscites agreed to in the Versailles Treaty. Others belonged to the food-relief and typhus-treatment teams of the American Polish Typhus Relief Expedition, formed by the War Department to help combat the public health crisis caused by Poland's war with Russia. A fairly large logistical support unit was stationed in Warsaw and Danzig to provide for the Americans and to aid the shipment of military goods to the Poles.

General Allen wanted Hay to observe every American activity in Poland except the embassy. Lacking precise details, and concerned about the safety of Americans and the stability of the country in light of a successful Russian offensive then in progress, Allen sought firsthand information on what was occurring and on what good U.S. units were doing.

---

[50] Rpt, Read to CofS, AFIG, 13 Sep, 19, sub: Killing of Private Howell Madsen, Co. L, 8th Infantry; Memo, Nudant to Pres, GerArmCom, 7 Nov 19. Both in Entry 1360, RG 120, NARA.

[51] Memo, Nudant to Pres, GerArmCom, 7 Nov 19, Entry 1360, RG 120, NARA.

Hay spent nearly three weeks in Poland, observing among other things the favorable influence on Polish fortunes of a French military mission headed by French General Maxime Weygand. He briefed Allen on the recently stabilized situation in early September, and there the matter rested. He was impressed by the activities of the U.S. medical teams, and his report prompted General Allen to write letters of commendation to several of the officers Hay had noted as deserving of praise.[52]

Such actions brought credit to Allen's command; others, only embarrassment. One case involving the personal misconduct of a few came to light in the late summer of 1922. To the surprise of the command, eight finance and quartermaster officers who had worked in Poland were all awarded the Polish Cross of the Brave—the equivalent of the Distinguished Service Cross. After the AFIG adjutant general could not find any record of their nomination or any of the follow-up correspondence cited by the Polish Ministry of War in its transmittal documents, he referred the case to the inspector general. The IG investigation revealed that one of the recipients, a finance lieutenant, had worked through one of the assistant adjutants general at the AFIG headquarters, who, in turn, had bypassed all channels by writing directly to the Polish government to request the awards. The Poles wished to be accommodating, and, assuming that General Allen must have desired the action, awarded the medals. The lieutenant and the assistant adjutant general were court-martialed, the other officers receiving only reprimands, and all the medals were disapproved for wear. The Polish government, however, was not advised of the action to avoid mutual embarrassment over the temporary success of a scheme that reflected poorly on both nations.[53]

It is often surprising to learn what sort of thing mobilizes the full investigative capabilities of a command. The biggest dragnet in the AFIG's history resulted when the Transportation Service lost Congressman Walter F. Lineberger's trunk in February 1922. The quartermaster and G–4 began the search, as did the Antwerp port commander. Soon, the recently reformed Provost Marshal's Department became

---

[52] Rpt, Hay to CG, AFIG, 1 Sep 20, sub: Inspection of American- Polish Typhus Relief Expedition, Entry 11, RG 159, NARA; Ltr, Magruder to Chamberlain, 23 Aug 20, Entry 1360, RG 120, NARA; Alfred E. Cornebise, *Typhus and Doughboys: The American Polish Typhus Relief Expedition, 1919–1921* (Newark: University of Delaware, 1982), p. 82.

[53] Ltr, Farman to AG, AFIG, 20 Dec 22; Rpt, IG, AFIG, to CoS, AFIG, 12 Feb 23, sub: Investigation Concerning Award of Polish Cross of the Brave. Both in Entry 1360, RG 120, NARA. See also Cornebise, *Typhus and Doughboys*, p. 145.

involved. Then the railway police of France, Belgium, and Germany were asked to investigate as well. When it became known that the trunk contained some sensitive official papers, both the American and French secret police took part in the investigation. Naturally, the Congressman and General Allen were concerned, but the pressure increased when General Harbord, now Pershing's Deputy Chief of Staff, inquired as to the status of the investigation during the final days of his European visit. Apparently, he wanted to bring good news back home to the Congressman.[54]

Finally, General Allen directed Major Magruder to gather all the threads of the investigation and attempt to determine the fate of the missing trunk. Magruder took nearly three weeks to digest the details of the other investigations and to complete his own findings. His sole achievement was to establish an audit trail, with a sequence of events pinpointing the time and place of loss to the Coblenz railyards on 2 February. His only recommendation was that everyone involved stay alert in case the trunk reappeared. Congressman Lineberger even gave Magruder $100 to hold as a reward. In January 1923, in one of his last acts as the AFIG inspector general, he returned the money, still without the trunk.[55]

By this time the occupation was ending, as far as the United States was concerned. The last troops marched out of Coblenz on 24 January, and General Allen turned over the American zone to the French on the twenty-seventh. Three weeks later he and a small staff left for home, and the AFIG joined the roster of other vanished forces in American military history.[56] To the very last, the ever-shrinking force maintained a reputation for discipline, courtesy, and appearance that challenged the forces of the other occupying powers. General Allen's high standards and strong command interest unquestionably set the tone, and his small IG office had proved to be a consistent source of reliable guidance, information, and analysis.

American Expeditions to Russia

During World War I American troops found themselves in places stranger than France and Germany. The collapse of czarist Russia early

---

[54] Rpt, Magruder to CG, AFIG, 20 May 22, sub: Loss of Trunk of Mr. W. F. Lineberger; Ltr, Lineberger to Magruder, 26 Jan 23. Both in Entry 1360, RG 120, NARA.

[55] Ltr, Lineberger to Magruder, 26 Jan 23, Entry 1360, RG 120, NARA.

[56] Henry T. Allen, *The Rhineland Occupation* (Indianapolis, Ind.: Bobbs-Merrill Co., 1927), pp. 536, 541.

Although theoretically the two U.S. expeditions to Russia were elements of a single scheme, the lack of any clear objective and the vast distance between them made their experiences completely different. Americans in northwestern Russia found themselves functioning as a major combat element of a mixed allied force. Those in Siberia, while attempting to carry out neutral security missions, more often were caught in a brutal diplomatic sparring match between Reds, Whites and the Japanese members of the allied expedition.

The U.S. forces sent to northwestern Russia consisted of the 339th Infantry, a battalion of engineers, and a field hospital. All had been part of the untested 85th Division, which had been staging in England for service in France. The regimental commander, Col. George E. Stewart, a former enlisted man and Medal of Honor recipient, found himself having to respond to orders from various organizations. At AEF headquarters he learned that his unit was to perform guard duty at Murmansk, but he subsequently received a War Department telegram directing him to take his orders from the senior allied officer there, British Maj. Gen. Frederick C. Poole. Then a few weeks after arriving in Russia, he received a State Department wire instructing him not to participate in offensive operations. It goes without saying that the colonel had no idea what he was supposed to do and, consequently, did as little as possible, virtually turning over control of his battalions to the British while he fruitlessly queried the War Department for guidance.[62]

Arriving early in March, General Poole had used his slender force of second-rate British and French troops to push southward, following the Dvina River and a railroad line, in the direction of Czech forces some 600 miles away in central Russia. When the Americans landed on 4 September 1918, his forces were having difficulty fending off Bolshevik counterattacks. The 339th doughboys were rushed straight from the Archangel docks into combat to stabilize the allied front. Not knowing why they were there, and with very little leadership from Colonel Stewart, they were committed to a miserable winter of exposure and fighting. The American forces, supported by a highly efficient Canadian field artillery battery, soon became the mainstay of the allied combat effort *(Map 4)*.[63]

---

[62] ABMC, *American Armies*, p. 443; E. M. Halliday, *The Ignorant Armies* (New York: Award Books, 1964), pp. 51, 77–78; John Silverlight, *The Victors' Dilemma: Allied Intervention in the Russian Civil War, 1917–1920* (New York: Weybright and Talley, 1970), p. 176; U.S. Congress, Senate, Committee on Veterans' Affairs, *Medal of Honor Recipients, 1863–1978*, 96th Cong., 1st Sess., p. 381.

[63] Halliday, *Ignorant Armies*, p. 73.

Map 4

In November General Poole was replaced by Maj. Gen. Edmund Ironside, a far better leader who recognized the errors of Poole's deployment. He adopted a defensive strategy, but could do little to

299

improve the difficult living conditions of the soldiers at the front. Ironically, the men of the 339th fought one of the worst battles of the expedition on the twelfth, the day they learned of the armistice. No one could understand why they were still there. At home, the War Department and President Wilson came under increasing pressure to withdraw the troops, since the reasons alleged for their presence had disappeared with the end of the war.[64]

By late January 1919 the pointlessness of continuing had become evident. Declining morale among the British and French troops and improving performance in the Bolshevik forces led General Ironside to recommend an allied withdrawal. The Whites in the area had done little to help themselves; the troops they raised had proven to be singularly unreliable. In February Secretary of War Baker announced plans to withdraw U.S. forces as soon as ice conditions permitted. Railroad units were sent to Murmansk to prepare for a withdrawal. Under Brig. Gen. Wilds P. Richardson, a small staff was dispatched to take charge of all U.S. units.[65]

Inspectorate in Northwestern Russia

Despite the fact that American units had received little support, even from the regimental headquarters, the troops had conducted themselves well. Among their allies, discouragement and mutiny had been rife. Russian units had mutinied and deserted; the French battalion had refused to go to the front; and the British battalion had to be severely disciplined before finally returning to the lines from a rest area. The only similar incident in the 339th received far more notoriety than it deserved.

In late March 1919 the men of Company I, at a rest camp near Archangel, complained to their first sergeant that they saw no reason to load up and return to the front. They felt that the numerous White Russian troops lounging around the rear area should be required to go before they did. The first sergeant reported this grumbling up the chain of command. Eventually, Colonel Stewart assembled the company in formation and read the Articles of War, one of which specified death for mutiny. Then, in what could only have been his finest hour in Russia, he told the troops that he, too, could not explain why they were there but that he knew they would be among the first to perish if the

---

[64] E. M. Halliday, "Where Ignorant Armies Clashed by Night," *American Heritage* (Dec 58): 26–29, 120–25.

[65] Silverlight, *Victors' Dilemma*, pp. 186–87, 197; Halliday, *Ignorant Armies*, p. 254.

Bolsheviks they were fighting triumphed. Seeing his logic, the men returned to duty without further incident.

This was the so-called mutiny of the 339th, which for reasons unknown was made the subject of a press release by the War Department. One of the few bits of news to emerge from northwestern Russia, the story got considerable exposure, unnecessarily staining the 339th's excellent reputation. The incident was investigated by the U.S. Military Mission, headed by Col. James A. Ruggles, and later by the Inspector General of the Army. Both agreed that it hardly merited the effort.[66]

The involvement of Colonel Ruggles' Military Mission in investigating the mutiny underscores the fact that the U.S. forces in northwestern Russia received little inspection support prior to the arrival of General Richardson. Ruggles relied on his intelligence officers to handle any problems. Needless to say, standards of discipline, appearance, and equipment suffered from the combination of deficient oversight with hard service in a mixed command. As General Richardson remarked in July 1919, "It was unfortunate for the interests of the Government and for the good name of the command in North Russia that a competent and energetic inspector was not appointed earlier."[67]

The new commander made haste to correct the deficiency. At the time of his appointment General Richardson asked Pershing to allow him to bring with him his inspector from his old command, Base Section No. 3, in London. This was Maj. Howard N. Scales, a temporary officer originally appointed into the Adjutant General's Department. Pershing agreed, and Major Scales assumed his duties on 9 April 1919, immediately initiating a series of inspections aimed at restoring morale and discipline. He stressed bearing, appearance, camp police, and sanitation, and he oversaw a generally satisfactory process of improvement.

The problems, he felt, were attributable "to a lack of attention by company and battalion commanders." He could have added inexperience as well. This was particularly the case in the area of funds management. Scales noted that virtually all of the unit funds were poorly maintained, and the fact that 90 percent of the money placed in sol-

---

[66] Halliday, *Ignorant Armies*, p. 238; U.S. War Department, *Annual Report of the Inspector General, 1919* (Washington, D.C.: Government Printing Office, 1920), p. 655; File 22–36.1, Morale and Mutinies, North Russian Expedition, Roll 1, Microfilm 924, NARA.

[67] File 22–66.1, Inspections, North Russian Expedition, Roll 2, Microfilm 924, NARA; 1st End (quotation), Richardson, 23 Jul 19, to Rpt, Insp to CG, AEF, N. Russia, 19 Jul 19, sub: Inspections and Investigations, Entry 26, RG 159, NARA.

Maj. Howard N. Scales Working in His Archangel Office

diers' deposits came from personnel in the supply company aroused his suspicion. His investigations led to the trial of three officers for "gross and inexcusable negligence" in handling various accounts. Poor management, he believed, on the part of the 339th's quartermaster had led to overstockages that, in turn, created unnecessary opportunities for black-marketing.[68]

Scales also looked into rumors of tension with the British and found them largely unfounded, mostly attributable to isolated instances of poor leadership on one side or the other. He recommended that the British ration should not be given to U.S. soldiers in future operations. Although nutritionally adequate, its differences from customary American rations "tended to cause a certain amount of discontent." Overall, Scales determined that the rumors of poor morale had no basis; in fact, in well-led units, such as those of the Engineer and Transportation Corps, he considered morale to be very high. Similarly, he judged that troop conduct was remarkably good, and like other investigating officers dismissed the Company I mutiny

---

[68] Rpt, Insp to CG, AEF, N. Russia, 19 Jul 19, Entry 26, RG 159, NARA.

as a minor incident that stronger company-level leadership could have nipped in the bud.[69]

The work of Scales and Richardson has been ridiculed by some historians as an unnecessary resort to Regular Army martinetism. But their by-the-book approach was needed to compensate for the inexperience of the National Army officers, who had been coping almost unaided with a difficult situation. The standards that they set were no different from those considered normal in the AEF in France or the Army of Occupation in Germany, and they were able to sustain the high level of discipline and morale necessary to achieve a smooth evacuation without incident in July 1919. The American forces had conducted themselves well in a virtually pointless situation, at the price of nearly 400 casualties.[70] Their fellow soldiers in Siberia were perhaps the only others who could understand the problems and frustrations of their task.

Americans in Siberia

U.S. forces landed at the eastern extremity of Russia better organized than their counterparts in the northwest, but equally unclear as to the reason for their presence. On 6 August 1918 the 31st and 27th Infantry, on duty in the Philippines, were alerted to move to Vladivostok. Their advanced parties set foot in Russia on the fifteenth, and within days the regiments were supporting Japanese attacks on Bolshevik strongpoints north of the port. Approximately 9,000 Americans, 70,000 Japanese, 1,000 French, and 1,000 British were in Siberia by the end of September.[71]

Meanwhile, Maj. Gen. William S. Graves had arrived in the region, accompanied by a complete staff, service units, and replacements for the infantry regiments. Graves immediately put a halt to U.S. offensive activity, viewing it as contrary to his instructions. An able officer with nearly thirty years of service, he had just assumed command of the former 8th Division in training at Camp Fremont, California, when he was tapped to lead the expedition. He was

---

[69] Ibid.

[70] Halliday, *Ignorant Armies*, p. 254; Richard Luckett, *The White Generals: An Account of the White Movement and the Russian Civil War* (New York: Viking Press, 1971), p. 208. The British lingered in North Russia until September 1919, when they left the place to the White Russians. In February 1920 the Bolsheviks overwhelmed the Whites.

[71] Manning, *Siberian Fiasco*, p. 94; Silverlight, *Victors' Dilemma*, p. 73; AEF Siberia Surgeon General's Report, Apr 20, Entry 5996, RG 394, NARA.

assigned in a most unusual way. Secretly meeting with Secretary Baker in the Kansas City railroad station, he was handed the President's diplomatic statement justifying intervention. Then Baker departed with the encouraging words, "Watch your step, you will be walking on eggs loaded with dynamite."[72]

After reading Wilson's document, Graves saw his mission as safeguarding allied property; helping the Czechs; and, above all, remaining neutral in any internal Russian conflicts. He consistently attempted to follow a policy of fairness toward all elements of Russian society, repeatedly ordering his troops not to take sides in any local trouble that did not directly threaten them—a policy that often ran contrary to those of the other allies. By April 1919 the effect was to restrict U.S. actions to providing security for parts of the Trans-Siberian railroad and the supply dumps in the Vladivostok area, which by that time had become targets for virtually every other player in the game *(Map 5)*.[73]

The allies did not dominate Russian politics in Siberia as they had in northwestern Russia. They were confronted with a kaleidoscope of strong and weak groups, all trying to gain control. Eventually, a series of White governments, supported by the Czechs, appeared at Omsk in central Siberia. Control was centered by November 1918 in the person of the former czarist admiral Alexander Kolchak. Personally honest and patriotic, Kolchak was a poor judge of character, and his government soon became more ruthless and corrupt than the old czarist monarchy. Despite this, the allies, including the United States, seriously considered recognizing the Kolchak regime because it seemed to have a chance of emerging as the dominant force in all Russia.[74]

Such a development was not favored by the Japanese. Ostensibly America's major partner and ally in the intervention, they saw opportunities for expansion in the continuing instability of Russian Asia and saw the American pressure as an obstacle to their goals. As their ambitions in Manchuria grew, they also began to consider possible annexation of Russian territory. But the American policy of neutrality, with its stress on the maintenance of existing territorial integrity throughout the changing Far East, ran counter to Japanese ambitions. The results led to tension and hostility with American troops, whose main mission had become securing the railroad upon which all parties depended. Moreover, since the railroad was largely in the hands

---

[72] William S. Graves, *America's Siberian Adventure, 1918–1920* (New York: Jonathan Cape and Harrison Smith, 1931), p. 4 (Baker quotation).

[73] White, *Siberian Intervention*, pp. 271–74; Kendall, *Soldiers in Siberia*, p. 190.

[74] White, *Siberian Intervention*, pp. 341–42; Luckett, *White Generals*, p. 216.

Map 5

of the Whites, Americans also were automatically the targets of Bolshevik partisans.[75]

The Japanese went out of their way to harass the Americans. Russian clergymen who married U.S. soldiers to Russian women were beaten up, and the brides' families were threatened. American soldiers en route through areas controlled by the Japanese or their surrogates were detained and interrogated. In several cases officers and their enlisted escorts were arrested, some of whom were brutally beaten before being released. Each such case was investigated and protests made to the Japanese high command, though to no avail. Fierce skirmishes erupted between American patrols and Bolshevik raiders or Japanese-sponsored bandits, and Company C, 27th Infantry, clashed sharply on one occasion with a Japanese unit of comparable size.[76]

General Graves had the responsibility of dealing with this tangle. With his headquarters in Vladivostok, most of his troops were deployed north of the city, along the railroad and at the nearby Suchan coal mines. Seven companies, however, were stationed 3,000 miles away, on the railroad just east of Lake Baikal in an area under Japanese control. The expe-

---

[75] White, *Siberian Intervention*, pp. 259, 383.
[76] Kendall, *Soldiers in Siberia*, pp. 202–06.

Col. Willis V. Morris

dition IG, Col. Willis V. Morris, played a prominent role in developing the information needed by General Graves to deal with the Japanese. Additionally, he labored to keep the command in the best possible shape in circumstances that were exceptionally difficult because of the divided forces, the ongoing civil war, the international complications, and the conditions of life in wartime Siberia.

Morris, a cavalry officer and a graduate of the U.S. Military Academy, had been the inspector on the 8th Division staff before coming to Russia with General Graves. Whenever his work load was heavy, acting inspectors were assigned to assist him. As a result, normally two officers performed inspection duties. One of the acting inspectors was Maj. Sydney C. Graves, the commander's son, who had come directly from France to serve first as his father's aide and then as an inspector from June 1919 to April 1920. The younger Graves received Britain's Distinguished Service Order for evacuating civilians from a wrecked train near Ussuri during the heated cross fire of the ambushers and defenders.[77]

The turbulent situation spared no one. The inspectors found themselves on the road a lot, visiting the dispersed U.S. units performing guard duty. The soldiers lived in tents during the warm season, bivouacking normally under the crudest of field conditions near tiny villages along the railroad. The IGs spent their time gathering information and facts necessary to describe each unit's situation. When American positions were attacked, an inspector went to the location to record the chain of events and to try to determine responsibility. Reports included data on the behavior and attitudes of Russian civilians and local unit policies toward both White and Red armed bands. Many

---

[77] AEF Siberia File 201, S. C. Graves, W. V. Morris, J. D. Leitch, Entry 5997, RG 394, NARA. Young Graves had earned a Distinguished Service Cross in France; he was a member of the class of 1915 at the Military Academy.

reports of atrocities were received and all were investigated, if possible; brutality was more often the rule than the exception in the Siberia of the time. One of the worst cases was the murder of nearly 300 unarmed Latvian soldiers by the Japanese. When confronted with the facts, the Japanese blandly replied that all Europeans looked pretty much alike to them, and their troops had thought the Letts were Reds.[78]

The inspectors also investigated instances of personal misconduct by American soldiers. The problems ranged from simple AWOLs and brawling to cases of desertion, in which men left their units to join the Bolsheviks. The small inspectorate handled many complaints from Russian civilians concerning theft, or the failure of soldiers to pay for goods and services. Most complaints about soldiers' conduct or duty performance were handled through command channels. Other investigations reflected the tension and danger routinely confronting American soldiers. Those that might have a broader impact on relations with Russian civilians or allied personnel were referred to Colonel Morris.[79]

Individual situations were often exceedingly complex. In one such case, Russian railway police accused an American sentry of attacking a local civilian. Investigation showed that the sentry had been under orders not to allow crowds to collect near his post. When a Russian began to give a speech and people gathered, the inexperienced soldier repeatedly asked the orator to stop. When the individual ignored him, the doughboy—after the sixth warning—struck him on the head with his rifle butt. Colonel Morris concluded that the sentry's action, "while unnecessarily severe," was excusable. General Graves agreed, saying he did not want anything done to discourage sentries from hesitating to act "when action might be critically needed."[80]

The conduct of inspections more nearly resembled standard IG practice. Unit inspections entailed typical reviews of administrative practice and logistical support, as well as detailed examinations of property records, morning reports, immunizations, and the soldiers' personal equipment and documents. A list of irregularities and deficiencies was given to the senior commander, who took corrective action and informed the IG of the results. When inspecting the camps where

---

[78] Rpt, Morris to Graves, 4 Jun 19, sub: Inspection of American Troops in Section Verkline—Udinsk to Mysovaya, Entry 5997, RG 394, NARA.

[79] AEF Siberia File 333, General Reference, Entry 5997, RG 394, NARA.

[80] Rpt, Morris to Graves, 8 Oct 18, sub: Investigation Concerning an Alleged Assault by an American Sentinel Upon a Russian Civilian, with Graves' notes in pencil, Entry 5997, RG 394, NARA.

U.S. troops were stationed, the same concern for administrative detail was maintained as in less harassed commands. Inspectors spent the bulk of these visits training inexperienced unit officers in requirements, such as ration accountability, maintenance of vouchers, and so forth. Recurring problems in finance and equipment records required painstaking reviews of unit ledgers to ferret out the inevitable errors.[81]

Complaints were accepted during each inspection visit from anyone who wished to speak out, including Russians and the remaining German and Austrian prisoners of war who were still under U.S. control. American soldiers complained about living conditions and discharge policies and what they viewed as instances of abuse of authority. Russians came to the inspectors with complaints about theft, misappropriation of property, and vandalism. In many cases, the U.S. command was the only form of authority able or willing to give a sympathetic hearing to complaints or claims. Colonel Morris heard many cases concerning injustices committed by the Whites or the Japanese, but could do little to correct them.[82]

In August 1919 the Kolchak government began to crumble, and even the most obtuse interventionists soon realized that the allies could achieve nothing by remaining in Russia. The British and French pulled out their token forces in September; the American units near Lake Baikal were pulled back to Vladivostok in December. At the same time, General Graves announced that the United States also intended to withdraw completely from eastern Russia in the near future.[83]

As the time approached, the demands on the small inspectorate swelled. The sale of surplus materiel that was to be left behind at campsites when the U.S. troops withdrew had to be supervised. Port activities and the condition of transports also became a matter of concern with the embarkation of the first group of soldiers in January 1920. A final surge of claims and complaints from Russian civilians required

---

[81] Rpt, Morris to Graves, 27 Jan 19, sub: Irregularities and Deficiencies Observed at Inspections of the 31st Infantry; Rpt, Morris to Graves, 25 Sep 19, sub: Inspection of U.S. Troops, Spasskoe, Siberia. Both in Entry 5997, RG 394, NARA.

[82] AEF Siberia File 321.3, Inspections—Consolidated Cross References, Entry 5997; Rpt, Sillman to Graves, 12 Oct 19, sub: Complaints of Men of Ambulance Company #4 at Spasskoe, Siberia, Entry 6012. Both in RG 394, NARA.

[83] There was growing opposition to the American presence in Siberia, led by Congressman Fiorello La Guardia and Senator Hiram Johnson (White, *Siberian Intervention*, pp. 355–58). Congresswoman Jeanette Rankin added to the pressure by proposing that the U.S. government buy land in Siberia, to be used as a reservation for the troops sent there. Rankin thought they would be too diseased and morally corrupted to be allowed to return to the United States (Kendall, *Soldiers in Siberia*, p. 229).

settlement, and more acting inspectors were added to handle the already heavy work load. Anti-American incidents increased as the Japanese and their bandit allies sought to hasten the American departure; the Whites felt betrayed and abandoned, and the Reds exploited the growing instability. Each incident of harassment, insolence, or outright assault had to be fully documented for General Graves, who would use the data to complain—although futilely— to the responsible commanders. Colonel Morris concentrated on the incidents and on closing out accounts, while other acting IGs saw to clearing billets, settling civilian claims, and disposing of surplus animals.[84]

In fact, American forces slowed their departure at the behest of the State Department, in an effort to deter any Japanese attempts to take advantage of the chaos. The American presence in Siberia helped to assure the preservation of eastern Siberia as part of Russia; it almost certainly prevented a Franco-British arrangement with Japan to conduct an all-out anti-Bolshevik campaign. On this count, the Siberian Expedition could be viewed as a diplomatic success. But from the perspective of the soldiers, success came at a high price. The last Americans pulled out of Vladivostok on 1 April 1920, ending a mission whose purpose General Graves later admitted that he had never understood.[85]

His inspectorate had performed conscientiously, if unspectacularly, in support of the expeditionary force. It had compensated for the inexperience of many of the officers and NCOs by assuring high standards in the administration of funds and supplies. Inspectors were instrumental in obtaining the information necessary for the headquarters to provide the best possible support to the isolated little garrisons strung along the railroad. They also kept General Graves more fully informed of the general situation than he could have been otherwise. Finally, it was their grim task to document many incidents of man's inhumanity to man. Solid, dedicated, and thorough, Colonel Morris proved the value of an inspectorate in a unique situation.

---

[84] AEF Siberia File 321.3, Inspections by the Inspector General, Nov 18–Apr 20, Entry 5997, RG 394, NARA; Graves, *Siberian Adventure*, p. 310.
[85] White, *Siberian Intervention*, pp. 187–88, 255; Judith A. Luckett, "The Siberian Intervention: Military Support of Foreign Policy," *Military Review* 64 (Apr 84): 54–63; Graves, *Siberian Adventure*, p. 354.

PART THREE

NEGLECT AND PRIVATION
1919–1939

9

The Problems of Peace

Soon after the armistice was announced, the War Department began to focus on demobilization and the structure of the postwar force. By mid-January 1919 over 700,000 soldiers had been discharged, followed by 500,000 the next month and another 800,000 during the three months after that—2 million men in half a year. This phase essentially ended with the return of the 1st Division from France in September.[1]

Simultaneously, the War Department began to grapple with issues of reorganization, modernization, and mobilization that were to consume much of its energies for twenty years to come. The changes brought by wartime to the National Defense Act of 1916 had been temporary. Yet the military system required structural reform, if only because American participation in the global conflict had made it apparent that a similar involvement might occur in the future. General March favored a 500,000-man force, supported by a large reserve based on peacetime conscription. The political feasibility of such a large peacetime Army was another question entirely.[2]

Future of the IGD

The role of the Inspector General's Department (IGD) also needed redefining. March himself favored the transfer of several IG functions. In November 1918 the War Department General Staff's War Plans Division (WPD), after its review of the IGD's history, proposed that its

---

[1] William A. Ganoe, *The History of the United States Army* (New York: D. Appleton and Co., 1924), p. 482; Erna Risch, *Quartermaster Support of the Army: A History of the Corps, 1775–1939* (Washington, D.C.: Quartermaster Historian's Office, Office of the Quartermaster General, 1962), p. 697.

[2] Russell F. Weigley, *History of the United States Army* (New York: Macmillan Co., 1967), p. 396.

functions be limited, with the General Staff assuming responsibility for training inspections and funds inspections. The study also recommended that the Judge Advocate General's Department or branch experts carry out investigations of misconduct and irregularities and that The Adjutant General take over the custody of inspection and investigation reports.[3]

When the WPD study was forwarded to the AEF for comment, General Spinks cautioned that eliminating the Inspector General's Department would not end the need for the functions it performed. He reasoned that somewhere in the War Department, assets would have to be consumed to continue the activities normally given inspectors. Spinks believed that the elimination proposal exposed a naivete and lack of understanding about the IGD mission. In sum, the command requirement for independent information was essential and that the WPD proposals would cause "injury to efficiency."[4]

Yet the WPD proposals reflected the views of the average line officer, whose opinion of the inspectorate was generally low. Too often in the period between the War with Spain and World War I excessive stress had been placed on blindly enforcing policies, instead of assessing and improving efficiency. One field artilleryman later told General Chamberlain that only once in twenty-one years had his units been inspected by a fellow gunner capable of discussing branch issues in detail.[5] Most officers had little understanding of the complete scope of IG activities and were unaware of Chamberlain's philosophy of providing assistance rather than merely citing problems. In turn, the inspectors' potential often went unrealized because senior commanders and senior staff officers failed through misunderstanding to use them properly.

General Chamberlain, in preparing his rebuttal, relied on the expertise of Lt. Col. Robert D. Palmer, a National Guard officer on duty in the Office of the Inspector General (OIG). In essence, Palmer argued that the Inspector General's Department had proven itself in war as a vital adjunct to the command and should not be altered. Without it, the Army could neither analyse its internal operations objectively nor, in

---

[3] Memo, White to Chief, WPD, 4 Dec 18; Memo, McIntyre to CofS, WD, 6 Dec 18, sub: General Outline of a Study on the Reorganization of the War Department. Both in Entry 296, Record Group (RG) 165, National Archives and Records Administration (NARA), Washington, D.C.

[4] Memo (quoted words), Spinks to CofS, AEF, 14 Dec 18, sub: Proposed Military Policy, Entry 588, RG 120, NARA; Memo, Fiske to CofS, WD, 21 Dec 18, sub: Extracts From Proposed Military Policy, 6 December 1918, Entry 26A, RG 159, NARA.

[5] Ltr, Scott to Chamberlain, 14 Nov 20, Entry 26, RG 159, NARA.

the absence of an independent oversight organization, retain credibility with other government agencies and the public at large. Despite the IGD's reputation for finding fault, he asserted that "instead of being an agent of destruction it was essentially and distinctly an agent of construction." Many of its inquiries were unknown, except to a select few, and could not have been given to any other agency to perform. Like General Breckinridge earlier in the century, Palmer quoted many distinguished former officers who had praised the department.[6]

Generals Chamberlain and Wood used Palmer's arguments, refining them with further examples of IG successes in the recently completed war and stressing Secretary of War Baker's use of the Inspector General's Department in such projects as the business methods survey. Chamberlain's formal reply synthesized the ideas developed earlier, emphasizing areas of IG activity overlooked by the WPD study. In his view, regardless of what happened, the inspection function was so necessary that it would survive somehow, somewhere. Efficiency and common sense dictated that it be allowed to remain in the form of the existing Inspector General's Department.[7]

Apparently, General Chamberlain submitted his January rebuttal in what could only have been a heated conference with the WPD officers who had drafted the study. The result was that they quickly backed down, explaining that their ideas were "experimental" and raised only for "consideration." A spokesman claimed that the WPD staff had not coordinated the study with the Inspector General's Department because of the press of time. The WPD staff agreed to consider Chamberlain's arguments in a revision, which was then under way. While General Chamberlain kept up his offensive, hoping to justify fully the need for an independent inspectorate, various plans of reorganization were reviewed more thoroughly by a WPD committee.[8]

Behind the apparent power grab by the General Staff may have been a fundamental disagreement between General March and Secretary Baker. March already had made it clear that, in his opinion, the General Staff could more appropriately perform training inspections and that only the Chief of Finance—not detailed officers—should

---

[6] Memo, Palmer to Chamberlain, n.d., sub: The Eyes and Ears of the Commander-in-Chief, Entry 25, RG 159, NARA.

[7] Memo, W. Wood to IG, 9 Jan 19, Entry 25; Memo, Chamberlain to WPD, WDGS, 22 Jan 19, Entry 26A. Both in RG 159, NARA.

[8] Memo (quoted words), Clark to Dir, WPD, 5 Feb 19, sub: Memorandum From Inspector General re Staff Organization; Memo, Brown to IG, 5 Feb 19, sub: Staff Organization. Both in Entry 296, RG 165, NARA.

oversee funds inspections. Secretary Baker agreed with March on the matter of training but was not in accord on the issue of financial inspections. The Secretary believed that the function of the Inspector General's Department should be a "corrective" to other elements' fiscal activities. Beyond that, he wished to have access to a "freelance, independent agency" that could look into any topic concerning any War Department component.[9]

General March contended that the Secretary could select any officer he wanted for such a service. Such power, however, existed only in theory. The Army was too large and the Secretary's tenure too transient for him to build his own list of trusted confidential experts in a variety of fields. It was the Inspector General's job to provide such a body of officers on an institutional basis. Hence, Baker felt that the inspectorate should be retained and saw no problem in keeping the Inspector General's Department as a separate element—not subordinate to the General Staff. Testifying before the Senate Committee on Military Affairs on 17 August 1919, Baker credited the department with serving as a "side window" to let in the light, remarking that "the process of coming through channels sometimes is so intricate and lengthy that it is almost impossible to know where this thing started and who is responsible for it. He concluded his testimony by stating that he considered the IG function essential to avoid what he called "staff despotism"—management without independent oversight.[10]

Meanwhile, discussion went on as to the form the Inspector General's Department should take, assuming that it survived as a part of the 500,000-man army proposed by General March. The Chief of Staff envisioned the creation of seven districts, each of which would contain two or more tactical divisions. For example, the First District, based in New York City, would cover New England and the Middle Atlantic States and contain three National Guard divisions; the Second District, based in Washington, D.C., would cover the upper South and contain one Regular Army and one National Guard division. The Seventh District, based in San Francisco, would include the Far West, Alaska, Hawaii, and the Philippines, and contain three Regular Army and one National Army division. Similar mixes prevailed in the remaining districts.

Substantial changes in the Inspector General's Department would be needed to support this scheme. One proposal had the Office of the

[9] Extract from Baker Testimony, Mil Affs Cmte, U.S. Sen, 17 Aug 19, Entry 26, RG 159, NARA.
[10] Ibid.

Inspector General providing support to the Washington-based district, with two inspectors and a field-grade accountant assigned to each of the other districts. A radical departure from the past appeared in a proposal that inspectors assigned to the field commands no longer be considered part of the department, but rather as staff officers exclusively serving their local commanders—a suggestion that would have the effect of keeping IGD strength low despite the proposed enlargement of the Army.[11]

General Chamberlain expanded on this concept by suggesting that all inspectors assigned to divisions no longer be considered a part of the inspectorate. Instead, they would sever their technical links with the Office of the Inspector General and work exclusively for the local commander. The Inspector General's Department, meanwhile, would develop regional offices answerable directly to the Chief of Staff, whose members annually would inspect all commands, depots, etc. These officers would operate under the direction of the Inspector General of the Army in response to the Secretary of War's requirements for information. Chamberlain justified his proposal by referring to the proven need for an inspectorate, as shown by wartime experience. He further stressed that it was unnecessary to reduce the number of inspectors during peacetime.[12]

In essence, the Inspector General's proposal would have made commanders or bureau chiefs responsible for virtually every type of inspection; but, at the same time, it would have made them subject to inspection by the centralized Inspector General's Department, with its direct line to the Secretary. Because the threat of placing Army elements under much closer War Department surveillance was so radical, Chamberlain surmised that it was unlikely that his proposal would be considered seriously. Instead, it established a bargaining position, in the expectation that a compromise could be achieved somewhat short of the other extreme of eliminating the department.[13]

Signs appeared that positions might be moderating. Secretary Baker assured General Chamberlain that he had not reached "any definite conclusion" as to the fate of the Inspector General's Department in any Army reorganization and that his mind was still open on the subject. General March retreated from his original views, and by July he was including an enlarged department as part of his plans for the 500,000-man force. Late that month General Wood advised him that, should the Army reach that size, 105 inspectors would be required—77

[11] Memo, Naylor to IG, 8 Apr 19, sub: Tables of Organization, IGD, Entry 26A, RG 159, NARA.
[12] Memo, Chamberlain to SofW, 15 May 19, Entry 26, RG 159, NARA.
[13] Ibid.

317

more than the 28 authorized in the 1916 legislation that had last defined the size of the permanent force.[14]

Despite the increasing support favoring retention of the Inspector General's Department, the elimination proposal had been included in the reorganization package sent earlier to the Congress. Consequently, General Chamberlain was required to defend his department before the largely sympathetic Senate and House Committees on Military Affairs. On 19 August 1919 he reiterated to the Senate committee the arguments developed by Colonel Palmer the previous winter and refined over the spring. The Inspector General stressed that the General Staff proposal had touched on only the most obvious of IG duties and failed to consider the more comprehensive special inquiries made by inspectors at every level. Once again contending that the Staff required an independent agency capable of determining the efficiency of Army activities, their relation to each other, and their coordination as a part of the whole, Chamberlain proffered as evidence the vast amount of work the inspectorate had performed for the Secretary and the Chief of Staff during the war and restated their continuing need to get the facts "no matter whom it hit."[15]

Several committee members agreed, citing examples of instances in which the IGD's thoroughness and detached professionalism had been important. The senators saw the inspectorate as an independent mechanism for correcting the mistakes of others. General Chamberlain raised the issue of credibility, saying that no organization could investigate itself objectively and reach conclusions that carried the same weight as those of a disinterested outside agent. His words were well received, with some of the committee members adding that an investigation of a hospital could better be carried out by an inspector than a surgeon. The Senate committee, already so inclined, was fully persuaded against making any radical changes in the IGD's structure. General Chamberlain expressed similar views to the House committee the next month and won solid support for the IGD's survival.[16]

Despite this, some field commanders continued to integrate their IGs into their functional staffs. Even when new Army regulations in 1921 specified that inspectors work exclusively for their comman-

---

[14] Memo (Baker quotation), W. Wood to Chamberlain, 5 Aug 19, Entry 26; Memo, W. Wood to CofPerBr, Opns Div, WDGS, 7 Aug 19, Entry 26A. Both in RG 159, NARA.

[15] Chamberlain Testimony, Mil Affs Cmte, U.S. Sen, 19 Aug 19, Entry 26, RG 159, NARA.

[16] Ibid.; Chamberlain Testimony, Mil Affs Cmte, HofReps, 29 Sep 19, Entry 26, RG 159, NARA.

ders, many continued to doubt their ability and to denigrate their function. The commander at Camp Sherman, Ohio, for example, revealed his bias; impressed by his IG's performance, he promised him an assignment "more in keeping with your abilities than your present duties." This continued lack of esteem for the duties of the inspectorate seems to be the basis for the fierce pressures against expanding the IGD's role encountered throughout the tenure of General Helmick, Chamberlain's successor in 1921.[17]

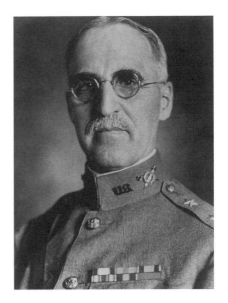

Maj. Gen. Eli A. Helmick

A major challenge in late 1922 served to clarify the issue further. That November, The Adjutant General told the Chief of Staff that he strongly objected to the Inspector General's ability to communicate directly with General Staff elements and recommended revocation of his authority to do so. At the time, a Chief of Staff memorandum had permitted the Inspector General to coordinate directly with any members of the Staff and to present papers in person to the Secretary of War and the Chief of Staff, or his deputy, on inquiries received from them. General Helmick also had direct access to the Deputy Chief of Staff on everything to do with officer discipline and conduct. The Adjutant General wanted all these contacts to be made through him so that he might review the paperwork for administrative correctness. On routine cases he felt that he could begin taking the Inspector General's recommended action while forwarding the papers to the Deputy Chief of Staff, and in doing so could "expedit[e] the transaction of business."[18]

General Harbord, the Deputy Chief of Staff, quickly rejected the proposal, ruling that The Adjutant General should have no power to

---

[17] Ltr (quotation), Smith to Austin, 1 Feb 19; Ltr, Helmick to Elmore, 12 Apr 22. Both in Entry 26, RG 159, NARA.

[18] Memo, Harbord to CofS, WD, 4 Nov 22, sub: Procedure in Disciplinary Cases, Entry 26B, RG 159, NARA.

review OIG recommendations beyond noting obvious policy or procedural errors. Furthermore, OIG recommendations were not a basis for any action until they had been approved by the proper authority. According to Harbord, The Adjutant General's relationship with the Inspector General's Department was intentionally vague, given the fact that certain "cases . . . cannot be handled according to any rule or policy" because they often required discreet and prompt referral to the Secretary of War or Chief of Staff for final action.[19]

This dispute averted any subordination of the Inspector General's Department to another General Staff element. The Office of the Inspector General was able to continue dealing directly with any part of the Army as necessary, although, as a concession to The Adjutant General, it had to include detailed implementing instructions for the action to be taken on a recommendation once approved. The last vestige of any questioning of the Inspector General's authority was resolved by Chief of Staff General Charles P. Summerall at a commanders conference a few years later: "The IGD is an independent agency of the Secretary of War, and of Corps Area commanders, self-contained and not affiliated with any other element of the military establishment."[20] By the end of the 1920s the IGD's status was settled unequivocally, and challenges against its mission and functions faded away.

This status was noted symbolically in 1924. General Helmick, along with several other department heads, was authorized to capitalize the word *The* in his title. A precedent for this practice was made in 1907, when General Ainsworth converted his office from Military Secretary back to Adjutant General. The general order directing this change specified that the word *The* would precede the title designation of the department head. Since then the heads of other similar departments periodically agitated for a similar distinction, achieving success in 1924. At this time General Helmick had the title of The Inspector General. Although the use of capitalization was restricted to the head of the department or agency, the office acronym reflected the change—for example, Helmick's office symbol changing from OIG to OTIG.[21]

---

[19] Ibid.

[20] Ibid.; Proceedings of Conference of Corps Area and Division Commanders (quotation), 1–2 Jun 27, Entry 26B, RG 159, NARA.

[21] WD GO 46, 1907, and GO 2, 1924. The other officers so distinguished in 1924 were The Judge Advocate General, The Quartermaster General, and The Surgeon General. Then in 1938 The Adjutant General confirmed a similar usage on their commissions. See Memo, TAG to Offs Div, AGO, 19 Jan 38, OTIG files, Pentagon (SAIG-ZXH).

National Defense Act and the Budget

During General Chamberlain's appearance on the hill in 1919, it had been clear from much of the questioning that what was really troubling the lawmakers was March's proposal for a 500,000-man force backed by universal military training. Subsequent congressional rejection of a large standing Army also affected the Inspector General's Department. And even while Congress debated the size of the Army, reductions had to be made in the active force. For a time Chamberlain hoped that his department might emerge stronger than before, or at least no weaker. To counter the confusion generated by a variety of legislative proposals and strength changes, the Inspector General began a practice of holding weekly meetings with OIG personnel, and by December was sufficiently optimistic to tell one of these gatherings that his successful defense of the IGD would probably increase its importance. "The General Staff has discovered that this Department is not something they can shove aside." He was confident that the Inspector General's Department was no longer in danger and expected it to emerge from his "little campaign" with a broader scope than ever before.[22]

Chamberlain's optimism proved to be unwarranted. What finally emerged from the legislative arena was the National Defense Act of 1920. The act authorized a peacetime Regular Army strength of 280,000 to provide the nucleus of a larger force, to be expanded in time of need by the National Guard and the Organized Reserve Corps (ORC). The Regular Army would man a large number of division, corps, and field-army units at skeleton strengths, to be filled up during mobilization. Implied in the law was reliance on conscription in case of a major emergency. Federal control over the National Guard increased in light of its role as the primary reserve for the active force. A Civilian Military Training Corps (CMTC) Program, similar to the prewar Plattsburg Camps, was launched to sustain public participation and interest in Army affairs. The act divided the country into nine corps areas for administration, training, and National Guard and reserve affairs *(see Map 6)*. Each area theoretically was to hold one regular, one guard, and three reserve divisions. The corps area functions, along with tactical responsibilities, were

---

[22] Memo, Jervey to IG, 23 Sep 19, sub: Allotment of Officers, Entry 26A; Notes of an Address by General Chamberlain at a Conference of All Officers of the IGD (quotations), 29 Dec 19, Entry 26. Both in RG 159, NARA.

Map 6

D   A

FIRST
• Ft. Ethan Allen

• Madison Barracks

SECOND   ⊛ BOSTON

SIXTH

THIRD   ⊛ GOVERNORS ISLAND (NYC)

CHICAGO   Ft. Jay
Ft. Sheridan •   • Ft. Dix

ok   FIFTH   • Ft. Hayes   Ft. Howard •
Ft. Myer • BALTIMORE
• Washington, D.C.

Leavenworth   INDIANAPOLIS
⊛ Ft. Benjamin
Jefferson   Harrison
Barracks   • Ft. Knox   • Ft. Monroe

ATLANTA • Ft. Gordon
⊛ • Ft. McPherson
FOURTH

CORPS AREAS
December 1920

•	U.S. Army Installations
⊛	Corps Headquarters
—	Corps Boundary
☐	Territory

*Note: Minor shifts in state assignments
occurred in subsequent years.*

1:15,900,000

B A H A M A S

CUBA

assigned to the three overseas departments in Panama, Hawaii, and the Philippines.[23]

The act mandated several structural changes within the War Department to meet problems that had surfaced because of the war. The original detail system was modified to provide for greater professionalism in the technical branches, such as the Ordnance Corps and Quartermaster Corps. Each of the combat arms finally was given a bureau-level branch chief, and the Finance Department, Chemical Warfare Service, Air Service (later Air Corps), and Chief of Chaplains became permanent bureaus. The act also enlarged the War Department General Staff from thirty-six to ninety-three officers in Washington and placed no limits on the number of its members serving in the field. The General Staff changed organizationally, with the establishment of four divisions. The addition of a fifth element, the resurrected War Plans Division, was mandated by regulation during a subsequent War Department reorganization; it focused on contingency plans, doctrine, and force estimates, serving also as a shadow headquarters staff for any major force that might be mobilized. The strong examples of General March and his successor, General Pershing, affirmed the Chief of Staff to be the Army's paramount officer as envisaged in the new law.[24]

Achieving the law's objective of a multicomponent Army required some complex adjustments that could only be accomplished over time. The Regular Army was the first "line increment," with a mission to provide post garrisons, an immediate strike force, and a training cadre for the reserve components. The second line increment, the National Guard, was to provide forces for peacetime domestic disturbances and to serve as a balanced supplement to the Regular Army in wartime. The

---

[23] Ganoe, *History*, p. 483; James E. Hewes, Jr., *From Root to McNamara: Army Organization and Administration, 1900–1963* (Washington, D.C.: U.S. Army Center of Militay History, 1975), p. 53; Mark S. Watson, *Chief of Staff: Prewar Plans and Preparations* (Washington, D.C.: Historical Division, Department of the Army, 1950), p. 25. As of December 1920 the nine corps areas were: First (New England); Second (New York, New Jersey, Delaware, Porto Rico); Third (Maryland, Pennsylvania, Virginia, District of Columbia); Fourth (Georgia, Florida, North Carolina, South Carolina, Alabama, Mississippi, Louisiana, Tennessee); Fifth (Kentucky, Ohio, Indiana, West Virginia); Sixth (Michigan, Illinois, Wisconsin); Seventh (Arkansas, Nebraska, Iowa, Kansas, Missouri, Minnesota, North Dakota, South Dakota); Eighth (Texas, Colorado, New Mexico, Arizona, Oklahoma); and Ninth (California, Oregon, Washington, Nevada, Utah, Idaho, Montana, Wyoming, Territory of Alaska). See WD GO 50 and GO 71, 1920.

[24] Risch, *Quartermaster Support*, p. 709; Hewes, *Root to McNamara*, p. 51; Watson, *Chief of Staff*, pp. 70, 73; Weigley, *History*, pp. 396, 403–05; James A. Huston, *The Sinews of War: Army Logistics, 1775–1953* (Washington, D.C.: Office of the Chief of Military History, United States Army, 1966), pp. 403–04.

Organized Reserve Corps was intended as the third line increment, to back up the other two with balanced units at a time of full emergency. The Army aimed at an incremental mobilization that would allow a 2-million-man force of six field armies, each with three corps of three divisions each, to be fielded within sixty days. The Regular Army would comprise one field army; the National Guard, two; and the Organized Reserve Corps, the final three.[25]

The new concept made the relationship between active-duty officers and part-time citizen-soldiers critical. Reserve, ROTC, and CMTC training duties also added to the Regular Army's sense of being a part of the greater society. However, it would require a large overhead to meet the demands imposed by the ambitious mobilization concept and the extended involvement with the reserve components. But the cost of such an overhead generally went unrecognized or at least unsupported by Congress, highlighting the Army's basic interwar problem. Because of the fact that avoidance of major war was avowed American policy, preparation for the Army's role in such a conflict proved to be difficult. The need to perform its training and mobilization duties while working within the limits of a shrinking budget prevented the Army from performing either task well. A further problem was the General Staff itself, ever consumed by matters of little substance and ineffective in translating theoretical plans and concepts into reality. Coordinating the efforts of the staff elements remained onerous, while the Chief of Staff's span of control was so great that demands on his time impeded his effectiveness.[26]

Congressional intervention soon compounded these flaws. In June 1922 the lawmakers cut the size of the Army from 280,000 to 175,000. The change required dropping or forcibly retiring 1,000 officers and demoting another 800 who wished to remain on active duty. The shattering effects led Congress to make some minor upward strength adjustments in January 1923, but the damage had been done. Most of the planning and preparations premised on the 1920 law proved unrealizable. The corps concept, for example, could not be implemented fully, and the extensive reserve training could not be carried out as contemplated. Beyond these practical consequences, the increasingly obvious

---

[25] WD Bul 25, 9 Jun 20; WD GO 48 and GO 50, 1920; Memo (quoted words), Hall to CGs, Corps Areas, 20 Sep 20, sub: Organization and Administration of Each Corps Area, Entry 26B, RG 159, NARA.

[26] Ganoe, *History*, p. 486; Watson, *Chief of Staff*, pp. 83–84; Robert A. Miller, "The United States Army During the 1930's" (Ph.D. diss., Princeton University, 1973), pp. 58–59.

national indifference to military affairs was to be a growing source of demoralization within the Army throughout the interwar period.[27]

Army strength was reduced further over the following years, reaching its low point of about 12,000 officers and 119,000 enlisted men in 1927, remaining constant until 1933, and then beginning to increase gradually thereafter. Besides the steady decline in strength through the 1920s, the Army was weakened by its huge stockpiles of deteriorating and outmoded equipment left over from the war and by its diminished funding, the bulk of military appropriations going to the Navy. With U.S. security policy focused increasingly on a sea defense, the steady decay and deterioration of the Army's capabilities continued unabated. The situation persisted late into the 1930s, despite repeated warnings about the Army's condition in the annual reports of the Secretary of War and the Chief of Staff and in their statements before Congress.[28]

The reductions in Army strength and the radical modification of many of the programs contained in the 1920 National Defense Act were attributable to a growing stress on economy throughout the government. The trend received additional impetus with the passage in 1921 of the Budget and Accounting Act, which created the Bureau of the Budget. The budget director, the aggressive Charles Dawes, a wartime general officer and former member of the Liquidation Commisson after the war, embarked on a highly publicized campaign for greater "business efficiency" in all government departments. He was supported in his efforts by a succession of conservative presidents, particularly Calvin Coolidge who stressed extreme economy in government expenditures. The frugal Harding and Coolidge administrations repeatedly forced agencies to cut their work force and reduce their scale of operations. Economy surveys became a matter of routine, and in the War Department the inspectorate was tasked with the responsibility of conducting the surveys.[29]

Before the establishment of Dawes' bureau, each Army element had been financially independent. No overall War Department coordination of appropriations had been attempted; each bureau and department dealt directly with the particular congressional appropriations committee that oversaw its activities. Once the 1921 law was passed, however, Army projections were processed through a War Department budget office that monitored requests for the Secretary of War. Then the

---

[27] Ganoe, *History*, pp. 484, 489–90.

[28] Watson, *Chief of Staff*, pp. 15–18; Weigley, *History*, pp. 400–01.

[29] Isabel Leighton, ed., *The Aspirin Age, 1919–1941* (New York: Simon and Schuster, Clarion Books, 1968), p. 145.

Secretary submitted a consolidated budget request for his whole department to the new Bureau of the Budget. It in turn set a ceiling, occasionally altering the military requests or returning them for adjustment before sending them to Congress. Eventually, the pressure of cutbacks led the Secretary to allocate the monies received to the various arms and services.[30]

Tight control by the Bureau of the Budget and its War Department counterpart, as well as the persistent paring of appropriations by Congress, had a profound psychological effect on the Army of the 1920s and 1930s. Officers adopted a conservative approach to their trade, focusing on economy and the avoidance of costly risks and innovations. Budget preparation within the Army eventually became a routine procedure, echoing earlier submissions with few changes. Officers viewed this approach as safer than making new proposals, which seemed more vulnerable to congressional inquiries and demands for justification. This attitude developed over time into a habit that made it difficult for the War Department to innovate, even when funding again became available late in the second Franklin D. Roosevelt administration.[31]

Diminishing Resources

The passage of the Budget and Accounting Act led General Helmick, then the Acting Inspector General, to have the act's financial oversight aspects reviewed for their effect on IGD activities. The act required the administration's Comptroller General to evaluate the adequacy of each executive department's system for inspecting its accounts and supervising its fiscal officers. Each department was supposed to provide the Comptroller General any information he requested about its financial activities, and his representatives were empowered to examine all relevant records and documents. By inference, the law allowed the Comptroller General to call on the Inspector General's Department, through the Secretary of War, for information on the inspection of War Department money accounts and to verify the information by direct inspection.[32]

---

[30] Weigley, *History*, p. 401; John W. Killigrew, "The Impact of the Great Depression on the Army, 1929–1936" (Ph.D. diss., Indiana University, 1960), ch. 1, pp. 8–9, and ch. 4, pp. 4–6.

[31] Killigrew, "Great Depression," Ph.D. diss., ch. 1, p. 1, and ch. 4, p. 2; Watson, *Chief of Staff*, pp. 21, 26, 37, 48.

[32] Memos, McKenney to Hunt, 27 Sep 21, and Hunt to IG, 29 Sep 21, Entry 26, RG 159, NARA. Helmick was slated to become the Inspector General of the Army at the conclusion of Chamberlain's terminal leave.

After reviewing the Budget Act, General Helmick concluded that the process would have no practical effect on IGD activities, except to increase the number of reports. The Comptroller was not given the power to direct corrections. So long as the Comptroller General worked through the Secretary of War, he foresaw no conflicts between the two organizations. These were accurate forecasts: The inspectors and the investigators from the Comptroller's General Accounting Office developed a harmonious and cooperative relationship, and the inspectors' work load increased as a result of the investigators' findings.[33]

The advent of the Great Depression in October 1929 had a major impact on Army funding. The resulting government deficits ensured that defense spending would continue to be minimal. President Herbert Hoover wanted military expenditures further reduced as part of an overall government austerity program, and his approach was endorsed by a Democratic congressional majority chosen in 1930 by an electorate disillusioned with Hoover's methods of dealing with the crisis. Adopting the view that the budget must be balanced, Congress slashed government payrolls in a vain attempt to restore prosperity. Meanwhile, the remaining stocks of World War I equipment were approaching final depletion.[34]

The possibility of using military expenditures to aid the tottering economy was discussed as early as the summer of 1930. The Bureau of the Budget began to explore this option seriously in December. All military outlays were subject to very close congressional scrutiny. Public airing of such expenditures added to public hostility towards the military as a useless expense in desperate times. Using the Army to provide relief came to be viewed as a means of justifying its cost, and various schemes were proposed to use military facilities and property to house the needy. A 1930 bill, for example, provided for the creation of a special reserve corps for the unemployed, whose members were to receive vocational training from the regulars. Army leaders were decidedly unenthusiastic regarding such proposals, and many civilians viewed them with suspicion, sensing the possible militarization of society. In 1931 corps area commanders were authorized to loan bedding and salvaged clothing to relief organizations. Otherwise, the Army remained aloof from relief activities.[35]

---

[33] Memos, McKenney to Hunt, 27 Sep 21, and Hunt to IG, 29 Sep 21, Entry 26, RG 159, NARA.

[34] Killigrew, "Great Depression," Ph.D. diss., ch. 1, pp. 1–6; Leighton, ed., *Aspirin Age*, p. 222; Watson, *Chief of Staff*, p. 4.

[35] Killigrew, "Great Depression," Ph.D. diss., ch. 3, pp. 1–5, and ch. 6, pp. 15–17, 24–25; Weigley, *History*, p. 402.

But the pressure resulting from the Depression was relentless. In May, as economy measures, President Hoover proposed cutting back Army personnel authorizations and closing thirty small posts. The War Department successfully resisted the across-the-board personnel reductions on the grounds that the Army would be left with too few men to meet its minimum obligations. But the need to economize led Congress early in 1932 to consider merging the War and Navy Departments. Chief of Staff General Douglas MacArthur vehemently opposed the consolidation, which proved to be an unsuccessful option. One result, however, was the creation of the Army-Navy Economy Board, with the mission of reporting periodically to the Joint Army-Navy Board on measures to reduce defense costs. The IGD executive officer usually was one of the Army representatives on the new board.[36]

With the Depression unconquered and a fall election facing him, President Hoover in September called for additional Army budget cuts. He focused again on the need to cut Army strength as a means to avoid paying the fixed pay and allowances costs that had been escalating as a result of more men staying in the Army since the onset of hard times in 1929. The President also hoped to trim reserve-component activities; he wanted National Guard drills be cut in half, and ROTC and CMTC strengths and training funds reduced sharply. The War Department resisted on the grounds that these measures, by critically impairing mobilization capabilities, were contrary to the intention of the National Defense Act of 1920. The General Staff worked closely with National Guard proponents to preserve a resource that was more important than ever because of reductions in the strength of the Regular Army. Such assaults on the core of the defense concept obliged the War Department to play the role of a lobbyist for the civilian reserve components. Despite its efforts, many ORC units had to be inactivated or cut back to minimal cadres.[37]

Following his inauguration in 1933, President Franklin D. Roosevelt took a strong, direct interest in managing Army affairs as he sought solutions to the economic crisis. The economic situation was so dark by the spring that Roosevelt announced that he would furlough 3,000–4,000 officers in order to save money. General MacArthur resisted, and the scheme was dropped as the need for officers in the newly activated Civilian Conservation Corps (CCC) became evident. Savings

---

[36] Killigrew, "Great Depression," Ph.D. diss., ch. 4, pp. 9, 19–20, and ch. 6, pp. 10–11; WD News Release, 18 Feb 32, Entry 26B, RG 159, NARA.

[37] Killigrew, "Great Depression," Ph.D. diss., ch. 4, p. 31, ch. 9, pp. 3, 6, 14, and ch. 10, p. 30.

were realized instead by reductions in training, target practice, and flight training. Virtually all arsenal and depot research and production stopped, as did most large reequipment programs.[38]

As a result, MacArthur directed that planning cease to adhere to the provisions of the National Defense Act of 1920. He was the force behind the preparation of a mobilization plan based on a Regular Army of 170,000, which was only slightly larger than the one that actually existed, backed by a 250,000-man National Guard. Known as the Initial Protective Force, this new approach became the basis for planning and requisitions until the beginning of World War II. The Organized Reserve Corps, of necessity, virtually ceased to exist, except as a man-power pool mostly of officers. MacArthur's more realistic plan won sympathy with the administration. After 1933 the strength of the Army increased moderately, and when the situation overseas worsened in the later years of the decade, Army budget projections trended upward.

Despite the gradual improvement, however, budget issues remained a bone of contention throughout the decade. Maj. Gen. Johnson Hagood, a corps area commander, was relieved and later reassigned for declaring at a congressional hearing in February 1936 that he found it more difficult to get five cents for a lead pencil than "to get $1,000.00 to teach hobbies to CCC boys." The continual stress on the need to economize and to achieve the greatest efficiencies with the limited resources available was a constant concern of everyone in the War Department. The Inspector General's Department, in particular, already deeply involved in disbursing and fiscal matters, was to find those issues dominating much of its time and absorbing its assets.[39]

Retrenchment and Growth

In contrast to General Chamberlain's hopes for a large and vigorous organization, the Inspector General's Department experienced the same steady decline in personnel as the rest of the Army during the interwar period. The 215 officers assigned on Armistice Day rose to 248 in June 1919, largely as a result of the special overseas inspections described earlier. Then the number plummeted. Within a year 87 officers and thir-

---

[38] Ibid., ch. 10, pp. 14–15; Watson, *Chief of Staff*, p. 5; Ltr, TAG to IG, 17 Jun 33, sub: Information To Be Compiled at Corps Area Headquarters as of June 30, 1933, mimeograph copy, Entry 26, RG 159, NARA.

[39] Killigrew, "Great Depression," Ph.D. diss., ch. 8, p. 7, and ch. 15, p. 31; Watson, *Chief of Staff*, p. 26; Weigley, *History*, p. 406; AP News Releases, 24 Feb (quotation) and 13 Apr 36, OTIG files, Pentagon (SAIG-ZXH).

ty civilians were all that was left of the wartime expansion; 33 officers were in the Office of the Inspector General, while 54 remained at camps or in the geographical departments.

The National Defense Act of 1920 fixed the strength of the department at 62 officers, including the Inspector General. The Secretary of War could raise or lower this strength by 15 percent without recourse to Congress. Inevitably, he selected the lower option, and department strength continued downward—to 56 officers in June 1922 and to 40 in 1923, supported by only thirteen civilians in the Office of the Inspector General. This average strength, which General Helmick considered an irreducible minimum, continued with little change. Only in 1939, when dangers of a new war caused the Army's rapid expansion, were ten vacant officer positions filled in the Office of The Inspector General and the field organizations brought up to authorized levels.[40]

The composition of the inspectorate underwent some changes as well. Before World War I the Inspector General's Department had consisted exclusively of officers of the combat arms. During the war, however, various specialists were admitted on a temporary basis and proved to be invaluable. The postwar stress on business efficiency and tight fiscal oversight made it natural that officers from the newly created Finance Department should be detailed to the corps areas as money accounts inspectors. Once on board, they were expected to audit virtually every financial activity. Of the six finance officers assigned in the fall of 1920, several were former AEF funds inspectors.[41]

Additional changes over the next few years included the arrival of one officer each from the Ordnance Corps, Quartermaster Corps, and the Corps of Engineers. Still, in 1930, more than two-thirds of the 41 detailed officers were infantry or cavalry, with the remainder members of the Coast or Field Artillery, except for one officer each from the Corps of Engineers, Finance Department, Ordnance Corps, and

---

[40] Ltr, Helmick to ACofS, G–1, WD, 16 Oct 22, sub: Revision of Allotment of Officers to Activities, Entry 26; Rpt, Chamberlain to Chair, Accts Com, HofReps, 12 Mar 20, Entry 26A. Both in RG 159, NARA. See also U.S. War Department, *Annual Reports of the Inspector General, 1919–1940* (Washington, D.C.: Government Printing Office, 1920–1940). IG strength distribution in August 1922 was: OIG, 10; Corps Areas, 17; Philippine Division, 3; Hawaiian Division, 2; Panama Division, 2; Combat Division, 4; Army War College, 2; Germany, 1; District of Washington, 1 (Helmick).

[41] Ltr, Chamberlain to TAG, 23 Sep 20, sub: Assignment of Accountants, Inspector General's Department, Entry 26, RG 159, NARA. The first Finance Department officers appointed were: Maj. Austin Brown, Maj. Arthur L. Webb, Maj. Thomas L. Clear, Maj. Frank M. Holmes, Capt. Thomas H. Chambers, and Capt. Lawrence Worrall. All were finance auditors during the war.

Quartermaster Corps. A final change in the branch mix occurred in 1936, with the assignment of an Air Corps officer. The changes reflected the IGD's growing need for broad expertise in a variety of fields.[42]

The fluctuation in commissioned strength was reflected in the experiences of the IGD civilian force. The peak OIG civilian strength was fifty-four at the time of the armistice. Then between 1919 and 1921 gradual reductions returned Army-wide IG civilian strength to the prewar total of fifteen. The National Defense Act of 1920 finally authorized the appointment of a chief clerk, something that inspectors had been urging since the time of General Breckinridge. The position was filled by the 61-year-old John D. Parker, who had worked in the Office of the Inspector General for forty-one years at the time of his appointment. These modest improvements did not, however, compensate for the ever-growing work load. In 1915 the office had handled about 9,500 actions, while in 1921 it was processing nearly 17,700, roughly a 55-percent rise, with no end in sight. Inspectors at all levels clamored for a proficient force of uniformed clerks to cope with what was proving to be a permanent increase in the demands on their department.[43]

An equivalent need for competent, permanent clerical support in the IG field offices remained a problem throughout the interwar period. Immediately after the war Army field clerks occupied the few existing clerical positions, but the National Defense Act of 1920 specified that the warrant officers in that occupational category would be phased out and, as vacancies occurred, replaced by administrative warrant officers, who, unfortunately, rarely had any clerical skills. However, the quality improved over time, and an OTIG survey conducted in 1930 indicated general satisfaction with administrative support in the field. By then most of the warrant officers were capable stenographers, and one or two of them were assigned to each field office. Their assignment to the Inspector General's Department was not approved by Maj. Gen. John F. Preston, The Inspector General in 1931, because he desired to have only detailed commissioned officers in the department. A satisfactory compromise was reached in 1932, when The Adjutant General agreed to allocate nineteen warrant offi-

---

[42] Ltrs, OTIG Insps to Ex Off, OTIG, 3 Feb 30, sub: Replies to Memorandum of Data Desired by General Drum, Entry 26A, RG 159, NARA. Three of the detailed officers were Maj. Harry R. Kutz, OrdC, 29 Jun 28; Maj. Leon M. Logan, QMC, 1 Jul 28; and, Lt. Col. Ernest D. Peek, CE, 22 Sep 30. On the Air Corps, see Reed Annual Rpt, 2 Sep 37, Entry 26C, RG 159, NARA.

[43] England, IG, Camp Benning, Annual Rpt, 5 Jul 20; Memo, Irwin to CofFin, FD, 10 Oct 21; Memo, Ex Off, OIG, to IG, sub: Status of Statutory Employees of the IGD, 1 Mar 22. All in Entry 26A, RG 159, NARA.

cers personally selected by General Preston for permanent rotation among IG positions.[44]

By late 1935 Preston's replacement, Maj. Gen. Walter L. Reed, sought ways to have more commissioned officers assigned to handle the OTIG's significantly heavy work load. Reed first wrote each corps area commander to determine if any of them would be willing to give up a position. All replied, however, that their inspectors, overworked because of CCC requirements, were barely adequate in number. In 1937 Reed resurfaced Preston's 1934 request that the Office of the Inspector General be authorized a permanent brigadier general slot. He wanted the officer to serve as chief of investigations and to supervise OTIG activities in his absence. The arrangement, he said, would facilitate senior officer investigations and would fill an "urgent and constantly felt" need to give more depth to the OTIG's capabilities.[45]

By 1937 the work load proved to be overwhelming because of several factors—the increase in Army strength, the continuing CCC requirements, and the ongoing special IG investigations. As a result, the informal practice of using officer augmentees was condoned officially. At first acting inspectors were authorized to be detailed wherever an assigned IG was unavailable; in this way two extra officers were added to the two detailed IGs at the Third Corps Area in Baltimore. Then later in the year assistant inspectors were detailed in each corps area, and plans were made to expand the Inspector General's Department up to its authorized full strength. By 1938 extra officers also were assigned to the Office of The Inspector General to deal with broadened tasks involving National Guard activities. The IGD strength reached sixty officers in October 1939, where it remained for some months. With the escalation of war tensions in Europe and Asia in 1940 and with the extended mobilization of the National Guard, the Inspector General's Department began to experience rapid growth.[46]

The Inspector General controlled the selection of officers for detail within the department. Those selected generally had more than twenty

---

[44] Ltr, Scott to Helmick, 7 Nov 24; Ltr, Conrad to Williams, 13 Dec 24; Ltr, Helmick to Scott, 29 Dec 24; Ltrs, OTIG to All Insps, 12 May 30, sub: Replies to Letter re Clerical Assistance to Inspectors; Ltr, Preston to Smith, 6 Oct 32; Ltr, TAG to All Corps Area, Dept, and Div Cdrs, sub: 26 Oct 32, sub: Allocation of Warrant Officers. All in Entry 26A, RG 159, NARA. See also WD Bul 25, 9 Jun 20.

[45] Memo (quoted words), Reed to ACofS, G–1, WD, 1 May 37, sub: Additional General Officers of the Staff, Assistants to Branch Chiefs; Ltrs, Reed to Corps Area Cdrs, 9 Jan 36, and Replies, various dates. All in Entry 26C, RG 159, NARA.

[46] Reed Annual Rpt, 2 Sep 37; Memo, W.L.R. to Babcock, 15 Sep 38; Ltr, Logan to Humber, 30 Sep 35. All in Entry 26C, RG 159, NARA. See also AReg 20–10, 1935.

years of service and were rated above average or better on their efficiency reports. Colonels usually were War College graduates, while the
other officers were Command and General Staff College graduates. The
Office of The Inspector General oversaw the assignment of IGs to the
field, coordinating with the gaining command and the chiefs of the
branches providing the individuals. Sometimes nominations came from
the commands, but more often the branch provided several names. The
OTIG would review them and forward those it approved to the field for
selection. Personnel changes occurred when details ended or units
deactivated, as well as when poor performance or other demands resulted in transfer.[47]

The duties of officer augmentees were varied. In 1919 the tasks
associated with demobilization had led to the appointment of so-called
special inspectors at the request of hard-pressed local commanders.
The augmentees functioned mostly at depots and ports, but also could
be found at posts and camps scheduled for closure. Some special
inspectors were approved by the Office of the Inspector General for
single actions, such as the disposal of the Indian School property at
Carlisle Barracks. Normally, however, these inspectors served a full
tour in a more general capacity at salvage points. By 1922 the special
inspectors had passed from the scene, but periodic surveys indicated
the continued use of locally appointed augmentees. When the 2d
Division inspector was reassigned in April 1928, for example, officers
temporarily detailed from division units took on his duties to prevent
a backlog of audits and property actions from accumulating before his
replacement arrived.[48]

An additional source of manpower was the Organized Reserve
Corps. IG reservists began to be selected within days of the armistice.
Those who applied had to be in the grade of captain or higher and have
had at least five years of commissioned service, three in a line unit.
Selectees filled specific mobilization positions in each corps area and
in Washington. By 1929 a total of 155 spaces, ranging from colonel to
captain, had been identified but only forty-three reservists had been
assigned. Because General Helmick wanted close links established
with the IGD's reserve officers, he launched a program under which the

---

[47] Ltr, Reed to TAG, 29 Aug 36, sub: Compilation of Policies Affecting
Commissioned Personnel, Regular Army, Entry 26C; File 210.2, Assignment of
Officers to 2d Corps Area, Entry 26A. Both in RG 159, NARA.

[48] Ltr, Cdr, Gen Hosp 31, to TAG, 26 Feb 19, sub: Special Inspector, Entry 26A;
Rpts, Stone to OTIG, 21 May and 18 Jun 28, sub: Surveys of Fort Sam Houston, Texas,
Entry 11. All in RG 159, NARA.

names and addresses of such reservists were given periodically to the corps area inspectors so that liaison could be maintained. These reservists were routinely provided with copies of all IG publications and guides and included in all aspects of mobilization planning. One OTIG officer monitored reserve activities, kept a list of mobilization needs, and maintained contact with the reservists through bulletins and other publications. The same officer developed and administered a modest series of correspondence courses for reservists after 1927.[49]

At first reserve officers were commissioned permanently in the IGD's Officer Reserve Corps, although after 1925 both the Organized Reserve Corps and the National Guard adopted the detail system. A detail in the IGD's Officer Reserve Corps was for four years, after which the officer had to return to his original branch for one year before eligible for a second appointment. All reserve appointments were in five-year increments, renewable until retirement so long as the physical and training requirements were met. However, reservists in the IGD's Officer Reserve Corps lost promotion chances, because they were not in a branch position with a promotion vacancy—a fact that explains the relatively small number of authorized positions actually filled. IGD reservists were assigned either to a regional assignment group controlled by corps area commanders or to a branch assignment group controlled by the Inspector General's Department. The latter were earmarked for corps and higher IG positions, while the former were destined for divisions or installations.[50]

Within the National Guard, fifty-five officers were assigned to IG duties in divisions or state headquarters. Unlike their IGD Officer Reserve Corps counterparts, these guardsmen could be redetailed indefinitely and could be promoted up to the grade authorized for their assigned position. The difference imposed a hardship on the IGD reservists, who had to find a branch slot to be eligible for promotion and barely had the chance to learn the nature of their IG duties before leaving them. When Maj. Gen. Hugh A. Drum became The Inspector General in January 1930, he directed a study of the reserve-component IG system, and the anomalies of the existing arrangements became apparent. Drum decided that it would be to the IGD's advantage to reduce the number of its Officer Reserve Corps incumbents. As an

---

[49] Memo, Wood to CofSelSubsec, Com Per Br, Opns Div, WDGS, 14 Mar 19, Entry 26; Ltr, Helmick to Corps Area Insps, 4 Jan 22, sub: Inspectors General, ORC, Entry 26; Rpt, Nugent to TIG, 13 Dec 27, sub: Survey of the OIG, Entry 11; and Ltr, Preston to Roberson, 16 Oct 29, sub: IG-Reserve Officers, Entry 26A. All in RG 159, NARA.

[50] Ltrs, OTIG Insps to Ex Off, OTIG, 3 Feb 30, Entry 26A, RG 159, NARA.

alternative, he proposed that a list of IGD-eligible reserve officers be compiled, to be drawn upon for call-ups required by mobilization. Thereafter, the reservists who were assigned in peacetime were volunteers on an indefinite tour.[51]

Gospel of Efficiency

Unlike its strength, the headquarters element of the Inspector General's Department was essentially stable throughout the interwar decades. At the end of the World War the Office of the Inspector General had six divisions. Two of these, Business Methods Survey and Field Inspections and Investigations, were dissolved by the end of 1919. The four remaining divisions were Inspections, Investigations, Money Accounts, and Miscellaneous and Personnel—the latter redesignated as the Administrative Division in 1921 and then as the Executive Division in 1927, with some functions reassigned in 1922 to form a small Records Division. Each division had a chief. The approximately fourteen officers not assigned as chiefs served in an investigations and inspections pool, conducting not only special investigations but also annual and accounts inspections. Each officer usually worked within a specialty, such as field artillery or supply.[52]

The demands on this small group were consistently heavy, starting with high-priority special demobilization inspections immediately after the war. The new mission to survey business methods promised to sustain the high postwar volume. The newly assigned finance specialists were required to inspect more than forty major War Department fiscal accounts, and the other officers averaged a like number of investigations each month. The disposal of surplus property received a great deal of attention in the years immediately after the war. A comprehensive survey was made of policies and methods of disposal, and safeguards against inefficiency and corruption were recommended. By direction of the Secretary of War, inspectors had to be present at all auction sales of sur-

---

[51] Memo, Merrill to TIG, 12 Feb 31, sub: Inspector General Reserve Officers; Memo, Bridges to TIG, 7 May 31, sub: Inspector General's Department Reserve. Both in Entry 159, NARA.

[52] OTIG Surveys, 1927, 1929, 1930, Entry 11; OIG Org Charts, [31] Jan 19 and 11 Nov 20, Entry 26A; Memo, Helmick to ACofS, G–1, WD, 21 Sep 21, sub: Estimated Requirements, Commissioned Personnel, Regular Army, Entry 26A; Memo, McKenney to OTIG, 28 Jul 21, sub: Name Change of Misc. & Pers. Div., Entry 26C. All in RG 159, NARA. The first structural changes since World War I took place in August 1941, when the Records Division was made a section of the Executive Division and National Guard and Procurement Inspections Division were created.

plus materiel to monitor procedures and adherence to law.[53]

The great interest in efficiency
and civilian business methods
resulted in new methods of improving Army efficiency. In 1922
Colonel Peck, now assigned at the
War Department, received a four-
month assignment with the large
commercial retailer Sears, Roe-
buck and Company. After carrying
out an in-depth study with the full
cooperation of the company, Peck
concluded that Sears' success lay in
its strict cost accounting methods
and its broad decentralization of
authority. His apprenticeship was
judged so successful that Maj. Gen.
William C. Rivers, when he
became The Inspector General in
1927, sought and obtained more

Maj. Gen. William C. Rivers

authorizations for civilian training. Two inspectors attended year-long
courses in business methods at civilian institutions in 1928, and four additional officers attended similar courses in 1929. After that, budget limitations brought an end to the promising experiment. As a result of both
training and practical experience on the job, inspectors were judged to be
desirable instructors in Army schools, and during the 1930s IG officers
lectured on funds management and business efficiency at the Army War
College and both the Adjutant General and Finance Schools.[54]

Training in key OTIG functions was also critical, especially for
those under consideration for The Inspector General position. The practice of naming the strongest contender as the executive officer became
the norm to assure continuity and the maintenance of standards. The
executive officer ran the daily routine of the Washington office, signed

---

[53] Ltr, TAG to IG, 21 Jan 19, sub: Inspection of Progress of Discharge of Enlisted
Men at Demobilization Centers and Ft. Sill, Okla.; Helmick and Irwin Testimonies, Mil
Affs Cmte, HofReps, 16 Jan 22, Entry 26, RG 159, NARA.

[54] Rivers Annual Rpt, 29 Sep 28, Entry 26, RG 159, NARA. In 1928 Maj. Franklin
Babcock attended Stanford, while Maj. Leo J. Ahern attended the Boston Institute. The
four officers in 1929 went to Harvard Business School. See Ltrs, OTIG Insps to Ex Off,
OTIG, 3 Feb 30, Entry 26A, RG 159, NARA. See also OTIG Lecture File 1937–1941,
Box 5, Entry 26C, RG 159, NARA.

most of the correspondence, and distributed the work load. He also prepared war plans and monitored War Department changes that might
affect IG mobilization, keeping close liaison with officers in the G–3.
Most significantly, the executive officer handled all personnel matters
throughout the Inspector General's Department. He maintained a roster
of officers considered suitable for detail, including both the names of
those who had done well as inspectors in the past and also of others
who had expressed a desire to be inspectors.

Every two years The Adjutant General provided the Office of The
Inspector General with a listing of field-grade officers rated by their
branch chiefs as above average or better and considered suitable for
inspector duty. Rarely was anyone selected below those ratings. Corps
area and department inspectors were usually picked from colonels who
had just completed a command tour. Inspectors were assigned from the
branch most strongly represented within their organizations. The executive officer selected officers from the Ninth Corps Area for rotation to
the Philippines and Hawaii, assigning an extra individual to compensate for the time consumed in trans-Pacific travel. Most new details
were made from among officers graduating from the Leavenworth
schools or the Army War College.[55]

General Helmick also made the executive officer responsible for
inspector training. Col. George Le R. Irwin, the first postwar executive,
prepared and issued the first course for newly detailed inspectors in
August 1921. The course was intended mostly for officers who were
unfamiliar with the Inspector General's Department, but could be modified depending on the experience of the prospective students. The
training was designed to be given at the Washington office, but could
be presented elsewhere if necessary. Students were required first to
review all Army regulations pertaining to the department and to inspectors. They then studied IG forms, publications, and policy statements.
Finally, they read those reports of inspections and investigations selected as fine examples of the art. The student then went on a "practical
phase," starting work as an assistant on an inspection and then moving
on, either to conduct a simple investigation on his own or to assist in a
more difficult one. The new officers then were given thorough training
in the inspection of money accounts and were briefed on IG administration and General Helmick's standards.[56]

---

[55] Memos, Williams to Ex Off, OTIG, 28 Sep 26, and Preston to TIG, 23 Jan 30,
Entry 26A, RG 159, NARA.

[56] Course of Instruction for IGs Newly Detailed in the IGD, 19 Aug 21, Entry 26,
RG 159, NARA.

The small Records Division, too, worked under the supervision of the executive officer. Consisting of one chief clerk and an assistant, the division maintained the IGD files and also kept the Washington office correspondence logs. A daily book of incoming cases, with a brief summary of each, provided a means to trace documents and served as a quick source for statistical summaries. The staff made all the indexes and cross- references necessary to keep track of related cases and provided a search service for other IG elements seeking old cases or precedents to support their current work. The inspection files, which dated back to pre–Civil War days, eventually included all of the AEF's IG office files.[57]

The day-to-day administration of the Inspector General's Department was carried out for the executive officer by the OTIG chief clerk. Inspection reports were sent first to the Inspections Division, where they were logged, reviewed, and cross-referenced, and then to the executive with a recommendation for action. Following his decision, correspondence for the appropriate bureaus or staff elements was prepared, after which the reports were forwarded and the suspenses monitored. Once the reports were returned, they were again reviewed for completeness or further follow up, their final destination being the Records Division for filing. All other cases were sent first to the Records Division for logging, indexing, and batching with similar material, if any. They were then given to the chief clerk for dispatch to the appropriate officer. The chief clerk handled all civil service matters and equipment requisitions on his own authority.[58]

OTIG divisions were small and set up on a functional basis. The Investigations Division decided what investigations were needed, made assignments, and reviewed completed investigations to assure sufficiency of coverage. The division kept close liaison with other War Department elements to locate quickly precedents, decisions, and policies affecting particular cases. Especially in officer disciplinary cases, the IG reports were scrutinized so that remedial, corrective, or disciplinary action would be the same in similar cases, the goal being to ensure uniformity throughout the Army. In seeking to protect officers from hasty or discriminatory adverse actions, the division amassed a large body of precedent decisions that remained relatively unknown to the rest of the Army, except to Judge Advocate

---

[57] Memo, OTIG to Insps, 28 Sep 26, sub: Records Division, Entry 26A, RG 159, NARA.

[58] Ltrs, OTIG Insps to Ex Off, OTIG, 3 Feb 30, Entry 26A, RG 159, NARA.

General officers who often relied upon it as a basis for their own decisions.[59]

Collateral duties often played a large role in the work of OTIG divisions. In addition to making inspections and reports, for example, the Inspections Division maintained the OTIG library; monitored exempted operations (those not under corps control); prepared and revised regulations and forms; and issued policy letters and guides to inspectors assigned outside the War Department. Many of the fifty-eight types of accounts inspected annually by the Money Accounts Division were in unexpected areas, including the fiscal activities of the District of Columbia monuments and buildings; the D.C. National Guard; the National Home for Disabled Volunteer Soldiers, especially its special expenditure funds; the Soldiers' Home; and the Bond Section of the Finance Department. The division also examined the countless unit, chaplain, mess, and similar funds throughout the Army and investigated various types of claims—for example, liberty bonds and payments lost in the mail and related problems involving War Risk Insurance.[60]

The Money Accounts Division, when required, could examine the books of firms making claims against the government and make recommendations as to the validity of the claim. Well into the 1930s, it continued to handle claims lodged against the unit funds of long-demobilized World War I organizations. The division reviewed the finance inspection reports of IGs in the field and was the office of record for filing the reports. Finally, it provided support to the Office of The Inspector General, preparing the budget and travel vouchers and serving as the point of contact for commenting on other agencies' finance-related proposals.[61]

Among the most unusual duties to befall Money Accounts Division officers was maintenance of the so-called Hixson Liquidation Fund. Set up in 1933 at the direction of the Secretary of War to liquidate the massive personal indebtedness of Lt. Col. Arthur G. Hixson, the fund consisted of thirty-nine personal debts to other officers, firms, financial institutions, as well as the obligations of his cosigners who had become indebted as a result of his default. The Fourth Corps Area IG,

---

[59] Memo, OTIG to Insps, 28 Sep 26, sub: Operations of Investigations Division, Entry 26A, RG 159, NARA.

[60] Memo, OTIG to Insps, 28 Sep 26, sub: Duties of the Inspections Division; Memos, Webb to Williams, 7 Nov 23 and 7 May 27, subs: Functions of Money Accounts Division. All in RG 26A, NARA.

[61] Memos, Webb to Williams, 7 Nov 23 and 7 May 27; Rpt, Chamberlain to Chair, Accts Com, HofReps, 12 Mar 20. All in Entry 26A, RG 159, NARA.

responding to numerous complaints, investigated Hixson's personal finances, and the Secretary had decided that extraordinary measures were necessary because—in the event of Hixson's bankruptcy—so many people would be hurt, to say nothing of the reputation of Army officers in general. Hixson agreed to have $160 a month taken from his pay, to be assigned to a fund managed by an OTIG officer to pay his debts. The Liquidation Fund disbursed over $10,000 before Hixson's death in 1938. The small remaining balance then reverted to the unfortunate officer's estate.[62]

When General Drum took over the Inspector General's Department at the beginning of 1930, he immediately ordered an extensive management survey of his office. The staff provided him with statistics on personnel, organization, and operating costs, as well as data on the types and frequency of War Department–level inspections and on every active and reserve officer in the department. Within a month, The Inspector General had a convenient overview of the status, procedures, and activities of each IGD element, as well as a listing of authorities and precedents. From this firm base Drum was able to embark quickly on changes he desired in inspection and investigation methods. In September each class or group of activities was assigned to a specified officer, who was instructed to build his expertise and become the IGD point of contact on his topic. Each specialist kept track of inspections done by IGs at all echelons and provided guidance to corps area IGs when they inspected units in his area of expertise. Using the lower-level reports, he extracted items for follow up and trends analysis. At the end of each fiscal year he also prepared a narrative overview of the situation in his field. General Drum's executive officer, Colonel Preston, assisted in developing this system, which he continued when he became the senior inspector a year later.[63]

General Drum also built on General Helmick's mobilization planning. Starting in 1922, Helmick had solicited from present and former inspectors comments on their wartime experiences, using the information as a basis for emergency planning. He warned that the mass of available data was too little utilized in planning for future crises—a weakness in the IGD system that invited an erosion of its functions in a time of emergency. Helmick's project languished during General

---

[62] Memo, Reed to TAG, 20 Apr 38, sub: Hixson Liquidation Fund, Entry 26C, RG 159, NARA.

[63] Ltrs, OTIG Insps to Ex Off, OTIG, 3 Feb 30, Entry 26A; Memos, Humber to TIG, [Aug] 31 and 12 Jul 32, Entry 26A; OIG/OTIG Org Charts, 1919, 1922, 1934, 1936, 1944, Entry 26C. All in RG 159, NARA.

Rivers' tenure as The Inspector General but thrived under the leadership of General Drum, who, by the end of his detail, had created a firm plan approved by the General Staff. His concept provided for a 150-percent increase in IGD military strength and an over 200-percent growth in civilian strength. On M–day (mobilization) one Regular Army inspector would augment those already assigned to divisions, while others would go to ports of embarkation.[64] Such preparations were timely in the decade that saw new wars break out in both Asia and Europe.

IGs in the Corps Areas

The corps area IG offices varied in strength in proportion to the number of units and War Department activities in their respective areas. Thus, New England's First Corps Area IG office in Boston was staffed by a colonel, a major, and a civilian clerk, whereas the Second Corps Area IG office at Fort Jay, New York, had three detailed inspectors (two for inspections, one for investigations and special inquiries); a captain attached to conduct audits and to inspect money accounts; and five military clerks. The IG office of the Fourth Corps Area in Atlanta was manned by a colonel and a major, who both carried out inspections, inventories, audits, and investigations. Because of the high volume of activity, two warrant officer clerks—one above the authorization—were assigned to the office.[65]

The volume of work was moderate in the first years of the new postwar organization. However, it grew year by year, and by 1924 corps area IGs found themselves in the position of having to repeatedly request additional clerks and officers, few of whom were available. The scope of their duties was broad, for they carried out inspections and investigations for not only their own commanders but also those required by the War Department (*Table 1*). By 1928 each of the eighteen IGs in the corps areas were averaging thirty inspections and investigations annually, in addition to the numerous finance audits and property actions that were required of them.[66]

---

[64] Ltr, Helmick to Elmore, 12 Apr 22, Entry 26, RG 159, NARA; Army War College File 160–621F, Mobilization Plan, OTIG, 1930, 1934, Revised to July 1, 1936, U.S. Army Military History Institute, Carlisle Barracks, Pa.

[65] Ltr, Ely to TAG, 26 Jan 28, sub: Survey of Headquarters, 2d Corps Area; Ltr, Patterson to AG, 4th Corps Area, 15 Feb 36. Both in Entry 11, RG 159, NARA.

[66] Ltr, Scott to Helmick, 7 Nov 24, Entry 26A; Rpt, Major to TIG, 3 Apr 24, sub: Annual Survey of the Nine Corps Areas Headquarters, Entry 11. Both in RG 159, NARA.

Table 1—Typical Corps Area Inspections and Investigations

Type	Level	Frequency	Authority
Subordinate commands	Corps Area	Annual	AReg 20–10
Items of interest	Corps Area	Special	AReg 20–10
Headquarters	Corps Area	Annual	AReg 20–10
Exempted commands	Corps Area	Limited	AReg 20–10
Property disposal	Corps Area	As necessary	AReg 20–35
NG armories	Corps Area	Annual	NGReg 48
Money accounts	War Department	Semiannual	AReg 20–10
Exempted commands	War Department	Special	AReg 20–10
Defects[a]	Corps Area	As necessary	AReg 20–5
Unit complaints	Corps Area	As necessary	AReg 20–5
Prejudicial complaints[b]	Corps Area	As necessary	ARegs 20–5/ 20–10/20–30
Referred complaints	Corps Area	As necessary	AReg 20–30
Misuse of public funds or property	Corps Area	As necessary	AReg 20–30

[a]Relating to mission conduct.
[b]Relating to the character, standing, or efficiency of any War Department member.

Source: Organization Chart, File 333.1, Entry 11, RG 159, NARA.

The area commanders' special demands imposed additional burdens. For example, in 1931 in one corps area both inspectors were asked to develop and monitor tactical exercises and map problems, and that duty, coupled with time-consuming local investigations, caused them to fall behind in performing and reporting required inspections. Maj. Gen. Fox Conner, while Hawaiian Department commander, used his inspector to prepare mess inspection standards and to help units meet them. Marked improvements resulted for the command, but again the inspector became tardy in his primary duties.[67]

---

[67] Ltr, Whiston to Parker, 24 Feb 31, Entry 26B; Rpt, Van Schaick to OTIG, 15 Feb 29, sub: 1929 Annual Inspection and Survey [of the Hawaiian Department], Entry 11. Both in RG 159, NARA.

The situation was no better in the IG offices of the tactical division headquarters. The inspector of the 2d Division, located at Fort Sam Houston with the division headquarters, spent most of his time auditing unit and post funds, making property condemnation inspections, and conducting investigations on such relatively minor matters as car accidents. He had little time left to spend on more substantive issues, let alone on the numerous larger inspections, surveys, and investigations that became common after 1929. Across the state of Texas at Fort Bliss, the inspector of the 1st Cavalry Division encountered similar problems. If anything, he was even more deeply embroiled in financial matters, in part because of the presence of several large Corps of Engineers civil works projects in his region.[68]

The nonmilitary aspects of the War Department's responsibilities consumed the energies of some inspectors, especially with the reactivation of the 1st Division at Fort Hamilton, New York City, in January 1927. Its elements scattered in small garrisons throughout New York and New Jersey, the new division spent much of its time supporting civilian components. It held a few small exercises, but the bulk of the division could not be assembled for maneuvers until the fall of 1931. The diversion from tactical concerns was reflected at all division IG offices, leaving the inspection of the tactical units to the corps IGs. The overall effect was a reduction in the amount of work at the division level and a dramatic increase at the corps area level. As a consequence, the division inspectors were later attached for duty to the corps area, working for their own commander as required. Not surprisingly, unit commanders in the 1920s and 1930s rarely gave thought to the tactical or wartime uses and needs of their IG sections. Inspectors themselves were so busy that they rarely raised the issue. There were, however, exceptions to the rule in the overseas departments, especially the Philippines.[69]

Inspecting U.S. Forces Overseas

During the war a series of acting inspectors, supported by temporarily detailed officers, had performed most inspection duties in the

---

[68] Rpt, Stone to OTIG, 18 Jun 28, Entry 11; Ltr, Dagley to TAG, 6 Feb 36, sub: Replacement of a Warrant Officer, Entry 26A. Both in RG 159, NARA.

[69] Rpt, Kaempfer to IG, 2d Corps Area, 23 Apr 28, sub: Annual Inspection and Survey of Headquarters, 1st Division, and Fort Hamilton, N.Y.; Rpt, Thompson to IG, 2d Corps Area, 24 Mar 32, sub: Inspection of the Headquarters, 1st Division, Fort Hamilton, N.Y. Both in Entry 11, RG 159, NARA.

Inspecting an AFIC Unit at Tientsin Barracks

Philippines. Staffing became more permanent after passage of the National Defense Act. At this time the Philippine Department IG office had a five-person staff—a colonel, a major, a warrant officer chief clerk, and two enlisted typists. The two commissioned officers shared the IG duties, except that most finance matters were handled by the major. The department inspector, based in Manila, was also responsible for the annual inspection of disbursing activities in Nagasaki, Japan, and for IG support to the American Forces in China (AFIC), based at Tientsin.[70]

General Helmick made an extensive tour of the Far East in 1925. A few years later an IGD team under the leadership of Colonel Van Schaick, the former AFIG inspector who was a reputed Philippine affairs expert, completed a detailed survey of the Philippine Department. The resulting reports, combined with those of the assigned inspectors, provide valuable insights into the condition of the department.

After his arrival in the Philippines in July 1925, General Helmick visited every post and unit throughout the archipelago, as well as most of the facilities in caretaker status. He was impressed favorably, for the most part, with the high levels of training and esprit shown by the units.

---

[70] Org Chart, Exh L of Rpt, IG, Phil Div, to CG, Phil Div, 4 Feb 26, sub: Survey of Headquarters, Philippine Department, Entry 11; Ltr, Austin to TIG, 10 Dec 26, sub: Inspections of U.S. Forces in China and Money Accounts Nagasaki, Japan, Entry 26. Both in RG 159, NARA.

One exception was the 31st Infantry, which Helmick severely criticized. The appearance and training of the troops and the condition of the livestock was very poor. Apparently, with its elements scattered in small garrisons throughout the city of Manila, the unit found training difficult. Helmick judged the cause of its overall problems to be the inept leadership of the regimental commander, whom he felt should voluntarily retire or be boarded. One of the few entirely American line units in the Philippines, this regiment—because of its highly visible location in the capital—should have been a showcase to set the standard for the entire department.[71]

The best of the many good units Helmick encountered was the 57th Infantry (Philippine Scouts). Located at Fort William McKinley, this regiment formed part of a large garrison that included a division headquarters and the headquarters of the 23d Infantry Brigade, commanded by General Donaldson, himself a former inspector. The 57th Infantry underwent a series of reviews, exercises, and facilities inspections, all of which Helmick rated as superior. A sister regiment, the 45th, similarly composed mostly of American officers and Filipino troops, was almost as good. Engineer, medical, and antiaircraft units were equally impressive in their own spheres. The only all-American unit at the post, the 1st Battalion, 15th Infantry, met the same high standards. Battalion members even had purchased tailored uniforms superior to the government issue. Helmick was measurably impressed, although he warned against possible improper command pressures on soldiers to buy non-issue uniforms.

The units stationed at another large post, Camp Stotsenburg, had American officers and Filipino troops. Helmick observed cavalry and horse artillery drills and exercises, all of which he praised. He was particularly fulsome in his description of the condition of buildings, facilities, and equipment. The guns of the 24th Field Artillery (Philippine Scouts), he said, were the best he had ever seen: "The steel looked like silver and brass parts shone like gold." Moving down to the southern islands of the Philippines, he found that the units there met the same high standards.[72]

The final two weeks were spent visiting the harbor defenses of Manila and Subic Bays. One of the three regiments assigned, the 59th Coast Artillery, was wholly American, while the other two were mostly Filipino. Helmick reserved most of his remarks for the condition of

---

[71] Rpt, Helmick to CofS, WD, 22 Oct 25, sub: Inspection of the Troops in the Philippine Department, Entry 11, RG 159, NARA.

[72] Ibid.

the defenses. The government's interpretation of the Washington Conference Naval Treaty had meant virtually no modernization for Corregidor, the key to the defense system. Helmick urged that the 60 miles of roads on the island be made all-weather and that underground quarters, hospitals, and storage space be developed. As matters then stood, the garrison would be unable to withstand any extended fighting, since less than a third of its men could be protected. Similar improvements were necessary in communications, transportation, and harbor craft.

Helmick was even more alarmed by a recent decision to raise the number of Filipino troops assigned to the defenses. Several times throughout his report he hinted at his doubts of Filipino reliability. Despite his conclusion that the Philippine Division was the best unit he had seen that year, he was concerned over the attitudes of the natives toward American rule. He urged that all important coast artillery fire control and communications positions be filled by Americans "so that no question as to loyalty may arise in any emergency." He went on to suggest that more American line troops be assigned so that a full brigade would be available "in time of emergency." Helmick claimed that Governor General Leonard Wood and the Philippine Division commander, Maj. Gen. James H. McRae, agreed with his concerns. Indeed, suspicion of the Filipinos formed the prevailing view at that time. Military intelligence officials in Manila judged that local sentiment for independence was strong, saw no way to change it, and believed that the only way to restrain its growth was to show progress toward independence for the Philippines.[73]

The Inspector General was so concerned that he made the political situation in the Philippines an item of special inquiry during his visit, raising the issue with senior officers, government officials, and businessmen wherever he went. Although impressed with the economic and social progress that had gone on since he had left the islands in 1903 as a young officer, Helmick did not feel that the Filipinos had made comparable political progress, still considering them impressionable, unsophisticated, and easily duped by propagandists. He predicted that there would be a decline in Filipino unit efficiency as the original American Constabulary and Scout officers began to retire—few senior Americans believed that Filipinos would make comparably good leaders—and that

---

[73] Ibid. (quotations); Ltr, Prosser to McIlroy, 24 Feb 26, Entry 26, RG 159, NARA. Wood retired from active service in October 1921, and he served as governor general of the Philippines from 1921 to 1927.

removal of American suzerainty would precipitate sectional, tribal, and religious strife, suggesting that the United States articulate a firm policy toward Philippine independence. In the meantime, he successfully pressed for more inspections to assure the maintenance of standards and to sense the mood in predominantly Filipino units. On his return trip home, Helmick prepared special reports for the Secretary of War and the Assistant Chief of Staff G–2 as well.[74]

Politics of another sort attracted Helmick on the next phase of his tour of the Far East. In September 1925 he visited the Chinese cities of Hong Kong, Shanghai, Tientsin, and Peking during a period of great unrest throughout the country, which he believed was due to Communist influence. He observed, with approval, the efforts of American officers stationed there to learn the Chinese language, but was disturbed by the poor relations between American Marine and Army personnel. He attributed the trouble to Marine resentment at serving under the command of an Army general. Judging "prejudice still prevailed between the two services," he noted that the senior Marine in Peking, a colonel, avoided paying him a courtesy call. Despite this pettiness, his overall impression of U.S. troops was favorable. But he also considered them vulnerable to the Japanese and left Asia with the impression that Japan was a growing threat to U.S. interests.[75]

Three years after Helmick's tour, the Inspector General's Department undertook detailed surveys of major commands. Once again the Philippine Department and its activities came under scrutiny. Colonel Van Schaick, an early advocate of Philippine independence, who had sustained a close interest in the islands since receiving the Medal of Honor in Batangas in 1901 and had advised both Theodore Roosevelt and Woodrow Wilson on the islands, led the effort. He and his team conducted the survey in late 1928 and early 1929. Van Schaick, cognizant that the Philippines were virtually indefensible against the Japanese, who regarded the American presence as a serious threat to their ambitions, nevertheless judged that the growth of autonomy at local and provincial levels was proof of the feasibility of self-government. Although treaties prevented any substantial military

---

[74] Memo, Helmick to SofW, 11 Dec 25; Memo, Helmick to ACofS, G–2, WD, 18 Dec 25, sub: Comments Affecting G–2 in the Philippines and China. Both in Entry 26, RG 159, NARA.

[75] Memo (quotations), Helmick to ACofS, G–2, WD, 18 Dec 25, Entry 26; Memo, Helmick to CofS, WD, 22 Oct 25, sub: Inspection of U.S. Forces in China, Entry 26C. Both in RG 159, NARA.

improvements, the islands were costing the War Department $10 million a year without contributing a great deal to either their own or American security. Granting the archipelago independence, he maintained, would meet a moral commitment to the Filipinos while reducing the chances for conflict with Japan.[76]

Despite his strong opinions about American policy in the Far East, Van Schaick found the Philippine Department to be exceptionally well run by MacArthur, then the department commander. Believing that MacArthur fully understood the Army's policies of operating efficiently and economically, he focused on identifying some of the problems inhibiting command efforts at economy. For example, large quantities of materiel in depots and warehouses remained on hand, despite being identified as unnecessary to the command. Since most of this was not worn out through "fair wear and tear," the department IG could not condemn it without the Secretary of War's approval. This took months to achieve. Meanwhile, the costs of safeguarding and storing the materiel continued. Often, by the time final approval to sell it was received, it had deteriorated beyond usefulness. In a related action, the department IG spent hours passing judgment on clothing turned in, "settling each case as if it were his own coat he was about to discard." This meticulousness kept serviceable clothing in the system longer and greatly reduced questionable turn-ins. In Van Schaick's view, it also showed that all salvage and condemnation authority could and should be delegated to the department commander.[77]

Another supply problem in the Philippines was the substantial delay encountered in completing requisitions. The fastest turnaround time that Colonel Van Schaick noted was five and a half months. He built an elaborate chart for his report, showing the average time consumed in completing requests for certain items. It took over a year for many requests to be filled, and two and three years were not uncommon; soldiers in the islands often had to wait such extended periods for simple items like metal polish and electric water heaters. Van Schaick recommended that the War Department G–4 study the matter, with a view to speeding up the process. A reverse problem in the supply system was that of automatic issue. Huge overages developed in some items, particularly

---

[76] Memo, Van Schaick to TIG, 2 Aug 29, Entry 26, RG 159, NARA. His views were not representative of his colleagues in the department, most of whom favored dominion status.

[77] Rpt, Van Schaick to CG, Phil Div, 12 Jan 29, sub: 1929 Annual Survey of the Headquarters, Philippine Department, Entry 11, RG 159, NARA.

rations, leading to forced issue of certain canned goods in contravention of Army policy to provide fresh food whenever possible. The need to rotate war stocks exacerbated the situation. Van Schaick suggested that the Philippines work solely on a modified requisition basis.

Despite these difficulties, everywhere Van Schaick went he found storage and warehousing to be exemplary. The concerns in this area had more to do with the structures available. Cost cutting over the years since the war had caused buildings to deteriorate. As Van Schaick observed, "If we are to guard against economic waste in supplies, roofs must come first." Part of the problem lay in the fact that until recently there had been nothing authorizing extensive permanent construction, for the official view had been that U.S. troops were in the Philippines only temporarily. As soon as this policy was changed, General MacArthur had proposed a ten-year $11 million program to construct decent housing and storage facilities. Van Schaick reviewed and agreed with the proposal, stating that it was the minimum necessary to meet the needs of the command and pointing out that tropical conditions required the best materials. He also added his views on how the government could save the value of rents paid within three years after building its own warehouses.[78]

Discussing administration, Van Schaick rejected a proposal that unit commanders be evaluated for the number of first-year enlistees lost through desertion and early discharges. He opined that the quality of the peacetime recruits was very low and the elimination of a large number inevitable. Enforcement of the proposed evaluation policy would result merely in the retention of unsuitable soldiers, with a consequent drop in overall morale and efficiency. In essence, Van Schaick was echoing General Helmick's earlier concern about the demographics of the officer corps of the Philippine Scouts. In 1928 there were sixty-four American and twenty-eight Filipino officers. Their routine promotion would create more senior officers than needed in the Scouts, while under the law the officers could not serve elsewhere. Van Schaick further alluded to the possible problem of senior Filipinos commanding junior Americans. As a solution, he proposed that the law be changed to allow the Scouts' American officers to be assigned elsewhere and no more Filipinos to be commissioned. The racism implicit in these views needs no comment, beyond noting that it was the prevailing view of the era.[79]

General MacArthur, in his endorsement to the survey, praised Van Schaick's report as "a constructive effort of great merit and value." His

[78] Ibid.
[79] Ibid.

lengthiest comments concerned the demoralizing effect of assigning officers to foreign service by roster; doing so smacked of picking a guard mount—and made no sense, being "based upon the false premise that the interest of the individual is paramount to that of the government." The system was unfair, with the total time an officer had spent overseas in his career the only basis for selection. As a result, senior officers who had been overseas during the Philippine Insurrection and World War I, when such duty was desirable, never received a postwar assignment outside the States. Younger, less experienced officers, on the other hand, got repeated tours, keeping them out of the United States for a large part of their careers. This rigid process had been adopted in 1922 over many protests, and MacArthur joined Van Schaick in urging its drastic modification. "It's an unquestionable axiom that military conditions which will not stand the test of war should not be adopted in time of peace."[80]

The concerns expressed by the senior inspectors of the Army during their various visits in the 1920s were echoed increasingly in the reports of Philippine Department inspectors during the next decade. The question of the Philippines' defense capabilities, first raised by General Helmick and discounted by Colonel Van Schaick, continued to be pressed by IGs. Concern for matters of security and combat readiness dominated inspection reports of the 1930s. The free use of native concessionaires on bases was criticized because of the opportunities it created for espionage and sabotage. The ammunition strength and equipment status of units often were detailed to show vulnerabilities and weaknesses. Inspectors, in many cases, were stating hard facts, which, although strongly endorsed by intermediate commanders, were not enthusiastically received at the War Department. Yet the emphasis on the weaknesses of American defenses in the Far East reflected the growing concern of many military professionals.[81]

The equally critical situation in China was revealed clearly in a response to a U.S. Senator concerning a complaint written by a soldier at Tientsin Barracks. According to the complainant, the barracks plumbing was inadequate but money was spent, not on the necessary repairs, but on a new wall around the compound to improve security. The construction of the wall, plus the issuing of fewer passes and new curfew hours, led the man to claim that he was in effect a prisoner in

---

[80] 1st End, MacArthur, 15 Jan 29, to ibid.
[81] Rpt, Dwan to IG, Phil Div, 31 Oct 36, sub: Annual Inspection, Fort Stotsenburg, P.I., including Clark Field, FY 1936, Entry 26C, RG 159, NARA.

the compound. He objected further to what he deemed was a loss of commissary privileges at a time when the troops had instructions to avoid native foods. One of the Philippine Department inspectors, Maj. Edward J. Dwan, prepared an information paper for the American Forces in China, addressing each topic in the complaint.

Dwan noted that the Tientsin Barracks, located in the former German Concession, was the only foreign military area that did not have extraterritorial status. Consequently, the facilities were leased from private owners, and all improvements had to be negotiated. Law enforcement in the neighborhood was a Chinese responsibility and was in practical terms nonexistent. Japanese activity over the years had displaced inhabitants from North China who drifted to Tientsin, attracted in part by the presence of well-paid AFIC soldiers. By 1930 the venereal disease rate was an amazing 283.5 per 1,000 troops, compared to an Army-wide average of 47.7. The command instituted strenuous efforts to reduce this rate, combining an education program with curfews and fewer passes. Further reviews showed that 65 percent of the soldiers at the barracks carried passes authorizing them to stay out overnight, which not only encouraged concubinage but also rendered the garrison unable to meet night time emergencies. Tighter control over commissary privileges was imposed to restrict their use to men with authorized dependents. All of these actions had been recommended previously by the visiting senior inspectors in their reports.[82]

In addition, recent Japanese aggression in North China had accented the indefensible character of the American facilities. Unlike most Chinese complexes of a similar nature, the American garrison lacked any substantial wall around it for defense. The owners had avoided the issue for years by maintaining a decorative picket fence. A new unit commander finally persuaded them to erect a proper wall, both for defense and to reduce theft. The Japanese threat also led the commander to require a percentage of the troops to be available on a 24-hour basis, and he tightened discipline in order to reduce the chance of any incidents that the Japanese could use to create "difficulties." Major Dwan reasoned that all of the actions were justifiable. The problem lay in the commander not keeping his men informed as to the reasons for the changes he had made.[83]

Throughout the world, the inspectors of the 1920s and 1930s were thus reporting on the cumulative effects of policies and conditions that

---

[82] Rpt, Dwan to IG, Phil Div, 18 Sep 36, sub: Information Pertaining to Quoted Allegations Contained in Letter From Senator Morris Shepperd re U.S.A.T. in China, Entry 26C, RG 159, NARA.
[83] Ibid.

had developed over many years. The adjustment to changing financial conditions, popular attitudes, new missions, and unexpected requirements strongly influenced the entire Army, making it by degrees an entirely different force in 1939 from what it had been in 1919. The gradual adoption of motor transport, wireless communications, and aircraft of all types generated new demands on the internal organization of the Army and its Inspector General's Department and, ultimately, produced a revolution in management that would shape their infrastructures in the conflict to follow.

10

The Managerial Revolution

Short on money and manpower, and overburdened with requirements, the Army was trying desperately to perform its mission within the constraints. As a result, to streamline a great variety of its operations, it made determined efforts during the 1920s and 1930s to learn from the management techniques that had been developed by the greater civilian society. In one form or another, this business culture and collateral economic issues influenced the diverse inspections and investigations that were carried out by the inspectorate during the interwar years.

Internal Controls

Much of the internal history of the Inspector General's Department (IGD) between the wars concerned The Inspector General's efforts to maintain uniform standards and procedures, using the technical chain for communicating with all inspectors. Just as it had before the war, the Office of The Inspector General (OTIG) required inspectors to send in copies of their travel orders, to avoid duplication, permit coordination, provide mutual support, and monitor travel costs. It also instructed them to submit monthly reports, each containing the expected completion date of the ongoing inspection and the closing statements of all funds examined. In addition, the senior inspector of each command was expected to submit a report on IGD activities at the end of each fiscal year.[1]

The bulk of most reports concerned the situation in the inspector's command, the effects of War Department policies, and recommendations for improvements. Future needs, such as new training or equipment, were identified. Topics ranged widely—anything of importance to the local commander might be considered. The report was prepared

---

[1] AReg 20–5, 1921, 1924, 1930.

in two copies, with the original being forwarded through normal command channels. Each echelon of command added remarks endorsing, rejecting, or amplifying the inspector's observations. At the War Department the report was reviewed, with extracts circulated among the responsible staff. After all action had been completed, it was filed in the Office of The Inspector General.[2]

The OTIG staff maintained contact with unit inspectors through the issue of numbered "neo-styles"—duplicates of letters and policy statements. The original Yellow Book had languished and disappeared after 1916, because of the rapid changes incident to the World War and its aftermath. Eventually, to supplement the periodic neo-style and circular updates, the pocket-sized guide "Helpful Suggestions to Inspectors" was developed. This small guide, aimed at newly detailed inspectors, not as a rigid outline but as a supplement to the requirements given by their own commanders, was divided into six parts, each outlining procedures and references for various types of inspections.[3]

In 1927 General Helmick tried to strengthen the rather disorganized and haphazard technical chain by directing the periodic issue of IGD policy statements to all inspectors. The need for tighter standards resulted from the War Department's emphasis on what was known as "dollar for dollar" efficiency. Inspectors were expected to scrutinize expenditures to see whether they were necessary and whether they achieved the desired objective at the least cost. Six policy statements had been issued by March 1929, when General Rivers created several inspection standards—short checklists and guides to ensure that inspectors covered all the necessary topics at each activity. The standards were made available to commanders, and generally were well received.[4]

Despite the blizzard of advice, there seemed to be no systematic flow of information coming from the Office of The Inspector General. Finally, under General Drum, the problem was addressed. True to character, Drum directed a complete survey of the matter in conjunction with the organizational overview that followed his appointment as The Inspector General in January 1930. He reduced the number of regulations pertain-

---

[2] Ibid., and 1932.

[3] "Helpful Suggestions to Inspectors, Particularly Those Serving Their First Detail in the IGD," 4 Feb 23, mimeographed, OTIG files, Pentagon (SAIG-ZXH). Seven pages deal with inspections, four with investigations, and thirteen with finance audits.

[4] OTIG Policy Statements 1–6, Boxes 213–14, Entry 26; Ltr, Rivers to Kilbourne, 8 Mar 29, Entry 26; Logan Lecture (quoted words) to QM School, 9 Apr 31, Entry 26B. All in Record Group (RG) 159, National Archives and Records Administration (NARA), Washington, D.C.

ing to IG activities from five to two and ceased the issue of neo-styles and policy statements, replacing them with functional inspection guides that consolidated the various bits of information in circulation. Each of the new inspections guides—ultimately twenty-six were issued—dealt with a separate subject, ranging from animal management to warehousing. The first gave general instructions, stressing that the guides were not intended to be followed slavishly. General Drum expected that the guides, once amended, would form the nucleus for a new IG manual akin to the old Yellow Book.[5]

Maj. Gen. Hugh A. Drum

Unfortunately, the project lost its momentum with General Drum's departure in November 1931. Although the guides continued to be used throughout the 1930s, undergoing revisions as regulations changed, the Office of The Inspector General also resumed the periodic issue of memoranda on trends noted by the War Department. Despite this deviation from Drum's structured system, better control was maintained over the technical chain and the overwhelming flow of miscellaneous advice and information inherited by Drum did not surface again.[6]

General Drum's legacy was even stronger in the area of inspection philosophy and focus. Drum considered inspectors to be the military equivalent of civilian efficiency experts. While the latter were concerned exclusively with matters of profit and loss, the IGs determined whether Army resources were being used in the best possible manner to support national defense objectives. Costs were a concern but not the sole consideration. Drum believed that the inspectorate's primary mission should be to "direct a searchlight into dark corners," to ensure the "preparedness of the army as an agency of national defense." He shift-

---

[5] Drum Annual Rpt, FY 1931, Entry 26; Inspection Guides 1–17 and 19–27, 1930–31, Entry 26A; Logan Lecture to QM School, 9 Apr 31, Entry 26B. All in RG 159, NARA.

[6] OTIG Miscellaneous Corresp Files, Box 1, Entry 26B; Memo, Merriam to OTIG Offs, 2 Nov 36, Entry 26C. All in RG 159, NARA.

ed the emphasis from a review of business methods and toward an analysis of equipment and systems maintenance for meeting mobilization or wartime requirements. As an aid to achieving change elsewhere in the Army, he urged inspectors to report positive innovations. Drum repeatedly stressed that "the IGD is a fact-finding, not a fault-finding, body" and that it existed to help commanders to meet their goals.[7]

Hoping to end the frequently adversarial relationship that had existed in the past between the Inspector General's Department and the General Staff, Drum saw two distinct levels of inspection within the Army. Unit inspections, conducted by the local commander and his IG, should focus on the efficiency and economy of post or commmand operations and on compliance with regulations. OTIG inspections should concentrate on the efficiency of broad systems, such as Army-wide hospitalization or heavy ordnance design and manufacture. Keeping such topics at the War Department level allowed closer contact with the staff elements responsible for making the systems work.[8]

To further his goals, Drum developed an Army-wide annual inspection plan. Each January the Office of The Inspector General would solicit other War Department officials for any topics of special interest they wished to see checked during the general inspections for the next fiscal year. Proposals were reviewed for appropriateness and then consolidated under broad headings, such as administration or supply. Items of concern to The Inspector General, the Chief of Staff, or the Secretary of War were treated under separate categories. The OTIG staff then developed a comprehensive inspection and special inquiry plan. After approval by the Chief of Staff, the plan became the basis for War Department–level IG activity for that year. The Adjutant General sent letters to major commanders, requesting that their inspectors look into the special subjects in addition to local matters.[9]

In principle, the integrated approach had merit. However, its practical application proved to be a great burden for the OTIG officers tasked with developing the lists of special subjects. In July 1938, after years of dealing with constantly changing topics, Col. Harry H. Pritchett, the chief of inspections, suggested that the practice of soliciting special inspection subjects be discontinued. He pointed out that

---

[7] Memo, Drum to OTIG, 16 Nov 31, sub: Relationship of OTIG to the Air Corps, Entry 26A, RG 159, NARA.

[8] Ibid.

[9] Ltr, Conley to CGs, Corps Areas, 18 May 35, sub: Special Subjects in FY 1936 General Inspections; Memo, TAG to TIG, 24 Aug 36, sub: Instructions re Harbor Boats. Both in Entry 26C, RG 159, NARA.

many requests essentially duplicated the types of coverage identified in the inspection guides. The need to consolidate the items submitted by the branches and bureaus represented considerable effort with relatively little return. Experience had shown that important issues were added outside the process in the course of the inspection year. The time spent organizing the special topics tended to limit the time available for general inspections, funds inspections, and investigations. General Reed, agreeing with Pritchett, directed that the practice be suspended in fiscal year 1940 to see if any adverse reaction followed. In fact, the change was barely noticed in the rush of activities associated with the war in Europe, and the practice faded away in the press of great events. General Drum's more organized approach remained, however, as did his philosophy of inspection, with its emphasis on teaching and its goal of efficiency as a means of preparing the Army for war.[10]

Decentralization

During the interwar period special topics dominated the inspectors' time. Redefining the IG function, gradually weeding out excess duties, and decentralizing much of the burden of inspection became major tasks. Passage of the National Defense Act of 1920 encouraged these trends. Inspectors were asked to comment, for example, on the decentralization that resulted from the establishment of the corps areas; on the surplus materiel at installations; or on the pretrial confinement of accused soldiers, for the purpose of identifying unnecessary delays. The Army's image, particularly on the latter issue, was a matter of growing importance. Civil-military relations were made a special item in 1922, for good public relations were seen as critical for building citizen support for the reserve components.[11]

---

[10] Memo, H.H.P. to TIG, 11 Jul 38, and Reply (pencil note), 18 Jul 38, Entry 26C, RG 159, NARA.

[11] Ltr, TAG to IG, 29 May 19, sub: Use of Motor Vehicles, Entry 34A; Ltr, Rivers to All Insps, 6 Jun 19, sub: Inspectors Required To Investigate System Under Which Rations Are Issued, Entry 34A; Ltr, TAG to IG, 29 Jan 19, sub: Fitting of Shoes, Entry 34A; Memo, TAG to IG, 9 Jul 19, sub: Enforcement of War Department Orders, Entry 34A; Ltr, W. Wood to Dept Insps, 4 Oct 19, sub: Shortages in Clothing, Entry 34A; Extracts from Aviation Repair Depot Insp Rpt, 15 Jun 20, Entry 11; File 323.6, GO 132 WD 1919 and GO 75 WD 1920, Entry 26; Memo, Peck to IG, 12 Jan 22, sub: Duplication of Reports on Surplus Property Activities, Entry 26; Neo-style 420, 2 Mar 22, Entry 26; Helmick Annual Rpt, 1922, Entry 26. All in RG 159, NARA. See also Neo-style 333, 8 Jul 18, Neo-style 370, 5 May 19, Neo-style 423, 23 Apr 23, Neo-style 345A, 30 Jan 19, and Neo-style 401, 8 Jun 20, OTIG files, Pentagon (SAIG-ZXH).

The steady growth of special items was one of the reasons that inspectors were overwhelmed with many forms of disjointed guidance. Most of this miscellany was rescinded in 1927 as part of General Helmick's changes. Despite his efforts, however, new special items began to appear almost immediately. Thus in 1927 the Secretary of War directed one of the many initiatives to identify the number of soldiers performing duties away from their assigned positions. Inspectors were to make inquiries during their scheduled inspection visits and then to prepare their findings in a separate report. The next year the names of soldiers away from their primary duties had to be listed, and the inspectors had to assess whether the absence was justifiable. The number of IG special investigation areas reached seventeen in 1927, sank to six in 1929, and then increased to nine in 1937. Of course, field inspectors had to deal with themes or topics assigned them by their own commanders.[12]

The primary difference after 1927 lay in the type and scope of the special items. Previously, almost every one had dealt with some kind of compliance requirement; inspectors were used as enforcers, duplicating the work of others and making it impossible for them to fulfill the role of teacher and helper as desired by the Office of The Inspector General. The overwhelming number of small requirements unquestionably distracted inspectors and diminished their efficiency. Helmick's policy changes during his last year on the job cleared the way for General Drum's reforms. During the 1930s more thematic special issues became the rule, and instead of compliance with official policy, inspectors sought to gather information and aid commanders on matters of current concern.[13]

The only IG duty in which consistency seemed to prevail throughout the interwar era was the conduct of tactical inspections and evaluations. Beginning in 1920, training and tactical inspections were supposed to be made by commanders and their staffs; inspectors no longer participated. In practice, however, the arrangement was not quite as clear as it seemed. Inspectors could observe and comment on field exercises that happened to be under way during an inspection visit, and they still

---

[12] Ltr, Helmick to TAG, 28 Jul 27, sub: Rescission of Certain AGO Letters, and Reply, 5 Aug 27, Entry 26; Helmick Annual Rpt, FY 1927, Entry 26; Rpt, Behr to OTIG, 16 Feb 19, sub: Inspection and Survey, Headquarters, 9th Coast Artillery District, Entry 11; Rpt, Cygon to CG, 3d Corps Area, 30 Apr 31, sub: Annual Inspection of Carlisle Barracks, Entry 11. All in RG 159, NARA.

[13] Themes in the Seventh Corps Area between 1931 and 1935, for example, included administrative efficiency, handling of requisitions, and work conditions. See 7th Corps Area Insp Rpts, 1931–35, Box 23, Entry 11, RG 159, NARA.

could hold formations of troops under arms to check on clothing and equipment. The new regulation ostensibly limiting IG activities in this sphere contained a significant loophole in that it allowed commanders to appoint qualified officers as their assistants. The practical result was that the whole inspection burden often devolved upon the local IG just as it had before the war. Moreover, because the senior commander's tactical inspection reports did not have to be forwarded beyond the major command headquarters, IG inspection reports continued to be used in Washington as a major source for unit evaluation.[14]

In 1928, when inspectors became exclusively involved in the conduct of economic surveys, all tactical inspection requirements were shifted in fact as well as in theory to command channels. The nearly concurrent reactivation of several major combat units, such as the 1st Division in New York, led to the practice of division or brigade commanders devising field exercises that included the tactical inspection. Accompanied by his G–3, the general observed his units in a variety of situations that he himself selected. Thus the 1932 inspections of 1st Division elements consisted of a unit parade, a field inspection, the establishment of a tactical camp, meeting engagements, night attacks, and a combined-arms attack-and-defense problem. These were conducted without any formal IG participation.[15]

General Drum's consolidation of the regulations governing inspections again raised some questions about the role of inspectors in tactical or training activities. In March 1931 a letter issued through The Adjutant General sought to clarify the situation. The regulations that made commanders responsible for tactical evaluations were cited again, emphasizing that IGs had no automatic role in such work. Yet inspectors were under the immediate and exclusive control of their respective commanders, who had the authority to decide the duties of their IGs, limited only by the latter's War Department requirements—that is, the time-consuming economic surveys. Commanders were enjoined to

---

[14] Memo, Chamberlain to Ex Off, 5 May 21, Entry 26; Memo, TAG to CsofBurs, WD, and CofMilBur, 27 Aug 21, sub: Instructions re Inspections by Chiefs of Branches and Other War Department Inspections, Entry 26; Logan Lecture to QM School, 9 Apr 31, Entry 26B; File 300.3, AR 20–10, Entry 26A; Helmick Annual Rpt, FY 1921, Entry 26. All in RG 159, NARA. See also AReg 20–10, 1922; Luther P. Call, Jr., "The History, Organization and Function of the Inspector General's Department," *Reserve Officer* 16 (Oct 39): 11.

[15] Rpt, Kaempfer to IG, 2d Corps Area, 23 Apr 28, sub: Annual Inspection and Survey of Headquarters, 1st Division, and Fort Hamilton, N.Y.; Rpt, Thompson to IG, 2d Corps Area, 24 Mar 32, sub: Inspection of the Headquarters, 1st Division, Fort Hamilton, N.Y. Both in Entry 11, RG 159, NARA.

keep inspections of all types to a minimum so "that inspecting may not be overdone and the morale of the Army personnel thereby lowered." For all intents and purposes, IGs were at last completely out of the business of tactical evaluation.[16]

At the same time, inspection responsibilities were shifting. Inspections entailed considerable travel and expense. Consequently, whenever money was tight, OTIG inspection functions were transferred temporarily to local inspectors. As the budget squeeze persisted, some of these duties became customary, almost permanent. This was especially the case with so-called exempted stations—the installations, including arsenals, airfields, and depots that were answerable to War Department authority rather than to the local commander. The exemption was no longer as total as it had been before the war; by 1921 corps area commanders could direct limited inspections of exempted stations located in their areas in order to familiarize themselves with conditions and personnel. The discipline and appearance of troops was added in 1924 as an appropriate topic. That same year mileage limitations coincidentally forced most OTIG inspections to be delegated to corps area personnel for the duration of the inspection cycle.[17]

The pressure to save travel money continued to grow, year by year. Finally, Chief of Staff Summerall directed in 1929 that exempted stations be made the responsibility of corps area inspectors. For the Office of The Inspector General, the order meant a possible loss of inspection continuity and uniformity at these installations. The problem was complicated by General Summerall's desire that War Department inspectorate continue to survey depots and arsenals and to inspect "big money" accounts. The OTIG executive, then Colonel Preston, seeking clarification, learned from the Chief of Staff that his basic intent was for corps area commanders to be able to direct inspections wherever soldiers were stationed in their areas. An understanding was reached. OTIG inspectors retained inspection responsibility for arsenals, depots, sea transports, and NHDVS facilities; corps area commanders assumed inspection responsibility of all other exempted stations. Additionally, the OTIG

---

[16] Ltr, McKinley to CGs, Corps Area, Depts, and Divs, 27 Mar 31, sub: Army Regulations and Guides, IGD, and Tactical and Training Inspections, Entry 11, RG 159, NARA.

[17] Memo, Bullard to Eastern Dept Motor Off, 13 Feb 20, sub: Exempted Stations, Entry 11A; Rpt, Stone to OTIG, 1 Nov 28, sub: Survey of the Tucson Municipal Airfield, Entry 11; Helmick Annual Rpt, FY 1924, Entry 26. All in RG 159, NARA. See also AReg 20–20, 1921 and 1924; Call, "Inspector General's Department," pp. 11–13.

executive would coordinate with the technical bureau chiefs to avoid duplication and excessive numbers of visits. In this way the special expertise needed to inspect these facilities was maintained at the Office of The Inspector General, while General Summerall's desire for greater corps area control was achieved as well.[18]

When General Drum became The Inspector General, he tried to concentrate his limited travel resources on the OTIG's remaining exempted station responsibilities, in part because of his desire to build extensive functional expertise in the War Department inspectorate. However, he found it difficult to achieve his goal because of

Maj. Gen. John F. Preston

the continued budget squeeze. Even financial inspections had to be passed down to the corps area levels for completion, and in 1930 and in 1931 many depots in the South and West came under local inspection purview. In 1932 the OTIG-level inspection of War Department offices was canceled so that the modest sum involved could be diverted to support IG travel. Similar economy measures in 1932 almost killed Drum's system, when the Chief of Staff considered having local inspectors make all the inspections in their areas. General Preston objected strenuously, arguing that some War Department–level expertise on technical facilities had to be maintained to preserve the effective control by the Army's leaders. After discussion, the Chief of Staff agreed, and the situation in respect to exempted stations remained the same.[19]

---

[18] Memo (quoted words), Summerall to TIG, 17 Jun 29, sub: Inspection of Exempted Station; Memo, Preston to Rivers, 19 Jun 29; Memo, Logan to TIG, 2 Jul 29, sub: Inspections and Surveys by Officers of the IGD. All in Entry 26B, RG 159, NARA. Exempted stations with troops were mostly schools and airfields.

[19] Rpt, Cygon to CG, 3d Corps Area, 21 Jul 30, sub: Inspection and Survey of Carlisle Barracks; Memo, OTIG to Insps, n.d., sub: Inspections Made by Officers in OTIG and Exempted Stations Assigned to Corps Areas for Inspections; Memo, Drum to Preston, 5 May 30; Memo, Preston to CofS, WD, 1 Aug 32, sub: Assignment of Inspectors. All in Entry 26A, RG 159, NARA.

Nevertheless, the tight budget continued to upset the intended division of inspection responsibilities. In essence, OTIG inspectors were required to take annual samples in areas that would have been their exclusive responsibility if funds had been available. The situation was recognized in 1935 by a change to the regulations. Corps area commanders were required to make The Inspector General aware of any inspections and findings made by their IGs at exempted stations, and The Inspector General was expected to reciprocate. The loss of firsthand information caused the Secretary of War to direct in 1936 that General Reed personally inspect all corps area headquarters. Starting in 1937, IGs from Washington inspected one corps area post in each command, specifically to give the Chief of Staff a sensing "for general conditions." That year corps area IGs evaluated nearly all the exempted facilities during their scheduled visits to review money accounts.[20]

The act of sending OTIG inspectors to the corps area headquarters made it apparent that decentralization had gone too far—in some instances IGs were inspecting their own superiors. An inspection report received at the War Department, in which an inspector had commended his own commander, provided the necessary impetus for change. Beginning in 1938, division and corps area inspectors no longer completed the annual inspection at their own headquarters. The situation had proven awkward and embarrassing, for the inspection report could require remedial actions from the inspector's own commander. Henceforth, corps area IGs had to examine the divisions, while OTIG inspectors did the same for the corps areas.[21] This was, however, the only case in which the long process of decentralization was reversed.

Paperwork, Paperwork

Army administration, on the other hand, was characterized by excessive centralization and excessive paperwork. In the opinion of critics both within the service and outside, too many organizational elements were

[20] Ltr, Pearson to CGs, Corps Areas, 2 Mar 36, Entry 11; Ltr, Reed to Corps Area Cdrs, 30 Jan 36, sub: Inspection of All Corps Area Headquarters, Entry 11; Ltr (quoted words), Reed to Spinks, 22 Apr 37, Entry 26C; Reed Annual Report, FY 1937, Entry 26C. All in RG 159, NARA. See also AReg, 20–10, 1935.

[21] Memo, TAG to Corps Area Cdrs, 7 Jun 38, sub: Assignment of Inspections, FY 1939, Entry 11; Logan Lecture to QM School, 9 Apr 31, Entry 26B; Memo, Reed to ACofS, G–1, WD, 6 Sep 38, sub: War Department Policy—Administrative Inspections, Entry 26C. All in RG 159, NARA.

engaged in monitoring others and shuffling documents. As the new efficiency experts for the Army, inspectors became deeply involved in attempts to control such excesses.

The vast amount of paperwork entailed in Army administration was both a product and a symbol of unnecessary supervision and excessive standardization. Even the most trivial action required endorsements through every level of command. The pressure to justify virtually every Army expenditure led, ironically, to an expensive accumulation of data in reports and records. One post commander estimated that almost 44,000 documents were needed to account for the fixed and movable property on his installation. The system, too complex to work in a time of emergency, had been waived in 1918 so that the Army went "from czarism to anarchy to czarism" as it moved from peace to war and back again.[22]

The subsequent proliferation of reports, blank forms, and complicated requisitions marked the resurgence of practices abandoned as unworkable during the war. Many of the inspections and inquiries carried out during the 1920s and 1930s had the aim of cutting paperwork while developing systems that would be applicable both in peace and in war. Inspectors viewed the current practice of issuing separate regulations as the primary cause for the increase. General Helmick predicted a time when no one would be able to read all of the regulations, and clerks would have to be assigned exclusively to filing and indexing. By 1922 the growth of regulations already meant that the average commander was unable both to administer and to command.

Bureaucratic habit contributed to the problem, with Helmick complaining that every time a form was eliminated another promptly took its place. But postwar turbulence was another factor. Allowances and authorizations were modified so often that few commanders could determine their unit's correct entitlements. "The result of this is to give a troop commander a feeling of helplessness," warned Helmick, "and to create a liability for the most careful, painstaking and hard working officer to be assessed with carelessness."[23]

Efforts to alleviate the problem generally had made it worse. In 1920 the General Staff was placed in direct supervision of the supply and administrative activities that once had been performed by the bureaus, thereby creating another echelon of correspondence and caus-

---

[22] Ltr, Hagood to TAG, 12 Sep 19, sub: The Appalling Burden of Paperwork, Entry 11A, RG 159, NARA.

[23] Helmick Annual Rpt, FY 1922, Entry 26, RG 159, NARA.

ing everyone involved to document his actions. In an early postwar effort to ease commanders' burdens, a personnel adjutant had been authorized at unit levels; the practical result had been to introduce even more paperwork by expanding the capacity to handle it. Helmick urged that staff procedures be simplified by requiring staff officers to deal with each other informally. Written records should be brief and should be made only when truly necessary.[24]

Helmick's findings, along with complaints from the field, led the Chief of Staff, General Pershing, to direct a special investigation of the entire situation in April 1922. A survey was undertaken worldwide. Inspectors in the field and each War Department bureau and staff element provided data; specialized commands, such as hospitals and depots, were examined to identify any practices that might be unique to them. A mass of information resulted, which an IGD group analyzed and subsequently coordinated its findings with other War Department elements.[25]

By 22 December, the day of Helmick's report to the Chief of Staff, about 138 reports, forms, or papers had been recommended for change or elimination. By the end of the month 73 were gone and 21 others were being simplified. The IGD findings were passed to a War Department board that had been established, on General Helmick's recommendation, to monitor the problem permanently. Col. Ora E. Hunt was named the IG representative to the board, when it became operational in March 1923.[26]

General Helmick, however, saw deeper causes for the glut of paperwork, declaring that much was due to the excessive number of staff officers at all headquarters and what he called the "overorganization of the War Department" because of the General Staff trying to perform the propriety functions of the bureau and service chiefs. He recommended an arbitrary 40-percent strength reduction of War Department staff officers, relocating them from Washington back to their units and thus drastically chopping the flow of paper, and also a 20-percent cut at corps area and department levels. Helmick further suggested that The Adjutant General's Office should insist on being the sole War Department channel to the field—as regulations required—and should be more critical of the material it forwarded.[27]

---

[24] Ibid.

[25] Ltr, TAG to Corps Area Cdrs, 10 Apr 22, sub: Reduction of Paperwork; Memo, TAG to IG, 6 May 22. Both in Entry 26, RG 159, NARA.

[26] Ltr, TAG to IG, 17 Feb 23, sub: Reduction of Paperwork in the Army, and Reply, 19 Feb 23, Entry 26, RG 159, NARA.

[27] Rpt (quoted words), IG to CofS, WD, 22 Dec 22, sub: Investigation Concerning Excessive Paperwork in the Army; Helmick Annual Rpt, FY 1923. Both in Entry 26, RG 159, NARA.

The volume of paperwork produced another unfortunate consequence in the tendency, noted by many inspectors, of General Staff officers becoming so absorbed in their office work because of the perceived need to document everything. Staff officers were functioning
more as operators than as planners and observers, and at unit level they
were buffering their commanders from proper contact with administrative and logistical personnel. Hence, Helmick suggested in 1924 that all
administration be centralized at the level of the unit adjutant and that
nothing be done at company level.[28]

Largely through General Helmick's efforts, the reform movement
began to show some progress. Regulations were changed in 1924 to
relieve commanders of personal liability for property accountability,
reducing greatly the need for extensive documentation. At the same
time, the War Department board successfully cut the number of blank
forms needed in supply and finance procedures. A major achievement
was the publication in 1926 of a new regulation restructuring the Army
personnel system. Administration was consolidated at the battalion
level along the lines Helmick had suggested two years earlier, theoretically freeing unit commanders and NCOs to focus on mission training.
Stock record accounting and clothing records also were simplified.
Although pleased with the reforms, Helmick pointed out that the total
volume of regimental-level paperwork had not really decreased but had
shifted to other echelons, making its impact less deleterious.[29]

Despite the best efforts and intentions, however, a growing number
of publications continued to be the bane of both inspectors and commanders in the field. Inevitably followed by changes, the regulations
represented a huge administrative burden. One corps area reported in
1928 that it had received 378 bulletins, regulations, and circulars, plus
123 changes to existing regulations. One depot commander told
General Rivers in 1928 that at the end of each fiscal year he had to submit sixty-two routine reports, most of them updating information
already available in some form at the War Department.[30]

General Drum made paperwork reduction a special item during the
1931 inspection cycle. He warned that the General Staff's efforts to
cover every possible administrative contingency with some sort of
guidance had stultified commanders' initiative. In violation of the War
Department's stated principle of decentralization, routine problems

---

[28] Helmick Annual Rpt, FY 1923; Memo, Helmick to TAG, 20 Feb 24, sub:
Reduction of Clerical Work in Organizations. Both in Entry 26, RG 159, NARA.
[29] Helmick Annual Rpts, FY 1924, FY 1926, FY 1927, Entry 26B, RG 159, NARA.
[30] Rivers Annual Rpt, FY 1928, Entry 26, RG 159, NARA.

were decided at the highest levels of command, although they could be better handled at a lower echelon. Drum urged that regulations be limited to policy statements and rules of procedures and that the General Staff refrain from attempting to control daily operations.[31]

General Drum continued to hammer away at the tendency to oversupervise throughout his tenure. Staffs at all levels managed subordinate elements too closely because of a misplaced zeal to remain fully informed. The result continued to be unnecessary documentation and busywork. The Inspector General declared that the cause of the problem was the failure of the General Staff to plan clearly and to articulate the standards desired. "The efficient executive knows that planning is an essential feature of organization; that centralized control is an essential feature of decentralized operation; and that methodical inspection is an essential feature of supervision—organize, decentralize, supervise."[32] This was good advice, based on contemporary management ideas, but it proved easier to enunciate proper principles than to halt bad practices.

The size of the senior-level staffs was another enduring issue related at least indirectly to oversupervision and excess paperwork. It, too, seemed resistant to reform despite intense, extended IG involvement. Immediately after World War I Secretary Baker had requested that IGs make special inspections throughout the War Department, with the aim of keeping the work force in proportion to a demobilizing Army. Although Baker used the information gathered to defend the Army against charges of idleness and overmanning, the special reviews were unpopular and perceived by many officers as threatening. In fact, the inspections had shown that much busywork was in progress, reflecting efforts to justify the strength of an officer corps that had become disproportionately too large for the shrinking Army.[33]

Little actual improvement occurred, despite the downsizing requirement of the National Defense Act of 1920. Finally, in February 1922 Secretary of War John W. Weeks, responding in part to congressional pressure and in part to Helmick's tough views, ordered a reduction in the number of officers assigned to the War Department, directing each bureau and staff department to halve its strength in two 25-

---

[31] Ltr, TAG to Corps Area Cdrs, 18 Jun 31, sub: Reduction of Paperwork; Drum Annual Rpt, FY 1931. Both in Entry 26, RG 159, NARA.

[32] Memo, Drum to OTIG, 16 Nov 31, Entry 26A, RG 159, NARA.

[33] Memo, Baker to Chamberlain, 9 Sep 19, Entry 26B; Notes of an Address by General Chamberlain at a Conference of All Officers of the IGD, 29 Dec 19, Entry 26. Both in RG 159, NARA.

percent increments and giving the affected elements only seven days to prepare plans for the reduction. The Inspector General's Department was directed to review each plan and inspect each agency for compliance with the directive. Inspectors also were to assess the effects of the reduction on operations and the degree of the General Staff's involvement in generating each agency's work. The Chief of Staff added the requirement that all officers be identified who had been on duty in Washington longer than four years and that the duties of enlisted personnel be checked to ensure that General Staff functions were not indirectly being performed by NCOs.[34]

The resulting report from General Helmick stated that, in general, even greater cuts were possible. However, the reductions had to be made judiciously. Some components, such as the new Office of the Chief of Chaplains and the Office of Public Buildings, clearly were overstaffed; others, such as the Office of the Chief of Infantry, were at or below minimum, and any further cuts would hamper efficient operation. Helmick actually recommended an increase in the staff of the Air Service, feeling that its performance was "crippled" by the lack of a sufficient number of officers. He found that most of the excess was in the Ordnance and Quartermaster Corps, both of whose leaders had embarked already on reorganization plans to reduce officer personnel. The Inspector General was successful in recommending that his findings, rather than the original across-the-board cuts, be used to prune the War Department staffs, a decision that allowed a more flexible and efficient reduction. Eventually, 164 positions out of an estimated 800 were eliminated.[35]

This substantial reduction, however, failed to end congressional criticism. Consequently, in May 1923 the Chief of Staff directed the Washington inspectorate to make annual surveys of all War Department branches and bureaus and all exempted stations throughout the United States. Now the objective was to assess the value of each activity to the Army and to determine whether it was being run as efficiently and economically as possible. Deficiencies were to be noted, and instances of exceptional management were to be identified and circulated. The

---

[34] Memo, TAG to IG, 8 Feb 22, sub: Reduction of Number of Officers on Duty in Washington, and Reply, 10 Feb 22; Memo, McKenney to Helmick, 18 Feb 22, sub: Instructions. All in Entry 26, RG 159, NARA.

[35] Rpt, IG to CofS, WD, 16 Mar 22, sub: Inspection of Office of the Chief of Infantry; Memo (quoted word), Helmick to CofS, WD, 21 Mar 22, sub: Reduction in the Number of Officers on Duty in Washington; WD News Release 1, 1 Apr 22. All in Entry 26, RG 159, NARA.

Secretary of War selected his own office as the first to be surveyed, and he enjoined all bureau and department heads to cooperate. An extensive analysis of General Staff operations was made by Col. Casper M. Conrad, Jr., who forwarded his report to the Secretary at the end of the year. Conrad noted a few areas where some positions could be cut, but on the whole he found strengths at the proper level for daily activities. A loss of personnel, in his opinion, would have "one of two effects—a reduction of routine or less time spent on planning—probably the latter."[36] This finding apparently reduced the volume of criticism, and for several years manpower changes were carried out by the General Staff with little IG involvement.

Despite continued command and political interest, as late as 1930 many posts still had not undergone as complete a reduction from wartime strength levels as the War Department. A special survey of corps area headquarters, prepared in 1929 with the object of reducing overhead and standardizing organization, resulted in the preparation of formal tables of distribution for each. Budget cuts and the effects of the Depression, however, renewed the pressure to reduce headquarters strengths still further. In June 1930 the Secretary of War asked the corps area and department commanders to have their inspectors survey post, depot, and garrison headquarters, with the aim of reducing personnel overhead to the absolute minimum that was necessary to conduct essential operations.[37]

The survey results indicated that military headquarters strength had increased by 300 percent over the March 1917 level and that operating costs had risen by 15 percent. General Drum used the information to develop a comprehensive remedy. Although critical of the high overhead on staffs at all levels, he recognized that the situation resulted in part from the refusal of members of Congress to close unnecessary Army posts and the lawmakers' tendency to heap many quasi-military tasks on the Army. Drum admitted that the Army had little control over being overcommitted and underresourced, but he believed that it could make much more of the resources it possessed.[38]

Drum supported a more thorough pruning of staffs to eliminate busywork and ease demands on troop units for nonmission support

---

[36] Memo, Wahl to IG, 3 May 23, sub: Survey of All Branches and Bureaus of the War Department and Certain Exempted Stations, Entry 11; Memo, Davis to CofS, WD, 26 Jul 23, Entry 26; Memo (Conrad quotation), IG to DCofS, WD, 13 Dec 23, sub: Report of Inspector on Activities of the General Staff, Entry 26. All in RG 159, NARA.

[37] Rivers Annual Rpt, FY 1929, Entry 26, RG 159, NARA; John W. Killigrew, "The Impact of the Great Depression on the Army, 1929–1936" (Ph.D. diss., Indiana University, 1960), ch. 2, pp. 12, 15.

[38] Drum Annual Rpt, FY 1930, Entry 26, RG 159, NARA.

requirements. Learning from the survey that maintenance funds were distributed more by precedent than by need, Drum successfully urged that allocations be made on a "fully scientific," or rational, basis. This reform allowed commanders, for the first time, to budget their annual repair expenditures and to make accurate projections for future materiel and personnel needs. To allocate funds, a board was set up at each echelon of command. A remaining weakness was officer turnover, which contributed to the lack of continuity for decision making and long-range planning. Moreover, although better resource management resulted from the survey, few personnel reductions were made because it was government policy not to add to the general unemployment. In consequence, only moderate curbs were imposed on the gradual increase in officer strength.[39]

The story was different at the top, with Congress and the Roosevelt administration still perceiving War Department strength as excessive. Responding to this pressure, the Chief of Staff in August 1937 directed The Inspector General to survey Washington operations to identify areas for manpower reductions. General Reed conducted the inquiry with the help of two of his officers and two from the General Staff. Working from a 1931 survey conducted by Lt. Col. Charles H. Patterson, who became The Inspector General in 1940, Reed discovered that by April 1937 only 40 of the 97 officer positions recommended by Patterson for elimination out of the total 644 had actually taken place. He attributed the slowness of the reduction to the addition of new missions, such as supervising the Civilian Conservation Corps, and to the growth of new planning and procurement activities. Reed concluded that the volume of work had grown while the number of War Department officers was dropping slowly and judged that any further cuts would impair efficiency.[40] There for the moment the issue rested.

Economic Surveys

Inspectors in their role as the Army's efficiency experts utilized economic surveys, which constituted the single greatest diversion from their customary IGD duties. Begun in May 1927 in response to a request from the Secretary of War, the surveys of branches, bureaus, and field activities and installations not under corps areas took prece-

---

[39] Ibid.

[40] Rpt, Reed to CofS, WD, 7 Jan 38, sub: Officers on Duty in Washington; Rpt, Reed to CofS, WD, 5 Oct 38, sub: Employment of Civilian Attorneys in Office of The Judge Advocate General. Both in Entry 26C, RG 159, NARA.

dence over other general inspections. Their purpose was to identify cost and management efficiencies for the Army.[41]

Like the earlier personnel survey, the first of the series of economic surveys came out of the Secretary of War's office, which set the pattern for a detailed management study of the entire headquarters. Commanders in the field concurrently were directed to have their IGs survey all of the activities and installations under their control. Inspectors were to determine which activities were essential and which were not. New and more economical methods of operation were to be identified and, when discovered, were to be considered for application elsewhere. A member of the activity being surveyed was to escort the inspector making the survey to assure that each understood the other's function. Corps area commanders were authorized to modify normal IG duties or to delegate them to other officers, thereby providing the inspectors sufficient time to conduct the surveys.[42]

The first surveys of the War Department were completed in 1927 and 1928 and consisted of analyses of more than nineteen bureaus and activities. The Office of The Inspector General consolidated the remarks and statistics in these surveys in an overview report on the Army's condition. Although little substantial action appears to have been taken as a result of this great effort, the first report nevertheless provided a comprehensive picture of the functions, organization, financing, and physical and personnel assets of each organization visited.[43]

Next, OTIG inspectors turned their attention to the large field activities, such as hospitals, depots, and arsenals. At the outset the Office of The Inspector General issued twelve inspection standards, ranging in subject from inspecting a headquarters to such topics as post exchanges, commissaries, and motor pools, to be used as preliminary guides for conducting the surveys. Subsequently, General Rivers

---

[41] Rpt, Nugent to TIG, 13 Dec 27, sub: Survey of the IGO, Entry 11; Helmick Annual Rpt, FY 1927, Entry 26; Ltr, TAG to TIG, 3 May 27, sub: Survey of All Branches and Bureaus of the War Department, and Certain Exempted Stations, Entry 26A. All in RG 159, NARA.

[42] Ltr, Collins to CG, Phil Dept, 3 May 27, sub: Survey of War Department Activities and Installations; Msg (Immediate Action), Wahl to Corps Area and Dept Cdrs, 5 Nov 27, sub: Survey of War Department Activities and Installations. Both Entry 11, RG 159, NARA.

[43] OTIG Cir Ltr 27, 8 Oct 27; Ltr, Wahl to Corps Area and Dept Cdrs, 14 Oct 27, sub: Survey of War Department Activities and Installations; Rpt, Nugent to TIG, 13 Dec 27, sub: Survey of the OIG; Memo, Rivers to TAG, 2 Oct 28, sub: Surveys of War Department Activities and Installations. All in Entry 11, RG 159, NARA. See also Rivers Annual Rpt, FY 1929, Entry 26, RG 159, NARA.

allowed each inspector to develop his own approach to the surveys, hoping that the variety of methods would enable him to select the best. The surveys quickly highlighted the fact that the Army had no standard system of cost accounting, making it difficult for inspectors to determine either costs or values received in some activities. In these cases, the IGs were obliged to make subjective judgments based on their own estimates of a unit's supervision, efficiency, and record of accomplishing its mission.[44]

The survey reports first were provided to corps area commanders and then referred to the chiefs of branches. These officers were required to report to the Office of The Inspector General any actions they took, based upon the reports, and what economies, if any, they achieved. Commanders in the field indicated that they found the surveys useful for improving their operations. War Department chiefs of bureaus and branches appreciated the surveys, saying that the studies served to keep them in touch with problems in the field. All agreed that the Army leadership's heightened concern over issues of efficient management had been beneficial.[45]

Troop and training installations underwent similar economic surveys. In their reports inspectors summarized the origin and development of such facilities; described in detail the property and buildings, noting the condition of storage facilities and motor vehicles; and provided a comprehensive outline of the activities of tenant organizations. The focus was to verify that the best practices were in use, to gather useful ideas for application elsewhere, and to ferret out inefficient practices, such as storing obsolescent gear rather than disposing of it. In 1928 one inspector found that the New York General Intermediate Depot was issuing expendable dental material with a 10-year-old expiration date. Other subjects covered in detail included property accountability and funds management.[46]

Later surveys did not contain the extensive details found in the earlier ones, but their emphasis remained the same—cost-effective administration of post and unit operations. New topics were added, such as the amount of troop labor used to sustain unnecessary overhead. Greater details were given on some topics, including the number of unprogrammed enlisted losses, and statistics were gathered in the hopes

[44] Memo, Rivers to TAG, 2 Oct 28, Entry 11, RG 159, NARA.
[45] Rivers Annual Rpt, FY 1929, Entry 26, RG 159, NARA.
[46] Rpt, Conrad to TIG, 2 Aug 27, sub: Survey of the Office of the Secretary of War; Rpt, Van Schaick to OTIG, 16 Jun 28, sub: Annual Survey and Inspection of the Medical Field Service School, Carlisle Barracks, Pa. Both in Entry 11, RG 159, NARA.

that ways could be found to modify this drain on the budget. Fire protection and electrical, water, and fuel arrangements were examined also. Yet too often the absence of funds prevented the necessary improvements from being made. For example, the ancient power plant at Carlisle Barracks, Pennsylvania, was marked down as inefficient in 1928. For lack of money for capital expenditures, however, replacement was not scheduled until 1934, by which time the cost of replacing the plant already had been expended on the excess fuel costs.[47]

The surveys also began to include subjects of special interest to the Chief of Staff. As the budget squeeze became more and more stringent, many began to deal with aspects of discipline and morale. Inspectors remarked on compliance with the proper wearing of uniforms and on the mental and physical fitness of officers to lead. Other topics by 1929 included the recycling of usable packing materials and the protection of classified and fiscal documents. Recreational facilities, messes, and post exchanges were evaluated for their positive effect on morale. After the pay freeze and later pay reduction in 1930, estimates on how Army personnel were coping were covered in the discussion on morale.[48]

The corps area surveys contained information on the region—its cities, populations, and so forth—and on the assigned military units, including statistics on their animals and vehicles. The same data was provided for exempted stations that were in the corps area. The distribution of military personnel was listed by category for each site in the region. The physical arrangement of the corps headquarters was analyzed for efficiency, and personnel costs were broken down by position and function. For example, the combined annual salaries of the colonel and warrant officer in the Third Corps Area IG office totaled $10,030 and that of the two officers, five enlisted men, and ten civilians in the signal office $35,147. Rental costs, mileage, supplies, transportation, and telephone expenses were reported and compared to previous fiscal years and projections.[49]

Some of the suggestions that were made for reducing personnel costs were not well received by the headquarters undergoing inspection. In the Third Corps Area, for example, the inspector suggested consolidating some staff functions and eliminating some positions. He

---

[47] Rpt, Rice to OTIG, 2 Jun 29, sub: Inspection and Survey of Carlisle Barracks; Rpt, Cygon to CG, 3d Corps Area, 26 Apr 33, sub: Inspection and Survey of Carlisle Barracks. Both in Entry 11, RG 159, NARA.

[48] See survey reports in Entry 11, RG 159, NARA.

[49] Rpt, Graham to OTIG, 2 Dec 27, sub: Survey of Headquarters, Third Corps Area, Entry 11, RG 159, NARA.

saw further savings in pooling secretarial support, rather than assigning typists to separate offices. He also recommended consolidating the duties of some officers in the field, such as having ROTC instructors serve also as local recruiters. General MacArthur, the corps area commander at the time, objected strenuously, pointing out that Army policy obliged the corps area headquarters to be sufficiently large to hold a full staff at mobilization. What was seen as overage by the inspector reflected the need to maintain war-strength levels in key staff elements. MacArthur judged that any more strength cuts would fatally impair his mobilization mission. Even in peacetime, as far as MacArthur was concerned, his staff was fully employed. He viewed travel and liaison—especially to reserve and National Guard units and mobilization sites—as essential to fulfilling the corps area's mission and concurred with the survey's finding that he should exercise greater control over the exempted stations in his region. MacArthur stressed, however, that the surveys, in their pursuit of economy, should not lose focus on the need for preparedness.[50]

Between November 1928 and March 1929 Col. Duncan K. Major, Jr., and Lt. Col. Ben Lear carried out, in addition to the regular schedule of surveys, a special comparative survey of the nine corps area headquarters at the request of the Secretary of War. The purpose was to provide data to guide changes in headquarters tables of organization. Colonel Major was detailed for the job because he had just completed a two-year tour as a corps area chief of staff, while Colonel Lear had considerable experience in the conduct of surveys. Each headquarters was visited for a week, during which statistics were gathered and each function observed. Major identified 37 officer and 237 civilian positions that could be eliminated—a cut described by General Rivers as "moderate." Standard tables were adopted by August 1929. Major also recommended increases in support to the reserves and the call-up of some reservists to work in the corps areas. His recommendations were accepted, and correspondence courses were readied to train the selected reservists.[51]

Freed of some routine IG duties under the pressure of the surveys, inspectors were able to develop more detailed reports on many activities, for example, large medical facilities, where the emphasis was on assuring the best possible service to patients in the most economical

---

[50] 1st End, MacArthur, 8 Dec 27, to ibid.

[51] Rpt, Major to TIG, 3 Apr 29, sub: Annual Survey of the Nine Corps Area Headquarters, with Rivers' marginalia, Entry 11, RG 159, NARA.

way. The normal problems, such as warehousing, stock accountability, and narcotics security, were addressed, and opportunities for savings were pointed out. Statistics gathered on hospitals included patient costs and the percentage of patients who were active-duty soldiers (about 42 percent). Although the means to save money were a central theme, inspectors remained open to ways to improve efficiency, regardless of cost. Thus, in 1928 Colonel Van Schaick, detailed to the Office of The Inspector General to conduct special surveys worldwide, recommended that the Walter Reed Guest House rates be reduced, thereby providing the families of patients an affordable and decent place to stay, and that greater expenditures be made on books and amusements as a morale measure. All inspectors repeatedly recommended an increase in the number of Army dentists, for everywhere they went they found that the size of the dental staff was inadequate for the services required. Because of budgetary constraints, proposals of this sort usually had to be deferred. Nevertheless, the fact that they had been raised permitted Army leaders to make overall projections of future medical capabilities and needs.[52]

The 1928 surveys of the sixteen ordnance depots by seven different inspectors also raised the issue of poor facilities management. Buildings and equipment were deteriorating prematurely because of a lack of funds to carry out basic maintenance and repairs. Based on this finding, additional funds were given the Ordnance Department to counter the trend. Another result of the depot surveys was an increase, at General Rivers' suggestion, in the depot commanders' authority to direct and coordinate the various bureau activities at their level.[53]

In fact, one major result of the surveys was the adoption in 1929 of scientific cost accounting procedures, based on commercial practice, at Army depots. The Ordnance Department incorporated the requirement for proper budgeting and cost accounting in its depot operations procedures, while the Air Corps developed its own system for determining and controlling equipment repair costs in its depots. A program developed in the Hawaiian Department recorded the costs and consumption of expendable supplies in an effort to eliminate waste or extravagance. The Office of The Inspector General continued to press

---

[52] Rpt, Van Schaick to OTIG, 2 Jun 28, sub: Annual Survey and Inspection of the Army Medical Center, Entry 11; Rpt, Rice to CG, 3d Corps Area, 22 Jun 27, sub: Inspection and Survey of Carlisle Barracks, Entry 11; Rpt, Cygon to CG, 3d Corps Area, 21 Jul 30 Entry 26A. All in RG 159, NARA.

[53] Memos, Rivers to TAG, 31 May 28, and Ames to TIG, 4 Dec 28, Entry 11, RG 159, NARA.

for the application of similar cost accounting in all supply and related activities, hoping to establish a pattern of efficient management throughout the Army.[54]

The emphasis on economy demonstrated the need for a more active role on the part of every headquarters in maintenance, facilities repairs, and property disposal. In 1928, based on The Inspector General's recommendation, funds allotments were processed through channels for disbursement to expending agencies. For the first time, this reform put each echelon in full control of its own budget. It also forced a better analysis of allotments. Hitherto, allocations had been made upon precedent and the convincing tone of the request, rather than upon actual need. The new policy required each level of command to better assess its needs in order to prepare accurate budgets.[55]

In the next survey cycle Colonel Van Schaick averaged six to eight weeks at each major depot, with briefer follow-up visits to gauge the response to his findings. He was accompanied by Maj. Frank Holmes, a Finance Department officer on IG detail, and by B. H. Simmons, a senior civilian accountant. The team not only identified problems but also helped the depot commanders resolve them—hence, the substantial amount of time spent at each site. The findings were passed informally to the Assistant Secretary of War by General Rivers. The visits resulted in warehousing improvements, more systematized inventory procedures, and greater physical security. Savings and efficiency were measured by the reduction in the time needed to fill requisitions. The New York Depot, for example, now took three weeks versus two–three months to fill an order.[56]

Other innovations proposed by the team brought about greater overall efficiency in operations. Productivity was maintained, despite civilian personnel cuts; security was improved and pilferage reduced because of the enhanced guard system; and better personnel practices were implemented, with hiring priority given to former soldiers. Systematizing procedures allowed much better cost accounting. This in turn produced quarterly savings of more than one-third over previous fiscal years. That the depot commanders sustained the momentum was proven during a series of follow-up visits by General Rivers, which verified the execution of Van Schaick's recommendations. The depots were working well by the summer of 1929, and Army leaders considered the

---

[54] Rivers Annual Rpts, FY 1928 and FY 1929, Entry 26, RG 159, NARA.

[55] Ibid., FY 1928.

[56] Memo, Rivers to Ames, 20 May 29; Memo, Rivers to OTIG, 6 May 29, sub: Beebe Report on San Francisco Depot. Both in Entry 11, RG 159, NARA.

survey reports, circulated throughout the War Department, as the definitive word on the condition of the Army's depots.[57]

As time went by, the surveys began to have an effect in other areas as well. The civilian work force of one corps area was reduced by 50 percent through attrition. Better laundry and family facilities were approved for installation on Army transports. Economies were achieved, not only in the depots but elsewhere through the redistribution of surpluses identified in the course of the surveys. The reorganization and consolidation of Quartermaster activities brought a major improvement in efficiency and economy. Petroleum purchases, including those of the Air Corps, were centralized under The Quartermaster General, to realize savings through bulk purchases. Finally, for the first time, standard tables of organization were developed for nontechnical elements, automatically capping their personnel rosters and forestalling unauthorized growth.[58]

In July 1929 the success of the surveys and the economies they generated led President Hoover to order a third series, with the objective of identifying more economies while preparing a realistic force development plan. The War Plans Division worked with the Office of The Inspector General because of the anticipated effect of the findings on the Army's mission capabilities. The report, completed in November, in essence revealed that very little further trimming was possible. It stressed the low level of preparedness of the Army, as a result of the cumulative effect of small budgets and the decline in strength. By the time of the survey the Army was at its nadir, unable to perform its mobilization mission as the core of an expanded force.[59]

The usefulness of the surveys seemed to decline thereafter, and in 1930 the Secretary of War directed that inspectors resume their customary IGD duties, asking that they maintain their current emphasis on economy and efficiency while conducting their general inspections. By June the transition back to the traditional system was complete. The nearly two and a half years devoted to the economic surveys were judged well worthwhile as a means of injecting modern business methods into the Army. Out of them came not only a greater sense of responsibility in the use of public assets but also a reduction of duplicate prac-

---

[57] Memo, Ames to TIG, 4 Dec 28, Entry 11, RG 159, NARA.

[58] Ltrs, OTIG to Insps, 3 Feb 30, sub: Replies to Memorandum of Data Desired by General Drum, Entry 26A, RG 159, NARA.

[59] Mark S. Watson, *Chief of Staff: Prewar Plans and Preparations* (Washington, D.C.: Historical Division, Department of Army, 1950), p. 23; Killigrew, "Great Depression," Ph.D. diss., ch. 2, pp. 2, 9, 18–19, 26.

tices throughout the Army. Despite reforms at the depots, however, the Army still had not devised an entirely satisfactory cost accounting system. Funds disbursement had become well regulated and controlled, but there was no simple way to evaluate expenditures at many different places. General Drum believed that standard cost accounting was a key element to efficient management. He cited the efforts made at the depots as "essential preliminaries" to imposing a like system on the entire Army. Until that was done, he judged that further business efficiency evaluations would be pointless.[60]

One of the achievements of the last cycle of surveys was the identification of the peaks and valleys in logistical operations. Most facilities were staffed and organized to cope with their maximum capabilities, and as a result personnel and assets were underutilized during slack periods. Inspectors' comments on these conditions led to improved facilities and resources management. For example, aircraft maintenance was scheduled evenly over twelve months, rather than just for the spring, leading to better workmanship and resource use over the year, with the same productivity from smaller staffs. General Drum, who relied on the survey findings to promote business efficiency, maintained that the surveys had stimulated interest throughout the Army in getting the most out of what was available.[61] His philosophy was perpetuated in the IGD's emphasis on economy and efficiency in the 1930s. The economic surveys had hit the right note at a time of very limited resources.

Depots

With too many unproductive positions and too much paper circulating, the Army of the interwar years also carried a heavy burden of useless and deteriorating equipment at its depots. As military technology advanced, supply administration became extremely complex—a fact that inspectors repeatedly noted. Considerable technical knowledge was required for preparing requisitions, and the system was completely unresponsive if the nomenclature listed was not accurate.[62]

---

[60] Drum Annual Rpt (quoted words), FY 1930, Entry 26; Logan Lecture to QM School, 9 Apr 31, Entry 26B. Both in RG 159, NARA.

[61] Memo, Drum to OTIG, 16 Nov 31, Entry 26A, RG 159, NARA.

[62] New York Depot Insp Rpts, 1922–23, Entry 11; Army Med Ctr Insp Rpts, 1936–39, Entry 11; England, IG, Camp Benning, Annual Rpt, 5 Jul 20, Entry 26; Helmick Annual Rpts, FY 1924 and FY 1927, Entry 26. All in RG 159, NARA. See also Neo-style 426, 14 Aug 23, Neo-style 428, 29 Jan 24, and Neo-style 433, 11 Oct 26, OTIG files, Pentagon (SAIG-ZXH).

Access to the depots did not become routine for inspectors until several years after the war. Depots in the United States whose functions were unique to a particular department or bureau, such as the Air Service, were not inspected by IGs until 1922. These inspections concentrated on operational costs. For example, reports submitted in the 1920s compared any changes in expenditures both to the previous report and to a 1919 base line, and any increases had to be explained. The emphasis on finances meant that the IGD accountant was always a team member during depot inspections.[63]

However, inspectors went beyond the balance sheet to discover problems that had eluded investigators with a narrower focus. For example, the Newark Depot was being kept open after the war because it contained acres of captured enemy artillery and other materiel held in open storage. No one had decided what to do with it. Ordnance inspections dealt solely with technical issues bearing on preservation of the hardware. An inspector successfully suggested a different approach. Legislative authority was obtained that allowed local governments and veterans groups to take items as trophies at their own expense; the remainder was scrapped. Concurrently, the IG's report led to the disposal or salvage of over 5,000 carloads of rapidly deteriorating ammunition. It was apparent that surveillance of the Army's storage system was needed if costs were to be reduced.[64]

Between 1921 and 1923 inspectors were required to make detailed special inquiries into the disposition of surplus property. Whenever they visited a holding area, they reported on the type, quantity and condition of the materiel and made recommendations for disposing of it. They rated the efficiency of the personnel, evaluated the materiel on hand, and estimated the cost of its maintenance and storage. Finally, the inspectors checked on accounting procedures, to assure that funds were managed properly and that payrolls for temporary-hire civilians were coming from sales proceeds rather than from regular appropriations.[65]

Inspectors repeatedly noted the Army's cumbersome storage operations throughout the 1920s and 1930s, with several recommending changes to simplify procedures. After the war the depots had remained

---

[63] Depot Insp Rpts, Boxes 67 and 69–70, Entry 11; Rpt, Rivers to OTIG, 28 Jun 22, sub: Inspection of New York General Intermediate Depot, Entry 11; OTIG Insp Guide 5 Notes, Entry 26A. All in RG 159, NARA.

[64] Rpt, Rivers to OTIG, 28 Jun 22, Entry 11, RG 159, NARA.

[65] Neo-style 409A, 30 Jul 21, Neo-style 425, 27 Jul 23, and Neo-style 415, 27 Jul 21 (all rescinded 1923), OTIG files, Pentagon (SAIG-ZXH). Temporary-hire civilians could not be used for any duties other than those for which they were hired. Later, IGs were required to report on what those duties were.

full of materiel that was no longer needed and, eventually, was obsolete. Some items were stockpiled in such great quantities that it was impossible to utilize them before they deteriorated. Other usable items were so expensive to store that it was cheaper to get rid of them and buy replacements whenever required. Aircraft engines, for example, were being maintained and stored when the planes using them no longer were in the inventory. The pace of technological developments made such situations increasingly common. The problem was aggravated by the fact that different storage criteria and cost-accounting methods were in use throughout the Army. The confusion encouraged continued stockpiling of unnecessary World War I era goods far in excess of needs, consuming maintenance and personnel resources while returning nothing to the government. In 1930 General Drum used the data from the first two economic surveys to show that reducing nonessential stocks and concentrating the remainder into fewer depots would save the Army half its warehousing costs.[66]

The stark evidence provided by the economic surveys gave impetus to serious cost reductions throughout the storage system. Inspectors urged item by item reviews of all stocks on hand. They recommended that all unessential war reserves be destroyed or, if possible, sold as surplus. The pressures of the economic surveys led to other cost savings as well. In 1929 the New York Depot commander pointed out he could achieve even greater savings if he could force-issue large quantities of generic items held in storage since the World War, including china, work clothes, and underclothing. But most requisitioners insisted on brand names, refusing to accept usable but nonstandard items. Colonel Van Schaick concurred with the depot commander, predicting complete loss of the material on hand under the existing system and huge savings through more vigorous substitution of brand names with generic products. Eventually, the regulations were adjusted, leading to a significant drop in storage and supply costs. Annual inventory adjustments thereafter continued to clear the warehouses of unnecessary stockage.[67]

---

[66] Rpt, Helmick to CofS, WD, 22 Oct 25, sub: Inspection of Troops in the Philippine Department, Entry 11; Drum Annual Rpt, FY 1930, Entry 26. Both in RG 159, NARA.

[67] Memo, Drum to OTIG, 16 Nov 31, Entry 26A; Memo, Williams to TQMG, 15 Aug 29, sub: Supplies on Hand at New York Depot, Entry 11; Ltr, TAG to TIG, 23 Aug 29, sub: Irregularities at Brooklyn Base, Entry 11; Ltr, Van Schaick to TIG, [25 Aug 29], sub: New York General Depot, Entry 11; OTIG Cir Ltr 54, 26 Aug 29, Entry 11. All in RG 159, NARA.

Property Disposal

Measures to dispose of unneeded materiel and facilities were implemented in the weeks after the armistice. Halting contracts, purchases, and new construction, the War Department ordered an inventory of everything in the system. A number of factors complicated the effort—the need to retain sufficient materiel overseas to support the occupation forces; the storage of 600,000 tons of supplies at the docks in France, with another 400,000 still en route; and the uncertainty over the size of the postwar Army. Despite these concerns, General Chamberlain in early December 1918 directed his inspectors to begin the processes of property disposal and the salvage or elimination of worthless items.[68]

The disposal of surplus equipment remained haphazard at best. Inspectors repeatedly urged better accounting methods and coordination between different War Department elements. For example, laundry and repair facilities that were needed to prepare other items for sale were among the first properties to be sold. Major delays in disposing of surplusage were criticized. System changes were implemented in 1920, when a special investigation revealed that a depot had sold cement to a civilian buyer who resold it—at double the price—to a local construction quartermaster. No one was culpable; the civilian had merely taken advantage of the Army's disjointed salvage system.[69]

In 1921 the War Department instructed all IGs to make a special inquiry into salvage operations as a part of their regular visits. The next year the Secretary of War directed that they attend auctions and public sales held in their respective areas. At that time the Army was operating twenty-six retail stores for such sales, realizing over $10 million annually. In each case the inspectors submitted separate reports, for the use of the Assistant Secretary of War and his director of sales. Findings continued to show a need for greater coordination. But in 1922, just as the system began to function, it was phased out on the grounds that it was no longer necessary because most of the large and expensive salvage items had been sold.[70]

---

[68] Erna Risch, *Quartermaster Support of the Army: A History of the Corps, 1775–1939* (Washington, D.C.: Quartermaster Historian's Office, Office of the Quartermaster General, 1962), pp 698–700; Ltr, TAG to TIG, 2 Dec 18, sub: Disposition of Useless Property at Abandoned Camps, Entry 34A, RG 159, NARA.

[69] Risch, *Quartermaster Support*, pp. 702, 705; Frederick Palmer, *Newton D. Baker: America at War*, 2 vols. (New York: Dodd, Mead and Co., 1931), 2:412; Peyton C. March, *The Nation at War* (Garden City, N.Y.: Doubleday, Doran and Co., 1932), pp. 181, 352–55; Chamberlain Annual Rpt, FY 1920, Entry 26, RG 159, NARA.

[70] Helmick Annual Rpts, FY 1921 and FY 1922, Entry 26, RG 159, NARA.

Yet the Army still retained enormous quantities of increasingly worthless property. The scale of the problem was difficult to determine. Inspectors found during a 1928 special inquiry that accurate balancing of stocks on hand against stock record cards was rarely achieved, because most of the accountable officers ignored the requirement to list overages. Auditors failed to detect the omission, for they rarely checked actual stockage if their totals on paper tallied. Some posts held excessive supplies that were not reported, and thus others went without items that were badly needed. Another flaw developed from the requirement that the Finance Department audit all property accounts annually, which meant that little, if any, oversight occurred during the intervening twelve months. As a result, many small accounting problems compounded needlessly before they were discovered. One of the solutions to resolve this was a tightening of inventory and inspection procedures.[71]

In 1928 a change in the regulations required nearly all surplus or salvage property to be listed on inventory and inspection reports, to allow the transfer of one post's surplus to fill another's needs. Inspectors had to check more items and to deface them before release to a buyer. General Drum simplified the condemnation procedure in a second policy change in June 1931, after which corps area commanders and IGs could take routine actions without referral to the responsible War Department bureau for approval. Condemnation criteria were published in an annual directive. Once property appeared in an inventory and inspection report, it could be inspected for condemnation either by an IG, by the local chiefs of supply, or by the services responsible for it. Corps area commanders could appoint special inspectors for emergency condemnations when no IG was available. Special property inspectors also were authorized at depots or arsenals, where materiel was condemned routinely as part of the manufacturing process.[72]

The property accountability and warehousing problem diminished gradually as the pressure generated by the Inspector General's Department began to show results. The advent of the Civilian Conservation Corps in 1933 speeded the consumption of inventories at various depots. This form of progress, ironically, gave birth to a concern among many officers over the shortage of war reserves in the late 1930s. General Preston at the end of his tour in 1935 had broached the issue, cautioning about insufficient appropriations and the impact on

---

[71] Rivers Annual Rpt, FY 1928, and Drum Annual Rpt, FY 1930, Entry 26, RG 159, NARA.

[72] AReg 20–35, 1917, 1929, 1931, 1935, 1937, 1941; Rivers Annual Rpt, FY 1928, Entry 26, RG 159, NARA; Call, "Inspector General's Department," pp. 11–13.

replenishing the war reserves. The little that was spent on moderniza-tion had the effect of impeding the process of standardization, which further impaired efficient and economical maintenance. The lack of funds also hindered proper maintenance of the materiel remaining on hand. Similar problems were encountered in each type of depot and logistical operation, especially transportation.[73]

Transportation

The Army's retention of a fleet of World War I motor vehicles proved to be costly. After the war the Quartermaster General's Department controlled all transportation because of the lessons learned in 1917, when several bureaus had tried to run their own transportation systems. As the Quartermaster General sought to assert administrative controls, IGs were instructed to check on compliance with official transportation policies during every inspection. Vehicles condemned in the United States were disposed of through Quartermaster channels; those in over-seas departments were processed through department channels, since it was more economical to sell them locally.[74]

Soon inspectors noted that the huge motor vehicle fleet could not be used fully. Minor problems often sidelined vehicles indefinitely, unable to be repaired because of the diminishing numbers of qualified mechanics remaining in the Army after demobilization. As early as 1922 inspectors urged the adoption of a gradual replacement program to forestall growing maintenance costs, but the fleet continued to dete-riorate from normal use and exposure. Economical operation no longer was possible by 1924, when a vehicular shortage was predictable because only 800 postwar motor vehicles were in the inventory and all wartime vehicles in storage—16,235—had been issued. As the condi-tion of the wartime vehicles worsened, General Helmick reported in 1927 that to ride in the old Dodge cars "was an affront to one's self-respect and a challenge to one's courage."[75]

The dilapidated condition of the motor vehicle fleet heavily over-burdened maintenance channels. Inspectors urged culling all the vehi-

---

[73] Preston Annual Rpts, FY 1933 and FY 1935, and Reed Annual Rpt, FY 1936, Entry 26C, RG 159, NARA. On the Civilian Conservation Corps, see Chapter 12.

[74] Neo-style 279A, 5 Jun 19, Neo-style 279B, 9 Jul 19, and Neo-style 385, 28 Oct 19, OTIG files, Pentagon (SAIG-ZXH).

[75] England, IG, Camp Benning, Annual Rpt, 5 Jul 20; Helmick Annual Rpts, FY 1922, FY 1924, and FY 1927 (quotation); Drum Annual Rpt, FY 1931. All in Entry 26, RG 159, NARA.

Sgt. John B. Tyler and His Truck. The ramshackle interwar vehicle fleet benefited from the skills of mechanics like Tyler, whose truck had no mechanical failures in fourteen years.

cles that were not cost-effective. The shortage of gasoline in June 1929 compounded matters, with the supply sufficient for operating only half of the vehicles in service—some 7,500, with another 1,000 on mothball status. The remaining half languished virtually unattended, with the increasing age of the vehicles forcing maintenance costs ever higher. Because of persistent reports by IGs and quartermasters, a few new passenger cars were issued in 1929 to offset the poor impression created by the use of dilapidated vehicles. Trucks had remained in better condition, largely because of the greater care given them by permanently assigned drivers. This principle was extended to the new cars through better training of drivers and mechanics and closer supervision of maintenance.[76]

The Army finally began to phase out wartime motor vehicles in great numbers by the end of 1930. Once the War Department imposed limitations on the amount that could be spent on repairing older vehi-

---

[76] Risch, *Quartermaster Support*, p. 717; Rivers Annual Rpts, FY 1928 and FY 1929, Entry 26, RG 159, NARA.

cles, all those requiring more were pulled out of inventory and sold as salvage. Appropriations were made to sustain only 55 percent of the aging fleet while new vehicles were being phased in. During 1930 inspectors condemned nearly 1,800 vehicles, which were sold for salvage. The unequal distribution of vehicle repair units in corps areas was noticed in the course of the exercise. As a result, several maintenance units were reassigned at the end of the fiscal year to provide better support geographically and at each maintenance level. The economic surveys had shown the pointlessness of trying to sustain the ancient fleet, giving impetus to renovation efforts.[77]

The Army Transport Service (ATS), which had drawn down rapidly after the war, was affected similarly by the tight economic situation. By mid-1921 the War Department had released all chartered ships, acquired only eleven of the seventy-five ships ordered before the armistice, and had only sixteen ships in commission by the end of the year. In 1928, because of the need to economize, the ATS fleet was reduced further to seven passenger, two freight, and one cable vessel.

Despite its small size, the fleet was a disproportionately rich source of inspection concerns for the inspectorate. By the end of 1921 inspection responsibility had reverted from port IGs to corps areas IGs. Complaints about service constituted the bulk of their investigations, which were unusually time-consuming since witnesses often were scattered throughout the country or were overseas by the time the complaint was received. Additionally, the money accounts of all transport quartermasters had to be inspected each time a ship arrived in port. The ships themselves were inspected on arrival and departure.[78]

Crowding on sea transports continued to be a major source of complaint. Because of the pressure to operate as economically as possible, ATS managers allocated the extra space that became available under peacetime conditions for transporting cargo. With the problem of crowding unresolved, inspectors continued to push for more realistic passenger space allocations. In 1928 General Rivers suggested empowering corps commanders to remedy the conditions reported by inspectors, thus taking some of the pressure off ATS personnel at the ports. This and several other IG suggestions implemented in 1929 brought immediate benefits. Transports also were required to obtain civilian safety certificates from the U.S. Steamboat Inspection Service, raising safety standards and improving lifesaving equipment.

---

[77] Drum Annual Rpt, FY 1930, Entry 26, RG 159, NARA.

[78] Risch, *Quartermaster Support*, pp. 715–16; Farmer, IG, New York Depot, Annual Rpt, 30 Jun 21, Entry 26, RG 159, NARA.

Post exchanges were established on each ship, along with post offices and better medical facilities for female passengers. Fairer accommodation policies were put into effect for officers. General Drum joined with the War Department G–4 to persuade The Quartermaster General to issue sheets, pillows, and mattresses to troop-bay passengers. Line officers were placed on board as permanent commanders of transient personnel, enhancing discipline and giving the men a spokesman. Finally, in 1931 the fourth, or bottom, tier of bunks was removed from the troop bays, taking temptation away from ATS planners and automatically cutting occupancy by a quarter. This move, combined with the new safety requirements, made the peacetime troop voyages at least tolerable thereafter.[79]

The Air Corps

At a time when fiscal considerations constrained every aspect of the line Army's existence, its airmen represented a special and baffling problem. The question of air power and the extent of its development dominated Army budget discussions throughout the interwar period. Supported strongly by Congress, the arm rapidly grew in significance, and in 1926 the Air Service became the Air Corps. But the new organization was expensive, and its needs had to be balanced against those of the hard-pressed conventional forces.[80]

All too often the airmen demonstrated that they were better aviators than administrators. The inspectorate often served as a brake on their excessive enthusiasm or administrative shortcomings. This relationship began in 1921, when General Helmick recommended reducing the number of Air Service facilities. As a result, the sixty-five activities then in existence nationwide were reduced to forty-four, and substantial consolidation took place. The Chief of the Air Service pledged further reductions as surplus was disposed of and depots closed down. Yet the airmen enjoyed much official and popular support. Some redundancy had to be allowed to continue, because of the need to keep Air Service units in each corps area to provide combined-arms training and support for reserve components. For the inspectorate, both the newness

---

[79] Memo, CofS, WD, to TIG, 19 Mar 30; Memo, TIG to TAG, 24 Mar 30, sub: Transport Service; Drum Annual Rpts, FY 1930 and FY 1931; Ltr, TAG to TQMG, 4 Jun 30, sub: Facilities on Army Transports. All in Entry 26, RG 159, NARA.

[80] Russell F. Weigley, *History of the United States Army* (New York: Macmillan Co., 1967), p. 413; Killigrew, "Great Depression," Ph.D. diss., ch. 1, p. 6; Barksdale Field Insp Rpts, 1933–36, Entry 11, RG 159, NARA.

and the expense of the Air Corps meant continuing interest in its activities; even when a large post underwent an installation-wide annual inspection, separate inspection reports were made on Air Corps operations and facilities. General Drum adopted the practice of reporting his impressions informally to the Chief of the Air Corps after each visit. He was particularly concerned with pilot selection and training, and he successfully advocated improved psychological testing.[81]

Despite the tightening economic pressures of the early Depression years, the Air Corps was able to sustain a comparatively higher level of spending than the rest of the Army by arguing that further cuts would damage severely the civilian aircraft industry. While it stressed materiel acquisition over manpower, the rest of the War Department pressed for trained cadres to provide a base for emergency expansion. Tensions smoldered as Air Corps strength increased at the expense of the other arms.[82]

General Drum particularly resented the Air Corps' failure to act in concert with the War Department in dealing with Congress. The airmen routinely did not participate in the budget process. Drum believed that internal debate and additional requests should end, once appropriations requests were consolidated and forwarded by the Secretary of War to the Bureau of the Budget. The Air Corps, however, saw things differently and continued to emphasize its own unique needs. Drum's findings while he was The Inspector General greatly influenced his actions while he served as the Deputy Chief of Staff. In 1933 he headed a board that led the way to a complete reorganization of the Air Corps two years later.[83]

In August 1935 OTIG's Col. William S. Browning was appointed to head a subsidiary board to survey personnel assignments and operations in the Air Corps. The board included representatives from the Office of the Chief of the Air Corps, from the new General Headquarters, Air Force, and from the corps areas concerned. Its primary mission was to validate Air Corps organization and support capability. Complaints had been received about the excessively complex base command structure. The Browning board recommended exempting all Air Corps facilities and operations, removing them from corps area control, and placing them directly under the Chief of the Air

---

[81] Helmick Annual Rpt, FY 1921, Entry 26; Memo, TAG to IG, 14 Jan 22, Entry 26; Memo, Drum to CofAC, 23 Apr 30, sub: Observations of Air Corps Installations, 8th and 9th Corps Areas, Entry 11. All in RG 159, NARA.

[82] Killigrew, "Great Depression," Ph.D. diss., ch. 3, pp. 11–12, and ch. 6, pp. 11–13.

[83] Ibid.; Weigley, *History*, p. 414.

Corps. The shift occurred in July 1936. While the arrangement was due in large measure to internal squabbles within the Air Corps, the restructuring implied a new inspection responsibility. Col. Roy C. Kirtland, an Air Corps officer, was assigned to the Office of The Inspector General to provide the necessary expertise. During 1936 and 1937 Kirtland personally inspected all Air Corps activities. After primary inspection responsibility reverted to corps area commanders as a result of another reorganization in 1940, he continued to monitor the corps area IG reports and made personal visits to selected air bases.[84]

One of the reasons for the turmoil in the Air Corps was a controversy over its procurement practices that led to the early retirement of its chief, the celebrated General Foulois. The issue began with disputes over interpretation of the Air Corps Act of 1926, a law that dealt with aircraft procurement in detail, but was unclear about many aspects of competitive bidding and negotiated contracts. Although Congress seemingly intended most contracts to be made as a result of competitive bidding, quantity purchases continued to be made through direct negotiation on the basis of an older law that had not been repealed. About 1930 Air Corps procurement officers began to monitor aircraft company profits derived from negotiated contracts. Later contracts were sometimes let below cost, specifically to reduce total profits.[85]

The amount of money available at the time, however, necessarily limited contracts to a few major producers, while lesser firms were ignored. The fact that this practice sidestepped the intent of the 1926 law was noted by Assistant Secretary of War Harry H. Woodring. In December 1933 he blocked Air Corps plans to spend $7.5 million in a negotiated contract to buy 100 aircraft of various types, directing instead that bids be solicited. The indirect effect of his order was that performance standards on some of the aircraft had to be reduced in order to enable at least two companies to compete—much to the chagrin of the Air Corps. Later, Woodring would testify that he honestly had not ordered any aircraft changes, while General Foulois would say with equal sincerity that the Assistant Secretary had done just that.[86]

---

[84] Ltr, TAG to Corps Areas CGs, CofAC, GHQ AF CG, and TIG, 22 Aug 35, sub: Survey of Personnel Situation of the Air Corps; Ltr, Reed to TAG, 29 Jul 36, sub: Assignment of Inspections, FY 1937. Both in Entry 26C, RG 159, NARA. See also John F. Shiner, *Foulois and the U.S. Army Air Corps, 1931–1935* (Washington, D.C.: Office of Air Force History, USAF, 1983), p. 210.

[85] Shiner, *Foulois*, pp. 151, 153–55.

[86] Edwin H. Rutkowski, *The Politics of Military Aviation Procurement, 1926–1934: A Study in the Political Assertion of Consensual Values* (Columbus: Ohio State University Press, 1966), pp. 98–101.

Meanwhile, rumors of aircraft company profits, combined with Woodring's procurement directives, caused congressional investigators to look into aircraft procurement. When Congress discovered that the Air Corps had largely ignored the intent of the 1926 law, Assistant Secretary Woodring and General Foulois were called to testify. Their testimony appeared to be contradictory and confusing. The investigating committee, as a result, decided to open a full investigation, in part at least because of a growing distrust in Foulois' judgment.[87]

The Military Aviation Subcommittee of the House Military Affairs Committee opened its investigation in March 1934 under the chairmanship of Congressman William N. Rogers. Rogers was suspicious of Foulois, and searching for someone to blame for Air Corps problems, he saw Foulois as a likely candidate. The general's natural lack of clarity caused the committee to suspect him of trying to mislead them; many of his rhetorical points could not withstand scrutiny, and his harsh criticism of the General Staff for impeding Air Corps development lost him many allies—particularly, the support of General Drum, by then the Deputy Chief of Staff, who resented Foulois' adverse comments. The Rogers committee had found enough inconsistencies in Foulois' testimony not only to charge him in May with violating the 1926 law and with mismanagement and dishonesty but also to ask Secretary of War George H. Dern to relieve him.[88]

Foulois was stunned by the committee report. On 18 June the problem reached Secretary Dern. Refusing to be hurried, despite congressional pressure, Dern referred the report to Foulois, who took six weeks to prepare a rebuttal protesting the lack of due process and stressing his right to see the evidence against him. The Secretary agreed. The impasse was broken in December by General MacArthur, the Chief of Staff, who suggested that The Inspector General include the Foulois case in an ongoing investigation of officer conduct requested earlier by the Rogers committee. This was an agreeable compromise, and the Secretary passed the additional requirement to General Preston on the thirteenth.[89]

In early 1935 Preston tasked Col. Walter L. Reed to interview many of the same officers who earlier had been critical of Foulois before Congress, including General Drum. Reed focused on the veracity of

---

[87] Shiner, *Foulois*, p. 158.

[88] Ibid., pp. 171–76, 182–83; Rutkowski, *Military Aviation Procurement*, pp. 81–83, 105–07, 113.

[89] Shiner, *Foulois*, pp. 190–92; Rpt, Reed to TIG, 10 Jun 35, sub: Investigation of Maj. Gen. Benjamin Foulois, Entry 26B, RG 159, NARA.

Foulois' somewhat flamboyant testimony, while the massive amounts of information he collected dealt almost exclusively with procurement practices and regulations. Included was considerable data on the air-mail service, which tended to show that the general had not lied deliberately about Air Corps capabilities. Testimony on Air Corps needs was gathered as well. The views expressed and the tone of much of the testimony showed a division within the War Department over the role and status of the Air Corps, with many senior officers stressing that Foulois was not a team player.[90]

Foulois, admitting to Reed that some of his rhetoric could have been misconstrued, emphasized that he had no intent to deceive. He provided affidavits from numerous members of Congress, attesting that they understood what he had meant to say and that they had not been misled. He further added statements from aircraft company executives, who praised his honesty and technical competence. The Foulois investigation took nearly six months, with Reed submitting his final report to Secretary Dern on 10 June. Four days later Dern released his findings, endorsing the view that Foulois had violated the spirit of the 1926 law by condoning closed contracts and that he had made exaggerated statements to the congressional committee. Dern, however, found no evidence of dishonesty. He gave Foulois a letter of reprimand, taking him to task for two unjustified statements. Foulois viewed the findings as a virtual acquittal but, recognizing that his usefulness and credibility had been exhausted, reached the same conclusion as most members of Congress— his departure was inevitable. Foulois retired in September.[91]

---

[90] Rpt, Reed to TIG, 10 Jun 35, Entry 26B; MFR, Preston, n.d., sub: My Remembrance of the Conference With Mr. McSwain at 5 PM, Wednesday, January 16, 1935, Entry 26C; Ltr, Strayer to TIG, 18 Jan 35, sub: Investigation of Maj. Gen. Benjamin D. Foulois, Chief of the Air Corps, Entry 26C; Memo, Humber to SofW, 26 Apr 35, sub: Investigation of the Chief of the Air Corps, Entry 26C. All in RG 159, NARA. See also Rutkowski, *Military Aviation Procurement*, pp. 126–30.

[91] Rpt, Reed to TIG, 10 Jun 35, Entry 26B, RG 159, NARA; Shiner, *Foulois*, pp. 190–92, 257; Rutkowski, *Military Aviation Procurement*, p. 131.

11

The State of the Army

The state of the Army during the interwar years was not encouraging in many respects, largely due to a lack of funds—even for necessities. The constraints worsened as the decade of change and retrenchment following the war gave way to the decade of national depression. At each echelon of command inspectors in their reports provided insightful commentary on the increasing difficulties and on the soldiers' response to them, and they undertook many investigations to resolve the variety of issues affecting the conditions of military life.

Investigations Continue

Many of the IG investigations that had commenced before the armistice lasted well into 1919, and wartime issues continued to be the subject of a large proportion of investigations into 1925. This was especially the case with improper allotment payments, with the lapse of time and the difficulty in finding witnesses making them almost impossible to resolve. Other wartime issues included paternity claims from France, the status of deserters, and the documentation required for less-than-honorable discharges.[1]

The work load was eased in part through the use of recruiting officers and advisers to civilian components to interview witnesses at various and distant locations. Regardless of who was doing the work, General Chamberlain insisted that inspectors be as open as possible in the course of their investigations. He made it policy that the senior offi-

---

[1] IG Special Investigations, Fort Monroe, Box 2, Entry 11A; Helmick Annual Rpt, FY 1924, Entry 26. Both in Record Group (RG) 159, National Archives and Records Administration (NARA), Washington, D.C. See also Memo, McIntyre to TAG, 8 Mar 19, sub: Report of Inspector General Relative to Conduct of SATC Unit, Mississippi A&M College, Entry 8, RG 165, NARA.

cer of a command or staff bureau be notified of any investigation going on in his area of responsibility and that those involved be kept informed with briefings and summaries. He saw the IG's duty as getting the facts within the "limits of justice and common sense. The moment we begin to gum shoe [*sic*] we would lose absolutely our standing with the Army." Openness, frankness, and fairness were the best guarantees of successful investigations.[2]

War Department–level investigations tended to become more specific after the war. For a time commanders had the latitude to decide where to refer certain types of cases. However, after June 1928 all cases of possible graft or improper property disposal had to be referred to the Inspector General's Department (IGD), for which inspectors had to inquire into the management of funds by anyone even remotely connected with a case and to reach "conclusions as to any liability." In addition, the department had to investigate all cases that might ultimately require action by the Secretary of War—that is, those involving the reputations or pocketbooks of military personnel or of the Army as a whole. War Department cases, of course, were brought directly to The Inspector General, while corps investigations were reviewed at that level and then the reports—an original and two carbons—forwarded, with recommendations, to the Office of The Inspector General (OTIG) for final action.[3]

Both situations required OTIG's Investigation Division chief to prepare a written review, which, along with the original report, was evaluated by the executive officer and by The Inspector General for comment. The report, the review, and The Inspector General's conclusions then were channeled through The Adjutant General to a reviewing officer on the General Staff—and perhaps also to The Judge Advocate General if legal issues were involved. After coordination had been completed, a General Staff action officer prepared a final review in the form of a staff study. The whole parcel went through the appropriate assistant chief of staff to the Chief of Staff, who presented it to the Secretary of War with his recommendation for final action.[4]

The fate of an IG's recommendation on an investigation could not be predicted. One inspector recalled having his views in some cases supported all the way through the elaborate review line. But in another case The Inspector General disapproved the suggestions of the field inspec-

---

[2] Notes of an Address by General Chamberlain at a Conference of All Officers of the IGD, 29 Dec 19, Entry 26, RG 159, NARA.

[3] AReg 20–30 (quoted words), 1928, and Change 1, 1929.

[4] Logan Lecture to QM School, 9 Apr 31, Entry 26B, RG 159, NARA.

tor, as did one of the reviewers; three others agreed, but the Secretary of War eventually upheld The Inspector General's position. In yet another case the IG's recommendations were approved at each level of review, only to be changed by the Secretary. If nothing else, the review process could not be considered perfunctory. Personal and meticulous attention was given to each investigation by everyone involved.[5]

By the 1930s the War Department inspectorate was averaging about sixty major investigations annually. A typical year was 1931, with a total of fifty-eight. Twenty-seven resulted in some form of disciplinary action. Another seventeen concerned funds management, specifically the noncompliance with procedural or regulatory requirements. Abuses and neglects of this sort were uncovered increasingly as the War Department sought more efficient and economical operations, and the rising totals reflected better auditing and supervision rather than a dramatic decline in integrity among the officer corps.[6]

Investigations also developed from service members' complaints. For dealing with them, inspectors first held a complaint session during each inspection, at which time they recorded the number and types of complaints and then summarized their findings and conclusions in a report. They were required as well to look into any complaints they heard in the course of their informal visits, and they were expected to give special attention to any problems brought to their attention by soldiers in confinement. As far as possible, inspectors were to resolve complaints during their visits.[7]

Complaints and requests for assistance that could not be dealt with satisfactorily within the command were written up in detail and forwarded to the Office of The Inspector General, where the information was extracted and processed for War Department action. Such cases were parceled out to inspectors by the OTIG executive officer, but it was not unusual for The Inspector General himself to resolve cases that had been addressed to him or had attracted his interest. Many cases were referred to other War Department staff elements for resolution, and the OTIG executive would notify the complainant of the referral.

How well this system worked in practice remains a question. A soldier who was assigned to Clark Field in the Philippines in the 1930s later recalled that an IG visited the post every month to hear griev-

[5] Ibid.; Preston Annual Rpt, FY 1933, Entry 26B, RG 159, NARA.
[6] Preston Annual Rpt, FY 1933, Entry 26B; Drum Annual Rpt, FY 1931, Entry 26. Both in RG 159, NARA.
[7] For a typical selection of complaint cases, see Box 131, Entry 26C, RG 159, NARA. See also AReg 20–10, 1922, 1927, 1930, 1939.

ances. However, no soldier "in his right mind" ever visited the inspector. "Whether a man had a legitimate grievance or not, just to see the IG automatically marked that man as a troublemaker," causing him to be singled out by his officers and NCOs for harassment. More often than not, this seems to have been the actual situation during the interwar decades.[8]

Complaints came from many sources other than service members. The Secretary of War passed those that he received to the Office of The Inspector General for resolution, including letters from relatives of soldiers, protests by lawyers of contractors, and problems raised by other elements of the government. In the immediate postwar period, such complaints frequently dealt with contract closings and difficulties of adjusting to the Army's peacetime procurement routines. The realignment of troops and garrisons also generated complaints, one of which again reflected the racial attitudes of the era.

During the war the Regular Army black combat regiments had been stationed along the Mexican border, where they remained after the armistice. When they were brought up to full strength with enlistees from demobilizing black units, several citizens complained about the increase in the number of black soldiers, calling them a community menace. In March and April 1920 Major Baer, who had returned to his regular grade in the peacetime Army, investigated the allegations. His findings were reminiscent of those made by then Colonel Chamberlain at Sacketts Harbor in 1908. Baer found that the troops had been maligned by a few prejudiced whites, even though most citizens appreciated their presence and their good behavior. He concluded that the black troops were not a menace, and he successfully recommended that the complaints be dismissed as unfounded.[9]

An enduring complaint was the movement of service members' household goods. The inspectorate often served as a court of last resort in these cases, when normal claims and insurance sources were unresponsive. In one investigation two complaints against the Washington Quartermaster Depot had to be resolved. One officer's goods had been damaged en route by fire, while another's had experienced abnormal breakage. Each had used the normal procedures to file claims against

---

[8] Charles Willeford, *Something About a Soldier* (New York: Random House, 1986), p. 152. For examples of cases handled by TIGs, see Complaint Files, Boxes 240–48, Entry 26C, RG 159, NARA.

[9] Rpt, Baer to OTIG, 23 Apr 30, sub: Investigation of Conditions at Stations Garrisoned by the 10th Cavalry, 24th Infantry, and 25th Infantry, Entry 11, RG 159, NARA.

the carriers for reimbursement, only to find in both cases that the carriers were unbonded and uninsured. Investigation revealed that the depot had taken the carriers' word that they were properly insured and bonded. Col. Thorne Strayer was assigned to investigate. He studied fully all the procedures involved in household goods shipments, concluded that the Army was at fault for not verifying the carriers' insurance status, and successfully recommended that the Chief of Finance approve the officers' claims.[10]

Civilians, both agencies and individuals, also could file complaints. IGD and U.S. Civil Service Commission officials conducted joint investigations on issues dealing with employment. Sometimes major questions were raised that concerned other government departments, as happened when the U.S. Post Office Department asked the Secretary of War to investigate allegations of mail mishandling in the Panama Canal Zone. Soldiers' mail was being pilfered. The case went to the local IG, Col. Franc Lecocq, who made an extensive investigation. He surveyed civil and military mail-handling procedures and identified the sites where the pilferage probably had occurred. After he had verified the allegations, he worked with Post Office inspectors on a joint endeavor that resulted in the arrest of a civilian postal employee for stealing from the mails. Lecocq successfully encouraged military commands to establish tighter mail-handling controls, while his office commenced periodic checks to spot trends in complaints about the postal service.[11]

Recruiting and Training

One of the problems turned up by the economic surveys was the continuing high cost of not only recruiting and training but also retaining enlisted personnel. Soldier turnover represented substantial annual financial losses. The problem first became apparent in the aftermath of the armistice, when the rapid discharge of wartime draftees suggested that increased recruitment efforts would be required for the Regular Army to meet the strength projections set with the passage of the

---

[10] Rpt, Strayer to OTIG, 19 Nov 35, sub: Investigation Into the Regulations and Procedure Governing Transportation by Commercial Van of the Household Effects of Officers on Permanent Change of Station, 19 Nov 35, Entry 26C, RG 159, NARA.

[11] Rpt, Graham to CG, 9th Corps Area, 12 Nov 38, sub: Investigation Into Alleged Irregularities in Civil Service Appointments at Rockwell Air Depot; Rpt, Lecocq to CG, Canal Zone, 3 Sep 35, sub: Investigation Report of Alleged Mishandling of Mail. Both in Entry 26C, RG 159, NARA.

National Defense Act of 1920. By 1924, however, the available manpower had dwindled to such a point that Army leaders were expressing serious concerns.[12]

The reasons were varied. Recruit depots had not been revived after the World War, in part as an effort to reduce the per capita cost of recruiting. They had performed a valuable service in screening out unsuitable recruits before the Army began to train its soldiers, committing major resources. The relatively low quality of men enlisting in the years prior to the Depression underlined the need for a better system. For a start, General Rivers recommended that the organization and administration of recruiting stations be standardized and that the pay and allowances of Army recruiters be brought on a par with their Navy and Marine counterparts. Rivers further suggested that recruiters be judged, not merely by the raw numbers of men enlisted from their stations, but by the percentage of them who were still in service after their initial training. Nearly one-third of the Army's enlisted strength turned over annually, and any measure that counteracted this trend would necessarily improve cost effectiveness.[13]

The numbers were sobering. In 1928 nearly 40,000 new recruits had to be brought in to keep the Army's enlisted strength at a paltry 115,000. Only about half the enlisted force remained in the Army for a full term, three years. The others either were discharged early for unsuitability or had purchased their discharges. Nearly all of the unprogrammed losses had exhibited physical or other flaws that should have been identified at the time of their enlistment. Yet the manpower drain could not be blamed entirely on the lack of effective screening by recruit depots. In 1928 inspectors spent the year investigating the reasons for the high loss rate, and they determined that the primary cause was the lack of remedial training for marginal recruits. Low pay, lack of recreation, and excessive nonmilitary labor duties added to the unattractiveness of Army life.[14]

The situation was, if anything, worse in 1929, when about 60,000 more recruits had to be brought in merely to maintain the Army's strength level. At General Rivers' request, the Eighth Corps Area IG undertook a special study of the situation. The inspector concluded that the annual discharge of 5,000 soldiers in the corps area cost the gov-

---

[12] WD Cir 169, 9 Aug 22; Ltr, TAG to TIG, 22 Jan 25, sub: Reports as to Measures Taken To Procure Enlistments. Both in Entry 26, RG 159, NARA.

[13] Rivers Annual Rpt, FY 1928, Entry 26, RG 159, NARA.

[14] Ibid. The Army spent $.60 per man annually on morale activities as compared to the Navy's $5.00 annual average.

ernment $3 million. Many soldiers left the Army so quickly that the service received no return on its investment. Inspectors believed that low pay and the lack of opportunity for advancement were the root causes for the dissatisfaction; low entry pay served to attract mostly unreliable and marginal types to the recruiter, and the situation went downhill from there. Once in the Army, many better quality recruits purchased their way out as soon as they could; the others simply deserted. Ironically, every summer regular units with their inexperienced recruits trained reserve units filled with men whose careers often went back to World War I.[15]

By 1930 the inspectors' attention to the low quality of recruits had begun to pay off. But even with recruiting stations screening applicants more thoroughly, the number of unprogrammed losses remained high. General Drum attributed the problem to what he termed the "surge approach." Months would go by with low requirements; then, usually in the summer, much larger recruiting quotas would be imposed. The Inspector General reasoned that the number of qualified applicants at any given station was fairly constant every month of the year but that recruiters had to lower their standards at surge periods, accepting marginal men to meet their quotas. Drum successfully recommended uniform monthly quotas, not only to increase standards but also to reduce recruiting staffs by eliminating the need to prepare for surges.[16]

Seeking to extend these modest reforms, Drum urged the assignment of surgeons to recruiting districts to cull men with physical defects. In October 1931 the regulations were changed to discourage the enlistment of married soldiers and to retain only those who could prove they had the means to support a family. Despite the Depression, turnover remained a problem until about 1935, when recruit depots were reopened and the force levels were stabilized. Inspectors now began to refocus their efforts on various issues, such as the composition of the Army, troop labor, low pay, and stagnant promotion opportunities. In the meantime, the Army was quite fortunate to have many NCOs and officers fully capable of serving several grades higher.[17]

A related issue involved both military training and nonmilitary instruction. Immediately after the war the Army had placed consider-

---

[15] Rivers Annual Report, FY 1929, Entry 26, RG 159, NARA.

[16] Drum Annual Rpt (quoted words), FY 1930, Entry 26; Preston Annual Rpt, FY 1935, Entry 26C. Both in RG 159, NARA.

[17] Drum Annual Rpt, FY 1931, Entry 26; Ltr, TAG to CGs, 5 Jan 32, sub: Marriage of Enlisted Men, Entry 26; Preston Annual Rpt, FY 1935, Entry 26C; Reed Annual Rpts, FY 1936 and FY 1937, Entry 26C. All in RG 159, NARA.

able emphasis on vocational and educational training, in part to keep the masses of men on hand occupied and in part to attract new recruits and justify the role of the military in peacetime. At the end of 1919, however, General Chamberlain came to the conclusion that this emphasis was adversely affecting morale and efficiency. He had heard rumors that the large number of students had unfairly shifted the bulk of garrison duties to the few "old soldiers" who were not participating. He directed all inspectors to be alert to the problem. Nevertheless, by June 1920 over 105,000 enlisted men were enrolled in some form of educational or vocational training.[18]

Apart from the successful training of those who were illiterate, the program itself had many defects. The War Department provided little overall direction, funds and equipment were insufficient, and few competent instructors were available. Many commanders simply resurrected the old garrison schools, in which officers and NCOs had memorized data while trying to stay awake. This was not universally true. For example, in 1920 the regimental commander at Fort Huachuca, Arizona, served as his own garrison educational and recreational officer, establishing first-rate programs in motor maintenance, carpentry, clothing repair, and English for illiterates; his men learned while they performed work necessary to post operations. The commander's interest meant that the program got the necessary attention from the entire chain of command. But Fort Huachuca was the exception to the rule.[19]

The failure to develop adequate training programs had unforeseen repercussions. The recruiting stations had promoted educational and vocational training as a lure to prospective enlistees long before garrisons were prepared to offer worthwhile courses. Recruits were thus dissatisfied and morale suffered. Unit efficiency also was impaired by the amount of time consumed in such programs. Disillusioned, many recruits took the one-year enlistment option that was offered at the time, and in consequence their whole term of service was devoted "to turn[ing] out an undisciplined soldier and a superficially trained artisan."[20]

Inspectors, critical of the negative aspects of the system, recommended that standardized training programs and instructional material be developed at the War Department level for use throughout the Army.

---

[18] Notes of an Address by General Chamberlain, 29 Dec 19, Entry 26, RG 159, NARA; Chamberlain Annual Report, FY 1920, OTIG files, Pentagon (SAIG-ZXH).

[19] Memo, Baer to IG, 25 Mar 20, sub: Education, Recreation and Morale at Fort Huachuca, Entry 11, RG 159, NARA.

[20] Memo, Baer to IG, 3 Aug 20, sub: Notes on Military, Educational, Recreational and Morale Training, Entry 26, RG 159, NARA.

They also urged that student-to-instructor ratios be specified and enforced. Many believed that they saw the solution to the problem in the establishment of centralized training centers and schools for soldiers, similar to the system that was already in place for officers. "It is no more difficult," said one inspector, "to instruct 1,000 men in one school than 100 in ten." And in fact, this policy was adopted at the end of 1920, when, to everyone's relief, the vocational program was dropped quietly in favor of broader schooling.[21]

The need to inculcate discipline through strictly military training remained. General Helmick in 1924 proposed a basic training period, to be followed by military occupational specialty training. Thereafter, the soldier would join his unit for "training in teamwork." Helmick argued that a green soldier could be militarized fully only through this three-tiered approach. He believed that the poor showing of many in drill, appearance, and military courtesy reflected deficient training that began with a soldier's induction. "The recruit of today is imbued with the spirit of the times—and this is an undisciplined and reckless era," he reflected.[22]

About 17 percent of the eighty major commands investigated by the inspectorate were considered unsatisfactory, and their poor performance was attributed to various factors—performing fatigue duties and supporting reserve components, among others. But the main cause was the lack of supervision on the part of officers and NCOs. Units whose leaders demonstrated interest in training continued to perform well, regardless of the extra duties imposed upon them. In such units police calls were treated as opportunities for drill; fatigue details were made competitive; and so forth. As Helmick demonstrated, good leadership ensured good discipline. He acknowledged, however, that substantial improvements could only be made by increasing funds for post maintenance in order to free soldiers for additional training.[23]

The use of troops as laborers, however, continued to be a problem. IGs recommended that the practice be reduced to the bare essentials of work that was necessary to troop welfare or otherwise of direct benefit to the men. But the situation had changed little by the time General Drum became The Inspector General, for he reported in 1930 that troop

---

[21] England, IG, Camp Benning, Annual Report, 5 Jul 20, Entry 26, RG 159, NARA.

[22] Logan Lecture to QM School, 9 Apr 31, Entry 26B; Helmick Annual Rpts, FY 1923, FY 1924 (quotations), and FY 1926, Entry 26. All in RG 159, NARA. See also AReg 20–20, 1921.

[23] Helmick Annual Rpt, FY 1926, Entry 26, RG 159, NARA.

labor and civilian-component support severely curtailed tactical preparedness in many units. He considered most units to be both untrained and unable to operate their equipment.

Other factors combined to worsen the situation. The dispersion of units, caused by the shortage of housing, reduced the chances for any large-scale combined-arms training. This, in turn, meant a diminishing number of officers and NCOs with experience in providing large-scale administrative and logistical support—a critical problem, exacerbated by the large annual turnover of officers that kept many units in constant turmoil. A special investigation revealed a turnover rate of 40–50 percent in line units and command tenures of less than four months. Drum hoped for an increase in stability, urging a much greater emphasis on standardized training and improved quality in the Army school system. But problems existed there also.[24]

Army Schools

Each Army school was visited annually by inspectors. Immediately after the World War school inspections were highly detailed, partly because the school system was being reestablished and partly because new approaches to vocational training—stressing practical application rather than lecture and theory—were being tried out. The IG reports listed the strengths of the faculty and troops, analyzed the quality of the students, and gave a brief account of the school and its origins. Inspectors described the facilities and recommended improvements, reviewed the establishment's logistical support, and evaluated the methods of instruction and the students' attitudes.[25]

Often the schools served as proving grounds for junior officers under consideration for Regular Army commissions. But there were some exceptions. The Chemical Warfare Service, for example, was found to be using its school to cull undesirable officers; its faculty had instructions to improve student quality and, simultaneously, to eliminate those that prove to be unfit. The War Department and the other bureaus also responded promptly and constructively to school inspection findings. Everyone agreed on the need to sustain a functioning

---

[24] Drum also felt that dispersion made quick mobilization impossible. The twenty-four infantry regiments were scattered at forty-five different posts, with a battalion or less at thirty-four. See Drum Annual Rpts, FY 1930 and FY 1931, Entry 26, RG 159, NARA.

[25] For example, see Rpt, Hunt thru CG, 3d Corps Area, to IG, 15 Jul 21, sub: Annual Inspection of Finance School, Entry 11, RG 159, NARA.

school system. Unfortunately, the lack of funds often prevented the implementation of necessary reforms.[26]

In other cases habit and inertia were at fault. General Helmick had long felt that courses in the psychology of leadership should be offered throughout the Army school system, and especially at the U.S. Military Academy (USMA). He confided that it had taken him five years to rid himself of the bad habits and attitudes he had learned as a cadet. He was impressed by the fact that a large portion of von Steuben's colonial era Blue Book had been devoted to basic aspects of small-unit leadership, and he believed that it was his duty as Steuben's successor to renew interest in the topic. Hence, he brought up the subject on every visit he made to West Point as The Inspector General. Receiving no response, he formally proposed in June 1924 that a leadership course be incorporated into the USMA curriculum.

Correspondence on the proposal circulated between himself, the West Point faculty, and the War Department for over three years. The main problem lay in the faculty's reluctance to make a space in the curriculum by sacrificing established courses. This, in Helmick's view, was merely an excuse for "doing nothing," and he kept the issue alive until his retirement. All he managed to obtain, however, was an agreement that the Military Academy would give added emphasis to leadership during tactical training. General Preston briefly renewed interest in Helmick's concept in late 1932, but the introduction of courses in the psychology of leadership at West Point was delayed until after World War II.[27]

This setback did not curtail IG interest in Army schools. At the Secretary of War's request, the Inspector General's Department carried out intensive surveys of the entire educational system between 1929 and 1931, uncovering many failings. At the conclusion of the first series in the late summer of 1929 Col. Pelham D. Glassford reported that substantial variations marked many supposedly equal programs. Moreover, most courses were geared exclusively to the needs of Regular Army officers; NCO training was insufficient; and the courses for reserve officers lacked any value. Glassford believed that the school

---

[26] Rpt, Baer to IG, 28 Jul 20, sub: Annual Inspection of Chemical Warfare School, Entry 11, RG 159, NARA.

[27] Ltr, Helmick to Superintendent, USMA, 2 Jul 24, sub: Introduction of a Course of Instruction in Leadership Into the Academic Curriculum at West Point, and Reply, 5 Sep 24; Memo (quoted words), Helmick to ACofS, G–3, WD, 18 Sep 24, same sub; Memo, Drum to Helmick, 28 Nov 24, same sub; Chronological History of the Effort of The Inspector General To Have a Course in Psychology Included in the Curriculum, USMA, 14 Dec 32. All in Entry 26, RG 159, NARA.

system was producing narrow branch specialists, with little sense of combined-arms operations. His observations led the Chief of Staff to direct General Drum to make another and more detailed inspection of the school system in 1930. In turn, Drum selected Col. Dana T. Merrill to lead the investigation.[28]

Colonel Merrill set up a special team and procured, through The Adjutant General, data from each school commandant on his organization and curriculum. Merrill asked for information on the number of personnel associated with the schools as faculty, students, or support troops, as well as for the student-to-faculty ratio for each course. His report, completed in June 1931, enlarged on Glassford's conclusions by using newly gathered statistics from thirty schools and from individuals studying at private institutions. In all, 28,713 officers were active in the Army school system and another 1,753 were on ROTC duty. Thirteen percent were serving as faculty or administrators, while 20 percent were students—an excessively high ratio, considering the maturity and experience of the student body. The fact that one-third of the officer corps was engaged in schooling had implications that affected the whole Army.[29]

The inspectors estimated that in the normal course of a career, an officer would be taken from his regular duties at least five times, for periods of up to two years—an average of eight years of training in all. Schooling was one of the primary sources of turbulence within the Army, and a basic reason why officers served an average of less than two years at each post. The implications for troop training were evident. The problem was compounded by the fact that very few of the graduating officers were assigned to positions where they could use their training.

Shifting to more practical matters, the inspectors analyzed course content at each training level. Officer basic training was supposed to be given in garrison schools, while the officers were serving in their first assignments. But, because turbulence among their seniors prevented any coherent programs from being developed, officer basic training was very uneven, rarely touching on all the required topics,

---

[28] Memo, Merrill to TIG, 12 Jun 31, sub: Army School System, Entry 26, RG 159, NARA.

[29] Information in this and the next five paragraphs based on ibid. Corps area officers were detailed to inspect ROTC units. They forwarded their reports through command channels to the Office of The Inspector General from 1925 to 1932 and thereafter to the War Department G–3. See Ltr, TAG to TIG, 3 May 27, sub: ROTC Units, Entry 11, RG 159, NARA.

especially unit administration and supply. Tactical training was reasonably sound at all types of schools. Leadership and management training, however, were deficient; this became apparent when young officers were assigned to reserve-component duties, where such skills were paramount. The lack of basic training also was reflected in IG inspection reports, which repeatedly noted problems in unit administration, supply, and messing. Few of the formal schools offered courses on these topics.

The inspectors noted a lack of coordination and standardization in advanced courses at the Army War College and the Command and General Staff College. In 1930 the two institutions were so parallel in their offerings that they could not provide the intended developmental progression. The inspectors suggested complementary course subjects, with the War College focusing on strategy and high-level staff work and the Staff College on operations and decision making. The same problems pervaded the Army school system, especially the schools run by the Air Corps. The latter were so similar that they could be consolidated.

Another dimension was the inappropriateness of some courses, which proved to be virtually useless to students. For example, the chaplains course at Fort Leavenworth was 50 percent equitation—horseback riding—and only 20 percent counseling and psychology. In fact, far too much time was being devoted to horsemanship throughout the school system, at a time when increased mechanization was understood to represent the future of the army. Other programs were cluttered with minutiae. For example, at the Quartermaster Subsistence School less than 100 hours were devoted to the subject of management, in contrast to 90 hours allotted for the subject of coffee and 105 hours for dairy products. Such courses seemed to be designed to produce officers who would be immersed in trivia and incapable of supporting large-scale operations.

The inspectors recognized that the small size of the Army prevented everyone from obtaining extensive practical experience, and they successfully urged that the schools adjust their curricula to provide substitutes through case studies and exercises. The War Department G–3 assumed the responsibility of coordinating and consolidating programs throughout the system, which reduced overhead and indirectly curtailed officer turbulence. A more progressive educational system thus gradually emerged, aimed at creating leaders who would be capable of performing command or staff functions commensurate with their grade or higher. The value of this transformation in Army education was to be proven a decade later during World War II.

Subsequently, inspectors confined themselves largely to scheduled inspections, paying little further attention to the curriculum. In 1936, however, the Chief of Staff requested a survey on the quality of USMA graduates, in response to complaints from corps area commanders that new lieutenants were not prepared to assume troop duties. Most believed that the USMA graduates needed to attend a basic course that would provide them practical, rather than theoretical, training. The Military Academy's position was that its mission was to produce future senior commanders and staff officers, rather than platoon leaders. Opinion was so divided that the Office of The Inspector General handed the issue to the G–3, where it was soon submerged by the crisis of World War II and the pressing need to obtain officers from any source.[30]

Morale Issues

Interest in morale continued in the postwar period, although measures intended to chart or otherwise manage it soon became suspect. A formal requirement for separate morale reports lasted only from January 1919 until August 1921. Inspectors found that the mandatory appointment of morale officers led many commanders to shirk their own responsibilities in this area, while some morale officers, in attempting to diagnose potentially demoralizing factors, became magnets for petty complainers. Hence, inspectors sought to reemphasize the time-honored command obligation, stressing individual character and unit pride.[31]

There were, however, practical steps needed to ensure a reasonable standard in such basics as food, clothing, and recreation. Soldiers' clothing presented a baffling dilemma for inspectors, despite the huge wartime stocks at the depots. Immediately after the war inspectors realized that something was amiss in the requisitioning process. Units were requesting clothing items properly, but their requests went unfilled. Reports to this effect went to the Quartermaster General, whose investigation surfaced several problems. Units were ordering clothing on prewar forms that listed thirty-two different clothing sizes, although during the World War only nine sizes had been made and, beginning in 1920, eighteen sizes had been approved for manufacture. Depot clerks

---

[30] Rpt, Martin to TIG, 15 Dec 36, sub: Annual Inspection of USMA, Entry 11, RG 159, NARA; File 333, Inspector General, 1920–45, USMA Archives, West Point, N.Y.

[31] Ltr, W. Wood to CofMoraleBr, WDGS, 11 Jan 19, Entry 11; Memo, OIG to Insps, 25 Aug 21, sub: Morale, Entry 25; Memo, Baer to IG, 3 Aug 20, Entry 26. All in RG 159, NARA.

had not been instructed to consider reasonable substitutes for requisitions made on the old form.

Furthermore, postwar recruits on average were smaller than wartime draftees, making the wartime stocks less useful than had been expected. Apparently, the Quartermaster General already had let contracts for new uniforms, but improvements were not realized until the end of 1920 because of the time required to manufacture the items. In the meantime, at the OIG's suggestion, the Quartermaster General had the requisition forms altered to reflect the new sizes and instructed the depots to be more helpful. Thereafter, inspectors reported equipment shortages and requisition dates after each visit to pinpoint responsibility for any delays in issuing supplies.[32]

The quality of the Army ration always had been a basic morale factor monitored by the inspectors for the Quartermaster General. Investigations of rations and messes thus consumed much of their time, as did commissary sales. In 1919 a series of complaints about food at Army hospitals led General March to request that IGs also examine hospital messes whenever they visited a post with medical facilities. But most ration-related reports at hospitals were brief, uncritical overviews, in which the inspectors noted mess hall visits, menu reviews, and cursory fund audits.[33]

A few hospital inspections, however, were much more thorough. Col. Robert C. Humber's inspection report of the messes at Fort Bayard, New Mexico, proved significant. He reviewed and evaluated mess operations, as well as followed up by examining supply methods and equipment. His work revealed not only an absence of close cooperation between quartermaster and medical personnel but also a greater need for coordination between physicians and dieticians. Much of the food service equipment was antiquated, making it virtually impossible to deliver a hot meal at bedside, for example. Humber recommended a complete survey to determine the type of equipment needed to cook and transport food properly. He also suggested more responsive supply procedures to assure fresher food and less wastage. His report added

---

[32] Rpt, Irwin to IG, 7 Jul 20, sub: Inspection of the Aberdeen Proving Ground; Ltr, Hanson to OIG, 16 Oct 20, sub: Clothing Sizes. Both in Entry 11, RG 159, NARA. See also Neo-style 383C, 30 Apr 20, OTIG files, Pentagon (SAIG-ZXH).

[33] Rpt, Kenan to IG, 20 Aug 19, sub: Inspection of Camp Hospital Mess; Ltr, TAG to IG, 23 Jul 19, sub: Inspection of General Hospitals; Rpt, Desobry to IG, 3 Mar 20, sub: Inspection of General Hospital 31 Mess; Rpt, Cummings to IG, 8 Aug 19, sub: Inspection of Camp Travis Hospital Mess. All in Entry 11, RG 159, NARA. See also AReg 20–5, 1921, 1924, 1931, 1935, 1942; Neo-style 379, 29 Jul 19, OTIG files, Pentagon (SAIG-ZXH).

momentum to initiatives begun earlier by The Surgeon General to improve the use of dieticians and to upgrade mess equipment. In cases where complaints proved to be justified, the reason was always inefficient or incompetent supervision, which could be rectified by either retraining or relieving unsatisfactory personnel.[34]

While inspections of hospital messes continued from 1919 to 1927, the focus gradually shifted to the Army ration and its procurement process, especially after the Office of The Inspector General issued a special report on the subject in 1924. Disparities in the ration between services, and even between Army components, represented a serious morale issue in General Helmick's view and was readily perceived at the summer camps, where ROTC or reserve-component rations were more generous than the less liberal Regular Army allowances. The dissatisfaction among the troops compelled regular units to improve their own rations, although improperly, by spending their unit funds—a practice condemned by inspectors because it curtailed spending for legitimate morale activities. Meanwhile, problems also had been detected in commissary operations. Colonel Johnson, the OTIG inspector who conducted several investigations in the Panama Department, concluded that the system needed reform. Apparently, nobody at supervisory levels knew how to check commissary operations in sufficient depth to determine whether they were being done properly. Johnson developed a guide—eventually used throughout the Army—that reduced complaints about the commissary just as major reforms began in the mess system.[35]

In 1928 the upgrading of ration allowances ended the existing disparities, took the pressure off unit funds, and assured a more balanced diet for the troops. New regulations required all mess purchases to be made at post commissaries, which produced savings through bulk purchases and also lowered rates of petty graft. Mess officers at first complained that the system impeded their flexibility in taking advantage of local price fluctuations, requiring them to anticipate future needs in time to allow the commissary to begin its purchasing process. Inspectors, however, favored the reform because it ensured greater efficiency and reduced opportunities for corruption.[36]

---

[34] Fitzsimmons General Hospital Insp Rpts, 1922–27; Rpt, Humber to IG, 12 Aug 19, sub: Inspection of Fort Bayard Mess, All in Entry 11, RG 159, NARA. See also Neo-style 379, 29 Jul 19, OTIG files, Pentagon (SAIG-ZXH).

[35] Helmick Annual Rpt, FY 1926; Memo, Johnson to TIG, 13 Jun 27, sub: Scope of Policy No. 1—Be Helpful. Both in Entry 26, RG 159, NARA.

[36] Rivers Annual Rpt, FY 1928, Entry 26, RG 159, NARA.

Mess operations continued to be an item of interest for inspectors in 1929 as the new purchasing system entered its second full year. Because the Chief of Staff showed his personal interest, mess officers made greater efforts. The centralized purchasing system proved itself by providing better rations at lower costs, and most objections to it faded away. Yet from this success came a new issue, that of standardized menus. IGs viewed better coordination between messes as essential if the full benefit of large-order purchasing was to be realized. Ideally, every mess should use the same food items at the same time. Although some commanders recognized the importance of standardization, too often the buying power of post quartermasters had been frittered away in efforts to accommodate the whims of each mess. Inspectors successfully pressed for menus to be coordinated at least to a degree, to ensure uniformity in basics while allowing purchasers to take advantage of local market conditions. But efforts to replace antiquated kitchen equipment proceeded slowly because of the lack of funds.[37]

Mess operations also failed to keep pace with the advances made in procurement. Just as in the hospital messes, better trained mess personnel and supervisors were needed. Company officers were encouraged to take special training at local cooks and bakers schools, and increased time was devoted during training to menu planning and teaching the value of nutrition and balanced diets. In 1931, however, a sudden cutback in funds threatened the whole process of reform. As an economy measure, the War Department lowered the value of the Regular Army ration by 24 percent, from $.50 to $.38, despite the fact that the general food index had dropped only 10 percent in response to the Depression and that the Navy Department ration remained steady at $.50. The more liberal allowances enjoyed by the Navy and Marines, as well as ROTC and CMTC participants, again threatened to demoralize the troops. Fortunately, the centralized purchasing system, by then in full operation, at least assured the men sufficient food.[38]

Housing was a never-ending problem. In part because of postwar reorganization, the size and stationing of the Army was so unsettled that little construction or maintenance was performed on posts until well after passage of the National Defense Act of 1920. The dispersal of so many officers to schools and civilian components deprived the regular force of much needed leadership and contributed to the problems that followed. By the mid-1920s living conditions at Army posts were a

---

[37] Ibid., FY 1929, and Drum Annual Rpt, FY 1930, Entry 26, RG 159, NARA.
[38] Logan Lecture to QM School, 9 Apr 31, Entry 26B; Drum Annual Rpt, FY 1931, Entry 26. Both in RG 159, NARA.

matter of great concern to Army leaders. In 1923 the Office of the Inspector General stated that most buildings were "becoming unfit and unsafe for occupancy." The critical deterioration of permanent structures was bad enough; worse was the decay of so-called temporaries built during the war, which were becoming uninhabitable. Keeping the temporaries even marginally livable imposed a constant drain on scant resources, with less and less to show for the effort. Continued use of such structures for living quarters both lowered morale and damaged the Army's image.[39]

The housing situation for troops began to make a slow improvement in the late 1920s, when a barracks-building program was implemented. Many wartime structures continued to be occupied, however, much to the distress of their inhabitants. Additional expenditures on upkeep were so uneconomical that only minimum sums were spent, with repairs performed by troop labor. Soldiers used a portion of their meager wages to buy cleaning and preserving materials that were on the Army's short-supply list. The general shortage of officers' quarters especially affected junior married officers, few of whom were able to afford suitable rentals. The problem was even worse for married junior NCOs and enlisted specialists, who lived too often in squalor in "unsightly colonies of shacks" that post commanders tolerated for lack of any alternative. General Rivers warned that this situation was the reason why the Army was losing personnel who were quite expensive to train. Nevertheless, the only result was a policy of restricting the acceptance and retention of junior married men—hardly a morale enhancer.[40]

Yet in the officer corps, the housing problem, grade stagnation, and turbulence were only secondary morale issues compared to pay. In 1927 General Helmick rated financial worries the biggest problem of most officers. By that year the majority of junior officers were finding it increasingly difficult to meet their obligations, forcing them to curtail the social activities hitherto expected of them in the name of community cordiality. In 1928, in the hopes of easing the situation, Rivers began to advocate twice-monthly pay for all personnel. The Marine Corps and Navy had adopted the practice some time previously, with no

---

[39] Helmick Annual Rpt, FY 1922, Entry 26, RG 159, NARA; Lenore Fine and Jesse A. Remington, *The Corps of Engineers: Construction in the United States* (Washington, D.C.: Office of the Chief of Military History, Department of the Army, 1972), p. 46 (OIG quotation).

[40] Helmick Annual Rpt, FY 1924, and Rivers Annual Rpt (quoted words), FY 1928, Entry 26, RG 159, NARA.

The Quality of Life. Support for units even of this size were an overwhelming problem for the Army.

adverse affects. In fact, the system had reduced personal indebtedness and credit purchases in exchanges. His proposal was rejected, however, on the grounds that it would make mandatory collections and deductions more difficult.[41]

Concern over morale issues led the Chief of Staff in July 1929 to direct The Inspector General to determine "the actual state of mind" of officers, soldiers, and local civilians. He also wanted IG reports to describe and evaluate the morale and recreational facilities that were available at each installation that inspectors visited. General Rivers suggested that the mental attitude of a command might be deduced from a variety of indicators: personal appearance; promptness in responding to orders; absence of discontent over minor matters; tolerance for the idiosyncrasies of superiors; use of recreational facilities; and extent of on- and off-duty socializing. He recommended that inspectors carry out individual and group interviews, and cautioned that they should reach conclusions about a unit only after comparing it with others under similar conditions.[42]

---

[41] Helmick Annual Rpt, FY 1927, and Rivers Annual Rpt, FY 1928, Entry 26, RG 159, NARA.

[42] OTIG Cir 51, 17 Jul 29, OTIG files, Pentagon (SAIG-ZXH).

The state-of-mind analysis continued to be an important element of inspection and survey reports throughout 1929 and 1930. The Chief of Staff was especially concerned over the effect of pay cuts and promotion freezes that were implemented by the Hoover administration to offset the effects of the Depression. There seemed a real possibility that the cuts, when added to poor housing and heavy administrative and labor burdens, would be the last straw in the process of demoralization. Officers, because they paid many of their own expenses, were especially hard hit. Corps area IGs now estimated that as many as 90 percent of their junior officers were in debt. Professional expenses, such as uniform, horse equipment, and the virtual necessity of owning a car—official vehicles were few and local travel authorizations were never granted—added to the burden. Declining morale in the officer corps inevitably affected the enlisted ranks as well.[43]

There were some palliative factors. The 1930 IG inquiry into the Army's state of mind revealed that morale was higher than expected, primarily because of the Depression, which underlined the importance of job security at the same time that it caused a moderate drop in the cost of living. The situation was fragile, however. Inspectors pointed out that such mitigating conditions were temporary and external to the Army. Most soldiers were being sustained by the hope that equitable pay and promotion legislation would be passed eventually. The long term solution was to increase their pay until its buying power equaled that enjoyed by similar grades before World War I, and the inspectors urged that remedial pay legislation be prepared for submission as soon as economic conditions gave it a chance of passage.[44]

Meanwhile, the continuing problems of officer pay were rendered more acute by Army demographics. In 1931, and for the next three to five years, a "hump" of captains emerged—those who had entered service in 1916–18. Their presence doomed younger officers who had come on active duty after 1918 to serving a minimum of sixteen to seventeen years as lieutenants, with correspondingly low pay and mounting indebtedness. The situation, which could only have an adverse affect on morale, led to a change in the retirement law in 1935, whereby officers with fifteen or more years of service could retire voluntarily. Dwindling government resources prevented any pay raises in future

---

[43] Helmick Annual Rpt, FY 1924, Entry 26; Rivers Annual Rpt, FY 1928, Entry 26; Drum Annual Rpt, FY 1930, Entry 26; Preston Annual Rpt, FY 1933, Entry 26B. All in RG 159, NARA.

[44] Drum Annual Rpts, FY 1930 and FY 1931, Entry 26, RG 159, NARA.

years, despite IG recommendations that were repeated without effect for the rest of the decade.[45]

Legal Issues

In an Army so ill-housed and underpaid, morale problems inevitably were reflected in the conduct of the troops. Both desertion and AWOL rates were high. Some AWOLs turned themselves in at more desirable stations, were tried, served their sentences there, and received new assignments on release. The principal force counteracting the desertion rate, which was high throughout the 1920s, was the advent of the Depression, aided by increased command interest in the problem.[46]

One issue that attracted IG attention was the Army practice of paying rewards for the apprehension of deserters. The Army continued to request appropriations for this purpose, even though a cutoff of funds in June 1932 seemed to have little effect on the number of either desertions or arrests. Senior commanders began questioning the value of rewards, arguing that returning deserters to military control was bad for discipline. In August 1934 the Secretary of War directed General Preston to study whether attempts to revive the program should be continued. The so-called deserter apprehension study lasted four months, under the supervision of Colonel Strayer. Taking a historical approach, the study showed that rates of desertion increased or decreased in proportion to the economic situation outside the Army. As the number of men volunteering for the service increased during periods of economic depression, recruiters were able to select the best of many good applicants. Desertion rates consequently declined from 1929 until 1934, when a slight rise was noted following the establishment of the Civilian Conservation Corps that paid higher salaries.[47]

Yet Colonel Strayer believed that the reward system should not be discarded. He was influenced by corps area commanders, the majority of whom opined that the appropriations request should continue because they foresaw the day when stronger measures against deserters might be necessary. All were pessimistic about rehabilitating offenders,

---

[45] Preston Annual Rpt, FY 1933, Entry 26B; Parkinson, IG, Phil Div, Annual Rpt (quoted words), 9 Nov 31, Entry 26C. Both in RG 159, NARA. See also Act of 31 Jul 35 (49 Stat. 507).

[46] Helmick Annual Rpt, FY 1924, and Drum Annual Rpt, FY 1930, Entry 26, RG 159, NARA

[47] Memo, Strayer to TIG, 15 Feb 35, sub: Deserters and General Prisoners, Entry 26A, RG 159, NARA.

judging that only a very small percentage would ever become valuable soldiers. Strayer agreed, yet considered it essential that the Army have an active policy against desertion, including the means to stimulate pursuit and apprehension if necessary. He recommended, however, that desertion be redefined; most of the men who were charged might more appropriately have been classified as AWOL. His views were accepted and, by mid-1935, were reflected in the regulations. Thereafter, the number of men dropped from the rolls, or listed as either deserted or AWOL, gradually declined.[48]

Cases of desertion continued to occur, however, and one became an object of high-level interest. For several years inspection reports on Fort Francis E. Warren, Wyoming, chronicled growing desertion and court-martial rates, which by 1939 were the highest in the Army. The post's problems were a concentrated version of those that had been plaguing the Army since the armistice. Barracks were overcrowded and recreational facilities poor. Each year the conditions were reported, and each year The Quartermaster General was forced to state that, although new construction was approved, funds were not available for anything except basic maintenance of the existing facilities. The situation was so bad that in May 1939 the Chief of Staff, responding to the cumulative evidence in IG reports and to the post commander's request, ordered a special investigation on crowding at the post.[49]

The inspector, Col. Charles F. Martin, documented the overcrowding once more, demonstrating its effect on morale with extensive medical and military justice statistics. He also reviewed the needs of the relatively isolated post above and beyond barracks. It was deficient in virtually every element of its infrastructure—few sewers, few garages, and very limited athletic facilities. Martin praised the efforts of the commander and chaplains to ameliorate conditions and to raise morale, but concluded that little improvement was possible without investment in new construction. The report, with strong endorsements from the chain of command, recommended that money be diverted from the Secretary of War's reserve fund to build new barracks and a gymnasium for the forlorn station.[50]

Many commanders believed that changes in the military justice system, brought about by the National Defense Act of 1920, were as

---

[48] Ibid.; Ltr, Hayne to TIG, 31 Aug 35, sub: Morals of Military Personnel, Entry 26A, RG 159, NARA.

[49] Rpt, Martin to TIG, 28 Jul 39, sub: Special Inspection of Fort Francis E. Warren, Entry 11, RG 159, NARA.

[50] Ibid.

much responsible for the erosion of morale and discipline as the lack of resources and facilities. The changes in question had been aimed at eradicating arbitrariness and providing greater protection for the accused. Many officers condemned the new court-martial procedures as cumbersome and unresponsive, arguing that the technical requirements for carrying out investigations and providing protection for the accused were too elaborate. The reforms in their view hindered quick justice and encouraged leniency to offenders. Inspectors reported these opinions, usually without comment. Their findings for the most part corroborated commanders' assertions that greater firmness was needed to reduce desertions and to prevent "change of station AWOLs."[51]

In 1926 General Helmick, judging the system to be "cumbersome, laborious and subversive of expeditious and effective justice," urged that administrative requirements be simplified. Many local inspectors proposed that unit commanders have greater powers to dispose of minor cases and that the process of investigating and reporting such cases be different than for major felonies—eliminating, for example, the requirement for verbatim transcripts of all procedures. They concurred with the line commanders that procedural delays were impairing discipline without enhancing justice. In fact, some of the stricter requirements had already been relaxed by the mid-1920s, although the new system remained a source of command complaint for many years afterward.[52]

Prison visits by inspectors continued as before, as did virtually all of the prewar requirements, such as Leonard Wood's 1911 policy of not having parties of garrison prisoners working under guard in public view. Every year an inspector visited the military prisoners held in the U.S. Federal Penitentiary at Leavenworth, Kansas. Between 1911 and 1935 their number ranged from 11 to 685. Each was accounted for, examined physically, and given the chance to voice any complaints. Specialized medical care requests were referred to the prison authorities; clemency requests were forwarded only if the prisoner produced new evidence, in which case a War Department review sometimes resulted. Favorable revisions of pay adjustments and copies of any proceedings were given to military prisoners. Many wanted to be transferred to the nearby Disciplinary Barracks. If possible, the transfers

---

[51] Helmick Annual Rpt (quoted words), FY 1924, Entry 26, RG 159, NARA; Neostyle 420, 2 Mar 22, OTIG files, Pentagon (SAIG-ZXH). See also Terry W. Brown, "The Crowder-Ansell Dispute: The Emergence of General Samuel T. Ansell," *Military Law Review* 35 (Jan 67): 1–45.

[52] Helmick Annual Rpt, FY 1926, Entry 26, RG 159, NARA.

usually were approved. In 1922, as a result of an IG report, 360 prisoners were relocated to the facility.[53]

In the 1930s the large Army prisons were closed and most of their occupants returned to post stockades, mostly through the efforts of The Inspectors General. The Disciplinary Barracks closed in 1930, and General Drum was able to show that the result was to increase labor resources at posts, reducing the use of troops for fatigue duties. General Preston agreed, believing firmly that military prison operations were not cost-effective and that the Army should get out of the business entirely. He built on Drum's work, urging a complete review in early 1932 that eventually resulted in the temporary end of the whole system. In June 1934 the Army prison at Alcatraz was transferred to the Justice Department.[54]

One morale and discipline issue affected the general society considerably more than it did the Army. In January 1919 the 18th Amendment to the Constitution made prohibition of alcoholic beverages a national policy. Ironically, the Volstead Act enforcing the ban had little practical effect on the Army. Various earlier laws had imposed limits on soldiers' access to alcohol. The sale of intoxicants in post exchanges had been barred since 1901, despite the objections of many officers. A law passed at the outset of World War I, prohibiting the use or importation of alcohol on all military installations, remained in effect afterward, a forerunner or supplement to the general prohibition imposed by the amendment. As a consequence, no new Army policies or regulations were issued until 1929, when a low-key policy statement resulted in minor changes to the relevant Army regulation for ensuring that military practice conformed to federal law.[55]

Because of current policy, the repeal of the 18th Amendment in December 1933 did not affect prohibition on Army installations. This was particularly galling because the Navy quickly changed its rules, and the general public was enjoying its new freedoms. Inspectors

---

[53] AReg 20–20, 1921; Memo, CofS, WD, to All Cdrs, 3 Feb 12, sub: Prisoners, in Neo-style Compilations, 15 Sep 21 and 12 Aug 27, OTIG files, Pentagon (SAIG-ZXH); Military Prisoners, U.S. Federal Penitentiary, Insp Rpts, 1911–35, Entry 11, RG 159, NARA.

[54] Drum Annual Rpt, FY 1930; Ltr, Preston to TAG, 8 Mar 32, sub: U.S. Disciplinary Barracks (and follow-up memos thru 6 Dec 33); Ltr, TAG to CG, 9th Corps Area, 20 Mar 34, sub: Transfer of Alcatraz. All in Entry 26, RG 159, NARA.

[55] Memo, Helmick to CofS, WD, 12 Jul 24, sub: Law and Regulations Covering Use and Possession of Intoxicating Liquor on Army Posts; Memo, Rivers to CofS, WD, 15 Jul 29, sub: Enforcement of the National Prohibition Act; OTIG Cir 61, 5 Dec 29. All in Entry 26A, RG 159, NARA.

stressed in their reports the installation commanders' concern about the morale of their troops, and General Preston recommended rescinding the Army's prohibition regulation and publishing a new policy. As a result, on 30 April 1934 the Army "went wet," joining the rest of the country.[56]

Post Exchanges

Despite the lack of alcohol, post exchanges became an increasingly important element in maintaining morale during the postwar years, and IG interest in their operations remained at a high level. Immediately after the war, however, their financing was in a state of confusion. Units customarily bought shares of the exchange on a per capita basis when they joined a new station, purchasing them from the departing units. The system had broken down during the war, partly because units moved about in haste and partly because newly activated units lacked funds to purchase the shares.

A typical example of the consequences may be seen in the conditions that existed at Fort Ethan Allen, Vermont, in 1919. The 2d Cavalry, in leaving the post in March 1918, had signed over its interest to the 310th Cavalry, a new National Army regiment that had no funds to pay for the shares. The 310th was later broken up to form other units, all of which were reassigned and demobilized at other posts. While it was in Vermont, its inexperienced unit officers had failed to keep accurate records. When a new Regular Army unit was assigned to the post in July 1919, it found the exchange accounts in disorder. An IG investigation showed that determining liabilities was virtually impossible, and yet it was clearly unfair to force the new unit to assume the exchange's debt. When a full audit had been completed, General Chamberlain successfully recommended that most of the exchange's liabilities be assumed by a War Department sinking fund, which had been set up to meet such contingencies. The remaining liabilities were to be repaid from future exchange profits.[57]

During the years that followed, General Staff elements waged a prolonged effort to reform the post exchange system, finally culminating in more centralized policy direction and funding. The actual opera-

---

[56] Memo (quoted words), Preston to TAG, 30 Apr 34, sub: Military Prohibition; Memo, Browning to TIG, 13 Apr 34. Both in Entry 26A, RG 159, NARA.

[57] Rpt, Chamberlain to SofW, 7 Aug 19, sub: Fort Ethan Allen Exchange; Rpt, OTIG to SofW, 31 Dec 27, sub: Claim of Mrs. Grace Rink, Cafeteria Concessionaire, Aviation Mechanics School PX, and Reply, 18 Jan 28. Both in Entry 26, RG 159, NARA.

tion of the post exchanges remained under the jurisdiction of local commanders, in part because of IG recommendations. By 1924 the exchanges, now the primary source of funds for post athletic and recreational activities, had become big business operations, governed by an increasingly complex body of regulations. As a result, their conscientious management entailed more time than one officer could be expected to give as an additional duty, and many inspectors began to suggest that qualified uniformed or civilian managers be appointed, at least for the larger exchanges.[58]

By 1930 over 200 post exchanges were being inspected throughout the Army. In that year a survey of the 83 largest revealed that they were doing a high volume of business, producing nearly $11 million in profits that were channeled into morale work or paid as dividends to stock-owning units. The dividend proceeds were used mostly for dayrooms and company recreational activities. When the War Department directed the larger exchanges to hire civilians to replace the soldiers on their staffs, inspectors noted a quick increase in efficiency that offset the cost of salaries. They urged that the policy be extended by hiring civilian managers at all exchanges, regardless of size, to assure greater expertise and continuity in case of individual or unit reassignments.[59]

The demand for stringent economy affected the post exchanges as it did all other activities. The War Department Appropriation Act for fiscal year 1933 sought to remove soldiers from the exchanges, where a few hundred still worked, and redirect them to military duties. It also sought to divert military personnel spending from the exchanges into local communities hard-hit by the Depression. Hence, the act limited the patronage of post exchanges to active-duty military personnel; the families of enlisted men, active or retired; and reserve-component members on active duty. Officers' family members could use the exchanges only with written authority from their sponsor, specifying purchases for each visit. The act also prohibited the use of any appropriated fund asset, such as an Army building, in support of exchange activities, and it required that the exchanges divest themselves of all elaborate merchandise and carry only ordinary expendable items.[60]

The act caused considerable hardship for military families and civilians working on Army installations. Discharged veterans of World War I receiving treatment at Army hospitals could no longer use the

---

[58] Chamberlain Annual Rpt, FY 1920, OTIG files, Pentagon (SAIG-ZXH); Helmick Annual Rpts, FY 1924 and FY 1927, Entry 26, RG 159, NARA.

[59] Drum Annual Rpts, FY 1930 and FY 1931, Entry 26, RG 159, NARA.

[60] WD Appropriation Act, FY 1933, Entry 26A, RG 159, NARA.

Post Exchange, 102d Engineers

exchanges; civilian employees could not patronize exchange cafeterias, even in remote country districts. The need for a signed permission for each visit by an officer's dependent was a great inconvenience. An even greater inconvenience for all was the limitation on the types of goods that could be sold at exchanges, especially when posts were located far from towns and town merchants. The difficulties imposed upon service families who lived on island posts, like Fort McDowell in San Francisco Bay, were almost insurmountable.[61]

The consequences of the act extended well beyond the military community. The restrictions on the exchanges were devastating to civilian concessionaires, many of whom were forced out of business. Merchants in surrounding communities were hurt by the loss of consignment sales. Low-paid soldiers and their families lacked the funds for not only making purchases without the exchange discount but also traveling to the nearest store. The exchanges, losing income, began to cut their work forces, releasing 300 civilian workers almost at once and scheduling another 1,000 for discharge over the fiscal year. On the other hand, all of the soldiers who had been working in the exchange system had to be retained—even though returning them to military duties was one of the law's stated objectives![62]

---

[61] Memo, OTIG to SofW, Aug 32, sub: Post Exchanges, and Draft Reply, Entry 26A, RG 159, NARA.

[62] Ibid.

The drop in exchange profits posed serious problems for morale in a variety of ways. The purchasing power of the already slim Army paycheck shrank still further. The activities that had been supported by the exchanges—including athletics and libraries—were threatened, as were educational facilities for enlisted men's children at many Army posts. The law failed to take into account the differences and unique needs of particular posts, from training camps to West Point, where civilian visitors were left without access to alternate facilities. The results embarrassed the Army at every level, while the economic effects in most cases proved to be the opposite of what the law's backers had hoped. A final loser was the taxpayer, who—as a newspaper in one town with an Army post pointed out—would now be obliged to pay for activities previously supported by exchange profits.[63]

Post commanders were quick to complain to The Inspector General of the problems engendered by the new policy. General Preston, calling the law's effects a classic example of the rule of unexpected consequences, was constrained to reply that the Army had no choice but to comply. The law itself required the Army to submit a report on exchanges to Congress. Using information collected by the local inspectors, the OTIG staff prepared an extensive report, detailing not only evidence of compliance with the act but also evidence of resulting hardships. The report emphasized the fact that the exchanges were nonappropriated activities, whose success reduced costs to taxpayers while creating jobs and improving morale. A second report six months later summarized major unit and garrison commanders' views on the law's effects. Sensitive to these findings, Congress at the end of 1933 eased some of the restrictions it had imposed. However, the basic principles of the law remained in effect until major changes were made as a result of World War II.[64]

Officer Conduct

During the time when the new exchange rules were taking effect, several cases of corruption on the part of Army officers had come to the attention of the House Military Affairs Committee. Such discoveries helped to fuel Congress' zeal for reform, while convincing it that corruption was rife throughout the service. In plain fact, enough cases involved well-known officers to sustain an aura of scandal.

---

[63] Ibid.; *Oswego (N.Y.) Palladium-Times*, 15 Dec 32, Entry 26, RG 159, NARA.

[64] Ltr, Stone to Preston, 15 Oct 32, and Reply, 19 Oct 32; Ltr, MacArthur to Garner, 23 Nov 32, sub: Post Exchanges. All in Entry 26A, RG 159, NARA.

Characteristic was a serious conflict-of-interest case that brought two major investigations of Lt. Col. Edward L. Hoffman, the officer responsible for parachute design in the Air Corps. General Preston personally conducted a month-long inquiry in January and February 1933, at which time Colonel Hoffman denied under oath all association with a firm in Cincinnati, Ohio, that manufactured parachutes. The case remained closed until early March 1936, when the president of a competing company complained to a member of the House Military Affairs Committee of Hoffman's close association with the Ohio company. A committee investigator verified the allegation. After the War Department was notified, the Chief of Staff called for a new inquiry on the ninth.[65]

Col. William W. McCammon reopened the case for the inspectorate. He reviewed the subpoenaed records of the suspect firm in great detail, reconstructing its activities, expenditures, and relationship with Colonel Hoffman from the time it was organized in 1927 to the time of the investigation. It turned out that Hoffman had been in charge of parachute development at Wright Field in Dayton since 1919. When he was reassigned as a reserve aviation adviser to Cincinnati, he persuaded a number of local businessmen to incorporate a parachute manufacturing firm. He became its principal engineer and was in fact, if not in name, its chief executive officer. From 1927 to 1929 Hoffman had himself detailed to the Commerce Department, ostensibly to advise that department's secretary on aspects of aviation safety. He actually worked full time for the newly founded company, using government facilities and equipment. Later, he was reassigned to Wright Field as the Engineering Section's parachute unit chief. He continued to draw a retainer from the civilian firm while on this duty. He tried to direct contracts in its favor, but without success. The firm was insufficiently capitalized to meet the government's requirements, in part because it had spent most of its money in payments to Hoffman over the years.[66]

By the time of the second investigation in 1936, the company had withered away and Hoffman had been reassigned to the Air Corps Tactical School. The statute of limitations precluded his being charged with influence peddling, but the Secretary of War reprimanded him for lying under oath during the earlier investigation.

---

[65] Blanton Testimony in U.S. Congress, House, *Congressional Record*, 72d Cong., 2d Sess., 1933, pp. 2263–65; Ltr, Reed to James, 5 Mar 36, Entry 26C, RG 159, NARA.

[66] Rpt, McCammon to TIG, 27 May 36, sub: Investigation of the Connection of Lt. Col. Edward L. Hoffman, Air Corps, With the Triangle Parachute Company, Entry 26C, RG 159, NARA.

Hoffman retired immediately thereafter. Hoffman's position as one of the most distinguished American parachute inventors brought the scandal considerable publicity and made it the object of prolonged congressional interest.[67]

An even more celebrated case of the time involved Brig. Gen. Alexander E. Williams, the Quartermaster Transportation Division chief, on whom the House Military Affairs Committee had evidence of his accepting kickbacks and bribes. Williams, an 1889 USMA graduate and a Silver Star recipient for action at Santiago, already had been the subject of three earlier investigations—in 1907, for disregarding procedures; in 1918, for involvement in the black market in France; and in 1921, for mismanagement leading to bankruptcy of the Munitions Office Cafeteria. In early 1935 the named investigators for the case—Colonel Reed, soon to become The Inspector General, and Lt. Col. Leo J. Ahern—carried out a complete audit of General Williams' numerous and complex bank accounts, tracking each check written and determining the source of every deposit. They verified that the general had received money and preferential prices from potential contractors and that he had misappropriated both government and USMA funds. Finally, he had lied about his associates and his conduct to Congress and a District of Columbia grand jury. The investigators successfully recommended a court-martial. In February General Williams was relieved of his position and reduced to his permanent grade of colonel, and after his trial in May he was dismissed from the service without entitlements.[68]

Not all officer conduct investigations had such high visibility. One began when the Office of The Inspector General received an advertisement for an economics book, which was severely critical of the Roosevelt administration's policies. The author, Edward C. Harwood, was a captain in the Corps of Engineers, but in a private capacity he served as director of the American Institute of Economic Research, a conservative group opposed to current policies. The captain's role raised issues of improper political activity and personal conduct. Nevertheless, the investigator, Lt. Col. Frank C. Mahin, proposed that the captain and his colleagues only tone down their criticisms as long as Harwood was director. General Preston disagreed, stating that Harwood had shown poor judgment in becoming so deeply involved in

---

[67] Ibid.

[68] Rpt, Reed to TIG, 28 Mar 35, sub: Investigation of Brig. Gen. A. E. Williams, QMC; Memo, Preston to SofW, 6 Apr 35. Both in Entry 26C, RG 159, NARA. See also AP News Release, 23 May 35, OTIG files, Pentagon (SAIG-ZXH).

such an organization and recommending his immediate reassignment. The Chief of Engineers, who considered Harwood to be necessary in his job supporting Works Progress Administration activities in the Boston area, interceded, and the two reached a compromise. After the Chief of Engineers explained his and Preston's views, Harwood agreed to disassociate himself from the institute.[69]

Under the rubric of officer conduct, the inspectorate reviewed or investigated many cases involving divorce and the child-support or custody agreements that resulted from marital breakups. Often the former spouse of an officer would write the Inspector General's Department, complaining of her ex-partner's failure to abide by the support agreements made at the time of the divorce or separation. The OTIG staff then forwarded the complaint and any documentation to The Judge Advocate General's Office for a judgment on the officer's legal obligation. If decided in the spouse's favor, the Office of The Inspector General would treat the case as a complaint of indebtedness and, using command channels, instruct the officer to meet his obligation or face disciplinary action.[70]

Homes and Cemeteries

As in the past, the inspectorate continued to oversee the operations of not only the retirement homes set up for veterans but also the cemeteries where they were buried. But the inspectorate's traditional oversight of the National Home for Disabled Volunteer Soldiers (NHDVS) underwent many changes after the war. In 1921 inspection of the home and its branches passed temporarily, for budget reasons, from a single OIG inspector to the corps area inspectors, who worked under OIG supervision rather than that of their commanders when examining NHDVS operations. Inspection by a single OTIG officer was resumed in 1925, because of the proven need for expertise and the necessity for saving time. The inspector continued to evaluate the finances and condition of the facilities, as well as the discipline and morale of the residents. Starting in 1928, however, Congress began to consider transferring the NHDVS to the recently created Veterans Bureau (later redesignated Veterans Administration). General Rivers objected to the idea, pointing out that the NHDVS was working well at little cost to the government and predicting an expansion of NHDVS overhead under Veterans

---

[69] Rpt, Mahin to TIG, 21 Sep 35, sub: Investigation of Possible Questionable Conduct on the Part of Capt. E. C. Harwood, CE, Entry 26C, RG 159, NARA.

[70] Ltr, Mallan to Reed, 29 Aug 38, with encls., Entry 26C, RG 159, NARA.

Bureau control. At Rivers' urging, a special committee, with at least one IGD member, was formed to study the issue. As part of this review, two Veterans Bureau hospitals, the NHDVS, and the Soldiers' Home were inspected in 1929 to provide a source of information for the eventual disposition of the NHDVS.[71]

In spite of these efforts, the need to pare the War Department budget made necessary the transfer of the NHDVS in July 1930 to the control of the Administrator of Veteran Affairs. The transfer left only the Soldiers' Home within the purview of the Inspector General's Department. The Inspector General continued to inspect the home personally, as required by law, assisted usually by another officer and the OTIG accountant. The inspection lasted about three days, with special attention given to compliance with requirements from previous visits, physical improvements, and financial and administrative operations.[72]

As before, inspection responsibility for the more than eighty remaining national cemeteries rested with the Office of The Inspector General. The routine nature had not changed, with inspectors noting the facilities' physical appearance and state of maintenance; evaluating the efficiency of the caretaker and his staff; and recommending improvements, if any were needed. In the 1920s the inspection reports were mostly brief summaries of the work necessary to get the cemeteries in good condition, accompanied by a comment on overall condition. Starting in 1930, however, the reports became much more thorough, as part of the move to monitor expenses. Each one gave a full physical description of the cemetery, with comments on its background. The cost of its upkeep was analyzed, and statistics on its operations were given.[73]

The value of these inspections was challenged in 1924. Maj. Gen. David C. Shanks, the Fourth Corps Area commander and a former inspector, was of the opinion that IG visits to the cemeteries were an extravagance, whose benefits could be achieved more easily through routine quartermaster activities. The Quartermaster General, Maj. Gen. William H. Hart, and General Helmick disagreed, sharing the view that the cemeteries had a strong potential for mismanagement if not monitored on a regular basis. In fact, at the time of Shanks' criticism the Assistant Secretary of War had just directed Helmick and Hart to

[71] Rivers Annual Report, FY 1928; Ltr, Humber to Peck, 20 Sep 21, sub: Inspection of NHDVS. Both in Entry 26, RG 159, NARA.

[72] Memo, OTIG to Insps, n.d., sub: Suggestions Pertinent to Soldiers' Home, Entry 26, RG 159, NARA.

[73] Cemetery Insp Rpts, Boxes 330–35, Entry 11, RG 159, NARA.

arrange their respective biennial visits to fall on alternating years so that the cemeteries could be checked annually. The Assistant Secretary's obvious interest, as well as the scheduling of other inspections in conjunction with the visits, indicated the need to continue them.[74]

Experience had often shown that cemetery activities were anything but routine. Sometimes they would uncover serious management problems, going well beyond the simple care of facilities. This was the case at Fort Barrancas, Florida, during the 1928 inspection. The inspector found that although routine maintenance was excellent, the procedures for reburials from other cemeteries were completely unsatisfactory. Corps area quartermasters failed to either coordinate their actions with the caretaker or keep adequate records. As a result, remains no longer could be identified, and extensive efforts were required to organize the cemetery records. A check throughout the corps areas revealed that a similar casual approach characterized other reburials when post cemeteries were closed. In the Fort Barrancas case one officer was disciplined, and improved procedures along with closer supervision became established policy for the future.[75]

During the period of economic surveys inspectors provided considerable detail on the histories of the cemeteries and on their operation. Major Pritchett, for example, listed the staff and their salaries when he visited the Custer Battlefield National Cemetery in 1928. He detailed the number of visitors and the degree of public interest shown in the site and cited the need for a telephone and better transportation. When he visited the site again fifteen months later, he followed up on actions begun as a result of his earlier report and reemphasized the need for items, such as telephones, which had not been provided. His approach was a great help to achieving improvements there, justifying expenditures beyond the abilities of the caretaker.[76]

Soldiers' lots in civilian cemeteries were supposed to be inspected in the same manner as the national sites. Often, however, they were overlooked, and The Quartermaster General would have to remind the Office of The Inspector General of the need to have someone check the graves at such places as Sitka, Alaska, and Mound City, Kansas. The inspec-

---

[74] Ltr, Shanks to TIG, 1 Nov 24, sub: Mileage, Entry 26, RG 159, NARA.

[75] Rpt, Bach to TIG, 19 Dec 28, sub: Inspection of Barrancas National Cemetery, Entry 11, RG 159, NARA.

[76] Rpts, Pritchett to TIG, 22 Jun 28 and 15 Oct 29, subs: Inspection and Survey of the Custer Battlefield National Cemetery; Ltr, Griffin to Superintendent, Custer Battlefield National Cemetery, 27 Jun 28, sub: Telephone Service. All in Entry 11, RG 159, NARA.

tions usually were made when the corps area IG requested a local officer to visit the sites and report informally on them. Soldiers' lots inspections were incorporated in Army regulations in August 1935, with the specification that they were corps area responsibilities. That same year the Secretary of War decided to include Confederate cemeteries in the inspection program on the same biennial basis as other cemeteries. The visits had the effect of keeping cemetery personnel attentive and in helping them get the assistance, funds, and equipment they needed.[77]

Through its cemetery work, the Inspector General's Department occasionally found itself saddled with related issues. Thus a congressional inquiry involved the inspectorate briefly with the American Graves Registration Service in Europe. After the war a permanent staff had remained overseas under the supervision of The Quartermaster General to support the work of the American Battle Monuments Commission. The agency bore responsibility for the cemeteries in Europe that contained the 40 percent of the American war dead whose bodies had not been returned to the United States.

In April 1930 Congressman David A. Reed wrote the Chief of Staff, relating rumors of problems in the graves program. General Summerall expressed surprise at the allegations, since the War Department had enjoyed a steady flow of praise for its graves registration activities. The Quartermaster General had visited the cemeteries in November 1929 and found them satisfactory. Summerall believed that the negative rumors came from persons precluded by law from participating in the gold-star pilgrimages, government-sponsored and -financed visits to European grave sites that were provided to the next of kin. However, the rumors and the lack of any formal audit program for the European graves service, led Summerall and The Quartermaster General to agree that the American Battle Monuments Commission should be inspected on a regular basis like all other Army activities. The Chief of Staff directed that inspection begin in the fall, as soon as the pilgrimage season ended.[78]

---

[77] Memo, OTIG to Insps, n.d., sub: National Cemeteries and Soldiers' Lots Remaining Under Jurisdiction of the War Department, Entry 11; Ltr, Gibbons to TIG, 21 Feb 39, sub: Inspection of Cemeteries, Entry 11; Ltr, TAG to CG, 6th Corps Area, 30 Oct 36, sub: Assignment of Inspections, Entry 26. All in RG 159, NARA. See also AReg 20–10, 1935.

[78] Ltr, Reed to Summerall, 1 Apr 30, and Reply, 16 Apr 30; Memo, Summerall to TAG, 16 Apr 30, sub: Inspection of Graves Registration Service; Memo, DeWitt to Drum, 26 Apr 30, sub: American Graves Registration Service in Europe. All in Entry 11, RG 159, NARA. See also Erna Risch, *Quartermaster Support of the Army: A History of the Corps, 1775–1939* (Washington, D.C.: Quartermaster Historian's Office, Office of the Quartermaster General, 1962), pp. 693–95.

Both the Chief of Staff and The Quartermaster General wanted General Drum, then The Inspector General, to make the first inspection. Although the inspection was scheduled for the fall of 1930, Drum, in his usual thorough way, immediately asked the Office of The Quartermaster General for information he needed to begin planning. By early May he had a roster of all employees and salaries, a summary of authorizing laws, and a recapitulation of capital expenditures going back to the beginning of operations in April 1923—a sum of $2.5 million on cemetery construction and improvements. Drum further asked that more detailed information on land acquisition, recent expenditures, and memorialization be available upon his arrival in Europe. His inspection lasted from mid-October to early December, during which time he visited all cemeteries and memorials under construction and completed a thorough review of expenditures and administration. The results of Drum's efforts completely vindicated the American Battle Monuments Commission.[79]

Parks and Monuments

Other IG duties concerned the so-called national military parks at battlefields or places that were considered important to the Revolutionary or Civil Wars. The parks had been placed under jurisdiction of the Assistant Secretary of War, who managed them through independent commissions. The first legislation stipulated that the commissioners for the Civil War sites would be veterans of the battle commemorated by the park. This arrangement worked reasonably well until the inevitable passage of time reduced the availability and energy of those who were qualified to serve. Consequently, the laws were changed in 1912 to allow the vacancies created by death or retirement to remain unfilled. The Secretary of War, or his representative, was named an ex officio member of each commission, fully empowered to act with the surviving members. With the passing of the veterans, management of each park shifted to the War Department, to be administered by a superintendent appointed by the Secretary of War.[80]

By 1922 superintendents were in place at all parks but that at Vicksburg, whose resident Civil War veteran was still the commission-

---

[79] Drum Annual Rpt, FY 1931, Entry 26; OTIG Memo, [1932], sub: Inspections Made by Officers in OTIG and Exempted Stations Assigned to Corps Areas for Inspections, Entry 26A. Both in RG 159, NARA. A few years later the inspection program lapsed because of budgetary problems.

[80] Memo, Helmick to ASofW, 26 Dec 22, sub: Administration of the National Military Parks, Entry 26, RG 159, NARA.

er. General Helmick wrote a memorandum to the Assistant Secretary of War in December, stating that the situation envisaged in the 1912 legislation had come to pass. He recommended that the military parks be brought under more formal War Department control, indicating that the 1912 law gave the Secretary of War the flexibility to manage the parks as he judged best. Helmick previously had coordinated his proposal with the Quartermaster General, who did not object to bringing the parks under his purview in the same manner as national cemeteries, subject to the same sort of biennial IG inspection. The Judge Advocate General foresaw no problem in such an arrangement.[81]

As a result, on 31 January 1923 the Secretary of War directed that by 1 April the operation of the national military parks come under the jurisdiction of the Quartermaster General. The Secretary's files on the parks were transferred to the Quartermaster General's Department in the ensuing weeks. The parks were listed in regulations as items for inspection, and the first IG visit was scheduled to be made in conjunction with the next regular cemetery visit to the local area. General Helmick had wanted an immediate inspection to assess the situation before the transfer, but travel funds were unavailable. Thus, the corps area IG in whose region the parks were located performed the first inspection. The Office of the Inspector General gathered copies of laws and policies governing the parks and distributed them to the field. Initially, the parks were to be inspected every other fiscal year, but in 1927 the schedule was changed to once every two calendar years to allow greater flexibility in combining the parks inspections with other scheduled visits in the same region.[82]

The scale of the endeavor increased in October 1924, with the designation of national monuments by Presidential Proclamation. These were sites, such as forts and memorials, that were significant historically. The Statue of Liberty on old Fort Wood was designated under this category, for example. The proclamation specified that these monuments would be administered and inspected in the same manner as military parks. Inspections began in 1925, with the first reports indicating considerable need for repairs and improvements. At their greatest number, there were ten monuments and twelve parks requiring inspection (*Table 2*).[83]

---

[81] Ibid.; Helmick Annual Rpt, FY 1923, Entry 26, RG 159, NARA.

[82] Orders, Weeks to QMG, 31 Jan 23; Ltr, Duyne to IG, 14 Mar 24, sub: Inspection of National Military Parks; Memo, Watrous to TIG, 21 Sep 27, sub: Inspection of Military Parks. All in Entry 26, RG 159, NARA.

[83] Memo, Davis to TIG, 23 Jan 25; WD Bul 24, 27 Dec 24, para. 3; Helmick Annual Rpt, FY 1926. All in Entry 26, RG 159, NARA.

TABLE 2—NATIONAL BATTLEFIELD PARKS AND MONUMENTS
SUBJECT TO INSPECTION

Name	State	Corps Area
Antietam National Battlefield Park	Maryland	Third
Castle Pinckney National Monument	South Carolina	Fourth
Chalmette National Monument	Louisiana	Fourth
Chickamauga and Chattanooga National Battlefield Park	Tennessee	Fourth
Fort Donelson National Battlefield Park	Tennessee	Fourth
Forts Marion and Matanzas National Monument	Florida	Fourth
Fort McHenry National Monument	Maryland	Third
Fort Niagara National Monument	New York	Second
Fort Pulaski National Monument	Georgia	Fourth
Fredericksburg and Spotsylvania National Battlefield Park	Virginia	Third
Gettysburg National Battlefield Park	Pennsylvania	Third
Guilford Courthouse National Battlefield Park	North Carolina	Fourth
Kenesaw Mountain National Monument	Georgia	Fourth
Lincoln Birthplace National Monument	Kentucky	Fifth
Meriwether Lewis National Monument	Tennessee	Fourth
Moore's Creek National Battlefield Park	North Carolina	Fourth
Mound City Group National Monument	Illinois	Fifth
Petersburg National Battlefield Park	Virginia	Third
Shiloh National Battlefield Park	Tennessee	Fourth
Stones River National Battlefield Park	Tennessee	Fourth
Statue of Liberty National Monument	New York	Second
Vicksburg National Battlefield Park	Mississippi	Fourth

Source: Inspections, Boxes 148–49, Entry 11, RG 159, NARA.

The inspections and, later, the surveys conducted on the parks and monuments focused on deficiencies in physical conditions that were beyond the abilities of local superintendents to correct, with inspectors commenting on roads conditions, rights of access across private property, and equipment needs and repairs. Occasionally, IG remarks would be more substantial, affecting policy. In 1932, for example, after Maj. Leon M. Logan objected in his report to the Confederate bias shown by the land purchasing policy of one park commission, increased appropriations were authorized to acquire land significant to federal operations. The inspectors'reports on parks and monuments were processed similarly to others originating at the corps areas. Following a review at that level, they were forwarded to the War Department inspectorate for circulation and file. The program seemed barely under way when the Army's association with the parks and monuments ended in 1933 as the result of a policy to reduce its nonmilitary activities. In March of that year responsibility for them and a few cemeteries began to be transferred by executive order to the Interior Department. The transfer was completed by the end of August.[84]

All in all, the complex duties carried out by the Inspector General's Department provided an excellent overview of the state of the Army during a difficult, prolonged period of adjustment. While some of the problems were perennial, many others reflected the dwindling resources and constricted opportunities that characterized the interwar years. Nevertheless, the inspectorate continued to carry out its traditional duty of attempting to provide for the welfare of the Army and its soldiers from the time of their recruitment until the time of their interment— indeed, even thereafter in the many memorials to their achievements.

---

[84] Rpt, Logan to IG, 25 Aug 21, sub: Biennial Inspection of the Fredericksburg and Spottsylvania [sic] County Battlefields Memorial; Ex Order 6228, 28 Jul 33; Ex Order 6166, 10 Jun 33. All in Entry 11, RG 159, NARA.

12

Guardsmen and Civilians

For both the Army and the inspectorate, the postwar era brought a number of entirely new responsibilities and duties. Some of the most important emanated from the closer relationship being forged between the Army's active and reserve components. As outlined by the National Defense Act of 1920, both the National Guard and the Organized Reserve Corps (ORC) would play a prominent role in any mobilization for some future war. And as these components began to receive a greater proportion of the Army's slim resources, The Inspector General's Department (IGD) began to take a closer look at the performance of these organizations.

Inspecting the Reserve Components

With the passage of the National Defense Act, the reserve organizations continued to be subject to IG inspections, for which the corps area headquarters had primary responsibility. Regular Army officers were detailed for temporary civilian-component duty at National Guard armories and facilities. Selected and supervised by the corps area National Guard affairs officer, they normally performed the inspections. In some commands the National Guard affairs officer himself conducted the inspection, assisted by the corps area IGs. The focus of each inspection dovetailed to the topics of interest listed on an IG checklist, which the Office of The Inspector General (OTIG) provided. The final inspection report recorded the funds allocated and disbursed, provided the statistics on equipment losses, and usually concluded with a summary of projected Guard expenditures.[1]

---

[1] Rpt, Townsend to OTIG, 25 May 28, sub: Annual Survey of National Guard Unit Activities, Entry 11; Helmick Annual Rpts, FY 1924 and FY 1926, Entry 26; Logan Lecture to QM School, 9 Apr 31, Entry 26B. All in Record Group (RG) 159, National Archives and Records Administration (NARA), Washington, D.C.

Other Regular Army officers were detailed to conduct annual inspections of federally recognized units during their summer training, usually with the aid of corps area IGs. Their purpose was to assist Guard commanders in correcting any problems that were reported. Beyond that, the inspectors' interest lay in determining the units' mobilization readiness. They submitted reports that listed each company-sized element and explained any variations from earlier strength reports. They also provided the names and duties of the Regular Army personnel who were serving as instructors, as well as information on federal expenditures and property disposals. Compliance with applicable Army regulations was checked and noted in the reports. The OTIG staff reviewed the reports and then forwarded them to the General Staff's National Guard Bureau, which used them as the basis for issuing or recalling equipment and property to Guard units.[2]

The ORC units, because of their federal status, at first were included in the annual corps area inspections. Yet they differed greatly from Regular Army units. Despite their tactical designations, these reserve organizations in reality formed administrative cadre for mobilization units. For example, the 66th Cavalry Division in Omaha, Nebraska, had only 286 officers and 49 enlisted men, while the lone unit that it supervised, the Regular Army 15th Cavalry (inactive), had 39 officers and 2 enlisted men. The command's job was to develop and give instruction to reservists in its area, provide them administrative support, and foster good relations between the Army and the public at large. Then in 1937 the tactical designations were changed to "regional reserve districts." Thus, the 66th Cavalry Division became the Western Missouri Reserve District. Its personnel retained duty positions in the division, should it ever be mobilized, and continued to provide branch training for cavalry reservists throughout the corps area.[3]

The ORC units were subject to additional inspections, performed by the corps area staff and coordinated by the area's civilian-component affairs officer with the local inspector. The only purpose of these inspections was to evaluate the work of the Regular Army personnel who were assigned to the ORC units as cadre. The inspection reports listed unit locations and the number of Regular Army advisers, as well

---

[2] Rpt, Townsend to OTIG, 25 May 28, sub: Survey of 184th Infantry Regiment, California NG, Entry 11, RG 159, NARA; AReg 20–20, 1921, 1923, 1924, 1925, 1929.

[3] Rpt, Austin to CG, 7th Corps Area, 22 Jun 28, sub: Economic Survey of 66th Cavalry Division, 7th Corps Area; Rpt (quoted words), Williams to OTIG, 26 Nov 37, sub: Annual Inspection of Headquarters, Western Missouri Reserve District. Both in Entry 11, RG 159, NARA.

as discussed any problems the advisers might have (for example, the high cost of living) and the value of the training they gave. The reports were submitted through channels to the Office of The Inspector General, where extracts were made and circulated among reserve officers on duty at the War Department. The closely supervised ORC units generally were found to be working well within the tight constraints of their budgets.[4]

The greater complexity of the National Guard establishment, with its ampler resources and fully manned units, naturally attracted more of the inspectorate's attention outside the inspection cycle. Many of the problems that were uncovered concerned the abuse of authority, the improper use of funds, or a combination of the two. Several cases proved to be extraordinarily complicated and time-consuming, requiring the temporary detail of many additional Regular Army officers. They surfaced, as a rule, either in complaints made by unit members or in audits made by other government agencies. The complaints were forwarded to the Chief of the National Guard Bureau and then, regardless of their source, to the Office of The Inspector General for resolution.

A typical case began when a former Georgia guardsman lodged a complaint with the local Justice Department office. It appeared that men who enlisted in the Machine Gun Troop of the 108th Cavalry automatically became members of a social group known as the Governor's Horse Guard, an incorporated organization that unit personnel supported with involuntary pay deductions. The complaint eventually was passed to the Fourth Corps Area IG for investigation. Apparently, everyone who joined the unit was aware of the conditions, and willingly did so for the chance to ride the troop's horses. The inspector determined that Governor's Horse Guard funds were kept carefully distinct from state and federal funds. The source of the problem turned out to be the fact that the best horses were being reserved for the relatively small number of unit polo players. The inspector found no illegal or incorrect actions. A legal review of the findings requested by the corps area commander led General Reed to opine that, although no law had been broken, he disapproved of the practice. The National Guard Bureau disagreed, however, ruling that the arrangement should be allowed to continue at the state adjutant general's discretion.[5]

Most troop complaints about abuse of authority by officers were unsubstantiated. In one such case the Chief of the National Guard

---

[4] See ORC Insp Rpts, Box 146, Entry 26C, RG 159, NARA.

[5] Rpt, Matthews to OTIG, 23 Dec 28, sub: Investigation of Alleged Irregularities in MG Troop, 108th Cavalry, Georgia NG, Entry 26C, RG 159, NARA.

Bureau referred a letter from some former Colorado guardsmen to the Office of The Inspector General. The guardsmen alleged that their unit commander had discharged them improperly and was mismanaging unit finances. The case passed through channels to the Eighth Corps Area IG, who made the investigation in Denver. In the letter the complainants had detailed a litany of abuses—padding payrolls, making loans to subordinates, and collecting fines, to name a few—and claimed that they had been dishonorably discharged without due process. The investigation, however, revealed that all of the complainants had been notorious troublemakers. The inspector found no evidence of financial irregularities in the unit or in the commander's personal affairs. Every allegation could be countered fully. Although the commander had acted incorrectly in striking out the word "honorable" on the discharge certificates, the inspector sympathized with him in light of the men's records and merely recommended that new certificates be issued. The state adjutant general supported the IG findings, joining the inspector in successfully recommending that the allegations be disregarded.[6]

However, not all investigations vindicated the authorities. Peculation seemed to increase as the Depression decade advanced. Many cases came to the attention of the Office of The Inspector General after they had been mishandled at local levels in an attempt to protect the reputations of those involved. Some cases extended over years, because of their complexity and the collateral issues they raised. Illustrative of the latter was the case involving a South Dakota National Guard unit. In August 1936 the Seventh Corps Area finance officer became suspicious of the processing of some payroll checks from the Headquarters Battery, 147th Field Artillery, and an investigation ensued. Interviews with one of the proper recipients showed that his signature had been forged, that he had never seen the check, and that he had not received the money. The matter was turned over to the Treasury Department's Secret Service, whose investigation proved that the commander was manipulating both the payroll and the drill attendance records. His scheme was to report absent or former unit members as present at all drills, to retain the government paychecks, and to pay the men with his personal checks for the times they actually were present. He then forged signatures to the government checks, and the difference went into his bank account. The officer was

---

[6] Rpt, Clarkson to OTIG, 6 May 38, sub: Investigation of Complaints Pertaining to Capt. Lou W. Appeldorn, 45th Tank Company, Colorado NG, Entry 26C, RG 159, NARA.

convicted of forgery and fraud in October 1938 and placed on probation for eighteen months.[7]

NCO Instructor Problems

Other major investigations involving the National Guard embraced
whole groups, forcing the Inspector General's Department to augment
its strength with temporarily detailed officers to cope with the tremendous work load. The first extended case of this magnitude began in
1934, with a check on the housing allowances paid to Regular Army
NCOs assigned to National Guard units as sergeant-instructors.
Problems with the allowances had been observed in each corps area and
in Hawaii, and as a result in April inspectors in the field were asked to
report all such cases to the Office of The Inspector General. By June it
was evident that a critical situation existed throughout the Army. Most
NCOs were circumventing the relevant regulation, which authorized
payments for housing costs up to a fixed maximum. Nearly all were
drawing the maximum, and many had made arrangements with their
landlords to document fictitious expenses in order to draw the largest
sum possible.[8]

The scandal was of great concern to the Army, because it marked
an ethical breakdown among a largely handpicked group of above-aver-
age NCOs. General Preston, after personally conducting the preliminary investigation and follow-up, attributed the root of the problem to
a confusing change in the regulation that had been issued in 1927.
Many finance officers were unable to understand or explain the new
language, and the obscurity had been exploited to create precedents for
making full payments that were followed by later supervisors. Innocent
NCOs, seeing others successfully manipulate the system, acted accordingly. The fact that housing allowances were often insufficient allowed
many to rationalize their conduct on the grounds that they were merely
receiving their traditional entitlement to rations and quarters in another
form. And the process of certification and monitoring was so complex
that in practice little or no supervision was being applied by accountable officers. Concluding that the War Department had to bear respon-

[7] Rpt, Wood to OTIG, 13 Dec 38, sub: Inspection of Headquarters Battery, 147th
Field Artillery, South Dakota NG; Ltr, Elliot to SofW, 26 Oct 38. Both in Entry 26C,
RG 159, NARA.

[8] Ltr, Preston to TAG, 27 Oct 34, sub: Irregularities in the Hire of Quarters for Use
of Sergeant-Instructors Detailed for Duty With the National Guard, Entry 26B, RG 159,
NARA.

sibility for such extensive confusion, The Inspector General success-fully recommended that a clearer revision of the rules be made and that no NCO be prosecuted or forced to reimburse the government, unless intent to defraud or to profit from the confusion could be proven.[9]

The latter recommendation, of course, meant that everyone who had drawn an allowance would have to have his finance claims reviewed. Despite the huge dimensions of the task, it became mandato-ry in January 1935, when the Comptroller General sent the Secretary of War a list with the names of forty NCOs who were assigned to the Pennsylvania National Guard. All of their finance records contained numerous housing allowance violations. The Comptroller asked the Secretary to look into the matter, with the implication that he would examine the matter himself if the Army failed to do so. Accordingly, General Preston tasked his executive, Colonel Humber, to conduct a comprehensive investigation of the problem throughout the Army. Each corps area was required to submit data on all the NCOs who had made rental agreements since 1 July 1927.[10]

The investigation that followed lasted until July 1937, at which time General Reed was The Inspector General. A total of 950 individual cases had been examined. Each landlord was sought out and the actual costs charged to the NCO were computed. Each corps area commander reviewed the cases in his region and made an administrative decision on each. The cases then were evaluated at the Office of The Inspector General and coordinated with the corps area IG, who spoke for his com-mander, until a reasonable Army-wide uniformity was achieved. The work load was heavy, for the War Department's policy was to analyze every case from the viewpoint of equity as well as law. NCOs who were found to have profited were required to refund any sum in excess of their minimum standard commutation (75 cents per day).[11]

The Inspector General's Department, however, continued to feel that much of the problem was the responsibility of the War Department. General Reed proposed legislation in 1937 to allow the Comptroller General to waive the requirement for full restitution in justifiable cases.

---

[9] Ibid.

[10] Ltr, McCarl to SofW, 7 Jan 35; Ltr, Torrey to OTIG, 26 Nov 35, sub: Regular Army Personnel on Duty With the National Guard; Ltr, Sullivan to CGs, Corps Areas, 2 Apr 35, sub: Information re Sergeant-Instructors on Duty With the National Guard. All in Entry 26C, RG 159, NARA.

[11] Rpt, Mahin to TIG, 4 May 36, sub: Investigation of Rental Quarters of Sergeant Earl Fletcher, Massachusetts NG; Rpt, Reed to SofW, 7 Jan 38, sub: Investigation of Officers on Duty in Washington. Both in Entry 26C, RG 159, NARA.

Although this measure reduced the total from $400,000 to about $40,000, the sums many NCOs owed continued to seem enormous when compared to their $65 monthly salaries. One NCO committed suicide at the prospect of having to repay his debt. In August, however, Congress passed a bill that permitted the use of discretion. From that time forward, once the OTIG staff and corps area commanders reached a consensus, their finding was validated at the Finance Department and the agreed-upon amount was deducted from the NCO's pay. Despite this lenient approach, one officer and seven NCOs were tried, eight NCOs were reprimanded, and thirty-seven officers and thirty-nine

Maj. Gen. Walter L. Reed

NCOs were admonished for their parts in the fraud—still a relatively small figure compared to the 950 who had been involved.[12]

In the course of the investigation, audits had revealed possible frauds as far back as 1922. But General Reed successfully avoided a second in-depth probe in favor of handling individually each case that was exposed through an audit or an inspection. It was fortunate that he did so, for soon an even larger investigation developed from another discovery made by the Comptroller General's General Accounting Office (GAO) staff.[13]

Another Scandal

This time the problem lay with the U.S. property and disbursing officers (USP&DOs) assigned to the states. The National Defense Act of

---

[12] Martin Testimony, Mil Affs Cmte, HofReps, 20 Jul 37, Entry 26C, RG 159, NARA. Boxes 98–200 of this entry contain all the individual cases and drafts of Public Law 326, 76th Congress, 1st Session. They give a good view of the life of the sergeant-instructors.

[13] Ltr, Elliot to SofW, 22 Oct 37, and Memo, Reed to TAG, 4 Nov 37, Entry 26C, RG 159, NARA.

1920 had placed USP&DO appointments under the Secretary of War's jurisdiction, but his prerogative had not been exercised, and by the late 1930s officials were being relieved and vacancies filled by state governors without securing War Department approval. When this was brought to the attention of the Chief of the National Guard Bureau, then Maj. Gen. Albert L. Blanding, he supported tightening the policy and suggested further that new appointees undergo a full background investigation. The War Department G–1 gave the responsibility to corps area commanders, who often used their IG or JAG officer for the task. The state adjutants general supported these reforms, urging that the Secretary be the only person to remove a USP&DO for cause.[14]

Unfortunately, the improvements arrived too late. In March 1937 the Comptroller General informed the Secretary of War that so many problems had been uncovered as to indicate the need for an investigation. The irregularities he cited included embezzlement; intermingling of personal, state, and federal funds; failure to deposit funds; improper use of federal property; and personnel hiring or contracting in contravention to federal regulations. General Reed was assigned investigative responsibility, and in the summer of 1937 officers from the Office of The Inspector General, the Office of The Judge Advocate General, and the National Guard Bureau completed a series of studies. By September they had reached a consensus on the need for reform, recommending that War Department inspections be increased. In the meantime, however, a mounting series of discoveries promised a major scandal.[15]

Typical offenses included paying substitutes to keep Guard units up to federal recognition strength and routinely forging signatures to pay checks. Some frauds were more complicated. For example, the Connecticut USP&DO had embezzled $8,500 in 1935 and taken kickbacks from contractors in 1936, and the Ohio USP&DO had used incorrect names and partial addresses on legitimate checks as a means to delay their cashing, thereby creating a floating fund that—with the addition of short payments on contracts—allowed him to hire his two

---

[14] Ltr, Smith to Roosevelt, 19 Feb 34, Entry 26B; Rpt, Perley to TIG, 27 Sep 34, sub: Investigation of Arkansas NG, Entry 26B; Memo, Gullion to TAG, 6 Jul 37, sub: United States Property and Disbursing Officers, Entry 26C; Memo, Blanding to CofS, WD, 11 May 37, sub: Investigations of Nominees for Appointments as USP and DO's, Entry 26C; Memo, Embick to ACofS, G–1, WD, 19 May 37, sub: Investigation of Nominees for Appointment as USP&DO's, Entry 26C; Memo, Beeke to Ex Off, OTIG, 11 Apr 38, Entry 26C. All in RG 159, NARA. See also AReg 20–10, 1935.
[15] Memo, Park to TIG, 28 Jun 37, sub: Inspection of the National Guard; Memo, Park to TIG, 20 Sep 37. Both in Entry 26C, RG 159, NARA.

sons, under false names, as surplus employees. IG action revealed the irregularities, eventually leading to conviction.[16]

An investigation in August 1937, prompted by a citizen's complaint, surfaced even greater problems in the Nebraska National Guard. From 1924 to 1933 firewood cut at Camp Ashland, a federal reservation used for Guard training, had been sold to the federal government for use during National Guard encampments. Both the USP&DO and the state adjutant general had condoned the practice, claiming that its purpose was to compensate the state for physical improvements to the camp that could not be funded otherwise. The actual transactions were made through a dummy contractor and credited to a so-called Quartermaster Fund in the adjutant general's office, but the money actually was used to feed livestock the two officers raised on the federal land and to maintain state property on or adjacent to it. The investigation by Col. William S. Wood exposed the fraud and further revealed that the USP&DO and the adjutant general were in a conspiracy to defraud the government.[17]

The findings were so stunning that General Blanding requested a second investigation to develop evidence on the extent of the personal gain made by the two officers. Maj. Everett C. Williams reviewed all state vouchers and identified eighteen more fraudulent transactions. He then developed an audit trail on each transaction, documenting how it was made, the sums involved, and who profited. Williams concluded that very little of the Quartermaster Fund went to the upkeep of Guard property; most ended in the pockets of the two conspirators. The case was referred to the Federal Bureau of Investigations and eventually the state adjutant general and the USP&DO were tried and convicted, long after they had been dismissed from the Guard.[18]

Not all investigations uncovered illegal practices. Some, after extensive probing, exonerated those involved of criminal intent but not of minor irregularities. A typical example was the Alabama National Guard investigation in 1938, generated by a GAO audit that found evidence of possible fraud in travel vouchers, food purchases, and local contracting. The Office of The Inspector General referred the case to

---

[16] Rpt, Hunt to TIG, 11 Dec 36, sub: Investigation of the Office of USP&DO Officer, State of Connecticut; Rpt, Park to TIG, 27 Jul 38, sub: Investigation of Alleged Irregularities and Deficiencies in the Accounts of USP&DO of Ohio; Memo, Reed to TAG, 22 Nov 38. All in Entry 26C, RG 159, NARA.

[17] Rpt, Wood to TIG, 16 Sep 37, sub: Special Investigation of Nebraska NG, Entry 26C, RG 159, NARA.

[18] Rpt, Williams to TIG, 18 Apr 38, sub: Continuation of Special Investigation of Nebraska NG, Entry 26C, RG 159, NARA.

the Fourth Corps Area IG, Col. Charles H. Patterson. Patterson assessed the problem to be a total disregard of regulations and procedures on the part of guardsmen and the USP&DO, such as using private cars for official travel without prior authorization and subsequently preparing the orders; paying for guardsmen's meals en route to summer camp and later fabricating receipts for reimbursement; and hiring workmen to repair unit buildings and then faking vouchers and contracts for reimbursement. All of these transactions were improper, but they were the result, not of criminal wrongdoing, but of uninformed guardsmen trying to get their mission done as best they could. Colonel Patterson successfully recommended that no criminal charges be made. Instead, the USP&DO received a letter of admonishment on proper finance procedures, and the state adjutant general began a program of education. The case was closed.[19]

Between 1937 and 1938 the Comptroller General's GAO teams had discovered major finance irregularities in eighteen states or territories. Embezzlement, nepotism, contract fraud, and a disregard of procedures were common, and probes into National Guard financial and property practices had begun in seven of the nine corps areas, most of them as a result of GAO audits. The biggest case of all was in the New York National Guard, which required the investigation of nearly 100 guardsmen, former guardsmen, and regulars, as well as 200 civilian firms.[20]

By January 1937 two USP&DOs in New York had been relieved, having a collective liability for 66,000 questionable vouchers. Hundreds of civilian firms or individuals, some possibly fictitious, were identified as payees or witnesses to actions connected with improper payments. The General Accounting Office assigned eight investigators on a special task force in New York to continue the investigation. The magnitude of the situation and the extensive involvement of so many key state fiscal officials ultimately led to a blanket sus-

---

[19] Ltr, Elliot to SofW, 16 May 38; Rpt, Patterson to TIG, 19 Sep 38, sub: Investigation of Alleged Irregularities in Payments Made by the USP&DO, State of Alabama. Both in Entry 26C, RG 159, NARA.

[20] Ltr, Boschem to CofNGB, 3 Nov 38, sub: In re Comptroller General Letter to Secretary of War; Memo, Martin to TIG, 8 Mar 40, sub: Investigations Now Being Conducted in the Second Corps Area of Matters Presented to the War Department by the Comptroller General . . . ; Memo, Martin to Peterson, 11 Mar 40; Memo, Reed to TAG, 19 Jan 39, sub: In re Accounts of M. A. Lee, J. Weston Myers, and W. A. Taylor. All in Entry 26C, RG 159, NARA. Irregularities were uncovered in California, Florida, Indiana, Kentucky, Minnesota, Montana, Nebraska, New Jersey, New York, North Carolina, South Carolina, Ohio, Pennsylvania, Rhode Island, Virginia, West Virginia, Wisconsin, and the Territory of Hawaii.

pension of their authority to certify and pay federal vouchers, a necessary action, but one that hindered the capabilities of the New York National Guard for nearly a year until new men could be appointed, trained, and bonded.[21]

A typical case involved units stationed in Brooklyn. In December 1937 seven certifying officers and two USP&DOs were implicated in various fraudulent practices through which they had embezzled sums of money. Erroneous names were carried on civilian payrolls, and the salaries were pocketed by the certifying officer. Vouchers were furnished for automotive repairs and services that were never rendered, and monies received were diverted to unit association accounts for unofficial or state activities. Other vouchers were submitted for tailoring fees that were wholly fictitious, profits again going to the certifying officer. Overpayments were made for other clothing and shoe repair services and the difference split between the merchant and the military contractor. In some cases false purchase documents had been prepared for building materials never provided, resulting again in checks going into private profits. In other cases contracts were given to relatives and friends of the certifying officer, instead of being opened properly for bids. This particular investigation, which lasted two months, required twenty-nine interviews and an elaborate tracing of the financial activities of four different regimental-sized units in Brooklyn.[22]

The collective effects of the New York investigations were felt throughout the country long before their completion. They led to a tightening of National Guard money accountability and accompanying IG inspections. The result was an immediate, noticeable improvement. The objective of the intense IG involvement had been to provide a basis for corrective and disciplinary action and to gather requests for reimbursement or relief from liability from persons involved. Policy decisions had been made by the end of 1939 as to the means of reimbursement. The Comptroller General agreed to allow voluntary repayment from officers not guilty of criminal activity and special legislation relieved USP&DOs of liability. Several senior guardsmen had their careers terminated by withdrawal of federal recognition and elimination by state board. Despite pressures from the Chief of Staff to complete the investigations as quickly as possible, they continued into 1941. By then the mobilization of the Guard and the statute of limita-

---

[21] Ltr, Jordan to CG, 2d Corps Area, 18 Feb 37, sub: Investigation of Alleged Irregularities in Accounts of USP&DO, State of New York, Entry 26C, RG 159, NARA.

[22] Rpt, Colvin to TIG, 3 Aug 38, sub: Investigation of Irregularities in Accounts of Former USP&DO's, Entry 26C, RG 159, NARA.

tions had obscured the issue to such an extent that all but a few cases were closed by December.[23]

Many inspectors were embarrassed by the fact that GAO personnel had uncovered the majority of the National Guard's problems. They recognized that the Inspector General's Department had not fully complied with the National Defense Act of 1920 in so far as the Guard was concerned. As one inspector explained it, "The IGD has never begun to function with reference to the National Guard . . . has fallen down on its job of keeping the Army honest." Partly at fault was the practice of designating special inspectors from corps area staffs to look at the Guard, instead of using detailed IGs. But responsibility of inspecting USP&DO accounts, a time-consuming task, had been transferred from the Office of The Inspector General to the corps area IGs only in 1935. More significant had been the lack of funding to support proper, all-encompassing inspections. Only during the brief era of economic surveys had there been any pretense at thoroughness. The moderate approach of the Inspector General's Department was in sharp contrast to that of the General Accounting Office, which provided its investigators sufficient per diem for whatever period was necessary to make a thorough inquiry. In one case a GAO crew of four spent over five months investigating the accounts of one USP&DO. By comparison, IG inspections had been superficial and of very little benefit. Increased manpower and resources alone could improve the situation.[24]

In March 1938, in light of the ongoing GAO investigations, General Malin Craig, the Chief of Staff, ordered General Reed to make a detailed survey of general conditions throughout the Guard. He wanted to determine the condition of federal property under Guard control; to discover how deep the corruption went; and to appraise the IGD role in Guard inspections, with an eye to improving it. The Chief of Staff requested the services of his brother, Lt. Col. Louis A. Craig, then assigned as the Third Corps Area IG, to perform the survey. The junior Craig, assisted by the OTIG expert accountant, Mr. Simmons, commenced the survey on 1 April. The Third Corps Area commander agreed to add Lt. Col. Roscoe C. Batson to Craig's team if the work became overwhelming.[25]

---

[23] Draft Ltr, Peterson for TAG, 18 Feb 41, sub: Investigation Regarding Irregular Vouchers and Questionable Transactions Reflected in the Accounts of Former USP&DO's for New York, Entry 26C, RG 159, NARA.

[24] Ltr, Logan to Reed, 17 May 37, Entry 26C, RG 159, NARA.

[25] Ltr, Reed to Lecocq, 5 Feb 38; Ltr, TAG to CG, 3d Corps Area, 8 Mar 38, sub: Survey of National Guard Disbursing and Property Functions With Particular Reference to Future Inspection Procedure; Memo, Martin to TAG, 21 Mar 38, sub: Irregularities in Accounts and Records of USP&DO's. All in Entry 26C, RG 159, NARA.

The findings of Colonel Craig's team corroborated the evidence already gathered by others and confirmed the existing suspicions about the poor quality of IG oversight of the Guard. He, too, found Guard practices to be characterized by a disregard of regulations and procedures, resulting in the loss of accountability, diversion of funds, and criminal actions unearthed by the General Accounting Office. The basic cause for the situation, in his view, lay in the legal status of the National Guard, which lacked an effective chain of command under the War Department. Since the Guard usually was not in federal service, the Army leadership dealt with it through state officials by way of a "chain of cooperative communication." War Department control was largely theoretical.[26]

The Regular Army instructors were War Department representatives, but the nature of their mission curtailed their effectiveness. Since their ability to function depended largely upon their acceptability to the Guard, "getting on" was a primary consideration, seen by many as likely to affect their future careers. Hence, they could not be expected to ferret out serious problems voluntarily. Another weak spot was the dual status of the Guard. One consequence was that some records and reports could be withheld from federal scrutiny; another was the confusion over the sources of its funds that had made accurate accounting so difficult.[27]

Colonel Craig acknowledged the failings of IG oversight as it had been practiced in the past. Inspections accomplished only a cursory review of USP&DO records, evaluating the bookkeeping for its administrative correctness rather than its substance. They were too limited in scope to be effective in identifying problems. The accuracy of the documentation was never questioned—for example, firms listed on vouchers seldom were verified to see if they and the recorded transactions were legitimate—and the routine approval of USP&DO procedures, in effect, fostered the fraudulent practices. In sum, the Inspector General's Department had failed to carry out its responsibilities for inspecting the Guard and no other agency had stepped in to fill the vacuum. Colonel Craig concluded his report with a number of recommendations, including that the number of inspectors be increased by ten to allow more thorough inspections; that procedures be revised to reduce the emphasis on administrative form and give more attention to substance; and

---

[26] Rpt, L. Craig to TIG, 15 Aug 38, sub: Survey of National Guard and Property Functions With Particular Reference to Future Inspection Procedure, Entry 26C, RG 159, NARA.

[27] Ibid.

that the Inspector General's and Finance Departments coordinate with the Treasury Department and the General Accounting Office to simplify numerous procedures.[28]

Based on Colonel Craig's findings, General Reed in October 1938 requested the additional manpower, which was approved. Concurrently, the National Guard Bureau released sufficient monies to launch the increased inspections immediately and also took action to fund in future budgets the travel of the ten new inspectors. The new system was in place by the spring of 1939. In May General Blanding informed the state adjutants general of the changes, praising the Inspector General's Department for taking the "broad view" in helping the Guard get back on the track as a component of the Army. At the same time, General Craig notified the corps area commanders that by the end of the year an extra officer would be assigned to their headquarters, specifically to inspect National Guard activities.[29]

Meanwhile, the Office of The Inspector General began to prepare new inspection guides, to revise others, and to develop a training program for the ten new inspectors. The first such class was scheduled in June 1939, with the goal of having all the inspectors in the field by the end of July. National Guard inspections had to be made by the corps area IGs under the general supervision of their commander. But the old practice of allowing the local inspector-instructors to inspect armories while the IGs restricted themselves to a brief review of the USP&DOs' books came to an end. Annual inspections of the property records were now required, in conjunction with the biennial money account inspections. Despite many problems with costs, manpower, training, and clerical support, the new policies tightened central control and brought closure to the era of scandals that had damaged the reputations of the Guard and the Army.[30]

The Army and the CCC

Perhaps the largest and most burdensome of the IGD's postwar duties involved the Civilian Conservation Corps (CCC), an organization con-

---

[28] Ibid.

[29] Ltr, Adams to TIG, 6 Oct 38, sub: Inspections of the National Guard, and Reply, 10 Oct 38; Memo, Blanding to TIG, 17 Oct 38, sub: Allotment of Funds, Fiscal Year 1940, Covering Travel and Per Diem of Ten Additional Inspectors for National Guard Activities; Ltr (quoted words), Blanding to State AGs, 27 May 39, sub: Inspection of the National Guard; Ltr, M. Craig to Corps Areas Cdrs, 18 May 39. All in Entry 26C, RG 159, NARA.

[30] Ltr, M. Craig to Corps Area Cdrs, 18 May 39; Ltr, Blanding to CG, Hawaiian Dept, 23 Sep 39, sub: Annual Armory Inspections of the National Guard. Both in Entry 26C, RG 159, NARA.

ceived by President Roosevelt for relieving the effects of the Depression by both promoting conservation and providing jobs for the unemployed. When he entered office in March 1933, Roosevelt directed the Secretaries of War, Labor, Interior and Agriculture to develop the mechanics for creating such an organization and to identify feasible projects for it to perform. The secretaries recommended that the Civilian Conservation Corps should be a distinct agency, focused on conservation projects that would not compete in any way with private industry or other government activities. Its primary mission was to ameliorate the unemployment situation among young men. The concept was generally well received, although some labor elements feared potential competition with its workers, and a few persons objected to another aspect of the scheme—the proposed involvement of the Army.[31]

On 31 March Congress passed the necessary legislation, specifying that the Civilian Conservation Corps should carry out useful public works, such as reforestation and flood control projects on federal and state lands. Congress also authorized the President to not only provide for the shelter, transport, and well-being of the persons hired to do the work but also to draw on the assets of any federal department or agency as necessary. On 5 April Robert Fechner, the vice-president of the American Federation of Labor, was named as the head of the Civilian Conservation Corps, with the title Director of Emergency Conservation Work. To support Fechner, the CCC Advisory Council was created and the Secretaries of War, Agriculture, Interior, and Labor were directed to appoint representatives. A former IG, Colonel Major, now a General Staff operations officer with many special projects to his credit, was selected to represent the War Department. He recognized early that the CCC's training benefits to the Army were greater than its drawbacks. The CCC program grew rapidly, thanks largely to Major's efforts.[32]

As first planned, the support provided by the Army to the program was to be extremely limited. Labor Department representatives were to select and hire the young men, who then were to be turned over to War Department personnel for administration and initial processing. The men were enrolled through the Army's recruiting organization and

---

[31] Erna Risch, *Quartermaster Support of the Army: A History of the Corps, 1775–1939* (Washington, D.C.: Quartermaster Historian's Office, Office of the Quartermaster General, 1962), pp. 728–29; John A. Salmond, *The Civilian Conservation Corps, 1933–42: A New Deal Case Study* (Chapel Hill: University of North Carolina, 1967), pp. 11–14 (hereafter cited as *CCC*).

[32] Salmond, *CCC*, p. 45; John W. Killigrew, "The Impact of the Great Depression on the Army, 1929–1936" (Ph.D. diss., Indiana University, 1960), ch. 13, p. 32.

transported to so-called reconditioning camps, which functioned like reception or replacement centers. There they were equipped and given some physical conditioning before being shipped to the work sites under the supervision of the Agriculture and Interior Departments. At that point, the Army's involvement was to end. In this way the first camp opened near Luray, Virginia, on 17 April.[33]

Initially, the Labor, Agriculture, and Interior Departments had been confident that they had the resources to develop and operate the work camps. Even before the first camp opened, however, the scale of the operations demanded by the President made it apparent they had undertaken an impossible task. The Chief Forester, Robert Y. Stuart, recommended that the Army assume the responsibility for building and equipping the camps and administering them. The technicians of the other departments would continue to select and supervise the work projects, and hence would also determine the work sites. The Army, however, had the right to veto any particular site.

Despite the misgivings of many Army and civilian leaders, the proposal had many good points. The Army was the only organization in the country with the ability to enroll the number of CCC men desired by the President at the speed he demanded, and the method proposed by the Chief Forester allowed the War Department to avoid the political pressures that would inevitably develop around decisions on where to locate projects. Although General Drum, now the Deputy Chief of Staff, wished to avoid embroiling the Army in routine CCC activities, an expanded role for the Army represented the best and cheapest solution. On 10 April the President thus enlarged the Army's mission to full responsibility for CCC camp operations under the general supervision of Director Fechner.[34]

Suddenly, the Army thus became responsible for everything to do with camp administration, supply, welfare, sanitation, and health care. Only the actual work projects would be under the technical representatives of the other federal agencies. When the President specified that the program absorb a total of 250,000 men by July, every available Army officer had to be diverted to the task. Service schools staged early graduations, and many faculty, incoming students, and officers detailed to the civilian components were diverted from their primary duties to CCC camp duties.[35]

In order to achieve Roosevelt's goals, standard contracting procedures had to be waived and wide authority over movement and disci-

[33] WD Prov Reg, 1933, Entry 26, RG 159, NARA; Salmond, *CCC*, p. 31.
[34] Salmond, *CCC*, pp. 26, 30, 40–41.
[35] Ibid., pp. 40–41.

pline given to local commanders. On the average, the Army processed 8,450 enrollees daily during May, June, and early July, a greater flow of men than during World War I. Over 1,300 camps were quickly established, and by 7 July a total of 274,375 men had been brought into the Civilian Conservation Corps.[36]

The effects of this rapid growth were reflected in the experiences of two representative posts. Jefferson Barracks, Missouri, had a permanent party of roughly 1,200, but processed 12,000 enrollees during the initial surge. The maximum number of CCC men on post at one time was 9,274 on 12 June. Six tent camps had to be prepared and hasty arrangements made to provide sewage and sanitary systems. The post commander, Col. Walter Krueger, won praise from an IG for his skill in gaining the willing cooperation of the selectees and the support of local politicians and the public. The garrison at Fort Sheridan, Illinois, processed 18,000 enrollees and provided cadre for 78 CCC companies. Then, like many others, it was confronted soon with the second CCC cycle. In October 4,200 of the enrollees who chose not to re-enroll for a second six months were processed and discharged. At the same time, 12,000 new men for the second increment were brought aboard, taxing the facilities of the post and the ingenuity of the cadre to the maximum to care for the new men while maintaining proper discipline. By early November 50,000 CCC men had been processed at Fort Sheridan—a situation that was typical of the Army as a whole.[37]

Yet this drastic reallocation of manpower proved insufficient to meet CCC needs. Furthermore, it could not be sustained indefinitely. General Preston pointed out that siphoning away so many leaders from the Regular Army made the service incapable of carrying out any other major mission. Recognizing the problem, the President in June 1933 authorized the call-up of 1,500 reserve officers. In September, when many of the regulars returned to their primary duties, another 4,400 officers had to be found for the Civilian Conservation Corps. Hence, as regulars were phased out, more reservists were brought in, especially reserve medical officers and chaplains. By October, when the transition

---

[36] Ibid., p. 32; Killigrew, "Great Depression," Ph.D. diss., ch. 12, pp. 7–10; Charles W. Johnson, "The Civilian Conservation Corps: The Role of the Army," (Ph.D. diss., University of Michigan, 1968), pp. 93–94 (hereafter cited as "CCC"); U.S. War Department, *Annual Report of the Chief of Staff, United States Army, 1933* (Washington, D.C.: Government Printing Office, 1933), pp. 3–5 (hereafter cited as *ARCS*).

[37] Rpt, Dwan to CG, 6th Corps Area, 29 Nov 33, sub: Annual Inspection of Fort Sheridan; Rpt, Dawn to CG, 6th Corps Area, 28 Nov 33, sub: Annual Inspection of Jefferson Barracks. Both in Entry 11, RG 159, NARA.

was substantially complete, only one regular was left on duty with each CCC company and one at each district headquarters. In time, even more reservists would be called up, allowing nearly all of the regulars to return to their primary duties. As incidental benefits, the call-up allowed a partial test of mobilization procedures to be made, while giving the reserve officers valuable experience on extended active duty. Indeed, the training opportunity was so good that the Army soon restricted CCC positions to officers in the active reserve, excluding those who were retired or on disability.[38]

General MacArthur, the Chief of Staff, welcomed the leadership opportunities and administrative challenges represented by the Civilian Conservation Corps. However, he cautioned that the program threatened national security in the short term by diverting leaders from their units, by making demands on stockpiles, and by forcing reductions in individual and unit training. Hence, to offset at least some of its deleterious effects, he decided on a decentralized approach to managing CCC operations by allowing local commanders the greatest possible flexibility. The corps area commanders were encouraged to "determine for themselves appropriate action in the problems that arise" and "whenever necessary to act contrary to War Department instructions or regulations." Each commander was to "follow unhesitatingly the dictates of his own judgement," while keeping the War Department informed to prevent controversy and confusion. The commanders were told to use whatever facilities they needed, but were cautioned not to give military training other than physical exercises and games because the enrollees were civilians, subject only to moral suasion and dismissal if they violated discipline. Liaison representatives from each of the other federal departments concerned were attached to each corps area headquarters to provide advice and to assist in camp site selection and assignment.[39]

Organization below corps area was equally flexible. Ordinarily, a number of companies assigned to camps would be grouped in a district embracing one or more states. The companies were approximately 200 strong and were staffed during the mobilization phase with one regular officer, three reserve officers, and four enlisted men (first sergeant,

---

[38] Ltr, TAG to Comdts, Svc Schools, 14 May 33, Entry 26; Ltr, AG, 9th Corps Area, to All CCC Dist Cdrs, 28 Jul 33, Entry 26; Memo, TAG to All Corps Area Cdrs, 19 Apr 33, sub: Civilian Conservation Corps, Entry 26; Preston Annual Rpt, FY 1933, Entry 26B. All in RG 159, NARA. See also Killigrew, "Great Depression," Ph.D. diss., ch. 12, pp. 23–24, and ch. 13, pp. 1, 5, 7; Salmond, *CCC*, p. 58; and Johnson, "CCC," Ph.D. diss., pp. 63, 68.

[39] Killigrew, "Great Depression," Ph.D. diss., ch. 12, pp. 16–17, 20; *ARCS, 1933*, pp. 6–10 (quotations on p. 6); WD Prov Reg, 1933, Entry 11, RG 159, NARA.

Sawbill CCC Camp, Tofte, Minnesota, August 1933

supply sergeant, mess sergeant, and first cook). Districts sometimes were divided into subdistricts to handle a large number of units. In either case, the intermediate commands normally were headquartered at an Army post close to the sources of supply and other support.[40]

The district or subdistrict commanders had a small staff consisting of an executive officer, adjutant, chaplain, and surgeon. These head-quarters were to interpret and channel the directives coming from Director Fechner and the corps area headquarters. The company camps, after the mobilization period, eventually were under the command of a captain or senior lieutenant, with a junior officer assistant. A camp commander's tour was six months, but it could be extended if both he and his superior at district headquarters mutually agreed. The com mander was responsible for camp operations and administration and the morale and welfare of the enrollees. In this latter category, an extensive program was developed under the general supervision of The Adjutant General. It included corps-wide athletic programs, camp libraries, and post exchanges, all of which over time entailed considerable expenses. The captain's authority was broad, to include issuing dishonorable dis-charges to enrollees who failed to measure up. The junior officers nor-mally supervised camp logistics, such as pay, transport, and rations, and a medical officer was assigned for every two or three camps.[41]

Nearly three quarters of the CCC camps were engaged in Agriculture Department projects, the majority of which were under the auspices of the U.S. Forest Service. Much of their work came under the

---

[40] Memo, TAG to All Corps Area Cdrs, 19 Apr 33, sub: CCC; CCC Cir 5, 29 May 33. Both in Entry 26, RG 159, NARA. See also Salmond, *CCC*, p. 84.

[41] Ltr, TAG to CGs and CofArms/Svcs, 18 May 33, sub: Religious Ministration for Civilian Conservation Corps, Entry 26, RG 159, NARA.

category of forest protection and improvement, the most spectacular duty being fire fighting. Insect and disease prevention was another major project. Forest improvement involved building trails, cabins, and shelters, as well as clearing land, building dams, and carrying out reforestation—considered to be the most important function, planting millions of young trees and reclaiming millions of acres. In addition, grazing land and soil conservation projects were undertaken, along with some wildlife management. CCC camps also supported the Tennessee Valley Authority and the National Park Service, while other CCC units fought underground coal mine fires in Wyoming and worked on large flood-control projects for the Army Corps of Engineers in Vermont and New York.[42]

The advent of the Civilian Conservation Corps posed numerous practical problems for the Army. One of the first was the effect on soldier morale due to pay discrepancies; CCC men drew $30 a month, while privates who trained them made but $18. Although War Department policy called for only senior NCOs to be assigned, this was often impossible, and the higher pay of CCC men caused General MacArthur to press for the return of detailed enlisted personnel even more quickly than officers. Fortunately, most soldiers were philosophical about the situation. When the local CCC camp was being established at Carlisle Barracks, Pennsylvania, the inspector reported that the soldiers performed their work "cheerfully and efficiently" and that their morale was high. Yet he expressed some concern about the effect on readiness. Regulars were diverted from their training, and reserve summer training had to be curtailed drastically because of the diversion of personnel, facilities, and resources to the Civilian Conservation Corps.[43]

The ill-defined relationship between the Army and Fechner's office caused some tensions and at times impeded operations. Fechner coordinated the efforts of the various executive departments involved in aspects of the Civilian Conservation Corps. His office staff consisted of a deputy, James J. McEntee; a legal assistant, Charles H. Taylor; and a publicity assistant, Guy D. McKinney. The office itself was divided into four sections: Statistical, Information, Safety, and Investigation and Correspondence. The latter section prepared inspection schedules, reviewed reports, and answered general inquiries for CCC inspectors.

---

[42] Salmond, *CCC*, pp. 121–23.

[43] Killigrew, "Great Depression," Ph.D. diss., ch. 13, p. 7; Rpt (quoted words), Logan to TIG, 26 Apr 33, sub: Annual General Inspection of Medical Field Service School, Carlisle Barracks, Pa., Entry 11, RG 159, NARA.

Problems soon developed with The Inspector General over the role of the CCC inspectors.[44]

The involvement of so many executive departments in CCC operations made it difficult for Fechner to assert his influence over the corps. He hoped to expand his authority by creating his own inspection service, believing that he could not manage effectively if he relied only on the weekly reports given him by the Army. Perceiving a need for his own independent sources, Fechner appointed three inspectors and instructed them to report only to him. The corps area commanders and General Preston, however, were disturbed by his action, which encroached on their own prerogatives and responsibilities. The War Department found that it could forestall use of the civilian inspectors by keeping Fechner fully informed. Since this was the director's objective all along, the arrangement proved to be mutually satisfactory.[45]

This cordial working arrangement was not without its upsets. On two occasions in 1937 Fechner clashed with the War Department over issues directly or indirectly involving IGD interests. That year, the education of enrollees was added to the CCC's basic mission of unemployment relief and conservation. Fechner wanted to place control of the new program in his office, reducing the War Department's involvement correspondingly. Army leaders rejected the plan, believing that it would intrude too greatly into the camp commanders' administrative responsibilities. A confrontation was averted when inspectors noted that the transfer of funds necessary to run an education program could not be made under the existing appropriation. Hence, supervision of the new program remained firmly under Army control.[46]

A more serious disagreement occurred over the issue of rotating Army officers. By 1937 the leadership training value of a camp tour was fully recognized, and the War Department wished to spread the benefit by replacing all officers who had been on the job eighteen months or longer, limiting subsequent tours to no more than twelve months. The new policy was put into effect over the objections of many of the incumbent reservists, as well as members of the corps area staffs. A former inspector, Col. Joseph A. Baer, now the Third Corps Area chief of staff, warned the Office of The Inspector General to expect a barrage of complaints as the program was carried out. Director Fechner strenuously objected to the policy, on the principle that it was foolish to tinker with a working system and unfair to the

<hr>

[44] Salmond, *CCC*, pp. 71–72.
[45] Johnson, "CCC," Ph.D. diss., pp. 34–35.
[46] Ibid., p. 110; Salmond, *CCC*, pp. 162–63.

officers affected, and went directly to President Roosevelt in an attempt to have it reversed.[47]

This action in turn upset the War Department, where officials believed that Fechner was trying to influence an internal departmental policy. The director heightened the confrontation further by criticizing aspects of the Army's CCC disbursement. He objected to the fact that only IGs inspected the accounts and asked that his inspectors be allowed to do the same. His proposals were rebuffed strongly by Assistant Secretary of War Louis A. Johnson, who referred the matter to the standing CCC Advisory Council. The council defused the issue, particularly when it became apparent that the President strongly supported the Army's view. The Chief of Staff, General Craig, restored more cordial relations by assuring Fechner that henceforth he would be advised on personnel changes in the CCC system.[48]

CCC Special Investigations

The concern over the effect of the Army's CCC responsibilities on defense capabilities was shared by the Chief of Staff and by many other high-ranking officers. General Preston predicted that training levels would decline to dangerous levels, and morale and discipline would falter after the novelty and excitement of the enrollment passed. The reserve call-up and General MacArthur's decision to press for the earliest possible release of enlisted men from the CCC camps in part reflected such worries. In June 1933 MacArthur's deputy, General Drum, asked Preston to prepare a detailed overview of the operation to document the effect on readiness and counter any future criticism of the Army.[49]

As a result, General Preston developed an inspection plan designed to gather the broadest amount of information with the least inconvenience to the commanders in the field. The inspections were to be informal, based on the belief that "personal interviews between officers of this office and the nine corps area commanders and members of their staffs, in addition to visits to important army posts," would provide the data needed. Their objective was to gauge "the effect the use of regular

---

[47] Johnson, "CCC," Ph.D. diss., p. 70.

[48] Salmond, *CCC*, pp. 172–74.

[49] Johnson, "CCC," Ph.D. diss., p. 14; Memo, Preston to Drum, 1 Jul 33, sub: Submitted as a Result of a Recent Verbal Interview Relative to CCC Activities, Entry 26A, RG 159, NARA.

officers for CCC work has had on the efficiency of the army." General MacArthur approved the plan on 5 July.[50]

Preparations for the inspections were unusually thorough. The inspectors were instructed to ensure that corps area leaders understood their objectives and the need for reliable data. They were to pay particular attention to deficiencies in training and maintenance caused by the creation of the CCC cadre. Elaborate guides and questionnaires were prepared for the use of IGs and unit commanders. Corps area commanders learned of the program through confidential letters, in which they were asked to nominate the CCC camps for unannounced inspections. They also were told that the inspections would require discussions with most senior corps officials. These letters were accompanied by lists of questions, to be answered by the corps and post commanders and returned to the Office of The Inspector General before the visits. Among the queries were requests for precise listings by branch of personnel detailed to CCC activities, the types of camps, and the effect of cadre work on normal activities.[51]

A five-man OTIG team conducted the actual inspections between 18 July and 18 August. After visiting each corps area headquarters, the IGs fanned out to visit the posts and depots that had been most directly affected by the CCC call-up. They also inspected a number of CCC district and subdistrict headquarters and visited eight-four company camps. Commanders and staff officers were interviewed at each location, as were Forest and Park Service representatives and many enrollees. On 21 August General Preston convened a meeting to discuss the inspection findings with representatives of all War Department elements involved in the CCC mission.[52]

The IGs reported that the program was running well and that the performance of units and personnel had been good. Relationships with the forestry, park, and agricultural services responsible for enrollee work were, for the most part, harmonious. The most sensitive issue raised by the civilian representatives was the question of how many

---

[50] Memo (quotations), Preston to Drum, 1 Jul 33; Memo, Drum to TIG, 3 Jul 33, sub: Inspection and Report on CCC. Both in Entry 26A, RG 159, NARA.

[51] Memo, Browning to Preston, 17 Jul 33, sub: Confidential Instructions to Inspectors General Who Inspect Civilian Conservation Corps Activities; Ltr, TAG to CGs, Corps Areas, 13 Jul 33, sub: Inspection, Civilian Conservation Corps. Both in Entry 26A, RG 159, NARA.

[52] Marcellus G. Spinks, "Major Problems of the Inspector General, AEF, and Their Solution" (Lecture delivered at G–1 Course No. 5, Army War College, Washington, D.C., 9 Oct 33), in Army War College Curriculum Papers, U.S. Army Military History Institute, Carlisle Barracks, Pa.

men were needed for camp overhead. The Forest Service especially complained that camp commanders were holding too many men for maintenance, mess duties, and similar work, and in some cases the complaint was valid. Already aware of the problem, they sought to resolve this and similar issues through compromise. In time, as routines and procedures became established, such issues disappeared. However, the IGs warned of similar problems in the future, when construction of side camps or new main camps became necessary.[53]

The inspectors credited the Army's success in the early phases of the CCC operation to General MacArthur's policy of decentralizing responsibility to the corps area level. The corps areas had adopted a district system, based on Army posts that served as supply bases for the camps. In all but the Sixth Corps Area, the districts provided command, control, and administration. The Sixth Corps Area commander retained command of all camps, using the districts to coordinate camp activities. In some areas where Army posts were few, districts had to be established to function like post headquarters; offices and warehouses in these cases often were either rented or borrowed from the state or municipality. Districts away from established posts were forced to use larger numbers of enrollees for housekeeping duties, in the process causing some of the friction that had developed with user agencies.

Many of the first CCC camps had been commanded by Regular Army field-grade officers. Around the time of the inspections company-grade officers had replaced them, and reservists were appearing in growing numbers. By midsummer most of the Regular Army enlisted men were returning to their units, to be replaced by enrollees who had shown they could perform supervisory functions in supply, mess duties, and so forth. The inspectors found the camps to be in good condition, considering their origins. Most had begun as tent camps, where administrative buildings and sanitary facilities were constructed first, followed by barracks. Many camp commanders expressed great pride in the speed with which they had improved conditions at their camps. By August most had such basic amenities as electricity and running water; a few already boasted hard-surfaced roads and railways, built with enrollee labor. Despite the necessary stress on camp development, some enrollees had begun work in forestry and other projects within a few days of arriving. Camp staffs, including every maintenance and support worker from orderly room clerks to KPs, formed only about 15

---

[53] Information in this and subsequent paragraphs based on Ltr, Preston to TAG, 8 Sep 33, sub: Inspection of Conservation Corps Activities of the War Department and the Army, Entry 26, RG 159, NARA.

percent of the total camp population, and the inspectors suggested that the size of the staff should continue to be resolved locally between commanders and their civilian counterparts.

Everyone the inspectors talked with agreed that the CCC mobilization had been a satisfying professional challenge. Mobilization principles had been tested and many junior officers had been given unprecedented opportunities to develop their leadership and initiative. The success of the rapid CCC buildup was the result of an intense effort on the part of the Army personnel involved. Many officers and men had worked all day, seven days a week, to fulfill their mission.

Inspectors verified, however, that the focus on the Civilian Conservation Corps had affected Regular Army training adversely. The proportion of officers engaged directly or indirectly in CCC activities ranged from 69 percent in the Second Corps Area to 49 percent in the Eighth Corps Area. Similar statistics prevailed for warrant officers and enlisted men. The prime determinant was the number of camps and enrollees, which ranged from a high of 379 camps and nearly 91,000 enrollees in the Ninth Corps Area to a low of 66 camps and 7,200 enrollees in the Second Corps Area. The high number of reconditioning camps in the Second Corps Area accounted for the large number of cadre required there.

The diversion of so many seasoned Army officers to CCC duty had impaired the effectiveness of their units. Even more important, the process threatened to reduce the quality of recruit training, extending discipline and training problems well into the future. Tactical training had virtually ceased, while practice in individual combat skills had lapsed. The problem was, not so much a lack of funds, but the inexperience of those left behind to plan and conduct such exercises. Although discipline and morale were high, the potential for future difficulties loomed large the longer experienced leaders were kept away from their units.

Readiness seemed to be seriously impaired in other ways as well. The IGs found that 139 officers not on CCC duty were commanding two or more units and that five commanded five units each. The supranormal taskings being placed on these officers, as well as the consumption of the war-reserve stocks of clothing, tentage, and personal equipment, were of great concern to senior commanders. In addition, because of the demands and distractions imposed by the CCC enrollment, they could not devote adequate time to training and policy matters. Hence, training camps for reserve and Guard forces had to be canceled or reduced in scope. As a result, the Army's combat readiness inevitably declined even as the demands of CCC duties, with their long family separations and extra personal expenses, adversely affected morale.[54]

The IGs also reported in depth on health and sanitation issues, especially the effect of the Civilian Conservation Corps on the medical care given to Regular Army personnel and their families. They successfully recommended contracting with local civilian physicians to care for the CCC enrollees during the absence of Army doctors. Nearly all dental service was provided in similar fashion. Two enrollees for each camp were given first aid training at the conditioning centers, further easing the burden, while arrangements were made with local hospitals to provide long-term care to camp personnel. Although inspectors considered the payment procedures for hospitals to be unnecessarily cumbersome, they had no real way of persuading the civilian facilities to adopt military methods.[55]

The IGs found that in most cases sufficient equipment had been issued to the CCC work companies prior to moving to their campsites. Inevitably, however, some shortages developed, which were either relieved through local purchase or by express shipments from distant depots. The situation became particularly acute at Fort Knox, Kentucky, where quantities of ration items had to be purchased locally to meet the demand created by the processing of 32,000 men. Complaints were universal about footwear and the quality of field cooking ranges. Inspectors offered various solutions, but in practice the problems usually faded once the decaying World War I stocks had been consumed and new issues could be made.[56]

Despite these and other technical and administrative problems, the IGs concluded that enrollee morale was high and that civilians generally admired the Army for its CCC role. Few major complaints were encountered. Cooperation with local communities was judged excellent. The only point of potential friction, they believed, might arise from the assignment of all-black work companies. The IGs suggested that racial friction be avoided by assigning the black units to duties on Army posts, wherever possible.[57]

In the late summer of 1934 a second inspection cycle on the same scale as the first was under way, with OTIG officers following up on

---

[54] Reliance on ibid. ends here.

[55] Ltr, Preston to TAG, 12 Sep 33, sub: Data Concerning CCC Activities Within Several Corps Areas, Entry 26, RG 159, NARA.

[56] Rpt, Allin to TIG, 31 Aug 33, sub: Inspections of CCC Activities, 5th, 6th and 7th Corps Areas, Entry 26, RG 159, NARA.

[57] Ibid.

their earlier findings. The adverse effects of the Civilian Conservation Corps on Army readiness were still apparent, along with some consequences that had not been discerned the year before. The underlying problem had not changed, namely, the large numbers of Army personnel on CCC duty, which was especially critical in line units at the smaller garrisons. Despite the increasing numbers of reservists called up to free the regulars, it was not uncommon to find 1933 West Point graduates commanding CCC work companies while first lieutenants were leading Regular Army battalions. Many officers continued to perform multiple major duties, and the IGs reported that the strain was beginning to tell. Unit efficiency continued to be impaired by the absence of NCOs. As noted earlier, the result was a steady decline in tactical training and an erosion of discipline and morale. The most evident practical effect of the Civilian Conservation Corps, however, was a sharp decline in reenlistments. Too many $18-a-month soldiers were leaving the Army to become $30-a-month CCC men.[58]

Because of the CCC's high priority for services, support to not only active-duty elements but also soldiers and dependents suffered as well. Motor transportation and maintenance operations were devoted almost exclusively to CCC support. Consequently, tactical vehicles deteriorated, and many of the World War I–vintage trucks in CCC service were abused past the point of retention. With Army hospitals and dental clinics operating far beyond their capacities, soldiers and their families became victims of a strained medical system, which was extremely demoralizing. A large percentage of soldiers experienced serious financial crises, resulting from the combination of pay cuts and the costs of CCC temporary duty, which lowered morale even further. The reduction in services extended to depot operations, where regular requisitions had been deferred sometimes for as long as a year while the installations coped with CCC requirements. The IGs considered the Army to be sound, but straining under the many demands placed on it. This report, along with the growing size of the Civilian Conservation Corps, led to increased reserve call-ups. By the end of 1935 the personnel crisis was over, and the Army settled into a more balanced routine.[59]

The IGD and the CCC

The CCC mobilization added new duties to the IGD's work load that went well beyond the major inspections, although no strength increas-

---

[58] Memo, Moses to TIG, 24 Dec 34, and Reply, 2 Jan 35, Entry 26A, RG 159, NARA.
[59] Ibid.

es were authorized in the Office of The Inspector General or elsewhere in the inspectorate. Part of the work derived from the speed demanded by the President, which assured that confusion would develop and that complaints would be heard from many quarters.

At first, all complaints were channeled to the War Department, where they were waived or held by the Office of The Inspector General until the mobilization surge had ended. This policy was intended to minimize distraction in the corps areas during the critical initial phases of the operation. Problems were dealt with as informally as possible; action officers contacted one another personally or by telephone; and paperwork was discouraged. The Chief of Staff required that all CCC-related questions be answered within forty-eight hours, and his staff issued a daily bulletin of decisions to keep everyone informed. Most of the conflicts that developed between the Army and the other involved federal departments were resolved in the corps areas, in keeping with the policy of decentralization.[60]

Many complaints dealt with money matters. Indeed, fiscal oversight proved to be a demanding task. The Army had close financial connections with the Civilian Conservation Corps because the Chief of Finance had been designated as its fiscal officer and as the Director of Emergency Conservation Expenditures. Army officers also acted as CCC disbursing officials. In this capacity they were subject to IG inspections on the same basis and frequency as those disbursing Army funds, even though most of the money came from Interior or Labor Department sources. For this reason, in May 1933 General Preston directed Major Parkinson, now OTIG's Money Accounts Division chief, to become the office expert on CCC finances.[61]

The relaxed procurement procedures intended to speed the mobilization process gave birth to a number of financial complaints and investigations. A five-cent error in the hourly rate for hiring trucks in the Shenandoah National Park led to one of the more extended inquiries, on which Col. Jesse D. Elliot spent nearly six months in 1937–38. The hourly rate in question turned out to have been a clerical error. But in the course of his review of four years of back vouchers, Elliot discovered thirteen that were fraudulent. Comparison of the vouchers with canceled checks revealed irregularities by one of the disbursers at the Army's regional finance office in Washington. When con-

[60] Killigrew, "Great Depression," Ph.D. diss., ch. 12, pp. 20–22, and ch. 13, p. 14.
[61] Ltr, SofW to SofI, 8 Nov 33, Entry 26; CCC Cir 1, 27 Apr 33, Entry 26; Memo, Humber to Parkinson, 18 May 33, Entry 26A; Memo, TAG to CofFin, FD, 13 Jul 33, Entry 26A; Ltr, Humber to Helmick, 25 Jun 34, Entry 26A. All in RG 159, NARA.

fronted with the evidence, the employee confessed to having forged vouchers since early 1934. The case proved that proper oversight of operations and internal review systems were lacking. As a result, the office was restructured and the officers responsible were admonished and ordered to make restitution. The investigation had required a painstaking review of contracts, vouchers, and procedures at numerous Army and civilian locations, growing in the process from a trifling issue to a fairly serious matter.[62]

One of the largest CCC fraud cases involved Reno E. Stitely, an Interior Department employee who routinely submitted fraudulent payrolls along with the legitimate ones that he collected as part of his job from Army disbursing officers. The fraudulent payrolls were so small in comparison to the others that they had escaped notice for some period of time. Then, in Stitely's absence on one occasion, an assistant turned in the regular payroll by itself. After checking with the assistant, it became clear that no separate small payroll existed. Subsequent investigation by Interior Department and IGD officials showed that Stitely had pocketed nearly $60,000 through his scheme. The Office of The Inspector General had become involved only at the request of the Chief of Finance, who feared that the Army disbursing officers might incur a liability for reimbursement. The IG investigator concluded that the finance officers had not established any suitable internal mechanisms against such fraud. A listing of all eligible payrolls, for example, would have shown something amiss, while a review of canceled checks could have been a backup. Stitely was tried and convicted, and two concerned finance officers were admonished.[63]

A collateral problem surfaced when Secretary of the Interior Harold L. Ickes asked for a copy of the IG investigation. Copies already had been given to the U.S. Attorney General for the District of Columbia and to the Comptroller General. Despite this, Ickes was turned down with a routine reply about the need to keep IG records confidential. Angry, Ickes personally pointed out to Secretary of War Harry H. Woodring that his investigators had willingly shared their work with the IGs, and he threatened to raise the issue with the President. The year-long Army IG investigation, he noted, appeared to

---

[62] Killigrew, "Great Depression," Ph.D. diss., ch. 12, p. 20; Rpt, Elliot to TIG, 13 Apr 38, sub: Investigation Covering Alleged Irregularities in the Army Finance Office, Washington, D.C., Entry 26C, RG 159, NARA.

[63] Rpt, Elliot to TIG, 13 Jul 38, sub: Investigation of Alleged Irregularities by the Finance Office, U.S. Army, in Paying Certain Vouchers of the National Park Service, Entry 26C, RG 159, NARA.

lack any sense of immediacy. Secretary Woodring quickly saw to it that Ickes got his copy of the report, while General Reed counseled his staff on the need for common sense in replying to cabinet members.[64]

Some investigations originated in complaints from the field. In January 1935 a CCC employee in Hawaii and his lawyer wrote separate letters to Director Fechner and The Adjutant General regarding problems in the worker's pay arrangements. Fechner, in turn, wrote the Secretary of War, demanding an investigation. He charged the Army disbursing officer with obstructive tactics, causing the dismissal of civilian employees, improper financial management, and failing to pay the complainant his due. The resulting inquiry, however, proved that Fechner was too quick to believe his employee.[65]

The case went to the newly assigned Hawaiian Department IG, Lt. Col. George R. Allin, an officer already familiar with the Civilian Conservation Corps. Allin interviewed eighteen witnesses, reviewed all financial records of the CCC's Hawaiian office, and analyzed the role of the Army disbursing officer. He found that the officer had held strictly to correct procedures in all transactions, sometimes delaying payments until he could verify their legitimacy. These delays apparently had upset the complainant. The finance officer had advised the local CCC head that he would not honor the vouchers of certain employees, because he did not consider them trustworthy. One was the complainant, who, the IG had learned, was a convicted embezzler. The money allegedly owed the complainant was being held up because of a GAO review into his associated irregularities. Colonel Allin concluded that the Army disbursing officer was extremely competent, indeed one of the few points of integrity in a corrupt system. Allin cited the officer for efficiently setting up CCC finances in Hawaii and recommended him for a commendation. General Preston and the Secretary of War agreed. While Fechner did not apologize for his earlier accusations, the undesirable employees were dismissed from the CCC's Hawaiian office, and Allin had the satisfaction of witnessing a total overhaul of its personnel and operations.[66]

The Hawaiian case underscored the encouraging fact that misconduct by members of the Army cadre assigned to the Civilian

---

[64] Ltr, Ickes to Woodring, 8 Oct 38, and Reply, 19 Oct 38, Entry 26C, RG 159, NARA.

[65] Rpt, Allin to CG, Hawaiian Dept, 19 Mar 35, sub: Investigation of Conduct of Captain Herbert Baldwin, F.D., With Respect to Administration of the ECW in Hawaii, Entry 26C, RG 159, NARA.

[66] Ibid.

Conservation Corps was rare. The few cases that did arise invariably concerned some form of funds mismanagement, and even these were usually low-level offenses. In a typical case, a corporal escorting enrollees on the train from Alabama to Maryland cheated his charges of their ration money by collecting their allowance at the start of the trip and then buying cheap food at bulk rates, pocketing the difference. At their destination the new men began to complain about the conditions of their trip. Their complaints came to the attention of the local IG, who opened an investigation. Because the men had crossed corps area boundaries, the Office of The Inspector General became involved in coordinating and processing the case. The corporal eventually was court-martialed.[67]

Financial inspections were the only ones prescribed on a regular basis, because CCC regulations did not provide for scheduled general inspections. Yet the IGD's reporting on the Civilian Conservation Corps remained quite extensive. In addition, officers of many other War Department elements interacted with CCC operations. For example, representatives of The Adjutant General visited the camps to check on administration and on morale and welfare programs; Colonel Major, the G–3 officer responsible for CCC oversight, made frequent tours; and corps area staff officers also made periodic visits. When IGs conducted an annual inspection of a post or garrison, they inspected all CCC activities on the post and prepared reports on them in the same manner as for other units, commenting on strength, functions, and mission performance; making recommendations for improvements; and proposing commendations for good work. In 1938 a resume of all CCC and Works Projects Administration activities on Army posts, including a brief description of the projects, their locations, and the dates they were undertaken, was added to inspection reports as an annex. The data from these various sources ultimately was forwarded to the Office of The Inspector General for filing.[68]

Inspectors also maintained oversight through special inquiries and investigations, which were ordered and conducted in the same manner as for any military unit. In fact, CCC regulations specified

---

[67] Rpt, Adams to CG, 4th Corps Area, 19 Aug 37, sub: Case of Corporal Columbus H. Hatton, Co M, 22d Infantry; Rpt, Batson to TIG, 23 Oct 37, sub: Continuance of Investigation of Allegations Against Corp C. H. Hatton. Both in Entry 26C, RG 159, NARA.

[68] Rpt, Herr to CG, 2d Corps Area, 21 Feb 36, sub: Annual Inspection of Madison Barracks; Rpt, Upson to CG, 2d Corps Area, 22 Apr 38, sub: Annual Inspection of Fort Wadsworth and Subpost Miller Field. Both in Entry 11, RG 159, NARA. See also Killigrew, "Great Depression," Ph.D. diss., ch. 12, p. 32; Johnson, "CCC," Ph.D. diss., p. 118.

that enrollees would have access to an IG for complaints and griev-ances. Occasionally, the IGD's interest allowed the informal resolu-tion of issues before they could develop into full-fledged investiga-tions. When complaints about CCC operations arose, corps area IGs usually dealt with them and, upon completion, forwarded their reports to the Office of The Inspector General for review and filing. High-level interest sometimes generated special inquiries, notably over the issue of race. Black activists were prominent in criticizing recruiting procedures that discriminated racially, and Emmett J. Scott, the Third Assistant Secretary of War for race matters during World War I, now an official of Howard University, strongly urged proportional black participation as CCC enrollees and leaders. His demand that black reservists participate fully in the program was especially forceful.[69]

In 1934 Director Fechner asked the Army to investigate the enroll-ment and placement of blacks in the Civilian Conservation Corps, after receiving numerous complaints of widespread discrimination. The investigation showed that wide variations in racial policy existed from one corps area to another. In the South the CCC units were strictly seg-regated, while in New England the relatively few blacks who enrolled were attached to white companies. Although the investigation con-firmed the allegations of unfairly reduced quotas for blacks, the Army failed to take a strong stand on fairness, citing the difficulty in placing black units and the need to allow each corps area commander to accom-modate local conditions. The investigation produced a slight increase in black enrollment, but Fechner was forced to tolerate artificial limits on the opportunities offered to blacks and to condone a policy of restrict-ing black companies to their home states or to duties on Army posts only. From the President down to the local communities, no support existed for a more equitable solution.[70]

Complaints about local hiring practices, contracting, and the like had to be investigated periodically. Again, such inquiries were almost invariably accomplished at the corps area level. The Second Corps Area IG, for example, investigated the commander of the Camden, New York, CCC camp, when local Democrats accused him of hiring only Republicans. The complaint proved to be accurate, and all the men

---

[69] Draft Memo, OTIG for TAG, 25 Mar 38; Ltr, Reed to Ford, 26 May 38. Both in Entry 26C, RG 159, NARA. See also Johnson, "CCC," Ph.D. diss., p. 159.

[70] Johnson, "CCC," Ph.D. diss., p. 159; Salmond, *CCC*, pp. 95–96, 100; Rpt, Wood to CG, 4th Corps Area, 26 Aug 37, sub: Special Investigation of CCC Camp 4735, Charlotte, Ark., Entry 26C, RG 169, NARA.

whose positions had been challenged were fired on the grounds that they lacked sufficient skill to hold their jobs. The Army officer in charge, who had taken the advice of a local Republican without adequately checking on the men, was admonished. Union labor practices and rules, nepotism in hiring, and favoritism also generated IG action from time to time.[71]

Complaints about mail handling at the camps arrived in a steady stream throughout the first years. In most cases pecuniary liability was at issue, its determination resting for the most part on an inspector's recommendation. The cause of the problems seemed to be the administrative inexperience of the junior reserve officers in charge of mail handling, who also were overwhelmed by many other responsibilities. In April 1934 General Preston successfully urged The Adjutant General to simplify requirements. Similarly, the handling of enrollee misconduct cases had to be modified from standard procedures. Such cases were forwarded through channels to the Office of The Inspector General for a review, which consisted of a procedures check and a recommendation for the disposition of the case. Since the enrollees were not subject to military justice, the OTIG staff addressed the question of whether the men should be discharged and which civilian law enforcement agency should be notified about the cases.[72]

Fortunately, with the exception of desertion, there were relatively few enrollee discipline problems throughout the existence of the Civilian Conservation Corps. A few disturbances, however, did require investigation In November 1937 a mutiny broke out in the five camps operating in the Shenandoah National Park. The enrollees were dismayed by the winter conditions in the Blue Ridge, and ten who refused to work had to be discharged. Fechner's staff, as well as the Third Corps Area IG, looked into the matter. The problem was attributed to the camp leaders' failure either to acclimate their charges or to explain grievance procedures to them. Many of the men, who had come from Pennsylvania coal mining areas, had assumed that striking was the way to get attention. Another case, this time in New York, concerned the theft and resale of CCC property. A serious riot in Luray, Virginia, in which Southern and Northern men clashed, also required investigation, as did liquor distribution in a Lexington,

---

[71] Johnson, "CCC," Ph.D. diss., p. 190; File 324.5, CCC Investigations, Box 251, Entry 26, and Box 23, Entry 26C, RG 159, NARA.

[72] Memo, Preston to TAG, 25 Apr 34, Entry 26; Ltr, Taylor to TAG, 18 Nov 35, sub: Alleged Improper Handling of Mail at CCC Camps, Entry 26C. Both in RG 159, NARA.

Indiana, camp. But such cases were exceptions to the generally order-ly operation of the camps, and never approached the scale or intrica-cy of the CCC's finance problems.[73]

As world tensions increased during the late 1930s, the corre-sponding growth of the U.S. armed forces made it increasingly diffi-cult to obtain qualified active reservists for CCC positions. As a result, all the camp cadre positions except the commander's were converted in June 1939 to civilian slots, with the War Department retaining its authority to select and appoint. But the outbreak of war in Europe brought increasing manpower pressures. In March 1940 inactive reserve officers were authorized to fill some of the remaining military slots, and in September civilians with no reserve affiliation began to be accepted for all camp leadership positions, subject to War Department approval.[74]

By now the growing threat of war in Europe and Asia was drasti-cally changing public perceptions of the military. The history of the Civilian Conservation Corps had been marked by constant low-level public criticism of the Army's association with it. Periodically, some journalist or member of Congress would voice fears about the milita-rization of American youth, and as a result CCC units had been unable to carry out many worthwhile projects on military installations. However, as the world situation worsened, calls began to be heard for using CCC units on defense projects and popular support increased for military training as part of the CCC program. In a sense, however, these changes came too late. The growth of employment opportunities in defense industries and draft calls on young men made recruiting for the Civilian Conservation Corps harder and gradually eroded its strength. The CCC program always had been perceived as a temporary measure to combat unemployment, and in April 1942 Congress voted to abolish the agency.

The heritage left by what was arguably the New Deal's most suc-cessful relief program proved to be broad and enduring. CCC refor-estation and soil conservation had helped to change the face of the country. Nearly three million youths were acclimated to the military, learning skills that they would apply during the great mobilization for World War II. In addition, thousands of reserve officers had acquired experience that would prove essential to their success in the greater test that was coming. The same may be said for the War Department and the

[73] Salmond, *CCC*, pp. 186–88; File 324.5, CCC Investigations, Box 251, Entry 26, RG 159, NARA.
[74] Johnson, "CCC," Ph.D. diss., pp. 88–89.

inspectorate, as both closed out the last of the unique missions that had been characteristic of the interwar period.[75]

---

[75] Ibid., pp. 207, 218, 226–27; Salmond, *CCC*, pp. 194, 196, 198, 213, 220–21; Killigrew, "Great Depression," Ph.D. diss., ch. 13, p. 25.

ENVOI

Unchanging Principles in Changing Times

The War Department's reliance on the Inspector General's Department (IGD) to monitor the Civilian Conservation Corps' impact in the 1930s was a mark of the hard-earned respect won by the inspectorate over the preceding decades. Under challenge at the beginning of the twentieth century, the Inspector General's Department had survived Secretary Root's organizational changes but remained in a sense on probation, obliged to prove its value to the new Army hierarchy. During this critical period of adjustment such strong capable leaders as Generals Chamberlain and Garlington, who served extended tours, preserved the IGD's high standards while successfully incorporating many temporarily detailed officers into the department. Through their committed, loyal support and the dedicated efforts of all inspectors, the Inspector General's Department became the locus of professionalism at a time when the Army desperately needed the stability to offset the centrifugal effects of innovation and recurring waves of reform.

The inspectorate remained as closely knit as it had been in the past. New officers themselves were selected carefully, to assure they measured up to the senior inspector's expectations, and either served an apprenticeship at the Washington office or attended a formal school to acquaint them with their duties. The Inspector General of the Army used his personal contacts, with both the inspectors and the commanders in the field, to ensure that high standards would be maintained. Uniform procedures were upheld through various IG publications, including the Yellow Book and General Drum's inspection guides. Such sources of information, in combination with the Army regulations, clarified the status and functions of inspectors, making it possible for the local IGs to become deeply involved in the unique concerns and programs of their commands.

The inspectors usually were high-quality officers, intent on helping and improving units. They functioned, however, very much in conformity with the wishes of their senior commanders. More often than not, inspectors were on the scene because of higher-level perceptions of failures or shortcomings. Inspected units or installations often forgot that IGs merely reflected the concerns of senior officers, and were not themselves responsible for the inspections that entailed a lot of extra work and were too often perceived as an embarrassing inconvenience.

While the inspectorate pursued its routine duties, it also became a key player in the modernization of the Army. From the beginning, the difference between observing the effects of reform and influencing its course was less than it seemed. By the end of General Wood's tenure as Chief of Staff the Inspector General's Department had matured beyond the stage of only making suggestions; it was enforcing the policies of the Army's leadership. This enforcement and evaluation role increased under such strong officers as Generals March and Pershing to the point that it threatened the inspectorate's image as objective evaluators of the Army's performance. By the end of World War I the department had acquired specific staff functions and exercised a degree of influence that was resented by other elements of the service.

The issues of training and command inspections were classic examples. Inspectors were called in every time the senior command lost confidence in the ability of subordinates to meet expected standards. They filled a vacuum that commanders appeared to avoid, and yet their involvement brought reactions from commanders that were sometimes hostile. In some cases where the command seemed to fail entirely in many of its functions, as the American Expeditionary Forces did, inspectors actually became the enforcers of theater policy. Their work did not endear them to many officers, even those who recognized that IG actions served to improve a chaotic situation.

The transformation from observers to enforcers had many roots, but one was basic. The pace of change and the later wartime expansion of the Army so diluted the leadership base that inspectors, as an elite group of professionals, had to supply the knowledge and experience that were otherwise lacking. As a result, they were propelled into aspects of tactical unit and leadership evaluation that were more appropriate to commanders. Commanders also tended to use IG information as an active element of management actions. On one hand, inspectors might assure fairness when officers had to be relieved; on the other, they might ruin careers indirectly by denying embarkation clearance to a deploying unit or failing it in a field exercise. The adverse consequences of IG actions often obscured the more numerous beneficial results.

After World War I, under the leadership of detailed officers, especially Generals Helmick and Drum, the inspectorate's role shifted to observing administrative and logistical functions and assessing compliance with policy. The Inspector General's Department increased its emphasis on teaching and helping, and was called on routinely to observe and report on the effects of government and War Department policies. Throughout the interwar era the department continued to be the source of suggestions for improvements in the condition of the Army. Often it was the only spokesman for the rank and file at a time when other War Department elements were mesmerized by programs and management techniques, with little regard for their effect on people.

Regardless of emphasis, the inspectorate's work throughout faithfully reflected the concerns and interests of the War Department leadership. The inspectors performed in the manner, style, and fields required by their superiors. In this light it is easy to see why they were so preoccupied with tactical operations in 1911, traffic in 1918, and business methods in 1923. The IGs were truly serving as the eyes and ears of the command, and sometimes also as its fist.

These were the big issues. At another level, the inspectorate performed a routine series of unspectacular but essential tasks that facilitated the Army's smooth daily operations. Every day an inspector helped some responsible individual do his job more efficiently and effectively. IG oversight in finance, property, and personal conduct matters made the inspectorate the conscience of the Army. Its involvement in these related issues perforce made the Inspector General's Department the most knowledgeable agency on matters of welfare and morale—and thus foremost in reforming the quality of life and improving conditions among all ranks. The department was an essential element in assuring the Army's modernization, effectiveness, and efficiency. It is hard to picture the Army developing or accomplishing what it did without the inspectors. At the same time, it is easy to see why too many soldiers neither understood nor valued their work.

The basic IG duties as formulated by General von Steuben continued to be to inspect, investigate, assist, and teach. Although subject to a varying emphasis during the forty years under discussion, none of these functions ever lapsed entirely, and each played a role in the way the inspectorate was seen and used. Experience showed that the inspectorate was most effective when its members in the field worked directly for the local commanders. Subordination to a staff element muted the inspectors' effect, while often concealing matters of importance. IGs saw their Army from a perspective different from that of their fellow officers and staff members. While responding to many pressures, they served a valuable function for their commanders and the Army. The record attests that as a group the IGs did all they could to improve and support the Army while assuring the nation the kind of military establishment it deserved.

The Inspector General's Department, like the rest of the Army, entered a new phase of its history in the years after 1939, bringing it new duties to perform in unprecedented situations. Despite this, the Army's need for expertise, teaching, and the maintenance of standards and integrity was to prove as great as ever. General Breckinridge's 1910 remark to General Garlington summarizing the IG role should be recalled: "Your Department is the army's litmus paper, making a test of our conditions and status—and the public is often the final court of appeals."[1]

---

[1] Ltr, Breckinridge to Garlington, 19 Sep 10, Entry 35, Record Group 159, National Archives and Records Administration, Washington, D.C.

Commands, Headquarters, and Inspectors, 1901–1940

Note: The named inspector was in the position on 31 December of each year. An asterisk indicates that the officer was not detailed to the Inspector General's Department. Commands marked *Vacant* were authorized an inspector but did not have one. Commands with no entry, or name, were not authorized an inspector.

1901

Division of the Philippines, Manila, Col. Joseph P. Sanger

Department of North Philippines, Manila, Lt. Col. Louis H. Rucker*
Department of South Philippines, Cebu, Maj. Frederick A. Smith

Department of California, San Francisco, Lt. Col. John L. Chamberlain

Department of the Colorado, Denver, Maj. James A. Irons

Department of the Columbia, Vancouver Barracks, Maj. Herbert E. Tutherly*

Department of Dakota, St. Paul, Maj. Alfred Reynolds

Department of the East, Governors Island, Col. Peter D. Vroom

Department of the Lakes, Chicago, Col. Ernest A. Garlington

Department of the Missouri, Omaha, Col. James B. Erwin*

Department of Texas, San Antonio, Maj. Thomas R. Adams

1902

Division of the Philippines, Manila, Col. Joseph P. Sanger

Department of the Visayas, Iloilo
Department of Mindanao, Zamboanga

Department of California, San Francisco, Lt. Col. John L. Chamberlain

Department of the Colorado, Denver, Maj. James A. Irons

Department of the Columbia, Vancouver Barracks, Maj. Herbert E. Tutherly*

Department of Dakota, St. Paul, Maj. Alfred Reynolds

Department of the East, Governors Island, Col. Peter D. Vroom

Department of the Lakes, Chicago, Col. Ernest A. Garlington

Department of the Missouri, Omaha, Col. James B. Erwin*

Department of Texas, San Antonio, Maj. Thomas R. Adams

1903

Division of the Philippines, Manila, Lt. Col. John L. Chamberlain

Department of Luzon, Manila, Maj. Hobart K. Bailey
Department of the Visayas, Iloilo, Maj. Charles H. Watts*
Department of Mindanao, Zamboanga

Department of California, San Francisco, Capt. Wait C. Johnson*

Department of the Colorado, Denver, Lt. Col. James W. Pope

Department of the Columbia, Vancouver Barracks, Maj. Lea Febiger

Department of Dakota, St. Paul, Lt. Col. Alfred Reynolds*

Department of the East, Governors Island, Col. Ernest A. Garlington

Department of the Lakes, Chicago, Col. Charles H. Heyl

Department of the Missouri, Omaha, Vacant

Department of Texas, San Antonio, Maj. Thomas R. Adams

1904, 1905, 1906

Philippine Division, Manila, Col. John L. Chamberlain

Department of Luzon, Manila
Department of Visayas, Iloilo
Department of Mindanao, Zamboanga

Atlantic Division, Governors Island, Col. Ernest A. Garlington

Department of the East, Governors Island
Department of the Gulf, Atlanta

472

Northern Division, St. Louis, Lt. Col. Frank K. Wood

Department of the Lakes, Chicago
Department of the Missouri, Omaha
Department of Dakota, St. Paul

Southwestern Division, Oklahoma City, Lt. Col. Frank West

Department of Texas, San Antonio
Department of the Colorado, Denver

Pacific Division, San Francisco, Lt. Col. Sedgewick Pratt*

Department of California, San Francisco
Department of the Columbia, Vancouver Barracks

Army of Cuban Pacification, Havana, Maj. Charles G. Treat

1907

Philippine Division, Manila, Lt. Col. Wilber E. Wilder

Department of Luzon, Manila
Department of the Visayas, Iloilo
Department of Mindanao, Zamboanga

Department of California, San Francisco, Lt. Col. George L. Anderson

Department of the Colorado, Denver, Maj. Charles G. Morton

Department of the Columbia, Vancouver Barracks, Vacant

Department of Dakota, St. Paul, Lt. Col. Francis H. French

Department of the East, Governors Island, Col. John L. Chamberlain

Department of the Gulf, Atlanta, Maj. Adelbert Cronkhite*

Department of the Lakes, Chicago, Col. George F. Chase

Department of the Missouri, Omaha, Maj. Jacob C. Galbraith

Department of Texas, San Antonio, Maj. Omar Bundy*

Army of Cuban Pacification, Maj. Charles G. Treat

1908

Philippine Division, Manila, Lt. Col. Francis H. French

Department of Luzon, Manila
Department of the Visayas, Iloilo
Department of Mindanao, Zamboanga

Department of California, San Francisco, Lt. Col. Charles G. Woodward

Department of the Colorado, Denver, Maj. Charles G. Morton

Department of Dakota, St. Paul, Maj. Samuel W. Miller

Department of the East, Governors Island, Col. John L. Chamberlain

Department of the Gulf, Atlanta, Maj. Frank G. Mauldin*

Department of the Lakes, Chicago, Col. George F. Chase

Department of the Missouri, Omaha, Maj. Jacob C. Galbraith

Department of Texas, San Antonio, Maj. Omar Bundy

Army of Cuban Pacification, Maj. William Lassiter

1909

Philippine Division, Manila, Col. John L. Chamberlain
Department of Luzon, Manila
Department of the Visayas, Iloilo
Department of Mindanao, Zamboanga

Department of California, San Francisco, Lt. Col. Charles G. Woodward

Department of the Colorado, Denver, Lt. Col. Wilbur E. Wilder

Department of the Columbia, Vancouver Barracks, Vacant

Department of Dakota, St. Paul, Maj. Samuel W. Miller

Department of the East, Governors Island, Lt. Col. William T. Wood

Department of the Gulf, Atlanta, Maj. Frank G. Mauldin*

Department of the Lakes, Chicago, Col. George F. Chase

Department of the Missouri, Omaha, Maj. James B. Erwin

Department of Texas, San Antonio, Maj. Tyree R. Rivers

1910

Philippine Division, Manila, Col. John L. Chamberlain
Department of Luzon, Manila
Department of the Visayas, Iloilo
Department of Mindanao, Zamboanga

Department of California, San Francisco, Maj. George Bell, Jr.

Department of the Colorado, Denver, Lt. Col. Wilbur E. Wilder

Department of the Columbia, Vancouver Barracks, Maj. Frank G. Mauldin

Department of Dakota, St. Paul, Maj. Walter H. Gordon

Department of the East, Governors Island, Col. George F. Chase

Department of the Gulf, Atlanta, Maj. Alfred M. Hunter*

Department of the Lakes, Chicago, Lt. Col. Charles G. Morton

Department of the Missouri, Omaha, Maj. Omar Bundy

Department of Texas, San Antonio, Lt. Col. Francis H. French

1911, 1912

Eastern Division, Governors Island, Col. Stephen C. Mills

Department of the East, Fort Totten
Department of the Gulf, Atlanta

Central Division, Chicago, Lt. Col. James B. Erwin

Department of the Lakes, St. Paul
Department of the Missouri, Omaha
Department of Texas, San Antonio

Western Division, San Francisco, Col. John L. Chamberlain

Department of California, Fort Miley
Department of the Columbia, Vancouver Barracks
Department of Hawaii, Honolulu

Philippine Division, Manila, Lt. Col. Charles G. Morton (1911)
                               Lt. Col. James B. Erwin (1912)

Department of Luzon, Manila
Department of Visayas, Iloilo
Department of Mindanao, Zamboanga

1913

Eastern Department, Governors Island, Col. Stephen C. Mills

1st Division, Governors Island, Lt. Col. William C. Brown*
    1st Brigade, Albany
    2d Brigade, Atlanta
North Atlantic Coast Artillery Corps District, Fort Totten
South Atlantic Coast Artillery Corps District, Charleston

Central Department, Chicago, Col. Henry P. Kingsbury
  3d Cavalry Brigade, Fort Riley
  2d Division, Texas City, Maj. Andre W. Brewster
  4th Brigade, Texas City
  5th Brigade, Galveston
  6th Brigade, Texas City
Southern Department, Fort Sam Houston, Maj. Alonzo Gray
  Cavalry Division, Fort Sam Houston
  1st Cavalry Brigade, Fort Sam Houston
  2d Cavalry Brigade, El Paso
Western Department, San Francisco, Col. John L. Chamberlain
  3d Division, San Francisco
  7th Brigade, Vancouver Barracks
  8th Brigade, Presidio of San Francisco
  Pacific Coast Artillery Corps District, Fort Miley
Philippine Department, Manila, Col. Jacob C. Galbraith*
Hawaiian Department, Honolulu, Lt. Col. John B. McDonald
  1st Hawaiian Brigade

1914

Eastern Department, Col. John L. Chamberlain
  1st Division
Central Department, Col. George K. Hunter
  2d Division, Maj. Ralph A. Van Dieman
Southern Department, Maj. Alonzo Gray
Western Department, Col. David C. Shanks
  3d Division
Philippine Division, Col. Jacob C. Galbraith
Hawaiian Department, Lt. Col. John B. McDonald

1915

Eastern Department, Governors Island, Col. John L. Chamberlain
  1st Division, Governors Island, Lt. Col. Frank L. Dodds
  1st Brigade, Albany

476

North Atlantic Coast Artillery Corps District, Fort Totten
South Atlantic Coast Artillery Corps District, Charleston

Central Department, Chicago, Col. George K. Hunter

3d Cavalry Brigade, Fort Riley
2d Division (Southern Department operational control)

Southern Department, Fort Sam Houston, Maj. John S. Winn

Cavalry Division, Fort Sam Houston
1st Cavalry Brigade, Fort Sam Houston
2d Cavalry Brigade, Douglas
2d Brigade, Laredo
5th Brigade, San Antonio
6th Brigade, Douglas
8th Brigade, Fort Bliss

Western Department, San Francisco, Col. Guy Carleton*

3d Division, San Francisco, Maj. John M. Jenkins
7th Brigade, Vancouver Barracks
Pacific Coast Artillery Corps District, Fort Miley

Philippine Department, Manila, Col. David C. Shanks

Hawaiian Department, Honolulu, Maj. Ernest B. Gose

1st Hawaiian Brigade

1916

Eastern Department, Governors Island, Col. John L. Chamberlain

1st Division, Governors Island, Col. Thomas Q. Donaldson
North Atlantic Coast Artillery Corps District, Fort Totten
South Atlantic Coast Artillery Corps District, Charleston

Central Department, Chicago, Col. George K. Hunter

Southern Department, Fort Sam Houston, Col. Frederick R. Day

Cavalry Division, San Antonio, Lt. Col. John S. Winn
1st Cavalry Brigade, Fort Sam Houston
2d Cavalry Brigade, Columbus
1st Brigade, Eagle Pass
2d Brigade, Laredo
5th Brigade, El Paso
6th Brigade, Douglas
7th Brigade, Douglas
8th Brigade, Columbus

Western Department, San Francisco, Col. John B. McDonald
  3d Division, San Francisco, Lt. Col. Frank M. Caldwell
  Pacific Coast Artillery Corps District, Fort Riley
Philippine Department, Manila, Col. David C. Shanks
Hawaiian Department, Honolulu, Maj. Herbert O. Williams
  1st Hawaiian Brigade

1917

Eastern Department, Governors Island, Col. Thomas Q. Donaldson
  1st Division, Governors Island, Vacant
  Mid-Atlantic Coast Artillery Corps District, Fort Monroe
  Panama Coast Artillery Corps District, Canal Zone
Northeastern Department, Boston, Col. Warren P. Newcomb, Ret.
  North Atlantic Coast Artillery Corps District, Boston
Central Department, Chicago, Col. George K. Hunter
Southeastern Department, Charleston, Maj. Jacob C. Johnson
  South Atlantic Coast Artillery Corps District, Charleston
Southern Department, Fort Sam Houston, Col. George O. Cress
  Cavalry Division, Fort Sam Houston, Lt. Col. John S. Winn
  4th Brigade, Nogales
Western Department, San Francisco, Col. John B. McDonald
  3d Division, Lt. Col. Frank M. Caldwell
  South Pacific Coast Artillery Corps District, Fort Miley
  North Pacific Coast Artillery Corps District, Seattle
Philippine Department, Manila, Col. David C. Shanks
Hawaiian Department, Honolulu, Maj. Herbert O. Williams
  1st Hawaiian Brigade

1918 (less tactical units)

Northeastern Department, Col. Edmund M. Blake
Eastern Department, Col. Frank E. Harris
Southeastern Department, Col. James M. Wheeler

Central Department, Col. Alexander L. Dade
Southern Department, Col. Samuel M. Rutherford
Western Department, Col. Ervin L. Phillips
Philippine Department, Col. Samuel E. Smiley
Hawaiian Department, Maj. Edward C. Wallington

1919 (less tactical units)

Northeastern Department, Col. Paul Hurst
Eastern Department, Col. Frank E. Harris
Southeastern Department, Col. Frederick W. Phisterer
Central Department, Col. Alexander Dade
Southern Department, Col. Lincoln F. Kilbourne
Western Department, Col. Guy Carleton
Philippine Department, Col. James M. Wheeler
Hawaiian Department, Col. Vincent M. Elmore
Panama Department, Col. Harry L. Hawthorne
               Col. Percy M. Kessler (as of June)

1920

First Corps Area, Boston, Col. George Blakely
Second Corps Area, Governors Island, Col. Frank L. Winn
Third Corps Area, Baltimore, Col. Frank E. Harris
Fourth Corps Area, Atlanta, Col. Frederick W. Phisterer
Fifth Corps Area, Indianapolis, Col. Charles H. Bridges
Sixth Corps Area, Chicago, Col. Frank M. Caldwell
Seventh Corps Area, Omaha, Col. Samuel M. Rutherford
Eighth Corps Area, San Antonio, Col. Lincoln F. Kilbourne
Ninth Corps Area, Presidio of San Francisco, Col. Guy Carleton
Philippine Department, Manila, Lt. Col. James M. Wheeler
Hawaiian Department, Honolulu, Lt. Col. Vincent M. Elmore
Panama Department, Quarry Heights, Col. Edmund M. Blake

1921

First Corps Area, Boston, Maj. Edgar S. Miller
Second Corps Area, Governors Island, Col. Tyree R. Rivers
Third Corps Area, Baltimore, Col. Frank E. Harris
Fourth Corps Area, Atlanta, Col. Frederick W. Phisterer
Fifth Corps Area, Indianapolis, Lt. Col. William A. Austin
Sixth Corps Area, Chicago, Col. Samuel M. Rutherford
Seventh Corps Area, Omaha, Col. William T. Johnston
Eighth Corps Area, San Antonio, Col. Lincoln F. Kilbourne
Ninth Corps Area, Presidio of San Francisco, Col. Ervin L. Phillips
Philippine Department, Manila, Col. George Blakely
Hawaiian Department, Honolulu, Lt. Col. Vincent M. Elmore
Panama Department, Quarry Heights, Col. Edmund M. Blake
District of Washington, Washington, D.C., Maj. Walter M. Robinson

1922

First Corps Area, Boston, Col. George D. Moore
Second Corps Area, Governors Island, Col. Tyree R. Rivers
Third Corps Area, Baltimore, Col. Clifton C. Kinney
Fourth Corps Area, Atlanta, Lt. Col. Ernest E. Haskell
Fifth Corps Area, Indianapolis, Col. Truman O. Murphy
Sixth Corps Area, Chicago, Col. Samuel M. Rutherford
Seventh Corps Area, Omaha, Col. William T. Johnston
Eighth Corps Area, San Antonio, Col. Lincoln F. Kilbourne
Ninth Corps Area, Presidio of San Francisco, Col. Ervin L. Phillips
Philippine Department, Manila, Col. George Blakely
Hawaiian Department, Honolulu, Col. Gordon G. Heiner
Panama Department, Quarry Heights, Col. Frank E. Harris
District of Washington, Washington, D.C., Maj. Walter M. Robinson

1923

First Corps Area, Boston, Col. George D. Moore
Second Corps Area, Governors Island, Col. William C. Rivers

Third Corps Area, Baltimore, Col. Alexander T. Ovenshine
Fourth Corps Area, Atlanta, Lt. Col. Ernest E. Haskell
Fifth Corps Area, Columbus, Col. Truman O. Murphy
Sixth Corps Area, Chicago, Col. Samuel M. Rutherford
Seventh Corps Area, Omaha, Lt. Col. George E. Goodrich
Eighth Corps Area, San Antonio, Col. Ernest D. Scott
Ninth Corps Area, Presidio of San Francisco, Col. Walter C. Short
Philippine Department, Manila, Col. George Blakely
Hawaiian Department, Honolulu, Col. William T. Johnston
Panama Department, Quarry Heights, Col. Frank E. Harris
District of Washington, Washington, D.C., Maj. Walter M. Robinson

1924

First Corps Area, Boston, Col. George D. Moore
Second Corps Area, Governors Island, Col. William C. Rivers
Third Corps Area, Baltimore, Col. Alexander T. Ovenshine
Fourth Corps Area, Atlanta, Col. Henry S. Wagner
Fifth Corps Area, Columbus, Col. Truman O. Murphy
Sixth Corps Area, Chicago, Col. Howard R. Hickok
Seventh Corps Area, Omaha, Lt. Col. Fred T. Austin
Eighth Corps Area, San Antonio, Col. Ernest D. Scott
Ninth Corps Area, Presidio of San Francisco, Col. Walter C. Short
Philippine Department, Manila, Col. Casper H. Conrad
Hawaiian Department, Honolulu, Col. William T. Johnston
Panama Department, Quarry Heights, Col. Frank E. Harris
District of Washington, Washington, D.C., Maj. Robert C. Goetz

1925

First Corps Area, Boston, Col. George D. Moore
Second Corps Area, Governors Island, Col. William C. Rivers
Third Corps Area, Baltimore, Lt. Col. Beverly F. Browne
Fourth Corps Area, Atlanta, Col. Henry S. Wagner

Fifth Corps Area, Columbus, Col. James M. Graham

Sixth Corps Area, Chicago, Col. Howard R. Hickok

Seventh Corps Area, Omaha, Col. Fred T. Austin

Eighth Corps Area, San Antonio, Col. Ernest D. Scott

Ninth Corps Area, Presidio of San Francisco, Lt. Col. Royden E. Beebe

Philippine Department, Manila, Col. Casper H. Conrad

Hawaiian Department, Honolulu, Col. Walter C. Short

Panama Department, Quarry Heights, Col. Jacob C. Johnson

District of Washington, Washington, D.C., Maj. Robert C. Goetz

1926

First Corps Area, Boston, Maj. Charles H. Patterson

Second Corps Area, Governors Island, Col. William C. Rivers

Third Corps Area, Baltimore, Lt. Col. Beverly F. Browne

Fourth Corps Area, Atlanta, Col. Henry S. Wagner

Fifth Corps Area, Columbus, Col. James M. Graham

Sixth Corps Area, Chicago, Col. Charles E. Stodter

Seventh Corps Area, Omaha, Lt. Col. William A. Austin

Eighth Corps Area, San Antonio, Col. Ernest D. Scott

Ninth Corps Area, Presidio of San Francisco, Col. William R. Smedberg

Philippine Department, Manila, Col. Fred T. Austin

Hawaiian Department, Honolulu, Col. Walter C. Short

Panama Department, Quarry Heights, Col. Jacob C. Johnson

District of Washington, Washington, D.C., Maj. Robert C. Goetz

1927

First Corps Area, Boston, Lt. Col. Charles H. Patterson

Second Corps Area, Governors Island, Col. Robert C. Humber

Third Corps Area, Baltimore, Lt. Col. Beverly F. Browne

Fourth Corps Area, Atlanta, Col. Henry S. Wagner

Fifth Corps Area, Columbus, Lt. Col. Raymond W. Briggs

Sixth Corps Area, Chicago, Col. Francis Le J. Parker
Seventh Corps Area, Omaha, Lt. Col. William A. Austin
Eighth Corps Area, San Antonio, Col. Charles B. Stone
Ninth Corps Area, Presidio of San Francisco, Col. William R. Smedberg
Philippine Department, Manila, Col. Fred T. Austin
Hawaiian Department, Honolulu, Col. Dana T. Merrill
Panama Department, Quarry Heights, Col. Charles E. Stodter
District of Washington, Washington, D.C., Maj. Robert C. Goetz

1928

First Corps Area, Boston, Col. Charles A. Romeyn
Second Corps Area, Governors Island, Col. Robert C. Humber
Third Corps Area, Baltimore, Lt. Col. Charles C. Burt
Fourth Corps Area, Atlanta, Col. Henry S. Wagner
Fifth Corps Area, Columbus, Col. Alexander T. Ovenshine
Sixth Corps Area, Chicago, Lt. Col. Nelson E. Margetts
Seventh Corps Area, Omaha, Lt. Col. William A. Austin
Eighth Corps Area, San Antonio, Col. Charles B. Stone
Ninth Corps Area, Presidio of San Francisco, Col. William R. Smedberg
Philippine Department, Manila, Lt. Col. Charles H. Patterson
Hawaiian Department, Honolulu, Col. Dana T. Merrill
Panama Department, Quarry Heights, Col. Charles E. Stodter

1929

First Corps Area, Boston, Col. Charles A. Romeyn
Second Corps Area, Governors Island, Col. Robert C. Humber
Third Corps Area, Baltimore, Lt. Col. Charles C. Burt
Fourth Corps Area, Atlanta, Col. Henry S. Wagner
Fifth Corps Area, Columbus, Col. Alexander T. Ovenshine
Sixth Corps Area, Chicago, Lt. Col. Nelson E. Margetts
Seventh Corps Area, Omaha, Lt. Col. William A. Austin
Eighth Corps Area, San Antonio, Col. Charles B. Stone
Ninth Corps Area, Presidio of San Francisco, Col. Herbert J. Brees

Philippine Department, Manila, Lt. Col. Charles H. Patterson

Hawaiian Department, Honolulu, Col. Dana T. Merrill

Panama Department, Quarry Heights, Col. Charles E. Stodter

1930

First Corps Area, Boston, Col. Charles A. Romeyn

Second Corps Area, Governors Island, Col. Robert C. Humber

Third Corps Area, Baltimore, Lt. Col. Albert B. Kaempfer

Fourth Corps Area, Atlanta, Col. Christian A. Bach

Fifth Corps Area, Columbus, Col. Alexander T. Ovenshine

Sixth Corps Area, Chicago, Col. William H. Burt

Seventh Corps Area, Omaha, Col. Harris Pendelton

Eighth Corps Area, San Antonio, Col. Charles B. Stone

Ninth Corps Area, Presidio of San Francisco, Col. Samuel T. Mackall

Philippine Department, Manila, Lt. Col. John M. Dunn

Hawaiian Department, Honolulu, Lt. Col. Jay L. Benedict

Panama Department, Quarry Heights, Maj. Edgar H. Thompson

1931

First Corps Area, Boston, Lt. Col. Lucian B. Moody

Second Corps Area, Governors Island, Col. Ernest D. Peek

Third Corps Area, Baltimore, Lt. Col. Albert B. Kaempfer

Fourth Corps Area, Atlanta, Col. Christian A. Bach

Fifth Corps Area, Columbus, Col. William E. Hunt

Sixth Corps Area, Chicago, Lt. Col. Charles H. Thuis

Seventh Corps Area, Omaha, Col. Harris Pendleton

Eighth Corps Area, San Antonio, Col. George D. Arrowsmith

Ninth Corps Area, Presidio of San Francisco, Lt. Col. Samuel T. Mackall

Philippine Department, Manila, Maj. Herman Erlenkotter

Hawaiian Department, Honolulu, Lt. Col. Jay L. Benedict

Panama Department, Quarry Heights, Col. Raymond W. Briggs

1932

First Corps Area, Boston, Lt. Col. Lucian B. Moody
Second Corps Area, Governors Island, Col. Ernest D. Peek
Third Corps Area, Baltimore, Col. Raymond W. Briggs
Fourth Corps Area, Atlanta, Col. Christian A. Bach
Fifth Corps Area, Columbus, Col. William E. Hunt
Sixth Corps Area, Chicago, Lt. Col. Charles H. Thuis
Seventh Corps Area, Omaha, Col. Harris Pendleton
Eighth Corps Area, San Antonio, Col. George D. Arrowsmith
Ninth Corps Area, Presidio of San Francisco, Lt. Col. Samuel T. Mackall
Philippine Department, Manila, Maj. Kenneth S. Perkins
Hawaiian Department, Honolulu, Lt. Col. Jay L. Benedict
Panama Department, Quarry Heights, Lt. Col. Edmund A. Buchanan

1933

First Corps Area, Boston, Lt. Col. Lucian B. Moody
Second Corps Area, Governors Island, Col. Ernest D. Peek
Third Corps Area, Baltimore, Col. William W. Taylor
Fourth Corps Area, Atlanta, Col. Christian A. Bach
Fifth Corps Area, Columbus, Col. William E. Hunt
Sixth Corps Area, Chicago, Maj. Edward J. Dwan
Seventh Corps Area, Omaha, Col. Harris Pendleton
Eighth Corps Area, San Antonio, Col. George D. Arrowsmith
Ninth Corps Area, Presidio of San Francisco, Col. Ben Lear
Philippine Department, Manila, Col. Henry C. Merriam
Hawaiian Department, Honolulu, Lt. Col. Jay L. Benedict
Panama Department, Quarry Heights, Col. Edmund A. Buchanan

1934

First Corps Area, Boston, Lt. Col. Lucian B. Moody
Second Corps Area, Governors Island, Col. Marcellus G. Spinks

Third Corps Area, Baltimore, Col. William W. Taylor
Fourth Corps Area, Atlanta, Maj. Harlan L. Mumma
Fifth Corps Area, Columbus, Col. William E. Hunt
Sixth Corps Area, Chicago, Maj. Edward J. Dwan
Seventh Corps Area, Omaha, Col. Harris Pendleton
Eighth Corps Area, San Antonio, Col. George D. Arrowsmith
Ninth Corps Area, Presidio of San Francisco, Col. Harry A. Wells
Philippine Department, Manila, Col. Henry C. Merriam
Hawaiian Department, Honolulu, Lt. Col. George R. Allin
Panama Department, Quarry Heights, Maj. Reuben N. Perley

1935

First Corps Area, Boston, Lt. Col. Frank C. Mahin
Second Corps Area, Governors Island, Col. Marcellus G. Spinks
Third Corps Area, Baltimore, Col. William W. Taylor
Fourth Corps Area, Atlanta, Col. Charles H. Patterson
Fifth Corps Area, Columbus, Col. William E. Hunt
Sixth Corps Area, Chicago, Col. William S. Wood
Seventh Corps Area, Omaha, Col. Harris Pendleton
Eighth Corps Area, San Antonio, Col. George D. Arrowsmith
Ninth Corps Area, Presidio of San Francisco, Col. Harry A. Wells
Philippine Department, Manila, Maj. Edward J. Dwan
Hawaiian Department, Honolulu, Col. George R. Allin
Panama Department, Quarry Heights, Col. Franc Lecocq

1936

First Corps Area, Boston, Lt. Col. Frank C. Mahin
Second Corps Area, Governors Island, Col. Marcellus G. Spinks
Third Corps Area, Baltimore, Col. William W. Taylor
Fourth Corps Area, Atlanta, Col. Charles H. Patterson
Fifth Corps Area, Columbus, Col. William E. Hunt
Sixth Corps Area, Chicago, Col. William S. Wood

Seventh Corps Area, Omaha, Lt. Col. Leon M. Logan
Eighth Corps Area, San Antonio, Col. George D. Arrowsmith
Ninth Corps Area, Presidio of San Francisco, Col. Harry A. Wells
Philippine Department, Manila, Col. Cassius M. Dowell
Hawaiian Department, Honolulu, Col. William W. McCammon
Panama Department, Quarry Heights, Col. Franc Lecocq

1937

First Corps Area, Boston, Col. William E. Hunt
Second Corps Area, Governors Island, Col. Marcellus G. Spinks
Third Corps Area, Baltimore, Col. William W. Taylor
Fourth Corps Area, Atlanta, Col. Charles H. Patterson
Fifth Corps Area, Columbus, Col. Harry A. Wells
Sixth Corps Area, Chicago, Lt. Col. Leon M. Logan
Seventh Corps Area, Omaha, Col. William S. Wood
Eighth Corps Area, San Antonio, Col. Charles P. George
Ninth Corps Area, Presidio of San Francisco, Col. James M.
    Graham
Philippine Department, Manila, Col. Cassius M. Dowell
Hawaiian Department, Honolulu, Col. William W. McCammon
Panama Department, Quarry Heights, Col. William R. Henry

1938

First Corps Area, Boston, Col. William E. Hunt
Second Corps Area, Governors Island, Col. Troup Miller
Third Corps Area, Baltimore, Col. Franc Lecocq
Fourth Corps Area, Atlanta, Col. Charles H. Patterson
Fifth Corps Area, Columbus, Lt. Col. Lathe B. Row
Sixth Corps Area, Chicago, Lt. Col. Leon M. Logan
Seventh Corps Area, Omaha, Col. William S. Wood
Eighth Corps Area, San Antonio, Col. William F. Robinson
Ninth Corps Area, Presidio of San Francisco, Col. James M. Graham

Philippine Department, Manila, Lt. Col. Oswald H. Saunders
Hawaiian Department, Honolulu, Col. William W. Hicks
Panama Department, Quarry Heights, Col. William R. Henry

1939

First Corps Area, Boston, Col. William W. Gordon
Second Corps Area, Governors Island, Col. Troup Miller
Third Corps Area, Baltimore, Col. Leo J. Ahern
Fourth Corps Area, Atlanta, Col. Charles H. Patterson
Fifth Corps Area, Columbus, Col. John G. Tyndall
Sixth Corps Area, Chicago, Col. Henry C. Merriam
Seventh Corps Area, Omaha, Col. John E. Mort
Eighth Corps Area, San Antonio, Col. William F. Robinson
Ninth Corps Area, Presidio of San Francisco, Col. James M. Graham
Philippine Department, Manila, Lt. Col. Benjamin C. Lockwood
Hawaiian Department, Honolulu, Col. William W. Hicks
Panama Department, Quarry Heights, Col. William R. Henry
Puerto Rican Department, San Juan, Col. Clyde R. Abraham

1940

First Corps Area, Boston, Col. Martyn H. Shute
Second Corps Area, Governors Island, Lt. Col. Frank B. Jordan
Third Corps Area, Baltimore, Col. Harry H. Pritchett
Fourth Corps Area, Atlanta, Col. Charles H. Patterson
Fifth Corps Area, Columbus, Col. John G. Tyndall
Sixth Corps Area, Chicago, Lt. Col. John W. Nicholson
Seventh Corps Area, Omaha, Lt. Col. John E. Mort
Eighth Corps Area, San Antonio, Col. William F. Robinson
Ninth Corps Area, Presidio of San Francisco, Col. John D. Reardon
Philippine Department, Manila, Col. Benjamin C. Lockwood
Hawaiian Department, Honolulu, Col. William W. Hicks
Panama Department, Quarry Heights, Col. William C. Christy

Roster of Inspectors, Headquarters, AEF and AFIG

Name	Command	Dates of Assignment
Agnew, Ernest H., Lt. Col.	AEF	20 Feb 18–2 Mar 19
Baer, Joseph A., Col.	AEF	29 Jul 18–Jun 19
Beeuwkes, Henry, Col., MC	AEF	18 Jun 18–31 May 19
Biddle, David H., Col.	AEF	5 Sep 18–31 Dec 18
Bradley, John J., Brig. Gen.	AEF	9 Feb 19–5 Jun 19
Brewster, Andre W., Maj. Gen.	AEF	26 May 17–Jun 19
Brewster, Daniel B., Capt., USMC	AEF	22 Nov 18–5 Apr 19
Brown, Laurence E., Capt.	AEF	22 Mar 19–20 May 19
Bull, Edgar L. Capt.	AEF	13 Mar 19 30 May 19
Burleson, Richard C., Col.	AEF	25 Mar 19–3 Jun 19
Carson, Clifford C., Col.	AEF	23 Feb 19–26 May 19
Chamberlin, Harry D., Lt. Col.	AEF	11 Apr 19–28 May 19
Clark, Robert S., Maj.	AEF	26 May 17–21 Nov 18
Conner, Fox, Maj.	AEF	26 May 17–10 Nov 17
Degen, John A., Lt. Col.	AEF	23 Jan 19–24 Feb 19
Fleet, Henry W., Lt. Col.	AEF	7 Apr 19–10 Apr 19
Grace, Joseph J., Col.	AEF	8 Apr 19–26 May 19
Hanley, Joseph L., Maj.	AEF	18 Mar 19–22 May 19
Haskell, Ernest E., Col.	AEF	23 Apr 19–31 May 19
Hay, William H., Col.	AFIG	19 Aug 20–9 May 21
Henry, T. Charleton, Maj.	AEF	19 Nov 18–29 Jan 19
Kinnison, Henry L., Col.	AEF	20 Mar 19–20 May 19

Name	Command	Dates of Assignment
Lewis, David, Maj.	AEF	19 Sep 18–30 Oct 18
McBride, Robert B., Col.	AEF	27 Sep 18–31 Oct 18
McDonald, Robert C., Col., MC	AEF	2 Jan 19–Jun 19
McIlroy, James G., Lt. Col.	AEF	28 Sep 18–20 May 19
McKenny, Richard I., Lt. Col.	AEF	9 Sep 18–5 Nov 18
Magruder, Lloyd B., Maj.	AFIG	3 Sep 19–10 Jan 23
Martin, Clarence A., Maj.	AEF	8 Apr 19–Jun 19
Matthews, Harry T., Col.	AEF	11 Feb 18–20 May 19
Millard, Charles M., Maj.	AEF	23 Sep 18–10 Mar 19
Moise, Leicester R., Lt.	AEF	8 Mar 19–15 May 19
Moore, George D., Col.	AEF	28 Mar 18–3 Apr 18
Morris, William H., Jr., Lt. Col.	AEF	16 Jan 19–15 Mar 19
Olmstead, Dawson, Maj.	AEF	26 Jan 18–30 Jun 18
Ovenshine, Alexander T., Col.	AEF	19 Apr 18–3 Sep 18 22 May 19–14 Jun 19
Parkinson, John L., Maj.	AFIG	14 Nov 19–19 May 22
Peck, Robert G., Col.	AFIG	16 Nov 18–12 Aug 19
Pendleton, Harris, Jr., Col.	AEF	28 Jan 19–21 May 19
Power, Henry C., Lt.	AEF	1 Mar 19–8 Mar 19
Read, Alvan C., Col.	AEF AFIG	20 Sep 18–12 Nov 18 13 Nov 18–19 Jan 20
Rice, Charles H., Lt. Col.	AFIG	13 Nov 18–27 Aug 19
Santschi, Eugene, Jr., Maj.	AFIG	28 Jan 22–19 May 22
Schudt, Charles O., Lt. Col.	AEF	20 Feb 19–31 May 19
Scott, Edgar, Lt.	AEF	20 Feb 18–20 Oct 18
Spinks, Marcellus G., Brig. Gen.	AEF	30 Jun 18–30 Apr 19
Stockwell, Fred E., Capt.	AEF	22 Mar 19–21 May 19
Streater, Wallace A., Maj.	AEF AFIG	11 Nov 17–Jun 19 12 Jan 20–20 Nov 20
Taggart, Matthew H., Lt. Col.	AEF	5 Jan 19–14 Mar 19
Taulbee, Edgar W., Lt. Col.	AEF	26 Feb 19–9 Apr 19
Taylor, Theodore B., Col.	AEF	27 Mar 19–19 May 19

Name	Command	Dates of Assignment
Thomas, Charles W., Jr., Lt. Col.	AEF	3 Sep 18–30 Jan 19
Tourtellotte, Neal E., Capt.	AEF	8 Mar 19–22 May 19
Van Natter, Francis M., Capt.	AEF	11 Feb 19–22 May 19
Van Schaick, Louis J., Col.	AFIG	24 Nov 19–19 Jul 20
Webb, Arthur L., Maj.	AEF	11 Nov 17–Jun 19
Wimberly, Albert C., Maj.	AEF	28 Feb 19–3 Mar 19

Biographical Notes on Significant Senior Inspectors

These biographical notes on individuals who served mostly as general officers in the Inspector General's Department, 1903–1939, are arranged alphabetically. The information in them goes beyond the scope of the story of the department but amplifies the record, providing further insight into the character and breadth of the personalities. Often, other aspects of their careers have been of greater significance or interest, and any summary of their lives given in response to an inquiry about them would need their inclusion. The companion volume, *The Inspectors General of the United States Army, 1777–1903*, contains biographical notes on other key members of the inspectorate.

BRADLEY, John J. (1869–1948)

The son of a lawyer, Bradley was born in Cook County, Illinois, on 20 April 1869. Graduating from the U.S. Military Academy in June 1891, he joined the 14th Infantry as a second lieutenant at Vancouver Barracks, Washington. Promoted to first lieutenant in April 1898, he deployed with his unit to the Philippines in June but soon was detached to be a temporary Quartermaster captain. After serving as a brigade quartermaster and sea transport supervisor, he saw action in January 1900 as an acting aide-de-camp to Brig. Gen. William A. Kobbe during operations in the southern Philippines, receiving the Purple Heart and Silver Star for his role. He then served as aide-de-camp to Maj. Gen. Elwell S. Otis and was promoted to captain in December 1900. Returning to the United States with his regiment in January 1901, he was stationed at various posts in the Department of the Lakes. In January 1903 Bradley returned to the Philippines, where he performed routine company duties on the island of Samar until March 1904.

That month Bradley was detailed to the Judge Advocate General's Department, with duty first at the Presidio of San Francisco and then at Vancouver Barracks. Concurrently, he began law studies leading to his 1908 admission to the Washington State Bar. Returning to the 14th Infantry in June 1905 as the regimental quartermaster, Bradley participated in the 1906 earthquake relief in San Francisco and the first maneuvers at American Lake, now Fort Lewis. From November 1906 to June 1910 he served as the judge advocate of the Department of the Columbia. His duty performance established him as fully knowledgeable in all aspects of supply and procurement and also as a man of sterling character and ability.

From 1911 to 1913 Bradley attended the Army School of the Line and the Staff College, both at Fort Leavenworth, Kansas. A major since May 1912, he was assigned to the 30th Infantry upon graduation in June 1913 and served with that regiment first in Alaska and on the Pacific coast and then, after March 1914, in the Canal Zone, where he was a member of the Canal Defense Board. As a newly promoted temporary lieutenant colonel, Bradley returned to the United States in June 1917, serving briefly as an inspector-instructor to the Maryland National Guard. He was promoted to temporary colonel in August, at which time he became the chief of the Training and Instruction Branch of the War Plans Division. There Bradley worked for nearly a year, receiving the Distinguished Service Medal "for initiating and standardizing the training and instruction of the Army during its formative period."

In June 1918 Bradley was promoted to temporary brigadier general and assigned to command a brigade in Maj. Gen. Eli A. Helmick's 8th Division, then training at Camp Fremont, California. Shortly thereafter, he left that unit to command a brigade of the 82d Division in France from mid-November until February 1919, when he was detailed to the American Expeditionary Forces IG. Because of his legal background, he was selected to head the massive morale support investigation then under way. He returned to the infantry and his permanent grade of lieutenant colonel in October 1919. After a brief stint at Camp Devens, Massachusetts, he was detailed to the New York Port of Entry, serving first as the maritime survey officer and then as the chief of transportation. Promoted to colonel in January 1920, Bradley next served as the chief of staff of the 77th Division from July 1921 to July 1923 and then commanded the 18th Infantry at Fort Slocum, New York, until his retirement on 28 December 1927. He entered the practice of law fully thereafter, specializing in foreign trade issues as well as teaching and writing. Active in veterans relief projects in his later years, General Bradley died in Detroit, Michigan, on 21 May 1948.

John J. Bradley, Cullum Files, U.S. Military Academy Archives; Association of Graduates, USMA, *Assembly*, Apr 49, pp. 8–10.

BRECKINRIDGE, Joseph C. (1842–1920)

The son of a Presbyterian minister prominent in the early Republican party, Breckinridge was born in Baltimore, Maryland, on 14 January 1842. He was raised on the family estate in Kentucky and attended Centre College and the University of Virginia before the Civil War. Although a nephew of Confederate general and former vice-president John C. Breckinridge, he entered the U.S Army in 1861 as a Kentucky volunteer for the Union. The young officer later received a Regular Army commission as a second lieutenant in the 2d Artillery as a result of gallantry at the Battle of Mill Springs. A first lieutenant since August 1863, he saw action in most of the battles fought in the Western theater before his capture near Atlanta in July 1864. After the war he served with his regiment on the Pacific coast and at various frontier stations, rising to captain in June 1874. In January 1881 he was promoted to major and assigned to the Inspector General's Department. Breckinridge soon gained a reputation as an untiring traveler, visiting every post in the West and rising through the ranks until appointed Brigadier General, Inspector General of the Army, on 30 January 1889. He continued his travels in the States and also made a special European tour, studying various armies.

During the War with Spain Breckinridge requested field duty. Appointed a major general in the volunteers, he accompanied Maj. Gen. (Vol.) William R. Shafter's V Corps to Santiago as an observer, displaying his usual bravery and receiving a citation. He later commanded the I Corps at Camp Thomas, Georgia, preparing it for a projected attack on Havana. At war's end he displayed considerable logistical skill in dispersing his large force to avoid a potential epidemic.

In 1899, reverting to his permanent grade of brigadier general, Breckinridge continued his habit of visiting units wherever they were stationed, thoroughly viewing those in Cuba, Puerto Rico, the Philippines, and even China and Alaska. At the same time, he kept close tabs on administrative developments in the Army and Congress that affected his department. Conservative, his focus was largely on the improvement of unit-level operations and specific items of individual equipment. Considered an effective defender of the functions of his bureau as shown by its survival through the Root reforms, Breckinridge strongly opposed plans to eliminate the inspectorate, a stand that ultimately precluded his continuation of service into the new era. Consequently, he was promoted to major general and retired on 11 April 1903. He lived in Washington, D.C., thereafter and was active in veterans and Presbyterian church affairs until his death on 18 August 1920.

"Recent Deaths: Joseph Cabell Breckinridge," *Army and Navy Journal*, 28 Aug 20, p. 1578; *National Cyclopedia of American Biography*, vol. 9, and *Who Was Who in America*, vol. 1, s.v. "Breckinridge, Joseph Cabell."

BREWSTER, Andre W. (1862–1942)

The son of a lawyer, Brewster was born in Hoboken, New Jersey, on 9 December 1862. He studied law at the University of Pennsylvania and was a member of the Pennsylvania and District of Columbia bars. He had been practicing law for three years when he accepted a direct commission as a second lieutenant in the 10th Infantry on 7 February 1885. After serving with the 10th at various stations in the West, he was promoted to first lieutenant in December 1891 and transferred to the 22d Infantry and subsequently to the 9th Infantry at Madison Barracks, New York. Commanding Company B when the 9th left for Florida in April 1898 and for Cuba in June, Brewster was cited for gallantry at San Juan Hill and saw action at Santiago, from where he was medically evacuated in August. He returned to duty in February 1899, received his promotion to captain in March, and served as a transport quartermaster until deploying with his regiment to the Philippines in October. Here he again was cited for his bravery in the battles at Panique and Tarlac.

The 1st Battalion, 9th Infantry, was part of the international force sent to China in June 1900 to relieve the Peking legations under siege by the Boxers. When the battalion commander, Lt. Col. Emerson H. Liscom, was killed early in the fighting at Tientsin, 13 July, Brewster assumed command and at one point rescued two of his men who were lying wounded in a canal, exposed to heavy fire. For his courage and inspiring conduct he was awarded the Medal of Honor, with one of his commanders stating that he was "one of the most competent, efficient and daring officers in the army . . . [who] always achieves success where success is possible." Brewster remained in China until 1905, first as a chief of police in Peking and then as commander of the legation guard. In 1903 he was assigned the additional duty of attache to China and Japan.

Brewster returned with Company B, 9th Infantry, in September 1905 to Fort Porter, New York, moving to Fort Wayne, Michigan, in May 1906. He spent most of his time over the next year on detail as an inspector-instructor to the Kentucky National Guard. His department commander, Brig. Gen. William H. Carter, singled him out as being particularly well suited to be an inspector general. Newly promoted to major, Brewster attended the Army War College from June 1907 to June 1908 and thereafter commanded a battalion of the 19th Infantry at Fort McKenzie, Wyoming, until detailed to the Inspector General's Department on 27 February 1909. He served in the Office of the Inspector General until September 1912, when he was transferred as an assistant inspector to the Department of the Lakes. He spent nearly all of 1913 in Texas as the 2d Division IG and then completed a six-month tour as executive officer of the Puerto Rico Regiment. However, in June 1914 Brewster, now a lieutenant colonel, was recalled to the Inspector General's Department for a second detail. After serving as the Eastern Department inspector until January 1915, he returned to the Office of the Inspector General to serve as Brig. Gen. Ernest A. Garlington's principal assistant.

In May 1917 General John J. Pershing selected Brewster, a temporary colonel, to be the IG of the American Expeditionary Forces in France, a role in which Garlington considered him "well equipped professionally to get the best there was from his men." Brewster held this position until early 1922, rising to the grade of major general. His reassignment to command of the First Corps Area in Boston closed the active books of the AEF. He retired on 9 December 1925 and remained in Boston, where he practiced law until his death on 20 March 1942. He was, in Garlington's words, an "excellent officer and high minded gentleman." Brewster also was a hard-driving, thorough professional, perfect in his role as the Iron Commander's eyes and ears.

File 5728 ACP 1884, Box 941, Record Group 94, National Archives and Records Administration, Washington, D.C.; Fred R. Brown, *History of the Ninth U.S. Infantry, 1799–1909* (Chicago: R. R. Donnelley and Sons Co., 1909); U.S. Congress, Senate, Committee on Veterans Affairs, *Medal of Honor Recipients, 1863–1978*, 96th Cong., 1st Sess., 1979.

DRUM, Hugh A. (1879–1951)

The son of a Civil war veteran and career officer, Drum was born at Fort Brady, Michigan, on 19 September 1879. He grew up living on various military posts and early set his sights on a military career of his own. He was commissioned a second lieutenant while a nineteen-year-old student at Boston College by a special act of President William McKinley in recognition of the death of his father, Capt. John Drum, 10th Infantry, who was killed at the battle of San Juan Hill in 1898. Soon afterward, he deployed with his regiment, the 12th Infantry, to the Philippines, where he experienced over four years of hard active service during the height of the Insurrection and achieved his promotions to first lieutenant and captain. He first met Capt. John J. Pershing there during the fighting at Lake Lanao. In the course of his campaigning Drum developed a lifelong liking and respect for enlisted soldiers, which became a consistent feature of his leadership and policies. After two years as a general's aide in Colorado, he was reassigned to the 23d Infantry in New York State. There, as an additional duty, he frequently inspected the training activities of the National Guards of New York and Massachusetts, gaining an appreciation for issues involving civilian volunteers. Following a third tour in the Philippines, he attended the Army School of the Line (1910) and the Staff College (1911), both at Fort Leavenworth, Kansas, which he completed with distinction.

While at Fort Leavenworth, the Army school system was the focus of intense scrutiny. The Inspector General himself, Brig. Gen. Ernest A. Garlington, criticized the Army School of the Line as being excessively competitive, which placed tremendous pressure on students to beat out their colleagues in class rankings. Drum remembered his experience at the school as the toughest but most important of his life. What he had learned was to assure him a significant place in the great events about to unfold. He was selected after graduation to serve on General Frederick Funston's staff on the Mexican border and later on the expedition to Vera Cruz. Funston had specifically requested Drum because of his growing reputation as an untiring worker and skilled staff planner. After the Vera Cruz expedition returned to the United States, Drum remained on Funston's staff at Fort Sam Houston. When the Funston died unexpectedly, the new commander, Brig. Gen. John J. Pershing, retained Drum as his chief planner.

In this position Drum worked out the plans for the defense of the Rio Grande frontier and the mobilization and concentration of the National Guard during the Pancho Villa crisis of 1916. Pershing was so impressed by Drum's performance that he selected him to be a member of the advance party that went with him to France after the United States declared war on Germany in April 1917. There, in less than two years, Drum rose from captain to brigadier general, finishing the war as the First Army's chief of staff. His accomplishments were responsible for much of the success of the American forces. He first drafted the disembarkation plans and selected the ports to be used by the American Expeditionary Forces. Thereafter, he headed a group that drew up the training programs for the officers and men arriving in Europe. Concurrently, Drum developed the U.S. strategy for deployment on the Western Front. He wrote the rules of engagement for the United States forces while also participating on several of Maj. Gen. Andre Brewster's inspection teams evaluating combat divisions.

While General Pershing dealt with his allied counterparts, Drum supervised the activation of the First Army. He had the primary role in both the planning for and the execution of the St. Mihiel and Argonne offensives. His handling of the complexities of the shift from one axis of advance to the other was instrumental in assuring effective American operations. Drum continued to play a major role when Maj. Gen. Hunter Liggett took over the First Army from Pershing's nominal command, successfully unraveling the numerous serious logistical problems encountered in the prolonged Argonne operations. At war's end Pershing rated Drum as being in the top 9 percent of all the generals who had served in the AEF.

Drum returned to the United States to spend three years as the director of training for the School of the Line at Fort Leavenworth. He was credited with being the major postwar influence on the curriculum and programs of the school, where he imposed the doctrine of open warfare that he and Pershing had adopted in France. He further expanded the philosophy of the school to embrace the concept of preparing officers for command as well as staff. After rejuvenating the staff colleges in 1922, Drum spent the last half of the year inspecting elements of the New York National Guard. Then came some schooling at Fort Monroe, Virginia, after which Drum was assigned to the War Department G–3. There he spent most of his time embroiled in the Col. William ("Billy") Mitchell affair and related investigations of the organizational relationships of the Army Air Corps. Drum was a strong advocate of Army control of air power, and he successfully persuaded Congress and the War Department not to create a separate air force. He then spent four years in the 1st Division stationed in New York City, ultimately rising to command it in 1929. On 12 January 1930 he was appointed Major General, The Inspector General of the Army, replacing Maj. Gen. William C. Rivers.

After General Drum left the Inspector General's Department, he commanded the Fifth Corps Area at Fort Hayes, Ohio, until he was recalled to Washington in February 1933 to serve as Chief of Staff General Douglas MacArthur's deputy. Again, the bulk of his time was spent on Army aviation matters, leading to the establishment of a separate air force general headquarters. On two occasions Drum was overlooked for the position of Chief of Staff, being beaten out by Malin Craig and then George C. Marshall. He was bitterly disappointed but continued to serve, first as the commander of the Hawaiian Division and then of the First Army in the early days of World War II. He retired from the Army in October 1943, shortly thereafter becoming the president of the Empire State Corporation. He was also appointed commander of the New York State Guard by Governor Thomas E. Dewey in 1944, a position he held until 1948. Drum died in his office in the Empire State Building on 3 October 1951.

Elliot L. Johnson, "The Military Experiences of General Hugh A. Drum From 1898–1918" (Ph.D. diss., University of Wisconsin-Madison, 1975); *Dictionary of American Biography*, Supp. 5, s.v. "Drum, Hugh Aloysius;" *Current Biography: Who's News and Why, 1941*, s.v. "Drum, Hugh Aloysius"; "General Hugh A. Drum Dies at Desk at 72," *New York Times*, 4 Oct 51, pp. 1, 33.

HELMICK, Eli A. (1863–1945)

Born near Terre Haute, Indiana, on 27 September 1863, Helmick migrated with his family by covered wagon in 1869 to southeastern Kansas, where his father farmed and served as the local doctor. In 1884 he graduated from the Kansas State Agricultural College in Manhattan, having performed so well as a member of the school's cadet corps that he was encouraged to apply to the U.S. Military Academy. Accepted, he entered West Point in August. While there, he began to form some of his ideas on leadership, mindful of the practices he did not approve of in the cadet corps. At graduation in 1888 he was commissioned a second lieutenant and joined the 4th Infantry at Fort Spokane, Washington, serving until mid-1893 in various capacities, to include commander of the Indian Scout Company. For the last six months of 1893 he served as the security officer at the World's Columbian Exposition in Chicago. He later said the need to handle large crowds with a few men introduced him to another style of leadership and persuasion, which added to his own growing views of how to manage people.

For several years he had an approved application for college duty on file. He had hoped to return to Kansas State but instead was sent to Hillsdale College in Michigan. He bumped the other contender for that duty assignment, Capt. George L. Brown. This must have influenced

Brown because, as Helmick's commander in the Philippines, he wrote the only critical report on his duty performance contained in his file. While this was going on, Helmick was transferred to the 10th Infantry, with which he was to serve for many years. He did a good job with the cadet corps at Hillsdale, consistently receiving praise from inspectors on their annual visits. However, the school was Baptist in its affiliation and largely pacifist in its attitude. In May 1896 Helmick, a first lieutenant since the preceding December, requested that he be relieved and that the military department be discontinued due to a lack of institution interest and support, with which the Department of the Lakes IG, Lt. Col. Peter D. Vroom, concurred. The military unit was closed on the Hillsdale campus, and Helmick was reassigned to the 10th Infantry at Fort Reno, Oklahoma Territory.

Working with the soldiers of the 10th Infantry further expanded his views on proper leadership. He later said it was there that he learned to appreciate the enlisted man's viewpoint, without which "it is not possible to lead or command him with the fullest success." His theories were put to the test when the regiment left Fort Reno for Cuba on 20 April 1898. While en route to Tampa, Florida, the port of embarkation, Helmick was appointed to his first staff job as regimental quartermaster. He would have preferred to have remained in the line, but characteristically did well in his new job. He served with the 10th Infantry in the early part of the operations against Santiago and then was reassigned as an engineer officer of the 2d Brigade, 1st Division, of Maj. Gen. (Vol.) William R. Shafter's Fifth Corps. He was cited for gallantry while performing those duties and later was awarded a Silver Star "for personal bravery and exhibition of iron fortitude and endurance."

At the end of hostilities he returned to Montauk, Long Island, New York, with the brigade headquarters, where he served as the camp ordnance officer until he was ordered back to Fort Reno on 30 September to close out the 10th Infantry's business. When two troops of the 6th Cavalry were sent to garrison the post, he was authorized to return to his regiment in Cuba, leaving on 6 February 1899. During his final brief stay at Fort Reno he had served simultaneously as the quartermaster, ordnance, post exchange, signal, commissary, and recreation officer.

Shortly after returning to Cuba, he was promoted to captain and assigned to the staff of the Department of Matanzas and Santa Clara, commanded by the able and magnetic Brig. Gen. (Vol.) James H. Wilson with whom he became lifelong friends. He performed a variety of duties, but most of his time was spent as the department's acting inspector and the Provincial Rural Guard inspector. This was the first of several assignments in the inspectorate, each of increasing scope. General Wilson considered him "first class . . . , a serious, sober, dignified and intelligent gentleman." Helmick said working for Wilson was one of the great experiences of his career. Under him he learned sound management and supervisory techniques, as well as the virtues of "organized" hard work.

Helmick was able to apply what he had learned when the 10th Infantry redeployed to the Philippines in February 1901. He became the military governor of Puerto Princessa on the island of Palawan. He filled a vacuum left by the fading insurrecto authorities and for a year and a half was the sole source of law and order on that part of the island. With little more than his family and a few soldiers to support him, he found he had to develop another style of leadership to handle the native population. In July 1902, after civil authorities assumed much of the Army's role in government, Helmick took his company back to regimental headquarters at Cotabato on Mindanao. This was more hostile country. After a month's adjustment, he was in active field operations for the remainder of the year. He commanded a provisional battalion in the operations around Lake Lanao. Helmick's regimental commander praised him for a good performance, remarking he was especially effective with both American and native troops.

The regiment returned to the United States in 1903, and that fall Helmick was sent to Springfield, Massachusetts, as a recruiting officer. Here he was exposed to another type of soldier, requiring a different type of leadership again. Finding his recruiting duties light, he did considerable work with the 2d Massachusetts Volunteer Infantry Regiment. He was impressed by the old traditions of the unit and the dedication of its members. He prepared several papers for them, one of which, "Remarks on the Instruction of a Company in the Field Service," was published as a brigade circular. He also was perfecting his German so that before his next assignment he could go on leave to Germany to observe a German garrison in training. He thus spent the winter of 1905–06 in Gottingen, attached to the 82d Kur Hessischen Regiment. His report on his experiences appeared in the October 1906 issue of the *Journal of the United States Infantry Association*.

He returned from Europe in time to deploy with the 10th Infantry to Alaska, where he spent two years as a post or company commander at Fort Liscum. The only excitement during the tour was when he had to take his company to Keystone Canyon on riot duty in September 1907. Otherwise, duties were normal, although he traveled a great deal, inspecting Army signal sites and living conditions among the Indians.

He also found the time to translate French and German military articles for the War Department General Staff's Division of Information. When he left Alaska in August 1908 for the Army School of the Line at Fort Leavenworth, Kansas, his battalion commander called him a "very desirable and efficient officer" in peace and war.

He did well at Fort Leavenworth, although he did not like the competitiveness and unnecessary pressure put on the students, and was immediately accepted for the Army War College after his June 1909 graduation. Before reporting, he spent the month of August as an adviser at a National Guard encampment, which again stimulated his thoughts on how to lead and motivate people over whom one had no direct authority. His performance was equally good at the War College, which he enjoyed a great deal more. He was recommended for duty as a service school tactics instructor or as an inspector general when he graduated in October 1910. Instead, he returned briefly to the 10th Infantry and then on 29 March 1911, recently promoted to major, was assigned as a brigade adjutant in the new Maneuver Division. He had no sooner learned his duties than he was picked up for a detail in the Inspector General's Department on 27 May. With the exception of less than three years, the rest of his service, until his retirement in 1927, would be as a member of the inspectorate. After orientation in Washington, he was assigned as an assistant inspector to the Central Division, based in Chicago.

The entire Army was still feeling the effects of the 1903 Root reforms, with their increased training and personnel standards. Inspectors, Helmick found, carried a major burden in explaining them to the field while evaluating and reporting on them to the War Department. This turbulence, coupled with the growing tensions with Mexico, made the Central Division an exciting place to be. The situation emphasized to Helmick how important to the commander a good inspector could be in a large complex organization. In May 1914 he was assigned as senior inspector to the newly formed 2d Division on the Texas coast. While his assistant, Maj. Alexander Dade, accompanied the division elements to Vera Cruz, Mexico, Helmick stayed behind to assure forward support and to cope with the effects of a devastating tropical storm on the division camps. When Maj. Gen. J. Franklin Bell replaced Maj. Gen. Frederick Funston as commander, Helmick devised a comprehensive inspection and training evaluation program for him. Bell remarked that Helmick ranked highest in ability, merit, and character of all the majors in the division. Helmick's experiences with Bell caused him to think seriously about systematizing tactical inspections and evaluations. His developed views were to prove invaluable during the 1916 and 1917 mobilizations.

Helmick next served as a battalion commander on the Mexican border with the 27th and 28th Infantry, receiving his promotion to lieutenant colonel in July 1916. In September he returned to the Inspector General's Department, this time on General Frederick Funston's staff in the Southern Department. Promoted to colonel in May 1917, he was transferred in June to the Southeastern Department under Maj. Gen. Leonard Wood. Both generals considered him dedicated and "excellent in drilling, instructing and handling men." At both commands and also at the Office of the Inspector General itself, he became actively engaged in the inspection and evaluation of National Guard and, later, National Army divisions and their cantonments. He developed an effective system to inspect an entire regiment in three days, without wasting any of the soldiers' time, which subsequently was published as a guide for other inspectors. On his judgment rested not only the careers of senior officers but also the determination of shipping priorities to France for the units he inspected.

His exceptional performance was recognized with rapid promotions to temporary brigadier general in February 1918 and to temporary major general in July, when he assumed command of the newly formed 8th Division at Camp Fremont, California. His tenure was marked by a rise in division morale and the initiation of numerous innovative training ideas. His successful techniques had the division ready for deployment in record time, and he took the advance party to France just before the armistice. Because of the end of hostilities the division's main body did not sail, and General Helmick and most of his staff were assigned to the huge Base Section No. 5 at Brest. Lt. Gen. Robert L. Bullard, wartime commander of the Second Army, later commented that soon after Helmick's arrival, things improved to the point that there was no basis for complaint. After the war he was awarded the Distinguished Service Medal for "brilliant administrative ability and energy in successfully directing the manifold activities" of the port, at which time he demonstrated his largess by crediting his inspector, Col. Walter L. Reed, a future The Inspector General, for ferreting out the problems and solving them while they were manageable.

In March 1921 Helmick was promoted to permanent brigadier general. His brilliant performance led to his appointment as the Acting Inspector General on 5 July 1921 and as Major General, Inspector General of the Army, on 7 November 1921, replacing Maj. Gen. John

L. Chamberlain. He was the first officer not a member of the old permanent department to become the senior inspector and, with the title change in 1924, the first to be known as The Inspector General. He served in this capacity until 27 September 1927. During his tenure he confirmed his reputation as a leading authority on the psychology of leadership and leadership techniques. Most manuals on the topics were referred to him before publishing. His lectures and views on the subject were often quoted in military and civilian publications. After his retirement in 1927, he entered the insurance business for several years and was very active in Washington civic affairs. He eventually moved to Honolulu, Hawaii, where he died on 13 January 1945.

Eli A. Helmick, "From Reveille to Retreat: An Autobiography of Major General Eli A. Helmick." custody of U.S. Army Military History Institute Archives (MHI), Carlisle Barracks, Pa., and copy at East Carolina University Archives, Greenville, N.C.; Interv, author with C. Helmick, 3 Feb 83, Inspector General Collection, MHI; File ACP 1888, Record Group (RG) 94, National Archives and Records Administration (NARA), Washington, D.C.; File 350.001, Entry 26B, RG 159, NARA; Eli A. Helmick, Cullum Files, U.S. Military Academy Archives; Robert L. Bullard, *Personalities and Reminiscences of the War* (Garden City, N.Y.: Doubleday, Page and Co., 1925), p. 335; Association of Graduates, USMA, *Assembly*, Jul 46, pp. 4–5; "Official Orders," *Army and Navy Journal*, 1 Oct 27, p. 89; "Promotions and Retirements," *Army and Navy Journal*, 12 Nov 21, p. 253; George W. Cullum, *Biographical Register of the Officers and Graduates of the U.S. Military Academy . . .* , various vols., No. 3276.

PETERSON, Virgil L. (1882–1956)

Peterson was born in Campbellsville, Kentucky, on September 1882. After graduating from Centre College in 1902, he taught school for two years before being admitted to the U.S. Military Academy. At graduation in 1908 he was commissioned a second lieutenant and joined the 3d Battalion of Engineers at Fort Leavenworth, Kansas, where he performed unit duties as well as some short map-making tours in Ohio and Indiana. In November 1910, after completing a fourteen-month course at the Engineer School then in Washington, D.C., he was assigned to the new Maneuver Division at Fort Sam Houston, Texas. Promoted to first lieutenant in February 1911, he began a three-year tour in November in the Philippines and completed numerous major engineering tasks there, including a topographical survey of the islands. He also served as Maj. Gen. J. Franklin Bell's aide from September 1913 to September 1914 while continuing to supervise various engineering projects.

At the end of 1914 Peterson returned to the United States, where he commanded engineer companies in Washington, D.C., and on the

Mexican border, rising to captain in February 1915. In April 1917 he went with his company briefly to Washington, receiving his promotion to temporary major in June. He subsequently assumed command of the 9th Engineers and later the 8th Engineer Battalion (Mounted), both at El Paso, Texas, earning his promotion to temporary lieutenant colonel in December. In the spring of 1918 he returned to the East. From April to August, when he was promoted to temporary colonel, he commanded the 4th Engineers Training Camp at Camp Lee, Virginia, and then the Engineer School now located at Camp Humphreys, Virginia, until June 1920. He became noted for his innovative techniques and was credited with improving engineer training while shortening the length of the course.

After reverting to his permanent grade of major in May 1920, he was assigned to various engineer districts in New England, serving most of his time as Providence district engineer. From 1924 to 1925 he completed the General Service Schools course at Fort Leavenworth, Kansas, where he remained as an instructor until July 1929. At this time he returned to Washington, D.C., to become the first National Capitol assistant director of public buildings and parks and subsequently the chief of the Miscellaneous Civil Section in the Office of the Chief of Engineers, earning his promotion to lieutenant colonel in November 1931. From August 1932 to June 1933 he was a student at the Army War College and, after graduating, became the Los Angeles district engineer. In February 1934 he assumed command of the 3d Engineers at Schofield Barracks, Hawaii.

He returned to the United States in 1936 to become the district engineer of the Detroit River and Harbor District, receiving his promotion to colonel in October. He was reassigned as the chief of staff of the Sixth Corps Area at Fort Sheridan, Illinois, in March 1937. The corps area commander at the time was Maj. Gen. Hugh A. Drum, who was impressed by Peterson's performance. Drum's recommendations were instrumental in Peterson's appointment to Major General, The Inspector General of the Army, on 24 December 1939, replacing Maj. Gen. Walter L. Reed.

Assuming his duties 9 February 1940, Peterson served as The Inspector General for the duration of World War II. He was credited with seeing more men, maneuvers, and facilities than any other officer in the Army. The scale and pressures of the job began to affect his health to the point that he agreed only to the extension of his detail until the war was over. After suffering a heart attack, he was reassigned in June 1945 to the Army Service Forces, serving as director of personnel until his medical retirement 28 February 1946. He lived in retirement in Washington, D.C., where he died on 15 February 1956.

"Obituaries," *Army and Navy Journal*, 25 Feb 56, p. 27; "Virgil L. Peterson," *New York Times*, 16 Feb 56, p. 29; "1100 Inspectors General Form Elite Corps of Army," *Washington Daily News*, 6 May 44, p. 7; "Virgil L. Peterson—Inspector General Reports on All Phases of Army," *Washington Post*, 11 Feb 43, p. B1; George W. Cullum, *Biographical Register of the Officers and Graduates of the U.S. Military Academy . . .* , various vols., No. 4644; Association of Graduates, USMA, *Assembly*, Jul 56, pp. 81–82; Biography File, Historian's Office Archives, U.S. Army Corps of Engineers, Fort Belvoir, Va.

PRESTON, John F. (1872–1960)

The son of a prominent lawyer, Preston was born in Baltimore, Maryland, on 5 November 1872. He completed his education at the City College in 1890 and subsequently attended the U.S. Military Academy, commissioned as a second lieutenant in 1894. He served with the 16th Infantry in Utah and Washington, spending part of the time as a quartermaster and commissary officer. Promoted to first lieutenant in April 1898, he deployed in June with his regiment to Cuba, where he saw action at San Juan Hill—he received the Silver Star for leading his men in the charge on the enemy's works on 1 July—and at Santiago. He remained in Cuba until September and then returned briefly to the United States. In May 1899 he deployed with his regiment to the Philippines, where he participated in five engagements against the insurrectos. From 1900 to 1901 he performed revenue and provost duties in the islands. A captain since February 1901, he took command of Company F, 26th Infantry, on 5 September. After six months with the company, he was appointed adjutant general of the 4th Separate Brigade.

In July 1903 Preston returned to the United States, where he performed various regimental duties at Fort Sam Houston, Texas; briefly commanded Fort Brown, Texas; and served at the 1904 St. Louis Exposition. In May 1907 he returned to the Philippines with the 26th Infantry, serving as a company and battalion commander. In June 1909 he was reassigned to command Fort Brady, Michigan. In March 1911 he was detailed to the Pay Department at Fort Sheridan, Illinois, during which time he served as paymaster for the Maneuver Division at Fort Sam Houston, Texas. He returned to Fort Sam Houston in November 1912, where he was post quartermaster. In March 1913 he became the quartermaster of the Southern Department, where he acquired extensive experience in finance and disbursing activities. He next joined the 4th Infantry at Galveston, Texas, in August 1914, serving with it on the Mexican border until he was appointed inspector-instructor of the Texas state troops in July 1916. He returned to the 4th Infantry, a major, and moved with it to Gettysburg, Pennsylvania, in June 1917.

Preston was promoted quickly to temporary colonel and transferred in September 1917 to Camp Devens, Massachusetts, to command the 303d Infantry, 76th Division. He organized, trained, and deployed to France with this unit in July 1918. He commanded the regiment at the St. Amand Training District until October, when he took over the 152d Infantry Brigade. His commander cited him for his thorough administrative knowledge and exceptional tactical abilities. The 303d was known for its sharp organization and good discipline. Preston was noted for his popularity, "pleasant personality and gentle manners." Shortly after the armistice he was assigned to command the 327th Infantry, 82d Division, which he led until returning from overseas with it in May 1919. He briefly commanded the 63d Infantry at Madison Barracks, New York, and then attended the School of the Line (distinguished graduate 1920) and the General Staff School (1921) at Fort Leavenworth, Kansas. Promoted to permanent colonel in July 1920, he remained as an instructor at the Staff School until August 1922. He subsequently attended the Army War College in Washington, D.C.

Graduating in June 1923, Preston was assigned to the Eighth Corps Areas headquarters at Fort Sam Houston, serving briefly as the G–3 and then as the chief of staff until October 1926. After infantry refresher training at Fort Benning, Georgia, he returned to Fort Sam Houston and assumed command of the 1st Infantry. He deployed with it to Fort Francis E. Warren, Wyoming, in June 1927 and then was detailed to the Inspector General's Department on 20 November 1928. He served as the executive officer in the Office of The Inspector General until appointed Major General, The Inspector General of the Army, on 1 December 1931, replacing Maj. Gen. Hugh A. Drum.

After his four-year detail, General Preston sought to be appointed as governor of the Soldiers' Home. When that failed, he reverted to his permanent grade of colonel and returned to Fort Sam Houston. There, he served as corps area civilian components officer until his retirement on 30 November 1936. He entered banking in San Antonio thereafter, eventually rising to become director of one of the largest banks in the city. He retired again in 1950 and died in San Antonio on

1 July 1960. Good natured, able, and well liked, General Preston brought an unusually broad range of experience to the Inspector General's Department.

John F. Preston, Cullum Files, U.S. Military Academy Archives; File AG 201, St. Louis, Mo.; George W. Cullum, *Biographical Register of the Officers and Graduates of the U.S. Military Academy . . .* , various vols., No. 3583.

READ, Alvan C. (1873–1920)

Although born in Marshall County, Tennessee, on 11 September 1873, Read came from an old Louisiana family and grew up in that state, the son of a Baton Rouge lawyer. He graduated from Louisiana State University in 1892 and taught school while earning a master's degree, which he received the next year. He entered the U.S. Military Academy in 1894 and graduated early with the rest of his class in April 1898, commissioned as a second lieutenant. He joined the 13th Infantry at Tampa in May, deployed to Cuba, and saw action at San Juan Hill and at Santiago. Diagnosed as having yellow fever on 12 July, he returned to the United States, finally rejoining his regiment at Fort Porter, New York, on 1 November. The 13th Infantry had suffered heavily in Cuba, leading to Read's promotion to first lieutenant in March 1899, a month before the unit deployed to the Philippines. Read fought in nine engagements in central Luzon, being cited again "for marked coolness, intelligence, efficiency and gallant conduct under fire." He further distinguished himself organizing civil government in the town of San Manuel.

He returned to the United States in May 1902 for a year's duty at the Alcatraz Disciplinary Barracks, earning his promotion to captain in December. In April 1903 he assumed command of a company in the 12th Infantry at Whipple Barracks, Arizona, and in September he accepted a four-year assignment as professor of military science and training at his old alma mater, during which time the visiting inspectors praised him in their reports for running an excellent, well-received program. In September 1907 he returned to the 12th Infantry at Fort Jay, New York, deploying with it to the Philippines in June 1909. He commanded his company for most of this period, occasionally acting as battalion or regimental adjutant. Read next attended the Army School of the Line at Fort Leavenworth, Kansas, from August 1911 to June 1912. In November 1912 he was assigned as a major in the Puerto Rico Regiment. In August 1915 he joined the 9th Infantry on the Mexican border at Laredo, Texas, serving there as executive officer until May 1917. He was promoted to temporary lieutenant colonel and reassigned to Fort Benjamin Harrison, Indiana, where he was senior instructor and later commandant of an officers training camp.

Read was detailed to the Inspector General's Department in November 1917, leaving for France the next month to become the 1st Division IG. He was promoted to temporary colonel on 9 May 1918. During June and July he attended the Langres General Staff College. Thereafter he worked at the Advanced Headquarters, American Expeditionary Forces, and in November became the Third Army and later American Forces in Germany IG. He served in that capacity until his untimely death from influenza on 19 January 1920. As Maj. Gen. Andre W. Brewster, the AEF IG, had remarked earlier, Read's "able handling of his important duties assured prompt and adequate means were always provided for improving conditions. . . ." The cheerful and well-liked inspector would have been pleased with such an epitaph.

Alvan C. Read, Cullum Files, U.S. Military Academy Archives; *Fifty-first Annual Report of the Association of Graduates of the United States Military Academy*, 14 Jun 20, pp. 117–21; "Recent Deaths: Alvan Chambliss Read," *Army and Navy Journal*, 7 Feb 20, p. 698.

REED, Walter L. (1877–1956)

The son of the famed Army doctor, Reed was born at Fort Apache, Arizona, on 4 December 1877. He traveled with his family and completed his education in the District of Columbia schools and at the Randolph-Macon Academy. He worked as a bookkeeper for a District of Columbia fuel dealer for over two years before entering the Army. In early 1898 Reed applied for a direct commission, but the advent of the War with Spain led him to enlist in C Battery, 2d Artillery, at Washington Barracks on 17 June 1898. He served with the battery for the next three months at Fort Warren, Massachusetts, rising to the grade of quartermaster sergeant. The battery deployed to Cuba in August for occupation duty, and in May 1899 Reed was transferred to N Battery as first sergeant. During that period he again applied for a commission. His battery and regimental commanders, both Civil War veterans and comrades of Secretary of War Russell A. Alger, enthusiastically supported his request. Other officers providing support included Surgeon General George M. Sternberg, Maj. Gen. Joseph Wheeler, and Col. Leonard Wood.

Although he asked to stay in the artillery, Reed was commissioned as a second lieutenant on 25 July 1900 and assigned to the 10th Infantry. His assignment to that regiment began a lifelong, warm association with Capt. Eli A. Helmick, who came to look upon the younger man as his protege. In February 1901 the unit returned from Cuba to Fort Robinson, Nebraska, where Reed was appointed quartermaster and commissary officer for the 2d Battalion. Deployed to the Philippines in March, his unit arrived in time to participate in the Lake Lanao operations, eventually going into garrison at Cotabato on Mindanao. There, Reed served as provost and town treasurer in addition to his assigned logistical tasks. At his own request, he was reassigned to Company G on 11 December 1902. He served with that company even after returning to the Presidio of San Francisco in September 1903. He was promoted to first lieutenant in January 1904 and in April assumed command of Company M and then in July of Company A at Fort Lawton, Washington. In February 1906 he received new orders for recruiting service at Columbus Barracks, Ohio, where he commanded a training company and escorted groups to their new units. He was cited for a superb job managing the huge general mess at Columbus Barracks.

In August 1908 he rejoined his own regiment at Fort Benjamin Harrison, Indiana. He served as regimental and post adjutant until December, when he was made post exchange officer. Along with the retail store and other concessions, he oversaw the management of a farm and diary. Throughout 1909 he periodically served as post or unit adjutant while continuing with his PX functions. The same held true after he was assigned in June 1910 to Company C. He finally shed his PX duties in March 1911, when the 10th Infantry relocated to Fort Sam Houston, Texas, to be part of the new Maneuver Division until June. In September the regiment next moved to the Canal Zone. Company C was stationed at Camp E. S. Otis, Las Cascades, where Reed, as the company executive, managed the unit funds and mess and, as cited in the inspectors' reports, demonstrated "excellent business sense." Promoted to captain in April 1914, Reed assumed command of his company in July. He held this position until October, when he left for the United States.

Reed had requested duty with the militia in Maryland or Virginia in order to be close to home. The best that could be done was to assign him as an inspector-instructor to the New Jersey National Guard, with duty station at Newark. He was so successful working with the Guard that he was elected major of the 4th New Jersey Infantry at the time of the 1916 call-up. He could not accept the state commission, so the governor issued it as an honor instead. Reed was on several inspection teams in 1916, observing mobilized guard units in Florida and Georgia and ended the year as a mustering officer, demobilizing New Jersey units. He reversed the process in the first months of 1917, recalling units. Promoted to temporary major in July, he remained with the New Jersey Guard until October, when he was assigned to the Inspector General's Department in Washington.

Receiving his promotion to temporary lieutenant colonel in May 1918, he joined the 7th Division at Camp MacArthur, Texas, in August, serving as its inspector. In September the unit deployed to France. In October, when Regular Army officers were taken from division-level IG positions, he became the assistant IG at the Second Army. In February 1919 he was transferred to Base Section No. 5 at Maj. Gen. Eli A. Helmick's request, serving as the inspector until the base was closed and receiving his promotion to temporary colonel in May. He then moved to the dwindling American Expeditionary Forces IG office and eventually became the American Forces in France inspector. He returned to the United States in 1920, becoming a permanent lieutenant colonel in July, and embarked upon several years of schooling—School of the Line, 1921; General Staff School, 1922; Army War College, 1923; and Naval War College, 1924. He remained at the Naval War College as an instructor until June 1928, when he was assigned as executive officer of the 29th Infantry at Fort Benning, Georgia. His promotion to permanent colonel was effective in May 1930. He assumed command of the 12th Infantry at Fort Howard, Maryland, in January 1933, serving in that position until detailed to the Inspector General's Department in October 1934. He served as its executive officer in Washington until 1 December 1935, when he was appointed Major General, The Inspector General of the Army, replacing Maj. Gen. John F. Preston. His tour ended 23 December 1939, and he retired 30 April 1940. General Reed was recalled to active duty in April 1942 as a member of the War Department Personnel Board, headed by former Chief of Staff General Malin Craig. He retired again on 25 June 1946 and lived in Washington, D.C. until his death on 1 May 1956.

File AG 197038, Record Group 94, National Archives and Records Administration, Washington, D.C.; "Obituaries," *Army, Navy, Air Force Journal*, 5 May 56, p. 32; Mark S. Watson, *Chief of Staff: Prewar Plans and Preparations* (Washington, D.C.: Historical Division, Department of the Army, 1950), p. 252; *Who Was Who in American History—The Military*, s.v. "Reed, Walter Lawrence."

RIVERS, William C. (1866–1943)

Rivers was born in Pulaski, Tennessee, on 11 January 1866. He graduated from the U.S. Military Academy in 1887, four years after his older brother, Tyree, for whom he was nicknamed. Commissioned as a second lieutenant, he began his service with M Troop of the 1st Cavalry as part of the first Army unit to assume control of Yellowstone National Park. He quickly learned a new style of leadership, dealing with tourists and recalcitrant ranchers and hunters over whom he held only the powers of persuasion. After performing as a unit supply officer in the field during the Ghost Dance campaign of 1890–91, he returned to the East for a two-year assignment as West Point's quartermaster. During his next tour as the Indian agent for the White Mountain Apaches in Arizona, he kindled a respect and empathy for native peoples that became a permanent part of his outlook, further broadening his capacity to cope with the unusual. He was promoted to first lieutenant in August 1894.

In June 1898 he deployed with his regiment to Cuba, briefly serving in the Santiago campaign until invalided home to Montauk Point, New York, with malaria. His first opportunity to influence the Inspector General's Department came in the fall, when he served as recorder on the board that developed the regulations for the new Army Transport Service.

Rivers, a captain since February 1901, achieved considerable prominence throughout the Army thereafter as the Military Academy's adjutant for the four years up to 1903. This was a time of major construction on the campus, and he was responsible for much of the administrative detail. It was also his lot to organize the spectacular West Point's centennial celebration in 1902, which involved graduates and foreign dignitaries from around the world. One of River's most pleasant achievements derived from this. Because of the anniversary he revived the virtually moribund Association of Graduates, personally writing letters and persuading most of the ex-Confederate graduates to return for the event, many of them for the first time since before the Civil War.

Rivers was among the first group of officers selected to serve on the newly created War Department General Staff in 1903 and was assigned to the Philippines. He arrived after the official ending of the Insurrection, but quickly noted numerous problems pertaining to civil affairs and pacification. Promoted to major in March 1911, he became increasingly involved with these issues. In 1912 he was transferred to the newly formed Philippine Constabulary as its inspector and later as its assistant chief, with the temporary rank of colonel. He served throughout the archipelago, participating in many minor engagements. During this period he gained a sympathy and respect for the Filipinos, which in later life was to make him an outspoken advocate for their independence. He rose to the rank of brigadier general when he was named chief of the Constabulary. But in 1914, under the provisions of the so-called Manchu law, he reverted to his permanent grade. He returned to the United States, assigned to the 2d Cavalry at Fort Ethan Allen, Vermont. In July 1916 he received a double promotion to lieutenant colonel and colonel on the same day and assumed command of his regiment.

When war was declared against Germany in April 1917, part of the 2d was organized as the 18th Cavalry. Rivers remained with the new unit as its commander when it was redesignated as the 76th Field Artillery and assigned to the 3d Division. In France he led the 76th in every action in which his division was engaged, from Chateau Thierry to the Meuse-Argonne. He was cited with the *Croix de Guerre* by the French for his exceptional leadership in command of an extemporaneous group of fourteen batteries during the 1918 Battle of the Marne. He received the Distinguished Service Medal from the United States and in October 1918 was promoted again to temporary brigadier general to command the 5th Artillery Brigade. Rivers returned to the United States in mid-1919, once again reverting to colonel, this time to command the 12th Cavalry and the Subdistrict of New Mexico. In 1920 he assumed command of the 3d Cavalry, his last branch assignment, during which circumstances thrust him to the fore in 1921 as he organized and conducted the ceremonies and security measures incident to the burial of the first Unknown Soldier and also the Washington Disarmament Conference.

His broad experience, flexible and sympathetic leadership, and strong organizational talents had marked him as a major candidate for high position. Accordingly, he was assigned as the Second Corps Area IG, based in New York City. This was traditionally the most important field office in the Inspector General's Department. On 27 September 1927 he was appointed Major General, The Inspector General of the Army, replacing Maj. Gen. Eli A. Helmick and gaining a general officer's commission for the third time.

On 11 January 1930, because of age, he retired from the Army, at the time the oldest and longest serving officer and last member of his Class of 1887 on active duty. During his retirement General Rivers remained active, working as a volunteer for the Bishop Brent Fund. He also became a prolific writer on military and political subjects, particularly on the issue of early Philippine independence. He died at his wife's home in Fletcher, North Carolina, on 10 July 1943.

Nathaniel F. McClure, ed., *Class of 1887, United States Military Academy: A Biographical Volume* (Washington, D.C.: P. S. Bond Publishing Co., 1937), pp. 163–65; George W. Cullum, *Biographical Register of the Officers and Graduates of the U.S. Military Academy . . .* , various vols., No. 3197; Frederic V. Hemenway, *History of the Third Division USA in the World War* (Andernach-on-the-Rhine, 1919), pp. 253–61; William C. Rivers, Cullum Files, U.S. Military Academy Archives; "Col. Rivers Succeeds Helmick," *Army and Navy Journal*, 27 Sep 27, p. 64.

SPINKS, Marcellus G. (1874–1943)

Born in Mississippi, Spinks was a coast artilleryman with extensive experience commanding units in his branch and with service on the War Department staff. His classmates from West Point in 1898 included Fox Conner and Alvan C. Read among several others who would become prominent staff officers in the American Expeditionary Forces. In September 1917 he was detailed as an inspector of the 90th Division at Camp Travis, Texas. In November he became 4th Division IG, and in March 1918 he was reassigned as an inspector in the Services of Supply, AEF, where the senior IG, Brig. Gen. John S. Winn, considered him to be "a superior officer in every way." On 1 July 1918 Maj. Gen. Andre W. Brewster, the AEF IG, designated him as his assistant, a position he held until returning to the United States in April 1919. Brewster judged him to be "an accomplished officer with excellent self-control . . . , a respected leader." In November 1930, after nearly ten years in branch assignments after the war, Spinks returned to the Inspector General's Department, where he served as Deputy Inspector General for four years and then as the Second Corps Area IG until his retirement in 1938. He was a strong contender for selection for the position of The Inspector General during that time. He died at Hampton, Virginia, on 28 November 1943.

File 201.6EE, Record Group 407, National Archives and Records Administration, Washington, D.C.; Association of Graduates, USMA, *Assembly*, Jul 44, p. 809.

WOOD, William T. (1854–1943)

The son of a Methodist minister, Wood was born in Irving, Illinois, on 19 June 1854. He graduated from the U.S. Military Academy in 1877, commissioned as a second lieutenant, and was assigned to the 18th Infantry. He served with the 18th at locations throughout the West, except for three years as a professor of military science at Illinois Industrial College and two years on recruiting duty. A first lieutenant since October 1886, he served as the regimental quartermaster during this period, for which he was cited for his business sense and organization that set examples and resulted in Army-wide changes in commissary operations. In May 1898 Wood, a captain for four years, deployed with his regiment to the Philippines, where he was wounded in fighting around Manila and later received the Silver Star for "fortitude and gallantry on the field of battle." He then served as chief of ordnance for the Philippine Division, seeing more action during the Insurrection. From November 1899 to June 1900 he was the collector of customs and assistant treasurer in the island government.

Wood returned to the United States for recruiting duty and then, as a major, was reassigned to the 20th Infantry at Fort Sheridan, Illinois. While there, he successfully requested a detail to the Inspector General's Department under the new 1901 detail law. His former Philippine Division commander, Maj. Gen. Elwell S. Otis, supported his application, saying Wood was "thoroughly qualified for any duty. . . . Whenever we had a particularly difficult labor to perform, we seem to have selected Wood to do it." Wood first was assigned from January 1904 to June 1905 as the assistant to the Atlantic Division IG, Col. Ernest A. Garlington. When Garlington was reassigned to Manila, he asked specifically for Wood to accompany him. He wanted his assistance because of his infantry background and also because of his knowledge of money accountability. When the poor health of the Inspector General of the Army mandated Garlington's early return home in July 1906, Wood, a lieutenant colonel since February, was named the Philippine Division IG. He held this position during the final phases of the Manila Depot investigation and was cited by General Leonard Wood for doing exceptional work. Colonel Wood was reassigned in August 1907 to be Garlington's assistant at the Office of the Inspector General in Washington. He served there until July 1909, running the inspectorate during Garlington's absences. Wood was the first of the detailed officers to have his tour in the Inspector General's Department extended with a second consecutive detail. He ended this second tour as the Department of the East IG from July 1909 to March 1910, at which time he was promoted to colonel.

He assumed command of the 19th Infantry at Camp Jossman in the Philippines, serving until July 1911. He then was reassigned to command the Recruit Depot at Jefferson Barracks, Missouri, where he established a reputation as a kindly disciplinarian, alert to the welfare of his men, and also was successful in several confrontations with commercial interests to assure fairness in contracts and services. He was recommended for promotion, but a routine physical found him to be physically disqualified, and he was forced to retire on disability in April 1913. He then served as treasurer of the Soldiers' Home in Washington, D.C., until recalled to active duty on 16 May 1917. Brig. Gen. John L. Chamberlain, the Inspector General of the Army, wanted Wood to run the office as he had done for Garlington. Wood was promoted to brigadier general on 18 February 1918. He continued to serve as the Deputy Inspector General until he retired again on 30 September 1920. He returned to the Soldiers' Home, where he was its secretary until 1931. He died in Washington on 18 December 1943. Characterized as a kindly man with a warm personality, he was known as well for his extreme efficiency. General Chamberlain said of him, "Whenever I am called away, I never have to think of my office. Wood is there."

File 4321 ACP 1877, Record Group 94, National Archives and Records Administration, Washington, D.C.; Association of Graduates, USMA, *Assembly*, Jul 44, pp. 3–4.

Bibliography

Archival Collections

The basis for any study of the Inspector General's Department in the first part of the twentieth century must be the extensive holdings of the National Archives and Records Administration in Washington, D.C. Record Group (RG) 159, Records of the Office of The Inspector General, is the greatest single source, for it includes copies of virtually all of the correspondence and the investigation and inspection reports, with supporting documents, generated during the period. A card index file developed by the Office of The Inspector General has survived, providing a good guide to the material. Knowledge of the Army's decimal filing system is essential to maximize use of the post–World War I files. Equally important to this study is RG 120, Records of the Office of the American Expeditionary Forces (World War I), which documents all IG and other operations in France during the war and in the postwar activities throughout Europe. IG correspondence or reactions thereto also can be traced in RG 94, Records of The Adjutant General's Office, 1780s–1917, and RG 407, Records of The Adjutant General's Office, 1917–. These are so voluminous that they should be used only to track particular points not fully addressed in RGs 159 and 120. Also of some help are RG 112, Records of the Office of The Surgeon General (Army); RG 165, Records of the War Department General and Special Staffs; RG 393, Records of the U.S. Army Continental Commands, 1821–1920; and RG 394, Records of the U.S. Army Continental Commands, 1920–1942.

These official records were greatly enhanced by various manuscripts and document collections in other repositories. The holdings of the U.S. Army Military History Institute (MHI), Carlisle Barracks, Pennsylvania, contain the personal papers of several important officers who served as inspectors during the period under study, particularly those of Marcellus G. Spinks and Eli A. Helmick. Student papers by these officers and lectures given by them later as senior members of the Army may be found in the Army War College Curriculum Papers. The

MHI Archives has in its custody General Helmick's autobiography, a copy of which is on file at the East Carolina University Archives, Greenville, North Carolina. It also has a special IG collection, where the researcher will find most of the documentation acquired for this volume, including the tape-recorded interviews. Both the MHI Archives and the Army Library at the Pentagon, Arlington, Virginia, have large collections of published congressional and military documents and regulations pertaining to the Inspector General's Department that were essential to this study. Finally, excellent biographical material on many inspectors may be found in the holdings of the U.S. Military Academy, West Point, New York, particularly in its Cullum Files.

Printed Documents

Department of the Army. Historical Division. *The United States Army in the World War, 1917–1919*. 17 vols. Washington, D.C.: Government Printing Office, 1948.

Hunt, Irwin L. "American Military Government of Occupied Germany, 1918–1920: Report of the Officer in Charge of Civil Affairs." Mimeographed, 4 vols. Coblenz, 1920. Copy in Army Library, Pentagon, Arlington, Va.

Ney, Virgil. *The Evolution of the U.S. Army Field Manual—Valley Forge to Vietnam*. CORG–M–244. AD820286. Cameron Station, Va.: Defense Document Center, 1966.

Parsons, John R., Jr. "History of Inspection in the Armed Forces." Mimeographed. Headquarters, USAF, 1981.

U.S. Army, American Expeditionary Forces. "Inspection of Administration, Disbursements, and Accounts." General Headquarters, AEF, 1918. OTIG files, Pentagon (SAIG-ZXH).

U.S. Army War College, Historical Section, *The Genesis of the American First Army*. Washington, D.C.: Government Printing Office, 1938.

U.S. Congress. House. Committee on Military Affairs. *General Johnson Hagood on National Defense and the Reorganization of the Army*. 73d Cong., 1st Sess., 1933.

———. *Hearing on Staff Service of the Army, Term of Enlistment in the Army, General Service Corps in the Army, Consolidation of Certain Branches of the War Department and the Army*. 62d Cong., 1st Sess., 1911.

———. *Hearings on Army Reorganization*. 66th Cong., 1st Sess., 1919.

————. *Hearings on a Bill To Increase the Efficiency of the Army.* 58th Cong., 1st Sess., 1902.

————. *Historical Documents Relating to the Reorganization Plans of the War Department and to the Present National Defense Act.* 69th Cong., 2d Sess., 1927.

————. *Relief of the Adjutant General of the Army From the Duties of His Office.* 62d Cong., 2d Sess., 1912, H. Doc. 508.

————. *Report of War Policies Committee.* 72d Cong., 2d Sess., 1932, H. Doc. 163.

————. *Reports of Inspections of Disbursements and Transfers by Officers of the Army. Letter From the Secretary of War Transmitting 1352 Reports.* 65th Cong., 3d Sess., 1919, H. Doc. 1559.

U.S. Congress. Senate. Committee on Military Affairs. *Additional Testimony Relating to the Brownsville Affray Taken by the Honorable Milton D. Purdy, Assistant to the Attorney General of the U.S., and Major Augustus P. Blocksom, IGD, U.S. Army.* 60th Cong., 1st Sess., 1908, S. Doc. 355.

————. *Affray at Brownsville, Texas. Hearings Before the Committee on Military Affairs Concerning the Affray at Brownsville, Texas, on the Night of August 13 and 14, 1906.* Vols. 1 and 3, 59th Cong., 2d Sess., 1907.

————. *Federal Aid in Domestic Disturbances, 1903–1922.* 67th Cong., 2d Sess., 1922, S. Doc. 263.

————. *Hearing on S. 3792 To Reorganize and Increase the Efficiency of the United States Army, and for Other Purposes.* 66th Cong., 2d Sess., 1920.

————. *Hearings Before the Committee.* 65th Cong., 2d Sess., 1918.

————. *Message From the President of the United States Transmitting a Letter From the Secretary of War Containing Additional Testimony in the Brownsville Case.* 59th Cong., 2d Sess., 1907, S. Doc. 155, pt. 2.

————. *Message From the President of the United States Transmitting a Report With Several Documents, Including a Letter of General Nettleton, and Memoranda as to Precedents for the Summary Discharge or Mustering Out of Regiments or Companies.* 59th Cong., 2d Sess., 1906, S. Doc. 155.

————. *Personal Narrative of the General Staff System of the American Army by Major General William Harding Carter.* 68th Cong., 1st Sess., 1925, S. Doc. 119.

————. *Politics of Our National Defense: History of the Action of Political Forces Within the United States Which Has Shaped Our*

Military National Defense Policies Form 1783 to 1940 Together With Document 107, 59th Cong., 2d Sess., 1906.

—————. *Reorganization of the Army*. 65th Cong., 1st Sess., 1917.

—————. *Special Committee Investigating the National Defense Program*. 80th Cong., 2d Sess., 1948, S. Doc. 440.

U.S. Congress. Senate. Committee on Veterans Affairs. *Medal of Honor Recipients, 1863–1978*. 96th Cong., 1st Sess., 1979.

U.S. War Department. *Annual Report of the Chief of Staff, United States Army, 1933*. Washington, D.C.: Government Printing Office, 1933.

—————. *Annual Report of the Inspector General*. Washington, D.C.: Government Printing Office, 1900–40.

—————. *Annual Report of the Secretary of War*. Washington, D.C.: Government Printing Office, 1900–40.

—————. *Final Report of Gen. John J. Pershing, Commander-in-Chief, American Expeditionary Forces*. Washington, D.C.: Government Printing Office, 1920.

—————. *A Manual for Courts-Martial, 1921*. Washington, D.C.: Government Printing Office, 1920.

—————. *Report of the Chief, Division of Militia Affairs, 1911*. Washington, D.C.: Government Printing Office, 1912.

—————. *War Department Decimal File System*. Rev. ed. Washington, D.C.: Government Printing Office, 1943.

U.S. War Department. Inspector General's Department. *Report of an Inspection of the Several Branches of the National Home for Disabled Volunteer Soldiers*. 10 vols. Washington, D.C.: Government Printing Office, 1896–1919.

—————. *A Guide for the Use of Officers of the Inspector General's Department, 1908*. Washington, D.C.: Government Printing Office, 1908.

U.S. War Department. Office of the Inspector General. *Affray at Brownsville, Texas, August 13–14, 1906. Investigation of the Conduct of U.S. Troops*. Washington, D.C.: Government Printing Office, 1906.

—————. *Catechism of Instructions for Keeping the Record of Correspondence in the Various Offices at the Headquarters of Military Posts, at Which the System of Record Keeping Prescribed Shall be Authorized by the War Department*. Washington, D.C.: Government Printing Office, 1909.

—————. *Compendium of Important Regulations, Orders, and Instructions of the War Department Relating to the Organization,*

Equipment, and Instruction of the Field Artillery. Washington, D.C.: Government Printing Office, 1906.

―――. *A Guide for the Use of Officers of the Inspector General's Department, 1911, Corrected to April 1, 1917.* Washington, D.C.: Government Printing Office, 1917.

Books and Memoirs

Allen, Frederick L. *Only Yesterday.* New York: Harper and Row Publishers, 1931.

Allen, Henry T. *My Rhineland Journal.* Boston: Houghton Mifflin Co., 1923.

―――. *The Rhineland Occupation.* Indianapolis, Ind.: Bobbs-Merrill Co., 1927.

Ambrose, Stephen E. *Duty, Honor, Country: A History of West Point.* Baltimore: Johns Hopkins University Press, 1966.

―――. *Upton and the Army.* Baton Rouge: Louisiana State University Press, 1964.

American Battle Monuments Commission. *American Armies and Battlefields in Europe.* Washington, D.C.: Government Printing Office, 1938.

Armstrong, David A. *Bullets and Bureaucrats: The Machine Gun and the United States Army, 1861–1916.* Contributions in Military History No. 29. Westport, Conn.: Greenwood Press, 1982.

Ashburn, P. M. *A History of the Medical Department of the U.S. Army.* Boston: Little, Brown and Co., 1929.

Association of Graduates, U.S. Military Academy. *Sixty-sixth Annual Report of the Association of Graduates of the USMA at West Point, New York.* Newburgh, N.Y.: Moore Printing Co., 1935.

Bach, Christian A., and Hall, Henry N. *The Fourth Division: Its Services and Achievements in the World War.* N.p., 1920.

Bacon, Robert, and Scott, James B. *The Military and Colonial Policy of the United States: Addresses and Reports of Elihu Root.* Cambridge, Mass.: Harvard University Press, 1924.

Barbeau, Arthur E., and Henri, Florette. *The Unknown Soldiers: Black American Troops in World War I.* Philadelphia: Temple University Press, 1974.

Barnett, Corelli. *Britain and Her Army, 1509–1970.* New York: William Morrow and Co., 1970.

Bayliss, Gwyn M. *Bibliographic Guide to the Two World Wars.* Ann Arbor, Mich.: R. R. Bowker Publishing Co., 1977.

Beale, Howard K. *Theodore Roosevelt and the Rise of America to World Power*. Baltimore: Johns Hopkins University Press, 1956.

Beaver, Daniel R. *Newton D. Baker and the American War Effort, 1917–1919*. Lincoln: University of Nebraska Press, 1966.

Bernardo, C. J., and Bacon, E. H. *American Military Policy: Its Development Since 1775*. Harrisburg, Pa.: Military Service Publishing Co., 1955.

Blumenson, Martin. *The Patton Papers*. 2 vols. Boston: Houghton Mifflin Co., 1972–74.

Bradley, John. *Allied Intervention in Russia*. New York: Basic Books, 1968.

Brereton, Lewis H. *The Brereton Diaries: The War in the Air on the Pacific, Middle East and Europe, 3 October 1941–8 May 1945*. New York: William Morrow and Co., 1946.

Brown, Fred R. *History of the Ninth U.S. Infantry, 1799–1909*. Chicago: R. R. Donnelley and Sons Co., 1909.

Bullard, Robert L. *American Soldiers Also Fought*. New York: Longmans, Green and Co., 1936.

―――. *Personalities and Reminiscences of the War*. Garden City, N.Y.: Doubleday, Page and Co., 1925.

Butt, Archibald. *Taft and Roosevelt: The Intimate Letters of Archie Butt, Military Aide*. Port Washington, N.Y.: Kennikat Press, 1971.

Carter, William H. *The Life of Lieutenant General Chaffee*. Chicago: University of Chicago Press, 1917.

―――. *The American Army*. Indianapolis, Ind.: Bobbs-Merrill Co., 1915.

A Chronicler [John Cudahy]. *Archangel: The American War With Russia*. Chicago: A. C. McClurg and Co., 1924.

Clark, Edward B. *William L. Sibert, The Army Engineer*. Philadelphia: J. P. Lippincott and Co., 1930.

Clary, David A., and Whitehorne, Joseph W. A. *The Inspectors General of the United States Army, 1777–1903*. Washington, D.C.: Office of The Inspector General and U.S. Army Center of Military History, 1987.

Clendenen, Clarence C. *Blood on the Border: The United States Army and the Mexican Irregulars*. London: Collier-Macmillan, 1969.

Coffman, Edward M. "American Command and Commanders in World War I." In *New Dimensions in Military History: An Anthology*, edited by Russell F. Weigley. pp. 176–96. San Rafael, Calif.: Presidio Press, 1975.

―――. *Hilt of the Sword: The Career of Peyton C. March*. Madison: University of Wisconsin Press, 1966.

————. *The War To End All Wars: The American Military Experience in World War I.* New York: Oxford University Press, 1968.

————. *The Young Officer in the Old Army.* Harmon Memorial Lecture in Military History No. 18. Colorado Springs, Colo.: U.S.A.F. Academy, 1976.

Cohen, Stan. *The Tree Army: A Pictorial History of the Civilian Conservation Corps, 1933–1942.* Missoula, Mont.: Pictorial Histories Publishing Co., 1980.

Coletta, Paola. *The Presidency of William Howard Taft.* Lawrence: University of Kansas Press, 1973.

Cornebise, Alfred E. *The AMAROC News: The Daily Newspaper of the American Forces in Germany, 1919–1923.* Carbondale: Southern Illinois University Press, 1981.

————. *Typhus and Doughboys: The American Polish Typhus Relief Expedition, 1919–1921.* Newark: University of Delaware Press, 1982.

Cosmas, Graham. *An Army for Empire: The United States Army in the Spanish-American War.* Columbia: University of Missouri Press, 1971.

Cramer, Clarence H. *Newton D. Baker: A Biography.* Cleveland: World Press, 1961.

Crowell, Benedict, and Wilson, Robert F. *The Road to France: The Transportation of Troops and Military Supplies, 1917–1918.* New Haven, Conn.: Yale University Press, 1921.

Cuff, Robert D. *The War Industries Board: Business-Government Relations During World War I.* Baltimore: Johns Hopkins University Press, 1973.

Cullum, George W. *Biographical Register of the Officers and Graduates of the U.S. Military Academy . . . .* Various class numbers.

Current, Richard N. *Secretary Stimson: A Study in Organization.* New Brunswick, N.J.: Rutgers University Press, 1954.

Dale, Ernest, and Urwick, Lyndall F. *Staff in Organization.* New York: McGraw-Hill Book Co., 1960.

Daniels, Jonathan. *The Time Between Wars: Armistice to Pearl Harbor.* New York: Doubleday and Co., 1966.

Deutrich, Mabel F. *Struggle for Supremacy: The Career of General Fred C. Ainsworth.* Washington, D.C.: Public Affairs Press, 1962.

DeWeerd, Harvey A. *President Wilson Fights His War: World War I and the American Intervention.* New York: Macmillan Co., 1968.

DeWitt, Harry M. *The General Staff.* Washington, D.C.: Government Printing Office, 1953.

Dickinson, John. *The Building of an Army: A Detailed Account of Legislation, Administration and Opinion in the United States, 1915–1920*. New York: Century Books, 1922.

Dierks, Jack C. *A Leap to Arms: The Cuban Campaign of 1898*. Philadelphia: J. P. Lippincott and Co., 1970.

Duffy, Francis P. *Father Duffy's Story: A Tale of Humor and Heroism, Life and Death With the Fighting Sixty-Ninth*. Garden City, N.Y.: Garden City Publishing Co., 1919.

Dupuy, R. Ernest. *The Compact History of the United States Army*. Rev. ed. New York: Hawthorn Books, 1961.

Dupuy, R. Ernest, and Baumer, William H. *The Little Wars of the United States*. New York: Hawthorn Books, 1968.

Dupuy, R. Ernest, and Dupuy, Trevor N. *Brave Men and Great Captains*. New York: Harper and Brothers, 1959.

———. *Military Heritage of America*. New York: McGraw-Hill Book Co., 1956.

Elting, John. *American Army Life*. New York: Charles Scribner's Sons, 1982.

English, George H. *History of the 89th Division*. N.p., 1920.

Fine, Lenore, and Remington, Jesse A. *The Corps of Engineers: Construction in the United States*. Washington, D.C.: Office of the Chief of Military History, Department of the Army, 1972.

Finnegan, John P. *Against the Specter of a Dragon: The Campaign for American Military Preparedness*. New York: Greenwood Press, 1974.

Fleming, Peter. *The Fate of Admiral Kolchak*. London: Rupert Hart-Davis, 1963.

Fletcher, Marvin. *The Black Soldier and Officer in the United States Army, 1891–1917*. Columbia: University of Missouri Press, 1974.

Flint, Roy K. "The United States Army on the Pacific Frontier, 1899–1939." In *The American Military and the Far East*, edited by Joe C. Dixon, pp. 139–54. Washington, D.C.: Office of Air Force History, USAF, 1980.

Foner, Jack D. *Blacks and the Military in American History: A New Perspective*. New York: Praeger Publishers, 1974.

Forsyth, George A. *The Story of the Soldier*. New York: D. Appleton and Co., 1905.

Fosdick, Raymond B. *Chronicle of a Generation: An Autobiography*. New York: Harper and Brothers, 1958.

Fraenkel, Ernst. *Military Occupation and the Rule of Law:*

Occupational Government in the Rhineland, 1918–1923. New York: Oxford University Press, 1944.

Frye, John H. II. *History of the Sixth Field Artillery*. Harrisburg, Pa.: Telegraph Press, 1933.

Ganoe, William A. *The History of the United States Army*. New York: D. Appleton and Co., 1924.

Goode, Paul R. *The United States Soldier's Home*. Richmond: Richard Byrd Press, 1957.

Gordon, Dennis. *Quartered in Hell: The Story of the American North Russian Expeditionary Force, 1918–1920*. Missoula, Mont.: Doughboy Historical Society and G.O.S., 1982.

Graves, William S. *America's Siberian Adventure, 1918–1920*. New York: Jonathan Cape and Harrison Smith, 1931.

Greene, Francis V. *The Revolutionary War and the Military Policy of the United States*. New York: Charles Scribner's Sons, 1911.

Hagedorn, Hermann. *Leonard Wood: A Biography*. 2 vols. New York: Harper and Brothers, 1931.

Hagood, Johnson. *The Services of Supply: A Memoir of the Great War*. Boston: Houghton Mifflin Co., 1927.

———. *We Can Defend America*. Garden City, N.Y.: Doubleday, Doran and Co., 1937.

Haines, Aubrey L. *The Yellowstone Story: A History of Our First National Park*. 2 vols. Yellowstone Park: Yellowstone Library and Museum Association; Denver: Colorado United University Press, 1977.

Halliday, F. M. *The Ignorant Armies*. New York: Award Books, 1964.

Hammond, Paul Y. *Organizing for Defense: The American Military Establishment in the Twentieth Century*. Westport, Conn.: Greenwood Press, 1977.

Hampton, Duane. *How the U.S. Cavalry Saved Our National Parks*. Bloomington: Indiana University Press, 1971.

Harbord, James G. *The American Army in France, 1917–1919*. Boston: Little, Brown and Co., 1936.

Hart, B. H. Liddell. *The Real War, 1914–1918*. 1930. Reprint. Boston: Little, Brown and Co., 1964.

———. *Reputations Ten Years After*. Boston: Little, Brown and Co., 1928.

Hassler, Warren W., Jr. *The President as Commander-in-Chief*. Menlo Park, Calif.: Addison-Wesley Publishing Co., 1971.

Heitman, Francis B. *Historical Register of the United States Army From Its Organization, September 29, 1789 to September 29, 1889*. Washington, D.C.: National Tribune, 1890.

―――. *Historical Register of the United States Army From Its Organization, September 29, 1789 to March 2, 1903.* 2 vols. Washington, D.C.: Government Printing Office, 1903.

Helmick, Eli A. "From Reveille to Retreat: Autobiography of Major General Eli A. Helmick." Custody of MHI Archives, Carlisle Barracks, Pa. Copy at East Carolina University Archives, Greenville, N.C.

Hemenway, Frederic V. *History of the Third Division USA in the World War.* Andernach-on-the-Rhine, 1919.

Hennessy, Juliette A. *The United States Air Arm, April 1861 to April 1917.* USAF Historical Study No 98. Maxwell Air Force Base, Ala.: Historical Division, Research Studies Institute, Air University, 1958.

Hewes, James E., Jr. *From Root to McNamara: Army Organization and Administration, 1900–1963.* Washington, D.C.: Government Printing Office, 1975.

Higham, Robin. *A Guide to the Sources of United States Military History.* Hamden, Conn.: Archon Books, 1975.

Higham, Robin, and Mrozek, Donald. *A Guide to the Sources of United States Military History: Supplement 1.* Hamden, Conn.: Archon Books, 1981.

History of the 332d Infantry. Akron, Ohio: 332d Infantry Association Reunion, September 1929.

Hittle, J. D. *The Military Staff: Its History and Development.* Harrisburg, Pa.: Stackpole Co., 1961.

Hoyt, Charles B. *Heroes of the Argonne.* Kansas City, Kans.: Franklin Hudson Publishing Co., 1919.

Huidekoper, Frederic L. *The Military Unpreparedness of the United States: A History of American Land Forces From Colonial Times Until June 1, 1915.* New York: Macmillan Co., 1915.

Huston, James A. *The Sinews of War: Army Logistics, 1775–1953.* Washington, D.C.: Office of the Chief of Military History, United States Army, 1966.

Huzar, Elias. *The Purse and the Sword: Control of the Army by Congress Through Military Appropriations, 1933–50.* Ithaca, N.Y.: Cornell University Press, 1950.

James, D. Clayton. *The Years of MacArthur.* Vol. 1, *1880–1941.* Boston: Houghton Mifflin Co., 1970.

Jessup, Philip C. *Elihu Root.* 2 vols. New York: Dodd, Mead and Co., 1938.

Johnson, Hugh S. *The Blue Eagle From Egg to Earth.* Garden City, N.Y.: Doubleday, Doran and Co., 1935.

Johnson, Virginia W. *The Unregimented General: A Biography of Nelson A. Miles*. Boston: Houghton Mifflin Co., 1962.

Jones, Wayne S. *Ben: The Life of Benjamin Seth Jones, 1877–1943*. N.p., 1984.

Karsten, Peter. "Armed Progressives: The Military Reorganizes for the American Century." In *Building the Organizational Society*, edited by Jerry Israel, pp. 197–232, 295–307. New York: Free Press, 1972.

Kellog, Walter G. *The Conscientious Objector*. New York: De Capo Press, 1970.

Kemble, C. Robert. *The Image of the Army Officer in America: Background for Current Views*. Westport, Conn.: Greenwood Press, 1973.

Kenamore, Clair. *From Vauquois Hill to Exermont: A History of the Thirty-fifth Division of the United States Army*. St. Louis, Mo.: Guard Publishing Co., 1919.

Kendall, Sylvian G. *American Soldiers in Siberia*. New York: Richard R. Smith, 1945.

Kohn, Richard, ed. *Military Laws of the United States From the Civil War Through the War Powers Act of 1973*. New York: Arno Books, 1979.

Kreidberg, Marvin A., and Henry, Merton G. *History of Military Mobilization in the United States Army, 1775 1945*. DA Pamphlet No. 20–142. Washington, D.C.: Government Printing Office, 1955.

Lacy, Leslie A. *The Soil Soldiers: The Civilian Conservation Corps in the Great Depression*. Radnor, Pa.: Chilton Book Co., 1976.

Lane, Ann J. *The Brownsville Affair: National Crisis and Black Reaction*. Port Washington, N.Y.: National University Publishers, Kennikat Press, 1971.

Lane, Jack C. *Armed Progressive: General Leonard Wood*. San Francisco: Presidio Press, 1978.

Lawton, Eba A. *History of the Soldiers' Home, Washington, D.C.* New York: G. P. Putnam's Sons, Knickerbocker Press, 1914.

Leckie, Robert. *The Wars of America*. 2 vols. New York: Bantam Books, 1968.

Leighton, Isabel, ed. *The Aspirin Age, 1919–1941*. New York: Simon and Schuster, Clarion Books, 1968.

Leopold, Richard W. *Elihu Root and the Conservative Tradition*. Boston: Little, Brown and Co., 1954.

Lerwill, Leonard L. *The Personnel Replacement System in the U.S. Army*. Da Pamphlet No. 20–211. Washington, D.C.: Government Printing Office, 1954.

Lettau, Joseph L. *In Italy With the 332d Infantry.* Youngstown, Ohio: J. L. Lettau, 1921.

Lewis, David. "A Short Account of My Experiences in the American Expeditionary Forces on Service in France, 1918–1919." OTIG files, Pentagon (SAIG-ZXH).

Lewis, George G., and Mewha, John. *History of Prisoner of War Utilization by the U.S. Army, 1776–1945.* DA Pamphlet No. 20–213. Washington, D.C.: Government Printing Office, 1955.

Liggett, Hunter. *A. E. F.: Ten Years Ago in France.* New York: Dodd, Mead and Co., 1928.

———. *Commanding an American Army: Recollections of the World War.* Boston: Houghton Mifflin Co., 1925.

Link, Arthur S. *Woodrow Wilson and the Progressive Era, 1910–1917.* New York: Harper and Row 1963.

Lockmiller, David A. *Enoch H. Crowder: Soldier, Lawyer and Statesman.* Columbia: University of Missouri Press, 1955.

Lord, Walter. *The Good Years: From 1900 to the First World War.* New York: Harper and Brothers, 1960.

Luckett, Richard. *The White Generals: An Account of the White Movement and the Russian Civil War.* New York: Viking Press, 1971.

McClure, Nathaniel F., ed. *Class of 1887, United States Military Academy.* Washington, D.C.: P. S. Bond Publishing Co., 1938.

McEntee, Girard L. *Italy's Part in Winning the World War.* Princeton, N.J.: Princeton University Press, 1934.

Manning, Clarence A. *The Siberian Fiasco.* New York: Library Publishers, 1952.

March, Peyton C. *The Nation at War.* Garden City, N.Y.: Doubleday, Doran and Co., 1932.

Matthews, William, and Wecter, Dixon. *Our Soldiers Speak, 1775–1918.* Boston: Little, Brown and Co., 1943.

May, Ernest R. *The World War and American Isolation, 1914–1917.* Cambridge, Mass.: Harvard University Press, 1959.

May, Ernest R., ed. *The Ultimate Decision: The President as Commander-in-Chief.* New York: G. Braziller, 1960.

Meinecke, Friedrich. *The German Catastrophe.* Translated by Sidney B. Fay. Boston: Beacon Press, 1968.

Merrill, James M., ed. *Uncommon Valor: The Exciting Story of the Army.* Chicago: Rand McNally, 1964.

Millett, Allen R. *The General: Robert Bullard and Officership in the United States Army, 1881–1925.* Westport, Conn.: Greenwood Press, 1975.

Millis, Walter. *Arms and Men: A Study in American Military History.* New York: G. P. Putnam's Sons, 1956.

————. *The Martial Spirit: A Study of Our War With Spain.* Boston: Houghton Mifflin Co., 1931.

Morison, Elting E. *Men, Machines and Modern Times.* Cambridge, Mass.: MIT Press, 1966.

————. *Turmoil and Tradition: A Study of the Life and Times of Henry L. Stimson.* Boston: Houghton Mifflin Co., 1960.

Mowry, George E. *The Era of Theodore Roosevelt and the Birth of Modern America, 1900–1912.* New York: Harper Torchbooks, 1958.

Muller, William G. *The Twenty-fourth Infantry, Past and Present.* 1923. Reprint. Fort Collins, Colo.: Old Army Press, 1972.

Munson, Edward L. *The Management of Men: A Handbook on the Systematic Development of Morale and the Control of Human Behavior.* New York: Henry Holt and Co., 1921.

Nelson, Keith L. *Victors Divided: America and the Allies in Germany, 1918–1923.* Berkeley: University of California Press, 1975.

Nelson, Otto L., Jr. *National Security and the General Staff.* Washington, D.C.: Infantry Journal Press, 1946.

Nenninger, Timothy K. *The Leavenworth Schools and the Old Army: Education, Professionalism and the Officer Corps of the United States Army, 1881–1918.* Westport, Conn.: Greenwood Press, 1978.

Palmer, Frederick. *America in France.* 1918. Reprint. Westport, Conn.: Greenwood Press, 1975.

————. *Bliss, Peacemaker: The Life and Letters of General Tasker Howard Bliss.* New York: Dodd, Mead and Co., 1934.

————. *Newton D. Baker: America at War.* 2 vols. New York: Dodd, Mead and Co., 1931.

Palmer, John M. *America in Arms: The Experience of the United States With Military Organization.* New Haven, Conn: Yale University Press, 1941.

————. *Washington, Lincoln and Wilson.* New York: Doubleday, Doran and Co., 1930.

Pappas, George S. *Prudens Futuri: The U.S. Army War College 1901–1967.* Carlisle Barracks, Pa.: Association of the U.S. Army War College, 1967.

Pershing, John J. *My Experiences in the World War.* 2 vols. New York: Frederick A. Stokes Co., 1931.

Pogue, Forrest C. *George C. Marshall: The Education of a General.* New York: Random House, 1963.

Pratt, Fletcher. *Eleven Generals: Studies in American Command*. New York: W. Sloane and Associates, 1949.

Pringle, Henry F. *Theodore Roosevelt*. New York: Harcourt, Brace and Co., 1931.

Reinhardt, George C., and Kintner, William R. *The Haphazard Years: How America Has Gone to War*. Garden City, N.Y.: Doubleday and Co., 1960.

Risch, Erna. *Quartermaster Support of the Army: A History of the Corps, 1775–1939*. Washington, D.C.: Quartermaster Historian's Office, Office of the Quartermaster General, 1962.

Root, Elihu. *Five Years of the War Department*. Washington, D.C.: Government Printing Office, 1904.

————. *The Military and Colonial Policy of the United States: Addresses and Reports by Elihu Root*. Edited by Robert Bacon and James Brown Scott. Cambridge, Mass.: Harvard University Press, 1916.

Roth, Russell. *Muddy Glory: America's Indian Wars in the Philippines, 1899–1935*. W. Hanover, Mass.: Christopher Publishing House, 1981.

Rutkowski, Edwin H. *The Politics of Military Aviation Procurement, 1926–1934: A Study in the Political Assertion of Consensual Values*. Columbus: Ohio State University Press, 1966.

Salmond, John A. *The Civilian Conservation Corps, 1933–42: A New Deal Case Study*. Chapel Hill: University of North Carolina Press, 1967.

Schaffer, Ronald, comp. *The United States in World War I: A Selected Bibliography*. Santa Barbara, Calif.: Clio Books, 1978.

Schley, Winfield S. *The Rescue of Greely*. New York: Charles Scribner's Sons, 1885.

Schulz, Gerhard. *Revolutions and Peace Treaties, 1917–1920*. London: Methuen and Co., 1972.

Scipio, L. Albert II. *Last of the Black Regulars: A History of the 24th Infantry Regiment*. Silver Spring, Md: Roman Publishers, 1983.

Scott, Hugh L. *Some Memories of a Soldier*. New York: Century, 1928.

77th Division Association, *History of the Seventy-seventh Division, August 25th, 1917–November 11th, 1918*. New York: 77th Division Association, n.d.

Sexton, William T. *Soldiers in the Sun*. Harrisburg, Pa.: Military Service Publishing Co., 1939.

Shanks, David C. *As They Passed Through the Port*. Washington, D.C.: Cary Publishing Co., 1927.

Shiner, John F. *Foulois and the U.S. Army Air Corps, 1931–1935*. Washington, D.C.: Office of Air Force History, USAF, 1983.

Silverlight, John. *The Victors' Dilemma: Allied Intervention in the Russian Civil War, 1917–1920*. New York: Weybright and Talley, 1970.

Skillman, Willis R. *The AEF: Who They Were, How They Did It*. Philadelphia: George W. Jacobs and Co., 1920.

Smith, Daniel M. *The Great Departure: The United States and World War I, 1914–1920*. New York: John Wiley and Sons, Inc., 1965.

Smythe, Donald. "General of the Armies John J. Pershing." In *The War Lords: Military Commanders of the Twentieth Century*, edited by Michael Carver, pp. 160–75. Boston: Little, Brown and Co., 1976.

Society of the Fifth Division. *The Official History of the Fifth Division, USA*. Washington, D.C.: Society of the Fifth Division: 1919.

Society of the First Division. *History of the First Division During the World War, 1917–1919*. Philadelphia: John C. Winston Co., 1931.

Spaulding, Oliver L. *The U.S. Army in War and Peace*. New York: G. P. Putnam's Sons, 1937.

———. *The Second Division, American Expeditionary Force, in France 1917–1919*. New York: Historical Commission, Second Division Association, 1937.

Speakman, Harold. *From a Soldier's Heart*. New York: Abingdon Press, 1919.

Stallings, Laurence. *The Doughboys: Story of the AEF, 1917–1918*. New York: Harper and Row Publishers, 1963.

Stanley, Peter W. *A Nation in the Making: The Philippines and the United States, 1899–1921*. Cambridge, Mass.: Harvard University Press, 1974.

———. *Sentimental Imperialists: The American Experience in East Asia*. New York: Harper and Row Publishers, 1981.

Steel, Ronald. *Walter Lippman and the American Century*. Boston: Little, Brown and Co., 1980.

Stimson, Henry L., and Bundy, McGeorge. *On Active Service in Peace and War*. New York: Harper and Brothers, 1947.

Strakhosky, Leonid M. *The Origins of American Intervention in North Russia (1918)*. New York: Howard Fertig, 1937.

Taber, John H. *The Story of the 168th Infantry*. 2 vols. Iowa City: State Historical Society of Iowa, 1925.

Thian, Raphael P. *Legislative History of the General Staff of the Army of the United States from 1775 to 1901*. Washington, D.C.: Government Printing Office, 1901.

Thomason, John W., Jr. *Fix Bayonets!* New York: Charles Scribner's Sons, 1926.

Toland, John. *No Man's Land, 1918—The Last Year of the Great War.* New York: Doubleday and Co., 1980.

Tompkins, Frank. *Chasing Villa: The Story Behind the Story of Pershing's Expedition Into Mexico.* Harrisburg, Pa.: Military Service Publishing Co., 1934.

Trask, David F. *The War With Spain in 1898.* New York: Macmillan Co., 1981.

Twichell, Heath, Jr. *Allen: The Biography of an Army Officer.* New Brunswick, N.J.: Rutgers University Press, 1974.

Unterberger, Betty M. *America's Siberian Expedition, 1918–1920.* Raleigh, N.C.: Duke University Press, 1956.

Vandiver, Frank E. *Black Jack: The Life and Times of John J. Pershing.* 2 vols. College Station, Tex.: Texas A. & M. University Press, 1977.

Watson, Mark S. *Chief of Staff: Prewar Plans and Preparations.* Washington, D.C.: Historical Division, Department of the Army, 1950.

Weaver, John D. *The Brownsville Raid.* New York: W. W. Norton and Co., 1970.

Weigley, Russell F. "The Elihu Root Reforms and the Progressive Era." In *Command and Commanders in Modern Warfare: The Proceedings of the Second Military History Symposium, U.S. Air Force Academy, 2–3 May 1968,* edited by William Geffen, pp. 11–27. 2d ed., enl. Washington, D.C.: Office of Air Force History, Headquarters USAF, and U.S. Air Force Academy, 1971.

————. *History of the United States Army.* New York: Macmillan Co., 1967.

————. *Towards An American Army: Military Thought From Washington to Marshall.* New York: Columbia University Press, 1962.

Weigley, Russell F., ed. *The American Military: Readings in the History of the Military in American Society.* Reading, Mass.: Addison-Wesley Publishing Co., 1969.

Wheeler, Joseph. *The Santiago Campaign, 1898.* Port Washington, N.Y.: Kennikat Press, 1971.

White, John A. *The Siberian Intervention.* Princeton, N.J.: Princeton University Press, 1950.

White, Lonnie J. *Panthers to Arrowheads: The 36th (Texas-Oklahoma) Division in World War I.* Austin, Tex.: Presidial Press, 1984.

Wiebe, William J. *The Search for Order, 1877–1920.* New York: Hill and Wang, 1967.

Willeford, Charles. *Something About A Soldier.* New York: Random House, 1986.

Williams, T. Harry. *Americans at War: The Development of the American Military System.* Baton Rouge: Louisiana State University Press, 1960.

———. *The History of American Wars From Colonial Times to World War I.* New York: Alfred A. Knopf, 1981.

Wright, William R. *A History of the Sixty-sixth Field Artillery Brigade.* Denver, Colo.: Smith, Brooks Printing Co., n.d.

Articles

Allen, Henry T. "The Organization of A Staff Post Adapted to the United States Army." *Journal of the Military Service Institution of the United States* 28 (Mar 01): 169–83.

———. "Proposed Reorganization For Our Central Staff." *Journal of the Military Service Institution of the United States* 27 (Mar 1900): 26–30.

Ansell, S. T. "Military Justice." *Military Law Review* Bicentennial Issue (Sep 75): 53–61.

"Army Increase To Cost a Billion." *New York Times*, 6 Nov 15, p. 4.

Brown, Terry W. "The Crowder-Ansell Dispute: The Emergence of General Samuel T. Ansell." *Military Law Review* 35 (Jan 67): 1–45.

Bush, Sterling C. "Eyes and Ears of the Commander." *Army Information Digest*, Jan 63, pp. 42–46.

Butler, Maria B. "The National Home for Disabled Volunteer Soldiers." *Harpers New Monthly Magazine* 73, no. 47 (Oct 1886): 683–95.

Call, Luther P. "The History, Organization and Function of the Inspector General's Department." *Reserve Officer* 16 (Oct 39): 11–13.

Coffman, Edward M. "The Battle Against Red Tape: Business Methods of the War Department General Staff, 1917–1918." *Military Affairs* 26 (Spring 62): 1–10.

———. "Sidelights on the War Department General Staff in Its Early Years." *Military Affairs* 39 (Apr 74): 71–72.

Colby, Elbridge. "Elihu Root and the National Guard." *Military Affairs* 23 (Spring 59): 20, 28–34.

Cooling, Benjamin Franklin. "Enlisted Grade Structure and the Army Reorganization Act of 1920." *Military Affairs* 31 (Winter 67): 189–94.

Cosmas, Graham A. "From Order to Chaos: The War Department, the National Guard and Military Policy, 1898." *Military Affairs* 29 (Fall 65): 105–21.

––––––. "Military Reform After the Spanish-American War: The Reorganization Fight of 1898–1899." *Military Affairs* 35 (Feb 71): 12–18.

Damon, Allan L. "The Great Red Scare." *American Heritage* 19 (Feb 68): 22–27, 75–77.

Deutrich, Mabel E. "Fred C. Ainsworth: The Story of a Vermont Archivist." *Vermont History* 27 (Jan 59): 22–33.

DeWitt, John L. "Brief Historical Description of the Organization of the War Department General Staff, United States Army." *Quartermaster Review* 12 (Sep–Oct 32): 29–32.

Ebstein, Fred H. E. "Twenty-first Regiment of Infantry." *Journal of the Military Service Institution of the United States* 12 (Jul 1892): 844–50.

Fleming, Thomas J. "Two Argonnes." *American Heritage* 19 (Oct 68): 44–45, 88–94.

"Further Promotion to General Officers." *Army and Navy Journal*, 21 Feb 03, p. 607.

Gallagher, Bernard J. "A Yank in the B. E. F." *American Heritage* 16 (Jun 65): 18–26, 101–08.

Garlington, E. A. "The Seventh Regiment of Cavalry." *Journal of the Military Service Institution of the United States* 16 (Jan 1895): 649–65.

Halliday, E. M. "Where Ignorant Armies Clashed by Night." *American Heritage* 10 (Dec 58): 26–29, 120–25.

Herring, George C., Jr. "James Hay and the Preparedness Controversy, 1915–16." *Journal of Southern History* 25 (Nov 64): 383–404.

Hewes, James E., Jr. "The United States Army General Staff, 1900–1917." *Military Affairs* 38 (Apr 74): 67–74.

Jackson, Chester V. "Mission to Murmansk." *United States Naval Institute Proceedings* 95, no. 2 (Feb 69): 83–89.

Jameson, Frank H. Letter to the Editor. *New York Times*, 13 May 1922, p. 12.

Johnson, Jacob C. "A Chain of Responsibility." *Army and Navy Journal*, Jul–Aug 27, pp. 1047–48, 1068, 1090, 1108, 1128, 1150; Sep–Oct 27, pp. 13, 34, 47, 67, 74, 92, 107, 132, 138, 152.

Lane, Jack C. "American Military Past: The Need for New Approaches." *Military Affairs* 41 (Oct 77): 109–13.

————. "Leonard Wood Leads His Team From Victory to Defeat" *American History Illustrated* 1 (Aug 66): 23–24.

Linn, Levon P. "Army Inspector General System." *Army Information Digest*, Oct 64, pp. 13–17.

Love, Edmund G. "The Case of the 'Fighting Irish': An Illustration of American Indifference to Regimental Traditions." *Military Affairs* 11 (Spring 47): 46–48.

Luckett, Judith A. "The Siberian Intervention: Military Support of Foreign Policy." *Military Review* 64 (Apr 84): 54–63.

McLaughlin, Patrick D. "Doughboy Diplomats: The U.S. Army in Italy, 1917–1919." *Army*, Jan 71, pp. 30–37.

McReynolds, G. B. "Notes on Some Random Activities of the Field Artillery Board." *Field Artillery Journal* 32 (Jul 42): 505–10.

Marx, Wilhelm. "Rhineland Occupation." *Foreign Affairs* 7 (Jan 29): 198–203.

Millett, Allan R. "The General Staff and the Cuban Intervention of 1906." *Military Affairs* 31 (Fall 67): 113–19.

Millett, John D. "The Direction of Supply Activities in the War Department." *American Political Science Review* 38 (Apr 44): 249–65; 38 (Jun 44): 475–98.

Morey, Lewis S. "The Cavalry Fight at Carrizal." *Journal of the U.S. Cavalry Association* 27 (Jan 17): 449–56.

"Newton D. Baker on Executive Influence in Military Legislation." *American Political Science Review* 50 (Sep 56): 700–701.

Preston, John F. "Inspector General's Department of the Army." *Army and Navy Journal*, 7 Oct 33, pp. 103, 116.

Ranson, Edward. "Nelson A. Miles as Commanding General, 1895–1903." *Military Affairs* 29 (Winter 66): 179–200.

"Recent Deaths: Alvan Chambliss Read." *Army and Navy Journal*, 7 Feb 20, p. 698.

"Recent Deaths: John Cabell Breckinridge." *Army and Navy Journal*, 28 Aug 20, p. 1578.

Reddick, L. D. "Negro Policy of the United States Army." *Journal of Negro History* 34 (Jan 49): 9–29.

Riepma, Siert F. "Portrait of An Adjutant General: The Career of Major General Fred C. Ainsworth." *Journal of the American Military History Foundation* 2 (Spring 38): 26–35.

Ruhl, Arthur. "What Is the Matter With the U.S. Army?" *Collier's Magazine*, 15 Apr 11, pp. 17, 39–41.

Semsch, Philip L. "Elihu Root and the General Staff." *Military Affairs* 27 (Spring 63): 16–27.

Spector, Ronald. "You're Not Going To Send Soldiers Over There, Are You!" *Military Affairs* 36 (Feb 72): 1–4.

Stallings, Laurence. "The War To End War." *American Heritage* 10 (Oct 59): 5–6, 84–85.

Stansfield, George J. "A History of the Judge Advocate General's Department, United States Army." *Military Affairs* 9 (Fall 45): 219–37.

Sutton, John L. "The German General Staff in U.S. Defense Policy." *Military Affairs* 25 (Winter 62): 197–202.

Tinsley, James A. "Roosevelt, Foraker and the Brownsville Affray." *Journal of Negro History* 41 (Jan 56): 43–65.

Todd, Fred J. "Our National Guard: An Introduction to Its History." *Military Affairs* 5 (Summer 41): 73–86; 5 (Fall 41): 152–70.

Tolley, Kemp. "Our Russian War of 1918–19." *United States Naval Institute Proceedings* 95, no. 2 (Feb 69): 58–72.

Triache, George N. "A Comparative Study of the United States Army." *Infantry Journal* 13, no. 7 (Apr 17): 615–25.

Van Piper, Paul P. "A Survey of Materials For the Study of Military Management." *American Political Science Review* 44 (Sep 55): 828–50.

Watson, Mark S. "First Vigorous Steps in Rearming, 1938–39." *Military Affairs* 12 (Summer 48): 65–78.

Wyche, Ira T. "Mission and History of the Inspector General's Office." *Armored Cavalry Journal* 56 (Apr 47): 38–41.

Yoshpe, Harry B. "Economic Mobilization Planning Between the Two World Wars." *Military Affairs* 15 (Winter 51): 199–204.

Dissertations and Theses

Baldwin, Fred D. "The American Enlisted Man in World War I." Ph.D. dissertation, Princeton University, 1964.

Brown, Richard C. "Social Attitudes of American Generals 1898–1940." Ph.D. dissertation, University of Wisconsin, 1951.

Franklin, Ben G. "The Military Policy of the United States, 1918–1933: A Study of the Influence of World War I on Army Organization and Control." Ph.D. dissertation, University of California–Berkeley, 1943.

Hacker, Barton C. "The War Department and the General Staff, 1898–1917." Ph.D. dissertation, University of Chicago, 1963.

Hampton, Duane. "Conservation and Cavalry: A Study of the Role of the United States Army in the Development of a National Park

System, 1886–1917." Ph.D. dissertation, University of Colorado, 1965.

Johnson, Charles W. "The Civilian Conservation Corps: The Role of the Army." Ph.D. dissertation, University of Michigan, 1968.

Johnson, Elliot L. "The Military Experience of General Hugh A. Drum From 1898–1918." Ph.D. dissertation, University of Wisconsin-Madison, 1975.

Jornacion, George W. "The Time of Eagles: United States Army Officers and the Pacification of the Philippine Moros, 1899–1913." Ph.D. dissertation, University of Maine, 1973.

Killigrew, John W. "The Impact of the Great Depression on the Army, 1929–1936." Ph.D. dissertation, Indiana University, 1960.

McKenna, Charles D. "The Forgotten Reform: Field Maneuvers in the Development of the United States Army, 1902–1920." Ph.D. dissertation, Duke University, 1981.

Miewald, Robert D. "The Stability of Military Managerial Doctrine: The United States Army, 1866–1941." Ph.D. dissertation, University of Chicago, 1967.

Miller, Robert A. "The United States Army During the 1930's." Ph.D. dissertation, Princeton University, 1973.

Nesmith, Vardell E., Jr. "The Quiet Paradigm Change: The Evolution of the Field Artillery Doctrine of the United States Army, 1861–1905." Ph.D. dissertation, Duke University, 1977.

Raines, Edgar F. "Major General J. Franklin Bell and Military Reform: The Chief of Staff Years, 1906–1910." Ph.D. dissertation, University of Wisconsin-Madison, 1976.

Roberts, William R. "Loyalty and Expertise: The Transformation of the Nineteenth-Century American General Staff and the Creation of the Modern Military Establishment." Ph.D. dissertation, Johns Hopkins University, 1980.

Rohl, James W. "The General Staff and American Military Policy: The Formative Period, 1898–1917." Ph.D. dissertation, University of Texas, 1967.

Sapp, Diane E. "Our Mission Our Future: The United States Disciplinary Barracks, Fort Leavenworth, Kansas." M.A. thesis, University of Minnesota, 1981.

Skelton, William B. "The United States Army, 1821–1837: An Institutional History." Ph.D. dissertation, Northwestern University, 1968.

Venzon, Anne C. "The Papers of General Smedley Darlington Butler, USMC, 1915–1918." Ph.D. dissertation, Princeton University, 1982.

537

List of Abbreviations

ABMC	American Battle Monuments Commission
Accts	Accounts
ACofS	Assistant Chief of Staff
Adj	Adjutant
Adv	Advanced
AEC	American Embarkation Center
AEF	American Expeditionary Forces
AFIC	American Forces in China
AFIF	American Forces in France
AFIG	American Forces in Germany
AG	Adjutant General
AGD	Adjutant General's Department
AGO	Adjutant General's Office
APM	Assistant Provost Marshal
AReg	Army Regulation
ARIG	*Annual Report of the Inspector General*
ARSW	*Annual Report of the Secretary of War*
Arty	Artillery
ASofW	Assistant Secretary of War
AWOL	absent without leave
Bn	Battalion
Bul	Bulletin
Bus	Business
Cdr(s)	Commander(s)
CE	Corps of Engineers
CG	Commanding General
ch.	chapter
CinC	Commander-in-Chief
Cir	Circular
Civ Affs	Civil Affairs
CMTC	Civilian Military Training Corps
Cmte	Committee

Co	Company
CO	Commanding Officer
CofAC	Chief of Air Corps
CofArms/Svcs	Chief of Arms and Services
CofBurs	Chief of Bureaus
CofF	Chief of Finance
CofMilBur	Chief of Militia Bureau
CofNGB	Chief of National Guard Bureau
CofPerBr	Chief of Personnel Branch
CofS	Chief of Staff
CofSecs/Svcs	Chief of Sections and Services
CofSelSubsec	Chief of Selection Subsection
Com	Commission, Commissioned
Comdt	Commandant
Comm	Communications
Cong.	Congress
comp.	compiler
Corresp	Correspondence
CSigOff	Chief Signal Officer
Ctr	Center
DA	Department of the Army
DCofS	Deputy Chief of Staff
Dept	Department
Dist	District
diss.	dissertation
Div	Division
ed.	editor, edition
encl(s).	enclosure(s)
End	Endorsement
Ex	Executive
Exh	Exhibit
FA	Field Artillery
FD	Finance Department
FY	Fiscal Year
G–1	Personnel officer or section of divisional or higher staff

G–2	Intelligence officer or section of divisional or higher staff
G–3	Operations officer or section of divisional or higher staff
G–4	Supply officer or section of divisional or higher staff
G–5	Training officer or section of divisional or higher staff
GAO	General Accounting Office
Gen	General
GerArmCom	German Armistice Commission
GHQ	General Headquarters
GO	General Order
Gov	Governor
GS	General Staff
HD	Historical Division
HofRef	House of Representatives
Hosp	Hospital
Hq	Headquarters
IAW	in accordance with
IG	Inspector General (Army), inspector general
IGD	Inspector General's Department
Inf	Infantry
Insp(s)	Inspector(s), Inspection(s)
Instrs	Instructions
Interv(s)	Interview(s)
JAG	Judge Advocate General
Ltr(s)	Letter(s)
LOC	Line-of-Communications
loc. cit.	in the place cited
Med	Medical
Memo(s)	Memorandum(a)
MFR	Memorandum for the Record
MG	machine gun
MHI	U.S. Army Military History Institute, Carlisle Barracks, Pa.

540

Mil Affs	Military Affairs, Militia Affairs
MilSec	Military Secretary
MP	Military Police
NARA	National Archives and Records Administration, Washington, D.C.
n.d.	no date
NG	National Guard
NHDVS	National Home for Disabled Volunteer Soldiers
Off(s)	Officer(s)
OIC	Officer-in-Charge
OIG	Office of the Inspector General
Opns	Operations
ORC	Organized Reserve Corps
OrdC	Ordnance Corps
Org	Organization
OTIG	Office of The Inspector General (1924)
Per Br	Personnel Branch
Phil	Philippine, Philippines
PL	Public Law
PM	Provost Marshal
pt.	part
Pres	President
Prov	Province, Provisional
Pun Exp	Punitive Expedition
PXReg	Post Exchange Regulation
QMC	Quartermaster Corps
re	regarding
RG	Record Group
ROTC	Reserve Officers Training Corps
Rpt(s)	Report(s)
Sec	Section, Secretary
Sess.	Session
SG	Surgeon General
SO	Special Order
SofI	Secretary of the Interior

SofW	Secretary of War
SReg	Special Regulation
Svc	Service
TAG	The Adjutant General (1907)
Telg	Telegram
TIG	The Inspector General (1924)
USMA	U.S. Military Academy
USMC	U.S. Marine Corps
USP&DO(s)	U.S. property and disbursing officer(s)
vol(s).	volume(s)
WD	War Department
WDGS	War Department General Staff
WPD	War Plans Division

Index

Miles, Lt. Gen. Nelson A., 11, 13
Military police, 175–76. *See also* Straggler control program.
  improper actions allegations against, 290
  quality of, 268
  traffic flow and, 203, 211, 216
Military Police Corps, 175
Military prisons, 101–04. *See also* Alcatraz prison; U.S. Federal Penitentiary.
Military Secretary's Office, 12
Militia, inspection of, 67–75
Militia Act of 21 January 1903, 67–68
Militia Affairs Division, WDGS, 67, 68, 69
Mills, Col. Stephen C., 25
Mitchell, Col. James B., 180, 184
Mitchell, Col. William "Billy," 192–93
Montfaucon, 208, 212, 222
Montgomery, Col. John C., 281
Monuments. *See* National monuments.
Morale. *See also* Fosdick, Raymond B.; Mail service; Post exchanges.
  effect of criticism on, 167
  impact of CCC on, 452, 455
  inspections of welfare and, 148–50, 241–42, 374
  issues, 406–12
Morale Branch, establishment of, 152
Morris, Col. Willis V., 306–09
Morrison, Maj. Gen. John F., 140, 144
Morton, Lt. Col. Charles G., 50
Mott, John R., 248
Mound City, Kansas, 425
Muir, Maj. Gen. Charles H., 221
Munson, Brig. Gen. Edward L., 152
Murmansk, 296, 298
Muster roll, elimination of, 14–15

National Defense Act of 1916, 24, 29–33, 111, 114, 313
  application to National Guard, 71–73
  and field artillery, 60
National Defense Act of 1920, 280, 285, 398, 431
  application to National Guard, 442
  division of country into corps areas, 321, 324n23
  strength of IGD set by, 331–32
  structural changes within War Department, 324
National Guard, 29–31, 33, 321, 431. *See also* Militia.
  inspections during WW I, 134–35
  peacetime adjustment, 324
  reduction of training funds, 329

National Guard—Continued
  sergeant-instructors housing allowance scandal, 435–36
  as a source of IGD manpower, 335
  during WW I, 121–24
National Guard Bureau, 438–39
National Home for Disabled Volunteer Soldiers (NHDVS), 105–06, 340, 423
National battlefield parks, 427–30
National monuments, 428–30
National Park Service, 450
Nebraska National Guard, 439
Neufchateau, 197
Nevers, 177
Newark Depot, 380
New York General Intermediate Depot, 373, 377, 381
New York National Guard, 440–41

Occupation army. *See* Third Army.
O'Connor, Col. Charles M., 86
Office of Public Buildings, 369
Office of the Chief of Chaplains, 369
Office of the Chief of Infantry, 369
Office of the/The Inspector General (OIG/OTIG)
  change from OIG to OTIG, 320
  collateral duties, 340
  decentralization, 359–64
  evaluation of Army's CCC responsibilities, 452–57
  guidelines for National Guard inspections, 444
  inspection standards for economic surveys, 372
  internal controls, 355–59
  officer evaluation by, 147, 229–30
  relations with War Plans Division, 142–43
  report on cemetery system, 107
  review of complaints, 87, 433–34, 462–63
  service schools inspections, 17, 47–51, 403–04
  subordinate divisions, 18–19, 336, 339, 340
  unit business practices inspections, 17
  WW I duties of, 115, 143–44
Office of The Judge Advocate General, 423, 438–39
Officer Reserve Corps, IGD, 117, 335
Officers. *See also* Reserve Officers Training Corps (ROTC) Program.
  appointment of welfare, 251
  evaluation of, 145–48, 229–30